Higher Stages of Human Development

HIGHER STAGES
OF
HUMAN DEVELOPMENT

Perspectives on Adult Growth

Edited by
CHARLES N. ALEXANDER
ELLEN J. LANGER

New York   Oxford
OXFORD UNIVERSITY PRESS
1990

155.6
H53

Oxford University Press

Oxford   New York   Toronto
Delhi   Bombay   Calcutta   Madras   Karachi
Petaling Jaya   Singapore   Hong Kong   Toyko
Nairobi   Dar es Salaam   Cape Town
Melbourne   Auckland

and associated companies in
Berlin   Ibadan

Copyright © 1990 by Oxford University Press, Inc.

Published by Oxford University Press, Inc.,
200 Madison Avenue, New York, New York 10016

Oxford is a registered trademark of Oxford University Press

Library of Congress Cataloging-in-Publication Data
Higher stages of human development / edited by Charles N. Alexander,
Ellen J. Langer.
p. cm.   Bibliography: p.   Includes index.
ISBN 0-19-503483-X
1. Adulthood—Psychological aspects.
I. Alexander, Charles Nathaniel.   II. Langer, Ellen J., 1947-
[DNLM: 1. Cognition.   2. Human Development.   3. Morals.
4. Psychological Theory.   BF 713 H638]
BF724.5.H53   1990
155.6—dc20   DNLM/DLC for Library of Congress
89-9314   CIP

2 4 6 8 9 7 5 3 1
Printed in the United States of America
on acid-free paper

Preface

Can dramatic advances in development occur after adolescence? What is the end-point or highest possible state of adult development? How we conceptualize the highest state of development is critical, for it shapes our understanding of the nature and limits of human growth. In this volume this issue of endpoint is addressed by some of the world's leading researchers and theorists in adult development.

Traditionally, developmental psychology studied the growth of children. More recently, the field also focused on the elderly and the process of aging. Now, there is growing recognition that human development comprises more than the beginning and end of life. There is still, however, a relative void in terms of major theoretical and substantive works that address development during the intervening period from late adolescence through the adult years (see chapter 1 by Daniel Levinson). This volume helps to fill that void by offering a comprehensive treatment of qualitative advances in adult development.

It was once widely held that cognitive development culminated during adolescence in a set of abstract reasoning abilities referred to by Jean Piaget as "formal operations." Contributors to this book suggest that mature intelligence may involve other forms of cognition and other domains of development (e.g., affective and moral) that are also fundamental to adult life. The authors explore a variety of higher stages, or states, beyond the ordinarily proposed endpoint of abstract reasoning or formal operations.

The book is divided into four sections. Section 1 focuses on nonhierarchical theories; section II on hierarchical stage theories of cognitive development; section III on stage theories of moral development; and section IV on stage theories of consciousness and self-development.

It is often said that stages of development beyond one's own are difficult to fully comprehend and describe. Some of the contributors to this book, by their own admission, are attempting to describe stages that they still are coming to understand more fully. Moreover, because these chapters focus on a wide range of developmental domains from a variety of perspectives, we have provided an introductory chapter that, in as straightforward a manner as possible, attempts to provide an integrative framework for understanding the various perspectives on the major issues explored in this book. In addition to the issue of endpoint, the introduction discusses the following corollary questions: Does growth in adulthood occur through distinct stages? What mechanisms undergird this growth? What domains get developed and how do they interrelate? As a point of departure, Piaget's ideas

and a critique of his positions on these central issues are presented. Next, the different viewpoints expressed in each of the book's chapters on these questions are summarized. Finally, the various theoretical positions presented in the book are compared and analyzed on these major issues. Especially for the reader who is not already familiar with adult development, we highly recommend that you begin by reading our introductory chapter to the volume.

This book is intended for the growing number of colleagues in the fields of psychology, gerontology, psychiatry, and social work, who are interested in adopting a life-span developmental approach to their discipline that takes into account the crucial period of the human life-cycle from late adolescence to late adulthood. It can also serve as a textbook for graduate and advanced undergraduate courses in cognitive, personality, and social development; adolescent, adult, and life-span development; and theoretical and philosophical developments in psychology. Because of the volume's focus on the highest stages of human growth, and on development of consciousness and the self (in addition to cognitive development), it may also be of interest to students of humanistic and health psychology.

Producing a volume of this size and scope is a collective effort, and many individuals have generously contributed their knowledge and skills. First, we would like to express our deep appreciation to the authors of these chapters, for the depth and originality of their contributions, and for their patient cooperation throughout the extended process of editing and producing this book. We thank Steve Druker, Roberta Oetzel, Mac Muehlman, John Davies, Carol Dixon, Lynne Israelson, and Rita Jacoby for the invaluable editorial advice and assistance that they provided at crucial junctures in the book's development. Susanne Gibbons devoted a great deal of time and effort overseeing practical concerns during the production stages of this book, for which we are most grateful. We also express gratitude to our editor at Oxford University Press, Joan Bossert, for her enthusiastic belief in this book. Without the encouragement of our families and close friends, completion of this book simply would not have been possible. We especially thank Victoria Kurth Alexander, who equally shared in these ideas and offered endless support throughout the project. Finally, C.N.A. would like to express a special debt of gratitude to Maharishi Mahesh Yogi, whose Vedic psychology provided the theoretical foundation for his own conceptual and empirical work on the highest possible stages of human development.

Fairfield, Iowa   C.N.A.
Cambridge, Massachusetts   E.J.L.
December 1989

Contents

Higher Stages of Human Development

Introduction: Major Issues in the Exploration of Adult Growth

Charles N. Alexander, Steven M. Druker, and Ellen J. Langer

What are the highest possible forms of human development? One's conception of the endpoint of development is fundamental, for it contains one's assumptions about the direction, possibilities, and dynamics of human growth. Moreover, all prior developmental stages will be viewed as progressive approximations of this goal. Contributors to this volume were asked to address this basic issue of endpoint. Answering this question generally requires examination of three related issues: Does development toward the endpoint proceed through qualitatively distinct stages? What mechanisms underlie this development? What major areas get developed (e.g., cognition and affect), and how do they interrelate? Based on recent theory and research, the chapters in this book provide expanded perspectives on these important issues.

Only recently have developmental psychologists directed significant attention to the study of adulthood. Developmental psychology has primarily focused on childhood, because it was believed that the most significant phases of growth occurred during this period. In fact, many psychologists assumed that development essentially ceases prior to adulthood. These thinkers may have recognized that change continues throughout the life span, but they chose to apply the term *development* only to qualitative changes involving growth of new capacities. In their view, change in adulthood is limited to the refinement and extended application—as well as degeneration—of existing capacities.

Jean Piaget was the most influential thinker advancing the view that human cognitive development attains its highest form in adolescence. His vision of the endpoint of human development at once inspired and delimited the endeavors of a generation of psychologists. Although many of the chapters in this book are in some way indebted to Piaget's insights, each goes significantly beyond him, and several present entirely new frameworks. Because these chapters represent diverse perspectives, this introduction furnishes the reader with a vision of the whole and a guide for apprehending the various parts. The introduction is organized into five sections:

1. As a point of departure, Piaget's ideas on the central issues of stage, end-

point, and mechanisms are summarized. (Readers well versed in Piagetian theory may skip this section.)

2. Major criticisms of Piaget's position on these issues are reviewed.
3. The sections of this book are briefly overviewed.
4. Each chapter is examined with respect to these three issues.
5. The various theoretical positions are compared and analyzed.

Summary of the Piagetian Theory of Cognitive Development

Developmental Stages

For Piaget (1970b, 1971b), stages are qualitatively distinct phases of development that have the character of a unified whole (*structure d'ensemble*). The unified character stems from an underlying structure—a stable organizational pattern of cognitive actions or operations. The structures are global in that, at a given stage, the individual is said to consistently process information and solve problems according to a general set of rules or logical strategies across all domains. Each structure is associated with a distinct conception of the world and distinct mode of cognitively interacting with it.

Piaget's (1971b) stages are hierarchical in that each successive stage is said to integrate the schemata of its predecessors within its more complex structure while also reorganizing and thus transforming them. In Piaget's theory the stages form an invariant irreversible sequence, and each serves as the necessary condition for development of the next higher one.

Endpoint

Piaget's proposed endpoint—"formal operations"—represents the logical culmination of the stages that preceded it. In Piaget's (1970b) initial "sensorimotor" stage, the cognitive processing modes are the schemes of sensation and overt action. During the subsequent "preoperational" transition period, action schemes are said to become mentally interiorized but are still largely rooted in direct perceptual experiences. Next, in the "concrete operational" stage, systematic internal actions called operations can be performed on mental representations of concrete objects and events. However, according to Inhelder and Piaget (1958), as long as operations remain centered on the concrete and the immediate, the system of their interrelations cannot achieve maximal equilibration (dynamic balance) and will have significant limitations. Because at this stage operations can be performed only on concrete components of *actual* experiences, one cannot mentally represent through propositions all *possible* combinations of variables in the devising of solution strategies. Further, the cognitive abilities that are available do not form a highly integrated system; consequently, the child cannot simultaneously integrate abstract operations in problem solving.

At the next stage, a higher order of operations becomes available that involves symbolic rather than concrete representations of objects. Piaget refers to concrete operations as "first-degree" operations, whereas he refers to the higher-order ones

as "second-degree" operations because they operate upon products of concrete operations. He holds that these "second-degree" operations involve propositions, in that these underlying thought processes in essence deal with binary combinations of declarative statements. It is because these "second-degree" operations coordinate abstract propositional forms rather than concrete manifestations that Piaget terms them "formal" operations (see Inhelder & Piaget, 1958).

Since thought now deals with symbolic objects, it can examine "the possible." Piaget states that a basic reorientation occurs in which the possible rather than the actual becomes the starting point for problem solving. The thinker systematically explores all possible combinations of propositions, and these various possibilities are treated as hypotheses to be tested. Piaget says that concrete operations exhibit an essentially "empirico-inductive" approach whereas this new level expresses a "hypothetico-deductive" one (see also Flavell, 1963, 1985). In Piaget's theory, 16 possible forms of propositions serve as the objects of formal operational thought. These propositions are systematically related through four types of transformational operations: identity, negation, reciprocity, and correlation (referred to as the "INRC group"). For a more technical treatment of the logico-mathematical models describing both concrete and formal operations, please see Richards & Commons' chapter.

Piaget believed that through these four transformational relations, the various propositions function as elements in an integrated system and that the fullest cognitive equilibration is achieved by organizing thought within this system. In his view, through fully developed formal operations, one can systematically analyze the totality of possible logical relations between all things that can be rendered in propositional form. For him, formal operations is the culmination of cognitive development: There is no further development of the organizational form of thought beyond this stage; remaining changes are in terms of increased competence with formal operations and their more comprehensive application in the accumulation of greater knowledge.

According to Piaget, given appropriate environmental experience, competence in formal operational thinking can be attained during the teen years. Thus, Piaget regards the formal operational stage as belonging to preadult development, even though full facility in this mode of thinking may not develop until adulthood—or may never develop (Piaget, 1972).

Mechanisms

As Piaget himself pointed out, a developmental theory does not so much rest upon its initial stage as hang from its highest one. One may conjecture that Piaget's proposed endpoint of the hypothetico-deductive reasoner, or experimenter, substantially influenced his conception of the origins and primary mechanism of development. Piaget appears to see all stages of cognitive development as phases of experimental investigation of the world guided by specific structures of logic. Thus, the infant can be viewed as a sensorimotor experimenter constructing knowledge of the world through his actions upon it (see Gardner et al. chapter).

Piaget (1971b; Ginzberg and Opper, 1979) considers sequential cognitive stages

not as primarily rooted in innate structures but as constructed through the process of spontaneous experimentation. Only a few automatic behavioral reflexes are said to be directly inherited, and these are quickly transformed into psychological structures through experience. Maturation of physiological structures is a necessary but not sufficient mechanism for cognitive development. For Piaget, the universal form of successive cognitive structures is not inherent in the mind or nervous system; rather, it results from invariant interaction of universal, genetically determined physiological structures with universal features of the environment.

In Piaget's (1977) theory, although the logical stage structures through which one progresses are qualitatively different, the mechanics through which these stages are generated are functionally invariant. As a result of general inheritance, all organisms display the functions of organization (the tendency to order activity) and adaptation. Adaptation may be further divided into the complementary processes of assimilation and accommodation.

Through *assimilation* the individual actively incorporates features of the external world into his existing structures. However, because the "fit" is not perfect, conflict inevitably arises. This causes the structures themselves to *accommodate,* or adjust, to achieve a greater *equilibrium,* or active state of balance between the cognitive system and the demands of the environment. The stability of cognitive equilibrium depends upon the ability to compensate through actions or mental operations for environmental changes without dismantling underlying structures. Each succeeding cognitive stage is said to achieve a more stable equilibrium than its predecessor.

This self-regulative process of equilibration is considered the primary mechanism of stage development and is said to occur spontaneously without need for conscious deliberation. This process of interaction between organism and environment is facilitated through three additional mechanisms (Piaget & Inhelder, 1969):

1. Physical experience through extraction or "simple abstraction" of physical features of the environment.
2. Logico-mathematical experience through "reflective abstraction" upon one's actions rather than through direct physical experience.
3. Social transmission of cultural materials, including, for example, language and number.

For further discussion of Piaget on these issues, see Flavell (1963, 1985); Furth (1981); Gardner (1982b); Ginzberg & Opper (1979, 1988); and Chapman (1988).

Critique of Piagetian Theory: Three Major Issues

Although Piaget's contribution to developmental psychology has been monumental, limitations in his framework are being increasingly recognized (e.g., Brainerd, 1978; Broughton, 1984; Sugarman, 1987; Toulmin & Feldman, 1976). This section briefly reviews general limitations that have been cited with respect to issues of stage, endpoint, and mechanism in preparation for review of these issues by contributors to this volume.

Limitations of Stage Theory

Piaget's conception of structural stages has come under attack. The increasingly prevalent information-processing approach (e.g., Siegler, 1983, 1986) generally questions the global nature of underlying stage structures as described by Piaget. Whereas Piaget spoke of stages as global in application, information-processing theorists typically hold that levels of skill vary across domains. For example, older children may appear more advanced because of increased domain-specific knowledge, or "expertise," rather than qualitative advances in cognitive mode (e.g., Bjorklund, 1987; Chi & Glaser, 1980). Such theorists, however, do not totally abandon the notion of cognitive structure, nor do they speak of mere compilation of knowledge. Instead, they may focus on development of elaborate networks of knowledge, which may be structural but not in a Piagetian sense.

According to Flavell (1985), the concept of global structural stages assumes there is relatively abrupt, qualitative (metamorphosis-like) change occurring concurrently among related cognitive entities. Although important qualitative advances do take place with age, Flavell suggests that they tend to be gradual and that within-stage changes are more extensive, significant, and less concurrent than initally proposed. Nevertheless, consistent with Wohlwill (1973), Flavell points out that the phenomenon of gradual consolidation does not invalidate the stage concept but requires its revision, so that a stage is viewed as a more dynamic, extended process. Further, whether or not cognitive components of a stage are temporally concurrent in their genesis, they do tend to become functionally related over time (Flavell 1971a, 1982). Concerning stage sequence, there is ample evidence that functionally meaningful relationships do develop between cognitive entities that occur early and those that occur late. Later-occurring "stages," however, may not necessarily hierarchically reintegrate or reorganize earlier ones in a strictly Piagetian way.

Overall, the concept of developmental stages continues to lead an active life. Most of the following chapters adhere to some type of stage theory, although the meaning of the concept is not the same for all. For the purpose of this volume, stages of adolescent and adult growth are considered hierarchical as long as they reflect a qualitative advance in capacity that encompasses and in some way reorganizes the gains of prior levels—even if their emergence is neither abrupt nor universally apparent in all adults. Alternatively, some contributors describe forms of "nonhierarchical" growth that can occur in adulthood.

Limitations of Endpoint Theory

Critics as well as defenders of Piaget admit that adolescents are typically more systematic and logical in problem solving than younger children (e.g., Braine & Rumain, 1983). However, the formal, logical models that Piaget has set forth to describe these differences have been criticized for their lack of appropriateness and completeness (e.g., Brainerd, 1978; Broughton, 1984; Bynum, Thomas, & Weitz, 1972; Flavell, 1982, 1983). Although some reject such efforts at formal modeling as reductive, others offer alternative models (e.g., Keats, Collis, & Halford, 1978).

Further, there has been an empirical challenge to Piaget's claims about the universality of formal operations. Certain studies indicate that perhaps less than half of the adolescents and adults in our culture can consistently solve formal operational problems across content domains (e.g., Capon & Kuhn, 1979; Keating & Clark, 1980). Moreover, some claim that it is virtually absent in nonliterate cultures (e.g., Super, 1980). If true, this suggests that formal operations may be culture or even subculture specific to technological societies that place a premium on scientific thinking. Others, however, have convincingly argued that formal operational capacities are evident within nontechnological societies when tasks appropriate to the culture are employed (e.g., Gladwin, 1970; Tulkin & Konner, 1973). Piaget himself later (1972) softened his original position, recognizing that emergence of formal operations is facilitated by formal education and that individuals may express formal operations only in areas of familiarity or expertise.

Authors of this volume focus on two other major shortcomings of formal operations. First, formal operations may too narrowly construe adult cognition in terms of deductive, syllogistic reasoning. Mature intelligence may involve other forms of knowing (such as contextual thinking) and other areas of life (such as affective development) that are critical to adult life and remained essentially unexplored by Piaget. Second, formal operations may represent a premature termination or endpoint of human growth. Piaget (1972) proposed that, under normal conditions, formal operations is attained between 15 and 20 years of age. As Souvaine, Lahey, and Kegan ask in their chapter, what about life after formal operations? Rather than engage in cataloging psychological and physiological decline that can occur in late adulthood, contributors to this volume ask the question, "Can further qualitative advance in human development occur after adolescence and, if so, under what conditions?" In addressing this concern, they explore a variety of potential endpoints for adult development.

Limitations of Mechanism Theory

Most developmentalists appreciate Piaget's emphasis on children as active participants in their own process of development. However, his emphasis on equilibration as *the* central mechanism of cognitive development has been questioned (e.g., Zimmerman & Blom, 1983). For Piaget, cognitive conflict is the propelling force for subsequent re-equilibration. But as Flavell (1985) points out, additional fundamental competencies not specified in Piaget's model would be required to initially recognize and subsequently resolve such conflicts. Also, it is difficult to see how cognitive conflict is critically involved in all major milestones of cognitive development. Further, Piaget's model tends to emphasize interaction with the external environment (Flavell, 1985), whereas internal interactions may be at least as important, especially in adult development. Flavell (1984) urges that we conceive more broadly of "what" gets developed and "how" this process occurs. Presumably not all mechanisms of development are age-independent, functional invariants. Some may require development themselves and only become available after a certain time.

Piaget did recognize that other factors contribute to development—biological, experiential, cultural—but he may not have given them due emphasis. His lack of

emphasis on the role played by inherent mental and corresponding biological structures and by environmental determinants may have been as much due to philosophical belief as to empirical observation. His commitment to the Promethean ideal of man as generator of his fate may have led him to reject what he perceived as the deterministic implications of either a preformationist–nativist or environmental view (Piaget, 1971c).

The ideal of the child as experimenter–philosopher constructing progressively more equilibrated theories of the world breaks down if those theories are prescribed either by the genome or the environment. A number of researchers now argue convincingly that various cognitive and perceptual structures are inherent features of the organism (e.g., Bower, 1982; Gibson & Spelke, 1983; Bornstein, 1988). A nativist position need not assume that inherent structures are fixed from birth; many nativists now recognize the significant role of experience in progressive expression of the genome (e.g., Aslin, Alberts, & Peterson, 1981).

Not surprisingly, Piaget also underestimated the contribution to development of automatic "figural" (as opposed to "operative") processes, such as memory, perception, and attention. The information-processing approach—whose very metaphor for the mind is an automatic digital computer—has more powerfully modeled the contribution of these mechanisms (e.g., Case, 1985; Sternberg & Powell, 1983). For example, this approach suggests that it may not be inadequate logical structures but rather constraints or lack of efficiency in information processing that prohibit younger children from solving formal operational problems (e.g., Siegler, 1983, 1986). Several processing-oriented approaches to the mechanisms of development are presented in Sternberg (1984) and Siegler (1989).

With respect to the issue of mechanisms, development beyond formal operations would require that either (1) the equilibration process continue in an expanded form, (2) other mechanisms relegated to a lesser role by Piaget become more significant than he anticipated, or (3) new mechanisms emerge. All these possibilities are considered by contributors to this volume.

Overview

The chapters of this volume are organized in sections according to their position on the issue of hierarchical stage development and their focus on "what" gets developed.

Nonhierarchical Theories

Levinson; Dittmann-Kohli and Baltes; and Gardner, Phelps, and Wolf appear to agree with Piaget that logico-mathematical development in childhood proceeds through hierarchical stages. Although they believe that genuine development also can occur in adulthood, they suggest that it is non-logico-mathematical and nonhierarchical in nature. Dittmann-Kohli and Baltes, and Gardner et al. specifically identify additional strands of intelligence that may develop in a more nonhierarchical fashion during both childhood and adulthood. McGuiness, Pribram, and Pirnazar, and Langer et al. adopt a more extreme position, questioning the existence

of global hierarchical stages of any kind in both childhood and adulthood. Although McGuinness et al. reject the notion of global stages, they do propose that micro-development of particular skills proceeds through an invariant sequence of processing levels. In contrast, Langer et al. emphasize the plasticity of the human organism and challenge the idea that any such observed hierarchical sequences are truly necessary features of human life.

Hierarchical Theories of Cognitive Development

These authors agree with Piaget in viewing development in terms of a hierarchical stage sequence. However, in addition, Richards and Commons, and Fischer, Kenny, and Pipp posit the potential for development of advanced stages of conceptual thought beyond formal operations. Further, Fischer et al. emphasize that actual cognitive competencies only arise through practice in specific domains and do not exist independent of the skills that express them.

Theories of Advanced Moral Development

These authors propose that cognitive stage development provides a necessary but not sufficient condition for hierarchical development of moral stages through childhood. Kohlberg and Ryncarz suggest that self-reflection can promote ethical–ontological development in adulthood but that the resulting "soft" postformal stage does not reintegrate its predecessors. Gilligan, Murphy, and Tappan suggest that two fundamentally distinct moral orientations can emerge during adolescence or adulthood but that these two perspectives can be further integrated in a hierarchical moral stage beyond the formal operational level.

Theories of Consciousness and Self Development

In the last section, the authors propose stages of consciousness or self development that are said to underlie all other aspects of development—cognitive, affective, and moral. Souvaine, Lahey, and Kegan, and Pascual-Leone posit postformal hierarchical stages of self development that are largely based in representational processes. In contrast, Alexander et al., drawing upon Vedic psychology (Maharishi, 1972), describe purely postrepresentational higher stages of consciousness that are said to hierarchically integrate all prior representational processes.

The position of each of the chapters in this volume on the issue of hierarchical stage development is summarized in Table I.1.

Review of Chapters in Relation to Major Issues

Nonhierarchical Theories of Adult Growth

Levinson. Levinson suggests that the "life course" interconnects growth across domains (e.g., cognitive, ego) and age levels. He posits that the life course unfolds through a "life cycle" consisting of four major eras: pre-, early, middle, and late

Table I.1 Position on Hierarchical Stage Issue

Theorist	Childhood	Adulthood
Piaget	H*	Non-H†
Levinson	H	Non-H
Dittmann-Kohli & Baltes	H	Non-H
Gardner et al.‡	Non-H	Non-H
McGuinness et al.	Non-H	Non-H
Langer et al.	Non-H	Non-H
Richards & Commons	H	H
Fischer et al.	H	H
Gilligan et al.	H	H
Kohlberg & Ryncarz	H	Non-H§
Souvaine et al.	H	H
Pascual-Leone	H	H
Alexander et al.	H	H

*H = Hierarchical; refers to theories in which later stages encompass and in some way reorganize their predecessors.

†Non-H = Nonhierarchical; refers to theories that may recognize qualitative as well as quantitative change but do not specify higher stages that encompass and reorganize their predecessors.

‡Refers only to development of non-logico-mathematical forms of intelligence.

§Refers only to ethical–ontological development.

adulthood. Although hierarchical development of logical thought takes place during childhood, Levinson claims that in domains significant to adult development no such stage hierarchy can be observed. Successive eras in adulthood cannot be considered "higher" than their predecessors. Instead, he refers to them metaphorically as "seasons" that have their own distinct character but that do not necessarily represent a progression in evolutionary form.

Thus, the endpoint of the life course involves interests and endeavors that typify the last season, but it does not necessarily reflect a logical culmination of capacities or fruition of potential. Levinson does recognize, however, that especially during transition periods both within and between eras, there are opportunities for "individuation" of the self.

He states that the key concept emerging from his work is that the life course has an underlying "life structure" that unfolds in an invariant sequence through the eras described earlier. Levinson states that the life structure differs from cognitive or self-structures as typically described. It is not "intraorganismic" but is said to be a structure of "self-in-relation-to-world" unfolding in a fixed sequence. Life structures are distinctly different for each person (unlike logical structures) and are built around significant and changing personal relationships with people, institutions, and objects (as opposed to invariant, environmental features said to be central to cognitive–structural development). According to Levinson, cognitive and personality stage development is generally held to be sequential but not highly age-dependent. (For exceptions see Fischer et al. and Pascual-Leone.) In contrast, Levinson observed an essentially age-linked (and apparently universal) sequence at the broader level of life-structure periods, with the onset for a given period varying within a range of three to four years.

Levinson suggests that Piagetians may tend to focus too exclusively on the properties of structured stages and not enough on transition processes that occur within and between stages. In studying development of the life structure he gives equal weight to "structure-building" and "structure-changing" periods and has observed that adults spend almost as much time in periods of transition as in those of structure. With respect to the mechanics of life structure development, he emphasizes that we must recognize the significant contribution of both "the psychobiological properties of the human species *and . . .* the general nature of human society at this phase of its evolution."

Dittmann-Kohli and Baltes. Dittmann-Kohli and Baltes also emphasize that adult development must be understood in terms of specific rather than universal features of the environment. However, whereas Levinson's focus is on the overall pattern of relations between self and world, these authors primarily examine one domain, that of cognitive development.

In their examination of adult cognitive growth, Dittmann-Kohli and Baltes propose two basic aspects of intelligence, the "mechanics" and the "pragmatics." The former are the fundamental context-free cognitive capacities, such as Piagetian operations, that develop relatively early in life and may be universal because of shared conditions of biological and social evolution. The authors believe that although this type of intelligence can be described in terms of hierarchical stages, pragmatic intelligence cannot. Pragmatic intelligence involves the application of the mechanics of intelligence in the construction or synthesis of context-specific, factual, and procedural knowledge of the world. Although it has some "features of universality" in that it encompasses some areas of widely shared knowledge, it includes a large component of particulars, with variation between individuals.

The authors state that mechanical intelligence is a necessary condition for growth of pragmatic intelligence but that it is not sufficient for it. Life experiences (e.g., types of social interaction) and aspects of the individual (e.g., social competence) not integral to mechanical intelligence are required for the synthesis of pragmatic intelligence. The major developmental period for mechanical intelligence is during childhood; although the pragmatic variety is also present in that period, its major growth occurs in adulthood. According to the authors, the central emphasis in adulthood is not on developing basic cognitive skills but on deploying existing skills in practical contexts and developing an *individualized* system of efficacy and knowledge. Thus, they believe that adult growth is particular and conditional, depending upon the pragmatics and context of adult life.

Though not explicitly presented as an endstate, the authors propose "wisdom" as one of the fullest expressions of synthesized intelligence. They state that it involves the integration of cognitive, affective, and reflective components and that it transcends mere factual and procedural knowledge to encompass means–end evaluation.

Gardner, Phelps, and Wolf. Gardner, Phelps, and Wolf also explore aspects of intelligence besides logico-mathematical (mechanical) intelligence. They study such domains as visual–spatial thinking, bodily–kinesthetic activity, musical

knowledge, and narrative thought. The authors note that each area involves "symbol systems," such as pictorial representation, dance, and music; and their research has led them to identify a sequence of capacities for symbolic expression that operate across diverse symbolic domains. These abilities are said to unfold as four "waves of symbolization," which emerge in an invariant sequence at approximately yearly intervals from two to seven years of age. As in Piaget's logical stages, these successive waves represent an increased ability to (1) function with relations and other abstract values and (2) generate greater complexity of symbolism. However, the authors use the term *wave* rather than *stage* because the impact in the various domains does not appear to be equal. Each wave has its crest of impact within a different domain accompanied by less elevated effects in other areas. Further, the particular character of each domain will influence the way in which the wave is expressed. Gardner et al. hypothesize that the waves are universal but that their pattern of expression within the various domains varies between cultures.

Gardner et al. theorize that across the entire life-span, three major stages of creative development can be identified: (1) "preconventional" (preschool age), characterized by free exploration uninfluenced by society's agenda and standards; (2) "conventional" (preadolescent), attentive to society's standards and concerned with mastering technical skills; (3) "postconventional" (from adolescence), evidencing a shift back to self-expression and freer experimentation on the basis of greater technical mastery.

Although they draw their terminology from Kohlberg's (1969) description of moral development, the authors recognize significant differences between creative development and the spheres of cognitive development studied by Piaget and Kohlberg. They state that in the latter, the adult's world view is qualitatively and irreversibly different from the child's but that through creative development the adult can gain access to earlier forms. They hold such access is often integral to fruitful innovation, whereas in logical reasoning, reversion to childhood forms would be dysfunctional.

Thus, although they employ the term *stage,* Gardner et al. do not conceive of their three major levels as typical hierarchical stages; rather, they believe creative development is more an epigenetic process, as described by Erikson (1963). In their view, although adult creativity may not involve new waves of symbolization, it does differ from childhood creativity in terms of increased technical skill and enhanced flexibility of movement between forms of knowing.

McGuinness, Pribram, and Pirnazar. McGuinness, Pribram, and Pirnazar agree with Piaget that there is a universal progression in cognitive development from a sensory level, through a concrete schema level, to an abstract level of symbolic transformations. However, they argue that recent research does not support Piaget's claim that this progression takes the form of age-related general stages applicable across domains. Rather, they posit that this progression recurs within each new learning experience or task domain at any age (e.g., in learning to read in adulthood). This learning sequence necessarily begins at a sensory level and progresses sequentially to an abstract one. The authors posit that most children develop certain logical capacities at similar ages not because of biology but because

of cognitive shifts that depend upon the accumulation of a threshold level of experience, with individuals of similar cultural backgrounds generally reaching the various thresholds at about the same age.

McGuinness et al. have thus created a nonstage "continuous state transformational model" that is nevertheless hierarchical in terms of microdevelopment in the acquisition of any specific skill. The states they identify form an invariant sequence, and each successor integrates its predecessor. Given such a model, adults do not develop qualitatively beyond the logical operations level but can laterally extend their intellectual powers through acquisition of more skills and knowledge.

Langer, Chanowitz, Palmerino, Jacobs, Rhodes, and Thayer. Langer et al. assert that developmental psychology should focus less on how life ordinarily unfolds and more on how it could possibly change at any time through alteration in underlying style of mental functioning. The authors propose that there are two basic styles of mental orientation, "mindfulness" and "mindlessness." Through the former, one actively constructs new categories about self and world; through the latter, one passively remains within the confines of previously formed distinctions. In their view, shifts in cognitive framework during childhood result from mindful interaction with the environment, but these shifts do not form hard-and-fast stages. The authors agree with McGuinness et al. that (1) general concurrence of age at which children make transitions in logical abilities is due to similarity in rate of accumulation of requisite experience, and (2) there are no overarching developmental stages. However, they do not, as do McGuinness et al., recognize a necessary, hierarchical sequence of states within task domains. From their perspective, mindfulness can come into play at any time in almost unlimited ways, yielding the possibility that human life can (1) leap ahead to a recognized state in a fashion that bypasses supposed intermediary states, (2) reverse direction and move to a previous state, and (3) move from a recognized state into a novel, unexpected state.

Langer et al. propose that stagelike phenomena do not necessarily involve universal cognitive structures as described by Piaget. What appear as stage structures are often actually mindless cognitive response sets. They contend that in a highly mindful mode, there would be frequent shifts to categories and operations other than the currently pervasive ones, allowing more adaptive behavior within specific contexts. They do not believe there is a developmental end state definable in terms of particular capacities. Instead, they hold that the concept "developmentally higher" applies only to a general increase of mindfulness as opposed to mindlessness. Because they postulate an essentially unlimited potential for increase of mindfulness, the current state can always be further transformed. Thus, for them, development is open-ended and, in its specific trajectories, multipathed and multidirectional (cf. Dittmann-Kohli & Baltes). They do recognize that a particular developmental sequence could be fixed, once the goal and path to it have become mindlessly accepted. However, if either the path or goal to it is mindfully modified, so too may be the developmental sequence.

Langer et al. agree with Piaget that disruption of equilibrium is necessary for development, but they believe at a mature level one must consciously and deliberately break it. They suggest that cognitive conflict is typically minimized because of mindless assimilation of experience to preexisting patterns. For them growth is

a process of mindfully breaking out of such molds. The authors hold that although greater mindfulness is potentially available in adulthood, in actuality children tend to be more mindful, because of greater inertial mass of cognitive habits in adults.

Hierarchical Theories of Cognitive Development

Richards and Commons. Richards and Commons focus on the realm of hypothetico-deductive thinking. They argue that formal operational logic is not an adequate model to explain the cognitive processes required for many significant conceptual advances in modern science—as exemplified by Darwin's creation of evolutionary theory and by Piaget's own work in generating his cognitive–developmental theory. The authors assert that formal operational thought cannot produce historical and developmental causal theories because such theories require notions of structure and structural transformation that cannot be generated through formal operations. They posit that this limitation of formal operations is due to the fact that the two causal logics of the formal stage—disjunctive and conjunctive causality—do not function interactively.

In their view, the application of one system of logic to the operations of another with which it previously did not interact is the general mechanism underlying the generation of higher stages of cognitive complexity throughout the course of development. They posit that just as concrete operations yielded formal operations through the integration of the logics of classes and relations, so the integration of the two causal logics of the formal stage yields a qualitatively distinct and higher stage in which (1) structure and transformation can be objects of operations, (2) complete causal systems can be conceptualized, and (3) operations can be iterative (reapplied to themselves).

The authors identify four stages of postformal operations. In the first (systematic), systems supplant propositions as the object of cognitive operations; in the second (metasystematic), the thinker constructs relations between systems; in the third (paradigmatic), the relations between systems come to be recognized as a unified paradigm; in the last (cross-paradigmatic), different paradigms come to be comprehended and related.

Fischer, Kenny, and Pipp. Fischer, Kenny, and Pipp suggest that if Piaget's basic hierarchical model is to be maintained, his theory of stages must be revised. Piaget originally posited that stage transformation in underlying cognitive competence entails synchronous change across domains. According to Fischer et al., although Piaget eventually acknowledged that research does not confirm such change, he revised his theory only minimally, holding that although structures are in principle globally applicable, specific content domains may in fact differentially resist such application. Thus, in Piaget's theory, competence is always present even though not always expressed in performance.

Fischer et al. hypothesize that stagelike shift in "capacity" only provides the potential for constructing a new "optimal level" of competence. Actual competencies only arise through practice in various domains, and they do not exist independently of the various skills that express them—skills that must be "built." It is only under optimal conditions (e.g., favorable environment, familiarity with a domain)

that optimal level is measurably expressed in terms of a spurt in competence or skill, and such circumstances ordinarily do not simultaneously exist for all domains.

Fischer et al. speak of discontinuity in performance primarily in terms of quantitative "spurts" in rate of skill expression. However, they also employ a qualitative criterion of discontinuity: level of skill complexity. The authors believe that skill structures can be hierarchically ordered in terms of complexity, falling within three major tiers—sensorimotor, concrete representations, and abstractions. They state there is empirical support for the position that (1) the emergence of qualitatively distinct skill levels is age dependent and (2) the entire sequence is a logical extension of the most rudimentary sensorimotor skills. In all, they posit four distinct levels within the tier of abstractions: the first (10–12 years) corresponds to the onset of formal operations; the second (14–16 years) corresponds with full competence in formal operations; the third, "abstract systems" (at about 20) is postformal and relates components of one abstraction to those of another; the fourth, "systems of abstract systems" (about 25), integrates two or more abstract systems in terms of some general theory or framework.

The authors appear to distinguish change within stages from change between stages by identifying two forms of complexity. In the first, two skills are combined to form a more complex skill still involving the same general level of capacity. In contrast, during a stage shift, two separate skills are interactively integrated rather than simply compounded (Richards and Commons recognize a similar integration), resulting in a qualitative change in complexity, with dynamic interrelation of skills supplanting their simple, quantitative aggregation. Such qualitative change in complexity cannot occur until a new capacity or optimal level becomes available. According to Fischer et al.'s "brain-growth" hypothesis, biological maturation acts as a major mechanism in the development of such capacity. They note that there appear to be age-linked biological spurts in characteristics such as synaptic density and global EEG pattern that correspond to occurrence of psychological spurts.

Moral Development

Kohlberg and Ryncarz. Kohlberg and Ryncarz postulate that although moral judgment proceeds through a six-stage hierarchical sequence associated with Piagetian logical stages, a level of ethical understanding exists that is both beyond formal operations and beyond linear extrapolation of the progression of prior stages. They hold that although stage progression in moral justice reasoning results from transformations in operational thought structures induced by the press for maximizing equilibrium in moral logic, the development of this final postformal stage involves a level of experience transcendental to operational thought.

They state that even at the highest principled level, justice reasoning is incomplete, because even though it can resolve dilemmas of conflicting rights, it cannot satisfactorily answer the basic question, "Why be moral?" They say that full justification for choosing particular actions and for being moral can only arise from a shift in underlying perspective—a shift from the perspective of the individual to

that of the cosmos as a whole. They propose that some type of transcendental, non-dual experience of unity between self and cosmos is integral in stimulating this shift to a "cosmic" perspective, or a "metaphoric stage 7."

They believe that the process of constructing this expanded world view occurs through self-conscious reflective thinking about transcendental experiences as well as about other distinctive, personal life experiences. Although a cosmic perspective stage may represent a more advanced level than that reached through the operational stage sequence, they believe that it is an "optional" endpoint rather than one toward which intelligence is universally directed. Although it does not improve on the quality of justice the individual can dispense, it does expand the meaningfulness of "being just" and increases the likelihood that one will act in a just manner.

Gilligan, Murphy, and Tappan. Gilligan believes that Kohlberg's theory of moral reasoning even at his highest stage (she does *not* address his "stage 7") may be limited because it deals primarily with one moral orientation (the justice perspective), an orientation in which rights and duties are determined in the abstract through logical operations and the primary motivation is to follow duty and avoid feelings of guilt (Gilligan, 1982). She agrees with Labouvie-Vief (1982, 1990) that formal operations represents a condition of excessive cognitive control of affect, and she theorizes that another important mode exists (the care perspective) in which affect plays a greater role and there is increased sensitivity to the concrete particularities of real-life situations. This latter orientation is not based in abstract reasoning ability, as are Kohlberg's higher justice reasoning stages, and its primary functional affects (such as love or care) are different from those primary in the orientation he describes.

In their chapter, Gilligan, Murphy, and Tappan suggest that the fullest level of moral judgment involves integration of these two perspectives and that progression toward such integration involves postformal cognitive stages beyond Kohlberg's schema. Gilligan et al. argue that moral character matures as one experiences the actual consequences of one's choices in real-life situations and comes to accept responsibility for them. They hold that in the process, one comes to recognize that the clear-cut categories and formulations of abstract formal logic are themselves too abstracted from the contextual complexities of life to serve as the sole basis for judgment. Thus, they state that mature adult morality is gained (1) by recognizing the contextual relativity of our moral knowledge, (2) by transcending primary reliance on formal operational logic and adopting a more dialectical style of thought, and (3) by compassionate commitment to responsible action—action geared to actual consequences.

Gilligan et al. believe that reason and affect become most integrated through this dialectical form of thinking at the highest stage. Yet this integration does not appear to be a state of harmonization. The authors suggest that there is an "irreducible tension" between justice reasoning and caring and that this tension is not transcended at the highest stage but is given freedom to reverberate fully between both poles. Kohlberg also believes that full morality incorporates caring, but his position is that the highest stage of principled justice reasoning does incorporate care.

Thus, both sets of authors hold that neither the commitment to be moral in

general nor the choice to follow a specific moral course can be fully grounded in or justified by reason and that formal operations must be superseded in structuring the highest ethical perspective. However, there are also important differences between them. Kohlberg and Ryncarz describe a process in which the highest level of universality (based in principled justice reasoning) is transcended to reach an even broader cosmic perspective in which one's moral choices are seen as increasingly harmonized with an absolute, objective natural order. Instead, Gilligan et al. speak of an expansion of perspective not in terms of experiencing a transcendental unity but as a recognition of all relevant competing perspectives. In their view, this entails epistemological uncertainty and recognition of the impossibility of aligning one's thought with an external objective moral order. They believe that attempts to maintain universality will, on the level of practical life, ultimately narrow morality rather than fully broaden it, since an approach that relies on universal, formal reasoning cannot adequately integrate caring and other affective factors and will thus be incapable of fluid response to concrete life situations.

Higher Stages of Consciousness and Self Development

Although modern "scientific" psychology arose as an empirical effort to understand consciousness (James, 1890), research soon became restricted to the study of observable behavior (Boring, 1950). Following recent advances in cognitive psychology and neurophysiology, psychologists are rediscovering the critical need for a scientific approach to the study of consciousness (e.g., Miller, 1981; Mandler, 1985; Pribram, 1986a; Sperry, 1987, 1988). Consciousness can be defined in a number of ways (e.g., Hilgard, 1980; Natsoulas, 1983). According to one or more of these definitions, consciousness could be considered a central theme of each chapter in this volume—especially the chapters on moral development by Gilligan et al., and Kohlberg and Ryncarz. However, only the final three chapters explicitly propose general hierarchical stages of consciousness or self development that are said to underlie and connect all other developmental domains—cognitive, affective, and moral.

From our perspective, a holistic theory of development of consciousness would embrace not only an understanding of processes of knowing (e.g., cognitive and moral reasoning) and the objects known (e.g., the physical world and social relations), but also the knower or self. Further, such a theory would not only investigate the knower as reasoner and information processor (i.e., the epistemic self), but also the knower as the locus or source of human consciousness and identity (i.e., the ontological self). The need for such an account is succinctly expressed in a literature review on the self by Markus and Wurf (1987, p. 328)): "The work reviewed here has yet to confront the perennially thorny issue of . . . who is this 'I' that is asking what is this 'me'?" (see Daman & Hart, 1988; Kihlstrom & Kantor, 1984; Kohlberg & Armon, 1984; McAdams, 1988; Mendelsohn, 1987).

Souvaine, Lahey, and Kegan explicitly attempt to identify qualitative changes in the subject–object relationship that underlie growth across several developmental domains. Pascual-Leone further enriches our understanding of the self by drawing upon the insights of the existential–phenomenological tradition of Western philosophy. For both, even at a mature level of development, the self can only be

known indirectly as an object of abstract thought processes (the "me"); indeed, the self is said to be "constructed" through such processes or operations. In contrast, based upon Maharishi's Vedic psychology, Alexander et al. describe higher stages of consciousness in which an inherent (i.e., not constructed) underlying Self can be directly experienced (as the "I" of awareness) without conceptual mediation.

Souvaine, Lahey, and Kegan. Souvaine, Lahey, and Kegan propose hierarchical stages that are much broader than the Piagetian logical stages and are associated with equilibrations of the self. They theorize that "deep structures" underlying cognitive, moral, and ego development are the sequential equilibria of the "living" subject–object relationship. In their approach, the crucial distinction is between the self's principle of organization (its "way of knowing") and that which gets organized. The subject is always embedded within and identified with the organizing principles (the cognitive structures), whereas the object is that which gets organized. They hold that a new stage arises when the subjective pole undergoes differentiation through the de-embedding of the self from the organizing structures. Standing outside of these structures, the self can systematically organize them and render them as objects. However, it can do so only through a higher level of organizing structures within which it in turn becomes embedded.

According to Souvaine et al., formal operations arises when the self acts through hypothetico-deductive structures (the level of the possible) to organize the "actual reversibilities" that had been the nonobjectified, subjective structures of concrete operations. They term such organization the "institutional self" because the self is the administrator of a closed system of self-defined and self-regulated goals. The limitation of this stage is that the self is a "sealed" system and cannot reflect upon and alter its self-selected values and purposes.

A transition in the self–object balance begins as the self, through extensive social interaction, recognizes the limitations of the institutional level. Eventually, a highly equilibrated "interindividual self" can be attained that is ultimately invested in the interaction between systems (viewpoints), each of which is seen as only one part of a larger whole. The self is identified with the motion between all the various systems of interpretation and meaning rather than any given position.

The authors view the basic mechanism of development as resolution of crises of meaning through a de-embedding process, which appears similar to Piaget's "reflective abstraction." However, whereas Piaget viewed conflict resolution through reflective abstraction as essentially an unconscious process, the authors imply that in reflecting upon the limits of the institutional self, one can become volitionally involved in negotiating a fuller equilibrium. Souvaine et al. state that the interindividual self may not be perfectly equilibrated, in which case it would be "vulnerable to adaptation" and the developmental process could continue.

Pascual-Leone. Pascual-Leone proposes that development of the knower has both a universal, nonoptional dimension and an optional one that can unfold during adulthood. He states that the former should be viewed as a stage hierarchy rooted in biological, organismic structures, whereas the latter is based not on the emergence of new biological structures but on the redeployment of those already present.

In Pascual-Leone's theory, although biological development provides the

energy for activation and coordination of schematic structures, it does not in itself cause their transformation. Pascual-Leone is a constructivist in that he believes structures will be transformed only when resistances are encountered that necessitate expenditure of effort in the direction of new accommodation. For him, adult self development is unique in that it is based not on increase in mental capacities, but on their degeneration, which serves as a major resistance that can stimulate structural "remodeling." Accordingly, he believes that the typical transitions in adulthood (as noted by Levinson) can be partially explained as reactions to progressive difficulty in mobilizing mental energy. Moreover, he feels that when inevitable biologically based resistances are coupled with extremely challenging circumstances, the resulting stimulation to the accommodative process can be strong enough to yield stages that transcend the ordinary adult level (see Meacham, 1990).

For Pascual-Leone the main structural changes in adulthood occur through mental effort and "mental macro-decentrations." He states that through such decentration, adults can develop higher modes of consciousness, each associated with a higher level of ego development. In Pascual-Leone's view, the higher ego stages are optional, and for most people the ordinary adult ego structure (which dates from late adolescence) remains unchanged. This is the "phenomenological ego," which is a product of interpersonal interaction. In contrast, he states that the "transcendental ego" ("ultraself") that some adults develop is structured solely in terms of internal interactions (e.g., coping with internal conflicts). The ultraself has four successive levels, each based on the coordination of a qualitatively distinct processing mode with its predecessors.

Pascual-Leone believes that the first transcendental ego structure ("empirical existence") can arise in the late formal period of 17–25 years, and the second ("conceptual existence") can typically develop between 25 and 30, in response to growing awareness of both intra- and interpersonal contradictions. It involves construction of general theories that, by largely ignoring particular variations in experience, allow one to cope with a growing information overload. He states that although the conceptual processing mode is mutually contradictory with its predecessor, both are necessary. Therefore, he sees this new ego structure as a "duality self" in which the two ego structures associated with the disparate processing modes are coordinated while not being directly integrated. This nonintegrated duality gives rise to awareness of contradictions within both world and self.

Pascual-Leone posits that biological decline first plays a significant role in the construction of the next level, which can occur between 35 and 40. A new processing mode arises because (1) there is not enough mental energy to sustain the current usage of the conceptual mode and (2) the conceptual models now appear too idealized and static in light of the dynamic texture of reality. This new mode ("temporal existence") is dialectical and can apprehend patterns of contradictory interacting theories, yielding appreciation of totalities in evolution. Again, Pascual-Leone sees this new mode as "incommensurable and pragmatically contradictory" with the preceding ones and thus views the new ego structure as a nonintegrated coordination of three "partial ultraselves."

Pascual-Leone hypothesizes that development beyond the "trinity self" can occur in response to actual hindrance in "action processing" with further biological decline. In these circumstances, he feels that the processing mode of "transcenden-

tal operations" can come to the fore. These operations involve a form of deep "meditative thinking" in which dialectical operations are performed upon dialectical operations, which means they do not occur during action processing and are directed solely within. This "realized self" level represents the endpoint of development for Pascual-Leone. He calls transcendental operations a "final" mode of processing that "has at last fully coordinated affect and cognition," and past, present, and future. However, the issue of whether this level represents a fully unified whole is left open, since, as with the preceding stages, Pascual-Leone refers to the new structure (the "quaternity self") as a collective that coordinates existing partial selves.

Alexander, Davies, Dixon, Dillbeck, Druker, Oetzel, Muehlman, and Orme-Johnson. Whereas Pascual-Leone's discussion of higher stages is organized around modern Western existentialist philosophies, Alexander et al. base their chapter on the ancient Vedic theory of consciousness as recently formulated by Maharishi Mahesh Yogi (e.g., 1972, 1986). Maharishi's Vedic psychology describes three "higher" stages of consciousness based in a purely transcendental, nonconceptual mode of experience. The authors propose that these stages reflect the natural continuation (and culmination) of the developmental process and constitute a postrepresentational tier of development, differing at least as much from the representational tier (which includes postformal representational processes) as the latter does from the prerepresentational, early sensorimotor period. The authors further propose a life-span developmental model that describes (1) the mental structures underlying commonly observed periods of development as well as the higher stages of consciousness and (2) the mechanisms underlying this developmental sequence.

According to Vedic psychology, the mind is hierarchically structured in layers from concrete to abstract: the faculties of action and sensation, desire, thinking mind (associative faculty), intellect (discriminative faculty), feelings and intuition, and experiencing ego, respectively. Alexander et al. posit that although all mental levels are operative to some degree throughout development, in the process of psychophysiological growth, conscious awareness becomes predominantly centered at each deeper level of mind. Sequential shifts in functioning of awareness through each subtler mental level are said to underlie progressive unfoldment of periods of cognitive development. For example, it is proposed that primary identification of awareness with the faculties of action and sensation gives rise to the sensorimotor period, whereas primary identification with the reflective intellect gives rise to an abstract reasoning period variously described by Piaget, Flavell, Fischer, and others.

Vedic psychology proposes that underlying all these levels is the completely abstract level of "pure consciousness" in which knower, known, and process of knowing converge in one unified field of awareness freed of all content (e.g., percepts, thoughts, and emotions). Stable identification of individual awareness with the field of pure consciousness is said to provide the foundation for development of the first higher stage of consciousness, termed "cosmic consciousness." At this stage the knower can finally know himself directly without representational mediation. This is because pure consciousness is held to be the essential nature of the

"Self"—a "self-referral" field in which consciousness is fully awake to itself. In cosmic consciousness the Self (functioning as a silent observer or "witness") becomes differentiated from all previous representational levels of mind. Alexander et al. suggest that differentiation of the Self in transition to the postrepresentational tier represents the emergence of subject permanence, which is even greater in its significance than emergence of object permanence in the transition from the prerepresentational to the representational tier.

Vedic psychology refers to the next higher stage as "refined cosmic consciousness," since it is said to involve further refinement of perception, which permits appreciation of finer values of the objective world. The final stage, or endpoint of development, is held to be a state of "unity consciousness" in which one experiences every object as an expression of the Self. The unified field of consciousness that was experienced only within oneself in cosmic consciousness comes to be experienced as underlying and permeating all of objective as well as subjective existence.

Alexander et al. propose that the primary mechanism of development is the spontaneous shifting of the locus of conscious awareness to progressively deeper inherent levels of mind. In this view, the stationing of awareness at each deeper mental level results in the increasing dominance and differentiation of a more abstract process of knowing, which allows more comprehensive understanding of the objects to be known. The authors propose that higher stages of consciousness are, in principle, no less "inevitable" than earlier stages: Both develop spontaneously and invariantly, given regular interaction with appropriate environmental support systems. They suggest that just as informal and formal instruction in symbolic systems such as language appears fundamental for development of representational periods, systematic exposure to an appropriate "postlanguage system," such as the Transcendental Meditation (TM) program, may be fundamental to permanent development of postrepresentational higher stages of consciousness.

The repeated process of *fully* transcending to the silent state of pure consciousness during TM is said to (1) normalize the nervous system, progressively freeing it from deep-rooted stresses that block development; (2) lead simultaneously to a major functional reorganization of brain processes; and thus (3) "unfreeze" psychophysiological development, which otherwise typically becomes arrested in adolescence or early adulthood.

Concluding Comparative Analysis of Positions on Major Issues

Mechanisms

Although a number of contributors posit novel stages beyond formal operations, often the primary mechanism proposed for generating higher stages does not depart substantially from Piaget's equilibrative mechanism. Unlike Piaget, however, they suggest that formal operations involves constraints that create further disequilibrium, leading to generation of still more equilibrated postformal structures. Other contributors emphasize additional developmental factors described to some degree by Piaget, or introduce entirely new mechanisms to account for adult development.

The various developmental mechanisms proposed in this volume are summarized in Table I.2.

Broadening of Equilibration. For Richards and Commons, as cognitive objects become more complex, the limitations of formal operations become increasingly salient. They suggest that through the equilibrative process, seemingly incompatible operations (i.e., the logics of conjunctive and disjunctive causality) come to be coordinated at the postformal level. To accommodate the unique demands of adult life, Gilligan et al. and Souvaine et al. further suggest that the equilibrative process can broaden to encompass affective and social processes.

Existential Experience and Self-Reflective Thought. According to Pascual-Leone, such structural change in adulthood represents an optional developmental track contingent upon self-reflective response to existential "limit situations" (e.g., loss of capacity). Kohlberg and Ryncarz hold that such adult growth is less structural and universal in nature because it results from a "metamode" of self-conscious reflection upon unique, existential life experiences rather than from the (largely unconscious) "primary mode" of equilibration responsible for universal structural stage change in childhood. Levinson also recognizes the contribution of existential experience (e.g., "mid-life crisis") to adult growth but does not posit more advanced developmental stages as a consequence.

From the perspective of Langer et al., existential dilemmas may stimulate development because they provoke "mindfulness"—a self-directive style of mentation through which new categories about self and world are actively constructed. According to Langer et al., what appear as increasingly stable developmental stages may result more from "mindless" adherence to previously formed distinctions than from an inevitable trend toward increased equilibrium. For Langer et al., the structure and direction of development are largely conditioned by mental presupposition and are alterable through mindfulness.

Skill Building. For Piaget, equilibration takes place both on a microlevel, in adjustment to each environmental event, and eventually on a macrolevel, through construction of higher, global developmental stages. McGuinness et al. agree that microdevelopment proceeds through an equilibrative process. They introduce a "continuous state transformational" model to describe a microgenetic sequence through which any specific skill is acquired. Consistent with the information-processing approach, however, they argue that this equilibrative sequence is applied anew in each domain that one enters, whether in childhood or adulthood. Thus, global, macrodevelopmental stages would not be constructed across skill domains. Whereas Fischer et al. posit that the *general* capacity to learn skills develops through a more discontinuous stage sequence, they also recognize that actual change in *specific* skills occurs through a more continuous microdevelopmental sequence described by "transformation rules."

Biological Factors and Inherent Mental Faculties. According to Flavell (1970), adult change does not display the "morphogenetic-type" qualitative features of

Table I.2 Proposed Mechanisms of Development

Piagetian Mechanisms (Childhood Only)	Extended or Additional Mechanisms (Childhood and/or Adulthood)
Biological factors. Set broad limits on cognitive development; primitive behavioral reflexes are the only directly innate antecedents of intelligence	*Inherent mental faculties corresponding to biological structures.* "Hardware operators" (Pascual-Leone); "Levels of the mind" (Alexander et al.); shift in "optimal level" of cognitive capacity (Fischer et al.)
Physical experience. Extraction or "simple" abstraction of features from environment	*Skill building.* Steps of skill development described by "continuous state transformation model" (McGuiness et al.); steps described by "transformation rules" (Fischer et al.); "waves of symbolization" in mastering symbolic skills (Gardner et al.)
Logico-mathematical experience and reflective abstraction. Knowledge acquired through "reflective" abstraction upon one's actions rather than through direct physical experiences	*Non-logico-mathematical modes of intelligence.* "Narrative thought, visual-spatial thinking, body-kinesthetic activity, musical understanding," and "creative processes" (Gardner et al.); "pragmatic" or "synthetic" intelligence (Dittmann-Kohli & Baltes); "caring orientation" (Gilligan, et al.); and "self-referral" process (Alexander et al.)
	Existential experience and self-reflective thought. Confronting existential "limit" situations through modes of "self-awareness" (Pascual-Leone); increased understanding of self and world through reflection on specific life experiences (Kohlberg & Ryncarz, Gilligan et al., Souvaine et al., Dittmann-Kohli & Baltes, Levinson); "mindfulness" (Langer et al.)
	Transcendental experience. Identification of awareness with "unified field of pure consciousness" (Alexander et al.); "nondual experience" (Kohlberg & Ryncarz)
Social Transmission. Influence of culturally transmitted information on development (including language and education)	*Symbolic–cultural environment.* "Symbol systems," including nonlinguistic systems such as play and music (Gardner et al.); "social–cultural world" (Levinson); technology of consciousness to "transcend" mental (symbolic) activity (Alexander et al.)
Equilibration. Primary mechanism integrating effects of other factors. Through "assimilation," and "accommodation," cognitive structures are dynamically adapted to the environment and cognitive conflict is reduced	*Expanded equilibration.** (1) Applied to more abstract cognitive objects (Richards & Commons, Fischer et al.), (2) also integrates self, affective, and social processes (Gilligan et al., Souvaine et al., Pascual-Leone)

*Only includes theories that explicitly describe higher stages of equilibrium.

child development primarily because biological growth stops relatively early in the life cycle. Even Piaget recognized the necessary role of biological factors in development. Thus, in the absence of further biological maturation, "momentous" stagelike change in adult development would appear difficult to achieve. This position is implicit in the chapters by McGuinness et al., Dittmann-Kohli and Baltes,

and Levinson, since they do not identify a major impetus for changing fundamental cognitive capacity in adulthood.

While apparently recognizing the role of biological factors in child development, Gilligan et al. and Souvaine et al. do not discuss their contribution to adult growth. They apparently presume that the demands of adult life are sufficiently great to stimulate further equilibration and that such change does not exceed the limits of available biological resources. Also these researchers may feel that there is insufficient information on child, let alone adult, biological development to include this consideration in their theories. For this reason Richards and Commons propose a formal model of cognitive development that explicitly requires minimal assumptions about the contribution of biological factors at any level.

In contrast, Fischer et al. and Pascual-Leone identify the organism as a biologically constrained information-processing system. They seek to locate biological correlates for age-linked changes in fundamental cognitive competence at every proposed stage of development. Fischer et al. explore possible neurophysiological changes in early adulthood that may correspond to shifts in "optimal level" necessary for postformal stages. Pascual-Leone posits cognitive "hardware operators" based in biological structures that expand in capacity at every stage through early adulthood. He views subsequent biological decline not as a restriction on growth but as a potential catalyst for further ego development.

Alexander et al. propose that the primary mechanism of development is not resolution of conflict through cognitive construction, but rather spontaneous shifting of functional awareness to deeper, inherent "levels of mind" (Maharishi, 1969) in the course of psychophysiological development. In contrast to the prevailing view, they posit that, under appropriate conditions, major psychophysiological development can continue in adulthood.

Transcendental Experience. Alexander et al. propose that repeated transcendental experience of a nonrepresentational unified field of consciousness, underlying the levels of mind, leads to a major functional reorganization of the brain necessary for development of stable higher stages of consciousness.

Kohlberg and Ryncarz also believe that "nondual" experience of unity between self and world, can play a significant role in postformal development. They suggest that even infrequent transcendental experiences can create a type of disequilibrium which induces construction of a new world view based on adoption of a "cosmic" rather than an individual perspective. This new view, however, is said to be primarily structured not through transcending representation, but through reflective thought about these and other distinctive life experiences. Construction of this new world view does not appear to require major physiological change. For Pascual-Leone "transcendental operations" generally refer to second-order dialectical thought processes that do not fully transcend the duality of thinker and thought.

Symbolic/Cultural Environment. Although allowing for the role of "social transmission" in development, Piaget may have substantially underestimated the contribution of such "cultural amplifiers" as language (Bruner, 1972) to conceptual development, especially in its later phases (see Flavell, 1971a; Vygotsky, 1962). Similarly, Gardner et al. emphasize the fundamental contribution of other "symbol

systems" (e.g., in music and art) to the development of non–logico-mathematical forms of intelligence and to the creative process in general. Finally, Alexander et al. suggest that systematic exposure to a technology of consciousness for "transcending" mental (symbolic) activity may be as fundamental to postrepresentational development as language learning is to representational development.

Stage and Endpoint

Each hierarchical model in this volume proposes stages that go beyond the constraints of the formal operational endpoint.

Constraints of Formal Operations. There appears to be increasing differentiation in development from the initial symbiosis of the newborn to the detached analytical reasoning of the formal operator, for whom a "maximal distance between the thinker and the thought" is achieved (Cook-Greuter, 1990). Although the formal operator gains in analytic power and objectivity of thought, it is apparently at the price of isolation from the world and himself. The self has become one more "object" to be reflected upon but cannot be directly known (Alexander et al.; Broughton, 1984). At this stage, concrete particulars become subordinate to abstract rules that organize them (Souvaine et al.). The individual attempts to hold an internally consistent theory about self and world, and conceptual or affective uncertainty is avoided (Gilligan et al.; Labouvie-Vief, 1982b).

Postformal Representational Stages of Development. Proposed postformal stages may foster a reintegration of the knower and the known through increased self-understanding, affective processes, sensitivity to context, and care and commitment in the world (Gilligan et al., Pascual-Leone, Souvaine et al.) Other theories, although not specifying hierarchical stages, also hold that similar qualitative changes can take place in adulthood—in the form of increased "pragmatic intelligence" and "wisdom" (Dittmann-Kohli & Baltes), "mindfulness" (Langer et al.), and "individuation" (Levinson).

Just as with formal operations, it appears that postformal operations can be divided into phases of acquisition. Labouvie-Vief (1981) proposed that early formal operations are characterized by "divergent production" of hypothetico-deductive ideas, whereas late formal operations involve "convergent thinking" in which such ideas are put to empirical test. More recently, Kramer (1983; cf. 1989, 1990) suggests similar phases in the acquisition of postformal operational thinking. Kramer identifies three general features of postformal operational thought, which may be viewed as possible steps through which the constraints associated with formal operations can be overcome. This three-phase process would involve one step of divergent thinking followed by two steps of convergent thinking:

1. Relativism (divergent thinking): recognition that one's personal perspective constitutes only one of many potentially valid viewpoints on reality (cf. Perry, 1970).
2. Acceptance of contradiction (first phase of convergent thinking): realization that contradiction, complexity, and dynamic flux may be inherent features

of reality that cannot be resolved simply by discarding opposing viewpoints; tolerance is gained through an appreciation of the "dialectic" relation between opposing systems.

3. Integration (final phase of convergent thinking): a synthetic form of thinking is evolved that integrates several opposing systems into an abstract whole that contains all particulars.

Although these three steps form a logical sequence, whether they temporally unfold in discrete hierarchical stages is an empirical question.

The various postformal stage sequences described in this volume are summarized in Table I.3 in relation to Kramer's three proposed features of postformal thought. Gilligan et al. and Souvaine et al. appear to collapse these three processes into one description of the growth and stabilization of a single postformal stage. Fischer et al. identify two stages, the second combining the two steps of the converging process. Pascual-Leone differentiates all three processes into distinct stages in the acquisition of postformal thinking. Richards and Commons also appear to describe the three steps, and in addition, divide the final convergent step into two phases of integration. Alternatively, it may be that the three-stage postformal models are not simply making a finer, temporal discrimination in the sequential development of convergent thought but are locating an additional distinctively higher-order thinking process not identified in the two and one stage models (e.g., Pascual-Leone describes his transcendental operations as dialectical operations to the second degree). This possibility awaits further empirical demonstration. Note that although there are interesting parallels among the various developmental models, there are also differences, and we do not mean to imply that they are formally equivalent. (See Richards & Commons for their version of a table summarizing development from concrete through postformal operations as described by a number of theorists.)

Advanced cognitive stages described by Richards and Commons and Fischer et al. are "postformal" in the *specific* sense that they propose more elaborate mental operations than those represented in Piaget's 16 binary operations and INRC group models. However, they do not appear to describe stages that go beyond formal thought in its *broad* definition. Piaget referred to his highest stage as "formal" to denote the capacity to reason with form abstracted from concrete content—to operate on propositions not only singly, but also interpropositionally. As Richards and Commons suggest, their postformal stages are still hypothetico-deductive and meant to accomplish the same functions as formal cognition, but involve patterns and objects of thought that are held to be more complex. Similarly, Fischer et al. describe their postformal stages in terms of increasingly abstract conceptual processes that complete the "tier of abstraction" begun with early formal operations. Thus, although such stages are postformal in the strict sense, they are clearly not postpropositional or postrepresentational.

On the other hand, those such as Gilligan et al. and Souvaine et al., who emphasize the growth of contextualism in adult thought, imply that concern with particularities of context render this form of thought nonformal, even in a broad sense. Yet Inhelder and Piaget (1958) state that formal operations also become more attuned to context in response to adult experience. If contextual thought is at basis

Table I.3 Proposed Stages of Adult Development Beyond Formal Operations

Theorist	Postformal Representational Stages			Postrepresentational Stages
Kramer (1983; cf. 1989, 1990)	Relativism (divergent thinking)	Acceptance of contradiction: dialectic	Integration: Synthesis	
		(convergent thinking)*		
Gilligan, Murphy, & Tappen	Transitional relativism	Commitment within contextual relativism stage		
Souvaine, Lahey, & Kegan	Transitional self-system	Interindividual self stage		
Fischer, Kenny, & Pipp	Abstract systems (relating two subdivided sets)	Systems of abstract systems		
Richards & Commons	Systematic stage	Metasystematic stage (relation between systems)	Paradigmatic stage (metasystems unified in paradigm)† Cross-paradigmatic stage	
Pascual-Leone	Predialectical operations stage	Dialectical operations stage	Transcendental operations stage† (Culminating in a realized self)‡	
Kohlberg & Ryncarz	Subjective relativism transition	Social contract legalistic stage	Universal ethical principles stage† Cosmic perspective stage‡	
Alexander et al. (based on Vedic psychology)	Development and integration of intellect, feeling, and ego			Three higher stages of consciousness

*Although she identifies the processes of both contradiction and integration, Kramer (1983) does not appear explicitly to divide the development of convergent thinking into two temporal steps.

†The third stage represents either a finer temporal differentiation within the development of "convergent thinking" or a distinctly higher-order thought process than that described in two-stage models.

‡Although temporary transcendental (i.e., postrepresentational) experience is considered a possible feature of this level, this stage is still based in representational processes.

still an interpropositional mode (although grounded in a looser logic than formal operations), then it would also still be "formal" in a broad sense. Consistent with this position, Richards and Commons (as well as Kramer, 1983) place relativistic-dialectical stages parallel to their postformal stages of cognitive development.

Proposed Postrepresentational Stages of Development. In contrast to Gilligan et al., Alexander et al., based upon Vedic psychology, propose a postrepresentational tier of "higher stages of consciousness" as qualitatively distinct from the representational tier (from preoperational through postformal representational stages) as rep-

resentation is from the sensorimotor domain. They suggest that to label such higher consciousness stages as "mystical" is a misnomer, for they "transcend" the representational domain in no more mystical way than the representational transcends the sensorimotor.

Just as the semiotic or symbolic processing mode of the representational tier supersedes the earlier sensorimotor mode, they suggest that an entirely new processing mode is introduced at the postrepresentational level. This "self-referral" mode is said to permit consciousness to (1) know itself directly without symbolic mediation and (2) de-embed from and integrate all previous, representational levels of mind.

Interestingly, this tier is also comprised of three stages that appear to follow a pattern of divergent and then convergent growth. In the first stage, the unified self-referral state of consciousness is experienced as transcendental to (divergent from) the other levels of mind and environment. The latter two stages provide first a virtual and then a complete convergence (or unification) of this self-referral state of consciousness with all levels of mind and environment. In the final stage the transcendental unified field is said to be experienced as underlying and pervading all aspects of both subjective and objective existence.

The "cosmic perspective" stage proposed by Kohlberg and Ryncarz, although not postrepresentational, might be transitional to the postrepresentational tier because it is constructed through representational thought about temporary transcendental experience. Similarly, Pascual-Leone recognizes the possibility for genuine transcendental experience as another possible object to be reflected upon at his highest representational stage. Other developmental theorists have also begun to recognize the potential for transcendental experience but have typically posited only a single stage rather than identifying sequential stages of increasing unification (e.g., Cook-Greuter, 1989; Koplowitz, 1984, 1990; for exceptions see Wilber, Engler, & Brown, 1986).

Meeting Criteria for Postformal Operational Stage Development

Are proposed postformal stages truly qualitatively distinct from formal operations? Kramer (1983) asserts that genuine postformal stages should satisfy three criteria of structural change: (1) greater abstraction of thought than in formal operations, (2) hierarchical integration of formal operations, and (3) broader equilibrium (see Piaget, 1971a; Inhelder & Piaget, 1958). We will briefly examine proposed postformal theories in this volume in relation to these criteria.

Abstraction. Kramer identifies two main features of increased abstractness of thought: (1) greater inclusiveness and (2) increased number of processing loops beyond immediate perception. Postformal modes described in this volume display these features, since they are said to include formal operations and to be "third-order" operations, which act upon second-order formal operations, thus involving an additional processing loop (or loops). However, Kramer states that these two characteristics alone are inadequate to demarcate structural change because one could always envision further orders of operations ad infinitum. She says that without specifying an additional type of change, a change in *kind* of thought, this prob-

lem of infinite regress renders vacuous the concept of structural change through mere increase of abstractness. Structural change must be gauged in qualitative terms and not simply reduced to quantitative change in number of processing loops and degree of inclusiveness.

It may be helpful to identify two different dimensions of abstraction: horizontal and vertical. Thought becomes increasingly abstract in the *horizontal* direction as number of processing loops increases and objects of thought become more abstract (inclusive), yet underlying mode of thinking remains qualitatively the same. Formal operations are said to be self-reflexive and capable of operating on propositions to render increasingly abstract propositions. This makes possible the generation of additional processing loops and more inclusive thought while horizontally remaining within the formal level because one can in principle always take a standpoint upon one's current standpoint (Fourcher, 1981; Miller, Kessel, & Flavell, 1970). Progressive looping in this direction would most likely soon result in cumbersome and maladaptive thought (see Fischer et al., 1984). It is only when increased abstraction involves qualitative change in mode of thinking with each new processing loop that it would be in the *vertical* direction.

To meet this criterion, cognitive models such as those of Richards and Commons and Fischer et al. must demonstrate empirically as well as conceptually that the difference between propositions and systems of propositions as objects is as qualitatively distinct as the difference between abstract propositions and concrete representations. It must be shown that this increase in inclusiveness of thought is not just a horizontal increase generated through formal operations but involves new processing capacities. Richards and Commons and Fischer et al. do specifically predict qualitative change through intercoordination of previously independent logics or skills, and they are engaged in testing their respective models (e.g., Commons, Richards, & Kuhn, 1982; Demetriou & Efklides, 1985; Fischer, Pipp, & Bullock, 1984; Fischer, Kenny, & Rose, 1987; Richards & Commons, 1990).

Several thinkers (Gilligan et al., Pascual-Leone, Souvaine et al.) propose that relativistic and/or dialectical thought may also involve new processing modes. However, Kramer (1983) states that it has yet to be conclusively demonstrated that formal operations cannot account for both these processes. She suggests that the main distinctions between these two types of mentation may lie more in their underlying epistemological assumptions than in the operations employed, with postformal thought resting in a world-view based on change and interdependence of variables and formal thought in a view based on stability and independence of variables. For promising research, however, on the potential postformal status of dialectical operations, see Basseches (1984a,b), Benack & Basseches (1989); Kramer & Woodruff (1986); Kramer (1989, 1990).

Hierarchical Integration. If a more abstract and qualitatively distinct mode of functioning can be identified and if this mode can be shown to reintegrate its predecessor, then the conditions for hierarchical integration are satisfied. When focus is on qualitative change in processing mode, researchers may be more likely to seek biological correlates for such change. In this regard, Flavell (1984) has cautioned against information-processing approaches decontextualized from biological factors, since he feels the organism conditions the nature of cognitive development

and sets limits to it. Infinite regress or developmental open-endedness could only exist in the vertical direction if either cognitive–structural change is not necessarily linked with physiological growth or physiological development is itself open-ended.

Those hierarchical theories that recognize a close connection between cognitive and biological development (Fischer et al., Alexander et al., Pascual-Leone) do propose endpoints in their developmental schemes. Although Souvaine et al. emphasize that the deep structures are the various subject–object relationships, they do not necessarily link them with physiological structure. Further, they appear to accept the possibility of developmental open-endedness due to their assumptions that (1) development may continue short of full equilibrium and (2) full equilibrium may not be reachable, since the self does not appear to know its current status fully or directly, nor the level of processing principles through which it knows objects. Langer et al., although they do not accept the notion of hierarchical stages, also recognize the possibility for open-ended qualitative shifts. They believe that the "mindful" mind can adopt new mental patterns that entail corresponding spontaneous reorganization on the physiological level.

There also remains the possibility that, although qualitative difference exists between specific forms of advanced adult thought and formal operations, proposed adult stages are not genuinely structural in a Piagetian sense. According to Kohlberg and Ryncarz, adult stages are "soft" stages built out of individual philosophies of life based on unique circumstances and do not hierarchically integrate formal operations.

In addition to the foregoing requirements for identifying hierarchical stages beyond formal operations, Flavell (1985) draws an empirical distinction that, if valid, poses even more rigorous standards. He asserts that evidence tends to weigh against Piaget's theory that the representational phase of development can be clearly divided into discrete hierarchical stages from preoperations through formal operations. He states that there may be only one major developmental discontinuity: the shift between sensorimotor and representational processes. If this is the case, then a major shift beyond formal operations would have to be as distinctive as the shift from the prerepresentational to the representational level.

In principle, Alexander et al.'s proposed tier of postrepresentational stages would meet such a criterion. They are said to be based in a totally new nonrepresentational "self-referral" processing mode that hierarchically integrates prior modes, enhances adaptive capacity, and involves major neurophysiological transformation. An extensive research program is under way to test these predictions derived from Vedic psychology (Maharishi, 1986): see reviews by Alexander, Boyer, & Alexander, 1987; Alexander & Boyer, 1989; Alexander et al., 1987; Dillbeck, 1983b; Dillbeck & Orme-Johnson, 1987; Orme-Johnson, 1988a,b).

Breadth of Equilibrium. Several postformal theorists posit that their higher stages achieve a broader equilibrium than formal operations. Some (e.g., Richards & Commons) focus on the cognitive domain, proposing that integration of apparently opposing logics yields greater equilibrium and power of thought. Others (e.g., Gilligan et al., Souvaine et al.) hypothesize that the formal operator cannot adequately integrate (1) affect with cognition, (2) internal self processes, and (3) self with environment; and they propose that more encompassing equilibria are reached through

postformal development. Dittmann-Kohli and Baltes emphasize how the development of wisdom integrates cognitive, affective, and self factors.

Because Piaget's portrait of the formal operational level emphasizes analytical reasoning in the context of scientific problem solving, it may be his description of formal operations that is too narrow rather than the actual style of functioning of the formal operator. Thus, it cannot be assumed that a person will have inadequately developed affective and social qualities simply because he or she functions at the formal operational level.

Concluding Observations

Many of the authors who delineate postformal stages agree about several of their main features, and it has been suggested (e.g., by Richards & Commons) that the alignment among these descriptions may reflect the universality of the underlying stages being described. However, it has yet to be demonstrated that an individual meeting developmental criteria for one proposed stage necessarily expresses the characteristics integral to the corresponding stages of the other theorists. For example, does capacity to reason about systems of systems on the level of abstract thought necessarily coexist with greater affective and self integration? This issue, as do many others raised by the expansive theorizing contained in this volume, promises to stimulate new directions and levels of developmental research.

One summary generalization can be safely made: Virtually all contributors agree that an understanding of adolescent development does not provide an adequate base for comprehending the breadth, depth, and richness of potential development in adulthood. Further conceptual clarification and research on the nature of development beyond formal operations should lead to significant revision of our understanding of the possibilities for fully "mature" forms of human growth. Ultimately, how we conceive of the endpoint of development will not only influence the direction of our research agendas but either restrict or encourage our own personal development as well.

I

NONHIERARCHICAL THEORIES
OF ADULT GROWTH

1

A Theory of Life Structure Development in Adulthood

Daniel J. Levinson

Until recently, it was taken for granted that the terms *human development* and *developmental psychology* referred to childhood and adolescence, roughly the first 20 years of life. Even today, when many psychologists apparently believe that development is a life-long matter, the Division of Developmental Psychology of the American Psychological Association still deals primarily with the preadult years. Research on the other end of the life cycle has been identified as the domain of gerontology—the study of the old and of the process of aging. In short, "development" has been associated traditionally with childhood, "aging" with the elderly. We have no division that focuses on the intervening years from roughly age 20 to 65, no consensus on the general character of "development" and "aging" within adulthood, and few examples of a developmental perspective on adulthood.

Adult development is beginning to establish itself as a defined field within psychology and the other human sciences, but its legitimacy is still uncertain. It does not yet have an established place within the structure of most psychology departments. It exists in the APA as an appendage to the Division on Aging and as an informal extension of the Division of (Child) Developmental Psychology. It is not specified as a funding category by government agencies or private foundations. There is no journal devoted primarily to this topic, no organized constituency of investigators, no integrated body of theory and research. There is probably not more than a handful of mature investigators for whom it is a major research interest.

Yet adult development is an idea whose time has come. The reasons lie primarily in the character of modern society. Increasing longevity has brought a rapid and continuing increase in the relative size of the adult population in the 40–65 age range. Major advances have been made in education, technology, and occupational specialization. Nations are becoming increasingly interdependent. As a result, adults are required to know more, to acquire progressively greater responsibility and judgment, to become more universal in outlook, to live in a world different from that of their parents—in short, to continue the process of psychosocial growth well beyond the level reached in adolescence. Society requires higher levels of adult development but is not yet very effective in fostering it. Greater understanding of the developmental process in adulthood is necessary if we are to make our institutions more humane and to reduce individual suffering.

In the last 20 years the idea of adult development has generated wide interest in the public mind and the mass media. It is increasingly represented in novels, plays, biographies, and other serious artistic–humanistic works. More and more academic programs are concerned with "life-span developmental psychology," and a growing number of graduate students and younger faculty members are eager to study adult development. Various fields of psychology (not only child development and gerontology but also personality, social, community, clinical, and counseling), as well as the social sciences and humanities, are becoming more aware that they need—and lack—an adult development perspective.

The seminal writings of Erik Erikson (1950, 1958, 1969) stimulated the human sciences to consider the importance of adult development. Erikson's most obvious contribution was his theory of stages in ego development. Less obvious is his view of development as being deeply grounded in his conceptions of the life cycle and the life course. Each ego stage has its primacy at a particular age level or segment of the life cycle, from infancy to old age. The sequence of age segments and ego stages thus provides a representation of the life cycle as a whole; the meaning of a stage is defined in part by its place in the total sequence. In addition, Erikson's developmental concepts arise out of his primary concern with the individual life course: the process of living, the idea of life history rather than case history, the use of biography rather than therapy or testing as his chief research method. Without abandoning the distinction between self (psyche, personality, inner world) and external world (society, culture, institutions, history), he gave first consideration to the life course—the engagement of self with world. It is time to build upon the landmark work of Erikson and establish an empirically informed theory of adult development that is rooted in a conception of the entire life cycle. New theory should draw upon the various relevant sciences as well as the humanities.

This chapter deals mainly with my conception of adulthood and of a developmental process within it. The theory originated in my initial study of men's lives (Levinson, 1977, 1978). It has evolved over the last few years, particularly through my current research on women's lives (Levinson, in press). It is supported by a number of other studies (e.g., Erlich, 1984; Filene, 1985; Gooden, 1980; Herbert, 1985; Holt, 1980; Kellerman, 1975; Levinson, 1984; Newton, 1984; Roberts & Newton, 1987; Ruffin, 1984; Stewart, 1976; Taylor, 1981); but a great deal must yet be done to test and modify it. I will discuss the following:

1. The concepts of *life course* and *life cycle,* which provide a framework for the field of adult development. Within this framework, studies of one process or age level can be connected to others; without it, we have a miscellany of findings and no integrated domain of inquiry.
2. The concept of the *individual life structure,* which includes many aspects of personality and of the external world but is not identical with any of these and evolves in its own distinctive way.
3. A conception of *adult life structure development* in early and middle adulthood. Life structure development is different from, and should not be confused with, the development of personality, social roles, or other commonly studied processes.

4. The concept of transition in its general sense and of transitional periods in life structure development.
5. Finally, I will briefly compare my theoretical approach to the approaches taken by other contributors to this volume. My nonhierarchical theory of adult development can, I believe, usefully be integrated with hierarchical theories.

The Life Course

Life course is one of the most important yet least examined terms in the human sciences. It is a descriptive term, not a high-level abstraction, and it refers to the concrete character of a life in its evolution from beginning to end. Both words in this term require careful attention.

The word *course* indicates sequence, temporal flow, the need to study a life as it unfolds over the years. To study the course of a life, one must take account of stability and change, continuity and discontinuity, orderly progression as well as stasis and chaotic fluctuation. It is not enough to focus solely on a single moment, nor is it enough to study a series of three or four moments widely separated in time, as is ordinarily done in longitudinal research. It is necessary, in Robert White's (1952) felicitous phrase, to examine "lives in progress" and to follow the temporal sequence in detail over a span of years.

The word *life* is also of crucial importance. Research on the life course must include all aspects of living: inner wishes and fantasies; love relationships; participation in family, work, and other social systems; bodily changes; good times and bad—everything that has significance in a life. To study the life course, it is necessary first to look at a life in all its complexity at a given time, to include all its components and their interweaving into a partially integrated pattern. Second, one must delineate the evolution of this pattern over time.

The study of the life course has presented almost insuperable problems to the human sciences as they are now constituted. Each discipline has claimed as its special domain one aspect of life, such as personality, social role, or biological functioning, and has neglected the others. Every discipline has split the life course into disparate segments, such as childhood or old age. Research has been done from such diverse theoretical perspectives as biological aging, moral development, career development, adult socialization, enculturation, and adaptation to loss or stress, with minimal recognition of their interconnections. The resulting fragmentation is so great that no discipline or viewpoint conveys the sense of an individual life and its temporal course.

The recognition is slowly dawning that the many specialties and theoretical approaches are not isolated entities but aspects of a single field: the study of the individual life course. This study is emerging as a new multidisciplinary field in the human sciences, linking the various disciplines. With the formation of a more comprehensive, systematic conception of the life course, the parts will become less isolated and each part will enrich the others.

The Life Cycle

The idea of the life cycle goes beyond that of the life course. In its origin this idea is metaphorical, not descriptive or conceptual. It is useful to keep the primary imagery while moving toward more precise conceptualization and study. The imagery of "cycle" suggests that there is an underlying order in the human life course; although each individual life is unique, everyone goes through the same basic sequence. The course of a life is not a simple, continuous process. There are qualitatively different phases or seasons. The metaphor of seasons appears in many contexts. There are seasons in the year. Spring is a time of blossoming, and poets allude to youth as the springtime of the life cycle. Summer is the season of greatest passion and ripeness. An elderly ruler is "the lion in winter." There are seasons within a single day—dawn, noon, twilight, the full dark of night—each having its counterpart in the life cycle. There are seasons in love, war, politics, artistic creation, and illness.

The imagery of the life cycle thus suggests that the life course evolves through a sequence of definable forms. A season is a major segment of the total cycle. Change goes on within each season, and a transition is required for the shift from one to the next. Every season has its own time, although it is part of and colored by the whole. No season is better or more important than any other. Each has its necessary place and contributes its special character to the whole.

What are the major seasons in the life cycle? Neither popular culture nor the human sciences provide a clear answer to this question. The modern world has no established conception—scientific, philosophical, religious, or literary—of the life cycle as a whole and of its component phases. There is no standard language that demarcates and identifies several gross segments of the life cycle. The predominant view, rarely stated explicitly, divides it into three parts: (1) an initial segment of about 20 years, including childhood and adolescence (preadulthood); (2) a final segment starting at around 65 (old age); and (3) the period between these segments, an amorphous time vaguely known as adulthood.

A good deal is known about the preadult years, which for a century have been the main province of the field of human development. The developmental perspective has been crucial here. The idea is now accepted that in the first 20 years or so all human beings go through an underlying sequence of periods—prenatal, infancy, early childhood, middle childhood, pubescence, and adolescence. Although all children go through common developmental periods, they grow in infinitely varied ways as a result of differences in biological, psychological, and social conditions. In its concrete form, each individual life course is unique. The study of preadult development seeks to determine the universal order and the general developmental principles that govern the process by which human lives become increasingly individualized.

Historically, the great figures in the study of child development, such as Freud and Piaget, have assumed that development is largely completed at the end of adolescence. Given these assumptions, they had no basis for concerning themselves with the possibilities of adult development or with the nature of the life cycle as a whole. An impetus to change came in the 1950s, when geriatrics and gerontology were established as fields of human service and research. Unfortunately, gerontol-

ogy has not gone far in developing a conception of the life cycle. One reason perhaps is that it skipped from childhood to old age without examining the intervening adult years. Our understanding of old age will be enhanced when more is known about adulthood, so that old age can be connected more firmly to the earlier seasons.

There is now very little theory, research, or cultural wisdom about adulthood as a season (or seasons) of the life cycle. We have no popular language to describe a series of age levels after adolescence. Words such as *youth, maturity,* and *middle age* are ambiguous in their age linkages and meanings. The ambiguity of language stems from the lack of any cultural definition of adulthood and how people's lives evolve within it. In the human sciences too we have no adequate conception of the nature of adulthood. We have a detailed picture of many trees but no view of the forest and no map to guide our journey through it.

My own view of the life cycle derives from my research and draws upon the work of earlier investigators such as Erikson (1950, 1969), Jung (1961), Neugarten (1968a), Ortega y Gasset (1958), and van Gennep (1960). (For a fuller review, see Levinson & Gooden, 1985.)

Eras: The Macrostructure of the Life Cycle

I conceive of the life cycle as a sequence of *eras.* Each era has its own biopsychosocial character, and each makes its distinctive contribution to the whole. There are major changes in the nature of our lives from one era to the next, and lesser, though still crucial changes within eras. They are partially overlapping: A new era begins as the previous one is approaching its end. A *cross-era transition,* which generally lasts about five years, terminates the outgoing era and initiates the next. The eras and the cross-era transitional periods form the macrostructure of the life cycle, providing an underlying order in the flow of all human lives yet permitting exquisite variations in the individual life course. Each era and developmental period begins and ends at a well-defined modal age, with a range of about two years above and below this average.

The first era, *preadulthood,* extends from conception to roughly age 22. During these "formative years" the individual grows from highly dependent, undifferentiated infancy through childhood and adolescence to the beginnings of a more independent, responsible adult life. It is the era of most rapid biopsychosocial growth. The first few years of life provide a transition into childhood. During this time the neonate becomes biologically and psychologically separate from the mother and establishes the initial distinction between the "me" and the "not me"—the first step in a continuing process of individuation.

The years from about 17 to 22 constitute the *Early Adult Transition,* a developmental period in which preadulthood draws to a close and the era of early adulthood gets under way. It is thus part of both eras, and not fully a part of either. A new step in individuation is taken as the budding adult modifies her or his relationships with family and other components of the preadult world and begins to form a place as an adult in the adult world. From a childhood-centered perspective, one can say that development is now largely completed and the child has gained

maturity as an adult. The field of developmental (i.e., child) psychology has traditionally taken this view. Taking the perspective of the life cycle as a whole, however, we recognize that the developmental attainments of the first era provide only a base, a starting point from which to begin the next. The Early Adult Transition represents, so to speak, both the full maturity of preadulthood and the infancy of a new era. One is at best off to a shaky start, and new kinds of development are required in the next era.

The second era, *early adulthood,* lasts from about age 17 to 45 and begins with the Early Adult Transition. It is the adult era of greatest energy and abundance and of greatest contradiction and stress. Biologically, the 20s and 30s are the peak years of the life cycle. In social and psychological terms, early adulthood is the season for forming and pursuing youthful aspirations, establishing a niche in society, raising a family, and, as the era ends, reaching a more "senior" position in the adult world. This can be a time of rich satisfaction in terms of love, sexuality, family life, occupational advancement, creativity, and realization of major life goals. But there can also be crushing stresses. Most of us simultaneously undertake the burdens of parenthood and of forming an occupation. We incur heavy financial obligations when our earning power is still relatively low. We must make crucial choices regarding marriage, family, work, and life-style before we have the maturity or life experience to choose wisely. Early adulthood is the era in which we are most buffeted by our own passions and ambitions from within and by the demands of family, community, and society from without. Under reasonably favorable conditions, the rewards of living in this era are enormous, but the costs often equal or even exceed the benefits.

The *Mid-life Transition,* from roughly age 40 to 45, brings about the termination of early adulthood and the start of middle adulthood. The distinction between these two eras, and the concept of Mid-life Transition as a developmental period that separates and connects them, is among the most controversial aspects of this schema. The research indicates, however, that the character of living always changes appreciably between early and middle adulthood. Similar observations, based on different methods and evidence, are given in the work of Jung, Ortega, Erikson, and others, noted earlier. The process of change begins in the Mid-life Transition (though the forms and degree of change vary enormously) and continues throughout the era. One developmental task of this transition is to begin a new step in individuation. To the extent that this occurs, we can become more compassionate, more reflective and judicious, less tyrannized by inner conflicts and external demands, and more genuinely loving of ourselves and others. Without it, our lives become increasingly trivial or stagnant.

The third era, *middle adulthood,* lasts from about age 40 to 65. During this era our biological capacities are below those of early adulthood but are normally still sufficient for an energetic, personally satisfying, and socially valuable life. Unless our lives are hampered in some special way, most of us during our 40s and 50s become "senior members" in our own particular worlds, however grand or modest they may be. We are responsible not only for our own work and perhaps the work of others, but also for the development of the current generation of young adults who will soon enter the dominant generation.

The next era, *late adulthood,* starts at about age 60. The *Late Adult Transition,*

from 60 to 65, links middle and late adulthood and is part of both. I will not discuss late adulthood here. My speculations regarding this era (and a subsequent one, late late adulthood) are given in Levinson (1978).

The Individual Life Structure

My approach to adult development grows out of, and is shaped by, the foregoing views regarding the life course and the life cycle. I am primarily interested in apprehending the nature of a person's life at a particular time and the course of that life over the years. Personality attributes, social roles, and biological characteristics are aspects of a life; they should be regarded as aspects and placed within the context of the life.

The key concept to emerge from my research is the *life structure:* the underlying pattern or design of a person's life at a given time. It is the pillar of my conception of adult development. When I speak of periods in adult development, I am referring to periods in the evolution of the life structure.

The meaning of this term can be clarified by a comparison of life structure and personality structure. A theory of personality structure is a way of conceptualizing answers to a concrete question: What kind of person am I? Different theories offer numerous ways of thinking about this question and of characterizing oneself or others (e.g., in terms of traits, skills, wishes, conflicts, defenses, or values).

A theory of life structure is a way of conceptualizing answers to a different question: What is my life like now? As we begin reflecting on this question, many others come to mind. What are the most important parts of my life, and how are they interrelated? Where do I invest most of my time and energy? Are there some relationships—to spouse, lover, family, occupation, religion, leisure, or whatever—that I would like to make more satisfying or meaningful? Are there some things not in my life that I would like to include? Are there interests and relationships, which now occupy a minor place, that I would like to make more central?

In pondering these questions, we begin to identify those aspects of the external world that have the greatest significance for us. We characterize our relationship with each of them and examine the interweaving of the various relationships. We find that our relationships are imperfectly integrated within a single pattern or structure.

The primary components of a life structure are the person's *relationships* with various others in the external world. The other may be a person, a group, an institution or culture, or a particular object or place. A significant relationship involves an investment of self (desires, values, commitment, energy, skill), a reciprocal investment by the other person or entity, and one or more social contexts that contain the relationship, shaping it and becoming part of it. Every relationship shows both stability and change as it evolves over time, and it has different functions in the person's life as the life structure itself changes.

An individual may have significant relationships with many kinds of others. A significant other might be an actual person in the individual's current life. We need to study interpersonal relationships between friends, lovers, and spouses; between parents and their adult offspring at different ages; between bosses and subordinates,

teachers and students, and mentors and protégés. A significant other might be a person from the past (e.g., Ezra Pound's vital relationship with the figure of Dante) or a symbolic or imagined figure from religion, myth, fiction, or private fantasy. The other might be a collective entity such as a group, institution, or social movement; nature as a whole, or a part of nature, such as the ocean, mountains, wildlife, whales in general, or Moby Dick in particular; or an object or place such as a farm, a city or country, "a room of one's own," a book or painting.

The concept of life structure requires us to examine the nature and patterning of a person's relationships with all significant others and the evolution of these relationships over the years. These relationships are the stuff of which our lives are made. They give shape and substance to the life course. They are the vehicle by which we live out—or bury—various aspects of ourselves and by which we participate in the world around us. Students of the life course seek to determine the character of each relationship, its place within the person's evolving life, and the meaning of this life for the person and his or her world.

At any given time, a life structure may have many and diverse components. We found, however, that only one or two components—rarely as many as three—occupy a central place in the structure. Most often, marriage–family and occupation are the central components of a person's life, although wide variations occur in their relative weight and in the importance of other components. The central components are those that have the greatest significance for the self and the evolving life course. They receive the largest share of the individual's time and energy, and they strongly influence the character of the other components. The peripheral components are easier to change or detach; they involve less investment of self and can be modified with less effect on the fabric of the person's life.

In terms of open systems theory, life structure forms a boundary between personality structure and social structure and governs the transactions between them. A boundary structure is part of the two adjacent systems it connects yet is partially separate or autonomous. It can be understood only if we see it as a link between them. The life structure mediates the relationship between the individual and the environment. It is in part the cause, the vehicle, and the effect of that relationship. The life structure grows out of the engagement of the self and the world. Its intrinsic ingredients are aspects of the self and aspects of the world, and its evolution is shaped by factors in the self and in the world. It requires us to think conjointly about the self and the world rather than making one primary and the other secondary or derivative. A theory of life structure must draw equally upon psychology and the social sciences.

The Sequence of Periods in Life Structure Development

In tracing the evolution of the life structure in the lives of men and women, I have found an invariant basic pattern (with infinite manifest variations): *The life structure develops through a relatively orderly sequence of age-linked periods during the adult years.* The sequence consists of an alternating series of structure-building and structure-changing (transitional) periods.

The primary task of a *structure-building* period is to form a life structure and maintain and enhance our life within it. A structure-building period ordinarily lasts

five to seven years. Then the life structure that has formed a basis for stability comes into question and must be modified. A *transitional* period terminates the existing life structure and creates the possibility for a new one. The primary tasks of every transitional period are to reappraise the existing structure, to explore possibilities for change in the self and the world, and to move toward commitment to the crucial choices that form the basis for a new life structure in the ensuing period. Transitional periods ordinarily last about five years. Almost half our adult lives is spent in developmental transitions. No life structure is permanent—periodic change is fundamental to our existence.

I have found that each period begins and ends at a well-defined average age; there is a variation of plus or minus two years around the mean. The discovery of age-linked periods in the adult development of the life structure is one of the most controversial findings of my research. Many psychologists and social scientists consider it impossible that development should unfold in so orderly a sequence during adulthood. They note that the available evidence goes against the hypothesis of age-linked stages in adult *personality* development. Moreover, *social roles* evolve in accord with institutionally defined timetables that vary widely among institutions and cultures. Some investigators regard adulthood as a series of *major life events* (such as marriage, loss, retirement) that may bring about changes in individual adaptation or personality. They maintain that these life events occur at widely varying ages, thus making impossible the kind of temporal order I have found. They have no conception of adult development as a source of order in the life course. I agree that neither individual personality nor social roles evolve through a standard sequence of age-linked stages in adulthood. I agree, further, that major life events occur at varying ages; but the study of events does not in itself provide a basis for a theory of adult development. It is abundantly evident that, at the level of specific events, roles, or personality, individual lives evolve in myriad ways. There is not much order in the concrete individual life course. Indeed, there is much more diversity and disorder than most researchers have been able to discover through their narrow theoretical lenses and methodological constraints.

I do propose, however, that there is an *underlying* order in the human life course, an order shaped by the eras and by the periods in life structure development. Personality, social structure, culture, gender, social roles, major life events, biology—these and other influences exert a powerful effect on the actual character of the individual life structure at a given time and on its development during adulthood. It is my hypothesis, however, that the basic nature and timing of life structure development are given in the life cycle at this time in human evolution. We cannot confirm or disconfirm a theory of life structure by studying changes in personality, social role, moral functioning, or the like. This theory can be tested adequately only by intensive studies that follow the evolution of the individual life structure over a span of years.

Within early and middle adulthood, the developmental periods unfold as follows (see Table 1.1). The first three periods of early adulthood, from roughly 17 to 33, constitute its "novice phase." They provide an opportunity to move beyond adolescence, to build a provisional but necessarily flawed entry life structure, and to learn the limitations of that structure. The two final periods, from 33 to 45, form the "culminating phase," which brings to fruition the efforts of this era.

Table 1.1 Developmental Periods in Early and Middle Adulthood

1. The *Early Adult Transition,* from ages 17 to 22, is a developmental bridge between preadulthood and early adulthood.
2. The *Entry Life Structure for Early Adulthood* (22–28) is the time for building and maintaining an initial mode of adult living.
3. The *Age 30 Transition* (28–33) is an opportunity to reappraise and modify the entry structure and to create the basis for the next life structure.
4. The *Culminating Life Structure for Early Adulthood* (33–40) is the vehicle for completing this era and realizing our youthful aspirations.
5. The *Mid-life Transition* (40–45) is another of the great cross-era shifts, serving both to terminate early adulthood and to initiate middle adulthood.
6. The *Entry Life Structure for Middle Adulthood* (45–50), like its preceding counterpart, provides an initial basis for life in a new era.
7. The *Age 50 Transition* (50–55) offers a mid-era opportunity for modifying and perhaps improving the entry life structure.
8. The *Culminating Life Structure for Middle Adulthood* (55–60) is the framework in which we conclude this era.
9. The *Late Adult Transition* (60–65) is a boundary period between middle and late adulthood, separating and linking the two eras.

A similar sequence exists in middle adulthood. It, too, begins with a novice phase of three periods, from 40 to 55. The Mid-life Transition is both an ending and a beginning. In our early 40s we are in the full maturity of early adulthood and are completing its final chapter; we are also in the infancy of middle adulthood, just beginning to learn about its promise and its dangers. We remain novices in every era until we have had a chance to try out an entry life structure and then to question and modify it in the mid-era transition. Only in the period of the Culminating Life Structure, and the cross-era transition that follows, do we reach the conclusion of that season and begin the shift to the next. During the novice phase we are, to varying degrees, both excited and terrified by the prospects for living in that era. To varying degrees, likewise, we experience the culminating phase as a time of rich satisfactions and of bitter disappointments, discovering as we so often do that the era ultimately gives us much more and much less than we had envisioned.

This sequence of eras and periods holds for men and women of different cultures, classes, and historical epochs. There are endless variations in the kinds of life structures people build, the developmental work they do in transitional periods, and the concrete sequence of social roles, events, and personality change. The theory thus provides a general framework of human development within which we can study the profound differences that often exist between classes, genders, and cultures.

The Concept of Transition in Adult Development

Many aspects of the theory of life structure development might be further elucidated here. I will focus chiefly on the concept of transition, which is central to many

developmental theories and certainly to mine. Consideration of the ways it is used in various theories may be helpful in clarifying their differences and in establishing links among them.

Let us begin with the general meaning of this term. A transition is a process of change that forms a bridge between X and Y. X and Y may be two subjects in discourse, two themes in a musical composition, two distinctive structures or modes of activity. During a transition we are "in transit" between the two: We are in some sense leaving X, separating from it; at the same time, we are moving toward Y and creating the possibility of being in, with, or part of it. The transition forms, as it were, a boundary region linking X and Y. We are not in this boundary region as long as we are primarily in X, and we leave it when we are primarily in Y. We are in a transition when we are engaged in both terminating X and initiating Y. This boundary space is not outside of, or independent of, the two adjacent regions; rather, it is part of both X and Y yet qualitatively different from them. A transition is thus a turning point, a transformation, a process of significant qualitative change.

The words *transition* and *crisis* are often used to convey similar meanings. Both carry the imagery of a turning point; a shift in course; a qualitative change; a process of cutting, sifting, separating; an attempt to resolve contradictions; a time of transformation (for better or worse) rather than stability. In Chinese, as many recent writers have noted, the characters forming the word *crisis* mean "danger" and "opportunity." This is part of the imagery of transition as well. Only by giving up what I now have at X do I create the opportunity to improve my life at Y. A transition is a time of promise, of hope and potential for a better future. But it is also a time of separation and loss, and of fear that I am giving up far more than I may actually gain. In contemporary usage, the term *transition* is generally given the connotations of both opportunity and risk, whereas *crisis* usually has more negative connotations of danger and disruption. Partly for this reason, I use *transition* as the most general term for a basic process of structural change, and *crisis* for a particular kind of transition, one that is relatively painful, tumultuous, or problematic.

In most structural or "stage" theories of development (e.g., Kegan, 1982; Kohlberg, 1969, 1973a,b; Loevinger, 1976; Piaget, 1970a; Werner, 1940), a transition is a bridge, a process of transformation, by which we move from one stage to the next. Each stage is identified, however, by a particular structure; a transition is not seen as a stage in its own right. The structures are connected by processes of transformation, but the times of transformation (transition) are not considered stages and are not given the same theoretical emphasis.

In contrast, some recent research on adult life has focused primarily on transitions following a major life event such as illness, the death of a loved one, a job promotion or retirement, the birth of a child, and the start or end of a marriage (Golan, 1981; Hareven & Adams, 1982; Lowenthal, Thurnher, & Chiriboga, 1975; Schlossberg, 1984). These events have certain common characteristics: They create moderate or great stress; they create problems of adaptation; they may lead to change in personality or life course. By and large, those who focus on specific life events are mainly concerned with adaptation and the process of transition. They

deal less with the developmental question, "To what extent does the transition contribute to a basic change in structure?"

The theory of life structure development gives equal weight to the *structures* (i.e., the periods of building and maintaining a life structure) and the *transitions* (i.e., the periods of questioning and modifying the structure). Both are periods in adult development. We spend almost as much time in the latter as in the former, and both are essential to our lives. Focusing solely on the structures will give no understanding of how they change. Focusing solely on transitions will give no sense of their products—the life structures that shape, enrich, and constrain our lives. The great challenge is to apprehend the continuous sequence by which individuals build, live within, modify, and rebuild the life structure over the entire course of life.

The Major Tasks of a Transitional Period
in Life Structure Development

A transitional period involves three main developmental tasks: (1) *termination* of the existing life structure; (2) *individuation,* and (3) *initiation*—making a start toward a new life structure. In a crude sense these tasks follow a temporal order. First, one must terminate the past; finally, one must initiate a new life. In between, as a basis for change, is the work of individuation. But development does not proceed in so logical a manner: All three tasks may continue throughout a transitional period, and they are intimately interwoven. I shall discuss each task briefly in turn.

Termination. The word *termination* is widely used but rarely examined. Its simple meaning is "an ending." However, the termination of a significant relationship plays an important part in our lives precisely because it represents not only an ending, but also a beginning. It is more realistic, and more fruitful, to conceive of a termination as a *major qualitative change* in the character of a relationship; it ends one form of the relationship and starts a new form. This view places the termination in a broader time perspective, regarding it both as an outcome of the past and as a starting point for the future.

The "other" in a significant relationship may, as noted earlier, be a person (living, dead, or imaginary), a group, institution, or social movement, symbol or place. If a relationship has little value or significance for me—if I lose a possession of no importance, if I lose contact with a person or group of only casual interest to me—it passes entirely out of my life with almost no consequences. The situation is very different for relationships that form major components of my life structure and in which I have made a great investment of self. The termination of such relationships is more painful and protracted and has far greater consequences for my future life.

The most dramatic terminations involve total loss of contact with the other: a loved one dies; a valued group is dissolved; the therapy ends and I no longer see the therapist; a bitter quarrel leads to permanent parting from a friend or mentor; a geographical move (voluntary or coerced) forces me to leave a world I shall never see again. I experience a profound loss and must come to terms with painful feel-

ings of abandonment, helplessness, grief, and rage. The other is no longer externally available to me. Yet the relationship does not die. Over time the lost other is more fully internalized and becomes available to me as an internal figure. The relationship continues to evolve in my self and my life; certain aspects of it are ended but other aspects survive and new ones are added. Losing the earlier relationship, I gradually create a new one, for better or worse.

In most cases, however, termination does not involve total separation from the other. We continue to have some contact, but a crucial change occurs in the character of the relationship. An intense mentoring relationship is followed by bitter conflict and withdrawal or by affectionate but distant acquaintanceship. A marriage ends in divorce and the relationship goes on in new forms.

A termination is thus not an ending but a turning point: the relationship must be transformed. There is sometimes, but not always, a clear-cut terminating event, such as a divorce, departure, geographical move, graduation, or the like. Such an event dramatizes one point in the termination process. The crucial thing to study, however, is not the event alone but the overall process. This always begins long before the identifying event and continues long after. The termination constellates anxiety over being left behind, guilt over deserting or betraying the other, fear of having to start out afresh on one's own. It is important for both parties to determine what they will keep in the relationship and what they will give up. They need time to see whether there is a basis for an improved relationship, whether the whole thing must go under, or whether they will, for whatever reasons, remain together in an essentially oppressive or dead relationship.

The termination of a single relationship is difficult enough. In a life structure transition the problem is compounded: It is necessary to terminate the overall pattern of one's life and, in a cross-era transition, an entire era. A particular relationship may be most problematic or most in focus during a transitional period, but closer examination will show that other relationships are also involved. The basic question is not simply, "What am I going to do about my marriage (or my work or my lack of leisure)?" It is, "What am I going to do about my life?" I may concentrate first on one particular component—the most painful one, or perhaps the one that seems most amenable to change—but in time I will have to deal with the others, and with the overall structure.

An example is the budding adult in the Early Adult Transition, at around 18 or 20, in the process of separating from parents. The developmental task is *not* to end the relationship altogether. It is important to reject certain aspects (e.g., being the submissive or defiant child in relation to all-controlling parents). But it is important also to sustain other, more valued aspects, and to build in new qualities such as mutual respect between distinctive individuals who have separate as well as shared interests. The parents, probably in their 40s and working on their own developmental tasks, are at least as involved in the effort to transform the relationship. If it cannot be modified in a way appropriate to the life season of both parents and offspring, it will become increasingly stressful and may even wither away. Moreover, the young adult's relationship with parents is but one component of the initial adult life structure. This component influences, and is influenced by, relationships to occupation, to friends and lovers, perhaps to the political, religious,

and cultural worlds in which the young adult is establishing her or his membership. In a transitional period, many relationships must be weighed, sifted, tested, and selectively incorporated into a fragile structure.

Individuation. Individuation, or the "separation–individuation process," is widely recognized as an important aspect of child development. During the first few years of life we take the first step in individuation, establishing a boundary between the "me" and the "not-me," and forming more stabilized relationships with the external world (Winnicott, 1965; Mahler, Pine, & Bergman, 1975). This is the first cross-era transition, the shift from life in the womb to the start of one's existence as a person in the preadult era. Individuation advances further in adolescence and the Early Adult Transition, with the initial consolidation of an identity, greater differentiation from parents, and preparation for future life as an adult. But despite the assertions of most textbooks on human development, our individuation is hardly complete by the end of adolescence. Jung (Campbell, 1971) has shown that a more advanced process of individuation may begin at about 40 and continue through the "second half of life." If we do not become more individuated in middle adulthood than we were in our twenties, our lives are limited indeed.

Individuation is often regarded as a purely intrapsychic matter, as a property of the self. It is broader than this: It involves the person's relationship both to self and to external world. With greater individuation of the self, we have a clearer and more complex sense of our identity; we are able to draw more fully on our inner resources (desires, values, talents, aspirations, conflicts, archetypal potentials); we are more autonomous, self-generating, and self-responsible; the self is more integrated and less rent by inner contradictions. Individuation exists as well in our relation to the external world. With more individuated relationships, we feel more genuinely connected to the human and natural world; we are more able to explore its possibilities and understand what it demands and offers; we give it greater meaning and take more responsibility for our personal construction of meaning; we accept more the ultimate reality both of our aloneness and of our membership in the cosmos.

What are the main elements in the individuation process? I conceive of individuation in part as a developmental effort toward the resolution of four polarities. These polarities are of fundamental importance in human evolution and in the individual life cycle. They are Young–Old, Destruction–Creation, Masculine–Feminine, and Attachment–Separateness.

Each of these pairs forms a polarity in the sense that the two terms represent opposing tendencies or conditions. Although they are in some sense antithetical, both sides coexist in every person and every society. At every age we are both young and old. At 40, for example, we feel older than we did in our youth but are not ready to join the generation defined as middle-aged. We feel alternately young, old, and in between. If we cling too strongly to the youthfulness of our 20s, we cannot establish our place in the generation of middle adulthood. If we give up on being young and on sustaining our ties to youth, we become dry, rigid, prematurely old. It is a problem of balance: The developmental task in every transitional period is to become Young–Old in a new way appropriate to that era in the life cycle.

The Destruction–Creation polarity presents similar problems of conflict and

reintegration. Every transition activates a person's concerns with death and destruction. In the Mid-life Transition of the early 40s, for example, we experience more fully our own mortality and the actual or impending deaths of others. We become more aware of the many ways in which other persons, even our loved ones, have acted destructively toward us (with malice or, often, with good intentions). What is perhaps worse, we realize that we have done irrevocably hurtful things to our parents, lovers, spouses, children, friends, rivals (again, with what may have been the worst or the best of intentions). At the same time, we have a strong desire to become more creative and loving: to create products that have value for self and others, to participate in collective enterprises that advance human welfare, to contribute more fully to the coming generations in society. In middle adulthood a person can come to know, more than ever before, that powerful forces of destructiveness and of creativity coexist in the human soul and can be integrated in many ways—though never entirely.

Likewise, all of us at mid-life must come more fully to terms with the coexistence of masculine and feminine parts of the self. The relative splitting of masculine and feminine cannot be overcome in early adulthood. It is a continuing task of middle and late adulthood. Finally, we must integrate the powerful need for attachment to others with the antithetical but equally important need for separateness. The integration of these and other polarities is a great vision that many have sought to realize but no one can fully attain.

We can work on these polarities at any time during the life course. During the transitional periods, however, both the opportunity and the need to attain greater integration are strongest. When the life structure is up for reappraisal and change, when we feel to some degree suspended between past and future, it is especially important to heal the deep divisions in the self and in our most significant relationships.

Initiation. As noted earlier, a termination is not only an ending but a beginning. As an ending, it presents the task of coming to terms with loss, separation, departure, completion. As a beginning, it presents the task of initiation: exploring new possibilities, altering our existing relationships, and searching for aspects of self and world out of which new relationships might evolve. The process of exploring, making and testing provisional choices, and questing in new directions may go on all through a transitional period. A choice made early in the period, no matter how enthusiastically, must have a provisional quality that stems from the character of a transitional period. Exploration requires tentativeness, an openness to new options.

As a transition comes to an end, it is time to make crucial choices, to give these choices meaning and commitment, and to start building a life structure around them. The choices mark the beginning of the next period. They are, in a sense, the major product of the transition. When all the efforts of the past several years are done—all the struggles to improve one's work or marriage, to explore alternative possibilities of living, to come more to terms with the self—we must make our choices and place our bets. We must decide, "This I will settle for," and start creating a life structure that will serve as a vehicle for the next step in the journey.

The choices made in a transitional period usually lead to moderate or drastic

change in life structure. A person may divorce, remarry, change job or occupation, make a geographical move, start new avocational pursuits that modify and enrich his or her life. A choice is often marked by an event that takes only a few days or weeks. The event is, however, embedded within a process of change that ordinarily extends over a span of several years. Thus, a divorce or a job change is the most conspicuous event within a complex transition that contains many other changes. In making this transition, a person destructures the existing life pattern, works on a number of basic developmental tasks, and restructures a new life.

Alternatively, a person may choose to reaffirm the commitment to an existing component of his or her life—for example, to remain in the marriage with the intention of making it work better, or to remain in the present job rather than make a drastic change entailing greater risks and discontinuity. If this is an active reaffirmation, significant improvement will occur in the meaning and character of this component of the life structure even if the spouse or job remain the same. However, the decision to stay put is not always based on a reaffirmed commitment. It may stem more from resignation, inertia, passive acquiescence, or controlled despair—a self-restriction in the context of severe external constraints. The spouse or job are unchanged, but the relationship and the life structure are different. This kind of surface stability leads to a long-term decline unless new factors intervene (perhaps in the next transitional period) and enable one to form a more satisfactory life structure.

A transitional period comes to an end not when a particular event occurs or when a sequence is completed in one aspect of life, but when the tasks of termination, individuation, and initiation have less urgency, and when the key tasks are to build, live within, and enhance a new life structure.

Life Structure Theory in Relation to the Other Theories Presented in This Book

There are several major differences between my theory and the theories of most other contributors to this book.

1. My focus is on the adult development of the life structure, which involves self-in-world and gives equal attention to both. The others, in contrast, deal chiefly with the development of the self or of specific aspects of the self (cognitive, ego, moral, spiritual). The study of adulthood takes us beyond the narrow focus on the self. It requires us to examine the life course in its complexity, to take into account the external world as well as the self, to study the engagement of self in world, and to move beyond an encapsulated view of the self. As we learn more about the lived life and the evolution of the life structure, we will have a sounder basis for studying the adult development of the self.

2. I conceive of development as a *sequential order that is not necessarily progressive or hierarchical;* it involves both growth and decline, a mixture of progression, stability, stasis, and dissolution. The other contributors, more true to a powerful tradition in academic psychology, tend generally to see development as a hierarchical order, a movement from a lower level (more primitive, less adaptive) to a higher one (more advanced, adaptive, fulfilling of inner potentials). Some, fol-

lowing Piaget, posit a hierarchy of stages (e.g., Fischer, Kenny, & Pipp; Richards & Commons). Others offer specific concepts, such as "mindfulness" (Langer et al.), or "wisdom" (Dittmann-Kohli & Baltes) that are presumably part of favorable development; but these concepts are not part of a more general theory of adult development.

This issue is of great importance in the study of adult development. The imagery of a hierarchy of developmental stages is prevalent in the study of childhood, where development takes primarily the form of positive growth. There are generally agreed-upon criteria for judging that one stage represents a "higher level" than another in preadulthood, where we make such dramatic advances in body shape and size, cognitive complexity, adaptive capability, and character formation. The variables that show such rapid growth until age 20 or so tend to stabilize in early adulthood and then gradually decline over the course of middle and late adulthood. At the same time, other psychosocial qualities may develop to greater maturity in middle and late adulthood.

It is essential to keep in mind that development is not synonymous with growth. Rather, it has the twin aspects of "growing up" and "growing down." Perhaps the best term for the former is *adolescing,* which means moving toward adulthood, and for the latter, *senescing,* which means moving toward old age and dissolution. The balance of the two varies from era to era.

In preadulthood we are mostly, though not only, adolescing. In late adulthood we are mostly senescing, though there is some vitally important adolescing to be done as we come to the culmination of the entire life cycle and attempt to give fuller meaning to our own lives, to life and death as ultimate states, and to the condition of being human. At the end of the life cycle, as we engage in the final process of biological senescing, we are also engaged in the final work of psychosocial adolescing, of growing up to our full adulthood. It is a costly oversimplification to equate childhood with growth and old age with decline.

In early and middle adulthood, adolescing and senescing coexist in an uneasy balance. Biologically, the forces of senescence come to equal and then gradually to exceed those of adolescence. Psychosocially, there are possibilities for further growth, but they are by no means assured of realization and they are jeopardized by external constraints as well as inner vulnerabilities. We must deal with this coexistence of growth and decline in our own lives and in our research on adult development. Simple models of growth do not hold in adulthood. It is inappropriate to study adult development with childhood-centered models. Adulthood has its own distinctive character and must be studied in its own right, not merely as an extrapolation from childhood. Erikson warned us of this long ago, and Jung even earlier, but it is a hard lesson to learn.

In studying the development of the life structure, we are not yet wise enough about life to say with precision that one life structure is developmentally higher, or more advanced, than another. We still know very little about the complexities and contradictions of the human life course. When we have learned much more about the kinds of life structure people build at different ages, under different conditions, we may be more able to evaluate, conceptualize, and measure the variations in developmental level among life structures.

3. The periods in life structure development are, according to my findings, rel-

atively *age-linked;* the age of onset for each period varies within a range of three to four years. The other theories generally describe a sequence relatively independent of age. Some of them posit stages that unfold with little connection to age; others see personal change as a response to life events that are not highly age-linked.

4. The final difference is a derivative of the first. Psychologists who deal with the development of the self generally assume that the primary determinants of any developmental sequence lie in a genetically given program within the organism. In this view, external conditions influence the concrete character and timing of the sequence found in any specific case, but the basic temporal pattern is given in the nature of the organism. The outside environment (society, culture, ecology, individual life circumstances) is considered to various degrees but is seen as extrinsic to the (intra-organismic) developmental process. The life structure, on the other hand, is not located within the individual. It is a property of *self-in-relation-to-world.* Self and society are thus conjointly involved in its intrinsic nature, in the origins of its developmental sequence, and in its evolution over the individual life course. There are wide differences in the kinds of life structures individuals build and in the changes they make during the transitional periods. My findings indicate, however, that the timing of the periods in life structure development varies only minimally across cultures, classes, and genders.

The theories are fundamentally different in these four respects. Are they irreconcilable, or can they be integrated to their mutual benefit? In my opinion, integration is possible and desirable. Efforts at integration will help to place the field of adult development on a sounder, more coherent basis. It is possible here only to comment briefly on some lines of convergence.

One major avenue for connecting the several approaches is through the concept of transitional periods in life structure development. These periods offer a developmentally given opportunity for psychological change and perhaps growth. Such change is possible but not automatically given or easy, and there are wide variations in the extent to which individuals change in a given period.

In their study of *early adulthood* (age 17–45), for example, several contributors to this volume have found significant (though far from universal) personal change. Souvaine, Lahey, and Kegan find a greater refinement of self that allows a more subtle understanding of social relationships and a fuller give-and-take with others who hold different values. Pascual-Leone observes a development of social values and interpersonal skills. Links could be forged between the theories by study of the *evolution* of these changes within early adulthood. My hypothesis is that greater inner change is likely to occur in the Early Adult Transition or the Age 30 Transition than in the structure-building periods. More concrete changes in attitudes and skills may occur in the structure-building periods, as the person seeks to establish a place and to acquire new modes of adaptation in a new social context. The thrust of my approach is to follow the course of change and to place changes in specific personal qualities within the framework of life structure development.

The same considerations apply in the study of *middle adulthood* (age 40–65). Less research has been done on this part of the life cycle than on any other. Pascual-Leone describes a mid-life crisis at about age 40—perhaps in the period of the Midlife Transition. His focus is on physiological changes that affect cognitive functioning. To the extent that a significant decline in certain cognitive capabilities and

their physiological substrate takes place at this time, it may play an important part in the future development (growth as well as decline) of personality and of life structure during middle adulthood. Again, one can imagine many ways of linking his views with my own and those of others.

Finally, my theory of the Late Adult Transition (age 60–65) and the era of *late adulthood* provides a framework for the study of psychological changes in the 60s and beyond. Dittmann-Kohli and Baltes offer the concept of "wisdom" as a significant form of cognitive–emotional change that may occur in middle or late adulthood. In their view, it involves an increased ability to reason with probabilities, an emphasis on context, and a relativity in judgment. Research on the course of change (and lack of change, as well as change in the opposite direction) would enable us to determine whether the growth of "wisdom" is at all shaped by the periods in life structure development. Similar considerations apply to Pascual-Leone's hypothesis that, as the youthful powers of cognitive functioning's diminish, one may develop other powers, including a more contemplative mode of thinking.

Alexander et al., Souvaine et al., and Pascual-Leone believe that growth in the self is a crucial element in (and perhaps cause of) progress in the adult life course. Although I am in agreement with this general principle, I give more emphasis than they to the importance of external conditions in determining the distinctive character of the lived life. In addition, they propose a standard, hierarchical progression of self-structures, though not through an age-linked timetable. They suggest that there are "optimal," higher states of self-development that can occur in adulthood but that these unfold only under appropriate internal and external conditions. For example, Alexander et al. assert that practice of Transcendental Meditation may provide such facilitative conditions. There appears to be no consistent evidence, however, that a sequence of stages of self-development universally unfolds in adults regardless of the circumstances under which they live.

It is important to clarify our thinking as to what constitutes "higher" versus "lower" levels of self-development in adulthood. Elsewhere (Levinson, 1978) I have presented some of my ideas about this, based on the concepts of individuation, polarities, and the partial (though never complete) resolution of polarities. There are truly remarkable variations, however, in the degree of self-development (and decline) that occurs during adulthood. There are equally remarkable variations in the degree to which the self is engaged in the life structure, enriching or depleting it. A more developed self is of little avail, and may become a source of deeper pain, when it cannot find expression in the life structure.

A central aim of the present book is to explore the ways in which favorable development may occur in adulthood. Our various ideas in this direction include individuation, mindfulness, transcendental consciousness, expansion of moral outlook, and many others. We need to generate such ideas and to explore their relevance in the actual lives of individuals over time. If it ignores the actualities of adult life, however, overemphasis on favorable development in adulthood can be as misleading as the traditional negative emphasis on decline and senescence. As we look more intensively at the realities of individual lives over time, we can begin to think in a more empirically grounded way about *what constitutes positive growth, in contrast to negative growth, and how the two are interwoven.*

2

Toward a Neofunctionalist Conception of Adult Intellectual Development: Wisdom as a Prototypical Case of Intellectual Growth

Freya Dittmann-Kohli and Paul B. Baltes

Objective

The field of adult development of intelligence is currently in a phase that is conducive to a major conceptual reorientation. In principle, such a reorientation can take many forms, depending upon one's conceptual interest and paradigmatic emphasis. The purpose of this chapter is to offer one such new conceptual approach for future research and theory and to apply this conceptual framework to the study of wisdom as a form of advanced cognitive functioning.

The specific starting point is the study of intelligence as conceived in the psychometric tradition. Following suggestions from psychometric research, we assume that intelligence is relatively plastic and that its course can evince differential trajectories or pathways, varying in level and shape, depending on the pattern of biological and environmental circumstances affecting a given individual. We outline what form the potential progression of intellectual aging can take. In general, adult intellectual development is conceptualized as a process of further change not so much in decontextualized cognitive skills but in real-life problem solving and synthesized pragmatic knowledge systems. In each individual life course, a pattern of general ontogenetic, social-structural, and idiographic conditions jointly define the form of intellectual aging. In addition, we take the position that intelligence should be seen in reference to its pragmatic and adaptive function. Furthermore, we assume that the development of adult intelligence can be best understood if seen in an extra-systemic context. Extra-systemic conditions of intelligence are those that are not inherently part of cognition *qua* cognition. The context of life-span personality and health development and many features of the sociological structure of the life course figure prominently as extra-systemic conditions in the later part of life.

The new orientation to adult intelligence we will proffer is a further development of nascent ideas contained in earlier or parallel articles (Baltes, 1987; Baltes & Baltes, 1980; Baltes & Dittmann-Kohli, 1982; Baltes, Dittmann-Kohli, & Dixon,

54

1984; Baltes & Kliegl, 1986; Baltes & Schaie, 1976; Baltes & Willis, 1979b, 1982; Dittmann-Kohli, 1981a, 1981b, 1982, 1984a, 1986, 1989; Dixon & Baltes, 1986; Willis & Baltes, 1980). Several theoretical elements are seen as central to our conceptual orientation. We approach the study of adult intellectual development by simultaneously applying three theoretical frameworks: (1) a life-span view of developmental tasks; (2) a cognitive-science view of knowledge, knowledge acquisition, and knowledge transformation in complex problem solving; and (3) an action-psychological view of intellectual functioning in a neofunctionalist perspective.

Together, these viewpoints emphasize the pragmatic use of intellectual resources for achieving successful life adaptation. Progressive development in select problem-solving strategies and knowledge systems is possible if performance-enhancing conditions exist. Among these performance-enhancing conditions are processes of personality development, participation in environments providing a life-long context of progression-enhancing role expectations, and opportunities for the practice of specialized (expert-type) competencies. Of special importance are abilities for self-development and self-directed learning (Dittmann-Kohli, 1981b).

Within this theoretical framework we present our emerging notion of wisdom and its relationship to social and practical intelligence. Wisdom is seen as one prototypical case of adult intellectual growth. The concept of wisdom is introduced by looking at its historical-cultural roots, by referring to other research efforts in the area of wisdom, and by describing its main features. The features advanced pertain to task characteristics, aspects of cognitive activities and products, the domain of knowledge, and concepts denoting the status of wisdom as a form of synthesized pragmatic intelligence. The domain of wisdom is seen as covering two main areas of intellectual competence: practical and philosophical wisdom.

Current Research on Psychometric Intelligence During Adulthood and Old Age

In past work, one of us argued that at least four salient findings and concepts need to be considered and coordinated when interpreting the existing body of data on adult intelligence (Baltes, 1987; Baltes & Willis, 1979a, 1982; Dixon & Baltes, 1986; Willis & Baltes, 1980). These four concepts are multidimensionality, multidirectionality, interindividual variability, and intraindividual plasticity.

1. *Multidimensionality* of psychometric intelligence reflects the notion that intelligence is not a unitary construct. Rather, intelligence refers to a multitude of abilities that are organized into an overall structure (Cattell, 1971; Horn, 1970; Jäger, 1967, 1982; Sternberg & Detterman, 1979).

Factor analysis and related multivariate models have often been used as research strategies. Extant multidimensional schemes representing the organization of abilities (number of abilities, levels of organization) vary markedly. However, in each case there is a common central posture: an attempt is made to distinguish between distinct (though possibly interrelated) classes of abilities when conceptualizing psychometric intelligence and charting its ontogeny (Anastasi, 1970; Baltes & Labouvie, 1973; Horn, 1970; Reinert, 1970).

2. *Multidirectionality* describes the varying course of quantitative development (age trends) of abilities. It indicates that developmental trends, instead of being unidirectional, can vary in direction.

In the developmental literature, the need for a concept of multidirectionality became exceedingly conspicuous when the study of intellectual development was extended beyond childhood and adolescence. Up to that age range, incremental trajectories or growth patterns were predominant findings for almost any intellectual ability considered (e.g., Bayley, 1970; McCall, 1979). As age-trend research was extended into adulthood and old age, however, results of negative age differences (decline) appeared. Different abilities appear to manifest rather distinct life-span trajectories. The different courses for fluid versus crystallized intelligence (Horn, 1970, 1982a, 1982b) or for verbal versus nonverbal dimensions (Botwinick, 1977) are perhaps the best-known examples.

3. *Interindividual variability* refers to the fact that individuals differ in regard to the course of development. The question of variability during adulthood and old age is not only one of directionality but also one of level and patterning. Some individuals increase in level of intellectual functioning, some display no longitudinal change, and others show decremental change, beginning to decline as early as the 40s and 50s (Schaie, 1979; Thomae, 1983). Interindividual variability in the course of intellectual development during adulthood and old age, then, is the third salient issue.

4. *Intraindividual plasticity* is the fourth issue we deem important in the study of psychometric intelligence during adulthood and old age. Plasticity in this context refers to the range of within-person or intraindividual functioning (Baltes & Willis, 1982; Baltes & Schaie, 1976).

The traditional view of psychometric intelligence emphasized abilities as largely invariant and fixed, "as attributes that have many of the properties of a trait, as this concept is used in general biology. That is . . . defined as an enduring characteristic by means of which one person can be distinguished from another" (Horn, 1977, p. 140). Such a trait view of abilities is in contrast to one that declares the study of the conditions for differential performance to be an equally important approach (Baltes & Schaie, 1976; Gollin, 1981; Willis & Baltes, 1980).

In research dealing with the conditions for modifiability or plasticity of intelligence it is important to distinguish between different indicators of the ability construct (e.g., potential vs. developed competence vs. performance). Similarly, a research emphasis on plasticity stresses the role of the context provided by an individual's life history in defining the level and rate of intellectual functioning. Indeed, when research on modifiability of adult and old-age intelligence is conducted (Baltes & Willis, 1982; Denney, 1979; Dittmann-Kohli, 1983; Sterns & Sanders, 1980), the results indicate considerable plasticity in functioning.

It is important to note that these four concepts do not imply that there is no regularity at all in the course of intellectual development during adulthood and old age, including the possibility of general late-life decline in some abilities. Rather, regularity and possible decline need to be seen in the context of other information. Thus, we hold only that any comprehensive interpretation of adult and aging intelligence needs to include multidimensionality, multidirectionality, interindividual

variability, and plasticity as salient features requiring integration. Together, these concepts emphasize a dynamic view of intelligence, a position that permits growth and decline to occur at the same time in the same individual and in persons of the same age (Baltes, 1987; Labouvie-Vief, 1985).

Psychometric Versus Cognitive Approaches to Adult Intellectual Development

In this section, we discuss first the relationship between our approach and Cattell and Horn's model of fluid-crystallized intelligence. The purpose is to show how our thinking affects the theory that, within the psychometric tradition, has been used most widely to describe and explain intellectual development during adulthood and old age. In addition, we sketch briefly some conceptions of intelligence as a form of problem solving as they have been advanced in cognitive psychology. Subsequently, we outline some general perspectives on adult intellectual development that emphasize the adaptive role of intelligence during life-span development from an action-theoretical posture. Together, these perspectives and conceptions permit us to offer some preliminary observations on the concept of wisdom.

Relationship to Cattell and Horn's Theory of Fluid-Crystallized Intelligence

It may be useful to explain further how our general approach is related to Cattell and Horn's theory of fluid-crystallized intelligence (Cattell, 1971; Horn, 1970, 1982a, 1982b). Our approach is similar, although we place different emphasis on the relative role and understanding of fluid versus crystallized intelligence. In particular, we view fluid and crystallized intelligence as being coequals in defining intelligence and its course of development. This is in contrast to Cattell's position, which defines fluid intelligence as the primary dimension and crystallized intelligence as a derived, or secondary, one. Furthermore, we believe that crystallized intelligence has been too narrowly defined and measured and that a cognitive-science approach helps to place what Cattell and Horn label crystallized intelligence into a larger and different context. Moreover, we believe that the role of crystallized intelligence and of personality-related domains of functioning looms larger and larger in indexing intelligence as individuals move into adulthood and old age.

The dominance of fluid intelligence in Horn's theory is reflected, for example, in his insistence on identifying decline as the central feature of intellectual aging. It may or may not be correct to interpret, as Horn (1982b) does, existing cohort-sequential data on fluid functioning with aging as evidence for average decline. However, elevating decline in fluid functioning to the dominant yardstick, in face of alternative trajectories for other dimensions of intelligence such as crystallized intelligence, is understandable only if fluid components of intelligence are seen as more basic and broadly relevant than other dimensions of intelligence.

It appears, therefore, that Cattell and especially Horn make fluid intelligence the master criterion on which age groups are compared. Their primary interest in fluid intelligence and related abilities probably explains why their test construction research has never reflected the necessity of developing more varied and comprehensive measures of crystallized intelligence. In fact, when it comes to crystallized intelligence-type measures, the test development work in Cattell and Horn's laboratories has been rather negligible; as a consequence, one is faced with a dearth of available instruments. In this vein, Cattell (1971) has pointed out that for many important domains of crystallized intelligence adequate tests have never been developed.

We argue that the products and cognitive activities of many adults (e.g., parents, educators, executives, therapists, scientists, artists, politicians) are difficult to judge by criteria of fluid intelligence alone, nor can they be judged adequately by existing measures of crystallized intelligence. On the contrary, it appears desirable to focus on the basic notion of crystallized intelligence as a "developmentally higher-level" factor covering culturally influenced, individually acquired and maintained abilities for understanding and thinking. Such acquired problem solving and understanding skills show developmental changes (expansion, modification, transformation) in childhood and adulthood and deserve major attention in their own right. They are not secondary to fluid functioning, as Cattell and Horn postulate, and they include many more of the kinds of tasks that adults face in their varying life careers. Such a focus on and expansion of crystallized intelligence demands a departure from the established practice (Horn & Donaldson, 1976), which is to evaluate aging intelligence primarily in terms of speed of information processing in the type of tasks used to measure fluid intelligence.

Because crystallized intelligence is so heavily attached to the factor-analytic scheme of Cattell and Horn and to relatively simple verbal reasoning tasks and abilities, we prefer to use the terms *synthesized* (Dittmann-Kohli, 1984a) or *pragmatic* (Baltes, 1987; Baltes et al., 1984; Dixon & Baltes, 1986) intelligence for those aspects of intelligence that concern the contextual and knowledge-based elaboration of intelligence.[1] We hope that the forceful consideration of synthesized intelligence will permit us increasingly to understand those aspects of adult intellectual functioning that scholars such as Erikson (1968b), Gruber (1973), Labouvie-Vief (1980, 1982b, 1990), and Dörner (1983) see as related to the highest forms of intellectual maturity and productivity.

We need an emphasis, therefore, on those problem-solving strategies and contexts that reflect the nature of cognitive functioning of adults in their natural settings. In particular, we need a focus on the adult's ability to deal with complex, important life tasks. To conceptualize and, in the future, to measure adult cognitive competencies, we judge cognitive science and action-psychological approaches as conceptually most compatible. In the long run and in the spirit of rapprochement between cognitive and psychometric endeavors (Resnick, 1976; Sternberg & Detterman, 1979), a psychometric treatment of such phenomena is desirable and necessary. Before we address cognitive-science and action-psychological approaches in more detail, we shall first comment on some further issues relating to a possible rapprochement between cognitive and psychometric endeavors.

Intelligence and Acquired Problem-Solving
and Knowledge Repertoires

Our general assumption is that fluid functioning à la Cattell is basic in the sense that performance in fluid tasks may reflect, if these tasks are overlearned, proficiency in elementary cognitive operations (Kossakowski & Otto, 1977). These elementary cognitive operations may be part of universal human capacities (like walking, perceiving, communicating by language, etc.). Whether and how well such elementary cognitive operations can be flexibly used out of context (i.e., outside everyday life tasks) and how well they can be performed in highly formalized tasks within tests or experiments seem to depend primarily on schooling or related socialization experiences (Cole, Sharp, & Lave, 1976; Laboratory of Comparative Human Cognition, 1982). However, interindividual differences within fairly homogeneous cultural groups or genetic differences in such basic abilities may also account for differences in performance (Scarr & Weinberg, 1978).

Elementary cognitive structures and operations develop early, may be universal, and constitute necessary conditions for the development of knowledge, expertise, and synthesized intelligence. However, elementary cognitive operations are not a sufficient condition for the development of synthesized intelligence: other experiences and processes need to occur in order to generate growth in complex knowledge and problem-solving abilities. Since these abilities are constructed over the course of many years, we refer to them as synthesized intelligence (Dittmann-Kohli, 1984a) or pragmatic intelligence (Dixon & Baltes, 1986). More specifically, synthesized or pragmatic intelligence reflects the acquisition and further transformation of cultural and individual knowledge and problem-solving repertoires applied to the demands associated with the life tasks of individuals.

Bower (1975) defined cognitive psychology as a science that "is concerned with how organisms cognize or gain knowledge about their world, and how they use that knowledge to guide decisions and perform effective actions" (p. 25). This definition of cognition illustrates the broad range inherent in our conception of intelligence and its inclusiveness beyond fluid functioning à la Cattell and Horn. Note also that Sternberg (1982) views abstract thinking as just one out of four "macro-components" of intelligence, whereas the other three components of Sternberg's conception stress learning from experience, adaptation to changing circumstances, and motivation for performance.

Which fundamental conceptions of cognition can be conceived as potentially useful for a developmental view of adult intelligence? One such alternative is associated with recent work in cognitive science and with research in complex problem solving. Conceptions used in this work make explicit the need to see intelligence, knowledge, and action in an integrated framework. Thus, concepts such as heuristics, strategies of inference, problem-solving repertoire, knowledge systems, metaknowledge, and reflectivity have become prominent (e.g., Aebli, 1980, 1981; Tversky & Kahneman, 1973; Weinert & Kluwe, 1984). These concepts can be used to describe higher-order intellectual systems and processes of problem solving in complex, natural situations.

With respect to development, we suspect that some aspects of acquired problem-solving skills and some domains of knowledge require an extensive ontogenetic history of experiences and cognitive activities. Long-term ontogenetic experience and cognitive activity seem important and perhaps even necessary conditions to achieve progress in some aspects of intellectual functioning. In contrast to fluid intelligence, which in industrialized and modernized societies, for both biological and societal reasons, is a hallmark of academic intellectual development during the first two decades of life, the unique characteristics of adult intelligence include other domains and reflect experiences and cognitions that also occur in adult life.

Although a later section deals in more depth with the concept, let us use wisdom as an example (Dittmann-Kohli, 1984a; Baltes & Smith, 1990). We see wisdom as a prototype of a highly developed, "synthesized" and "pragmatic" form of intelligence or potential for problem solving dealing with important (existential) aspects of real-life situations. The ontogeny of wisdom is postulated to require extensive experience with complex life tasks. In contrast, fluid abilities involve solving clearly limited, decontextualized problems with clear-cut answers similar to what we have called in another context the "mechanics" of intelligence (Baltes et al., 1984). Following our discussions of fluid intelligence, we assume that wise persons must not necessarily excel in level of fluid functioning. It is unlikely that fluid functioning, if above the average level of performance of the adult population, is in itself a powerful predictor or generator of synthesized adult intelligence of the wisdom type. In contrast to fluid abilities, wisdom does not become relevant vis-à-vis problems that are well-defined, clearly limited, and decontextualized and that have clear-cut answers.

Cognitive Models, Schemata, and Knowledge Systems

A conception of intelligence that goes beyond a structural view of "elementaristic" abilities dealing with fairly abstract and content-free tasks is, of course, not new. Moreover, we need to acknowledge that Cattell (1971) himself has emphasized that available intelligence tests fail to index some domains of real-life problem situations. Nevertheless, it appears as if the effort to capture such real-life problem situations is more evident in recent work in cognitive psychology and in life-span developmental psychology than in the quarters of psychometric study.

Concepts from cognitive psychology (e.g., see Aebli 1980, 1981) possibly fertile for a new look at adult development of intelligence include declarative (factual) and procedural *schemata* that can be conceived of as the structural and dynamic elements of knowledge systems (synthesized intelligence). Such schemata and their organization (interconnections) are also constituents of the problem-solving repertoire of individuals and reflect the shared knowledge of a culture as well as the unique dimensions of a person's life history. The developmental process by which schemata are established and become organized into larger units has been described as "chunking" (e.g., see Mandler, 1983, p. 17). Another concept potentially useful is that of *content domains of knowledge.* An explicit concern with content (Shaw & Bransford, 1977) makes obvious that intellectual processing deals with both the *how* and the *what.*

Brown's (1982) effort at integrating salient aspects of cognitive models is particularly noteworthy in this context. Her theoretical approach contains the following features, all relevant to a comprehensive model of synthesized intelligence: (1) A distinction is made between declarative or *factual knowledge* and *procedural knowledge* (see also Anderson, 1982); (2) both factual and procedural knowledge range from highly *specific* to *generalized schemata* (see also Carver & Scheier, 1982; Meichenbaum, 1980); (3) knowledge systems can be distinguished by *content domains* and associated operative strategies (see also Hacker, 1978); (4) developed problem-solving strategies and factual knowledge in particular content domains define a category of efficacy or ability labeled as *expertise* (see also Chi, Glaser, & Rees, 1983; Ericsson & Crutcher, in press; Hoyer, 1984; Kliegl & Baltes, 1987).

Structure and differentiation of the various features of a knowledge system are important in defining whether and how a given problem—or what German action psychologists (see Dittmann-Kohli, 1982, 1987) call "action space"—is represented in the cognitive system of an individual and whether adequate problem-solving strategies are present or can be generated. In other words, the mark of synthesized or pragmatic intelligence is the quality of the individual's factual and procedural knowledge as well as his or her ability to combine general with specific schemata (see also Reither, 1981).

Particularly prominent with respect to general schemata are those described by the term *metacognition. Metacomprehension* is the awareness of whether or not something is being understood (Brown & French, 1979); *epistemic knowledge* is a term chosen by Kitchener (1983; Kitchener & Brenner, 1990) to denote reflective thinking (higher-order metacognition) about problem understanding and solution in cases where problems are ill-defined and have no clear-cut solution. The conception that cognitive activities may be regulated by higher-level, transsituational (general) procedural skills and by higher-order reflective thinking is in agreement with the hierarchical concept of action (see Gallistel, 1980, esp. Chap. 12) and with self-regulation of internal (cognitive) and external actions through attention or consciousness (e.g., Leontjew, 1979; Mandler, 1983; Norman & Shallice, 1975; Tomaszewski, 1978; Volpert, 1980, 1982).

An Action-Psychological and Pragmatic View of Adult Intellectual Development

An Action-Psychological Perspective

The action-psychological approach is another orientation to psychological research that is relevant to reconceptualizing adult intelligence. The concept of action (in contrast to "mechanistic" conceptions of a response or behavior) has a longstanding social science tradition in the United States and Europe.[2] Historically linked to functionalism (James, Dewey, Parsons), some more recent approaches in American cognitive psychology and contextually oriented life-span developmental psychology demonstrate compatible conceptualizations (e.g., Baltes, Reese, & Lipsitt, 1980; Dixon & Baltes, 1986; Norman & Shallice, 1980; Rumelhart & Norman, 1978).

Action psychology focuses on using action rather than response or reactive

behavior as the central unit of analysis. In activity theory (as well as in schema approaches of cognitive scientists, see Norman and Shallice, 1975), one conceptualizes the individual as an agent who is capable of goal setting, planning, and achieving effective functioning. The paradigm is intentional, active, and interactionistic in the strong sense of these words (Brandtstädter, 1984; Ford & Ford, 1987; Dittmann-Kohli, 1982, 1986). For some (e.g., Kaminski, 1981), the action-psychological framework is one strategy aimed at achieving a holistic perspective on man as a system. It follows from an action-theoretical perspective that intelligence has an instrumental character and that its development occurs in the context of human activity (Boesch, 1976; Kossakowski & Otto, 1977). Goals, plans, processes of regulation, outcomes, and transition to subsequent actions are the central factors determining cognitive activity and problem solving. In action theory, problem-solving and thought processes are inherently interwoven with the task of human activity in everyday life, its planning, execution, and evaluation (Dittmann-Kohli 1982, 1987). Thus, for intelligence to be understood it is imperative to analyze its structure and function in the context of real-life activities and the respective goal structures and ecologies of individuals (Dittmann-Kohli, 1984a).

Such action-theoretical orientations suggest that, as one charts adult intellectual development in terms of knowledge systems and problem-solving schemata, it is important to consider these as emanating from the action systems and societal contexts that characterize the individual life course. Thus, the goals, life experiences, and ecological demands that individuals exhibit or face as they move through adulthood are connected with external actions as well as with internal cognitive activities. The interplay between real-life settings (work, family, leisure) and cognitive activities has been consistently highlighted in action-theoretical endeavors (Hacker, 1978; Kossakowski, Kühn, Lompscher, & Rosenfeld, 1977; see Kohn & Schooler, 1978, for American counterpart work in sociology). Action theorists emphasize, as do others (e.g., Charlesworth, 1983; Schank & Abelson, 1977; Shaw & Bransford, 1977; White, 1974), that cognition is an essential part of human adaptation and that changes in intellectual functioning reflect the specifics of the action contexts and ecological conditions of everyday life.

An emphasis on the role of action and ecology in the formation and transformation of problem-solving repertoires and knowledge systems not only exemplifies how progression in intellectual functioning during adulthood can be understood, but suggests the conditions under which progressions will not take place or, on the other hand, conditions under which movement toward less effective cognitive functioning may occur. If the dominant life activities of a given person do not contain a sufficient amount of cognitive demands and supports, cognitive structures and functions will tend to regress (see also Smith's, 1968, concept of benign and vicious circles of development).

The structure and sequence of life activities, then, can result in such life-span developmental change patterns as (1) development (expansion, modification, or constriction) of pragmatic intelligence; (2) differential but cumulative development or decline of factual and procedural knowledge in the sense of selective optimization and differential loss; and (3) age-grading (sequencing) in relative foci of factual and procedural knowledge. Before we add some more observations to these latter

points by furnishing illustrations for sources and patterns of life activities, we want to elaborate the notion of neofunctionalism, another historical tradition in relation to the development of intelligence in adulthood (see also Dixon & Baltes, 1986).

The Neofunctionalist View of Adult Intellectual Development

The neofunctionalist paradigm in psychology includes both the cognitive-science concepts cited earlier and the action-psychological framework. Neofunctionalism represents a general orientation that emphasizes and possibly coordinates the various facets of mind and action highlighted in the previous sections. A concern with functionalism, then, serves as another vehicle by which we can illustrate and communicate our position on adult intelligence and its development.[3]

In our view, and within our focus on intellectual competence, the essential goal of a neofunctionalist approach is to locate intellectual functioning and competence within an action-in-context perspective (Dittmann-Kohli, 1982, 1984a, 1984b, 1986; Dixon & Baltes, 1986) and to emphasize the role of acquired and synthesized intelligence in human adaptation and activity during adult development. This neofunctionalist view of intellectual development is also evident in other discussions about the general concept of intelligence (Aebli, 1980; Baltes, Dittmann-Kohli, & Dixon, 1984; Glaser, 1981) and its ontogeny (Beilin, 1983; Labouvie-Vief, 1982, 1990; Pascual-Leone, 1983, 1990).

How does a functionalist approach influence work on intelligence? Historically, the concept of intelligence had been identified as part of a general process of human adaptation. It appears that subsequent conceptualization of intelligence and its development has dealt primarily with basic cognitive skills and contexts such as school achievement and logical problem solving. Relatively little work has been done, however, to identify the typical cognitive processes and the tasks to which intelligence can be applied at later stages of life or in problem-solving contexts outside of school life (Dittmann-Kohli, 1987; see also Baltes & Willis, 1979a; Schaie, 1977–1978). With a focus on a different age group (adolescence), the first author has presented a taxonomy and interview study on the problem-solving context of older adolescents in apprenticeship training. In this study, person–environmental and person–self transactions were analyzed as real-life problems and their solutions were seen as dependent on problem understanding and problem definition (Dittmann-Kohli, 1986; Dittmann-Kohli, Schreiber, & Möller, 1982).

The quest to recapture the original intent of viewing intelligence as part of a process of adaptive performance is seen, for instance, in the work of Charlesworth (1979, 1983). He stresses the necessity of collecting empirical data to shed light on the environmental factors involved in cognitive change and adaptational success. In his research with children and adults he attempts to gather data on problems and problem-solving behaviors. He places special emphasis on the contexts and consequences of problem-solving behaviors in order to examine the possible functional value of problem solving. From his ethological perspective, cognitively mediated behavior is a significant form of human adaptation to environmental conditions. However, Charlesworth believes that the extent to which particular learning or thinking processes are effective means for adapting to the natural envi-

ronment has never been adequately studied. Sternberg (1982) also argues that traditional research on intelligence has neglected those aspects of intelligence dealing with adaptation and motivation. An important link between motivation, intelligence, and mastery of life is to be seen in the transformation of vague need states into goals, plans, and behavioral projects (Nuttin, 1984).

A Developmental Dual-Process View

Cognitive-science, action-psychological, and ethological approaches have not placed their main emphasis on specifying the conditions and forms of cognitive development during adulthood and old age. We have recently formulated a dual-process model to account for the development of intelligence across the life-span (Baltes et al., 1984; Dixon & Baltes, 1986). In this *dual-process* model, two interrelated types of cognitive developmental processes are postulated. The first concerns developmental changes in cognition *qua* cognition or the *mechanics of intelligence*. This developmental process is seen as dealing with the ontogeny of basic forms of thinking as contained in such cognitive operations as classification, perceiving relationships, and logical reasoning. Ideally, measurement of this first process is content-free (ideally in the sense of a Weberian typology).

The second developmental process is called the *pragmatics of intelligence*. This second process of intellectual development deals with content and knowledge (i.e., with the construction of factual and procedural knowledge through the use of the mechanics of intelligence) and results in what we describe in the present paper as synthetic or pragmatic intelligence. It includes the development of abilities dealing with varied domains of substantive knowledge, systems of acquired (synthesized) general and specific cognitive procedures, as well as knowledge and skills relevant for the activation of intellectual resources and their application in different situations (performance factors as well as metacognition and epistemic knowledge).

On the one hand, then, we acknowledge in the first component of the dual-process model (cognition *qua* cognition) the existence of a system of ontogenetic processes in basic cognitive functioning. Within the realm of research on information processing, cognition *qua* cognition implies notions such as the basic architecture or mechanics of information processing. Cognition *qua* cognition is implied also in cognitive-developmental structuralism à la Piaget and derivatives thereof (e.g., Labouvie-Vief, 1980, 1982a; Pascual-Leone, 1983; see Pascual-Leone chapter). This first system of developmental processes may be fairly universal in form and function because it reflects shared conditions of biological and societal evolution.

On the other hand, we add to this "traditional" developmental perspective on cognitive structure and functioning a focus on a second class of processes and abilities that we judge to be contextual or extrasystemic in origin. This second process has features of universality as well (e.g., dealing with knowledge that is widely shared), but it includes a solid dose of particularisms. Feldman (1980), for example, has focused his analysis of developmental stages on such nonuniversal cognitive growth processes. The functional considerations that are particularly relevant for specification of this second process address the pragmatics of intellectual development. Factual and procedural knowledge evolves as a function of the goals and

contexts of individual lives—in our present case, those characteristic of adulthood and old age.

From a dual-process, neofunctionalist perspective, then, intelligence is seen as involving first a system of cognition *qua* cognition. In addition, however, there is an emphasis on viewing intelligence as one component of a larger system of human functioning, not as an end in itself. To concretize the essentials of such a neofunctionalist approach, we are focusing on action and the pragmatic use of intellectual resources as the first guiding principle to organize our understanding of the role and development of intelligence during adulthood and old age. A second guiding principle is a life-span view of the tasks or problem situations that individuals face as they age.

We believe that a dual-process, neofunctionalist perspective obtains particular importance for conceptualizing intelligence during adulthood and old age. Why is our emphasis on the role of the second process (i.e., the pragmatics of intelligence) particularly appropriate for adulthood and the second half of life?

As has been mentioned earlier, we believe that the acquisition and extension of basic abilities to reason (cognition *qua* cognition) is a widely shared developmental goal in the first decade of life. The emergence of this first class of cognitive processes is very much a reflection of fairly general evolution-based biological (e.g., genetic) programs, shaped by societal conditions (e.g., familial socialization and education). In subsequent segments of the life course, the central emphasis is less on exercising and improving basic cognitive skills. Instead, the relative emphasis is on putting these skills to use (e.g., in professional life) and on evolving a more individualized system of intellectual efficacy and knowledge for different domains of life. Whether and how use is made of earlier developed cognitive skills will be determined by external demands as well as by the individual's personality and actions. For instance, schooling does not specifically prepare individuals for interpersonal tasks at home or work, but many women seem to be motivated to develop social intelligence for use in family life (Dittmann, 1978; Dittmann-Kohli, 1980).

When juxtaposing the two developmental processes for the adult phase of life, then, our basic position is that the second one is relatively more important than the first. The primary force and directionality for intellectual development during adulthood and old age are not seen in further changes of the basic processing capacities, but in the tasks and directionality given by the pragmatic dynamics and contexts of adult life. In Baltes et al. (1984; see also Baltes, 1987; Dixon & Baltes, 1986), we discuss further the interplay between the two processes as they interact over the life course, particularly during aging. It is shown how growth in one process is possible in face of decline in the other (e.g., cognition *qua* cognition). The model of "selective optimization with compensation" is used to illustrate this possibly prototypical interplay between growth and decline.

Illustration: Conditions for Adulthood Change in Intellectual Functioning

We now offer some observations on environment- and person-related variables and action systems that may affect the course (directionality, differentiation, rate, etc.) of adult intellectual development. Although we favor an interactionist conception

of the person-environment transaction, for heuristic reasons it may be useful to offer these observations separately for environmental-external and person-internal conditions.

Environmental-External Conditions. The sociostructural organization of the life course involves both sequential or age-graded (normative) and differential (social stratification) aspects. In addition, there are historical differences in the life course within a given society to be considered as well as differences between cultural entities to be taken into account (e.g., Featherman, 1983; Kohli, 1986; Mayer & Müller, 1986; Riley, 1983; Rosow, 1976). Such differences in the social organization of the life course may relate to conditions that either (1) promote or interfere with development of intellectual functioning or (2) generate distinct and differential courses of change in cognitive abilities and cognitive processes.

The following illustrations are examples for (1) age-related and (2) differential social structuring. There is growing evidence that the ecology for aging persons is, on the average, increasingly one that is deficient in cognitive stimulation (Baltes & Baltes, 1980; Langer, 1982; see Langer et al. chapter; Perry & Slemp, 1980). The developmental tasks faced by aging individuals appear to entail an increasingly stronger dose of privatization (Meyer, 1986) as well as a correlated decreasing demand and support for public, wordly accomplishments (Featherman, 1980; Kuypers & Bengtson, 1973). At the same time, the social structure of the life course contains elements of differential directionality and differential support for intellectual change. For example, members of higher social classes continue to benefit more extensively from societal resources conducive to intellectual efficacy than members of lower social strata (Thomae, 1983). Kohn and Schooler (1978) have demonstrated such effects in the context of the work environment (see also Hoff, Lappe, & Lempert, 1982). Similar observations can be made for society-based differences in intellectual support when considering other social-structural conditions, such as gender (e.g., Shanan & Sagiv, 1982; Smelser, 1980), educational level (e.g., Baltes & Labouvie, 1973; Botwinick, 1977; Thomae, 1983), and ethnic-subcultural membership (Berry, 1981; Laboratory of Comparative Human Cognition, 1982).

Another illustration of the role of environmental-external conditions relates to differentiation and specialization effects associated with the commitment to particular life careers. It is in the nature of social structure and age-graded role differentiation that individuals acquire distinct patterns of expertise. Maintaining and evolving such expertises involves devoting a considerable amount of time and motivation to the relevant tasks. There is naturally a correlated reduction of alternative pathways available to an individual who is engaged in a particular career trajectory. Specialization is by definition selective and, by and large, incompatible with maintaining a high level of general intellectual efficacy and achieving alternative forms of expertise. The structure and sequence of work careers, then, is a persuasive example of how specializing and restrictive features of social-structural conditions influence the level, rate, and course of intellectual abilities and the type of cognitive skills and knowledge acquired. Depending on their location in the social structure of the life course, individuals differ in regard to the likelihood of exhibiting further progress, decline, or individualized patterns of selective but restricted optimization in intellectual functioning.

Personal Conditions. Developing individuals are shaped by more than external environmental conditions. In the framework of an active-organism, action-theoretical paradigm, individuals are also producers of their own development (Dittmann-Kohli, 1982, 1986; Lerner & Busch-Rossnagel, 1981). An action-theoretical perspective also emphasizes the view that developmental or life tasks are to be defined in terms of how the individual interprets and feels about those tasks. Therefore, cognitions that reflect subjective representations of goals and demands and their transformation into action must be taken into account. The definition and construction of specific life tasks are influenced not only by perceived immediate demands but also by beliefs about reality, generalized goals and values, expectations about the future, and possibilities. By processes of assimilation and accommodation, the individual's construction of self and life changes throughout adulthood. The implied changes in beliefs and goals can be seen as personality changes and as a reorganization of personal meaning systems. What is seen as a problem and what kind of knowledge and problem solving skills appear as useful and desirable will be related to these more comprehensive meaning systems (Dittmann-Kohli, 1989, 1990).

Other person variables mark more stable interindividual differences. For instance, beliefs about control, self-efficacy, and expectations for the future (e.g., Baltes & Baltes, 1986; Bandura, 1982a; Brim, 1974; Weisz, 1983) influence the selection and mastery of intelligence-demanding life tasks. The role of self-efficacy, for instance, determines whether and how individuals make use of existing opportunities, including the occurrence of chance encounters or nonnormative life events (Bandura, 1982b; Brim & Ryff, 1980; Howe, 1982). The life-span ontogeny of such belief systems (Lachman, 1985; Seligman & Elder, 1986; Weisz, 1983) is expected to play a major role in determining the manner in which individuals engage in cognitive activities aimed at expanding both their factual and procedural knowledge.

A host of other person variables may be among the conditions for continued growth (or decline) of intellectual functioning. Among them are achievement motivation (Dittmann, 1973; Dittmann-Kohli, 1981a; Heckhausen, 1980, 1986) and other achievement-related attitudes and values (Dittmann, 1973; Featherman, 1980). Because of the dearth of longitudinal data, the evidence for the long-term role of such personality variables for subsequent intellectual development is scarce. A recent analysis of the Berkeley–Oakland studies (Eichorn, Hunt, & Honzik, 1981), however, offers support for such a long-term effect from late childhood into middle age. One of the salient predictor variables for adult IQ change was a complex personality variable in early adolescence labeled Cognitive Investment. Cognitive Investment was indexed by a composite score of cognitive competence and motivational commitment. It was found that investment in oneself and one's growth during adolescence was a major driving force in achieving high levels of intellectual functioning during adulthood.

Another set of repertoires suggested by action-theoretical perspectives as possible facilitators of adult intellectual growth concerns self-directedness in learning. Examples are self-guided learning projects (Tough, 1971) and the availability of strategies or techniques of autonomous learning (Bransford, Stein, Shelton, & Owings, 1981; Dittmann-Kohli, 1981b; Flechsig, 1980). Such techniques of self-

directed learning can be seen as part of more generalized styles of life planning and life management. As discussed by Thomae (1968), such styles (*Daseinstechniken*) are important determinants of the extent to which individuals continue to seek and process new information.

It may be useful for researchers to focus on criterion groups of experts and outstanding individuals as models to study the conditions and mechanisms of continued growth in intellectual functioning and productivity (Chi et al., 1983; Cole, 1979; Ericsson & Crutcher, in press; Howe, 1982). Understanding how such criterion groups, collectively and individually, expand and apply their knowledge and how individuals differ in the emphases and strategies they utilize (e.g., specialization versus generality of knowledge) may offer clues for further understanding the development of adult intelligence in the larger population as well.

Forms of Progressive Intellectual Development: Wisdom as an Example

A Glimpse of the Past

The concept of wisdom and the life course has a long history in the philosophical and religious thought of ancient cultures (Clayton & Birren, 1980; Baltes & Smith, 1990; Dittmann-Kohli, 1984a). Aristotle was the first, or at least the best known, thinker in Greece whose notions of practical and philosophical wisdom were introduced into Western thinking. Western notions of wisdom are concerned with the quality of thought and judgment about the external world and human behavior therein. Eastern notions of wisdom are, however, much older and often stress quite different aspects of man's relations to the world. For instance, Indian philosophy addresses the development of higher states of consciousness (Alexander, 1982; see Alexander et al. chapter; Coan, 1977; Sprockhoff, 1979). In ancient Vedic philosophy, awareness of the innermost nature of the Self is held to be synonymous with direct experience of existence as a unified field of natural law that is at the basis of both subjective and objective life. According to this view, wisdom lies in living in full attunement with this inner nature of the Self and hence with the universal laws of nature underlying man and the world (Alexander et al., in press; Dillbeck, 1983a). In various forms of Buddhist philosophy, wisdom is the state of knowing and enlightenment to be attained by developing one's mind and transcending the boundaries of self-centered consciousness (Coan, 1977; Govinda, 1961).

In their review of the literature on wisdom, Clayton and Birren (1980) have emphasized that "wisdom has always enjoyed a positive association with the later years of life; in the past, it has also had social significance as a model for adults and as a guiding principle for ancient societies" (p. 129). Clayton and Birren also emphasize that one dominant tradition has been to consider wisdom as a type of knowledge involving an understanding of ontological issues and that an extended period of tutelage and passage of time in life were necessary conditions for the acquisition of this type of knowledge. Finally, they argue that wisdom not only deals with cognitive skills, but involves the integration of cognitive, affective, and reflective components.

In recent years, the topic of wisdom has been addressed by a small group of

scholars in the context of life-span psychology (e.g., Baltes & Dittmann-Kohli, 1982; Clayton, 1975, 1982; Clayton & Birren, 1980; Dittmann-Kohli, 1984a; Holliday & Chandler, 1986; Meacham, 1982, 1990; Smith, Dixon & Baltes, 1989; Sowarka, 1989).[4] Thus far, however, there is little agreement on the conceptualization and operational definition of wisdom and a corresponding lack of empirical work.

Wisdom as a Prototypical Concept of Adult Intelligence

In this section, we offer some preliminary observations on one possible form of progressive intellectual growth, wisdom. In general, we view wisdom as an individual's ability to exercise good judgment about important but uncertain matters of life. It is a highly developed aspect of synthesized or pragmatic intelligence in a particular domain accessible to everybody, that is, human life and the conditions of existence.

In the context of the present paper, with its focus on action-theoretical and neo-functionalist perspectives on intelligence, how could one approach the study of wisdom? Proceeding from our working definition of wisdom as an "individual's ability to exercise good judgment about important but uncertain (ill-defined) matters of life," we propose a number of characteristics for further delineation of the concept. We do this by specifying five features of wisdom or wisdom-related knowledge and problem solving.

General Characteristics of Wisdom and Wisdom-Related Tasks. Five features characterize our general theoretical orientation to the study of wisdom. Wisdom as an ability and/or wisdom-related tasks involve (1) a high level of efficacy in the sense of an *expertise* (including descriptive and procedural knowledge); (2) existential situations and the fundamental *pragmatics of life* as knowledge domain as well as interpretative and evaluative knowledge about the significance of this content domain; (3) attention to *life-span contexts* in problem definition and solution; (4) *uncertainty* as a characteristic of problem definition and solution; and (5) awareness of *relativism* in judgment and recommendation involving action. We acknowledge that these criteria are preliminary and in need of careful scrutiny and research.

What is the meaning of these definitional features? First, classifying wisdom as a form of *expertise* connotes that it is an ability and process involving a highly developed form of (abstract as well as concrete, general as well as specific) factual and procedural knowledge. This definition is similar to the treatment of expertise in other areas such as physics, the arts, or chess (Chi et al., 1983; Hoyer, 1984), as it involves long-time experience and a particular quality of the knowledge system that enables superior problem definition, evaluation, solution, and optimal judgment.

The use of the term *expertise* as a first characterization of wisdom, however, may be misleading to those who identify expertise with factual and procedural skills in fairly well-organized and contained knowledge domains such as chess and physics. The study of expertise has proceeded predominantly in such domains. In principle, however, the concept of expertise can be applied to domains that are not

well organized. In the case of wisdom, for example, as described by the entire set of five criteria mentioned, procedural and factual knowledge involves uncertainty and issues of interpretation and evaluation of human values. Thus, the expertise of wisdom is not limited to proficiency in the use of formal logic and to coherent, explicit, and socially organized knowledge domains. Rather, it requires knowledge in a content area that by definition is not part of an established and closed body of knowledge. Yet in its highest form, wisdom-related knowledge is highly differentiated as well as integrated and well organized. Wise persons, because of their expertise, will possess heuristics and find solutions that are judged by others to demonstrate quality of judgment. As a consequence, wise persons are sought out by others and viewed as advisors (Clayton, 1975) in select domains of life.

Wisdom as a form of expertise, then, is not focused on societally standardized tasks and well-known domains of knowledge. One may want to hypothesize that certain aspects of wisdom refer to an area of human reality where highly general and abstract understanding and procedures must be related to specific problems and situations. Thus, the expertise related to wisdom is not that of a specialist who has acquired a very limited set of operations and concepts for a specific subject matter already available in standardized form and taught to only a few people. In principle the "subject matter" of wisdom is accessible to most people as it is defined by one's own life or human existence in general. In the usual course of life, such knowledge is accumulated, and its accumulation is regulated by internal as well as external conditions. The domains of knowledge and cognitive skills particularly relevant for wisdom-related performance are further described later.

Second, we propose that the substantive domain of wisdom-related performance consists of the existential aspects and the fundamental *pragmatics of life*.[5] The fundamental pragmatics of life entails knowledge about questions of life adjustment (life planning, life management, life review). The knowledge is not only factual and procedural, but also reflective and involves means-end evaluations of goals in the larger meaning context of life. The term *pragmatics* is not used in the narrow sense of *practical* but in the philosophical sense (Bridgewater & Kurtz, 1963, p. 1714) of involving "thought. . . . as an instrument supporting the life aims of the human organism." Not all tasks of life call for wisdom. Rather, the contextual domain activated for wisdom-related performance is probably one that focuses on fundamental (existential, ontological) features of life, in regard to both the individual life course and societal functioning at large. Thus, the domain of wisdom is very extensive but does not include all possible contents or problems to which human thinking can be applied.

Tasks calling for wisdom are likely to include problems and crisis situations that are defined by the structure and sequence of major life events. Baltes and Dittmann-Kohli (1982; see also Baltes & Smith, 1990), for example, have argued that it may be possible to identify wisdom-related problem situations by reference to the patterning and sequencing of age-graded, history-graded, and nonnormative life events. Thus, wisdom would be needed to find superior problem definitions and solutions for those life tasks that are connected to important and/or long-term goals and values (cf. Dittmann-Kohli, 1982, 1984b, 1986). In defining relevance, one needs to consider both the individual (e.g., salience of the problem in the context of developmental tasks à la Havighurst or Erikson) and his or her salient partners

(in the sense of a life convoy; Kahn & Antonucci, 1980) and one's larger group, or even humanity. Thus, defining wisdom as dealing with the realities and pragmatics of life includes understanding ramifications, antecedents, and consequences of issues of life as well as availability of criteria that would permit judgments about degrees of life significance.

The wise person is likely to penetrate through the surface of a problem to its essentials, to sort out the short- from the long-term problem, to separate ideology and rhetoric from core components, and to identify the salient dimensions, alternatives, and solutions. As already indicated, many wisdom-related problems are issues of life-long significance for human existence or have long-term consequences in terms of suffering and happiness. In regard to societal issues, fundamental problems are those concerning collective solutions to human existence and conditions of distress and well-being. Because the domains of wisdom are the fundamental pragmatics of existential situations, the development of superior understanding and problem-solving capacity for this domain will often touch on social values and prohibitions as well as emotional problems and conflicts in self and others. In this respect, our understanding of wisdom includes the integration of cognitive, affective, and reflective components as seen by Clayton and Birren (1980). Thus, we expect wise judgments usually to be enhanced by reflectivity about one's emotions and cognitions as well as by an understanding of the origins and functioning of social norms and values.

Third, wisdom is strongly *life-span contextual* in problem definition and solution. We expect wise problem-solving behavior to begin with a "field"-oriented search toward identifying the meaning of the problem in its larger context and the course of life (Arlin, 1975; Tomaszewski, 1981). Such a search for the contextual meaning of a problem maximizes and at the same time focuses on the ecological, social, or human relevance of the problem at hand. As a consequence, the steps of procedural implementation of the problem solution are delayed until wisdom-related problems have been identified or constructed. The phase of problem identification (i.e., the understanding of problem ramifications and its context) gain in relative importance vis-à-vis the solution process in the narrower sense (Dittmann-Kohli, 1982, 1984b, 1986).

Fourth, wisdom acknowledges *uncertainty* in the problem, its definition, and its management. Uncertainty in problem definition is generated by a number of conditions. Uncertainty is involved because problem-solving tasks dealing with the pragmatics of life are likely to have a strong dose of ambiguity and complexity; the tasks are interdependent and ill-defined (Dittmann-Kohli, 1982, 1986; Dörner & Reither, 1978; Kahneman, Slovic, & Tversky, 1982; Kitchener, 1983; Scriven, 1980). The problems cannot always be clearly identified; they involve explication of possible interconnections, and solutions are not fully determined, nor are they based on complete information.

Fifth, forms of *relativistic* and *reflective thinking* and epistemic knowledge are part of higher levels of cognition toward which there is possibly progress in adulthood (Kramer, 1983; Labouvie-Vief, 1980; Meacham, 1982). For example, there is recognition of large interindividual variability in how individuals lead successful lives and define their interests. Varied sequences and multiple endpoints are acceptable. Wisdom-related judgments, therefore, are prone to have to reconcile

contradictory information (Clayton, 1975), to recognize the unknown (Fitzgerald, 1980; Meacham, 1982), to estimate the epistemological basis of one's own and others' knowledge and conclusions (Kitchener, 1983), and to offer conclusions of the conditional type. Thus, relativistic and reflective thinking is closely intertwined with the complexity and relative uncertainty of real-life situations and pragmatics.

Distribution and Possible Measurement of Wisdom as Ability. When is wisdom attained in life-span development and is it an attribute of a small elite? Wisdom is not *necessarily* a phenomenon that is entirely unique to adulthood. On the contrary, there may be precursors of wisdom in earlier periods of life-span development. Note, for example, that there are age-specific life crises in preadulthood (e.g., teenage pregnancy, death of parents) during which certain age mates may be prompted to acquire or demonstrate wisdom-related insight. Because wisdom is considered as an expert body of knowledge, however, its presence should be rare. Furthermore, we are uncertain about the distribution of wisdom across social strata. We do not consider "mainstream" worldly success and cleverness to be a *sine qua non* for wise judgment. Patterns of life tasks and repertoires may differ markedly for distinct cultural groups and subgroups. Thus, factual and procedural knowledge systems relevant for wisdom-related judgments on such life tasks must differ, at least in part, between members of different cultures and social strata (such as age, gender, and social class).

Finally, we are aware of the perhaps most troublesome dilemma in our attempt to define wisdom: the problem of criterion-referenced validity or scoring. We have not offered any definite prescriptions for assigning scores denoting quality to wisdom-related judgments (see however, Baltes & Smith, 1990). We have offered only a set of criteria that circumscribe the general approach. Measurement poses particular problems in the case of wisdom because its tasks do not have clear solutions and the problem definition itself is part of the task solution. As is true for many tasks dealing with complex matters involving a dimension of socioculturally defined value judgment (e.g., Kohlberg's system of moral-judgment levels), we do expect the task of measurement construction of wisdom to be challenging.

Domains of Wisdom

In conclusion, we consider some suggestions for differentiation within the concept of wisdom, thereby further solidifying the meaning of wisdom. We begin by briefly describing some domains of intelligence already in the literature that are amenable as a starting point for further specification in wisdom-related terms: social intelligence and practical intelligence. In addition, we add brief characterizations of two additional domains of wisdom *proper:* practical wisdom and philosophical wisdom.

Related Knowledge Domains: Social and Practical/Everyday Intelligence. Both a long-standing tradition and recent research have aimed at expanding the scope of intelligence to include domains other than academic intelligence. In some instances, the basic intent of such work has been similar to our interest in articulating a progressive form of adult intelligence, that is, wisdom. The major difference

is that we view wisdom as carrying specification beyond that given to areas such as practical and social intelligence.

Social intelligence and judgment constitute the domain with the longest history of work (e.g., Dittmann, 1978; Dittmann-Kohli, 1980; Keating, 1978; Spivack, Platt, & Shure, 1976; Thorndike, 1920; Trower, 1980). The substantive domain of this form of intelligence or ability is interpersonal relationships (not societal issues). Criteria and content used to define social intelligence vary but usually include (1) the ability to decode social information (role taking, interpersonal awareness, etc.), (2) the ability to solve tasks involving interpersonal and social problems, and sometimes, (3) measures of the effectiveness of one's social understanding and interactive achievements.

The separation of cognitive and sociocognitive development has a long-standing tradition (Berndt, 1981; Gelman & Spelke, 1981). Empirical evidence for the existence of a separate and coherent domain of social intelligence is, however, scant within the psychometric tradition. This may be due to the fact that existing tasks are inadequate. The traditional picture may be altered, however, based on work by Ford and Tisak (1983; see also Spivack et al., 1976). Ford and Tisak were able to show in factor analyses a distinct factor of social intelligence. Spivack et al. (1976) did not find any correlations between intelligence test measures and social problem-solving measures, whereas the latter were related to general life adjustment in children, adolescents, and adults. Cantor & Kihlstrom (1987) worked for many years on issues of social intelligence and its relation to personality and self-related knowledge and thinking, which they subsume under the social knowledge domain. Gardner (1983) has taken the position that social (interpersonal) and personal (intrapersonal) intelligence should be considered as two different basic human abilities which in their turn are separate "intelligences" from other types of thinking and knowing, like logical or spatial intelligence.

Practical or everyday intelligence is the second example of an existing domain focus that is relevant. Practical intelligence is contrasted often with the term *academic intelligence,* and work in this area reflects the general dissatisfaction with extant models of intelligence and their primary focus on fluid and decontextualized problem solving. Practical intelligence is often understood as problem solving directed toward tasks of daily living with an emphasis on technological or managerial demands.

Work by Sternberg, Conway, Ketron, and Bernstein (1981) provides a meta-perspective on this issue. Based on experts' ratings, they were able to show that different patterns of intellectual behaviors were associated with the concepts of academic versus everyday intelligence. As expected, academic intelligence was characterized by variables such as (academic) problem solving, verbal ability, and motivation. Everyday intelligence, however, was defined by variables such as social competence and practical adaptive behavior.

Practical and Philosophical Wisdom. Research in the two domains of social intelligence and practical, everyday intelligence is not aimed directly at operationalization of wisdom itself. However, such work is indicative of a significant trend relevant for alternative conceptions of adult intelligence (i.e., the consideration of forms of synthesized intelligence and of factual and procedural knowledge typical

for adult life). Such efforts, as is true for Sternberg's (1981) conception of four "macroprocesses" or our own concern for a dual-process model, reflect the search for an expansion of the concept of intelligence beyond its traditional heavy emphasis on fluid functioning and decontextualized thinking.

It is possible to make some further observations on the domains and evaluative criteria of wisdom. Within the domain of wisdom, two prototypical concepts can be distinguished with respect to abilities (expertise), tasks, and activities of problem definition and solution: practical wisdom and philosophical wisdom.

Practical wisdom is a concept that refers to the praxis of life and can be closely tied to action-theoretical concepts. In this vein, the *Shorter Oxford English Dictionary* (Onions, 1965) defines *wisdom* as, "The capacity of judging rightly in matters relating to life and conduct; soundness of judgment in the choice of means and ends; sometimes, less strictly, sound sense, especially in practical affairs."

In the context of action theory and life-span development, such a general definition may be operationalizable. Practical wisdom would entail what has been described under the notions of extrapersonal, interpersonal, and intrapersonal competence by Dittmann-Kohli (e.g., 1982, 1984b, 1986), that is, knowledge used to understand and master personally relevant real-life situations, including interpersonal interactions, performance in social roles, and person-self transactions. Within the different life tasks and reality domains of the life space, practical wisdom can be exercised with respect to the following: (1) knowledge and organization of action goals in the framework of a lifelong view of development (Gehmacher, 1975); (2) placement of individual decisions and action plans in the larger context of supraordinate goals and action systems (e.g., Wilensky, 1981); (3) consideration in each individual case of the existing personal resources and of external conditions and action outcome possibilities (Tomaszewski, 1978, 1981); (4) attention to conditions of individuality and the particular ecologies (Bronfenbrenner, 1979) defining the "action potential" of a given individual. Furthermore, (5) practical wisdom can be thought to involve problem-solving patterns related to cost-benefit analysis and the application of other concepts concerning the evaluation of effectiveness and efficiency of actions (Gasparski, 1969; Zieleniewski, 1966).

From a life-span developmental framework—based especially on knowledge about adulthood changes in personality (Jung, 1933; Neugarten, 1968)—it is important to distinguish carefully between *internal* and *external* outcomes (Dittmann-Kohli, 1982, 1984b, 1986) of "effect-directed behavior" (Dörner, 1982). External outcomes are located in the environment, whereas internal outcomes refer to intrapersonal psychological changes. Thus, practical wisdom would need to reflect the observation that for many individuals there may be, with advancing adulthood, a greater concern for internal than for external outcomes. A concern for internal outcomes may be the consequence of reevaluations involving external benefits and possibilities for goal attainment and realization of life expectations or standards of achievement (Dittmann-Kohli, 1989). Mid-life crises and internal changes described for socially successful men (Chew, 1976; Farrell & Rosenberg, 1981; Levinson, 1980; see Levinson chapter) can also be interpreted to reflect such processes and to result in a new system of criteria dealing with meaning and satisfaction in life (Brim, 1976; Kohli, 1977; Neugarten, 1968b).

This example illustrates the important role that personality plays as an objec-

tive and as a system context for wisdom-related thought. Consider the "self" as a pertinent example. A concern with the "self" as a regulatory and developmental system for assessing the quality of practical wisdom or of other forms of cognitive progression in adulthood appears attractive (see also Edelstein & Noam, 1982; Labouvie-Vief, 1985; Smith, 1968). Such an approach links practical wisdom to general conceptions of life-span personality development such as Erikson's epigenetic model (1968a) and Dittmann-Kohli's (1988, 1990) research on the reorganization of meaning of self and life in adulthood.

In Erikson's model (1968a; see also Staude, 1981), practical wisdom would involve judgments that facilitate optimal transitions at all stages of development. (Erikson's stages can be conceptualized as domains of factual and procedural knowledge.) In this process of optimization of stage transitions, the continuing construction and transformation of the self would represent a cornerstone for progressive development of practical wisdom. Thus, when it comes to old age and Erikson's last stages, practical wisdom would include consideration of the increasing limits on societal and personal resources associated with growing old (e.g., Kuypers & Bengtson, 1973). Because of such a reduction in certain personal, interpersonal, and societal resources, it is necessary and advantageous to develop new cognitive and affective resources through progression in practical wisdom. In Erikson's conception, practical wisdom in old age would consist of a construction of the self and the world that permits, for instance, the anchoring of one's increasing losses and one's finitude into the context of intergenerational transmission and cultural movement. Dittmann-Kohli (1988, 1989) has investigated self- and life-related cognitions of both young and elderly adults using systematic content analysis of self-descriptions. The results show that the elderly (1) show awareness of vanishing personal and temporal resources, (2) that their motivational cognitions (goals and evaluations) are adjusted to perceived limitations, and (3) that they construct satisfaction on the basis of self- and life acceptance.

Philosophical wisdom refers to a dimension of knowledge, cognitive activities, and genuine concern that goes beyond one's own self and specific environment and place in life. It is a more general concern with societal and cultural solutions for human existence. Philosophical wisdom includes cognitive activities on such topics as the conditions and barriers to collective attempts to resolve contradictions of interest and claims for truth.

In terms of the criteria specified earlier for wisdom-type cognition, the expertise of philosophical wisdom must entail, in addition, a high level of abstraction and generalization. The domain of philosophical wisdom may extend to transhistorical, transcultural, and transspecific aspects of life and its variable occurrence. The issues of life involved in philosophical wisdom are more fundamental and more general than those described for practical wisdom. They would include the essence of being and the relationship of the self and others to the world at large. The emphasis on uncertainty and relativity would be further accentuated and taken beyond the life course of a given individual and the variation within his or her culture. Philosophical wisdom would also include epistemological knowledge and understanding (Kitchener, 1983). For example, individual biases associated with distortions of human judgment and the conditions of critical thinking, the importance of historical and cultural differences in understanding the world and intelligence itself,

societal ideologies, and the general limits of the human mind would be explicitly recognized.

As we reflect about this attempt at a psychological definition of philosophical wisdom, we feel pushed toward certain limits, either our own limits or those of the scientific approach and our discipline. It is acceptable to most empirical scientists that there are forms of knowledge other than science and that some phenomena may not be amenable to scientific analysis. Thus, unless there is a high level of interdisciplinary cooperation, including the social sciences and humanities as well as applied professions, progress in the understanding and definition of philosophical wisdom will be hampered. In principle, it seems desirable that such interdisciplinary cooperation should be attempted. An adequate understanding of the highest forms of cognitive processes and knowledge cannot be the monopoly of one discipline or of one method.

Conclusion

We have proposed alternative approaches to the conceptualization of intelligence and intellectual development in adulthood by examining psychometric findings. These findings point to the necessity of defining a broader concept of intelligence than that for much current work on intelligence. This broader concept includes the developmental synthesis of factual and procedural knowledge in adulthood and the adaptive (pragmatic) functioning of intelligence in the context of everyday living and lifelong adaptation.

The terms *synthesized* and *pragmatic intelligence* are used to describe this extended conceptualization of intellectual competence.[5] Synthesized pragmatic intelligence refers to systems of factual and procedural knowledge used in problem solving and in coping with life in general. As with crystallized abilities, the development of synthesized intelligence depends on the individual's interactions with his or her culture. Unlike crystallized abilities, however, synthesized pragmatic intelligence is not restricted to verbal abilities and simple reasoning skills but, in addition, provides the intellectual resources for complex problem solving and the production of complex and creative achievements. These achievements are possible only as a result of the selective integration of long-term experience into successively better-organized knowledge systems.

This expansion of the concept of intelligence is linked to a dual-process conception of the development of intelligence. The first process is the development of cognition *qua* cognition or the mechanics of intelligence, whereas the second is the development of pragmatic (synthesized) intelligence as a class of resources to be acquired and employed in human actions related to the adaptive tasks of human functioning during the life course. In the dual-process scheme, growth and decline occur simultaneously. During adulthood, decline may apply primarily to the first process. Growth, on the other hand, is possible primarily in the second process leading to an increase in select facets of synthesized or pragmatic intelligence. It can be understood as the increase of select domains of expertise. Among such expertises are domains in which problem definitions and solutions involve everyday living as well as more fundamental issues in human life.

Thus, we propose that the potential for intellectual growth during adulthood is related to continued evolution and reorganization of factual and procedural knowledge. This process is associated with the developmental tasks and life conditions of adulthood. We conclude that the primary force and directionality for intellectual development during adulthood can be seen not in the basic properties of intelligence as a logical system, as would be true for Piagetian theory (in our conception part of the first process), but in the tasks and demands given by the pragmatics and context of adult life.

This conceptualization of the dynamics of adult intellectual development is proffered within a neofunctionalist paradigm. Such a neofunctionalist paradigm is consistent with and can be elaborated by two other theoretical orientations that are used as a framework: cognitive psychology and action psychology. Cognitive psychology contains concepts and methods relevant for the study of synthesized intelligence. Action psychology specifies the behavioral context in which intelligence is employed. An action-theoretical approach focuses on the individual's goals and actions within a societal context. A life-span developmental view of goals and action systems provides an organizational framework for the content and likely sequence of cognitive activities. Because of interindividual differences in the structure of the life course, the life-span approach contains also statements about differential conditions for growth and decline.

These views and concepts imply that there are differential courses of intellectual development with respect to growth and decline as well as domains of knowledge. Under beneficial circumstances with respect to both personal and environmental conditions, growth may occur in knowledge domains (and thus in problem-solving abilities) pertaining to social roles and everyday functioning as well as to fundamental aspects of individual and collective life. In this sense, we present wisdom as a prototypical case for lifelong growth in intellectual functioning. Such lifelong growth leading to wisdom may occur only under certain favorable conditions.

A set of five criteria has been used to define the prototypical features of wisdom-related cognitions: expertise, fundamental pragmatics of life, contextual richness, recognition of uncertainty, and awareness of relativism. These criteria are also relevant to wisdom-related tasks. We further differentiate between practical wisdom as related to one's personal life and life course, on the one hand, and philosophical wisdom as related to the general nature of human life and existence, on the other. These considerations may help to pave the way for further work on the concept of wisdom, with the goal of operationalization and empirical study.

Acknowledgments

We thank a number of colleagues who have either read an earlier version of this manuscript or have discussed with us some of the ideas presented: Michael Chandler, Michael W. Chapman, Steven W. Cornelius, Fergus I. M. Craik, Roger A. Dixon, Rita de S. French, Reinhold Kliegl, Deirdre Kramer, Jutta Heckhausen, Daniel Keating, Margie E. Lachman, Richard M. Lerner, Ellen Markman, John A. Meacham, Carol A. Ryff, Jacqui Smith, Doris Sowarka, Ursula Staudinger and Hartmut Zeiher. The essence of this manuscript was completed in 1982 while the second author was a visiting fellow and professor at Stanford University (Center for Youth Development and Department of Psychology); a revision and updating was

completed in 1987 and 1989. More recent work has used the theoretical framework outlined in empirical research on wisdom-related knowledge associated with tasks of life-planning and life review (Baltes & Smith, 1990; Smith & Baltes, in press; Staudinger, 1989).

Notes

1. A terminological note regarding the terms *synthesized* and *pragmatic* intelligence is necessary because the authors in their own independent work use different concepts for similar but not identical phenomena. Dittmann-Kohli (1984a) speaks of "synthesized" intelligence. Baltes uses the concept "pragmatics" of intelligence and juxtaposes it with the "mechanics" of intelligence (Baltes et al., 1984; Dixon & Baltes, 1986).

2. Recently, in German-speaking countries, the concept of action has been emphasized as the centerpiece of psychological research and theory (Boesch, 1976; Brandtstädter, 1981, 1984; Chapman, 1982; Dittmann-Kohli, 1981b, 1982, 1986; Eckensberger & Silbereisen, 1980; Kaminski, 1981; Lenk, 1981; Leontjew, 1979; Tomaszewski, 1978, 1981; von Cranach, Kalbermatten, Indermühle, & Gugler 1980). Boesch's conceptions of action psychology are derived from a joint consideration of several French lines of scholarship (Janet, Piaget, Rey). Within the Soviet and East European tradition, action-theoretical orientations have been used for many years as core conceptions in a person-environment model that stresses goal-oriented behavior (e.g., work, learning activities) as the main adaptational feature of the human species for solving existential tasks. The human capacity for intentional self-regulated behavior is seen as the most important device for planning and implementing complex action systems that serve individual and societal goals within a historically changing cultural context. This theoretical framework is referred to as action psychology (*Handlungspsychologie*) or activity theory (*Tätigkeitspsychologie*). Within the framework of activity theory, the process of acquiring and synthesizing factual and procedural knowledge occurs within the context of human actions that function as a link between individuals and their environment (Kossakowski & Otto, 1977; Mehan, 1981).

3. Beilin (1983) has specified the neofunctionalist features of information processing research as well as other approaches (e.g., social learning theory), in contrast to earlier functionalism (Heidbreder, 1933). He also points out that Vygotsky (1962, 1978) has been the inspiration for a number of neofunctionalists and that Vygotsky's attraction has at least in part resulted from the emphasis he placed on interpersonal interaction and the cultural context of cognitive development. In line with Vygotsky's standing in East European scholarship, the stress on the interactive and cultural context of cognitive development and its dependence on planful learning and thinking activities has been elaborated, for example, in East German work on educational psychology (e.g., Kossakowski et al., 1977).

4. The reader interested in the history of developmental psychology may enjoy the fact that G. Stanley Hall, one of the great pioneers of developmental psychology, though better known for his work on childhood and adolescence, published in his late life a book on aging (Hall, 1922). In this book Hall devoted considerable attention to the concept of wisdom—after having published an anonymous essay on the same topic in the *Atlantic Monthly* the year before (January 1921).

5. A historical note may be helpful. In line with a functionalist orientation, the term *pragmatics* as used here is much influenced by one of the philosophical counterparts of functionalism, that is, pragmatism. In pragmatism (e.g., Bridgewater & Kurtz, 1963), thought is considered instrumental to the aims of an individual. Occasionally, it is also assumed that when using the term *pragmatic* the aims or matters involved are "important" ones. An example is the term *pragmatic sanction* in political history. Pragmatic sanction involves a decision of state that deals with "matters of great importance to a community or state having the force of fundamental law" (p. 1714).

3

The Roots of Adult Creativity in Children's Symbolic Products

Howard Gardner, Erin Phelps, and Dennie Wolf

Adult and Child Creativity

In his *Critique of Practical Reason* (1956/1788) Immanuel Kant spoke of two experiences that filled him with awe: the starry heavens above and the moral law within himself. To Kant's list, one might consider adding a third miracle—the young child engaged in creative artistic activity. Consider children the world over, building intricate castles in the sand, then knocking them down and reconstructing them; making an imaginative drawing, then showing it to other individuals or displaying it upon a wall; listening to stories or songs and then creating novel instances of these compositions themselves; mastering a simple computer programming language and then using it to create and play various kinds of traditional and invented games. The confidence, skill, and flair with which young children execute these activities is certainly worthy of careful investigation, if not Kantian hyperbole.

Equally miraculous in their own way are the creations of talented adults at the height of their powers. Whether it is Picasso executing *Guernica,* Mozart composing *Don Giovanni,* Shakespeare drafting *Hamlet,* or Newton ferreting out laws of the universe, these events represent creativity in all of its fullness—the miraculous forging of powerful symbolic products.

Once the creative products of the young child and those of the mature artist, scientist, or inventor have been juxtaposed, an insistent set of questions leaps to mind. How similar are the products fashioned by these contrasting populations and are there discernible similarities in the processes whereby each is achieved? How deep are the resemblances? Do insights into children's artistic or scientific products shed light on the activities of the adult creative individual as he devises a new theoretical system or an artistic masterpiece? Or to reverse the direction of insight, can the adult creator help us to understand better what the young child is about? Might there even be a U-shaped curve of development capturing special affinities that obtain between the creative products of the young child and the mature artist? On this U-shaped hypothesis, the differences between the individual of 10 or 15 years of age and the mature artist would emerge as more pronounced than those

that obtain between the preschooler and the adult (Strauss, 1982). In short, how do the symbolic products and processes of the young child stack up against those fashioned by the mature creative adult?

Even to approach these questions requires initial spade work. To begin with, one needs a working notion of adult creative work, its principal characteristics and its favored manner of operation. Next, one wants an equivalent portrait of the development of the creative process in young children. Only armed with these bodies of knowledge can one initiate a comparison to see whether there are indeed revealing similarities between the two target populations. Of course any argument of this sort should build on what has already been established about the relationship between child and adult thought. And once this question has been raised, all roads lead inevitably to the momentous work of Jean Piaget (1970b).

Piaget's Contribution

It is to Piaget that we owe many, if not most, of the key working concepts in the area of cognitive development. To mention just a few, there is the conviction that one must begin by positing an end state of adult competence and then trace the various steps through which children pass en route to this adult competence. There is the notion of the child as an active, constructing hypothesis generator and problem solver—one continually seeking to make sense in his own way of the objects, persons, and products about him. There is the general view of thought as commencing in overt activity but consisting eventually of various kinds of internal actions—operations, transformations, and the like. Finally, there is Piaget's insightful though elusive form of interactionism, with the child's inherent biological and psychological proclivities constantly guiding his actions upon the environment, even as the environment is shaping his thoughts and behaviors through the particular objects and experiences encountered by the child. It is indeed a tribute to Piaget that researchers working in this area, whether or not they ostensibly agree with his specific themes and contributions, have almost without exception adopted his agenda for the study of cognitive development. For the most part they adopt his image of the child and approach the kinds of issues and concepts in which he was interested, though often in instructively different ways.

Not even Piaget could consider all issues from every angle. And so when one turns to a study of creative process, one encounters genuine limitations in his formulations. One obvious (and readily conceded) characteristic of Piaget's contribution is its focus on logical–rational thought. Piaget pointedly took as his end state the developed scientist; accordingly, the kind of thought whose development he singlemindedly traced was logical-scientific thinking of the sort engaged in by the work-a-day scientist. Moreover, Piaget believed that this form of thinking unfolded in predictable fashion, with its major outlines being completed by early or middle adolescence: He had virtually nothing to say about innovative scientific work of the sort in which he himself engaged.

But our own work, and that of an increasing number of other researchers, raises

questions about whether it suffices to study the development of one form of intelligence. There is increasing evidence to suggest that intellect is better thought of as composed of a variety of domains, including not only logical-mathematical thought and linguistic knowledge, but also such relatively unstructured forms as visual–spatial thinking, bodily-kinesthetic activity, musical knowledge, and even various forms of social understanding (Allport, 1980; Fodor, 1983; Gardner, 1984; Rozin, 1976). To be sure, development occurs in each of these domains, and a Piaget-type model may prove adequate for some or even all of them (Feldman, 1980). But there is no necessary identity of intellectual progression across these distinctive domains. At the very least, transdomain similarities constitute an empirical issue, not one that can be settled by fiat. Further, it is not at all clear that the kind of symbolic products an individual fashions in such disparate areas as language, logic, or bodily expression come about by virtue of the same kinds of processes and entail analogous critical capacities.

A further issue that remains unresolved in the Piagetian corpus concerns the ways in which creative work is actually carried out. Clearly, Piaget's prototypical child is engaging in creative problem solving. Even though the problems the child is addressing (such as the permanence of objects or the conservation of liquids) have previously been confronted by countless other individuals, he must still construct solutions himself. In that sense at least, we may credit Piaget with insights about original creative activity. Yet because Piaget deals principally with the solution to naturally encountered problems that individuals normally negotiate by adolescence, he perforce leaves uninvestigated the fashioning of highly complex and often idiosyncratic products by the mature adult creator. In Piaget's scheme there are no notions of problem finding, of forging a new area of study, of constructing a finished artistic work or a complex scientific theory. Instead, Piaget has been interested principally in the processes with which youthful individuals attack limited problems with clear-cut solutions and has shown relatively little concern with how the aforementioned completed products might be fashioned.

Of course, Piaget himself was aware of these lacunae. In a 1972 paper in *Human Development,* Piaget conceded that formal thought did not necessarily obtain across all domains, but in fact might be found only in those lines of practice where an individual worked steadily. Here was a tacit recognition of a plurality of domains in which humans can be competent, as well as acknowledgment of the possibility that the processes or products involved in one domain might not be identical to those that figure in others. Piaget also said of the creative imagination that it is "a magnificent subject which remains to be investigated" (Piaget & Inhelder, 1966, p. vii). And in a telling warning to his colleague, Howard Gruber, he once said of creativity, "it touches everything." It seems clear to us that any scientific study of creativity in children and adults should build upon Piaget's path-breaking work, and his seminal ideas. We have relied heavily on his clinical method and his notions of organized stages of development. Yet, because of the problems just noted, it seems equally evident that we cannot develop a scientific study of creativity solely through an uncritical application of Piaget's insights into the development of logical–mathematical thought.

Adult Creativity

Efforts to elucidate adult creative powers have been undertaken for many years by psychologists, but progress in this area has been elusive. An initial wave of studies, some decades ago, focused particularly on an ability dubbed *divergent thinking*— the capacity to come up with an indefinite number of meanings for a word, uses for an object, associations to an idea. The fascination with divergent thinking seems to have been based on a belief that such "cocktail party fluency" might in fact provide the key to understanding more elaborated forms of creative behavior (Guilford, 1959; Torrance, 1965; Wallach & Kogan, 1965;). But the virtual discontinuation of this line of research is the strongest evidence of its generally perceived inadequacy. The face validity of such associative ability has never been convincingly established, particularly since the correlation between performance on such tests of fluency and creativity of a high order has yet to be demonstrated. Perhaps such fluency is helpful for middle-range inventiveness, but it seems far removed indeed from the forging of significant symbolic products.

A step forward was taken in the past two decades by investigators who focused on more molar kinds of problem solving. Abjuring artificially simplified laboratory stimuli, investigators like Herbert Simon and Allan Newell (Newell & Simon, 1972) have examined the creative activities involved in playing chess or solving geometrical proofs. They have used the protocols of skilled subjects engaged in these kinds of problem-solving situations as a major source for devising "intelligent" computer programs. The Simon team and others working in the tradition of artificial intelligence have done a yeoman's service in demystifying the creative process; they have provided evidence that, far from being a mystical "eureka" experience bathed with affect, problem solving can be properly viewed as a regular, systematic, and rational process wherein an individual (or a program) armed with a goal can steadily reduce the distance between the information initially given and the specifications of a solution.

In an allied tradition, several investigators, including Catherine Patrick (1935) and our colleague David Perkins (1981), have engaged in "process-tracing" studies of the creative mind in operation. Rather than focusing particularly on the relationship between the initial and the final steps in problem solution, they have examined the microstructure of moment-to-moment problem solving, especially in less-well-defined areas, such as the editing of a poem. Once again, this line of activity has helped to demystify the creative process by demonstrating its step-by-step and often quite mundane nature. In this view, the creative person is not a special species, but someone who has sharply honed the kinds of routine noticing, reasoning, and problem-solving processes that characterize all normal individuals.

Though clearly an advance upon the earlier experimental studies of creativity, much of the work growing out of the artificial intelligence tradition still strikes us as targeted to relatively specific kinds of problem solving carried out in overly circumscribed periods of time. In actuality the most impressive creative processes involve a fully developed individual who has been working for many years, with the result that he is able to create products of great intricacy, power, complexity, and novelty. In the long run, it may be essential to study such a creative process directly rather than trying to simulate or capture it in the laboratory. In this con-

text, we find especially intriguing the recent efforts by Howard Gruber and his associates to study ongoing problem solving and problem finding over a substantial period of time by creative individuals of the indisputably highest order.

In his path-breaking study of the notebooks of Charles Darwin, Gruber (1981) shows how the biologist's creative activity entails the pursuit of a whole series of projects—a network of enterprise—over a long period of time. The creative individual is guided, even defined, by an overall sense of purpose or purposes to achieve these ends; he will involve himself in many activities that to an outsider may exhibit only a loose connection to one another. He acquires new methods and skills as he needs them and, in good "executive" fashion, draws flexibly upon them to solve problems that arise in the course of the larger mission.

Other characteristics frequently found in creative individuals include easy access to the details in an area of expertise, the use of various organizing metaphors or images of wide scope, the capacity to perceive connections and patterns among a wide and apparently disparate set of facts, and a genuine passion for the materials with which the individual is working (see Gardner, 1982a, Chap. 32; Lorenz, 1966). But for the purpose of a study of creativity, what comes out most clearly in the work of Gruber and his associates is a sense of the elaborateness of the enterprise in which the creative individual is engaged: Such an enterprise takes many years to achieve fruition, involves the monitoring of an incredibly large amount of information that the individual is continuously sifting, reordering, thinking through, until he finally arrives at a perspective that makes sense to him and that realizes his mission. Only at this point can the individual produce a symbolic product that matches his own specifications.

Adopting Gruber's perspective, we see creative individuals as not merely solving but also finding problems, not just answering questions raised in the world they inherited but creating their own worlds (Getzels & Csikszentmihalyi, 1976). Nor is this spirit restricted to scientific work. As Charles Rosen has commented, "Since the Renaissance at least, the arts have been conceived as ways of exploring the universe, as complementary to the sciences. To a certain extent they create their own field of research. Their universe is the language they have shaped whose nature and limits they explore and, in exploring, transform. Beethoven is perhaps the first composer for whom this exploratory function of music took precedence over every other: pleasure, instruction, and even at times expression" (1972, p. 445). Igor Stravinsky put it more succinctly in *Expositions and Development:* "A new piece of music is a new reality" (Stravinsky & Craft, 1981).

In surveying this literature, we arrive at a provisional picture of adult creative process. We encounter a fully developed adult at the height of his powers working within a domain in which a considerable degree of expert knowledge is essential. The individual has worked for many years to master the relevant materials and skills. He displays great flexibility in how he accesses relevant information and he is willing to countenance unusual connections, juxtapositions, and patterns and to play with them. He resists the conventional wisdom. In addition, the creative individual is marked by a clear agenda, a sense of purpose, a goal, as well as a large number of projects in which he deliberately engages as a means of bringing himself closer to this goal. In his constant involvement in this mission, he exploits many of the mundane problem-solving capacities that each of us uses every day. But he

does it with an enhanced intensity, extending over a wider body of knowledge, and with a more pervasive goal in mind than most of us can realize (or even envision) in our everyday workings.

Thus described, our creative adult at work seems quite remote from the daily activities of the young child. Certainly there is no way in which the four- or the seven-year-old can magically acquire the knowledge base, or the technical skills, on which an adult artist or scientist routinely relies. Yet in the manner in which he approaches his own activity with symbols, the young child may well bear more than a superficial resemblance to the accomplished adult creator. Before we can effect a full comparison between child and adult creativity, however, it is necessary to take a closer look at what has been established about the roots of creative activity in the young child.

Creativity in the Child

As with adults, there are several traditions of research on creativity in children. Some work probes divergent and fluent processes in the child (Wallach & Kogan, 1965), but like the adult investigations, this line of research has not generally been credited with any breakthroughs. Within the personality and psychoanalytic areas (Greenacre, 1959), a search has been conducted for traits that seem associated with creative children—imaginary compositions, unresolved Oedipal conflicts, and permissive households are candidates for early indicators of eventual creative achievement. These latter lines of investigation have informed our understanding of possible differences between those children who become involved in highly creative activities and those who do not. But because of their focus on affective and personality facets of development, they leave unilluminated those cognitive facets of creativity that constitute our particular focus here.

Perhaps for these reasons, a rather different perspective upon youthful creativity has more recently come to the fore (Bates, 1979; Werner & Kaplan, 1963). This approach focuses on the way in which young children first become engaged with, and eventually come to master, the building blocks of creative work, the various symbol systems of their culture. It is this particular approach that marks our own examination of child and adult creativity.

An interest in symbol systems is a child of this century. As Susanne Langer argued persuasively in *Philosophy in a New Key* (1942), a major preoccupation of researchers over the past 50 years has been the nature of the various systems evolved by human beings to create, capture, and communicate meanings. Current interest in language, art, and science, all reflect an increased awareness of what human beings create: various kinds of symbols that, through their syntactic, semantic, and pragmatic properties, capture and convey important kinds of information.

From our own point of view, a focus on symbol systems takes on additional significance (Gardner, 1979, 1983). The symbol systems of a culture represent a crucial mid-point between the individual's "raw" computational powers, on the one hand, and the ensemble of roles and values endorsed by the culture on the other. The individual is constrained by his biologically grounded ways of knowing; the culture is constrained by the roles and functions that must be realized if that

culture is to endure. In our view, evolutionary processes extending over many thousands of years have enabled an individual to partake of his culture's agenda; and the favored means for achieving this goal has been various symbol systems in his culture.

Let us say a bit more about this special intermediate role assumed by symbol systems. On the one hand, symbol systems have been so constituted that they can be perceived and comprehended by the human nervous system: in other words, as biological creatures, we are able to process and make sense of language, pictures, music, and the like. On the other hand, symbol systems are also capable of capturing the principal values and knowledge of the culture and to do so in such a way that (whether successful or unsuccessful) their operation is apparent to other members of that culture. The particular forms in which such symbol systems are apprehended are various symbolic products—the stories, songs, paintings, mathematical problems, scientific theories, and the like—that individuals have forged over the centuries in an effort to make sense of the meanings of their experiences. It is through monitoring the mastery of these forms that the culture can assess its own vitality and endurance. An individual who would participate in his culture and eventually express himself creatively must first master these symbol systems; only then does the opportunity arise for the creation of new forms of meaning, for the imaginative deployment of symbol systems.

Reflecting trends in philosophy, psychologists have also turned their attention to the development of competence in various symbol systems. For the most part this work has focused on particular symbol systems. As a result, we have learned a significant amount about the development of linguistic (Brown, 1973) and mathematical-logical capacities (Gelman & Gallistel, 1978), though considerably less about other forms of symbolic competence, such as those involved in various art forms. We have also attained some insight into individual differences in symbolic facility, differences that affect the child's interest in the rules of particular symbolic systems and ability to assimilate them readily (Kogan, 1976; K. Nelson, 1973). In short, as in many other areas of developmental psychology, one finds a number of well-populated settlements that, when combined, yield at least a preliminary sketch of the development of symbolic competence in the child.

Notably absent from the developmental literature, however, has been a coordinated effort to synthesize our knowledge about the development of different symbolic competences and to see how in fact they relate to one another. Nor has there been sufficient consideration of the relationship between the acquisition of work-a-day symbolic competence and the capacity to engage in novel or creative activity. To fill part of this gap, our research group at Harvard Project Zero has been engaged over the past decade in an intensive study of early symbolic development. On a regular basis, we have visited a group of nine children, from the age of one to seven, and we have documented their progress in coming to know a variety of symbol systems—language, symbolic play, music, number, drawing, block building, and bodily expression or dance. Our effort has been to provide a portrait of symbolic development in each of these several domains, but even more, to establish what commonalities might obtain across different symbol systems. (For details, see Gardner & Wolf, 1983; Wolf & Gardner, 1979, 1981.)

Part of our effort, then, has been to sketch out the development of competence

within specific symbolic domains. We have looked, for example, at drawing and we have discerned a sequence from early scribbles to the development of specific but nonrepresentative geometric forms; we have gone on to observe the child's emerging ability to relate these forms to objects in the real world, initially with prompting from others, and then on his own to forge two-dimensional equivalents of three-dimensional objects. Going beyond the representational stage, we have studied children's ability to represent less prominent aspects of visual experience, such as occlusion of one object by another, as well as their nascent capacity to organize elements within a drawing so that the resulting product exhibits a sense of balance and composition (Gardner, 1980a; Gardner and Wolf, 1979).

In the area of music we have observed an analogous sequence (Davidson, McKernon, and Gardner, 1981). From an undifferentiated matrix of linguistic sounds and tonal sequences, the child proceeds in the second year of life to practice various pitch patterns, including those intervals that eventually constitute the music of his culture. Next, the child produces spontaneous songs that, by the third year of life, feature characteristic bits obtained from the songs of the culture. In a parallel to the onset of representational drawing, a child at the age of three or so becomes increasingly influenced by the songs sung in his culture; by the age of four, he displays the ability to sing the culture's songs, which have now become dominant over the production of spontaneous song. Within another year the child is able to convey not just the overall pattern of a song (its general shifts in contour and dynamics), but the precise pitch patterns, intervals, and meter. He has a first-draft knowledge of music.

A somewhat parallel pattern can be discerned in the area of storytelling (Rubin & Wolf, 1979; Scarlett & Wolf, 1979). Initially, one can identify two separate streams. There is the development of language proper, which commences with individual words and gradually shifts to words in meaningful duos, simple sentences, and, before long, sentences exhibiting grammatical complexity. The companion stream involves narrative competence. This can be observed first in simple play constructions: The child carries out elementary sequences where an agent's actions have consequences for an object or another person. By the age of three the child can use his burgeoning language skill to guide these elementary narratives. And so one notes the onset of simple stories, where a good and an evil character vie for control. Initially, the child exhibits difficulty in respecting the boundary of the story. He seeks to solve problems via a *deus ex machina* rather than through the exploration of elements implicit in the plot of the story. For instance, he rescues a trapped doll simply by announcing that an impediment has been removed rather than by having an appropriate character come to the doll's aid. Or he inserts himself into the action of the story rather than respecting the "boundedness" of a fictive entity. But again, by the age of four or five, the child has achieved sufficient command over narrative, as well as sufficient linguistic subtlety, to allow him to produce a story that adheres to many principles of narrative in his culture.

Much of what happens within each symbol system proves peculiar to that symbol system. Thus, laws of perspective are important to the realm of drawing and have no interesting reverberations in other symbol systems; similarly, the mastery of pitch in music, or of the narrator's role in storytelling, also proves specific to these particular symbol systems. Part of the story of symbol development is an

account of the ordinal scales in each of these particular symbolic domains—what we have elsewhere labeled the "streams" of symbolization (Gardner & Wolf, 1983).

Yet, as already suggested, there are definite parallels across development in particular symbolic domains. For instance, one finds a steady growth in complexity of organization, and a steady increase in faithfulness to "approved" cultural products, in each of the previously mentioned realms—drawing, singing, and storytelling. Moreover, in our investigations, we have also found evidence for deeper continuities that operate across diverse symbolic domains. We believe that we have uncovered a set of underlying psychological processes that emerge at approximately yearly intervals during the first quinquennium of life (Wolf & Gardner, 1981, Gardner & Wolf, 1983). These "waves of symbolization" arise initially in one or two symbolic systems but rapidly spread to other symbolic systems, including ones in which they are not necessarily appropriate. In our view, these waves of symbolization constitute an important, perhaps central, part of the course of symbolization in the young child. Moreover, they may assume crucial importance in later creative activity of the individual. Thus, they command our special attention.

The flavor of these psychological processes can perhaps be best conveyed by an example. Consider the child who is given a marker and asked to draw. At the age of one and a half, when asked to draw a person, a child may employ the strategy of grabbing the marker and pretending to *be* that person, walking the marker across the page. At the age of two and a half, the child may make two blobs (one larger than the other), or a "tadpole" blob with two appendages, and have this stand for a person. At the age of four, we find the child able not only to draw some blobs, but actually to produce the correct number of fingers and facial features. Finally, by the age of six or seven, the child can make a map in which the locations of several elements (e.g., a group of houses) can be represented by the same abstract symbols (e.g., a set of dots), or he can write out the words *boy* or *man* using alphabetic letters.

We may observe a similar sequence in the area of music. Asked to sing a song, a child of a year and a half or two will simply re-create the activity during the course of which that song is usually sung. At the age of three, his vocal effort will capture whether the song gets louder or softer, faster or slower, but will not be sufficiently fine to re-create the pitch or metric relations characteristic of the particular song. At the age of four or five, the youngster will get the number of notes and intervals between pitches at least approximately right. By six or seven, he can capture in a simple notation some of the principal events that occur in a song.

In observing parallels of this sort, we became convinced of the existence of the aforementioned *waves of symbolization*. We term the first wave, which occurs toward the end of the second year of life, *role* or *event structuring*. This "wave" is found most straightforwardly in the area of narrative, where it entails the child's ability to capture in words or gestures the basic structure of an event: Typically, there is an agent who, in the course of donning a particular role, carries out actions that have particular consequences. Thus, a child, capable of event structuring can have a doll put another doll to bed, or he can say, "Mommy, go store" or "Daddy, eat cookie."

There is method in our use of the term *wave*. Each wave features certain symbol systems—in this case language and pretend play—where its eruption is most exten-

sive and appropriate; but it is in the nature of a wavelike process that it is also manifest less appropriately in other areas, for example, in drawing and music. Thus, the two-year-old asked to draw a truck will clutch the marker, push it back and forth against a surface, and growl "RRRR" or "Vroom."

The second wave—*topological or analog mapping*—occurs around the age of three. At this point, the child is able to capture in his symbolic display the relative size, shape, or temporal relations presented in a given referent. This is the point at which the child can first carry out representational drawing or block building by juxtaposing a few forms with correct size ratios. Thus, depiction of a human being involves a smaller form placed atop a larger one. It is also a time when he can capture two or three trends in singing or storytelling, such as a melody ascending or a narrative becoming more violent. Yet this wave of symbolization is in several ways distinct from the next wave, which occurs around the age of four. For in *digital mapping,* the child becomes able to produce a far more accurate rendering of a referent; in particular, he can capture up to 10 elements involved and their precise systematic relationship to one another. Thus, in drawing a human figure, the child can include the correct number of features; in singing one hears the correct number of pitches and their appropriate intervals; and in stories, the number of characters, their outstanding traits, and their relationship to one another can be maintained.

Finally, at the ages of five, six, or seven, the child can take his "first-draft" symbolic knowledge and capture important aspects of this knowledge in one or another *notational* systems. Not only does the child learn how to read, write, and do mathematics (if he resides in a schooled society), but, particularly if he is living in a culture where notations are favored, he becomes motivated on his own to try to develop and use various kinds of notational systems to aid his memory, to simplify and codify experience (Vygotsky, 1978). And so we have the spontaneous devising by children of various notational systems, including maps, diagrams, and other self-cuing mechanisms. Sometimes these notational systems can become dysfunctional—in attempting to capture certain key elements the child's understanding of a domain may appear less accurate than it had been in a prenotational phase (Strauss & Stavy, 1979). As Jeanne Bamberger has put it, "formal knowledge" sometimes interferes with a more direct "figural knowledge" (Bamberger, 1978).

In the long run, however, these notational capacities are a decided asset. They allow the individual to process large amounts of information and to engage readily in a recursive process, where bodies of already mastered knowledge can themselves become elements in more complex systems of knowledge. Indeed, this susceptibility to recursion lies at the core of mathematical thinking. As Alfred Adler (1972) has formulated it, one begins in mathematics with numbers, but then shifts to algebra, where the specific numbers are replaced by the general idea of variables. Variables themselves are simply specialized cases of mathematical functions; these functions in turn need not be restricted to real values (such as length or width) but can give meanings to more abstract mathematical objects as well. One can eventually have collections of functions, functions of functions, and the like. In short, by abstracting and generalizing the concept of number and, subsequently, the concept of variable and function, it is possible to arrive at extremely abstract and general levels of thought, all possible courtesy of notational symbolization.

What, then, can we conclude from this sequence of waves of symbolization?

We can see an ordered series of psychological processes used by children as a means of negotiating their way through the various symbolic domains with which they come in contact. The notion of waves indicates that the particular thrust of one psychological process occurs in one area at one age, whereas the thrust of another process occurs in another area at another age. Thus, event structuring crests particularly in the areas of language and symbolic play before the age of two; digital mapping has its greatest impact in the areas of music and number at the age of four or four and a half. As genuine psychological processes, these waves do not stop at the gates of alien symbolic domains; rather, they can be discerned, if sometimes in less appropriate fashion, across a range of symbolic domains.

But the symbolic waves are a psychologist's convention (and invention). From the point of view of the child (and his elders), he is learning to fashion the various products of his culture: to sing a song, make a drawing, tell a story. This is important, for in the absence of these culturally valued products, it is doubtful whether the child would be motivated to activate the relevant "wave" processes and to progress in each domain. The child makes these products because he likes them and enjoys them, but also because he is rewarded for doing so and because they occupy a niche of some centrality in his culture. Indeed, we need only observe a symbol system de-emphasized in our culture—for example, dance for the young male—to see that relatively little symbolic development unfolds in that domain. Were one to visit a culture where dance was emphasized, one would presumably encounter much more elaborate symbolic development in that particular sphere.

And after age five? Our studies have not clarified with the same degree of confidence the course of symbolic development in the years following entry to school. Nonetheless, we can at least suggest some of the broad outline of symbolization after the first half decade of life.

Between the ages of five and seven, we behold a flowering of the child's symbol-making activity. This is the age when the child's symbolic products exude a great deal of charm, originality and flair. In fact, such output at this age gives rise to the frequent observation that the young child seems capable of significant creative activity. Consider, for example, these musings by the noted American novelist Alison Lurie:

> All young children, we know, are imaginative and creative: and while they remain young, these qualities are usually fostered. The grubby but delightful paintings and naive verses are extravagantly admired, shown to visitors, tacked to the kitchen walls. But as children grow older, encouragement of imaginative creation is often quietly replaced by encouragement of what have begun to seem more important traits: good manners, good marks, good looks; athletic and social success; and a willingness to earn money mowing lawns and babysitting—traits that are believed to predict adult success (Lurie, 1982, p. 13).

And indeed, by the age of seven to 12, the agenda of the culture comes much more to the fore. This is exemplified in the child's desire to master the various cultural notations, particularly writing and mathematics. As already suggested, this notational skill is important for ultimate accomplishment, but it may, at least in the beginning, appear to retard the child and to suppress more figurative forms of knowing.

Mastery during this period involves far more than notationality. In most cases, the child is interested in producing symbolic products just the way that adults do (Gardner & Winner, 1982). For this reason he becomes preoccupied with acquiring skills—learning to write a poem that rhymes and scans properly, make a drawing that has appropriate perspective, dance according to the precepts of the square dance or the ballet stage. This is a time of rules, regulations, principles—a kind of narrow but dogged skill building across all aspects of social and cognitive growth as the child attempts to go beyond the status of the novice to the level of apprentice or even journeyman. The mastery of details is impressive here, though sometimes it undermines the possibility of making an overall symbolic product of depth, subtlety, and comprehensiveness. In comparison to the less self-conscious creations of the four-, five-, or six-year-old, the products of the middle-school child are often considered tedious and conventional, especially during an era that admires spontaneity.

With the advent of adolescence, the agenda of the growing child (and of the culture) changes once again. No longer content simply to acquire skills, the youth becomes quite self-critical, and if his own products fail to attain a certain level of competence, he is likely to stop creating altogether and rest on his laurels as a mere observer or connoisseur. Second, the youth's personal and emotional characteristics become more central components of creative activity. No longer is he satisfied simply to ape the products of the external culture. The youth now wants to fashion an object that makes sense in light of his own feelings and beliefs, that captures his own emotional center. Sometimes, this change of perspective gives rise to an unthinking relativism where "anything goes." Sometimes, the youth's feeling that he is "expressing himself" overwhelms the need to express meanings to other individuals. But in other, more desirable instances, the youth succeeds in melding some aspects of his own personality and well-being with appropriate aspects of the culture's agenda—in particular, its notions of meaningful symbolic products. He may then succeed in creating products that are not only significant to himself but also able to communicate successfully to others.

To the extent that this thumbnail sketch has validity, it suggests that the very notion of a symbolic product changes repeatedly and dramatically during the course of symbolic growth. The child's own notion of what he is trying to do, his own sense of goals and rewards alters even as the kind of interpretation placed by the culture upon the child's activity alters with the onset of each new developmental epoch. Adult masters do not particularly employ the "rhetoric of *products*" in their own analyses; in fact, today the overt emphasis falls almost entirely on *processes* of creation, and there is little discussion of what a finished drawing or theory should be like. Yet even a moment's consideration of the adult's activity indicates the extent to which it is actually governed by the imperative of fashioning a viable product.

The adult makes decisions regarding which activities to engage in; when to start, stop, revise, and edit; when to persist and when to move on to something else. Even though his own pleasures may be derived from "processing" considerations, there is no question that he is continuously assessing the product in terms of its potential impact upon others and its relation to an earlier tradition. Indeed, the decline of egocentrism, reflected in the emerging ability to serve as one's own best critic, is a

crucial criterion for an individual who would eventually achieve success in a symbolic domain. Unless you can speak to other individuals, unless you can don their ears, their eyes, and their interpretive systems, you are unlikely to attain success as a human creator.

Children and Adults as Symbolic Creators

The differences between child and adult creation are certainly considerable. Just to mention a few, there is the scope and the overall quality of the symbolic products; the technical knowledge upon which the adult can draw; the sense of time and scale captured in a work; and the critical faculty that allows the adult to reject those elements that, however attractive he may regard them, are unlikely to make sense to a wider community. All these stand in striking contrast to the younger child's moment-to-moment behavior, concern with local detail, spontaneity and (at best) partial knowledge of the skills required for symbolic fluency.

It is possible to consider the relation between adult and childhood creativity in another way, however, and should one do so, the relationships between these two forms of creation turn out to be far more intricate. Armed with our opening sketch of the creative adult (in both the arts and the sciences), we can revisit our portraits of children of different ages and determine the extent to which and the manner in which such children partake of certain features of the adult creator. The resulting picture indicates that the trajectory of creative development, unlike most other developmental trajectories, is nonlinear: At each age there are clear resemblances between child and adult creativity; indeed, in some ways the young child bears an especially intimate connection to the adult creator.

Turning first to the preschool child, we see an individual who is proceeding along a developmental course that is still relatively insulated from the external culture. Rather than taking tasks and problems from other individuals, the child is engaged in exploring symbolic media chiefly in his own way, finding problems where he does, drawing lessons from his own solutions. Still in the process of defining the symbolic domains and fixing the line between them, he has no reluctance to cut across symbolic domains, to create new figures of speech, to combine forms and colors in innovative ways, to juxtapose elements that are normally kept asunder. He has the fluency and the fluidity, the willingness to take chances, the adventurousness, the proclivity toward synthesis, and the patience to immerse himself with materials for long periods of time that also characterize the mature worker in various symbolic domains. Not least, in a manner reminiscent of the adult artist, he gains pleasure from playing and experimenting, from adhering to his own standards and fulfilling certain emotional needs, from the feeling that what he wants to say is best conveyed through a specific symbolic medium fashioned in a particular way. Finally, he is remarkably unreflective about what he does, and although this means that some of his work will be egocentric and therefore unclear to others, it also means that, like an adult creator, he is more willing to follow his own inclinations, and far less likely to become crippled by an excessively critical spirit.

Proceeding next to the child of school age, roughly 7–12 years old, we encounter a youngster whose agenda has shifted radically, to the point where in some respects

he stands distant from both the young child and the adult artist. Where the preschool child was insensitive to domain boundaries and to cultural dictates, the school-age child is exquisitely sensitive to both. He abjures metaphors, the collapsing together of areas, and indeed any effort to blur the distinctions that he has recently (and perhaps painfully) learned to make. He rejects novelty, the search for new problems, in favor of effective faithful solutions to the problems the society has posed for him. In seeming contrast to the young child, he lacks a feeling for the "whole picture," for large-scale problems or solutions, preferring instead to master the details of one corner of a domain before moving on to the next. Perhaps these are all necessary steps in the course of human growth, but they represent, at least from some vantage points, a detour from the path of creativity.

In other ways, however, our school-age child bears a stronger resemblance to the adult creator. He is beginning to master in earnest the materials on which he will eventually have to draw as an accomplished adult. His interest in building skills and in acquiring a rich knowledge base is an important prerequisite for later flexibility. His mastery of details on a step-by-step basis provides a useful model for the later building up of a network of enterprise. His attention to environmental feedback and to the criticism of informed others helps to ensure that his symbolic products will not be excessively egocentric. And his doggedness en route to the solution of problems teaches him what it is like to reduce the distance between the "initial" and the "final" stages. He is developing the habits of mind and daily toil that will enable him to be a competent creator and critic.

Arriving finally at adolescence, we confront yet another juncture in the trajectory of creative development. Having now constructed domains to the culture's satisfaction, and achieved some mastery in them, the youth is in a position once again to flout convention. He need no longer be overly concerned with the "right way" to do things, since he has already mastered that; he can begin to think about the way in which *he* wants to execute something for his own purposes. He has worked his way sufficiently through domains so that he can now (or once again) have that invaluable "view of a whole" that seems necessary if truly innovative work is to result. He is able to pursue a long-term goal and to orchestrate many skills and subgoals en route to the final destination. Further, he may have traced through past developments and products within a given domain and so find himself in a favorable position to figure out what the next plausible steps should be. Finally, he has sufficient sense of self that he can appreciate his own efforts and their limitations, and so can make an informed decision as to where (and whether) he should direct his symbol-using skills.

Of course, this portrait is an idealization, and most particularly so in its final strokes. For most adolescents, at least in our society, never achieve sufficient mastery of skills, knowledge of a domain, or awareness of self to be able to make innovative products: They remain impaled by the "literalness" of earlier stages, or perhaps cease altogether to participate in the creative process. Furthermore, it must be stressed equally that growth continues past adolescence: In few areas of science, and in even fewer areas of art, is the individual of 19 capable of truly innovative contributions. Nonetheless, even this brief sketch should indicate that each period of symbolic development makes its own contributions to eventual creative output and that distinctive ties exist between children of various ages and creative adults.

The vocabulary developed in another context may be helpful in summarizing the view that we have just put forth (cf. Kohlberg, 1969; see Kohlberg and Ryncarz chapter in this volume). We can speak of the kind of symbolization found in a young child as *preconventional:* that grasp of symbol use that can proceed independent of mastery of the culture's agenda. In middle childhood the cultural demands of symbolic competence come to the fore. The child comes to know what is required to achieve symbolic mastery in an area like literature or painting, and he may be thought of as at a *conventional stage.* The capacity emerging in the adolescent years can be thought of as *postconventional:* here, although keenly aware of the culture's notion of what counts as a product in particular domains, the young adult is willing to suspend this template and to experiment once again in terms of his own values, beliefs, and standards. Moreover, freed of convention's dictates, the adult has the option of reverting to earlier forms of expression and understanding, including those once favored in childhood.

In its passage from preconventional to postconventional, the trajectory of creative development bears analogies with other lines of development. However, certain differences between creative and other forms of development merit further comment. In the areas of cognitive development that have been most carefully studied, it seems apparent that individuals gain important forms of competence with age, even as very little of importance seems to be lost in the passage from childhood to adulthood. Even those who dispute the existence of different stages in the course of cognitive development usually concede that the older individual has a qualitatively different view of the world than the young child, a world view that is decisively altered by access to concrete and formal logical–mathematical operations. However, the course of creative development should be thought of as a more gradual or epigenetic process. On such an epigenetic account (Erikson, 1963), earlier constituents are never truly lost but are instead absorbed into each successive stage and remain available to be drawn upon at higher stages of development. Indeed, what may characterize the especially creative adult is precisely the capacity readily to gain access to earlier forms of knowing and understanding that may be dysfunctional in certain contexts but that prove of the essence in highly innovative work.

In trying to understand what allows certain symbol-using adults to be highly creative, we turn to the processes that occur in the first years of life. It is our contention that the waves of symbolization play an important, perhaps pivotal, role in ultimate adult creativity. Initially, the waves of symbolization are nature's way of allowing the child to gain an initial hold, a *first-draft mastery* of the skills needed in particular symbolic domains. Once these have clicked into place, the child is capable of acquiring mastery within particular domains—that, in fact, constitutes the agenda of the years following early childhood. But once this agenda has been mastered, the individual is thrown back once again largely on his own resources, if he is to produce original, creative kinds of products. It is here, thanks to the processes of epigenesis, that the waves of symbolization can once again be marshalled into service.

In their initial appearance, the waves of symbolization are obligatory. The child has no choice but to use them, and to do so in the order in which they emerge. However, by the adult years, the waves of symbolization—now in place—have

undergone considerable further evolution and can be drawn on voluntarily. The adult artist or scientist has the option of invoking, when he so chooses, the processes of event structuring, topological mapping, digital mapping, or notating in order to carry out his task and reach his goals. Thus, the adult painter can resort as he chooses to the re-creation of the structures of events, the presentation of global or topological similarities, the capturing of specific or digital similarities, the use of notations, the recursive embedding of systems of visual meaning within other systems. To use a contrasting example, the adult computer scientist is no longer restricted simply to a linear solution to problems, where he first devises one part of the program to deal with subproblem 1, then a second part to deal with subproblem 2, and so forth. Instead, proceeding from a "top–down" as well as a bottom–up or left–right fashion, he has the option of using programming procedures that involve or capture topological, digital, event structuring, or recursive kinds of functions. And the creative scientist similarly has the option of choosing among these various ways of sense making. He may (and according to scientists' testimony, often does) move back and forth among them, trying to find the best way to conceptualize the problem in which he is involved and, eventually, to communicate his theories or findings, images or models, to other individuals.

Such processes can most readily be observed in an individual who is an avowed polymath, such as Leonardo da Vinci, Johann Wolfgang von Goethe, or William Blake. In the actual words and remarks of these individuals, one beholds recourse to different forms of symbolization, alternative ways of representing meaning, explicit use of narrational, topological, digital, or notational forms of sense making. We also gain evidence for the co-occurrence of disparate modes of symbolization in the introspections of individuals concerning their own creative processes, reflections that stress the fluidity of associations, the utility of multiple assaults on a problem, and the exploitation of analogies between disparate domains of experience (see Ghiselin, 1952; Koestler, 1964; Perkins, 1981, for numerous examples). Some individuals who work exclusively within one symbol system may be restricted to a single symbolic wave, but it is our own guess that more innovative individuals turn as a matter of course to a multiplicity of forms of symbolization, which take advantage of the epigenetic sequence that we have outlined.

It has often been remarked that the creative adult is that person who retains access to his experiences as a child. Editing this characterization, we suggest, instead, that the adult creator maintains access to all the child's ways of knowing, access to those waves of symbolization that initially were brought to bear by every normal child in an effort to make sense of the various symbolic and expressive systems in his surroundings. The experiences of the first years of life are a special kind of capital, a form of sense making that perhaps all of us can (at least potentially) access following childhood: Creative individuals seem to specialize in returning to and exploiting this access, presumably because of their caring, because of their intense immersion in their subject matter, and perhaps by virtue of a special talent at retaining access to more primitive ways of knowing (Schachtel, 1959).

We suggest, moreover, that the waves of symbolization may well have life beyond early childhood. To begin with, each wave may be recapitulated in microgenetic fashion when an individual invades a new area. Our own observations of

initial attempts to learn notation suggest, for example, that in learning to notate performances, children begin with an event-structural or enactive form of notationality, move next to a topological form, and only later become able to employ notation in a digital or recursive way. Furthermore, our studies of symbolic development suggest that each of the waves has its own developmental history. To be sure, event structuring may have its moment of isolated glory in the second year of life—but the developed storyteller may be validly portrayed as an individual who has brought event structuring to its highest level of realization. So, too, we find in the artist, the musician, or the painter a superlative sense of topological mapping, even as we find in the mathematician, architect, or scientist the most highly developed forms of digital and recursive notation. Thus, the waves of symbolization may exhibit developmental histories as lengthy as an individual's life as a symbol user and may also be brought to bear in incipient form whenever an individual invades a new area of learning.

Let us summarize the thrust of our remarks. Every individual must learn to deal with those symbol systems and to forge those symbolic products that are of importance in his culture. We have been equipped by our biological heritage with mechanisms—here termed streams and waves of symbolization—for making preliminary sense of these symbolic systems. It is our speculation that those streams and waves arise in rather similar ways in human beings around the world and are brought to bear on the range of meaning systems derived by diverse cultures. In particular, the waves of symbolization are the processes that allow human beings to master symbol systems and to make symbolic products at various levels of competence demanded at different points in the life cycle, culminating in the creation of novel symbolic entities by a few gifted individuals.

Cognitive-symbolic development does not consist of a single strand. Rather, it comes in multiple lines that reflect the particular domains that cultures may stress at various phases of development. The waves are brought to bear in each domain, but the importance of each wave, and the time at which it makes its maximum impact, will depend upon the particular symbolic domain in question.

This way of thinking may offer hope for reconciling an increasingly severe split in developmental psychology (cf. Gardner, 1980b). We have come to think of Piaget, on the one hand, as focusing on the most general aspects of development and presupposing that there is one pivotal domain, that of logical–rational thought. Chomsky (and others influenced by the "modularity hypothesis") have been cast as embracing the contrasting view that development occurs differently in each of a number of domains (if development occurs at all). Our waves suggest that certain general wavelike psychological processes may occur across domains but that the particular way in which they are realized may well reflect the nature and the structure of particular domains. Were this theory to help reconcile two seemingly conflicting structuralist approaches, it would be a desirable theoretical outcome indeed. Moreover, because our approach suggests *which* aspects of the young child resemble the highly creative adult and which aspects stand in need of much further development and training, it also points the way toward reconciling another prevailing tension—that which obtains between those who believe that important knowledge is innate and those who believe that knowledge can only be constructed painstak-

ingly over many years. The roots of creativity may be part of our birthright, but the routes to its achievement can only be negotiated with considerable support throughout childhood from the culture in which we live.

Acknowledgments

The work described in this paper has been supported by grants from the Spencer Foundation, the Carnegie Corporation, the National Science Foundation (BNS-79-24430), and the Bernard Van Leer Foundation. We are grateful to Ellen Winner and to the editors of this volume for their comments on an earlier draft.

4

Upstaging the Stage Model

Diane McGuinness, Karl H. Pribram,
and Marian Pirnazar

Marie Jahoda once remarked that after 40 years of research on Freud's model of psychological development with few concrete results, "Freud will still not go away." This is because Freud asked the fundamental questions that psychology has so far failed to answer. There is a direct parallel between Freud's puzzle over psychosocial behavior and Piaget's concern with the development of human cognitive capacities, for despite all the criticism that has been aired concerning Piaget's methods and his stage model, we have no more sophisticated model to put in its place. No one has as yet answered the fundamental question that Piaget raised: What is the nature of the cognitive process that leads to competence in complex problem solving? Not only did both men pose the key questions, but they worked in a very similar style, building a model from painstaking and meticulous observations. Although both inductive thinking and their subjective methodology are currently unfashionable, their contribution looms large.

In this chapter we attempt to bring Piaget's insights in line with new data from psychology and the brain sciences. Our fundamental premise is that Piagetian "stages" are not unidimensional, applying globally to every cognitive ability. However, *each* unique cognitive domain will require the *same* progression from sensorimotor to symbolic or logical transformations. In addition, age must be factored separately from these cognitive progressions. Children and adults undertaking a completely novel task must begin with its sensorimotor properties, though to some extent the facility with which a sensorimotor process can be attained will be different, depending upon age and experience. Therefore, what exists beyond logical operations is both a lateral extension of existing cognitive structures through the refinement of skills and increasing knowledge *and* the possibility of acquiring completely new cognitive abilities, by running through the stages from the beginning.

One of the more intriguing aspects of Piaget's work is that both his genetic epistemology and his stage model were formulated in terms of biological systems. Despite the evidence that has accrued over the past 40 years, he only began to attempt to specify the biological processes for his "logical" mechanisms toward the end of his life. This beginning has proved extremely valuable, because it highlights the similarities and the distinction between his epistemology and his stage model that are so often obscured.

First and foremost, although Piaget has been credited with developing a philosophical system of epistemology, his theory of knowledge is a biological theory, not a philosophical one. Piaget never really inquires into the central philosophical question of what a knower knows, the *contents* of knowledge. He asks instead, "*How* do organisms know?"—a question more related to the mechanics of knowing. His genetic epistemology appears philosophical because of his extraordinary capacity for logical analysis, and it is powerful because it is logically consistent, rather than because it is "scientific." It suggests the way things must "go" if they are to make any sense at all, and it leads the way to a search for mechanism.

By contrast, Piaget's stage model is derived from observational data. It is not a biological model, but an inductive theory based on a set of phenomena. What is puzzling about Piaget's stage theory is that it seems to have so little in common with his epistemology. There is no way one could predict the nature of his genetic epistemology from his stage model, or predict stages from his epistemology. In fact, one of Piaget's frequent assertions is that the acquisition of knowledge is continuous: "knowledge is a continuous construction" (1970a), which appears on its face to contradict the notion of age-related abrupt changes in "state."

To address the question of whether or not a stage model can continue to apply at levels beyond logical operations, we will attempt to reassess Piaget in three ways. First, we will discuss his genetic epistemology in the light of our interpretation of recent data. Second, we will explore the evidence for an age-related theory of stage. Finally, we will attempt to show how "stages" become redeployed as context-dependent "states" invoked in every new learning experience irrespective of the age of the subject.

Genetic Epistemology

Equilibration

The central concept in Piaget's epistemology is that of equilibration. In Piaget's description of this concept he refers to two fundamental issues. The first is the question of biological versus environmental determinism, the quintessence of the nature–nurture debate. In dealing with this issue he refers to the process of environment–structure *interaction.* Here the organism serves as the field for multiple interactions or *transformations,* while maintaining stability in overall form through a set of invariant relationships, through what he terms *conservation.* Whereas "transformations" represent his solution to a biological–environmental interaction, "conservation" is much more akin to Cannon's notion of homeostasis. The purpose of equilibration is to achieve a stable state in an open environment–organism interaction.

Equilibration is a "process," a cycle of approximations to a state that is never totally satisfied. In common language, equilibration has three characteristics: (1) It entails active compensations to environmental change; (2) it operates to maintain internal coherence; and (3) it represents an ongoing search beyond the current status quo (an aspect that makes equilibration a misnomer). Piaget has stated that the process of equilibration can take place by means of these three "mechanisms,"

which he names (1) *autoregulation,* which ensures that the organism remains stable while adapting to the environment; (2) a mechanism for *action,* which is both a condition for and a consequence of behavior and which operates on the environment to adapt it to the organism; and (3) *decentration,* which operates to extend behavior away from stability.

Cognition enters the picture as the result of the transformations and constructions that occur in the cycles of "assimilation" (determined by autoregulation) and "accommodation" (determined by action) by which the organism interacts with the environment (1936, 1952c). The relationship between assimilation and accommodation and neural systems has been discussed in detail (Pribram, 1969; Pribram & Melges, 1969).

Autoregulation

In his writing from the mid-1960s to the early 1970s, Piaget began to specify in more detail exactly how he conceived the mechanism of autoregulation. He saw this as a set of dynamic, endogenously organized processes rather than as static endogenous "structures" as he believed Chomsky and Lorenz conceived them. The notion of autoregulation is much more in keeping with Waddington's (1975) idea of homeorhesis, which is a continuously changing self-organizing process. And although Piaget uses the term *equilibration,* his meaning is closer to that of Prigogine and Stengers (1984), who have identified processes characterized by temporary stabilities "far from equilibrium," which depend on fluxes constrained by initial conditions and the context in which they occur.

Autoregulatory mechanisms are involved at all levels of the system and include cognitive operations. These mechanisms set the overall pattern of constraints on the whole that operate downward in the system on its parts. This is true both at the level of the cell, where as Paul Weiss (1969) had noted, the totality of the cell is more stable than the activity of its elements, and in higher levels of organization, where there is a continuing balance between the open program of parts of a system and the more closed and stable properties of the whole. Piaget's view of the autoregulatory process is more related to cybernetics, with interlocking feedback systems, than to a balance of "forces" as conceived in classical physics. Ashby (1960) and Pribram (1971, Chaps. 5 and 14) have proposed formal models of such self-organizing autoregulatory processes based on the ubiquitous parallel processing connectivities of the nervous system. These have the property of integrating feedback closed-loop processes, which gives rise to open-loop feed-forward mechanisms that make voluntary action possible. An example of a feed-forward process is the temperature regulator on a thermostat. A thermostat ordinarily acts as a negative feedback mechanism, entirely regulated by the changes in the room temperature effecting the expansion and contraction of two metal tips. However, by adding an external regulator that controls the position of the metal tips, the circuit can be manipulated independently and in parallel with the effects produced by the temperature in the room. The system, in other words, comes under "feed-forward" voluntary control.

The internal neural organization of organisms imposes constraints on this

assimilative process. Piaget quotes Waddington (see also Pribram, 1971) to the effect that, just as tissue must be "competent" to respond to an inductor in embryonic development, neural systems must be "competent" to process signals from the environment. It will not be lost on some readers that in the example of tissue competence in induction, Piaget has one possible mechanism for his stage model in the concept of "critical periods." This issue will be taken up below, but Piaget's failure to seize on this idea is a puzzling example of how his epistemology and stage model have not been brought into harmony.[1]

Piaget in 1972 also refers to Pribram's work on the central regulation of input to the senses in the context of autoregulation, suggesting that he saw autoregulation as governed by two sets of constraints. The first represents the competencies of the sensorimotor systems to respond to events in the environment (an information processing system), and the second, the competencies of control systems to filter out unwanted events (an attentional mechanism). Piaget saw these as two parts of a single process, whereas we have come to view them as independent processes originating in different neural systems (Pribram & McGuinness, 1975).

Action

So far we have discussed autoregulation only in terms of its impact on sensory and attentional processing, but one of the key aspects of Piaget's epistemology is the great importance he places on action as a critical variable in the development of cognitive systems. In 1967 he states that the most manifest characteristic of life is that it is the "creator of forms"; it is "invention." Action accommodates the environment in the sense that the environment can provide constraints or "totalities," within which the organism behaves. Action is the essence of creation and invention because it is an operator by which a self-organizing system changes its environment. At the same time, action is integral in the formation of competencies, in that competence is demonstrated by its response-ability, the ability of a system to "respond" (i.e., to be challenged and changed). Competencies regulate both the range of possibilities and the actual configuration of a response.

At the most primitive level actions are generated by neurobehavioral rhythmicities and emerge in reflexes, which are the earliest observable actions. A major turning point in the development of acts is the onset of coordinations. Both ontogenetically and phylogenetically, the connection between stimulus and response weakens with time and with evolution. In the most primitive systems the response is temporally bound to the stimulus. The S–R connection is truly reflexive. In higher organisms, control systems make it possible to impose a *delay* between the input and the reaction. The delay allows the organism to block reflex action either by stopping the behavior entirely or by the substitution of a new response. In other words, control systems allow for *reflection* instead of reflexion. (The similarity to Freud's concept of ego functions is striking; see Pribram & Gill, 1976, Chap. 2.) Intentional acts, in particular, depend upon the coordination of means and ends. Means are determined by intentions, but intentions must be in accord with possible action. Piaget discusses two mechanisms that are necessary for coordinated action. The first is an energizing element; the second is the existence of structure in both

neural and physical systems that allow the action to occur. How structures become energized is developed in the concept of decentration.

Decentration

Decentration involves the coordination of autoregulation with action. Decentration is invoked to account for the fact that the boundaries of action continue to increase. That is, although the organism retains an essential stability or "integrity," action can go beyond this stability and need not function solely to bring the organism back to equilibrium. The capacity of action systems to go beyond stability means that new problem-solving capabilities can emerge. Had Prigogine's insights into the creation of stabilities far from equilibrium been available to Piaget, the concept of decentration would undoubtedly have had a greater mathematical and biological foundation. Nevertheless, Piaget was able to see the importance of the coordination of autoregulation and action as the critical factors initiating the process of intentionality, or the awareness of self. In the same sense, action (including speech and thought) forms the basis for new stages of development.

Neural Mechanisms of Control

Neither Piaget nor neuropsychologists working on brain models have, until recently, had access to Prigogine's discoveries. As noted earlier, Piaget used the concept of "equilibration" incorrectly. Similarly, neuroscientists studying cognitive brain function have generally used the concept of "control," rather than framing their theories in terms of extensions away from equilibrium to new stabilities. Prigogine's solutions could provide a far more powerful explanation of how hierarchical cognitive processes come to be established. Not only this, but viewing novel organizations of subsystems as new "stabilities" could help to explain how certain of these organizations take on a life of their own and appear as "abrupt changes in state."

It is not appropriate here to present a detailed account of the neural structures involved in autoregulation, action, and decentration. However, it has been possible from research using animal models to distinguish three major systems that operate as controls on attention and learning (Pribram & McGuinness, 1975). These are systems anchored in corebrain systems and operate outward onto cortical systems. One system, centered on the amygdala, responds to changes or shifts in recurrent regularities of input, often thought of as "novelty." This is called an "orienting–habituation" system or an "arousal" system and has many of the properties of Piaget's autoregulation mechanism. A second system, which has a brain stem reflex component, comes to be centered on the basal ganglia of the forebrain. This system regulates action, in Piaget's sense of the word, by establishing a set or bias to respond and is called a "readiness" or "activation" system. These two systems act reciprocally on the functions of the primary sensorimotor projection systems (Spinelli & Pribram, 1966, 1967; Lassonde, Ptito, & Pribram, 1981), and in young infants, when most stimuli are "novel," they work more or less in tandem.

Over time the primary sensorimotor systems come to regulate habitual behav-

ior without the intervention of these two control mechanisms. Instead, a third system, the hippocampus, comes to operate as a high-level override on the reciprocal relationship between the orienting and the activation systems. This third system, called an "effort" system, increases flexibility by biasing behavior toward risk (Spevak & Pribram, 1973). This system shares the properties Piaget attributes to decentration.

Cognitive Development

It can be seen from this brief overview that the mechanisms Piaget sought do exist and that they fulfill his requirements of how the processes must operate. However, for Piaget, as for most cognitive neuropsychologists, the problem of how these separate systems effect the development of complex cognitive organizations has not been solved. This seems to be the central problem in the schism between the neurosciences and cognitive psychology per se, as it is between Piaget's *own* difficulties in reconciling his genetic epistemology with his stage model.

Before we move on to a discussion of this issue, it is of interest to consider the role that development played in Piaget's epistemological theory. He was very specific in his view that the affective domain was anchored in an energy concept, or in his terminology: "energetics." About this domain Piaget had little to say (in contrast to Freud and his followers). It was a shortcoming in his model that he acknowledged. Cognitive development, on the other hand, received much more careful attention and was conceived of as largely due to structures that developed during an interaction with the environment. As noted, Piaget's definition of structure differed from that of Chomsky and Lorenz. For Piaget, structure or schema simply embodied a *system of transformations.* These transformations constituted "wholes" in which various elements are organized according to laws. However, the laws are never specified. During cognitive development, three categories of schemata play a predominant role.

The first he called *inversions,* which are structures arising from rhythmic or repetitious movement, based largely upon autoregulatory processes. These movements subsequently lead to "habit schemata" involving coordinated actions. Ultimately, the child is able to gain conscious control over these actions in what Piaget calls secondary or tertiary circular reactions. These are "procedures which make interesting things last." In other words, Piaget is describing the point at which the child achieves voluntary control over reflexive movement.

Second are *inventions,* or "action schemata," wherein an action arising from reflex organization moves through voluntary control of repetitive movement to the initiation of a completely novel act. Experimentation, defined as employing a variety of means to the same end, is one way that secondary and tertiary circular reactions are accomplished. For Piaget the concept of an "act" always included the totality of the action schema, that is, the stimulus to be operated upon, the behavior, and the outcome. This need not always involve physical movements. As Piaget noted (1936, 1952c) "operations" are "acts" that are carried out symbolically. They are "mental inventions." In 1972 he made the distinction between an operation and an object schema: "An operation is not the representation of a transformation, it is in itself an object transformation, but one that can be done symbolically, which

is by no means the same thing. Thus an operation remains an action and is reduced neither to a figure nor to a symbol."

Finally there is *reality construction,* which arises from decentration. This leads to the separation of self from objects in the world and ultimately to abstract schemes such as object permanence, schemes of space–time, and schemes of causality. Piaget makes it very clear that abstract schema develop from the capacity to *distance* oneself from events, rather than by being incorporated into them. It might be noted that this idea has interesting philosophical implications, especially as it has become popular to view modern man as overly "distanced" or "alienated" from his environment. Piaget would consider this "distance" or "objectivity" to be a sign of a higher cognitive level.

The Stage Model

From the preceding discussion it can be seen that current evidence is compatible with Piaget's biological epistemology, and we have no quarrel with his approach. A problem does arise, however, when one uses his genetic epistemology to predict how age-dependent stages might be organized or indeed whether they even exist. In addition, apart from the fact that his epistemology and his stage model of development have an uneasy fit, there are further problems with Piaget's stages. First, Piaget employs the notions of cognitive development, intellectual development, and development of logico-mathematical operations interchangeably throughout his writings. In general his stage model is based upon his observations of logical operations, and this is too limited to have broad implications. As he himself points out:

> The states of intellectual development form a privileged case and we cannot generalize them to other fields. If, for example, we take the development of a child's perception or the development of language, we observe a completely different and much greater continuity, than in the field of logico-mathematical operations [1972, p. 49].

This of course raises the immediate problem of whether or not logico-mathematical thinking can be separated from other forms of thought and if it can, how one would draw the appropriate boundaries. But the major difficulty here is that in using the terms *cognitive* or *intellectual* rather than *logico-mathematical,* Piaget has misled many scholars into believing that his stages were representative of all cognitive development.

A second problem arises from the results of research that seriously challenges the sequence of the landmarks that Piaget adopts for his stages and substages. Not only this, but research findings have also challenged the characteristics of the schemes that Piaget claims to have identified (see Flavell, 1985). Recall that the sensorimotor period consists of six stages that follow one another in a specific order. Object permanence is expected to arise at stage 4 and imitation at stage 6. Studies by Bower (1966, 1982) and by Charlesworth (1966), however, show that object permanence is established as early as stage 3. Meltzoff and Moore (1977)

have evidence that imitation, presumed to require "symbolic representation," can be demonstrated shortly after birth at 12–21 days.

Furthermore, in a summary of studies on psychotic children performing Piagetian tasks, Cowan (1978) points out that a re-examination of the "notion of necessary sequence" is essential to explain how "older psychotic children and adults achieve beginning conservations (concrete operations) without having established schemes of object permanence (sensory-motor period)" (p. 337).

Some of this confusion is due to the fact that object permanence has at least two meanings. One refers to "object constancy," or identification, and the other to "permanence" in memory during distraction. Thus, Bower and Wishart (1972) found that infants who failed the standard version of the object permanence test did reach for the vanished object when the room lights were off. This suggests that one of the problems children face in learning about the world is their high distractibility (i.e., failure to habituate an orienting reaction) and that failure in Piaget's task occurs for entirely different reasons than the ones he specified (see also Anderson et al., 1976). Also, Uzgiris and Hunt (1975) report a different and larger set of landmarks in the sensorimotor stage when they were constructing scales for infant assessment. It does not appear possible at this point to determine whether landmarks or stages of development (other than perhaps reaching, walking, and talking) are *real,* or merely a product of the investigator's own categorizing system and imagination. In all the various ways of demonstrating object permanence (pulling away the cloth, showing surprise, or reaching in the dark) are we measuring distractibility, motor skills, emotionality, or visual short-term memory? That is, does object permanence arise not because of achieving some higher-order abstraction, but because of the development of some lower-level capacity?

Finally, even when a particular skill is investigated, regardless of the sequence in which it appears, it has been observed many times that the demonstration of the scheme may not be simultaneous with its construction. This is an old problem in developmental psychology and is especially familiar to psycholinguists. It has been suggested by one of us (Pirnazar) that as differentiation between qualities of objects (object constancy) begins at birth, this differentiation process may ultimately underpin object permanence. For example, an infant comes to discriminate the sensory and motor distinctions he experiences when sucking at his mother's nipple and on his thumb. After several repetitions of finding the thumb and sucking it, it soon becomes a fixed habit. The images of the thumb in terms of sensations of movement, taste, comfort, and so on, remain when the sensations are absent (permanence), and the real experience can be reinstated. The fact that he can voluntarily locate his thumb and bring it to his mouth indicates that he has a sense of the permanence of an object. It does not guarantee, however, that he will be able to pass any test designed to measure this aptitude.

This example suggests that object constancy and resistance to distractibility are not related to one another in a linear progression, but develop in parallel. This suggestion is supported by neurophysiological data that clearly dissociate constancy, the extraction of invariances in the formation of object percepts, from permanence, the maintenance in awareness of these percepts. Distractibility during the performance of an object permanence task (temporarily hiding a piece of food) is

increased by lesions of the far frontal cortex (Anderson et al., 1976), whereas constancy (e.g., of size) is impaired by posterior lesions to the peristriate cortex (Ungerleider et al., 1977). The developmental "sequence" of performance based upon these competencies occurs as follows: The function of neural systems of the posterior cortical convexity enters in the formation of percepts of three-dimensional objects, irrespective of the angle of view, by means of automatic cross-correlations of a large number of visual images. In other words, this part of the brain extracts invariances (Pribram, 1990). Once the brain has coded these invariances (thumbs do not turn into nipples), object permanence is a necessary consequence. But object permanence is also affected by distraction, and the ability to resist distraction develops more slowly, because the frontal lobes are late to mature in comparison with the posterior visual systems (see review article by Pribram, 1986b). This maturation process is more in accord with a stage model. Object categorization, on the other hand, is dependent upon the *amount* of exposure to stimulus patterns and their reinforcement history.

Cognitive Operators

Because of the problems with Piaget's Stage Model, we wish to develop a somewhat different approach to "stages," one that is more akin to Piaget's genetic epistemology. A central difficulty with the term *stage,* as used in Piaget's theories of behavioral development, is that it confounds two distinct aspects of development. First, developmental changes that occur as a function of age cannot simply be dismissed. The slow maturation of the frontal lobes is matched by the finding that certain problems are solved with different strategies at different ages. At the same time this effect is dependent upon the sequential nature of development in which each stage of a sequence is contingent upon a prior stage of processing.

In addressing cognitive development, we would like to suggest that all cognitive processes, or some subsets, such as problem-solving routines, undergo "stages" and that these occur independently of maturation. An example might be the development of software for a computer system. "Machine language" could be thought of as analogous to a sensorimotor stage; the creation of "assemblers," as involving operational processes; and the creation of high-level languages, as akin to transformational structures.

The dissociation of cognitive stages from age-related developmental stages has several consequences. First, it allows for the fact that as children become skilled processors, they can run through stages more rapidly and in certain contexts can even skip a stage. For example, an adult "dyslexic" remediated for sensorimotor deficiencies could advance immediately to an adult reading vocabulary. A second and related fact is that the utilization of an appropriate stage depends as much on context as on age. Finally, only the *elements* of classes of cognitive skills would be expected to show plateaus. This would result in the failure to find support for fixed stages when the elements essential to successful performance on any task had not been correctly identified by the investigator.

In short, we are suggesting that *in addition* to age-related developmental stages

(critical periods, and the timing of maturation of specific brain systems), there are also cognitive stages that are specific to certain problem sets. These stages are so intertwined in each culture's educational process that they appear inseparable.

Identifying Elements

Several examples will illustrate how a difficulty in any specific domain is independent of other cognitive operations and will spell failure whatever the age of the subject. The most cogent example is that of reading failure in subjects who are well beyond the level of logical operations. In fact, studies have shown that in families with a predisposition to dyslexia across several generations, visuospatial reasoning (concrete and logical operations) is actually *superior* to that in control subjects who show normal reading skills (Decker & DeFries, 1980; Smith, 1982). Clearly, the predisposition to dyslexia cannot be accounted for by a failure to achieve the appropriate cognitive stage for learning to read—for example, the misapprehension of symbolic representation or some related cognitive deficit. The evidence is now conclusive that reading failure is in large part due to a deficiency in sensorimotor processing. Poor readers of all ages consistently fail in tasks that measure phonemic discrimination in both written and spoken language (Calfee et al., 1973; Liberman & Mann, 1981; McGuinness, 1981; Blachman, 1982; Smith, 1982). Moreover, these same subjects show a deficiency in sequential motor fluency both in purely manual operations and in speech and decoding (Smith, 1982; Badian, 1982).

Training programs designed to improve phonemic decoding, especially in conjunction with training in articulatory regulation, have been uniformly successful in teaching subjects to read (see McGuinness, 1981, 1985). The most dramatic results have come from those programs that *integrate* the perceptual and motor tasks. This allows for the development of new transformations and enhances the fluency with which the operations can be executed, thus reducing the load on short-term memory. The result is a change in competency that allows larger units, or "chunks," to be encoded into short-term or working memory. Pribram (1971) has argued that, once developed, attention span or the *capacity* of working memory remains relatively fixed and that what appears as a change in capacity is in actuality a change in competence, or the ability to chunk the operations into more complex units. This is supported by the fact that short-term memory studies reveal that the absolute number of items retained in a sequence varies between modalities *within* each individual, depending upon their competence to process information in that mode (Tallal & Stark, 1982).

Of course, what we are saying is not incompatible with an age-related stage model in the sense that no advanced stage can be achieved prior to the more primitive stage, in this case sensorimotor coding. It could be argued that this is merely another example verifying Piaget's theory of "invariant sequences." Yet one has a very uncomfortable feeling about a stage model in which adults, after years of schooling, have bypassed the sensorimotor period but nevertheless are fully aware of the "logical" properties of a writing system, that it is symbolic, phonemic, and so forth. A writing system is a *code* and belongs in Piaget's category of logical-mathematical operations. Nor is it any more convincing to argue that Piaget's stages only

apply in some circumstances, such as tangible real-world situations, but not in others; otherwise "Piagetian Stages" would apply only to Piagetian tasks, and a general theory of invariant stages would collapse.

More pertinent is the example of the failure of many college women to find the correct solution to Piaget's water level task, in which subjects are expected to draw a line representing water in a tilted pitcher. The solution is supposed to emerge between the ages of 7 and 11 years, during the stage of concrete operations. This failure is not due to a misunderstanding of the "concrete" aspects of the task, because even after the principle has been thoroughly explained, and the women appear to understand, they still cannot perform accurately (Thomas et al., 1973; Liben & Golbeck, 1984). So far, the only evidence that can account for this sex difference comes from two sets of data. First, there is a high correlation between tests of visuospatial ability (exemplified by 2-D drawings of 3-D shapes) and Piaget's water-level problem. Females from the ages of about 12–14 years tend to score between one half to one standard deviation below the males on these visuospatial tests. Second, females score below males on tests requiring the construction of three-dimensional objects from about four years of age (McGuinness, 1985), despite the fact that they perform equally well on two-dimensional constructions.

Our explanation of this sex difference is that there is a failure on the part of females to create the appropriate sensorimotor scheme of object movement in three dimensions, initially. That this is due to the lack of sensorimotor *integration* seems more likely, as no tests of primary visual processing (acuity, convergence, stereopsis, depth perception, etc.) have been found to correlate with visuospatial ability (McGuinness & Brabyn, 1984; McGuinness & Pribram, 1978).

Finally, hyperactive children, whose main problem appears to be that they continue to want to learn by putting their hands into the world, show by this behavior an extreme tendency to remain in the sensorimotor stage. Yet these children have no deficit in Piagetian tasks or any other cognitive tasks, and in some studies they have actually been found to be superior to their controls on abstract reasoning (Kroener, 1975).

We would suggest that in learning *any* cognitive operation a new sensorimotor scheme must be evolved. First, the relevant invariant units essential to the solution of the task must be discriminated through repetition or interest. Second, the appropriate action patterns or skills must be acquired. Third, these perceptions and actions must be coordinated and integrated to the point where a transformation has been achieved. This transformation is initiated through decentration, which allows a higher level of abstraction (hierarchical) to emerge in which the sensorimotor components of the task become one integrated unit, or chunk, and the process runs off automatically without conscious effort. This is the essence of what Piaget describes as "autoregulation."

Over time these higher-order abstractions can be integrated into further abstractions, so that the initial operations required by the scheme are lost to immediate awareness or even to memory. If you ask mathematicians "how" they think when they are solving problems in algebra or geometry, they will usually be unable to tell you. This may seem like typical behavior on the part of inarticulate mathematicians, until one considers questions closer to home, such as, "How did you learn

to read?" "What is it that you *see* when you look at that word?" The fact is that good readers don't actually "see" the word at all; they are only aware of its meaning.

It is important to note that we have not been describing minute pockets of the population. About 15 percent of all boys are diagnosed as dyslexic. Approximately 50 percent of college women fail Piaget's water-level test. We have cited these extreme examples rather than using the cross-cultural data that show large discrepancies between the ages at which children of different cultural backgrounds reach various Piagetian stages. The Geneva counterargument has always been that the necessary experience had not taken place for the various schemes essential to each stage to emerge. This is taken to indicate that the same sequence of stages would be found irrespective of the large delays in children of some cultures. This argument becomes less valid when applied to adults who have been raised in the same culture, attended the same schools, and had identical educational bgackgrounds. In fact, an across-the-board theory of invariant sequences determined merely by exposure becomes completely untenable, and such a stage model must collapse. When using Piaget's epistemological model, however, we find no contradiction. As interpreted by us in the suggestions of cognitive specific stages, this model is sufficiently flexible to allow for failure to arise in any one component of a particular process at any age.

Covariation

We cannot construe any of the preceding to mean that we can ignore age changes as a factor in cognitive development. Too many talented and shrewd observers of behavior have independently come to the conception of stages—including Freud (1949), Sullivan (1953a), and Berne (1961)—to dismiss the concept entirely. Furthermore, these stages are remarkably similar in essential respects. For example, Freud's oral stage, Sullivan's prototaxic and Berne's "child" are essentially sensorimotor in character. Freud's anal, Berne's "parent," and Sullivan's parataxic stages are essentially devoted to developing voluntary control. Finally, Freud's sexual, Berne's "adult," and Sullivan's syntactic stages all involve communicative transformations. However, just as in the case of cognitive development, recent stage models, most especially Berne's, emphasize that these stages are really "states" that depend more upon context than upon age.

So far our account cannot explain the fact that by and large *most* children do appear to develop certain logical capacities at certain times. There are two ways that this characteristic of "stages" could be explained. The first is simply due to *concurrence*—that is, given similar cultural and educational backgrounds, children will begin to integrate (transform) certain types of sensory and motor experience at the same time. Once these transformations are sufficiently internalized and become automatic, they lead to a shift in logical thought that is qualitatively different. By this explanation, there would be periods of continuous development, followed by sudden shifts to a new level of understanding, a new "stage." This process would be largely independent of age but would entail "invariant" sequences.

For example, in a comparison of the performance of children in two cultures who were asked to construct a replica of a model built from 3-D blocks, Ghanaian

children were equal to Scottish children in accuracy. Yet when asked to build a replica from a 2-D pictorial representation, many of the Ghanaian children could not complete the task (Jahoda, 1979). This illustrates that the capacity to perform at the level of concrete operations can be demonstrated to be equivalent cross-culturally under one set of stimulus conditions but nonequivalent in another. Obviously, the Ghanaian children had had less exposure to pictorial representations. But the same argument might be applied to the 3-D blocks, which were equally novel to these children. How, then, does one determine which "stage" the Ghanaian children had reached? Quite apart from these data, lengthy exposure to specific materials does not guarantee that higher stages will automatically be reached, if the initial sensorimotor programs are not developed. We have already discussed severe reading delays, and the same problem arises in mathematics. College students often begin geometry or calculus with no understanding of the *concrete* principles involved. The most efficient and lasting teaching method, as pioneered by Davidson at the University of Massachusetts (see McGuinness, 1985), is to teach the entire course in the concrete mode, or, in other words, at the sensorimotor level.

Second, we have a good deal of evidence of the importance of "critical periods" in the developmental progression. Critical periods for visual perception have been worked out in detail in the rat and the cat and are found to be extremely reliable. Furthermore, unit recordings in cat visual cortex have shown that each cell in the brain has specific innate sensitivities to certain properties in the environment, such as velocity of movement and orientation, and that with use the "tuning" in these cells becomes sharper and sharper (discrimination). In highly constrained environments, or freak environments, these cells either lose their original sensitivity or set up new sensitivities. In extreme conditions, such as the absence of light, the cells stop functioning, and if this occurs at certain periods of time, the animal becomes functionally blind (Hubel & Wiesel, 1963).

Not only this, but complex cognitive functions in humans show the effect of extreme environments. Perhaps the best example is Genie, who when found at the age of 12 years in a Los Angeles bedroom had no language and had heard no one speak. After several years of training, Genie's language skills were identical to those of the great apes, with a severely restricted vocabulary employed in two- to three-word strings (Curtiss et al., 1974). The "critical period" for language development appeared to have passed, and although she had spent as much if not more time in language training than the ordinary five-year-old, she could not even come close to a five-year-old in language skills.

Piaget tended to avoid an emphasis on maturational theories, because he wished to promote his central thesis of a biological–environmental interaction. Perhaps Piaget, like Freud, although trained in biology, wished to avoid the problems inherent in a strict biological or genetic determinism that underpinned social Darwinism. Not only does such an extreme position have profound social consequences, but it negates the impact of the environment in shaping cognitive development. Yet both Piagetian and Freudian theories are essentially theories of "mechanism," and a truly "interactive" approach has to take into account the inbuilt constraints of the machine. One of these constraints is that neurons are primed for certain types of input. When this input does not materialize, aggregates of these cells are adopted into other neural networks.

Conclusion

In conclusion, we would like to suggest that Piaget's genetic epistemology provides a compelling set of constructs to account for developmental change, especially in terms of our more continuous cognitive specific state–transformational model. Shifts that occur in any cognitive process are produced by the self-organizing and autoregulatory properties of sensorimotor schemes, which by virtue of action and decentration come to function as subsets in a new whole. Furthermore, biological data indicate that critical periods must be factored separately from concurrent covariation among these self-organizing properties. It is likely that both multiple transformational and multiple maturational processes are operating simultaneously and that this has been one of the reasons the data from studies on Piaget's tasks have been so difficult to disentangle. What is clear, however, is that the continuous and recurring state-transformational process, cast in the framework of genetic epistemology, applies at all ages and can account for cognitive growth.

The implications for human cognition beyond logical operations lead to a restructuring of our thinking and research goals. First, are there critical or sensitive periods after childhood and what operations would they entail? So far the most compelling evidence for early critical periods comes from extreme cases. We know that permanent amblyopia can result from a sufficient absence of patterned light in infancy and that language not only will fail to develop in the absence of another species member, but cannot develop fully after a specific time period has elapsed. From the limited number of cases that have been observed, it is possible that logical operations, involving advanced analytical thought, may not function in the absence of language. However, we know neither the timing parameters nor the precise critical period during which such profound effects can be produced. Furthermore, we cannot set up any research programs on humans that could answer such questions. The importance of these abnormal phenomena is to alert us to the possibility that the efficiency of certain psychological processes may be dependent upon the right input at the right time. This is not a new problem in educational psychology, but the approach has been more by trial and error than by any rigorous assessment of sensitive periods, and no one has explored the possibility of critical or sensitive periods past puberty.

A less dramatic illustration of the impact of sensitive periods relates to skilled performance. Certain high-level skills that we might consider indicative of cognitive ability, such as musical performance, are closely tied to early critical periods. It appears from a long history of training musicians that aptitude in performance depends to a large degree upon an early commitment of certain neural structures to specific motor routines (habits). If these skills are not acquired before the neural networks are committed, then a facility in performance can rarely be obtained, no matter how long practice continues. This might occur despite a high musical intelligence. The same situation applies to second-language learning, where early critical periods play a role in the degree to which accuracy in perception and production of speech can be developed. This ability declines rapidly after the age of six to eight years, when the phonemic structure of the primary language appears to coopt most of the neural networks engaged in linguistic processing. Learning a second language later in life appears to be more of an intellectual exercise, wherein conscious anal-

ysis replaces the effortless and semiautomatic processing characteristic of childhood.

The second and related issue, that of the continuity of state-transformational processes, concerns the problem of sequential timing rather than absolute time dependent upon chronological age. One interesting facet of the research on this issue is that the results of such studies can shed considerable light on the question of sensitive periods. It has been suggested that failure in certain higher-order aptitudes is created initially by poor sensorimotor processing. If these skills can be *taught* at any age, by the process of exclusion, one can obtain a clearer picture of which cognitive abilities are more related to absolute time than to sequential time. Take for example, the problem discussed earlier on adult dyslexics. New techniques have revealed that the deficit is due almost entirely to the failure to develop the fine discrimination in both sensory and motor domains that is required during the initial learning stage. Unlike language-deprived children and those learning a second language, these adults learn to read once the missing subroutines are in place. Furthermore their reading rapidly catches up to normal limits if they are of normal intelligence in other respects (McGuinness, 1985).

Does this ability to catch up apply to other cognitive domains? What are the subroutines underpinning mathematical competence? That this also depends upon sensorimotor competencies that can be mastered in adulthood is suggested by Davidson's work. In addition, visuospatial problem solving is known to be highly correlated to ability in higher mathematics, yet despite a number of studies that have demonstrated this correlation, no programs have been established to discover how these visuomotor subroutines are set up initially. Such questions might lead to a more precise definition of cognition, one that relates more directly to some innate competence for abstract reasoning or problem solving that is independent of sensorimotor skills but that cannot be demonstrated unless these skills are in place. This definition would imply that there is some truth in the notion of Spearman's "G" factor, an inherent ability to find "intelligent" solutions, irrespective of the means by which these solutions are obtained.

Many of the examples cited earlier are negative cases that are intended to highlight those situations in which a stage model would be less viable than a continuous transformational model. However, most children proceed through their educational experience without deprivation, even of piano lessons! The question still remains, especially when dealing with Piaget's final stage of logical operations, what weight to place upon experience as opposed to neural maturation. Piaget and Inhelder were insistent that both were equally important in their discussion of logical operations. Yet they had considerable difficulty in reconciling these two domains. This struggle is highlighted in the following quotation.

> Given that in our society the 7–8 year old child (with very rare exceptions) cannot handle the structures which the 14–15 year old adolescent can handle easily, the reason must be that the child does not possess a certain number of coordinations whose dates of development are determined by stages of maturation. In a slightly different perspective, the lattice and group structures are probably isomorphic with neurological structures and are certainly isomorphic with the structures of the mechanical models devised by cybernetics in imitation of the brain. For these reasons, it seems clear that the development of formal structures in adolescence is

linked to maturation of cerebral structures. However, the exact form of linkage is far from simple, since the organization of formal structures must depend on the social milieu as well.—Moreover the history of formal structures is linked to the evolution of culture and collective representations as well as their ontogenetic history.—Thus the age of 11–12 years may be, beyond the neurological factors, a product of a progressive acceleration of individual development under the influence of education and perhaps nothing stands in the way of a further reduction of the average age in a more or less distant future.

In sum, far from being a source of fully elaborated "innate ideas," the maturation of the nervous system can do no more than determine the totality of possibilities and impossibilities at a given stage. A particular social environment remains indispensable for the realization of these possibilities. It follows that their realization can be accelerated or retarded as a function of cultural and educational conditions. This is why the growth of formal thinking as well as the age at which adolescence itself occurs—i.e., the age at which the individual starts to assume adult roles—remain dependent on social as much as and more than on neurological factors.

For, if the social milieu is really to influence individual brains, they have to be in a state of readiness to assimilate its contributions. So we come back to the need for some degree of maturation of individual cerebral mechanisms (Inhelder & Piaget, 1958, pp. 336–338).

Unless one were to assume that, following adolescence, which Inhelder and Piaget have characterized as extending from puberty to the late teens, a new neurological departure took place, one must conclude that at the point of logical operations, the ultimate structure of cognitive operations is in place. In fact, their description of the final form of logical operations as the capacity for deductive and inductive reasoning is scarcely a commonly applied aptitude even in the adult members of any society. Indeed, whenever a totally novel problem is encountered, this inductive reasoning is brought to bear *only* at the conclusion of a sequence of prior operations, such as discrimination, categorization, and so forth, which constitute the application of sensorimotor strategies and concrete operations. The greater the amount of information acquired through past experience, the faster and more flexibly this sequence will be performed.

Therefore, it appears that what is beyond logical operations are processes of lateral extension rather than forward extension in terms of the available intellectual tools. Such a lateral extension makes possible greater powers of reasoning by virtue of a larger matrix of available skills and knowledge. In short, what is beyond logical operations is simply more of the same.

Appendix

Baerbel Inhelder was kind enough to read our chapter in two versions. She made three specific comments, which support the theme we are developing:

1. Piaget wrote in 1975 a major book titled *The Equilibration of Cognitive Structures* (translated by T. Brown and K. Thampy. Chicago: University of Chicago Press, 1985) in which he developed a dynamic conception of equilibration through the description of three compensatory mechanisms (labeled as Alpha, Beta,

Gamma). Thus, the shift towards a view closer to that of Prigogine (i.e., stability far from equilibrium) comes more easily. In fact, on his 80th birthday in 1976 Piaget's thinking was related to that of Prigogine, Paul Weiss, and others. This set of interchanges was published in *Epistémologie Génétique et Equilibration* edited by Inhelder (Neufchâtel and Paris: Delachaux et Niestlé, 1977).

2. Inhelder states that her epigenetic model is clearly an interactive one: both biology *and* culture interweave to form stages in development:

> In sum, cognitive progress as observed in our learning research, cannot be interpreted according to a maturationist model or according to an empiricist theory. Since neither external factors nor purely internal factors are sufficient by themselves to explain the dynamics of acquisition of knowledge, and since there is no absolute beginning, only a model that reflects the continuity between the biological genesis and the development of the cognitive functions is appropriate. Such a model is provided by the concept of an epigenetic system where each new state incorporates the preceding ones, and where the influence of environment becomes progressively more important.

3. ". . . according to my [Inhelder's] still unpublished results it seems questionable as to whether microgenesis (the completion of a cognitive act) is in some [nontrivial] sense simply a foreshortened macrogenesis."

We look forward to the publication of Inhelder's results on the process of microgenesis.

Note

1. The example remains puzzling. One of the most interesting results in Inhelder's experiments is that a task given at one age and solved at that age with a cognitive strategy appropriate to that age, when given at a later age with no intervening practice, is immediately solved with a "more advanced" strategy. Is this the result of a change in age or of concurrent experience? Piaget and Inhelder both felt that it is age related but failed to make a good case for this.

5

Nonsequential Development and Aging

Ellen Langer, Benzion Chanowitz, Mark Palmerino,
Stephen Jacobs, Mark Rhodes, and Philip Thayer

Traditionally, developmental theories have presumed that the performance of skills and psychological and physical health are curvilinearly related to age. The individual grows to maturity (during adolescence in most instances) and then lives out the adult years of life adjusting to diminishing capacities. More recently, there has been an emphasis in developmental theory on incorporating the growth of wisdom into any account of human aging. This view is appreciative of the fact that our knowledge in important areas continues to grow as life progresses. This continuing growth of wisdom, however, which synthesizes cognitive and affective schema with the collected body of the individual's life experience, is seen as a stream of development that is essentially independent from or even, in part, occurs in reaction to a process of decline that is taking place in other areas (see chapters by Levinson, Dittmann-Kohli & Baltes, and Pascual-Leone in this volume).

In this chapter, we will propose a broader perspective on aging, one in which ongoing growth in all areas is recognized as a viable continuing possibility. While chronological age increases in linear fashion from birth to death, attributes associated with age may change monotonically or even nonmonotonically. Sometimes ill health, that characteristic most strongly associated in people's minds with aging, becomes the motivation to become healthy again at 50 and stay that way thereafter until death (cf. Rowe & Kahn, 1987). We all know that some people look, act, and feel younger (or older) than their cohorts, or even than people who may be a decade younger (older). Chronology aside, age is relative. We review some of our research in gerontology that indicates that decline and debility are not inevitable features of human aging and that, more important, when this decline does occur, it may be reversible.

In recasting the character of human aging as a domain in which growth is possible on more fronts than has hitherto been accepted, we are led to reconsider traditional models of human development and presuppositions that shape our theories about human growth. Thus, revisions in our portrait of human aging may inevitably lead to revisions in our encompassing portrayal of human growth. To that end, we first present some research that shows that aging is not a process of irreversible psychological and physiological decline. At the same time, we present other work that clarifies how persons generally come to follow this escapable rut in later life when other, more productive paths of development are available. The

strategies that this work suggests could provide a vehicle for avoiding decline and debility in later life.

Next we examine the broader issue of human development. In particular, we examine widespread presuppositions about the split between body and mind, about the determining role that the body plays in shaping the direction that the whole person takes, and about the nature of time as an all-pervasive container that inevitably wears down all that it contains as it inexorably proceeds in a linear fashion. Conjointly, these assumptions condition the prevalent view of human development. They lend credibility to the portrait of aging as a process where the body (and, consequently, the person) is inevitably and lawfully worn down over time after it has reached its peak efficiency in the earlier stages of development.

We feel it is necessary to subject these presuppositions to a critique that yields an alternative understanding of the roles that body, mind, and time play in shaping the process of human aging and development. In this alternative view, the physical aging process need not operate like a force of gravity, inevitably dragging the person downward toward the end of life. Rather, the path that persons traverse from birth to death, encapsulated by time, may take on the character of a series of goal-directed mini-trajectories that are relatively independent of each other. In principle, earlier episodes can have a less determining influence on the form of later episodes, since greater force is attributed to the potential role of the willful mind in shaping the development of the whole person within the current period (e.g., within late adulthood). Conversely, the body may diminish in importance as an active determining factor in the development of the person later in life. An experiment is described in which we sought to empirically demonstrate the viability of these ideas. We conclude by relating the broad implications of these notions to altering our treatment of development and aging.

Within the life-span approach the term *development* applies to changes over the entire life cycle of the person. This is in contrast to psychologists, including many Piagetians, who apply this term only to qualitative change in cognitive structuring during the first two decades of life. The influence of this attitude is persistent. Despite the recent emphasis on a life-span perspective, young persons are still described as "developing," whereas persons changing in their later years are typically described as "aging," even though we all understand that in a formal sense, "developing" describes the entire span. Children develop, but grandparents age. It is like day and night, where "day" might formally refer to the entire 24-hour span, but it is informally used to refer to the brighter side of day. So, too, "aging" has come to refer to the darker side of development. In this case, however, the nominal distinction has great consequence. To make changes in later life one must fight against all sorts of consensually held preconceptions before they are "recognized" as growth. This struggle for legitimate recognition would be less strenuous if development were cast in other frames.

Accordingly, in this paper we will argue that, in principle, human development should be viewed as virtually limitless with respect to its potential expressions. When the human agent is viewed in this light, structural theories of human development appear short-sighted to the extent that they either explicitly or implicitly recognize inflexible boundaries or limits to human growth.

The sequential character of development and the endpoint toward which it is

moving become less determinate once we question theories of development. In our view, it is only when people are behaving "mindlessly," and thereby are relying on categories that were drawn in the past, that change appears necessarily sequential and endpoints seem fixed. In such a situation, the individual is like a projectile that is moving along a calculable trajectory. However, we feel that a "mindful" mind continually creates categories and thus creates expanded possibilities and that this alteration in the mind influences the state of the body as well. Therefore, we postulate that by virtue of mindful involvement in any process within one's larger lifespan, one becomes less like a projectile propelled along a predetermined trajectory and more like a free-flying bird. If this is so, then the process of aging does not necessarily have a single endpoint and, in principle, development can proceed nonsequentially rather than decrementally as the person ages. By nonsequentially, we mean that the order people ordinarily assume to exist between stages and substages in any developmental process is not inevitable. Moreover, we believe it is possible both (1) to move bidirectionally from a given "stage" to any other "stage" without passing through intermediate ones and (2) to construct any number of new and different stages or states. We do recognize that a particular developmental sequence could be fixed once the goal and path to it have been mindlessly accepted. If either the path or the goal, however, is mindfully modified so too may be the developmental sequence. This view opens the possibility of positive growth in late adulthood.

Aging Without Decline

Any theory of aging must begin by defining old age. This should present no difficulty. Everyone knows an old person when they see one. Or do they? We set as our first task to find the biological markers of aging. The questions we posed to 10 of the leading research geriatricians in the country are rather straightforward: If there were a 50-year-old in one room and a 70-year-old in another, how could you reliably tell them apart? If a treatment were supposed to make someone younger, what measures would you take to be convinced of its success? Interestingly, this turned out to be more difficult than expected. No one was able to tell us what characterizes old age. There were several physiological markers that are correlated with chronological aging, such as decreases in forced vital capacity (depth of breath), auditory thresholds, near-point vision (vision acuity), but improvement on any of these or other measures would *not* lead to judgment that the individual had in fact gotten any younger with respect to "real" age. The geriatrician would simply assume that the measure was not an adequate or reliable marker of real aging. In other words, if there was anything looking like a reversal of the familiar signs of aging, the measure, rather than the familiar view, would be found to be at fault. Clearly, the assumption of irreversible decline is firmly embedded in prevailing views of old age.

Some geriatrician believed that the best measure of age was how old the individual looked. The correlation between apparent age and chronological age, however, is likely to be exaggerated. In fact, it is probably because of an illusory correlation effect that this measure appears so strong (Chapman & Chapman, 1967). That is, although older people are probably more likely to have gray hair than younger persons, for example, we can all think of exceptions. Nevertheless the

strangers we see every day are typically taken as confirmation of the hypothesis; young people with gray hair are taken to be chronologically older than they actually are, and old people with dark hair are assumed to be younger. So the correlation may not be nearly as high as we presume (Rodin & Langer, 1980). The same would be true, of course, for other characteristics and abilities as well. It is interesting that in such an ageist society all we can be sure of is that a 70-year-old has lived 20 years longer than a 50-year-old.

In any case, in several investigations we found that psychological and physical debilitations at least typically associated with old age in fact were malleable. The debilitations could be slowed and in some cases reversed by subtle variations in the environment. In each case, our population was the institutionalized elderly (see Piper & Langer, 1984, for a review). In the first study, we encouraged decision making and found that residents became more alert, more active, happier, and healthier (Langer & Rodin, 1976). Follow-up data 18 months later revealed that the experimental group also lived longer than comparison groups. By the time of the follow-up, 15 percent of the experimental group had died versus 30 percent of the comparison group (Rodin & Langer, 1977). In a second study we increased the cognitive demandingness of the environment for the residents in the experimental group (Langer, Rodin, Beck, Weinman, & Spitzer, 1979). Here too we found improvement. Short-term and long-term memory improved, as did general alertness and adjustment. Moreover, follow-up data again showed that fewer people in the experimental group had died relative to comparison groups (14 percent vs. 47 percent) (Langer, Beck, Janoff-Bulman, & Timko, 1984).

The cognitive work that subjects in the experimental group of both these studies engaged in may be conceived of as mindfulness (see Langer, 1982; 1989a and b). Mindfulness is the type of cognitive activity that occurs when an individual actively deals with a novel environment or deals with an old environment in new ways. People are mindful when they are creating new distinctions rather than relying on distinctions that have already been drawn. These new distinctions need not be radical interpretations; for instance, in one of these experiments, we had subjects learn (among other things) the names of nurses they did not already know by name. This represents creating a new distinction in that someone in the environment changes from merely a nurse to a person viewed as a distinct individual.

Mindlessness, on the other hand, refers to a relative absence of cognitive activity where the person abstains from creating new distinctions. Action is guided by already-made distinctions, and the apparently routinized character of life dulls the person's sense of vital involvement. Mindful involvement has an enlivening effect upon the person, whereas mindless involvement has a deadening one.

Although we did not originally conceive of these aging experiments within the mindfulness framework, each treatment required that subjects mindfully deal with their environments. Further, follow-up data from the last study presented clearly suggest this reinterpretation. Subsequent to the intervention, the experimental group was better able to find novel uses for familiar objects and describe them in greater detail than the control group (Langer, Beck, Janoff-Bulman, & Timko, 1984).

A third, prospective experiment that we conducted lends additional credibility to this interpretation (Alexander, Langer, Newman, Chandler, & Davies, 1989). In

this study mindfulness was experimentally investigated in one of two ways. An active distinction-making mindfulness group and a "restfully alert" group practicing the transcendental meditation (TM) program (predicted to enhance mindfulness *after* meditation practice) were contrasted with a no treatment and a low-mindfulness control group. Again, the results provided striking confirmation that debilitations highly correlated with age could be reversed. Both mindfulness-producing groups showed marked enhancement in intellectual functioning as well as physical health. They also exhibited an increase in perceived control, felt significantly younger, and were rated by nurses as improved on mental health. Further, both groups appeared to live longer during the three-year follow-up period: none of the subjects in the TM group and 12.5 percent in the active distinction-making mindfulness group died, as opposed to 28.8 percent of those in the comparison groups and 37.5 percent of the remaining elderly adults ($N = 478$) in the institutions studied during the three-year follow-up period (Alexander, Langer, Newman, Chandler, & Davies, 1989; cf. Alexander et al. chapter in this volume).

Thus, despite the assumption that growing old is an irreversible process of physiological decline, important improvements can be induced through creative mental functioning that is under voluntary control. And these changes are both psychological and physical in nature. However, given that such changes are positive and are not difficult to produce, one might wonder why they are not more prevalent.

Such so-called positive change may not be seized upon because it appears mutually exclusive with another framework through which the individual is currently operating. All will admit that behavior is multiply determined and potentially ambiguous. We give it a label that hides its ambiguity while adding some stability to our lives. The elderly have taken their potentially ambiguous responses and rigidly cast them in an unflattering light. All of us may do this when we "need" to view our behavior as unidimensional in order to reduce ambiguity in our lives, even when the only frame available for stabilizing our lives is a demeaning one. It is single-minded, however, to view the changes that occur in old age as indicative of a diminution of cognitive functioning and productivity. People believe their behavior is largely rational and well intentioned. When someone (some group) behaves differently from them, they conclude that it must be for negative reasons (cf. Ross, 1978). However, different concerns may make different forms of behavior rational in the same setting. Similarly, identical behaviors do not necessarily arise from common bases, nor do they necessarily convey the same information. What may be desirable to younger persons may be undesirable or uninteresting to an elderly person.

Consider, for instance, being taught how to produce widgets more quickly. If one is not interested in widgets any longer or is interested in developing a better-quality widget rather than more widgets, this new information would fall on deaf ears. The person's focus on developing certain skills relevant to his or her current concerns might lead unwittingly to the diminution of other skills that have greater value in an alternative framework adopted by the majority of society.

This may often be the situation for the elderly: They are frequently not aware of how what they are gaining may be *causing* what they are losing. That is, they may be gaining something valuable that in itself causes a corresponding loss, yet they (and the rest of society) are only aware of the loss. For example, elders tend

to focus on the *process* of engaging in activity, whereas younger adults often value an activity for its *outcome*. It is likely that one can produce a lot of widgets when one implicitly believes that one's status will improve with the production of each new widget. By standards of an outcome orientation, however, a process orientation may yield lower levels of productivity. The younger person, who single-mindedly values outcomes, may not appreciate a process orientation that values the way in which things are done. The quality of experience in the aged may be ignored by younger adults in the same way that the adults' quality of experience is egocentrically ignored or misunderstood by the child.

Regardless of which orientation "really" has more value, the disparity of performance between younger and older adults might be explicable in terms other than the alterable psychological disability in the elders. Rather, it may result from different psychological orientations of younger and older adults. This difference may lie in the process versus outcome distinction or in some other distinction as well. One more analogous case might help to make this point.

The same behavior may be labeled negatively as field dependent or positively as field sensitive. Take the situation of a woman wishing to become more autonomous while not losing her receptivity or sensitivity to her environment. She may wish to become more field independent because of the rewards such behavior occasions. However, she may not seek these rewards because of other rewards for being field sensitive. But because she may not be aware of her competing motivations to maintain field sensitivity, she may feel unnecessarily deficient in her inability to achieve autonomy (field independence). This phenomenon of noticeable deficiency in one that is due to unnoticed development in another may well be a basis upon which politically less powerful groups (women, children, the old, gays) come to be perceived as the more debilitated by themselves and others. Thus, what a younger outsider often perceives as absolute decrements in the elders may be only differences in performance levels that are induced by voluntary involvement in an alternative framework for activity (cf. Langer, 1989a).

Another reason improvements are not more prevalent, given that we can so "readily" induce them experimentally, is that they may be blocked by premature cognitive commitments about old age that people make in their youth. (This explanation is appropriate to the extent that one has accepted the idea that the differences one initially observed in the elderly are indeed decrements.) Premature cognitive commitments are like photographs of information where action (meaning) is frozen. When individuals are first presented with information it may be mindlessly processed in this way (as, for example, when information is personally irrelevant). In this instance, the information is taken at face value. If at a later time the information became relevant, it usually would not occur to the individual to reexamine it, even if it would be personally advantageous to do so. Thus, the way information is initially processed ordinarily determines how it subsequently may be used. If a child attended to the outcome of walking and was mindless of his style, later as an adult it would not naturally occur to the person to consider whether to change the way he walks. The relevance of this notion to aging will become clear.

We conducted an experiment testing this idea. We presented subjects with information about a disease under conditions where they would process information mindlessly or mindfully. This was done by framing the information about the

symptoms of the disease in such a way that subjects believed that the information was, respectively, either not relevant or relevant to themselves. All subjects then "discovered" that they had the disease. The results were striking. Those subjects who mindlessly, unwittingly, initially accepted the relationship between symptoms and disease displayed those symptoms when they found that they had the disease. Those who initially processed the information mindfully did not fall victim to it (Chanowitz & Langer, 1981).

In a later investigation, we assessed the relationship between premature cognitive commitments one made about aging and the success of one's own aging. We compared elderly subjects who had lived with a grandparent before they were two years old with those who had lived with a grandparent after they were 13 (age of parents was held constant). For the former group, the grandparents were likely to be younger and to "look bigger" than for the latter group. Thus, the former group should have more "youthful" premature cognitive commitments about old age than the latter group; therefore, the younger group should "act out" a "younger" version of old age. Indeed, we found this to be true. Our elderly subjects were independently evaluated by raters unaware of our hypothesis; those whose earliest premature cognitive commitments were youthful, were considered more alert. There was also a tendency for them to be more active and more independent. The results suggest that many of us inadvertently may have been taught to grow old inadequately (Langer, Perlmuter, Chanowitz, & Rubin, 1988).

Hence, elderly adults may be caught up in a premature cognitive commitment to a single-minded way in which it is appropriate to be old. They shape their behavior and they understand its significance in light of single-minded conceptions of agedness that they absorbed much earlier in their lives, when the character of old age was irrelevant to them. These same conceptions are now also used by younger adults to make sense of the elder's different behavior and reinforce the elder's response pattern. The old are kept in this place, by themselves and others, simply because alternative forms of behavior are outside their imaginative reach. Less "debilitated" behavior is within reach once the elder realizes *how* he or she fell prey to these debilities (e.g., the process of making premature cognitive commitments), *that* there are other possibilities, and *what* those other possibilities are. In seeing these possibilities, the path of development that was absolute and predetermined becomes relative and more a matter of choice. The behavioral rut of elders' performance decrements, then, may be more a function of alterable psychological factors than of unalterable physiological ones.

In summary, our assertion is that to the extent that the so-called biologically necessary changes (i.e., "debilitations") of old age arise from the two sources discussed earlier—different interpretive schemes and premature cognitive commitments—they may be reversed through psychological intervention. Although premature cognitive commitments to a certain way of behaving may be to some degree stabilizing, they also can be demeaning. Therefore, it might be appropriate to label such behavior as debilitated. However, it is a difficult situation when elders adhere to these so-called low levels of functioning because, from their own perspective, these patterns are viewed as rewarding. In this case, it might be inappropriate to refer to the disparity in behavior as a decrement, since it must be valued in a distinct context. In either case, the difference should not be regarded as the irreversible

effect of physiological aging, since research suggests that "improvement" in behavior (or alternative forms of apparently more "normal" behavior) may be within the reach of the elder.

This perspective becomes theoretically more coherent if we reconceptualize the relation "between" mind and body. The typical conceptualization of this relationship may represent another premature cognitive commitment that may mislead one into thinking that decline is inevitable in later life.

Putting Body and Mind Back Together

Twentieth-century science, as well as everyday parlance, is replete with examples that imply a deep-rooted belief in a division between mind and body. Typically, the intimate interrelation between these two aspects of the human being is not fully acknowledged. Further, it is common for scientists to assume that the body is somehow more real and a more apt object of study than the mind. In extreme, such a tendency ends in relegating the mind to the status of an epiphenomenon. This materialistic view became prevalent as modern science increasingly focused on the physical world as the more appropriate realm for objective, rigorous investigation and as modern social science increasingly placed emphasis on that which is concrete and more easily quantifiable. However, for most people throughout most of history, consciousness was seen to involve more than merely something derived from the matter of the body. Indeed, the idealist tradition of philosophy—which until this century was extremely influential—clearly advocated the primacy of mind.

Ironically, as science has continued to probe into the deepest aspects of matter, its physical character, as *physical* has traditionally been understood, has disappeared. The eminent physicist Ernst Schrödinger stated that the materiality of matter dissolves at the underlying level of the quantum mechanical wave function. Others have suggested that at the basic level of the universe, "things" do not really exist at all, only relationships (Bohm & Hiley, 1975). The physicist Sir James Jeans (1943) was led to conclude that, "The universe seems more like a great idea than a great machine" and that the cosmos may essentially be a vast mind.

Although sharply distinguishing between the mind and body can serve useful purposes in many contexts, we argue that it is time to reconsider the ways in which we conceive of their relationship. In our view, in most instances attempts to study or deal with the physical body without considering corresponding mental states constitute a necessarily limited approach. Alternatively, we suggest that (1) the mind and body represent different dimensions or levels of analysis of one fully integrated system, (2) the mental aspect of the mind–body system is at least as ontologically "real" as the physical, and (3) the mind can exert powerful control over physiological processes.

In the three studies cited earlier, we found that changes in physical health occurred as a result of psychological intervention. In fact, a vast literature on seemingly anomalous phenomena, when taken collectively, also strongly supports the potentially powerful influence of mental processes or procedures on health problems ordinarily thought to be outside of conscious control. For example, it has been

found that hypnosis may remove warts (Surman, Gottlieb, Hackett, & Silverberg, 1973); cognitive reappraisal may provide relief from the pains of major surgery (Langer, Janis, & Wolfer, 1975); placebos are effective in alleviating many illnesses, including multiple sclerosis, epilepsy, and Parkinsonism (Haas, Fink, & Hartfelder, 1963); faith healing may lessen intense pain (Katz, 1982); relocation of an elderly patient may lead to premature death (Krantz & Schulz, 1980); "voodoo deaths" do occur (Cannon, 1942), as do parasympathetic deaths that result from extreme learned helplessness (Seligman, 1975).

The full practical import of these findings is obscured while researchers devote their energies to finding mediating links between such "psychological" interventions and "physical" consequences. The problem may be insoluble because of the way it is conceptualized. If there is assumed to be a split between the mind and the body, then one asks what can connect the two. If the two are conceived as one integrated whole, then the question itself loses meaning and other questions can be addressed. Too much research attention has been sidetracked from accepting the fact of influence of mind on body and then going on to ask how this influence can be further explored and beneficially maximized. In consequence, there may be vast areas of human potential, ordinarily latent, that have remained outside of our conscious influence. By focusing our research on what the full potential of the mind–body whole actually is, we could perhaps learn how to achieve much richer levels of human development. "Development" here refers to the process of expanding (rather than contracting) our range of available mental and physical possibilities.

In this chapter, for heuristic purposes, we will assume that the mind–body is a single system and that every change in the human being is simultaneously a change on the level of "mind" *and* "body." We will proceed pragmatically, attempting to induce change in "body" by intervening at the level of "mind." For us the amount of change that can be manifested remains an open, empirical question. Our early research, guided by this pragmatic perspective, has proved to be quite useful in demonstrating that mental and physical improvement are possible for the elderly (see Piper & Langer, 1984).

Taking the preceding cases (e.g., placebos) as illustrative evidence of psychological change measurable in physical parameters, or vice versa, we are led to ask, "How else might we change the mind if we wanted a change in the body or vice versa?" and, "How would we change the body if we could?" An intervention at the level of mind may be more likely, since the mind is a more plastic medium. Clearly, our proposed heuristic view of mind–body unity would more easily lead one to question presently accepted physiological and psychological limits. This perspective has led us to the radical view that "old age" may be a premature cognitive commitment and that changes in mindset can radically affect the apparently aging body.

The results of two conditioning experiments provide us with important clues about how we might effectively induce change in the mind–body system. Ader and Cohen (1982) reported a study that investigated whether or not immune function could be behaviorally conditioned in rats. Specifically, they were interested in the extent to which the longevity of rats that were genetically disposed to a fatal autoimmune disease (systemic lupus erythematosus) could be prolonged with a placebo treatment. Group 1, the standard treatment group, received a weekly injection of

an immunosuppressive drug (cyclophosphamide) immediately following consumption of a novel drinking solution. (Research has shown that the immunosuppressive effect of this drug prolongs longevity of animals with lupus.) Group 2, the conditioned placebo group, received the same treatment as Group 1, except that an inert saline injection was substituted for the immunosuppressive drug half of the time. Thus, Group 2 received only 50 percent of the total amount of the immunosuppressive drug that Group 1 received over time. Group 3 was identical to Group 2, except that the injections and drinking solution were administered on different days; injections were not paired with consumption of the novel solution. Finally, the control group received a weekly contingent administration of drinking solution and saline injection, but at no time was it administered the immunosuppressive drug. The critical comparison, for our purposes, is between Group 2 and Group 3. If the autoimmune disease developed more slowly in Group 2, the rats were somehow eliciting an additional immunosuppressive response that could not be attributed to the drug. Focusing especially on the rate at which the first half of each group died, the results were striking. Not only was the mortality rate significantly lower in Group 2 as compared with Group 3, but Group 3 did not differ from the control group. Moreover, the mortality rate of Group 2 (i.e., the placebo group) was not significantly different from that of the group that always received the immunosuppressive drug.

Let us also consider a study that Pavlov (1927) conducted on the perception and meaning of pain over 50 years ago. He observed that whereas the usual response of a dog to strong electric shock administered to one of its paws is violent and indicative of pain, the dog can be conditioned to respond as if it felt no pain (e.g., salivation, tail wagging, eagerness) by presenting it with food after administering the shock. The conditioned behavior was observed, however, only when the same paw was shocked. When a new paw was shocked after conditioning, the dog again reacted violently.

What do these studies have in common? First, in both studies, there was an association between the occurrence of some external agent (the drink, the electric shock) and some bodily process (immunosuppressive effects, salivation). Second, upon closer inspection, it is clear that the embodied response, after conditioning, was not a function of the external agent per se, but of the meaning that it had acquired. Pavlov's dogs, for instance, apparently felt no pain when the electric shock signaled something positive. Third, the research animals were presumably unaware of any other way of interpreting and responding to the external agent in a given context. That is, the occurrence of the agent automatically resulted in a context-consistent embodied response.

These observations together support our understanding of the relationship between mind and body. Embodied responses do not reflect a one-to-one correspondence to stimuli in the external world because there is no one-to-one correspondence between the external world and how we perceive it. There is a reciprocal interaction between one's internal cognitive structure and perceptual apparatus and the particular contextual givens; and it is one's perceptual response or cognitive interpretation that in turn remediates embodied response. The meaning of any situation and the corresponding way in which the organism responds to it result from this interaction. Thus, according to the view espoused here, *when the "mind" is in*

one context, the "body" is necessarily also in that context. Therefore, to arrive at a different embodied state, perhaps "all" one needs to do is to place the mind in the preferred context. No one is surprised that an injury incurred while playing football may not hurt, whereas a similar injury if incurred in the home would hurt and would be nursed attentively. Interestingly, people try to take the at-home "victim's" mind off the injury in order to ease the pain. We suggest that this be turned around just a bit. Rather than take the mind out of one context, what would be the effect of intentionally putting it in another context?

Placebos, hypnosis, sudden voodoo deaths, and the like are all linked, in that each places the individual in a new context. Their effectiveness relies on the individual's premature cognitive commitments. The body responds in a way commensurate with those commitments. For example, an individual has a premature cognitive commitment for what it means to be an unhealthy person. When one, for whatever reason, is led to believe that he or she is unhealthy, the behavior (on all levels) that is taken as true for that unhealthy context may unfold. In these instances the individual is basically "fooled" into the new mindset.

The interesting empirical question is, "Can individuals intentionally put themselves completely in a new context to produce embodied change?" To do so, subjects must do more than role-play. To be sick and to role-*play* a healthy person, for example, by this reasoning, would not work as long as the person was aware of playing a part—caught somewhere between current self and ideal role self. Instead, the subject must, intentionally or unintentionally, role-*be* a healthy person or whatever else was demanded by the context.

Changing Our Perception of Time

The experienced flow of time is relative, varying with psychological state, changes in this perceived flow may mediate changes in mental and physical functions. This suggests that specific, systematic, and sustained changes in psychological state could significantly alter the pace and character of the life cycle, leading to a dramatic change in human development.

All of us share the notion that the aging process and the physiological deterioration that accompanies it are the inevitable results of the passage of time. To challenge this assumption is to challenge commonly held notions about the nature of development itself. Yet if dimensions of time exist that we do not ordinarily experience or comprehend, there could be facets of development that are likewise not ordinarily experienced and comprehended. Further, when we encounter ways of perceiving time as something no longer highly fixed, we have additional reason to seek alternative perspectives on other commonly held "fixed" phenomena such as aging.

Of course, one nonordinary dimension of time would be the timeless. Numerous world views recognize such a dimension as a basic level of reality. Various Eastern philosophies postulate "timeless," "mystical" states in which the individual transcends the world of space and time. In the "mystical" experience it is commonly reported that the individual is outside (or at least experiences oneself as outside) the normal flow of time. Western religions share notions of timelessness

as well. Heaven is thought to be a timeless place, and God is thought to exist outside the normal flow of time. In the West this timelessness is typically conceived of as being accessible only in the hereafter. However, timeless transcendental experiences have been reported by certain Westerners as well, such as Emerson, Thoreau, and Whitman. (Many examples are provided by James, 1902, and Huxley, 1945.)

To most Westerners, the timeless is difficult to conceive; however, even within the realm of time, there are more possibilities than commonly grasped. For instance, whereas in classical physics and common sense, space and time are distinct, Einstein has demonstrated that they can be seen as reciprocal phenomena. In his understanding, because of this reciprocity it is most appropriate to consider them as a whole: space–time. In Einstein's famous example, events occurring in the same place but at different times in a moving system (such as a train) will be perceived by a stationary observer as occurring at different places. Likewise, events taking place at the same time but in different places in a moving system will be perceived by a stationary observer as different times. Further, he showed how the flow of time is itself relative, depending on the reference frame. For example, he showed that although a trip to the center of the galaxy at the speed of light would take 40,000 earth years, upon return, space travelers would be only 30 years older.

Einstein's theory points out that from one physical reference frame to another, time is relative. Psychological experiments have demonstrated that within a given physical frame, the *perceived flow* of time is also relative. This relativity is due to the fact that there are many possible psychological reference frames, with time seeming to flow at different rates within them. These experiments speak to a fundamental philosophical question: Is there really a phenomenon of time that exists apart from any individual, or is it a phenomenon that is dependent upon one's perceptions of it? A growing body of empirical studies is available in which perceptions of the passage of time are affected by real-world events. By varying the context of a situation, one can alter an individual's perceptions about the passage of time (see Fraisse, 1964; Orne, 1969). This work has shown what the layman knows— that some periods of time "seem" longer or shorter than other "objectively" equal periods, depending on context. For example, time seems to pass quickly when a task is interesting or challenging, while unfilled time intervals seem longer. For example, Langer, Wapner, and Werner (1961) showed that when subjects were asked to sit on electric carts moving toward a precipice and to stop the cart after five seconds had elapsed, those subjects headed for danger constantly overestimated the passage of time.

A number of individual differences have been associated with the perception of time. For instance, psychological measures of introversion–extroversion, authoritarianism, "dissociation," and anxiety have been shown to differentiate those with fast "internal clocks" from those with slow ones. McClelland (1976) has stated that the need for achievement serves to "relate present in terms of a wider context." Motives, he asserts, "tie the present and future together." His investigations have shown that need for achievement relates to an active future orientation. For those who are high on need for achievement, the present is a state to be tolerated on one's road to the future. For example, people with a high need for achievement tend to put their clocks or watches ahead as if to anticipate or catch up with the future.

If the perceived flow of time is variable, might not processes that are considered time dependent also show some unexpected variation? In other words, through psychological intervention that changes the perception of time, can important rhythms of the life cycle be changed? This question is central to the thesis of this chapter. We have postulated that by altering subjects' psychological state in certain ways, both psychological and physiological changes will occur. If in fact this is the case, then it would have significant consequences for current notions of human development as an invariant and limited sequence of growth that is bounded by linear time. Viewed in such a context, people have the opportunity to create their own development as they respond to the environment. Traditional learning theorists understand the significance of the environment differently. For them, the individual is a passive receiver reacting to a "given" environment. We are advocating a view of the individual as an active organism who is able to "take" the environment in one meaningful way or another. We postulate that in exercising this choice and acting mindfully, people are able to take part in *directing* the course of their development.

Several studies are supportive of this view. Lewis and Lobban (1957) took subjects to an isolated location during Arctic summer, in which day and night are indistinguishable. Subjects were provided with wristwatches that moved through 24 hours of time for every 22 hours of "real" time. Results showed that, despite the persistence of cyclic metabolic activity, there was some tendency for urine production to follow cycles of perceived, rather than "real" time. Craik and Sarbin (1963) investigated the effects of covert alterations of clock rate upon time measures of personal tempo. Results showed that when the clock rate was altered, tapping and dotting rates shifted in the direction of the clock rate, both when the clock rate was increased relative to ordinary clock time and when it was decreased.

A series of studies by Albert (1978) also found an influence of perceived time rate on various psychological measures. In one study, Albert showed that by altering the perception of time through the manipulation of clock speed, the forgetting curve could be altered. That is, subjects appeared to be forgetting memorized words according to the rate of clock time rather than that of "real" time. In another study Albert showed that the temporal effects on person perception could be altered by manipulating perceived time duration. Subjects were placed in a situation in which they heard either a positive or a negative description of a stimulus person. Results showed that both positive and negative information occurring "three hours ago" in subjective time had less effect on impressions of the stimulus person than information acquired "45 minutes ago." In fact, these two time periods were "objectively" equal. Thus, the ordinary temporal effects on person perception were shown to be secondary to subjective time.

Although many of the previously noted studies support the view that systematic changes in psychological and physical state follow changes in perceived time, it is clear that research in this area is still in its early phases. Understanding that many key studies remain to be done, we would like to report one of our recent investigations that adds additional credibility to the assertions that (1) psychological factors make an important contribution (positive or negative) to the way humans age/develop and (2) the aging process is less fixed than has hitherto been suspected.

In our experiment we attempted to invoke a state of mind in a group of elderly subjects that they had experienced 20 years ago in order to determine if their physical health and cognitive competencies would also "backtrack" to a somewhat more youthful status. To test these notions of context control, we enlisted the help of elderly men who agreed to try to place themselves in a new psychological context and to participate in physical as well as psychological assessment. A striking test of context control is to have the new context be an earlier time in the lives of the men. These men's bodies were approximately 75 years old and the "new" mind we were going to encourage was their own mind when they were 55 years old. This seemed to be a context change that subjects would be willing and motivated to make.

Mindset and Aging: An Empirical Perspective

We initiated our study to test the hypothesis that subjects could be induced to adopt their own mindsets of 20 years ago and that, consequently, they would be drawn into a more youthful physical and mental state. We tested this by comparing the effects of two manipulations: One had subjects attempt to *be* psychologically where they were about 20 years ago; the other had subjects *reflect upon* the past of 20 years ago but (implicitly) included the recognition that they were now here, 20 years later. We supposed that, in terms of content, the two groups would be occupied with broadly the same thoughts. The only difference between the two groups that could account for any difference in results would be the frame that the two groups adopted for contextualizing those thoughts. The experimental group would adopt a frame for experience that outsiders would recognize as one of 20 years ago, whereas the control group would adopt a frame representative of the present.

We believe this experimental manipulation is achievable because subjects do potentially have available a rigid framework or mindset that represented the world as it was 20 years ago. The only problem was to get them "into" it and then to get them to act routinely. We felt this could be done by exploiting subjects' mindless attitude about this prior time period. The control group, on the other hand, would be acting through the routine frame of reminiscence, gazing at the past from the present.

The two groups of elderly subjects were taken to a retreat where they were to be isolated for five days and where they were encouraged either to step back into the past of 20 years ago (e.g., all conversation about the past was to be in the *present* tense) or to view the past from the present (e.g., conversation about the past was in the *past* tense). Psychological and physical measures were taken before and after the intervention to see if such a mental context change could produce observable improvements in physical health and cognitive capability. Because of the unusual nature of this experiment it is worthwhile going into detail about the procedure.

Subjects

Volunteers 70–75 years old who responded to advertisements in local newspapers and senior-citizen circulars were selected for initial consideration. Each volunteer

was given two questionnaires to assess their health and interests. These were identical, except that the second questionnaire asked the volunteer to complete it as he would have "20 years ago." The questionnaires had three purposes: to help us form two comparable groups of subjects, to ensure that those selected were not less healthy approximately 20 years ago than they are today, and to help us plan the discussions and activities for the experimental week. Any respondent who failed to complete the second questionnaire as if he were responding 20 years ago was not included in the pretest sample. All participants ($N = 17$, nine in the experimental group and eight in the control group) were middle class, educated, and in relatively good health. They were administered a range of measures before the experimental week actually began and on day 5 of the experimental week. In addition, a subset of measures was administered throughout the week.

Measures

The tests measured physical strength, perception, cognition, and gustatory, auditory, and visual thresholds. The particular measures used were a summary of the "biological markers" recommended by the geriatrician discussed earlier. The subjects also answered questions concerning personal values and behavior. In addition we took a series of anthropometric measurements of the body, including the following: triceps skinfold, finger length, weight, height, gait, and posture.

Vision was measured with and without eyeglasses by a standard eye test that assessed acuity, accommodation, and contrast (binocularity). Scores were collected for each eye separately and for both together. To determine gustatory sensitivity, a modified version of the method of limits technique was employed, involving two sets of trials for sucrose and saline. In the first trial, subjects were asked to sample two cups of liquid. One cup contained distilled water and the other contained 0.015 M concentration of sucrose or saline. (Less sensitive thresholds for taste of salt and sweet are correlated with age.) Subjects then were asked to respond to whether the solution tasted salty, sweet, or had no taste. An incorrect response on one trial was followed by the next strongest solution concentration on the next trial. A correct response was followed by the next weakest solution concentration. Concentration levels (M) were sucrose 0.001–0.080 and saline 0.0001–0.080. This procedure was repeated until a sensitivity threshold was determined.

Cognitive measures included the Digit Symbol Substitution subtest from the Wechsler Adult Intelligence Scale (WAIS), which was administered in accord with the standard WAIS instructions, and a series of paper and pencil mazes that would assess speed of completion and accuracy under evaluation conditions. Subjects were also administered the Visual Memory Test excerpted from the Dementia Screening Test. They were asked to look at a figure drawing for 10 seconds and then wait 10 seconds before producing the figure from memory with paper and pencil.

Finally, each subject also was asked to fill out a SYMLOG self-rating form (Bales, 1979). SYMLOG is a system of rating and scoring both behaviors and values according to a three-dimensional factor-analytic space. The three behavioral dimensions are Dominant–Submissive (U–D), Friendly–Unfriendly (P–N), and

Task oriented-Emotional expressive (F–B). The three value dimensions are Dominant-Submissive (U–D), Egalitarian–Individualistic (P–N), and Conventional–Unconventional (F–B).

Procedures

Subjects selected for the study were sent an information packet in the mail. The information packet included several items—general instructions, an outline of the schedule of the week (mentioned testing, meals, discussions, and each evening's activities), a floor plan of the retreat marking the location of their room, and a request for subjects not to bring any magazines, newspapers, books, or family pictures that were more recent than *1959*. Copies were made from the photographs that subjects sent of themselves from the recent past and from 20 years ago. A set of photographs of each of their fellow group members was included in the information packet. The experimental group was given pictures of each group member as they were approximately *20 years ago,* whereas the comparison group was given *recent* photographs. Information in the packet also included suggestions about what clothing to bring.

Discussions were scheduled for each day on defined topics, although there was also plenty of free time available. In addition, we scheduled various types of entertainment, including a movie night, a game night, live music, and a party. Rooming assignments were made randomly and each subject had his own room. Subjects were told that, although the five-day retreat had a vacation atmosphere, it was fundamentally a research study designed to explore the relationship between reminiscing and well-being. Therefore, they were strongly discouraged from contacting family and friends. In case of emergency, we required the name of their physician and two friends, and we allowed them to give the telephone number of the retreat to whomever they wished.

Subjects were required to prepare an autobiography for the first day of orientation. The instruction read: "Specifically, the autobiography should describe you (your likes, dislikes, activities, jobs, relationships, joys, worries, etc.) as you were about 20 years ago. In fact, please focus on 1959. Please note that it is important that you be accurate. Begin with the day you were born and work up to the present." These directions were the same for each group. However, the experimental group was further asked to "write (and talk) in the *present tense* even though you are describing the past. Remember that the 'present' means 1959. So do not include any of your history past this date." We elaborated on the importance of this instruction before the experiment began, since speaking in the present tense was to constitute our primary experimental manipulation.

Orientation

Experimental and control subjects had no interaction with each other, were oriented separately, and participated in the study during different weeks. Subjects arrived at Harvard early on the first morning of the study, were introduced to one another, and awaited a brief orientation meeting. We told the subjects that one

purpose of our study on reminiscence was to gather information about people in their late 50s, and we said that we believed one way to get new information about this age group was to question older people about their experiences at that earlier time in their own lives. They were told that, to encourage memory of their personal histories, we wanted to create interactions among similar people. Hence we brought them together. As part of the Day 1 pretest, subjects were administered a maze test. The maze used for the experiment was fixed so that there was only one path to travel. Subjects were informed of this and told that their task was to complete the maze quickly in the time allotted but not to go out of the lines. Thus, it was a test of *dexterity* rather than one of path finding. The same would be true for the maze test that would be administered each day at the retreat. While medical measures were being taken for some subjects, others were photographed. Finally, subjects individually and at various times were instructed to go into a different room to pick up another questionnaire. Their gait and posture were unobtrusively video-taped as they entered the room. The questionnaire to be completed was a SYM-LOG questionnaire.

After this pretesting was completed, subjects were joined together for the final orientation comments before departing for the retreat. The control group was told once again that they were to concentrate on the past. They were asked to help each other do this. Further, they were told that we had reason to believe that the discussions we had planned for them, coupled with the other activities that would take place in a very beautiful environment, might have very positive effects on them. They were told that we had good reason to think that they might improve their physical health as well as their psychological well-being. "In fact," they were told, "you may feel as well as you did in 1959."

In contrast to this, the orientation remarks for the experimental group stressed that the best way to learn about the past may not be through simple reminiscence. Rather it may best be achieved by returning as completely as possible in our minds to that earlier time. "Therefore, we're going to go together to a very beautiful retreat where we will live as if it were 1959. Obviously, that means no one can discuss anything that happened after September, 1959. It is your job to help each other do this. It is a difficult task since we are not asking you to 'act as if it is 1959' but to let yourself be just who you were in 1959. We have good reason to believe that if you are successful at this you also will feel as well as you did in 1959." This was elaborated upon as they were told that *all* of their interactions and conversations should reflect the "fact" that it is 1959. "It may be difficult at first, but the sooner you let yourselves go, the more fun you'll have."

All subjects also were asked to use the photos they were sent in order to help them come to know each other. Thus, for the experimental group, subjects would be looking for the 20 years younger man in each other person. Both groups were equally led to expect improvement over the course of the next five days. With this information, subjects boarded the van to the retreat. The experimental group was told that once they left for the retreat, it was no longer the present, but 1959. In keeping with this, a tape of music that was popular in 1959, along with commercials advertising products of the time, was played on the van's "radio." The following week the control group left for the retreat in the van and heard radio from the current time.

Intervention

The retreat is located on approximately 10 acres of tree-covered rolling hills, set off the main road, so that it appears as a world unto itself. Because subjects were from various ethnic backgrounds, religious icons were removed and what remained was a building decorated in rather timeless fashion. To this we added many props for the experimental group, including magazines, put in their rooms, for the week of the study in 1959. For the comparison group there were also old magazines available; but these were from various past years, and not solely that week in 1959.

The experimental treatment was largely enforced through the twice-daily structured discussions that the subjects had. After breakfast, each day would begin with a brief (15-minute) testing period and a group discussion period, followed by lunch, and then another discussion. Dinner and free time in the evening was then followed by a planned activity. The discussions involved rigorously defined topics and were led by moderators who were prepared in advance. Each discussion was initiated by a three-minute audiotape about the past played through an old radio (the experimental group) or a new radio (the control group). Subjects had been given the questions to be discussed the night before. After the radio broadcast the moderator would engage subjects in discussion of the issues for 45 minutes. After this, subjects were randomly assigned to one of two four-person groups, where they came to a decision relevant to the preceding discussion. Subjects then met again as a larger group. All the while, the experimental group had been having the discussions in the present tense, whereas the comparison group had been free to discuss the issues in the past tense. Each topic had been woven into the activity from the night before, which helped provide a context for remembering.

The evening activities that were woven into the next day's discussions were designed to accomplish several ends. First, they were supposed to be entertaining. Second, they were supposed to prod memories of the past and thereby facilitate the following day's discussion. Third, they provided the opportunity to take several dependent measures. The first evening's activity was a movie, "Anatomy of a Murder." During the morning discussion of the second day, subjects discussed "old" movies. In the afternoon, they discussed sports. That night they had a game night and played a version of "The Price Is Right." The following day they discussed financial matters. In the afternoon they heard a speech by Eisenhower and then discussed politics. That night they were entertained by musicians. The following morning they discussed some general aspects of music. And finally, that afternoon they discussed television situation comedies of the past. Late in the afternoon of the fourth day of the trip and on the last morning, all the dependent measures were readministered.

Much of the five day trip was preserved on videotape. However the tapes were not very clear so many of the subtleties were lost. Nevertheless, subjects' gait and posture were recorded to be compared to pretesting where they traversed a similar distance. Discussions were videotaped to see how active participating and ease of conversing changed over time. Meals were recorded to ascertain how much and how vigorously participants ate. Moreover, it allowed us to assess how dependent they were by noting whether they took what they needed from the kitchen without

waiting to be served, whether they cleaned up after themselves, etc. Videotapes of the evenings' activities allowed us to assess amount and kind of participation.

Results

Results fall into two classes. First, there were measures on which the experimental and control groups did not differ from each other but together showed significant improvement at the end of the intervention compared to their baseline level of performance prior to the intervention. These data are noteworthy insofar as we usually associate irreversible psychological and physical *decrements* with aging. The change of context in this study seems to have yielded, at least short-term, improvements on these measures. Second, there were measures on which the experimental group showed significantly greater improvements than the controls. We will present the two classes of findings in order. The results presented represent statistically significant differences.

Four raters blind to our hypotheses each rated a randomly presented subset of the facial photographs taken before (time 1) and on the last day of the experiment (time 2), where raters saw either the before or after photo of the subject but not both of them. Even though lighting and printing were held constant subjects were rated as appearing younger (mean = 63.95 years) at time 2 than at time 1 (mean = 66.38 years). There was a uniform tendency for hearing to improve. Threshold sensitivity to 1000 Hz tended to increase in the right ear, and sensitivity to 6000 Hz tended to increase in the left ear. Improvement in psychological functioning was evident in both groups, as indicated by steadily improved performance on the figure memory task over the course of the experiment.

Subjects in both groups ate heartily, as can be attested to by a weight gain of approximately three pounds over the week. Bideltoid and tricep skinfolds also increased. And, finally, hand strength increased steadily over the week for the two groups. It is noteworthy that by the second day all subjects were actively involved in serving their meals and cleaning up after they finished. With respect to this measure, conformity effects made statistical analysis inappropriate. Nevertheless despite their obvious dependence on relatives who initially brought them to us, they were all functioning independently almost immediately upon arrival at the retreat.

We were not able to find a comparable "vacationing" comparison group, nor could we afford to bring other groups to the retreat to isolate various potentially contributing factors. It is promising, however, that we found increments in performance for a group for whom such baseline measures typically remain the same or show decrements. We cannot be sure to what we can attribute these changes. Subjects in both groups were vacationing, were given expectations of positive outcome, and were treated with more respect and given more responsibility than is typical for the old. Other research (Rodin & Langer, 1977; Langer, Rodin, Beck, Weinman, & Spitzer, 1979; Schulz, 1976) suggests this latter variable can be quite powerful. Making demands on these elderly adults, as we did here, and in these earlier studies, may apparently reverse many debilitations of old age.

Differences between groups were also found. However, given the relatively small sample sizes and the shared positive impact of the weekend retreat on both

groups, these differences were not always substantial enough to reach statistical significance. Nevertheless, the following reliable results did emerge.

Joint flexibility (finger length) increased significantly more for the experimental group than for the control group. Finger length *increased* for 37.5 percent of the experimental group and remained the same for the rest of the group, whereas 33.3 percent of the comparison group actually *got worse* on this measure. Only one person in this latter group improved. There was also an increase in sitting height for the experimental group when compared with the sitting height of the control group. Those in the experimental group were able to sit taller, and they also had gained more weight, as revealed in measures of body weight, tricep skinfold, and bideltoid breadth. Performance on the mazes, our measure of manual dexterity, also discriminated between the two groups. Subjects traversed the same distance; however, the number of times per second that they went out of the line significantly differed. At the pretest the two groups' performance was virtually identical. At the posttest the experimental group decreased in the average number of errors while the average number of errors for the comparison group increased.

Near-point vision also showed the expected difference. In testing without eyeglasses, vision in the right eye improved for the experimental group and slightly worsened for the comparison group.

In addition to these physical changes, there were improvements on psychological tests. The most important of the differences occurred on the digit symbol substitution test. Again, the experimental group improved from pre- to posttest, whereas the control group's performance somewhat worsened over time. More specifically, 63 percent of the experimental group improved, 12 percent remained stable, and 25 percent declined. In contrast to this, 44 percent of the control group improved and 56 percent declined.

The status of the person in middle age is not uniformly better than the status of that person during later life. Indeed, Levinson, Darrow, Klein, Levinson, McKee (1978) and Levinson (chapter in this volume) tell us that middle age is often a time of particular crisis and malcontentedness compared with other periods in the lifespan. If our subjects returned to this earlier time, then there may be some indication of this malcontentedness in the self-ratings of behavior and values using the SYMLOG methodology (Bales & Cohen, 1979). Although the control group changed toward greater friendliness and emotional expressiveness, the members of the experimental group rated themselves as increasingly unfriendly. Of course, this may also reflect the fact that they had to work somewhat harder to maintain the time orientation than the comparison group.

Taken together, these results are encouraging, given typical views of aging. Although a few measures did not show reliable differences, enough did to suggest that more than chance was operating here. However, they provide only preliminary support for our radical hypothesis that humans have the capacity to shift discontinuously to an "earlier" context. This context change should have consequences for the person's body. Although we were not sure what to expect in this short time period, the strong prediction from this view would be instant return to the body of the 50-year-old if the mind were *truly* the mind of the 50-year-old. Nevertheless, there were meaningful differences between subjects in the experimental and control groups, and they were all in the right direction.

We realize in retrospect that one reason results were not more extreme may have been that we too were victims of age bias. Surely, a 50-year-old who cherished his self-perceived mature consciousness would feel ambivalent about giving up his current identity to return to who he was at 30 years old. In the same way, the 70-year-old may feel ambivalent about completely returning to the world of the 50-year-old, even though some of the health and strength of the earlier time is desirable.

Although the design of our study was motivated by the hypothesis that the state of a person's body could be "turned back" if we could shift that person's mind to where it was 20 years ago, there is an alternative hypothesis. The alternative also stems from the mindlessness–mindfulness framework. This hypothesis presumes that it took a certain measure of mindfulness for subjects in both groups to comply with the experimental instructions and that a greater degree of mindfulness was required of the experimental group, since it had to comply with a set of instructions that were more involving than those given to the control group.

Conclusion

Regardless of which mechanism produced these outcomes, the results have important practical implications for revising current views of time, aging, and development.

If significant differences between the two groups were produced as a result of two mindless patterns of activity—one centered in the past versus one centered in the present looking back at the past—then the results would show that humans may be capable of willfully thrusting themselves into a supposedly (because of presuppositions about body, mind, and development) inaccessible context and that the body will automatically follow suit. It just may be that humans won't consciously concede this capacity. They won't (or they don't believe they can) discontinuously switch from one context to another when that switch violates certain constraints that have been consensually adopted (e.g., irreversible aging). The "regular" and "irreversible" cycles of development that we psychologists witness are shaped by these constraints that may, in fact, be dissolvable. If this is the correct interpretation of how our results were achieved, then it has implications for what "must" develop during the process of aging and development.

As we said earlier, however, there is another process that might account for the results of the study. In the effort to comply with the instructions for the experiment, both groups could have been responding mindfully. Given the research we cited earlier that mindful activity has a significant beneficial effect on a person's health, the measured improvement in both groups could be attributed to this required mindful activity, and the significantly greater improvement of the experimental group could be attributed to the greater mindful activity that was required to comply with the instructions. If this were the case, then any mindful activity (e.g., composing an opera) could have served as a substitute in order to achieve our results. In either case, the broader point is that the objectively measured, "irreversible" signs of aging and "development" have been altered as a result of a psychological intervention.

Another test of the mind–body hypothesis was recently conducted (Langer, Dillon, Kurtz, & Katz, 1989). The data are very promising. In an attempt to improve vision, we took advantage of the premature cognitive commitments people have about airplane pilots. ROTC students served as subjects in two studies and were asked to assume the mindset of an airforce pilot. They were dressed in fatigues and flew an airplane simulator. Comparison subjects, also ROTC students dressed in fatigues, were asked to role-play a pilot rather than "be" a pilot. For them the simulator was broken, but they were asked to go through all the same motions anyway, from this more distant perspective. An eye test was given before the intervention as part of a general examination and then again when subjects were in the simulator, where the eye chart was disguised, and they were asked to read the markings on the wings of the airplane ahead. Vision improved for 40 percent of the group asked to "be" pilots. No improvement was found in the comparison group. This differential improvement was replicated in a second similar study.

When the results of this study are taken in conjunction with the many findings of our research that were cited earlier, we feel there is enough evidence to suggest that the "inevitable" decay of the aging human body may, in fact, be reversed through psychological intervention. However, the word *reversed* concedes too much in this domain, since it presumes that there is something natural about the progressive decay of the developing human body.

Instead, the seemingly irreversible cycle of decline observed in later stages of life may be the *product* of a certain sort of psychological participation—a mindless participation in certain premature cognitive commitments about how one is supposed to grow old. If people didn't feel "compelled" to follow through on these commitments (or, in other words, if they could see the alternative possibilities that are available as vehicles for growing old), then we psychologists might not have the data that we now marshall to validate the claim that late adulthood is a period of inevitable debilitation. In one of our most recent studies, for example, we found a correlation between mindfulness and hearing capacity among groups of elderly. Without these kind of data it would be harder to argue that changes that seem so clearly one-sided are not (Langer, Stoddard, Brown & Park, 1989). Age-related decrements may be less inevitable than they are made out to be, and the parameters of change that are observed during the aging process may be in part self-imposed through psychologically mediated factors. Our movement through time is bogged down by the sense of development that we use to guide and shape such movement—a sense of development as a sequential process that after adolescence involves decline.

What does all this suggest about development? Certainly, a concept of *developmental* psychology is to be commended, especially when it is compared with other frames of psychological theory that presume the reality of a status quo and that devote their energies to "understanding" and "explaining" it. An intrinsic element of developmental psychology's theorizing is the notion that *change* is what has to be understood and explained. Developmental psychology presumes that human beings are changing creatures. An underlying theme of this chapter is that much of the work in developmental psychology, however, is dominated by a conservative notion of change. There is too easy an understanding of what the next stage is going to be. "Development" is perceived as a time-dependent continuity

where the articulation of later stages "follows through" from participation in earlier stages. And there is an all too definite idea of what stages and possibilities lie ahead as persons make their way through development.

This is an unnecessarily *constraining* concept of development. As psychologists, it constrains our ideas about the limits of human capacity. As human beings, it constrains our idea about the limits of our personal growth. New theory and research suggest that there may be many more possibilities than we can now know.

II

HIERARCHICAL THEORIES OF ADVANCED COGNITIVE DEVELOPMENT

6

Postformal Cognitive-Developmental Theory and Research: A Review of Its Current Status

Francis A. Richards and Michael L. Commons

It is important to distinguish between approaches that define developmental end-points as states and those that define them as abilities. In the first approach, a developmental endpoint might be described as the state of maturity. An account of the state of maturity might include how mature people feel and what their attitudes or values are, but it does not necessarily describe what a mature person can or should be able to do. The second approach does so, conceptualizing developmental end-points as a system of abilities.

In the second approach, abilities are detected in activities, making abilities the explanatory cause of actions. The explanatory cause of the abilities that define developmental endpoints begins with the description of the abilities that are active before the endpoint abilities appear. The explanation of these abilities, in turn, lies in predecessor abilities, which are themselves explained by predecessor abilities, and so on, back to an initial set of abilities. Descriptions of such sequences are incomplete without some specification of the *successor–predecessor* relation that exists between the abilities that constitute a developmental sequence. Specifying a successor–predecessor relation necessitates a description of how abilities at a higher level come to replace those at a lower level.

These additional requirements make the abilities approach more theoretically adequate than the state approach. Abilities are defined at a level of greater generality than the activities, or tasks, that are used to detect them. Defining an ability is an analytical attempt to express parsimoniously and powerfully what is central to a set of activities. These generalized expressions can also be called models, since they explain how a competence, or ability, can produce observable performances, or a set of activities. To test an explanation, models can be used to formulate new tasks for detecting abilities. This increases the validity of the endpoint construct by expanding its empirical detectability and, possibly, practical importance.

Focusing on abilities facilitates formulating and testing the predecessor–successor relation between abilities in a developmental sequence. Specifying the type of relation that holds between abilities in a developmental sequence is of particular importance because it bears critically on what can be called the properly psychological components of developmental theory. These are the components that

explain how, not what, a developing organism learns. For example, Piaget (Beth & Piaget, 1966) has argued that the *hierarchical* relation between abilities supports his interpretation of learning as a complex process of assimilation and accommodation, autoregulated by equilibrium. However, if abilities are simply *different from* other abilities, this relation can support more traditional learning theory (Brainerd, 1978).

The foregoing remarks serve as an introduction to the review of a body of developmental research examining the *postformal* period of the life-span (Commons, Richards, & Armon, 1984; Commons, Sinnott, Richards, & Armon, 1989; Commons, Armon, Kohlberg, Richards, Grotzer, & Sinnott, 1990). The work of the researchers—Alexander, Arlin, Armon, Basseches, Commons, Demetriou, Efklides, Fischer, Hand, Kohlberg, Koplowitz, Labouvie-Vief, Pascual-Leone, Powell, Richards, Sinnott, and Sternberg—can be called *post*-Piagetian because it attempts to resolve contradictions perceived within Piaget's framework and between Piaget's and other researchers' frameworks, with what is variously perceived as the "true" core of the Piagetian framework. The methods employed are structural, analytical, dialectical, and empirical (see Alexander et al.; Fischer, Kenny, & Pipp; Gilligan, Murphy, & Tappen; Pascual-Leone; and Kohlberg & Ryncarz chapters).

The common goal of this body of research is to describe postformal stages of cognitive development. The common approach is to specify a group of intellectual abilities that develop *out of* those described by Piaget (1952b) as *formal-operational* or out of related abilities, such as moral reasoning, at a parallel level. This means that the predecessor abilities, formal operations, are in some way necessary to the development of their successor abilities, postformal operations.

This chapter consists of two sections. Since close familiarity with Piaget's work is not assumed, the first section begins with a review of basic notions entailed in the formal operational stage of cognitive development. This section also explores some issues involved in specifying the relations between abilities at different developmental levels. It then describes central features of Darwin's (1855) theory of evolution, to show how this theory depends upon the utilization of reasoning abilities that are *higher than* formal operations. At the very least, these abilities are not detectable by using Inhelder and Piaget's (1958) formal-operational tasks. The second section reviews the research on postformal thought by those people already mentioned.

Piaget: Logic as an Empirical Construction

A common interpretation of Piaget's central theme is that cognition develops as a sequence of developmentally related logics. Here the term *logic* is used in a primitive sense and refers to the way entities are put together, or to the structuring principles that form cognitive objects and acts relating those objects. Logic, then, refers to the principle, or principles, that organize incoherent elements into coherent wholes and means what the Greek term *logos* meant (Heidegger, 1962, pp. 201–204). In Greek usage, the truth of logic rested on the perceived adequacy of its

description and explanation of a complex phenomenon. That is, a logic is true when it succeeds in constructing the reality behind a phenomenon. In this usage, *logic* does not refer to any particular logic, such as the Boolean logic. For it to refer to any more specific and less primitive logic, the structuring actions and the entities that are structured must be specified.

The radical aspect of this approach is often obscured by a tendency to give a priori status to logic. This occurs in a Platonic approach, where logic is conceptualized as a complete and adequate form existing outside the phenomenal world. When such status is assigned, logic becomes true in itself, because it could not be otherwise. To illustrate, a logician develops a particular logic that may or may not prove to be a logically consistent interpretation of a problem in the world. If it is a logically consistent interpretation, the logician has correctly captured a part of logic in its true form. If it is not, the detail and confusion of the phenomenal world has clouded the logician's apperception of its true logical form.

More specifically, the proposition "two spaces equal to a third space are equal to each other" illustrates the difference between conceiving logic as true a priori and as true by construction. To an a priorist, the proposition is self-evident by the logic of relations, specifically the relation of equality. In particular, it is true independent of the activity of measuring the spaces in question. The logic of the proposition is based upon a truth about relations, rather than a truth about experience. The relation is prior to the entity that it orders: *Any* entity must conform to this relation to be considered equal.

This line of reasoning contrasts with an alternative line of reasoning, developed principally by Mach (1906), Maxwell (1871), and Helmholtz (1950), that assigns a posteriori status to logic. In this approach, space and the relations of spaces are defined by measurement procedures, or actions. For example, Helmholtz argued that equivalent magnitudes (spaces) are those "in which there can occur the same processes under the same conditions in the same period of time" (quoted in Enriques, 1929). Helmholtz used the notion of rigid body motions to determine this equivalence; if the same rigid body can make the same motions in the same time in two spaces, then the spaces are equivalent.

As a consequence, space is defined in terms of coordinated actions, in particular the group of rigid body motions (see Piaget, 1954, pp. 108–112 for the psychological application of this philosophic principle). In addition, logical relations are defined in terms of a further coordination of those actions (e.g., the one-to-one comparison of sets of rigid body motions that results in the discovery of equivalence between the actions defining two spaces). The reasoning that assigns a priori epistemological status that had held sway (Kant, 1975) is inverted, creating an epistemology in which the axioms of logic are built out of the coordination of simpler experimental actions.

This is why the specification of structuring activities and the elements to which they are applied is of central importance in Piaget's attempt to describe the development of cognition through a sequence of stages. At each stage these activities, or abilities, are coordinated into a whole that can be called a logic in its primitive sense. Each of these logics is based on abilities to detect, measure, and relate the features of an environment.

The Predecessor–Successor Relation Between Formal and Concrete Operations

Given the notion of the nature of logic, it is helpful to arrive at the particular logic of formal operations by way of the logic of concrete operations, its developmental predecessor. Piaget (Beth & Piaget, 1966) ties the logic of concrete operations to the phenomena of classes and relations. In accord with the preceding definition of logic as a construction of actions in an environment, it can be anticipated that the logic of concrete operations will be some sort of coordination of detecting, measuring, and relating operations on entities.

In fact, two distinguishable kinds of coordinations constitute concrete operations. The first has to do with classes, which are defined (Beth & Piaget, 1966) as collections of objects organized by their partial equivalences. Classes are organized into classifications. An example of a simple classification appears in Figure 6.1.

The preceding classification is composed of classes (**A**, **B**, **C**) and their complements (defined by the relation *not* **A** = **A′**, *not* **B** = **B′**, *not* **C** = **C′**, and so on). Each class contains objects that are qualitatively equivalent, or equivalent in the sense that their distinguishing features are overlooked. Cognitive operations then relate classes into coordinated classifications. Specifically, these following operations construct and deconstruct classifications:

1. Addition of any class and its complement creates the next higher class (e.g., **B** + **B′** = **A**).
2. Subtraction of any class from its next highest class creates that classes's complement (e.g., **A** − **B** = **B′**).

However, the operations of addition and subtraction are limited to classes that are vertically contiguous in Figure 6.1. They do not apply to classes separated by more than one level. They are further limited because any class added to itself results in that class (e.g., **A** + **A** = **A**, a tautology). This differs from addition with numbers, where, for example, 1 + 1 = 2. For these reasons, associativity, a basic property of addition, is limited in the addition of classes to those cases of addition between contiguous classes that are not tautological.

The second kind of coordination has to do with relations. Relations are defined on elements that are distinct from one another from the viewpoint of one common

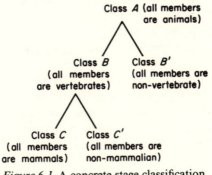

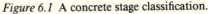

Figure 6.1 A concrete stage classification.

characteristic, such as height, weight, and so on. Given two objects, the relation between them has certain properties. If the two objects are the same object, then there is an identity relation, $\equiv$, between them. If the two objects are different but equal, then there is an equivalence, $=$, relation between them. If the objects are different and unequal, there is an inequality, $\neq$, relation between them.

These relations divide pairs of objects into different classes in which different orderings can occur. Of these different types of orderings, those pertinent to the inequality relation, $>$ or $<$, are given most attention by Piaget. This relation is asymmetric (if $A > B$, then it is not true that $A < B$) and transitive (if $A > B$ and $B > C$, then $A > C$). It can be coordinated into orderings that Piaget calls seriations.

Classes and relations are closely related; in classes objects are grouped in terms of similarity across differing characteristics; in relations objects are distinguished from one another in terms of a common characteristic. Relations, like classes, are coordinated by addition and subtraction, which results in seriations, or organized sets of relations. Like the arithmetic of classes, the arithmetic of relations is subject to the limitation of tautology and contiguity. These limitations in turn limit associativity in this logic.

At the end of the concrete stage, the subject develops operations that relate objects in classifications and seriations. Formal operations arise out of the integration of these two systems of operations. Beth and Piaget (1966) claim this occurs by *abstraction,* a term with two related meanings. In terms of physical objects, abstraction refers to the removal of physical features from objects. This would occur if the class "mammals" in Figure 6.1 were replaced by an equally numerous collection of blank disks.

In terms of operations, or organizing activities, abstraction refers to dissociating the organizing activities of addition and subtraction from any particular classification or seriation. Here abstraction results in an awareness of operations, which previously had been wholly associated with the objects to which they were applied. It might be recognized, for example, that class inclusion is similar to an inequality relation. Commons and Richards (1984a) make the case that operational abstraction separates the stage of concrete operations from a successor stage they call *abstract operations.*

When physical abstraction occurs, neither the logic of classes nor the logic of relations can function independently. To illustrate this, imagine a classification in which physical abstraction has taken place. This would be equivalent to replacing the items in each class of Figure 6.1 with an equal number of blank disks. In this situation, the only way to preserve the configuration of the classification is to preserve the numerosity that defines each class, that is, to count how many members are in each class. However, counting within a class depends on being able to distinguish the members of a class. In the absence of distinguishing physical characteristics, this can only be done by imposing an order structure on the members of the class. This order structure ensures that a class member will not be counted twice because it is distinguished by its position in the structure. Such an order structure within a classification can be represented as $A_1 > A_2 > A_3$, where ">" denotes the successor relation.

However, constructing an order relation across a class requires the construction

of a classification structure. Once an element is assigned to the initial position in an order structure, it must be kept in that position so that it cannot reenter the assigning process. To do this, the first element in the order structure is equated with a class that contains that element, $A_1 = (A)$. The second element is equated with a class that contains the original element on a second element, $A_2 = (A + A)$, and so on, until all the elements in the class are contained in a class that is equated with the final element in the order structure.

This integration can be conceptualized as the embedding of a logic within another logic. This means that one system of logic is applied to the products, or operations, of another system of logic. Applying one system of logic onto another can thus be thought of as the action that generates new stages of cognitive complexity (Richards & Commons, 1984). Identifying this generating process accounts, at least hypothetically, for the hierarchical predecessor–successor relation between stages in Piaget's cognitive sequence, because it explains why those stages must build on one another.

When the logical structures of classes and operations are integrated, the operations of addition and subtraction are abstracted from their concrete form and become more general and flexible. In their abstract form, the restrictions of contiguity and tautology are lifted. In a classification of blank disks, adding class **A** to class **C** becomes meaningful, and amounts to simply adding the cardinal numbers representing the classes. Adding class **A** to class **A** is also meaningful and amounts to multiplication, a special form of addition. Finally, with these restrictions lifted, the operations become associative. At this point, concrete operations become formal operations.

Propositional Operations as the Model of Formal Operations

Piaget uses propositional logic as a model of this integration. Here he follows a direction established earlier by Frege (1950) and Peano (1894), who attempted to generalize propositional logic in order to represent other forms of reasoning, most notably arithmetic. Because propositional logic was developed to reason about other forms of reasoning, it can be used to reason about the logics of classes and relations. Propositional logic can represent statements about both relations (e.g., **p** is heavier than **q**) and classes (e.g., **x** is a member of the class **A**). However, in this form, propositions can be treated as objects in themselves, rather than as the direct reflection of some concrete reality. Hence, propositions have formal properties that are different from the properties of objects, and the actions that organize propositions are different from the actions that organize concrete reality.

Propositions are statements to which the truth values *true* (**T**) or *false* (**F**) can be assigned. The actions that organize propositions work under the basic constriction of this bivalent system of truth values. For example, the truth values impose a restriction on the operation of negation: A proposition and its negation cannot both be true. To negate a proposition is to change its truth value.

Piaget ties the logic of propositions to the Boolean system of combination, a system in which *nuclear* propositions are combined into larger *molecular* propositions using the connectives *not*, $-$; *and*, &; *or*, **v** (*ver* = *and/or*); *if . . . then*, $\rightarrow$; *if and only if*, **y**. All these connectives are operations. The connective *not* was just

Table 6.1 Classification of Animal by Type and Habitat

	Animals	Nonanimals
Vertebrate	**AB**	**AB′**
Nonvertebrate	**A′B**	**A′B′**

discussed in connection with the operation of negation. The connectives *and* and *or* join nuclear propositions into molecular propositions of unlimited length. If one of the propositions in a string constructed only with the connective *and* is false, then the entire molecular proposition is false. Only one member of a string connected by *or* need be true for the molecular proposition to be true.

To demonstrate how propositional operations are applied to reasoning about objects, one of the more complex organizations of concrete operations, a multiple classification appears in Table 6.1.

In multiple classifications (here a two-way classification), objects are simultaneously classified by at least two systems of classification. This organization is reflected in the nuclear propositions (**AB, AB′, A′B, A′B′**). Hidden in these are the connective *and*. Each nuclear proposition is a pair of statements about reality connected by *and;* thus, **AB = A&B**. Each pair of nuclear propositions is connected by *and;* thus, **AB, AB′ = (A&B) & (A&B′)**. There are 16 possible ways the nuclear propositions can be joined by *and;* any single entry in the table may be true, or any compound of two or three entries may be true. Finally, all four entries taken together may be true or false. These, then, are the minimal elements of formal operations.

Out of these, a second set of coordinating relations can be constructed using the Boolean connectives. These are the *identity, negation, reciprocal,* and *correlative* relations. These relations connect every nuclear proposition to the three remaining nuclear propositions. Furthermore, they relate larger compound propositions to create the logic of hypothetico-deductive reasoning. These relations can be shown using the proposition **AB**, "there are vertebrate animals" and its truth value:

$$\mathbf{A\&B} = \mathbf{T}. \tag{1a}$$

By the law governing the Boolean connective *not,* the following is an *identity transformation* of 1a:

$$\mathbf{-(A\&B)} = \mathbf{F}. \tag{1b}$$

If 1a is true, it may imply that **A&B′, A′&B**, and **A′&B′** are false:

$$\mathbf{(A\&B)} \ \mathbf{v} \ \mathbf{-(A\&B')} \ \mathbf{v} \ \mathbf{-(A'\&B)} \ \mathbf{v} \ \mathbf{-(A'\&B')} = \mathbf{T}. \tag{2a}$$

Again, by the law governing *not,* this is *identical* to:

$$\mathbf{(A\&B)} \ \mathbf{v} \ \mathbf{(A\&B')} \ \mathbf{v} \ \mathbf{(A'\&B)} = \mathbf{T}. \tag{2b}$$

which is the *correlative* of 1a.

When the truth value of 1a is reversed, its *negation* results:

$$\mathbf{(A\&B)} = \mathbf{F}. \tag{3a}$$

which by the identity transformation is:

$$-(A\&B) = T. \tag{3b}$$

This proposition may imply that **A&B′**, **A′&B**, and **A′&B′** are true:

$$-(A\&B) \text{ v } (A\&B') \text{ v } (A'\&B) \text{ v } (A'\&B') = T. \tag{4a}$$

This reduces to:

$$(A\&B') \text{ v } (A'\&B) \text{ v } (A'\&B') = T. \tag{4b}$$

This is the *reciprocal* of 1a.

In the more concrete terms of Figure 6.1, this chain of reasoning begins by asserting the truth of the proposition that there are vertebrate animals. Thus, it is false that there are not vertebrate animals. The existence of vertebrate animals might imply the existence of nonvertebrate animals (since the animals exist) or might imply the existence of vertebrate nonanimals (since vertebrates exist). Note that this latter possibility lies outside the concrete classification. The truth of the negated proposition asserts the existence of nonvertebrate nonanimal entities, which also lies outside the possibilities afforded by the concrete classification. It implies the same additional categories as the original proposition, but by a reverse line of reasoning.

There are then four important relations constructable in formal operations: *identity, negation, correlativity,* and *reciprocity.* The novelty of this group is that negation and reciprocity appear together (Piaget, 1952). Using concrete operations, adolescents can reason about classes or relations. Consequently, they can construct negation (subtraction in classes) or inverse relations (subtraction in relations), but not both simultaneously. The ability to construct negation and reciprocal relations opens the door to reasoning about a vast range of more complex phenomena among which are combinations, proportions, mechanical equilibrium, and controlled experiments (Piaget, 1952b, pp. 21–22).

Propositional Operations and the Mechanics of Reasoning

Piaget often uses the term *hypothetico-deductive* to describe formal operational thinking. Presumably, this term refers to a style of reasoning, heavily used in the sciences, that is not truly deductive. Galileo, for example, was one of the earliest proponents of this style of reasoning, and it was his rupture with classical methods of logical argument, as much as his results (Drake, 1970), that ran counter to the grain of the church scholars of his age.

In classical, or deductive, reasoning a conclusion follows strictly from a major and minor premise. The conclusion is true because the major premise is known to be true and the a priori status of logic is granted. However, in hypothetico-deductive reasoning, the major premise is not known to be true; it is a hypothesis. Given the hypothesis, a chain of minor premises, or deductions, leads to conclusions about what would be true if the hypothesis were true. Observing such evidence leads to a conclusion that the hypothesis is true. Since Locke (1966), the truth

claims of this mode of reasoning have been couched in more cautious terms, but its essential *modus operandi* remains robust.

Hypothetico-deductive reasoning has been successful because it attempts to integrate deductive ways of knowing with empirical ways of knowing. This is very much the role, and significance, of formal operations in Piaget's genetic epistemology. Formal operations is a tool of both deductive truth and empirical confirmation. To distinguish these two sets of tools more clearly, an artificial dichotomy can be constructed between those situations that only contain information, and apply to deductive truth, and those that only contain evidence, and apply to empirical confirmation.

In this dichotomy, information refers broadly to rules of combination and formal elements to which those rules apply. To maintain the distinction between deductive truth and empirical confirmation, it must be specified that the formal elements have no meaning outside of the ways in which they can be combined. Thus, the rules of deductive truth can be conceptualized as a set of directions that specify how to get from one location to another, where the defining *grid* is the axioms of the system. In contrast, the rules of empirical confirmation refer only to the *things in themselves*. The rules of empirical truth can be conceptualized as a set of *recipes* that specify what a thing is in terms of combinations of more basic *ingredients*.

When the rules of combination are applied to the formal elements, they produce an outcome. If, as in formal operations, one of the rules of combination is "true plus false equals true" (disjunctive addition), the elements are true and false, the outcome true, and the rule of combination is plus.

One of the sources of power of the tools of deductive truth finding is its capacity to compose complex statements (theorems) that are consistent with rules of combination. Another is to decompose complex statements to determine whether they are consistent with a set of simpler rules and elements (proofs). Each of these activities is, formally, the reverse of the other. To integrate or go from one activity to the other, the operations of one must be reversed. Producing formal deductions and proving formal deductions requires an *operational reversibility* that can be associated with Piaget's reciprocity, the form of reversibility applicable to operations.

Empirical confirmation provides evidence, rather than information. Evidence supplies neither laws of combination nor elements, but is instead a possible instance of both. As an instance of both, evidence requires accumulation and induction from accumulation. Induction establishes hypotheses about how evidence is generated, and any subsequent observation can weaken a hypothesis based on previous evidence, as the hypothesis "x causes y" based on 100 observations would be weakened by an observation of a y without an antecedent x. Here evidence reverses hypothesis by negation, a *hypothetical reversibility* that can be associated with Piaget's inversion, the form of reversibility applicable to classes.

Of course, the cardinal feature of formal operations is that the hypothetical and deductive forms of reasoning are not distinct, as above, but are integrated. The two forms, as well as their characteristic forms of reversibility, are distinguishable moments of opposed direction in a larger process.

Objections to Formal Operations

For all its formal and empirical power, objections have been made to Piaget's model of formal operations and the cognitive mechanics it implies. One argument, advanced and expanded by Broughton (1977, 1984), has to do with the nature of the integration of formal and empirical reasoning at this stage. Simply put, Broughton argues that there is no integration; rather, there is domination of the latter by the former. The formal structure of reasoning becomes preeminent at formal operations, and the empirical structure can no longer function in its negating, and ultimately dialectical role. As a result, formal operations cannot be used to reason about certain types of phenomena, notably those of a non-Boolean nature. Perhaps they cannot even be used to observe such phenomena. Broughton concludes that if Piaget's developmental sequence leads to such a barren endpoint, it ought to be abandoned altogether.

Piaget (1970a) seemed to counter Broughton's contention about the *closure* inherent in formal operations. Specifically, he discussed the activity of negating key axioms in formal structures as a method of transforming and keeping open hypothetico-deductive structures. He provided an example of this activity in the negation of axioms in Euclidean geometry that led, during the nineteenth century, to the development of several non-Euclidean geometries. In addition, he discusses the *decomposition* of systems into more basic systems, and the subsequent *recombination* of basic systems into new systems, as cognitive activities that keep the formal-operational structure from ossifying.

However, these latter activities can be considered to be postformal rather than formal. Their appearance can then be explained as a cognitive development necessitated by limitations of the formal cognitive structure. This argument is advanced in the body of research under review. Generally, the argument runs that formal operations, instantiated in propositional operations and employing the system of Boolean connectives mentioned, are adequate to formulate and analyze linear logical and causal relations. The latter are particularly useful for reasoning about situations in which dependent and independent variables are postulated to exist. Together, they create a kind of reasoning that will be referred to as *functional analysis.*

However, developmental conceptions of phenomena require the representation of states of phenomena as systems. Systems are characterized by relations that are not only functional but transformational. Such transformations require nonlinear conceptions of causality. At this level of complexity, formal operations are not sufficient. (For a detailed discussion of this point, see Commons, Richards, & Kuhn, 1982; Richards & Commons, 1984; and Commons & Richards, 1984a.)

Postformal operations, which form, relate, and describe different systems, can formulate developmental conceptions of phenomena. This is because these operations arise out of an integration of structural and functional modes of analysis into transformational modes of analysis. The coordination of systems cannot be reduced to formal operations (Commons, Richards, & Kuhn, 1982) because notions needed to describe systems cannot belong to formal operational systems.

Formal operations must be rigorously transformed and extended in such a way that they can be shown to account for the ability to relate different states of complex

phenomena, and hence the more imaginative and exciting products of (at least) scientific thought. Otherwise, sequences of cognitive development ending with Piaget's formal operations can correctly be thought of as ossified in formalism.

The Coordination of Function, Structure, and Transformation

One example of the transformation and extension of formal operations is found in Darwin's (1855, 1877, 1897) account of evolution. (See Gruber, 1984, for a discussion of the development of Darwin's theory.) Darwin's theory resembled theories advanced by earlier evolutionists, such as Lamarck (1873), in that it maintained that the environment plays a role in the evolutionary process and that there is an overall direction to the evolutionary process. However, Darwin conceptualized the causal mechanism at work between organism and environment very differently from earlier theorists. Furthermore, he tied the overall direction of evolution to this causal process, eliminating the supernatural causality that Lamarck, for example, had assumed.

In a broad sense, structure can be said to exist at three critical locations in Darwin's theory. The first location is in the individual organism. Unlike Lamarck, Darwin did not think of the organism as highly labile. Instead, he thought of organisms as relatively stable, because they were highly organized integrations of biological parts. The shape of a beak, for instance, could not change radically in a few generations, because it was integrated into a total system in which wings, claws, and other biological components formed a structure capable of relatively specific behavior. Certain finches, for example, gather a particular kind of food in a particular way, and in these finches the various physiological features are highly adapted to the food-gathering activity. If rapid environmental alterations made these food-gathering activities inefficient, Darwin believed that the species would perish rather than change.

On the other hand, there was evidence that strongly suggested the transformation of one species into another. Darwin realized from his study of animal husbandry that within a species the vast majority of offspring differed slightly from their parents. In stock breeding, this meant that only a minority of a second generation would breed true and that a pure breed was maintained only by careful and constant selection from the offspring. This pointed out the location of a second regulatory structure in the breeding population.

A breeding population, or species, can be considered a structure in the sense that it is composed of parts (individuals) that are related by their ability to breed with each other. This relation not only connects the parts of the structure but is necessary for the survival of both the parts and the whole. The species cannot survive unless individuals breed, and individuals within a species can form communal behaviors that help ensure the survival of the individuals.

Darwin reasoned that, in the large number of individuals that comprise a species, some of the variations that constantly appear in individuals would create small, favorable differences in the structure and behavior of those individuals. These differences would be preserved in the species because these favored individuals would be more likely to breed. In this way, a species simultaneously preserved individual structure and created changes in those structures.

Finally, the totality of species and the physical environment can be considered a location of structure in Darwin's theory. Darwin had learned from Malthus (1798) that populations increased more rapidly than food supplies. This would result in a crisis of overpopulation, during which those individuals in a species with adaptive differences would be able to exploit new food supplies. These individuals would increase more rapidly than the less adaptive individuals, and the differences between the two groups would become more pronounced as adaptive differences tended to concentrate in the new group. This would eventuate in a new species, defined as the moment when individuals in the two groups no longer interbred in natural conditions.

Initially, organisms with minimally complete structure would exploit the most readily available food supplies. But as these sources dwindled, new forms of structure would arise that would be more complex because they were adapted to exploit less available food supplies. Consequently, the relation of species to species and of species to environment would tend to shape the course of evolution in the direction of increasing diversification and structural sophistication.

These three kinds of structures can be modeled by a group of integrated series. At the individual level, the transformations between parents and offspring can be represented by a random series. In a random series there is a fixed number of terms (e.g., the numbers between 0 and 9), each of which has an equal probability of appearing as the next term. In a random series each term will appear an equal number of times over the long run, whereas, over the short run, there is no pattern in the appearance of the terms. If the terms of an organism were considered to be its biological components—say, beak, claws, and wings—then variation would appear in these components in an unpredictable sequence that would nonetheless balance out over a long period of time.

At the species level, change between generations can be modeled by a geometrically increasing series: Two parents produce four offspring, these offspring produce eight offspring, and so on. This series has to be combined with an arithmetically increasing series to model the relation between species and food supply. Originally, food supply is much larger than species size, but this difference rapidly diminishes in the relation between the two series. A monotonically increasing series models the relation between species. In a monotonically increasing series each term is at least equal to the last term. It may also be larger than the last term, but is so by an unspecified amount. When overpopulation occurs, a new species may completely displace an old species, in which case the new term is equal to the old term. A new species may also leave remnants of the old species, and an old species may transform into more than one new species. In this case, the new term is unspecifiably larger than the old term. Darwin's theory integrates all these generational processes into an explanatory framework that is above the level of all formal-operational thinking mentioned so far because it embeds explanatory schemes in three levels.

Formal Operations and Historical Science

As this example shows, there is a general transformation of formal operations in the explanatory system used by Darwin. In cognitive terms, this transformation is

based on the integration of causal and historical modes of explanation. Formal-operational causal explanation formulates laws that primarily describe how short-term transformations take place in physical entities, whereas historical explanation formulates laws primarily describing how long-term transformations take place.

This integration is based on the ability to conceptualize and integrate several types of fundamental regularities. These regularities and the applicability of historical–scientific explanation were not immediately apparent, even to the greatest thinkers: "But it is not to be conceived that mere mechanical causes could give birth to so many regular motions, since the comets range over all parts of the heavens in very eccentric orbits. . . . this most beautiful system of the sun, planets, and comets, could only proceed from the counsel and dominion of an intelligent and powerful Being" (Newton, 1960, pp. 543–544). However, by the end of the nineteenth century, historical explanation based on the "intelligent and powerful Being" had been banished from the natural, the biological, and increasingly, the social sciences. The inexplicable irregularities of phenomena which had previously been explained by divine intervention, began to be conceptualized as regularities by more complex, nonlinear causal reasoning. The majestic regularities of nature, previously explained by divine design, began to be explained by more complex serial reasoning that built irregular series by combining simpler series. As these cognitive schemes increased in sophistication, the distinction between scientific and historical explanation blurred. Historical data (e.g., records describing the past appearance of comets) played a role in the formulation of complex functions. Causal relations played a role in explaining processes that produce historical series. In the face of this convergence, reviewing Inhelder and Piaget's isolation of variables and the combinatorial schemes (see Inhelder & Piaget, 1958, pp. 46–66, 107–122) helps show how to distinguish formal from postformal reasoning.

Disjunctive Causality and the Elimination of Variables

In the elimination-of-variables task a set of rods of variable composition, length, thickness, and cross-section form is set up in such a way that they bend when different weights are attached to their ends. The task is to associate these different independent variables with the dependent variable, flexibility, and formulate a functional relation between the two types of variables. A fully formal operational performance holds all but one of the independent variables constant and varies the remaining independent variable to determine whether it has an effect on the dependent variable. As the effect of each variable is determined, the subject moves systematically to the next until all variables are tested.

This procedure can be represented propositionally by dichotomizing the values of each variable (e.g., long and short [not long] rods) and representing this dichotomization by propositions and their negations. In this example, the proposition $\mathbf{p}$ would represent long rods and its negation, $-\mathbf{p}$ would represent short rods. Associating the independent variables with observed outcomes would be represented as:

$$(\mathbf{p} \cdot \mathbf{q} \cdot \mathbf{r} \cdot \mathbf{s} \cdot \mathbf{t} \cdot \mathbf{x}) \; or \; (-\mathbf{p} \cdot \mathbf{q} \cdot \mathbf{r} \cdot \mathbf{s} \cdot \mathbf{t} \cdot -\mathbf{x}) \tag{5}$$

Here changes in length $\mathbf{p}$ produce changes in flexibility $\mathbf{x}$, when all other variables are held constant. In shortened form, the association of $(\mathbf{p} \cdot \mathbf{x}) \; or \; (-\mathbf{p} \cdot -\mathbf{x})$ is the

formal operation of *equivalence,* which asserts that length has an effect that is equivalent to asserting that flexibility changes because of length.

This propositional reasoning is also a simple form of multivariate analysis, as can be shown by representing the procedure as the solution of a set of simultaneous equations:

$$\rightarrow p + q + r + s + t = x \tag{6}$$

$$\rightarrow -p + q + r + s + t = -x \tag{7}$$

$$\rightarrow p - q + r + s + t = -x \tag{8}$$

$$\rightarrow p + q - r + s + t = -x \tag{9}$$

$$\rightarrow p + q + r - s + t = -x \tag{10}$$

$$\rightarrow p + q + r + s - t = -x \tag{11}$$

The solution for this set of equations can be represented as the regression equation $Y' = ap + bq + cr + ds + et$, where the terms a, b, c, d, and e represent the regression weights (the causal value) of the variables. In this equation there are no interaction terms because there are no interactions; the combined effect of any two variables is exactly the same as the effects of those variables taken one at a time. This is a disjunctive concept of the relation between variables. With a disjunctive relationship the variables are independent, or have no effect on each other. This type of simple causality is compatible with the concept of causality in which internal structure plays no role in transformational relations. If internal structure did make a difference in transformations, this would be indicated by an interaction indicating that a different principle governed the behavior of combined variables.

Conjunctive Causality and the Combination of Colorless Liquids

In the bending rods experiment, all variables are combined in the experimental apparatus. The colorless liquids task presents the opposite problem of combining variables to produce an outcome. In this task five colorless liquids are provided, and it is demonstrated that an unknown combination of these liquids will produce a pink liquid. In an ideal formal-operational performance, all combinations of two, three, four, and five liquids are tested, which reveals that one combination of three and one combination of four liquids will produce a pink liquid. These two "potent" combinations can be represented propositionally as:

$$(p \& q \& r \& -s \& -t \& x) \ or \ (p \& q \& r \& s \& -t \& x) \tag{12}$$

This can be shortened into the association $(-s \& x) \ or \ (s \& x)$. This is the formal operation "independence of s in relation to x," and it eliminates the liquid s as a causal agent. In this causal analysis, none of the variables would have a regression weight in the preceding equation. The only term that would have a weight would be the interaction term (pqr), and the regression model would be $Y' = a(pqr)$. This indicates that a causal relation only occurs when the three variables are connected conjunctively. As Piaget says, a conjunctive conception of cause is different from a disjunctive conception of cause, because "cause is no longer sought in one or another of the elements, but in their being brought together" (Inhelder & Piaget,

1958, p. 119). This is a conception of cause that implies internal structure, and only internal structure, plays a role in causal transformations.

There are strict limitations on reasoning about causal relations that employs only conjunctive or disjunctive (but not both) modes of analysis. These two conceptions of causality are incompatible in the sense that variables must be either directly or interactively causal. To have a causal logic in which both conceptions function, causal systems have to be conceptualized in which the same variable can function in different processes. This amounts to differentiating the causal process into multiple causal processes. Next, the way these causal processes affect one another must be specified to integrate the multiple causal processes into a causal system.

Accomplishing this differentiation and integration creates a specification of structure and transformation that is on the postformal level. At this level the two causal logics of formal operations are integrated in a way that recapitulates the integration of the logics of classes and relations at the formal stage. This logic would be capable of representing embedded causal relations, as in Darwin's theory of evolution, because variables in one causal process could reappear in another causal process. It would also be capable of representing the reiterative processes that characterize the *feedback loops* of equilibrational and open-ended historical processes.

Piaget's construal of formal operations makes them logical, mathematical, and scientific, but not historical. They are eminently useful for determining causal relations and generating predictive knowledge, but they do not place these in historical context. The operations, without some mechanism for making them apply to entities more complex than propositions, are not capable of creating notions of structure and structural transformation. Without these notions, formal operations are unable to formulate developmental interpretations of phenomena.

Piaget and Postformal Theory

It is important to distinguish between Piaget's theoretical framework and the products of that framework. Although the argument has just been made that formal operations are inadequate for detecting, measuring, and relating developmental phenomena, the same claim is not made about his theoretical framework when suitably modified by weakening his assumptions as to the particular form of the developmental endpoint. Piaget advanced a complex theory of processes of assimilation, accommodation, and autoregulation that could only be formulated out of a developmental–historical logic. If Piaget's explanatory system is explicable in terms of a higher-level logic than that of formal operations, then it is the developmental logic not the formal-operational logic that is of use to psychologists attempting to understand adult cognitive development.

Piaget's achievement in explaining cognitive development rests on his attempt to synthesize two major paradigms, the historical and the scientific. He attempts to show how logical structure is transformed by the construction of schemes for ordering the environment by the application of a historical–biological paradigm. This synthesis accounts for the changes in performance in children as they develop. Because this synthesis unites two fields, giving rise to a new paradigm, it is at the cross-paradigmatic stage, as shown in Table 6.2.

Table 6.2 Stage Sequences from Concrete through Postformal

Piaget Stage Name	Commons & Richards*		Levels to be Detected	Fischer, Hand & Russell†			Sternberg	Kohlberg‡		Armon‡	
	Stage Name	Entity		Tier Level	Level Sublevel	Characteristic	Stage Name	Stage Number	Characteristic	Stage Number	Characteristic
Concrete II-B	3b Concrete		1.M-FA 2.H-FA 3.M-CR 4.H-CR	2-IV	6-1 6-2 6-3 6-4	System of representations		2/3	Instrumental	2/3	Instrumental
Formal III-A	4a Abstract	Variables or single abstractions	1.M-Fa 2.H-FA 3.M-CR 4.H-CR	3-I	7-1 7-2 7-3 7-4	Single set or variable values		3	Mutuality	3	Affective
Formal III-B	4b Formal	Relations among variables	1.M-FA 2.H-FA 3.M-CR 3.M-CR	3-II	8-1 8-2 8-3 8-4	Mapping (relating two sets)	First-order relational reasoning	3/4	Logical social	3/4	Logical individuality
	5a Systematic	Systems of relations	1.M-FA 2.H-FA 3.M-CR 4.H-CR	3-III	9-1 9-2 9-3 9-4	Systems (relating two subdivided sets)		4, 4/5	Social system conscience	4, 4/5	Individuality
	5b Meta-systematic	Super system: Relations among systems	1.M-FA 2.H-FA 3.M-CR 4.H-CR	3-IV	10-1 10-2 10-3 10-4	Systems of abstract systems	Second-order relational reasoning	5	Prior rights and responsibilities	5	Autonomy
	6a Paradigmatic	Fields: Systems of supersystems	1.M-FA 2.H-FA 3.M-CR 4.H-CR					6	Universal processes	6	Universal categories
	6b Cross paradigmatic	Relations between fields	1.M-FA 2.H-FA 3.M-CR 4.H-CR								

Commons & Richards* Stage Number	Pascual-Leone§ Stage Name	Powell Stage Name	Labouvie-Vief Stage Name	Arlin Stage Name	Sinnott Stage Name	Sinnott Characteristic	Basseches Phase	Basseches Dialectical Schemata	Koplowitz Stage Name	Alexander‖ Level Name
3b	Late concrete	Advanced concrete	Symbolic	2b—High concrete	Concrete		1a	Preformal early foundation		Dominance of thinking mind
4a	Early formal	Early formal		3a—Low formal (problem solving)						
4b	Formal and Late formal	Formal	Intra-systematic	3b—High formal	Formal		1b	Formal	Formal	Dominance of reflective intellect
5a	Pre-dialectical empathy	Stage 4a, Interactive	Inter-systematic	4—Postformal a. problem finding	Relativistic	Relativised systems, meta-rules	2	Intermediate ds	Systems	Growth of feeling and intuition
5b	Dialectical	Category operations	Autonomous	b. relativism of thought c. overgeneralization d. displacement of concepts e. dialectical	Unified theory	Interpenetration of contradictory levels	3 / 4	2/3 out of General advanced ds / All clusters: framework coordinated	General systems	
6a	Transcendental								Unitary concepts	Differentiation of individual ego / Three higher stages of consciousness

Adapted from M. L. Commons, F. A. Richards, and C. Armon (1984), *Beyond formal operations: Vol. 1. Late adolescent and adult cognitive development*, with permission of the editors and Praeger Publishers.

*See Richards & Commons chapter. The level name characterizes a subject's performance vis-a-vis the entities to be detected for the stage in question: M = Miss; FA = False Alarm; H = Hit; CR = Correct Rejection.

†Sublevels for levels supplied by Commons, Richards & Armon (1984).

‡Adapted by Armon (personal communication, May 4, 1989) and Commons from Kohlberg (in press); Commons & Grotzer (in press).

§Pascual-Leone (1984; Personal communication, May 1, 1989), see Pascual-Leone chapter.

‖Based on Vedic psychology, Alexander et. al. (see chapter) propose an additional post representational tier of higher stages of consciousness.

155

Consequently, current assumptions about reality and causality that appear in different variants of postformal theory can be seen as a species of developmental-historical logic. In addition, the specific reasoning systems that seem to be at work in adulthood (see the following descriptions) rest on the integration of concepts of structure, function, and transformation. For this reason, more specific models of adult postformal thinking are likely to resemble some particular variant of post-formal reasoning.

A Review of Some Postformal Research

Among the authors reviewed next, the most common method of extending cogni-tive theory into the postformal area is to locate limitations in formal operations, then to describe a kind of thinking that enables the individual to transcend these limitations. Authors use examples of thinking already developed in other domains, such as the dialectical tradition (Basseches, 1980, 1984a,b; Benack & Basseches, 1989; Kramer, 1990), relativity theory (Sinnott, 1984, 1988, 1989), moral philoso-phy (Armon, 1989), philosophy of science (Chinen, 1990), general systems theory and Buddhism (Koplowitz, 1984, 1990), music (Funk, 1982, 1983, 1989), or Vedic psychology and unified field theory (Alexander, Chandler, & Boyer, 1990; Alex-ander et al. chapter; Orme-Johnson, 1988a) as models for postformal thinking.

Another method of extension is based on analyses of the nature of the devel-opmental process, rather than on the limitations inherent in formal operations. Instead of concentrating on a demonstration that change does occur, this approach attempts to show *how* it occurs. Piaget (1970a) had proposed a general process of *equilibrium* and a somewhat more specific process of *reflective abstraction* to account for cognitive development. Commons and Hallinan (1989); Commons, Richards, and Kuhn (1982); Commons and Richards (1984a, 1984b); Fischer, Hand, and Russell (1984); Labouvie-Vief (1990b); Fischer et al. chapter; Pascual-Leone (1984, 1990, see chapter); Richards (1990a, 1990b); Sternberg and Downing (1982); Sternberg (1984) and others (Kitchener & King, 1990) all focus explicitly on the mechanism of intellectual development. They attempt not only to clarify proposed mechanisms of cognitive development in a systematic, formalized-math-ematical manner, but also to show how the continued operation of these mecha-nisms should result in postformal thinking.

Either of these approaches leads to the claim that adult thinking contains the formal-operational framework, but employs at least one other encompassing framework as well. This kind of development results in multiple-system models of cognition. The common claim is that some adults develop alternatives to, and per-spectives on, formal operations. These adults use formal operations within a "higher" system of operations and transcend the limitations of formal operations.

Basseches (1984a,b; Benack & Basseches, 1989) attempts to balance the idea of historical particularity with the idea of general structures in postformal cognitive development. He begins with the assumption that change is the basic feature of cognitive, social, and natural phenomena. To comprehend change, postformal thinkers use the idea of *form* rather than the idea of *thing*. Forms are structures

whose fundamental function is to change. Things are structures whose fundamental function is to maintain their stability or identity. As such, structure can never be temporally crystallized, but it can still be used to interpret society, nature, and the self as organizations in constant transformation.

Arlin's concept of postformal operations (1975, 1977, 1984, 1989) is based on the hypothesis that a radical change occurs in the way formal operations are used. While accepting the idea of formal operational structure, she proposes that the whole function of that structure changes. Her argument is that a replacement process takes place whereby problem-solving operations disappear and problem-finding operations appear.

The next group of researchers maintains that postformal cognition attempts to accomplish the same functions as formal cognition but that the complexity of the patterns of thought, and the complexity posited in the objects of thought, is at a new level. One approach to describing this new level of complexity is to use the analogy of *unfolding dimensionality* (see Fischer, 1980b; Fischer, Hand, & Russell, 1984; Fischer et al. chapter; and Sternberg, 1984).

The concept of unfolding dimensionality uses dimensions in space to convey the idea of the new size and complexity of postformal cognition. Although size may be thought of as quantitative, dimensional increase in size generates complexities that must be thought of as qualitative. It is important to realize that different arithmetics, geometries, and algebras are variously possible and impossible in different dimensions. For instance, adding a dimension to two-dimensional space makes it possible for the angles of a triangle to sum to more than 180 degrees and for parallel lines to intersect, illustrating that the complexity of geometric systems increases unpredictably as the dimensionality of the space containing them increases.

In another approach, sets of axioms, or other system properties, are used to describe the increased complexity of postformal reasoning (see Commons & Richards, 1984a,b; Koplowitz, 1984, 1990; Labouvie-Vief, 1984; Powell, 1984; Richards, 1990a, 1990b; Richards & Commons, 1990; and Sinnott, 1984, 1989). For instance, Labouvie-Vief (1980, 1984) uses the properties of different systems of logics. She describes the limitations of different logics and asserts that these limitations are due to their *strength*. A *strong* logical system is one that has several limiting assumptions. When a logic contains many restricting assumptions, it seems clear, but causes confusion when applied in areas that do not conform to those assumptions. Postformal reasoning arrives at an understanding of the inflexibility involved in thinking "overlogically." It locates the limitations of excessive assumptions and formulates a more flexible, *weaker* logic containing fewer assumptions. Although this logic is weaker than the logics it replaces, it contains them because, with further restrictions, it directs their use in appropriate situations. By releasing formal thinking from overly restrictive strong logics, a weaker logic allows the development of new kinds of thinking.

Sinnott (1984, 1989) uses the concept of relativity (Einstein, 1950) in a similar way. As weaker logics contain and coordinate stronger logics, so relativistic frameworks contain and coordinate more localized frameworks. Each framework can be thought of as a system of relations among elements. A relativistic framework would then be a more general system for relating systems. Sinnott uses the concept of

system metaphorically, so a system need not be attached to concepts of energy, mass, speed, and so on. It could be a system of relations that coordinates people, allowing application in the moral reasoning domain. Although a person who thinks in a formal-operational manner could reason within one such system, a person who thinks in a postformal manner deals with the problem of integrating local systems into a framework, and deals successfully with the relativity of the systems.

A variant of this argument appears in Koplowitz's description of unitary operations (1984, 1990). He argues that, as thinking becomes more developed, the perceived boundaries between people become less useful. A child, for example, cannot be understood outside of its family. In a real sense, a child is part of a larger whole, from which that child cannot be disassociated. Koplowitz's *unitary operations* are used to comprehend wholes that have internal parts. Consequently, they organize and bring those parts into relation with one another.

The idea of postformal development resulting in cognitive unification also appears in Alexander et al. (see Alexander et al. chapter). These authors refer to recent work in physics where theorists have postulated a unified field theory for all known force and matter fields. According to Alexander et al., Vedic psychology (Maharishi, 1969) describes the potential development of higher stages of consciousness in which an underlying unity can be directly experienced within and between both the subjective and objective domains of existence. They propose that this direct experience may represent a "veridical" appreciation of the unified structure of the physical universe as currently described in unified quantum field theories. Further, they propose that the mechanism of development toward psychological unity lies in technologies of consciousness, principally meditation, which are employed directly in continuing a process of achieving subtler levels of mind.

Commons & Richards (1984a, 1984b) likewise describe the new complexity of postformal thinking in terms of systems that unify formal operational relations. However, they describe such systems formally. Their argument for the qualitative nature of change is consequently less tied to the particular nature of either logics or physics. This argument is based on the notion that higher-stage thinking is irreducible to lower-stage thinking. This means that in the process of stage transformation, new objects of thought appear that cannot be successfully thought about at a lower stage. In particular, the operations that coordinate formal operations are not themselves formal operations. Considerable attention is devoted to defining irreducibility in Bickhard (1978, 1979) and in Commons and Richards (1978, 1984b).

A different perspective on this argument appears in Powell's (1984) description of *category operations*. Category operations have been developed in mathematics, partly in response to the Bourbaki (1939) program. One of the concerns of the Bourbaki program has been to place the various branches of mathematics in relation to one another. Their approach has been to locate mathematical *mother structures* that can be transformed and combined to produce the various mathematical disciplines (discussed in Piaget, 1970).

Category operations were invented to reach the same goal, but do so by examining the nature of mathematical operations rather than mathematical structures. Since category operations characterize the nature of mathematical activity, they

model postformal thinking as an understanding of the ways cognitive activity can be related.

The relation of biological and cognitive development influences the concept of postformal development. Piaget (Inhelder & Piaget, 1958) acknowledged the biological factor in cognitive development, although he argued that it is not the critical factor. Nevertheless, there is a strong parallel between his sequence of cognitive development and the sequences of biological maturation. In biological maturation, adolescence is the last great period of growth. In parallel, great intellectual disequilibrium also occurs during adolescence. Piaget argued that the subsequent equilibration, formal operations, persists throughout the remainder of the life-span. Pascual-Leone (1984) creates an interesting twist to this argument, claiming that postadolescent cognitive development results from the degeneration of this equilibrium. Fischer, Hand, and Russell (1984) straightforwardly argue that there are physiological limitations to cognitive growth.

Alternatively, Alexander et al. (see Alexander et al. chapter) suggest that inward deployment of attention to increasingly abstract levels of mind through a postconceptual means such as meditation may facilitate the "unfreezing" of maturational and ontogenetic processes that otherwise become fixed in adolescence or early adulthood. Less specifically, Commons and Richards (1984b) conceive of stages as arising from the analysis of tasks. They assume that there are necessary biological aspects of cognitive development. Differences in brain structure among various organisms may be reflected in differences in the cognitive stage achieved, given appropriate environments.

The problem of specifying what is meant by a stage and a stage sequence remains a critical issue in cognitive developmental theory. Elsewhere, Piaget (1953), Flavell and Wohlwill (1969), Kohlberg (1969, 1981b), Flavell (1971b, 1972, 1977, 1982, 1983, 1985), Bickhard (1978, 1979), and Campbell and Richie (1983) have devoted considerable attention to it. This specification is centrally important in the work of Kohlberg and Armon (1984), Kohlberg (1990), Kohlberg and Ryncarz chapter; and Commons & Richards (1984a, 1984b). The concern of Kohlberg and his colleagues is to distinguish *functional, soft,* and *hard stages. Functional stage* refers to the Eriksonian model in which each stage develops in order to perform a new task or function. *Soft stage* refers to development that is conditioned by particular experiences. These experiences could arise from differences in personality characteristics, education, class, age, and so on. *Hard stage* refers to developmental sequences that occur universally, arising out of the overall reorganization of an underlying intellectual framework. Kohlberg and Armon argue that the idea of a hard stage of adult development may be neither theoretically useful nor empirically justifiable. Their argument can be seen as reiterated insistence that a postformal stage be a demonstrably new mode of cognitive reality.

On the other hand, soft stages play an important part in conceptualizing adult development. A diversity of postformal soft stage proposals includes Baldwin (1906), Perry (1968), Levinson et al. (1978) (see Levinson, chapter), Loevinger (1976), Erikson (1978), Fowler (1981), and Langer (1982); among others. For instance, Langer et al. (see Langer et al. chapter) challenge the hard-stage approach to understanding adult development by postulating a nonhierarchical pattern in

cognitive growth. They postulate a general cognitive mechanism for growth referred to as mindfulness, which involves active participation in the construction of new categories about self and world. These categories are different from categories that are transmitted, or mindlessly accepted, but they do not form a logical structure that is internally organized in a way that could be called necessary.

Thus, Langer et al. argue that development, as a process of becoming mindful, need not follow a predetermined or universal sequence. To the extent that people choose to participate mindfully in the process of their own development, the direction of that development becomes labile. Consequently, adult development as mindfulness is a species of "liberational psychology," and the potential of adulthood lies in its capacity to determine the nature and course of human growth. For example, Langer and her colleagues (Langer, 1982; Langer et al., 1984) have provided empirical evidence that deteriorization of cognitive functioning is not an inevitable consequence of growing old. To the contrary, some cognitive decrements can be reversed by enhancing mindfulness.

Commons and Richards' concerns lie more with the general specification of any empirical task that could possibly be used to demonstrate either the presence of, or the development into, a postformal stage. They de-emphasize the reconstruction of the "reality" of a person "at a given stage" and attempt to develop a general way to specify the structure of tasks in any domain that a person "at a given stage" can do. They suggest development proceeds, postformally, through systematic, meta-systematic, paradigmatic, and cross-paradigmatic stages. Other attempts to specify what it means to be at a postformal stage can be found throughout the work reviewed here.

Conclusion

Reviewing his career, Piaget (1952, p. 256) remarked, "My one idea . . . has been that intellectual operations proceed in terms of structures-of-the-whole. These structures denote the kinds of equilibrium toward which evolution in its entirety is striving; at once organic, psychological and social". In part, the work of all the authors mentioned here is a response to this one idea. Their work represents part of a broad attempt to grow out of the form Piaget gave to a wide variety of nineteenth-century thought.

The question remains whether the growth of postformal theories is itself proceeding in terms of some sort of structure of the whole. Broughton (1984) argues that this is not the case and suggests abandonment rather than revision. Another approach to this question is to assume that postformal research does not talk about many different stages, but about many different manifestations of the same stage. Table 6.2 shows one way that the stage sequences presented here can be aligned across a common *developmental space*.

The harmony in the alignment shown in Table 6.2 suggests a possible reconciliation of theories of stages, both hard and soft. Although many of these stages may be soft stages, taken as a whole, they indicate some hard-stage development. The results of this development are seen in domains where the sequences initially

appear soft. The general stage model implies that hard stages underlie all soft stages if there is anything developmental about those soft stages.

The true extent and nature of these postformal stages cannot be determined from the chart. Their extent may range beyond the developmental arenas so far described. Their nature will only emerge with a clearer understanding of the similarities and differences of the various stage conceptions (cf. Broughton, 1984). For this to happen, the nature of elements and operations must be communicated across the various developmental sequences that appear in Table 6.2. Part of what this suggests for the future is that the postformal constructs proposed must be formalized in order to facilitate comparison. Similarly, theories of stage generation must be formalized.

The adequacy of these theories depends on at least two major criteria, accountability and predictability. The extent to which each theory accounts for adolescent and adult developmental phenomena in many areas must be examined, and this dictates the continued development and assessment of instruments. Likewise, the similarities and differences in the predictions made by each theory have to be clarified. Initial steps in these directions have been taken. Yet they are by no means complete. With 14 developmental sequences, there are 91 different possible pairwise comparisons between these theories. As this makes clear, the task is huge. Nevertheless, it should create the differentiation and integration that characterize all developmental movement.

Acknowledgments

The authors thank Joan L. Richards for suggesting some historical references for our analysis, and Cheryl Armon, who participated in the early stages of the preparation of this manuscript. A graduate student read drafts of the manuscript and suggested stylistic clarifications for numerous passages. This work was supported by a grant from the Dare Association, Inc.

7

How Cognitive Processes and Environmental Conditions Organize Discontinuities in the Development of Abstractions

Kurt W. Fischer, Sheryl L. Kenny,
and Sandra L. Pipp

There is a major contradiction in the literature on adult cognitive development. Most studies seem to show that adults cannot perform the complex abstract tasks that Inhelder and Piaget (1955/1958) and others use to measure advanced thinking (Flavell, 1970; Horn, 1976; Neimark, 1975). Yet everyday beliefs suggest that many adults can reason in sophisticated ways about abstract concepts. In recent years, evidence has accumulated contradicting the findings of low-level thinking in adolescents and adults. In later adolescence and early adulthood, people seem to show major cognitive-developmental advances (Commons, Richards, & Armon, 1984; Fischer & Lamborn, 1989; Kitchener, 1982; Kitchener & King, 1990; see Richards & Commons chapter).[1]

The contradiction between these two sets of findings can be readily explained. What is needed is a theory that treats cognitive development as arising from the collaboration of person and environment. That is, both organismic and environmental components must be included in the central constructs of the theory. Then cognitive development is seen to involve both the great heights of abstractions and normal variations below those heights. That is, the two sets of findings not only are both correct but are fully compatible with each other: On the one hand, adolescents and young adults develop new levels of abilities to understand abstract concepts and relations. On the other hand, most behavior during this period does not show these cognitive advances.

Within the collaborative framework called skill theory (Fischer, 1980b), these apparently contradictory findings are explained by the systematic variations in people's level of performance. Under ordinary environmental conditions, people routinely function below their highest capacity. Yet high-level performance—and true cognitive-developmental levels—are strikingly evident under specific environmental conditions that optimize performance.

Cognitive–Developmental Levels as Discontinuities

One of the central problems in cognitive-developmental research has been that the criteria for what constitutes a stage have been unclearly specified. Piaget (1957) argued that the fundamental criterion for a stage is synchronous change across domains: The child's abilities in diverse domains should move nearly simultaneously into a new logical stage, such as concrete operations (Broughton, 1981b). Yet research has shown overwhelmingly that such synchrony does not obtain (Fischer & Bullock, 1981; Flavell, 1971b, 1983), as Piaget himself gradually acknowledged (e.g., Piaget, 1941, 1972). With the failure of this straightforward criterion, investigators have fallen back on a loose, poorly articulated criterion: Some sort of qualitative change indicates a new stage or level (Fischer & Silvern, 1985). As a result, ways of detecting stages or levels have remained unclear. Indeed, if observers were to happen upon a genuine stage or level, how would they know they had found it?

One straightforward criterion for a cognitive-developmental level is a discontinuity or sudden alteration in the pattern of developmental change. The simplest form of discontinuity is a spurt in performance during a limited age period, as shown in Figure 7.1: A person shows a sudden improvement in performance during a relatively short time interval. To test for such a spurt, a number of methods are available, as outlined by Fischer, Pipp, and Bullock (1984). The fundamental requirements of all the methods are the use of a ruler and a clock. The ruler can be any scale that provides an approximately continuous measure of the ability hypoth-

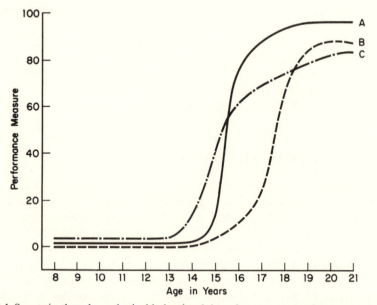

Figure 7.1 Spurts in three hypothetical behavioral domains as a result of the emergence of a new developmental level. Note: A, B, and C are different behavioral domains. The spurts were chosen to represent the emergence of Level 8 abstract mappings. (Reprinted with permission from Fischer, Hand, & Russell [1984]. Copyright Dare Association and Praeger Publishers.)

esized to change. The clock can be age or any other measure that can specify the length of the interval during which change takes place. A discontinuity is evident when a large change in performance occurs in a short time.

According to skill theory (Fischer, 1980b; Fischer & Farrar, 1987), the emergence of a new cognitive-developmental level produces a cluster of such spurts in performance. Within some limited age period, spurts can be detected in a wide range of different domains. For example, one level hypothesized by skill theory typically appears between 14 and 16 years of age, as shown for three hypothetical domains in Figure 7.1. The spurts do not all occur at exactly the same age, nor do they take exactly the same form. Adolescents do not suddenly metamorphose on their fifteenth birthday. Instead, the change is only relatively rapid, occupying a small interval of time.

For such spurts to occur reliably, people must be performing at or near their optimal level, the most complex skill that they can control. Complexity is defined in terms of a developmental scale of hierarchically ordered skill structures involving the coordination of sources of variation in behavior. For the cognitive levels that develop in adolescence and adulthood, the sources of variation are based in a structure called an abstraction, which typically specifies an intangible characteristic for coordinating some of the sources of variation in representations (concrete characteristics of people, objects, or events). Examples of abstractions include concepts such as justice, honesty, law, and responsibility, as well as arithmetic operations such as addition and division (Fischer & Lamborn, 1989).

Environmental conditions determine when people perform at their optimal level. Only with practiced skills in familiar domains and with environmental support for high-level performance will most people perform at optimum and thereby show a spurt in performance with the emergence of a new level. Most of the time, people do not encounter such environmental circumstances, and so they do not usually show spurts in performance. Levels are therefore evident only under special environmental conditions. Most conditions are likely to produce slow, gradual, continuous improvements in performance, even when people are performing exactly the same tasks that show discontinuities under optimal conditions.

Evidence for Continuous, Gradual Change

The typical pattern of slow, gradual change is evident in most developmental and educational research. Study after study demonstrates that with age, children, adolescents, and young adults typically show small improvements in performance or no change at all (Brown, Bransford, Ferrara, & Campione, 1983; Chi, 1978; Fischer & Silvern, 1985; McCall, Meyers, Kartman, & Roche, 1983). However, it could be argued that many of these studies do not provide appropriate tests for stagelike change because they do not assess developmental sequences. Colby, Kohlberg, and their colleagues (1983) carried out a longitudinal study that does not suffer from these problems and so provides a particularly clear test of the hypothesis that most cognitive development is slow and gradual (see Kohlberg & Ryncarz chapter).

Kohlberg (1969) devised a structured interview comprised of a series of moral dilemmas for assessing ideal types that were found to form a sequence of stages in

the development of moral judgment. The stages were formulated within the Piagetian tradition to reflect changes in thinking about morality and were hypothesized to form what Piaget (1957) called structured wholes. Consequently, they should emerge in a stagelike manner, appearing relatively suddenly and permeating the child's moral thinking.

According to the optimal-level hypothesis from skill theory, on the other hand, performance on Kohlberg's interview should demonstrate slow, gradual, continuous improvement over many years rather than abrupt, stagelike emergence. Gradual change is predicted because the interview is administered in such a way that it does not encourage optimal performance: Each dilemma is given only once, subjects are never told what is a good answer, and no contextual support for high-level performance is provided.

Groups of normal boys were originally tested on Kohlberg's interview at 10, 13, or 16 years of age, and they were retested on the same interview several times over the ensuing 20 years. Results showed that the stages did indeed form a developmental sequence, such that people consistently demonstrated later stages after they had first shown earlier ones. Because Kohlberg's research was designed to detect Piagetian-type cognitive–structural stages and because the stages have been shown empirically to form a developmental sequence, the study provides a strong test of the two competing hypotheses: Will the stages show abrupt emergence, or will their development be slow and gradual because the subjects were tested under nonoptimal conditions? With the longitudinal design, it is possible to determine not only whether the group as a whole showed spurts or gradual change in moral stage but also whether individual subjects demonstrated such spurts.

We analyzed the published data (Colby et al., 1983) to test for spurts versus gradual change in performance. The results were clear. Movement from stage to stage was continuous—slow and gradual. There was no evidence at all for relatively sudden change from one stage to the next. The development of Stage 4 offered a particularly good case, because no Stage 4 moral reasoning was evident at the youngest age in the study and virtually all subjects produced extensive Stage 4 reasoning by the end of the study. As shown in Figure 7.2, Stage 4 moral reasoning

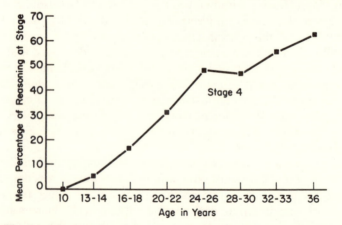

Figure 7.2 The development of stage 4 reasoning in Kohlberg's longitudinal study. Based on data in Colby et al. (1983).

first appeared at approximately 13 years of age, and the frequency of Stage 4 reasoning increased very slowly throughout the entire course of the study. Most subjects did not produce a preponderance of Stage 4 reasoning until they reached their 30s. The pattern was the same for individual subjects—a slow, gradual increase in Stage 4 moral reasoning over many years.

This study of Kohlberg's stages clearly demonstrated continuous change, not discontinuous, and the pattern of continuous change is typical of most other research. Nevertheless, a few studies do provide evidence of developmental spurts during adolescence and early adulthood (e.g., Martarano, 1977; O'Brien & Overton, 1982). We propose that the optimal-level hypothesis will predict how spurts appear and disappear as a function of environmental conditions and will thus explain the cases in which spurts have been found. To show how this explanation will operate, we first need to elaborate our skill-theory analysis.

Building and Using Skills: The Importance of Practice and Environmental Support

It takes work to build a skill. When a person develops a general capacity to build skills at a new developmental level, there is no automatic transformation of all skills to the new level. The human information-processing system follows what might be called a Calvinist principle: The person must actively construct every new skill. Skills do not emerge for free, without effort.

In general, at least two circumstances are necessary for a person to build a new skill. First, the environment must provide a context that induces and supports performance of the behaviors that comprise the skill. Second, the person must practice the skill until he or she has mastered it.

When stated so directly, the Calvinist principle about skill building may seem sensible and obvious; yet it has not been included in the central principles of traditional cognitive-developmental theories such as Piaget's (1970b). Once it is included, stagelike change can no longer be expected across all domains of behavior. Even if Piaget could magically touch the head of an 11-year-old and instantaneously transform him or her to formal operations, the child would have to take time and effort to use the new capacity to build specific formal-operational skills. Only with time, then, would the new capacity become evident. And while the child was expending time and effort on building new skills in one domain, such as arithmetic, little progress would be made in building skills in other domains, such as morality. Consequently, even an instantaneous transformation of capacity would result in a gradual transformation of skills occurring during some interval of time. Relatively, this transformation would involve spurts in performance, but absolutely, it would still take time.

Furthermore, if the environment must induce and support the building of a new skill, then the levels of a person's skills will inevitably vary across domains. After a new capacity emerges, the environment will happen to induce the building of skills at the new level in certain domains and not in others. The person will experience the environmental contexts necessary for inducing the building of some

skills, such as those for arithmetic reasoning, and not for the building of others, such as those for moral reasoning. It is physically impossible within a limited time period to encounter the contexts needed to induce all possible skills. Consequently, even if capacity were transformed instantaneously, the actual skills a person possesses would vary across domains.

According to skill theory, the environment not only induces the transformation of a skill to a new level but also affects the level of performance of a skill more directly. The environmental context provides varying degrees of support for high-level performance (Fischer & Bullock, 1984). A skill is not simply present or absent, but it is internalized to a certain degree. The more it is internalized, the less environmental support is required for a person to perform it. Conversely, the less it is internalized, the more environmental support is required for performance. The gap between the person's optimal level and his or her level of functioning with low support is called the developmental range (Lamborn & Fischer, 1988).

In Kohlberg's moral judgment interview, little support was provided for high-level performance: Subjects were not shown a good answer or given any other aids for high-level performance, nor were they allowed to work out an answer over a period of time. Without environmental support or the opportunity to work out a high-level skill, people do not typically function at or near optimum. They function at the bottom of their developmental range.

Detection of the discontinuities predicted to appear with a new developmental level, then, requires the following sort of skill assessment: People must be tested (1) in familiar domains, where they have had the opportunity to construct high-level skills; (2) under environmental conditions that provide contextual support for high-level performance; and (3) with the opportunity to practice the tasks they must perform. In familiar domains, relatively short periods of practice will suffice, such as hours, days, or weeks. But in unfamiliar domains, optimal performance will be possible only after long time periods for practice and instruction.

Traditionally, developmental and educational researchers have not assessed behavior under conditions for optimal performance (Feuerstein, 1979). As in Kohlberg's study, testing conditions have provided little contextual support for high-level performance, and there has been little opportunity for practice. Also in some cases, the domains tested have not been familiar. Inevitably, performance under such conditions will show slow, gradual, continuous change.

In a study of the development of arithmetic skills, we have tested this interpretation by varying both degree of contextual support and opportunity for practice (Fischer et al., 1984; Fischer, Kenny, & Rose, 1987). Subjects were tested individually in two sessions, with two conditions in each session. In the first session, a series of arithmetic tasks was administered to them with no support or practice. The subjects were shown each task for the first time, and they were encouraged to give an immediate answer. Later in the same session, they were given each task again, but now environmental support was provided. The experimenter first showed them a sample good answer and allowed them time to read it over and ask questions about it. Then the sample answer was taken away, and they provided their own answer. At the end of this session, they were reminded that they would be tested on the same tasks in two weeks and that they should think about them

during the interim. In the second session, the two conditions from the first session were repeated—first, assessment with no support, and then assessment with the support of first seeing a good answer.

Eight subjects were assessed in each grade between third grade and college. The tasks in the arithmetic study were designed to test several of the levels of abstract skills that are predicted by skill theory to develop during adolescence and early adulthood.

Four Levels of Abstract Skills

According to skill theory, abstractions first develop at about 10–12 years of age, the period when formal operations are said to begin (Inhelder & Piaget, 1955/1958). This new capacity for abstractions is built upon a series of earlier levels involving first reflexes, next sensorimotor actions, and then representations. First, young infants come to control reflexes at successively more complex levels until they can ultimately control single sensorimotor actions. Next, older infants build sensorimotor actions at successively more complex levels, until eventually they can control single representations. Children in turn build more complex representations, moving through a series of levels that culminate in the control of single abstractions at 10–12 years. The developmental levels involving actions, representations, and abstractions are presented in Table 7.1, along with the simplest algebraic representation of the skill structure for each of the 10 levels. All the developmental levels are described in detail in Fischer (1980b).

The first level of abstractions (Level 7) involves only the simplest level of abstract skills. Three additional, more complex levels (Levels 8–10) develop over the next 15 years. These four levels of abstractions continue the hierarchical series of levels that started in early infancy. The cycle of the four levels of abstractions is the focus of the present section.

Each level is defined in terms of a skill structure that is specified algebraically. For Level 7, the structure is a single abstraction, which arises from the intercoordination of two or more representational systems. To avoid having to elaborate upon the structural definitions for each abstract skill level in this chapter, we will define these levels in terms of one type of abstraction, the intangible category. Many instances of abstractions involve intangible categories and the relations between them, and they seem to have been investigated more than any other type, not only in our laboratory but in most research on cognitive development in adolescence and early adulthood. In describing the levels, we will focus on our arithmetic study as well as several other studies from the literature dealing with the following intangible categories: intention and responsibility (Fischer, Hand, & Russell, 1984; Hand & Fischer, 1981), political concepts (Adelson, 1972), moral concepts (Kohlberg, 1969; Rest, 1983), and reflective judgment about knowledge (Kitchener, 1982; Kitchener & Brenner, 1990).

In the arithmetic study, tasks were designed to assess each of the four levels of abstractions, although thus far we have collected data only for the first two levels. All the tasks involved using, defining, and relating the four basic arithmetic operations—addition, subtraction, multiplication, and division. For each task, the sub-

Table 7.1 Ten Levels of Skill Structures*

Level	Name of Structure	Sensorimotor† Tier	Representational† Tier	Abstract Tier	Estimated Age Region of Emergence
1	Single sensorimotor set	[A] or [B]*			3–4 mos.
2	Sensorimotor mapping	[A − B]			7–8 mos.
3	Sensorimotor system	$[A_{G,H} \leftrightarrow B_{G,H}]$			11–13 mos.
4	System of sensorimotor systems, equivalent to a single representational set	$\begin{bmatrix} A \leftrightarrow B \\ \updownarrow \\ C \leftrightarrow D \end{bmatrix} \equiv$	$[R]$		20–24 mos.
5	Representational mapping		$[R - T]$		4–5 yrs.
6	Representational system		$[R_{J,K} \leftrightarrow T_{J,K}]$		6–7½ yrs.
7	System of representational systems, equivalent to a single abstract set		$\begin{bmatrix} R \leftrightarrow T \\ \updownarrow \\ V \leftrightarrow X \end{bmatrix} \equiv$	$[\mathcal{E}]$	10–12 yrs.
8	Abstract mapping			$[\mathcal{E} - \mathcal{F}]$	14–15 yrs.
9	Abstract system			$[\mathcal{E}_{A,B} \leftrightarrow \mathcal{F}_{A,B}]$	19–21 yrs.
10	System of abstract systems, equivalent to a single principle			$\begin{bmatrix} \mathcal{E} \leftrightarrow \mathcal{F} \\ \updownarrow \\ \mathcal{G} \leftrightarrow \mathcal{H} \end{bmatrix}$	24–26 yrs.‡

*Boldface capital letters designate sensorimotor sets; italic capital letters designate representational sets, and script capital letters designate abstract sets. Multiple subscripts designate differentiated components of a set; whenever there is a horizontal arrow, two or more subsets exist by definition, even when they are not expressly shown. Long straight lines and arrows designate a relation between sets or systems. Brackets designate a single skill.

†Sensorimotor structures continue after Level 4, and representational structures after Level 7, but the formulas become so complex that they have been omitted. To fill in the sensorimotor structures, simply copy the pattern in the representational tier, replacing each representational set with the sensorimotor formula for Level 4. Similarly, to fill in the representational structures, copy the pattern in the abstract tier, replacing each abstract set with the representational formula for Level 7.

‡Since little research has been done on development at this level, this age region must be considered highly tentative.

ject calculates a simple arithmetic problem or two, such as 7 + 3 = ?. Then he or she answers a general question about the operations used, such as "Explain what addition is, and show how the definition applies to this problem." In all cases, the problems dealt only with positive whole numbers. Each type of task was given in two different forms, one involving general verbal explanation without any visual props and one involving an explanation using the number line for positive whole numbers (a line along which the numbers are displayed at equal intervals). Table 7.2 provides an example for each of the four abstract levels taken from the arithmetic study.

In *Level 7 single abstractions,* which first appear as early as 10 or 11 years of age, the child controls individual intangible categories, such as intention and responsibility, law, society, and justice. Children with single abstractions can coordinate two or more concrete instances to form an intangible category, but they can-

Table 7.2 Arithmetic Examples for Four Developmental Levels of Abstract Skills

Level	Name of Structure	Skill Structure	Examples from Arithmetic Study*
7	Systems of Representational Systems, Which Are Single Abstractions	$[\mathscr{E}]$	*General Definitions of Arithmetic Operations and Application to Problem* "Addition is when you put together two numbers, and you end up with a bigger number called the sum. Like you put together the numbers 5 and 7, and you get the bigger number 12."
8	Abstract Mappings	$[\mathscr{E} - \mathscr{F}]$	*General Relations of Two Closely Related Arithmetic Operations and Application to Problems* "Addition and multiplication are similar operations. Both put numbers together to get a larger number, but the numbers are put together in different ways—by single numbers in addition and by groups of numbers in multiplication. Multiplication is really addition repeated a specific number of times. In 5 times 7, the first number, 5, tells you how many times to do the second number, 7, so you have a group of five sevens. In addition, you take the single number 7 and put it together with another 7, and another, and another, and another."
9	Abstract Systems	$[\mathscr{E}_{A,B} \leftrightarrow \mathscr{F}_{A,B}]$	*General Relations of Two Distantly Related Operations* "Addition and division are opposite operations in two ways. Addition increases by single numbers, while division decreases by groups of numbers. The fact that one increases and the other decreases is one way they are different, and the way they increase or decrease by single numbers or groups is the other way. Repeated addition can be used to express a division problem like $35 \div 5 = 7$. Five added seven times yields 35, so we know there are seven fives in 35."
10	Systems of Abstract Systems, Which Are Single Principles	$\begin{bmatrix} \mathscr{E} \leftrightarrow \mathscr{F} \\ \updownarrow \\ \mathscr{G} \leftrightarrow \mathscr{H} \end{bmatrix}$	*Principle Unifying the Four Arithmetic Operations* "Addition, subtraction, multiplication, and division are all operations, which means that they all transform numbers by either combining or separating them and doing so either in groups or one number at a time. There are relations between all possible pairs of operations. Some pairs are closely related, and others are more distantly related . . . (Elaboration explaining the pairs, as diagramed in the table below, and applying them to concrete arithmetic problems, such as $5 + 7 = 12$, $12 - 7 = 5$, $5 \times 7 = 35$, and $35 \div 5 = 7$.)"

	Single Number	Group of Numbers
Increase	Addition	Multiplication
Decrease	Subtraction	Division

Note: Script capital letters designate abstract sets. Subscripts designate differentiated components of the respective set. Long straight lines and arrows designate a relation between sets of systems. Brackets designate a single skill.

*The arithmetic concepts deal only with positive whole numbers.

not relate one intangible category to another. There were eight arithmetic tasks for assessing Level 7 skills. All tasks required providing a general definition of one of the four operations, as illustrated in Table 7.2, and showing how it applied to an arithmetic problem the child had calculated.

With *Level 8 abstract mappings* emerging at about 14–16 years of age, adolescents relate one intangible category to another in a simple way. Examples include the relation of intention to responsibility, of liberal to conservative, and of one type of knowledge to another type. What is not possible at Level 8 is dealing simultaneously with several components or varieties of each intangible category, such as relating two types of intention to two types of responsibility. There were eight arithmetic tasks for assessing Level 8 skills, two each for the four following pairs of closely related operations: addition and subtraction, multiplication and division, multiplication and addition, and division and subtraction. To pass each task, the person had to explain in general terms how the two operations in the pair relate to each other (how they are similar and different) and how that relation is evident in specific arithmetic problems, such as $7 + 3 = 10$ and $10 - 3 = 7$.

The findings from a number of studies support the emergence of the new capacities described by Levels 7 and 8, but there are not many studies relevant to Levels 9 and 10 (Fischer, Hand, & Russell, 1984). Nevertheless, a few studies do suggest the emergence of the hypothesized capacities of Levels 9 and 10 in early adulthood (see Broughton, 1978; Commons et al., 1984; Fischer & Lamborn, 1989; Jaques, Gibson, & Isaac, 1978; Kitchener, 1982). Also, the theories of Case (1980) and Biggs and Collis (1982) predict levels of abstraction similar to those of skill theory. Because of the dearth of data, the description of the nature of these two levels and the ages associated with them should be considered tentative.

Level 9 abstract systems, developing initially at approximately 20 years of age, introduce more complex relations between intangible categories. The young adult can relate several components or varieties of one abstraction, such as intention, to several components or varieties of another, such as responsibility. For example, systems relating several types of intention to several types of responsibility seem to be common in the legal system, where intention and responsibility are two of the essential components for determining guilt and punishment. In arithmetic, one such system for relating several types of arithmetic operations involves the two pairs of distantly related operations: addition and division, subtraction and multiplication. The relation of each pair constitutes a Level 9 skill, in which the pair is related by variations in two distinct components—direction of change and type of unit (see Table 7.2). We devised a series of arithmetic tasks for assessing Level 9 skills based on these two distantly related pairs of operations.

The final reorganization, *Level 10 general principles,* involves the integration of two or more Level 9 abstract systems in terms of some general theory, ideology, or framework. A reasonable estimate is that this level first appears at approximately 25 years of age. Examples include an epistemological framework for coordinating variations in knowledge systems, such as the reflective-judgment framework outlined by Kitchener (1982), and Darwin's principle of evolution by natural selection (Gruber, 1981). More modest principles also occur at Level 10, including the one integrating the relations among the four arithmetic operations: The four operations involve the possible combinations of the two different types of transformations of

numbers implied by the components in the distantly related pairs assessed at Level 9: direction of change (increase or decrease) and type of unit (single numbers or groups of numbers), as outlined in Table 7.2. At Level 10 the person can fluidly use this principle relating these transformations to analyze how the four operations relate to each other.

Empirical Criteria for Levels

With the arithmetic tasks devised for testing the four levels of abstractions, it is possible to test the skill-theory analysis of the effects of environmental conditions on the pattern of developmental change. Under optimal conditions, performance on these tasks should demonstrate discontinuities upon the emergence of each new level. Under ordinary (nonoptimal) conditions, performance should demonstrate slow, gradual, continuous improvement. This hypothesis specifies several empirical criteria for levels.

Spurt in Tasks for a Particular Level

The most obvious empirical criterion for the emergence of a new level is a spurt in optimal performance. In the arithmetic study, such a spurt occurred for both Level 7 and Level 8.

Between third and fifth grades, Level 7 performance under optimal conditions spurted from near zero to over 50 percent correct. Figure 7.3 shows the data for the two extreme conditions: no support or practice (the first condition in the first session) and both support and practice (the second condition in the second session). The latter, the optimal condition (practice and support), produced the spurt in per-

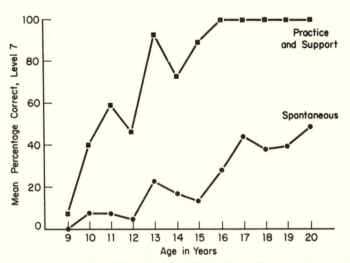

Figure 7.3 Development of level 7 arithmetic skills under ordinary and optimal conditions of support.

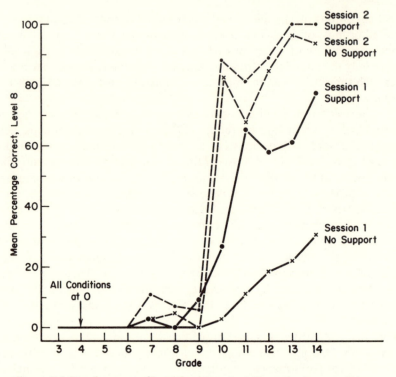

Figure 7.4 Development of level 8 arithmetic skills under four conditions.

formance, whereas the former, the nonoptimal ordinary (spontaneous) condition, produced slow, gradual improvement on the same tasks. The nonoptimal condition is like most standard cognitive and educational assessments, which employ similar testing procedures. Under each condition, children performed eight tasks assessing Level 7 skills, but two of the tasks dealt with division, which is not taught until late in elementary school. Consequently, only the six tasks for addition, subtraction, and multiplication are included in the analysis for Level 7.

Between ninth and tenth grades, Level 8 performance under the optimal condition spurted from near zero to over 80 percent correct. Figure 7.4 includes all four assessment conditions, ranging from spontaneous to optimal. For every condition, each subject performed eight tasks assessing Level 8 skills, as described earlier.

For both Levels 7 and 8, the spurt was closely tied to age and grade: In the optimal condition, Level 7 was marked by a spurt that occurred for all subjects between third and fifth grades (approximately 9 and 11 years of age), and Level 8, by a spurt for all subjects between ninth and tenth grades (approximately 15 and 16 years).

To meet the criterion for a discontinuity, however, such a close tie to age and grade is not necessary. All that is required is that every subject show a spurt in the tasks for a given level at some point; different people can demonstrate the spurt at different ages. To test for such a spurt, the researcher can use either a longitudinal or a cross-sectional design: The fundamental pattern of data predicted is that under

optimal conditions most subjects will either fail all or most tasks at a given level or pass all or most of them. In a cross-sectional design, this pattern will produce a bimodal distribution of scores for each level. In a longitudinal design, it will produce not only the bimodal distribution but also a relatively abrupt change at some age for each subject from failing most tasks to passing most of them (Fischer, Pipp, & Bullock, 1984).

The spurt criterion applies to performance in a single domain, such as the understanding of arithmetic operations. When tested across domains, people's optimal performance will demonstrate a cluster of spurts in a given age region, as shown in Figure 7.1 for Level 8. According to skill theory, every person will produce the spurts, although they will occur only for optimal performance in familiar domains (Fischer & Pipp, 1984). It is possible that all normal people will show the cluster of spurts within the same age region, such as 13 to 16 years for Level 8, or there may be substantial variation across people. If there is substantial variation, however, what will vary is (1) the exact age interval when the cluster of spurts occurs and (2) the specific domains that show spurts. Across these variations, there will be a universal phenomenon, the cluster of spurts itself. That is, every individual will show such a cluster for each level at some limited age interval. For example, one person might spurt to Level 8 at 13–15 years, and another might do so at 18–20 years.

Note that the cluster of spurts is predicted only for optimal performance in familiar domains. Spurts will not occur consistently for ordinary, nonoptimal performance, or for performance in unfamiliar domains. Except for optimal performance, the norm for development is slow, gradual change, with discontinuities occurring only under limited circumstances.

Spurt upon Emergence of the Next Level

The data from the arithmetic study allow a partial test of the cluster hypothesis. Different tasks were used to assess each level, and the tasks for one level can in some cases be used to test not only for a spurt at that level but also for one at the succeeding level. When two such spurts occur, they should cluster within an age region.

For example, with the spurt in optimal performance upon the emergence of a given level, such as Level 7 in Figure 7.3, performance may not reach 100 percent. In that case, the opportunity still exists for substantial improvement in performance, and so a second spurt can be predicted upon emergence of the next level. When Level 8 emerges, performance on the Level 7 tasks will spurt again as the new capacity produces consolidation and differentiation of the Level 7 skills. The findings in Figure 7.3 support the second-spurt hypothesis. After the initial spurt in Level 7 performance, performance leveled off at 50–60 percent correct. Level 7 performance then showed a second spurt beginning at 13 years. Performance reached 100 percent by age 16, the age at which the spurt in Level 8 occurred (Fig. 7.4). According to these results, the age region for the two spurts indexing the emergence of Level 8 was 13–16 years.

For performance on Level 8 tasks, a similar second spurt can be predicted at approximately 18–20 years, when Level 9 emerges. The data in Figure 7.4 suggest

such a spurt, although performance in the optimal condition was already so high that the magnitude of the increase is necessarily small.

In general, then, the arithmetic study supports the skill-theory hypothesis that development shows spurts in optimal performance with the emergence of each new cognitive level while showing gradual, continuous change in performance under ordinary, nonoptimal conditions. Further tests of the hypothesis seem warranted by these initial encouraging results.

In addition to investigating the effects of different testing conditions on the form of developmental change, researchers also need to assess the relation of change across domains. The spurts found in the arithmetic study were simple first-order discontinuities. More complex discontinuities should also occur, such as second-order discontinuities involving an abrupt change in the relation between performance in different domains. There are straightforward empirical criteria for detecting these second-order discontinuities, based on measures of the relation between performance in different domains (Fischer, Pipp, & Bullock, 1984; McCall, Eichorn, & Hogarty, 1977).

The Brain-Growth Hypothesis

The emphasis on the environmental conditions for detecting developmental levels highlights the environmental side of skill development, but the organismic side needs to be taken seriously as well. Optimal level is a property of a specific combination of organism and environment—a person under specific environmental conditions. Several researchers have suggested that the emergence of developmental levels may be accompanied by major biological changes in the child, including changes in brain waves and neural networks (Emde et al., 1976; Epstein, 1980; Kagan, 1982; White, 1970). Indeed, a number of these changes involve developmental spurts in biological variables, spurts that seem generally to parallel the spurts in behavior documented in psychological research.

Despite the paucity of knowledge about how brain functioning relates to cognitive-developmental changes, we have put forth a simple hypothesis about a possible neural basis for the change in levels—the brain-growth hypothesis (Fischer, 1987). Each level is hypothesized to correlate with a spurt in the formation of a new type of neural network. That is, with each level, the brain grows a large number of new networks that facilitate performance at that level. The networks are then gradually pruned to form efficient neural systems.

Early Development

Synapses are a fundamental component of neural networks, since they are the primary junction between neurons. Consequently, a straightforward interpretation of the neural network is that a spurt in synaptic growth will be associated with the emergence of each cognitive-developmental level. The existing evidence is limited, but it provides enough data to allow us to begin to articulate what these spurts might look like.

In early infancy, there is evidence for a dramatic long-term growth surge in synaptic density throughout all major areas of the cortex. The surge lasts over many months, reaches a peak at approximately twice the density level of adult cortexes, and then gradually decreases over a very long period to the adult level. The decrease indicates that "excess" synapses are gradually being pruned away.

The most extensive data are from infant macaque monkeys (Goldman-Rakic, 1987; Rakic, Bourgeois, Eckenhoff, Zecevic, & Goldman-Rakic, 1986). For human beings the data are more sparse, but they indicate the same sort of surge: Synaptic density in the visual cortex seems to increase throughout the first year of life to approximately 200 percent of its eventual adult level (Huttenlocher, de Courten, Garey, & van der Loos, 1982). After the peak at one year of age, it gradually decreases over several years until it reaches the adult level during the grade school years. In the frontal area, which is associated with high-level cognitive functioning, the growth surge seems to last even longer: Synaptic density seems to sustain its peak to five or six years of age and then begins gradually to drop down to the adult level (Huttenlocher, 1979).

The general surge in synaptic growth does not mark the emergence of a cognitive level, because it occurs over a long period when a number of levels are emerging. It is analogous to the familiar general increasing curve for cognitive skills, like that in Figure 7.2. Where levels will be evident is in discontinuities in the general curve, points where the curve shows short-term spurts or drops (Fischer, Pipp, & Bullock, 1984).

Since synapses play such a crucial role in neural networks, discontinuities in the synaptic-growth curves can be hypothesized for each emerging cognitive level. During the period of the general surge in synaptic growth in infancy, several cognitive levels develop. For each of them, discontinuities in the growth curve are predicted at the approximate age of emergence of the new cognitive capacity. Unfortunately, existing data do not allow reliable detection of the predicted sudden changes in the growth function, although there are some suggestions of such discontinuities in the data for monkeys (Fischer, 1987). The apparently long growth period for synapses in the human frontal area suggests that synaptic spurts could be correlated with the emergence of all cognitive levels before those involving abstractions.

Development of Abstractions

The synaptic growth curves make it unlikely that there are spurts in synaptic density in adolescence, when the levels of abstractions develop. However, other changes in networks could still produce discontinuous increases in the formation of networks during these ages. Factors that increase the speed of neural transmission are likely candidates, because speed is a crucial determinant of neural network functioning (Grossberg, 1980). For example, myelin, the insulation around neural axons, not only grows in infancy and childhood but also continues to grow into early adulthood (Yakovlev & Lecours, 1967). Spurts in myelin formation or in other factors contributing to effective neural-network functioning could produce the hypothesized spurts in network formation during adolescence and early adulthood.

Changes in Brain Electrical Activity

Although it is not yet possible to test the brain-growth hypothesis directly, it is possible to test for changes in brain activity associated with the ages of emergence of the developmental levels. Data are available for both the electroencephalogram (EEG) and the evoked potential, two measures of brain electrical activity. These data, collected by independent researchers, were analyzed to determine whether spurts appeared at appropriate ages for each level.

Brain activity does seem to spurt in the appropriate age region for every level for which we could find relevant data (nine levels—from single sensorimotor actions through abstract systems in Table 7.1). The most extensive data are available for the EEG. Global measures reflecting the entire spectrum of activity waves typically show a discontinuity (spurt or drop) for each new developmental level. Figure 7.5, illustrating one such measure based on data collected by the Swedish neuroscientists Matousek and Petersen (1973; John, 1977), shows statistically significant spurts for Levels 4, 5, 6, 7, and 8, starting at approximately ages 2, 4, 8, 12, and 15. There is also a possible spurt for Level 9 at about 19 years, but because of the great variability of the measure during that age period, the spurt is not statistically reliable.

Measures of relations between electical activity in different parts of the cortex seem to be especially promising because they may relate directly to the functioning of neural networks. For example, links between activity in the frontal and occipital area of the cortex are likely candidates for detecting neural-network changes associated with the later developmental levels. A recent study with an American sample by Robert Thatcher and his colleagues found spurts and drops in several measures of such links. These discontinuities occurred at the approximate ages for Levels 5, 6, 7, and possibly 8 (Thatcher, Walker, & Guidice, 1987). The data did not allow tests of the other levels.

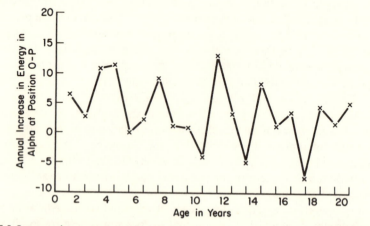

Figure 7.5 Increase in percentage of energy in alpha waves of the electroencephalogram as a function of age. The electroencephalogram was measured in the occipital-parietal area, and the percentage of energy was calculated by dividing the amount of energy in alpha waves by the total amount of energy in all waves.

Studies of evoked potentials also show discontinuities at the expected ages. When people were exposed to flashes of light, the brain electrical potential that resulted showed discontinuities at the ages for Levels 6 and 7 (Dustman & Beck, 1969). It was not possible to test for the other levels.

Of course, these data can only be taken as suggestive, since there have been no studies systematically examining both brain electrical activity and cognitive changes in the same people. Nevertheless, the evidence is strong enough to indicate that the brain-growth hypothesis is worth pursuing further. It at least provides a basis for beginning to investigate relations between cognitive levels and brain development. In our opinion, the major danger to avoid in developing the hypothesis further is thinking of the biological changes as prerequisites in any simple sense for the cognitive changes (Fischer & Silvern, 1985). Just as it is necessary to avoid neglecting organismic influences when testing environmental hypotheses, so is it necessary to avoid simplistic biological hypotheses that neglect environmental influences.

How Optimal Level Functions

According to the optimal-level hypothesis, then, development is *both stagelike and gradual at the same time.* When people are functioning at their upper limit, development spurts in a relatively short period to a new level of skill, and correlated brain changes may spurt roughly simultaneously. When people are not performing at their limit, change occurs gradually over a longer period. Most of the time, people do not perform at their optimal level; consequently, most development is gradual.

During periods in which a new optimal level is emerging, developmental changes in familiar domains can occur at a rapid rate. After the optimal level has emerged, skills in those same domains will show slower, less dramatic change in complexity and generalization. The periods of slow change in optimal performance do not indicate developmental stasis, however. The person never lacks additional skills to learn, because there are always new domains to master. The emergent capacity must be extended to many diverse domains, and it must be internalized to the point that the individual can use it even when there is little environmental support. This extension and internalization of the capacity both consolidates the person's skills and prepares for the emergence of the next optimal level.

The way that a new optimal-level capacity is extended to diverse domains highlights a major difference between skill theory and competence–performance models such as those of Piaget (1957, 1971b) and Chomsky (1965). In the latter approaches, a general structure is present in the mind and can be straightforwardly applied to new domains. For instance, Piaget's *structure d'ensemble* (structure of the whole) for concrete operations emerges at six or seven years and is said to be automatically applicable to any content. The reason that it does not generalize to all contents immediately is that objects and events differentially resist application of the structure. The competence is thus present, but sometimes the child cannot demonstrate it in performance (Bullock, 1981; Stone & Day, 1980).

Optimal level functions very differently. When people develop a new optimal

level, they have the capacity to construct skills at the new level, but they do not actually have any competences at the level until those skills are built. An individual must always work to construct particular skills in specific domains. There are no powerful competences that are somehow being prevented from eventuating in performance.

In summary, although much research remains to be done, a number of independent strands of evidence do support the optimal-level hypothesis, including the particular levels postulated in skill theory. The upper limit on the complexity of skills that a person can construct seems to develop through a series of qualitatively different levels, each of which is characterized by a cluster of spurts in optimal performance. Most of the systematic changes in behavior that constitute development, learning, and problem solving, however, are affected only modestly by this upper bound. Optimal level, after all, specifies only a limit on skills that can be mastered. To explain the many systematic changes in skills below the upper limit, another set of developmental processes must be invoked—processes of skill acquisition.

Transformation Rules for Analyzing Skill Acquisition

Skill theory gambles that thought and behavior can be fruitfully described structurally and that development, learning, and problem solving can be explained by transformations of these structures (Fischer, 1980a). The transformations can be characterized in terms of a limited set of rewrite rules, which specify how given skill structures can be transformed to produce new skill structures.

The transformation rules constitute one of the most important mechanisms by which skill theory predicts and explains sequences in development. New skills are mastered in a succession of many small steps, each of which is specified by a transformation rule. The sequence of skill acquisition within a domain can thus be described by reference to the initial skill structure and the series of transformation rules used. Development, learning, and problem solving all involve these same basic transformations.

Five different transformation rules have been specified, and we suspect more will be discovered. There are four rules for predicting steps within a developmental level: substitution, focusing, compounding, and differentiation. The fifth rule, intercoordination, deals with movement to a new level—how skills at one level are combined to produce a new skill at the next level. All the rules have been formally defined as algebraic rewrite rules for skill structures, and principles for ordering the results of the transformations have also been explicated (Fischer, 1980b).

A Developmental Sequence Involving the Transformations

To illustrate four of the transformation rules, we will analyze a developmental sequence for the two levels of representations that immediately precede abstractions. Three Level 5 representational-mapping skills for social roles are rewritten by the four transformations, and the results are ordered according to skill-theory principles to produce the sequence shown in Table 7.3. This sequence has

Table 7.3 Examples of the Transformation Rules in the Domain of Social Roles

Step	Type of Transformation	Cognitive Level	Role-Playing Skill	Example of Behavior	Formula for Transformation	Skill Structure
1	Initial skills	5: Representational mappings	Social role of doctor	The child pretends that a doctor doll examines a patient doll, who responds appropriately.		$[R_D - S_P]$
			or			
			Social role of nurse	The child pretends that a nurse doll examines a patient doll, who responds appropriately.		$[T_N - S_P]$
			or			
			Social role of father	The child pretends that a father doll takes care of a child doll, who responds appropriately.		$[R_F - S_C]$
2	Substitution		Doctor role with woman patient	The child pretends that a doctor doll examines a woman doll, who responds appropriately.	$\mathrm{Sub}[R_D - S_P] \quad =$	$[R_D - T_P]$
3	Focusing		Shifting between doctor and nurse roles	The child pretends that a doctor doll examines a patient doll, who responds	$\mathrm{Foc}[(R_D - S_P),(T_N - S_P)] = $ $[(R_D - S_P) > (T_N - S_P)]$	

			Behavior	Formula
			appropriately; and then she switches to having the nurse doll examine a patient doll, who responds appropriately.	
4		Compounding	Social role of doctor with complementary roles of nurse and patient	The child pretends that a doctor doll examines a patient doll and is aided by a nurse doll. Both patient and nurse respond appropriately.	$[R_D - S_P] + [T_N - S_P] = [R_D - T_N - S_P]$
5	6: Representational systems	Intercoordination	Intersection of doctor and father roles and their complements	The child pretends that a doctor doll examines a patient doll and simultaneously acts as a father to the patient, who is his son or daughter. The patient doll acts appropriately as both patient and offspring.	$[R_D - S_P] \cdot [R_F - S_C] = [R_{D,F} \leftrightarrow S_{P,C}]$

Note. In the formulas, the italicized capital letters stand for the child's representation of a particular doll as an independent agent: R for a man doll, S for a child doll, and T for a woman doll. The subscripts designate the role or roles that the child represents for each doll, as follows: C = child; D = doctor; F = father; N = nurse; P = patient. See Fischer (1980) for elaboration of the notation. The sequence has been tested and confirmed in several studies (Watson 1981; Watson & Fischer 1980).

been tested and confirmed in several studies (Watson, 1981; Watson & Fischer, 1980).

The initial Level 5 mappings deal with the social roles of doctor–patient, nurse–patient, and father–child as shown for step 1 in Table 7.3. A social role always involves a relation between a primary role, such as doctor, and a complementary role, such as patient. For the doctor–patient role, for example, a girl pretends that a doctor doll examines a patient doll, who interacts appropriately. For the nurse–patient role she pretends that a nurse doll examines a patient doll, who interacts appropriately. For the father–child role she makes a man doll treat a child doll as his daughter, who interacts appropriately.

The simplest of the within-level transformation rules is *substitution,* a type of generalization in which a skill is mastered through one task and then transferred to a second, similar task. An individual may show such transfer when all but one of the components in the second skill structure are the same as those in the first structure, and when the single different component can be generalized to the second task. The Level 5 skill for doctor/patient shows an instance of such transfer when the type of patient is changed, as shown in step 2 of Table 7.3. The child first learns to make a doctor interact with a girl patient and then transfers that skill to the interactions of a doctor with a woman patient.

In the transformation called *focusing,* a person uses two related skills in succession, shifting from one to the other within a single task or situation (Gottlieb, Taylor, & Ruderman, 1977; Hand, 1982; Harter, 1983b; Watson, 1981). The example in step 3 of Table 7.3 uses the two skills of doctor–patient and nurse–patient. The child first has the doctor doll examine the patient doll, who interacts appropriately. Then the child simply shifts her focus from the doctor to the nurse: The nurse doll examines the patient doll, who interacts appropriately. There is no integration between the two types of social roles: They are simply strung together.

Like all transformations, focusing arises from the collaboration of person and environment. The person possesses two or more related skills for a given situation but can apply only one of the skills at a time. Nevertheless, the situation tends to elicit both skills. The result is that the person effectively links the two skills together by focusing on first one skill and then the other.

The two Level 5 skills can be integrated by another type of within-level transformation, *compounding.* Two skills at a given level are combined to form a more complex skill at the same level that unifies the components. With the play example, the child may combine the two role skills, doctor–patient and nurse–patient, to form a new compounded structure, doctor–nurse–patient, as shown for step 4 in Table 7.3. With this new structure the child makes the doctor doll and the nurse doll jointly examine the patient doll, who responds appropriately to both of them. Note how this skill is different from the one based on focusing. In compounding, the three actors are made to carry out an integrated interaction, but in focusing, the two initial skills remain separate and are only linked temporally.

The final transformation, *intercoordination,* is the one rule that describes how combination moves behavior to a higher level. In conjunction with optimal level, it specifies how a person's skills at one level are transformed to the next level. At the beginning of the process, the child has two well-formed skills at a given level. The two skills function separately from each other until some object or event in

the world induces the child to relate the two skills. If at this point the child is capable of the next developmental level, she will unravel the relationship between the two skills, gradually intercoordinating them.

For example, two Level 5 social roles can be intercoordinated into a Level 6 understanding of the intersection between social roles. In one Level 5 skill, a child pretends that a doctor doll examines a patient doll, who interacts appropriately. In another Level 5 skill, the child pretends that a father doll interacts with a daughter doll, who responds appropriately. By intercoordinating these two social roles, the child constructs a Level 6 role intersection (step 5) in which a doctor who is also a father interacts appropriately with a patient who is also a daughter. As a result of the intercoordination, the child can control the relations between the several social roles and so can understand that two people interacting can fulfill two complementary roles at the same time. Once this simple Level 6 role intersection has been mastered, more complex intersections can be built by means of the other transformations, such as the addition by compounding of a nurse who is also the patient's mother.

These four transformation rules specify different ways of rewriting skills. Within a domain the rules can be used to analyze and predict sequences of skill acquisition, including both steps that must be ordered in a sequence and steps that cannot be consistently ordered with respect to one another. It is no trivial matter to predict developmental sequences (Bertenthal, 1981; Flavell, 1972; Fischer & Bullock, 1981; Siegler, 1981), and the transformation rules seem to provide a useful framework for doing so.

Many Paths from a Few Transformations

Cognitive developmentalists, especially Piagetians, commonly assume that there is one and only one path for development in any domain (e.g., Piaget, 1970a,b). That is, all children are believed to pass through the same steps or stages of development. Skill theory postulates, to the contrary, that when specific skills are considered, different people follow different developmental paths (Fischer & Corrigan, 1981; Fischer & Farrar, 1987; see also Bullock, 1983; Flavell, 1982; Kuhn & Phelps, 1982). The steps that people move through in mastering a domain may vary enormously in detail from one person to the next.

Variations in the environment alone will produce such differences, because every person's specific experiences are different from every other person's. For example, the types of dolls available to a preschool child will influence the types of social roles the child will construct when playing with those dolls. The child who plays with a baby doll and a mommy doll is likely at an early age to construct a skill for acting out a mother–child relationship, whereas the child who plays with a doctor doll and a nurse doll will construct different role skills. Likewise, various nine-year-olds will master the skills of addition through different paths, depending on their experiences with numbers and arithmetic tasks (see Lawler, 1981).

Similarly, variations in the person alone will produce differences in developmental paths. People seem to differ widely in the facility with which they can master certain kinds of materials, as illustrated by wide variations in verbal, spatial, and mathematical abilities (Horn, 1976; Sternberg, 1980). When variations in other

person factors such as motivation and activity level are considered, it is evident that individuals will demonstrate important differences in developmental paths.

Since skills always involve influences from both person and environment, the degree of variation in developmental sequence will inevitably be large. It will be difficult to find two children who spontaneously develop through exactly the same steps in any domain.

There are, of course, important equivalences of skills across individuals, especially when those skills are analyzed globally. Various nine-year-olds, for example, have skills for addition that typically produce the same answers to simple addition problems. Likewise, in pretend play, preschoolers living in similar environments show many equivalences in the general types of developmental paths they demonstrate, as illustrated by the sequence outlined in Table 7.3.

The general developmental levels postulated by skill theory describe one highly general type of equivalence. When sequences are described in more detail, however, every child will show a different developmental path. In other words, people show wide variations in developmental paths because the specific skills they build are different. On the other hand, their skills all pass through the same general developmental levels.

Although developmental paths may vary widely, the transformation rules underlying them do not vary, according to skill theory. The many paths can all be characterized by the same small set of transformation rules. Both the skills that individuals start with and the way in which they use the transformation rules do vary, and therefore developmental paths vary. Yet all skill acquisitions at all ages involve the same limited group of transformation rules. This postulate of skill theory is similar to the position taken by many information-processing theorists that the same fundamental acquisition processes occur in development, learning, and problem solving at all ages (see Goodman, 1980; Klahr, 1984; Klahr & Wallace, 1976; McGuinness, Pribram, & Pirnazar chapter; MacWhinney, 1978; Sternberg, 1980, 1984).

How Optimal Level Limits Transformations

The transformation rules specify how skills can be changed and thereby predict which sequences of skill acquisition can occur, but there is an important limit on application of rules—the person's optimal level. The type of transformation that can be applied to existing skills is restricted by the highest level of which the individual is capable.

The most basic form of this restriction involves the transformation rule for moving to a higher level, intercoordination. With two skills that are already at the person's optimal level, intercoordination cannot occur because the person is not capable of building a skill beyond her upper limit. In the social role example, a four-and-one-half-year-old who has several Level 5 skills for social roles can make those skills more complex via the other transformations; but she cannot intercoordinate two of the skills to form a Level 6 role intersection.

Another form of limitation is hypothesized to occur when a new optimal level is first emerging: The person cannot yet apply the within-level transformations to

the simple skills just built at her new level. For focusing, the period of this limitation may be brief; but for compounding it is probably longer. Consider a six-year-old girl who has just began to be capable of Level 6 and has constructed a simple role intersection such as the relation of doctor–father to patient–daughter. Because of the hypothesized limitation, she cannot extend that intersection by compounding, by adding, say, nurse–mother. For all within-level transformations, the duration of this limit is brief relative to the age interval between levels. By the time the girl becomes six and a half or seven years old, she will be able to compound her skill to include three role intersections.

For each optimal level, then, there is development of the limitations on transformation. As the level initially emerges, the person cannot apply the within-level transformation. This limitation gradually recedes, first for the simpler rules and finally for compounding. At that point the within-level limit no longer exists, and the only restriction is on moving to a higher level. This upper bound remains until the next optimal level begins to emerge.

Adult Functioning Below Optimal Level

Developmental research suggests that after the first few years of life, children typically function below optimal level (Fischer & Elmendorf, 1986). The size of this developmental range between functional and optimal levels seems to grow especially large during adolescence and adulthood (Fischer, Hand, & Russell, 1984). In the arithmetic study, for example, the ordinary or spontaneous testing conditions generally produced performance far below optimum.

This conclusion is supported by a vast array of research, including studies of Inhelder and Piaget's (1955/1958) tasks for assessing formal operations. Many adolescents and adults can readily pass a few of the easiest of Piaget's formal-operations tasks, but they fail the rest of them (Martarano, 1977; Neimark, 1975). Most of the tasks they fail seem to require the higher levels of abstractions, beyond Level 7 single abstractions (Fischer & Lamborn, 1989). Adults, it seems, routinely function at the lowest levels of abstraction. Only under special circumstances do they demonstrate abstractions at the highest levels.

Conclusion

Both data and theory indicate that cognitive development does not end with early adolescence but continues into adulthood. New capacities develop that allow the individual to relate abstractions in increasingly complex ways. These capacities are hypothesized to develop through four successive levels—single abstractions, abstract mappings, abstract systems, and principles integrating abstract systems.

Two different types of processes are involved in developmental transitions and in many other systematic changes in the organization of behavior. (1) Optimal level is the upper limit on the complexity of skills that the person can construct, and it develops through the series of hierarchically organized levels for abstractions. (2)

Skill acquisition processes are the rules by which a skill can be transformed into something more complex or advanced. Together these two types of processes account for both large and small changes in cognitive development.

Stagelike change to a new optimal level is most evident when a person is tested under environmental conditions that produce optimal performance. With the types of testing conditions typically used in psychological research, optimal performance is not assessed; consequently, developmental change appears to be slow and gradual. When environmental conditions such as practice, instruction, and support are thus taken into account, it becomes evident that stagelike and gradual changes can both occur in the same person.

Organismic factors contribute to the optimal levels too. According to the brain-growth hypothesis, each new optimal level is associated with spurts in the growth of neural networks in the cortex of the brain. Research evidence supports an association between cognitive levels and spurts in the growth of brain electrical activity.

The optimal-level effects for abstract capacities have powerful implications for education, as well as for any other enterprise involving adolescents or young adults. Apparently, there are certain kinds of concepts and relations between concepts that will pose great difficulty for students who have not yet reached the highest developmental levels. Of course, intelligent individuals will be able to learn parts of these concepts and thus mimic high-level functioning, but only at the highest levels will students be able to master such concepts in a straightforward manner.

When people develop a new optimal level, what changes is the most complex skill they can construct and control. Their general cognitive functioning does not change abruptly, because to function at the new level they must actually build specific skills at that level. The building of such skills takes time and effort and proceeds according to skill-transformation processes. Even when students have the capacity to function at a certain level, they cannot be expected to do so easily or automatically. They need both time for constructing the needed skills and environmental support to stimulate and guide the construction.

The environment plays an important role in supporting not only the construction of skills but also their internalization and use. The construction of an optimal-level skill in a specific domain is insufficient to lead to functioning at that level in that domain. There is a gap, called the developmental range, between people's optimal level and the level at which they ordinarily function. This gap seems to grow larger at the highest levels. Although environmental support is required for optimal functioning at any developmental level, it seems to be especially important at the highest levels of abstraction. One of the most important roles of educational institutions may well be to provide the support that is necessary for functioning at high levels of abstraction.

Indeed, people may be virtually incapable of routinely using high-level skills without supportive environments like those provided by educational institutions such as high schools and colleges. At lower cognitive levels, the ordinary environment seems to provide infants and children with the support they need for functioning near optimum. At the highest levels, the ordinary environment will no longer suffice. Socially constructed environments designed to facilitate abstract thinking seem to be essential (Fischer & Bullock, 1984; Rest, 1983).

Note

1. Preparation of this article was supported by grants from the Spencer Foundation, the Carnegie Corporation of New York, and the Foundation for Child Development. The statements made and views expressed are solely the responsibility of the authors. The authors would like to thank Daniel Bullock, Helen Hand, Karen Kitchener, and Malcolm Watson for their contributions.

Portions of this chapter are reprinted, with permission of the publishers, from articles appearing in:

R. Mines & K. Kitchener (Eds.), *Adult cognitive development: Methods and models* (pp. 57–75). New York: Praeger.

R. J. Sternberg (Ed.), *Mechanisms of cognitive development* (pp. 45–80). San Francisco: W. H. Freeman & Co.

III

THEORIES OF ADVANCED
MORAL DEVELOPMENT

8

Beyond Justice Reasoning: Moral Development and Consideration of a Seventh Stage

Lawrence Kohlberg* and Robert A. Ryncarz

In 1958 I began longitudinal and cross-cultural research defining and validating a sequence of six stages of justice reasoning (Kohlberg, 1958). These stages conform not only to strict empirical criteria of stages but to a philosophic model of moral rationality as conceived by Western philosophers such as Kant and Rawls, a "rational reconstruction of ontogenesis" in Habermas' terms (Habermas, 1983).

Since 1973, I have also speculated about mystical forms of experience and religious or metaphysical concepts that articulate these forms of experience, conceptions I have referred to as a metaphoric *Stage 7* (Kohlberg, 1973a,b; 1974; 1981a; 1984; 1987). At this level a sense of unity with the cosmos, nature, or God is expressed in such a way as to resolve such ultimate ethical questions as, "Why be just in a universe filled with injustice, pain, and death?" This approach takes the form of what may be termed a *natural law* orientation toward ethical questions, an area that has been enriched by James Fowler's (1981) empirical study of stages of *faith*. In this article I have summarized my thinking concerning this issue. Although I do not believe that the same level of empirical or philosophic precision can be reached on the issue of Stage 7 as can be achieved on the stages of justice reasoning, theorizing about a Stage 7 still falls within the domain of science if science is broadly defined and conceived.

Six Stages of Moral Reasoning

Over the past 25 years, the stage theory model of moral development has received considerable empirical and theoretical attention while at the same time undergoing conceptual and methodological refinement (Kohlberg, 1969; Kohlberg, Levine, & Hewer, 1983; Colby & Kohlberg, 1986; Kohlberg, 1986). Built upon the seminal ideas of Dewey (Dewey & Tufts, 1932) and Piaget (1932/1948) and incorporating the characteristics of cognitive-developmental stage theory, it traces the progression of moral development through six stages of justice reasoning. This progression is marked chiefly by changes in sociomoral perspective: beginning from a self-inter-

*Deceased

ested egoistic social perspective, leading to one that is consciously shared by other group members or by society as a whole, and culminating in an autonomous, *prior-to-society* perspective where the individual rationally defines his or her own values and principles in a universalizable way. Table 8.1 outlines a current formulation of the six stages of moral judgment along with a description of the social perspective taken at each stage.

A Metaphorical Stage 7

Even after attainment of Stage 6's clear awareness of universal principles, a fundamental ethical question still remains, namely, "Why be moral? Why be just in a universe that appears unjust?" This question asks whether there is any support in reality or nature for acting according to universal moral principles. This is, of course, one of the problems thought to be unanswerable at the stage of transitional relativism, Stage 4½ in Table 8.1. The Stage 5 answer, the social contract, is essentially a compromise answer, the answer that I pursue my own happiness socially or with due regard to the rights and welfare of others. Although Stage 6 ethical principles offer a more complete solution to the problem of relativity of values than those of Stage 5, they have an even less complete solution for the problem, "Why be moral?" The answer to this question entails the further question, "Why live?"; thus, ultimate moral maturity requires a mature solution to the question of the meaning of life. This, in turn, is hardly a moral question per se; it is an ontological one. Not only is the question not a moral question, but it is not a question resolvable on purely logical or rational grounds, as moral questions are. Nevertheless, I have posited a purely metaphorical notion of a Stage 7 as pointing to some meaningful solutions to these questions that are compatible with rational science and rational ethics. The central characteristic of all these Stage 7 solutions is that they involve experience of a nonegoistic or nondualistic variety. The logic of such experience is sometimes expressed in theistic terms, but it need not be. Its essence is the sense of being a part of the whole of life and the adoption of a cosmic, as opposed to a universal humanistic (Stage 6) perspective.

According to many accounts described in religious and metaphysical literature, movement toward a cosmic perspective often begins with experience of despair. This state can arise when we first begin to see our life as finite from some more infinite perspective. Here questions arising about the meaningfulness of our life are questions about the meaningfulness of the finite from the perspective of the infinite. The resolution of this state, which I call *Stage 7,* represents a continuation of the process of taking a more cosmic perspective that began with the realization of the finitude of our individual self. It represents, in a sense, a shift from figure to ground. In the first state, we are the self seen from the distance of the cosmic or infinite. In the state of mind I metaphorically term Stage 7, we identify ourselves with the cosmic or infinite perspective and value life from its standpoint. Spinoza, a believer in principled ethics and in a science of natural laws, described this state of mind as the "union of the mind with the whole of nature." Even persons who are not religious may temporarily achieve this state of mind in certain situations, such as when on a mountaintop or before the ocean. At such a time, what is ordinarily back-

Table 8.1 The Six Stages of Moral Judgment

Level A. Preconventional Level

Stage 1. The Stage of Punishment and Obedience

Content

Right is literal obedience to rules and authority, avoiding punishment, and not doing physical harm.

1. What is right is to avoid breaking rules, to obey for obedience' sake, and to avoid doing physical damage to people and property.
2. The reasons for doing right are avoidance of punishment and the superior power of authorities.

Social Perspective

This stage takes an egocentric point of view. A person at this stage doesn't consider the interests of others or recognize they differ from actor's, and doesn't relate two points of view. Actions are judged in terms of physical consequences rather than in terms of psychological interests of others. Authority's perspective is confused with one's own.

Stage 2. The Stage of Individual Instrumental Purpose and Exchange

Content

Right is serving one's own or other's needs and making fair deals in terms of concrete exchange.

1. What is right is following rules when it is to someone's immediate interest. Right is acting to meet one's own interests and needs and letting others do the same. Right is also what is fair; that is, what is an equal exchange, a deal, an agreement.
2. The reason for doing right is to serve one's own needs or interests in a world where one must recognize that other people have their interests, too.

Social Perspective

This stage takes a concrete individualistic perspective. A person at this stage separates own interests and points of view from those of authorities and others. He or she is aware everybody has individual interests to pursue and these conflict, so that right is relative (in the concrete individualistic sense). The person integrates or relates conflicting individual interests to one another through instrumental exchange of services, through instrumental need for the other and the other's goodwill, or through fairness giving each person the same amount.

Level B. Conventional Level

Stage 3. The Stage of Mutual Interpersonal Expectations, Relationships, and Conformity

Content

The right is playing a good (nice) role, being concerned about the other people and their feelings, keeping loyalty and trust with partners, and being motivated to follow rules and expectations.

1. What is right is living up to what is expected by people close to one or what people generally expect of people in one's role as son, sister, friend, and so on. "Being good" is important and means having good motives, showing concern about others. It also means keeping mutual relationships, maintaining trust, loyalty, respect, and gratitude.
2. Reasons for doing right are needing to be good in one's own eyes and those of others, caring for others, and because if one puts oneself in the other person's place one would want good behavior from the self (Golden Rule).

Social Perspective

This stage takes the perspective of the individual in relationship to other individuals. A person at this stage is aware of shared feelings, agreements, and expectations, which take primacy over individual interests. The person relates points of view through the "concrete Golden Rule," putting oneself in the other person's shoes. He or she does not consider generalized "system" perspective.

Stage 4. The Stage of Social System and Conscience Maintenance

Content

The right is doing one's duty in society, upholding the social order, and maintaining the welfare of society or the group.

Table 8.1 (Continued)

1. What is right is fulfilling the actual duties to which one has agreed. Laws are to be upheld except in extreme cases where they conflict with other fixed social duties and rights. Right is also contributing to society, the group, or institution.
2. The reasons for doing right are to keep the institution going as a whole, self-respect or conscience as meeting one's defined obligations, or the consequences: "What if everyone did it?"

Social Perspective

This stage differentiates societal point of view from interpersonal agreement or motives. A person at this stage takes the viewpoint of the system, which defines roles and rules. He or she considers individual relations in terms of place in the system.

Level B/C. Transitional Level

This level is postconventional but not yet principled.

Content of Transition

At Stage 4½, choice is personal and subjective. It is based on emotions, conscience is seen as arbitrary and relative, as are ideas such as "duty" and "morally right."

Transitional Social Perspective

At this stage, the perspective is that of an individual standing outside of his own society and considering himself as an individual making decisions without a generalized commitment or contract with society. One can pick and choose obligations, which are defined by particular societies, but one has no principles for such choice.

Level C. Postconventional and Principled Level

Moral decisions are generated from rights, values, or principles that are (or could be) agreeable to all individuals composing or creating a society designed to have fair and beneficial practices.

Stage 5. *The Stage of Prior Rights and Social Contract or Utility*

Content

The right is upholding the basic rights, values, and legal contracts of a society, even when they conflict with the concrete rules and laws of the group.

1. What is right is being aware of the fact that people hold a variety of values and opinions, that most values and rules are relative to one's group. These "relative" rules should usually be upheld, however, in the interest of impartiality and because they are the social contract. Some nonrelative values and rights such as life, and liberty, however, must be upheld in any society and regardless of majority opinion.
2. Reasons for doing right are, in general, feeling obligated to obey the law because one has made a social contract to make and abide by laws for the good of all and to protect their own rights and the rights of others. Family, friendship, trust, and work obligations are also commitments or contracts freely entered into and entail respect for the rights of others. One is concerned that laws and duties be based on rational calculation of overall utility: "the greatest good for the greatest number."

Social Perspective

This stage takes a prior-to-society perspective—that of a rational individual aware of values and rights prior to social attachments and contracts. The person integrates perspectives by formal mechanisms of agreement, contract, objective impartiality, and due process. He or she considers the moral point of view and the legal point of view, recognizes they conflict, and finds it difficult to integrate them.

Stage 6. *The Stage of Universal Ethical Principles*

Content

This stage assumes guidance by universal ethical principles that all humanity should follow.

1. Regarding what is right, Stage 6 is guided by universal ethical principles. Particular laws or social agreements are usually valid because they rest on such principles. When laws violate these principles, one acts in accordance with the principle. Principles are universal principles of justice: the equality of human rights

Table 8.1 (Continued)

and respect for the dignity of human beings as individuals. These are not merely values that are recognized, but are also principles used to generate particular decisions.
2. The reason for doing right is that, as a rational person, one has seen the validity of principles and has become committed to them.

Social Perspective

This stage takes the perspective of a moral point of view from which social arrangements derive or on which they are grounded. The perspective is that of any rational individual recognizing the nature of morality or the basic moral premise of respect for other persons as ends, not means.

Source: This table was reprinted from L. Kohlberg, *Essays in Moral Development,* Vol. I, *The Philosophy of Moral Development* (New York: Harper & Row, 1981a), pp. 409–412.

ground becomes foreground, and the self is no longer figure to the ground. We sense the unity of the whole and ourselves as part of that unity. This experience of unity, often treated as a mere rush of mystic feeling, is also associated with a structure of conviction.

The reversal of figure and ground felt in the contemplative moment has its analogy in the development of belief. This development, in turn, has some parallels to the movement of moral thought. The adolescent crisis of relativism, Stage 4½, can occur only because there is a dim apprehension of some more universal ethical standard in terms of which the cultural code is relative and arbitrary. To explore the crisis of relativism thoroughly and consistently is to decenter from the self, reverse figure and ground, and see as figure the vague standpoint of principle that is the background of the sense of relativity. Similarly, one may argue that the crisis of despair precipitated by the recognition of one's finite character from the perspective of the infinite, when thoroughly and courageously explored, leads to a figure–ground shift that reveals the positive validity of the cosmic perspective implicit in it.

Stage 7 and Natural Law Theory

The concept of such a Stage 7 is a familiar one in our Western philosophic tradition, one form of which has appeared within natural law doctrines. Natural law theory generally holds that human responsibilities, duties, and rights are not arbitrary or dependent upon social convention but are objectively grounded as laws of nature. It further holds that individuals can apprehend these laws of nature through the exercise of reason. This natural law theory has been the theory held by many exemplars of education for justice. Two great moral educators who lived their lives as educators for justice are Socrates and Martin Luther King, Jr. Both Socrates and King held a natural law theory in their ethical–ontological beliefs. Their willingness to live by moral principles was partly based on their faith in moral principles as an expression of human reason and partly on their faith in justice, which was rooted in a cosmic perspective. Their resoluteness came from seeing principles of justice as not only a social contract to resolve conflicts in a civil society but as the reflection of an order inherent in both human nature and the natural or cosmic order.

Socrates and King recognized that their own questioning of society's laws must

occur in a context in which civil disobedience was civil, public, and informed by respect for law. Both recognized, however, a natural higher law grounded in human reason and prescribing respect for human personality. In his "Letter from Birmingham Jail," King (1963/1976) explained his conception of the relation of civil law to natural law principles of justice: "One may well ask, 'How can you advocate breaking some laws and obeying others?' The answer lies in the fact that there are two types of laws: just and unjust. One has not only a legal but a moral responsibility to obey just laws. Conversely, one has a moral responsibility to disobey unjust laws . . . [though] one . . . must do so openly, lovingly and with a willingness to accept the penalty" (p. 215).

King agrees with St. Thomas Aquinas' assertion that "an unjust law is a human law that is not rooted in eternal law and natural law." He concludes that "any law that uplifts human personality is just [and] any law that degrades human personality is unjust" (p. 215).

A first translation of King's natural law assumption into the theory developed in this chapter would state that Stage 6 moral principles enjoining the uplifting of human personality are *eternal and natural law* in the sense that they are the universal outgrowth of the development of human nature. From the perspective of a psychology of human nature, moral stage theory states that human conceptions of moral law are not the product of internalizing arbitrary and culturally relative societal norms. They are, rather, outcomes of universal human nature developing under universal aspects of the human condition, and in that sense they are *natural*. King is assuming more than a psychology, however. He is also making an ontological or metaphysical assumption. He is assuming that our consciousness of justice or moral law is parallel to, or in harmony with, our consciousness of the ultimate power or laws governing the larger cosmic order.

King's natural law assumption is not specific to a particular philosophy or creed. Other proponents of natural law theory, such as the Stoics and Spinoza, equated ultimate power, being, or reality with the whole of nature and natural law known by rational science. From this perspective, human moral law is a part of the larger natural order or law embodied in the cosmos. Kant, who in a broad sense held a natural law theory, found the only *knowable* objects of reverence to be the "starry sky above and the moral law within" and felt that the consciousness of moral law required a faith in a parallelism between our consciousness of moral law and the nature of ultimate reality.

Divine Command and Emotivist Theories of Morality

Stage 7's natural law perspective stands in sharp contrast to two other major theoretical perspectives on morality and the moral order we will now consider. The first, divine command theory, is a fundamentalist theory that states that morality is ultimately defined or rests upon divine command as revealed by the Bible or other documents of revelation. The second, emotivist theory, states that morality is in part, and religion is altogether, an "illusion" born of irrational human fantasy and conflict.

Divine Command Theory

In the *Euthyphro,* Plato records a dialogue between Socrates and Euthyphro that illustrates the incompatibility of rational inquiry with divine command theory. Euthyphro, a believer in divine command theory, has denounced his father for what Euthyphro believes is an act of impiety. Euthyphro believes his own denunciation of his father is an act of piety. Socrates asks Euthyphro to define piety, and Euthyphro defines it as "acting in a way the gods approve (or what the gods command)." Socrates attempts to get Euthyphro to clarify whether an act is virtuous or pious because the gods command or approve the action or whether the gods approve the action because it is virtuous or pious in the light of some standard or quality of the action independent of the gods' approval. Euthyphro is totally unable to address the question and gets lost in confusion as a result.

The logical confusion in Euthyphro's mind, as well as in the minds of modern proponents of divine command theory, is the confusion that can be identified as a form of the *naturalistic fallacy,* which is the general fallacy that *ought* statements can be derived directly from, or reduced to, *is* statements. The particular form of the fallacy involved in divine command theory is the fallacy that "*X* ought to be done" or "*X* is just" can be derived from the statement "*X* is a command of God," "*X* is in the Bible," "*X* is one of the Ten Commandments," "*X* will be rewarded by God," and so on.

At first, one might think that the natural law perspective I describe represents another form of the naturalistic fallacy, like the divine command theory just critiqued. One may argue that natural law theories commit the naturalistic fallacy insofar as they deduce moral prescriptions from "facts" about the natural order. The natural law assumption that I endorse, however, is not the derivation of moral principles from factual generalizations but is, rather, the assumption that there are certain shared features of the natural order as known by science or metaphysics and of the moral order as known by moral philosophy. From this point of view, moral principles are autonomous; they cannot be derived from or reduced to scientific laws or metaphysical statements. Moral principles, however, are structures that have features that parallel ontological and scientific structures; that is, well-developed moral intuitions parallel intuitions about nature or ultimate reality. These intuitions inform a general natural law, ontological orientation and support principles of justice.

Emotivistic Theory of Morality: The Freudian View

Another perspective on morality that contrasts with the Stage 7, natural law perspective is emotivistic theory. Emotivism is an offshoot in ethics of the general philosophy called *positivism* or *logical positivism*. Emotivists say that moral judgments have no meanings as statements of truth or falsity, in contrast to scientific judgments or statements that have meaning as predictors of sense data. Denying kinds of meaning and validity other than scientific truth meaning, emotivists say that the only meaning of moral judgments is as expressions of emotional states of approval and disapproval.

Probably the most important and knowledge-producing emotivist theory of

morality is that of Freud. According to Freud, moral judgments are primarily expressions of the constellation of emotional structures termed the *superego*. The superego is conceived of partly as culturally universal in its direction against incest and aggression in the family, partly as arbitrary and relative in incorporating the arbitrary norms of the culture and the parents. In any case, the foundations of moral judgment are considered to be irrational and relative (Gilligan, 1976). Although the superego and the sense of guilt that arises from its moral judgments have no direct rational basis, the superego serves a necessary function, the control of antisocial impulses and desires. The superego and its guilt are according to Freud the origin of both "civilization and its discontents" (Freud, 1930).

A generation of neo-Freudian development has softened the impact of Freud's harsh view of morality. In the hands of Erik Erikson, neo-Freudian interpretation gives rise to a sensitive psychology of adult moral and ethical development in individuals such as Martin Luther and Mohandas Gandhi. Philosophically, however, Erikson does not really provide a way out from Freud's reduction of moral judgments and meanings to emotive states rooted in childhood illusions and conflicts. The implications of an emotivist theory of morality becomes similar to that of divine command theory in that they both agree that morality is not psychologically founded in rationality.

Natural Law Theories of Ethical and Ontological Orientation

I have rejected two theories of the relation between morality and religious or ontological orientation: divine command theory and emotivist theory (in its Freudian form). I have suggested that there is a class of theories about the relation between morality and ontological orientation that I do accept: theories of natural law. The following section illustrates two different expressions of natural law theory in the metaphysics of Marcus Aurelius and Benedict de Spinoza.

Natural Law Justice—Marcus Aurelius

An example of an individual who held a natural law perspective is the Roman emperor Marcus Aurelius. I choose him because in the world of the Roman empire, in which absolute power corrupted absolutely, this man with absolute power was the only man who was absolutely incorruptible, absolutely principled.

Aurelius, by nature a philosopher who hated war and killing, felt compelled by his sense of principle to exile himself from Rome to lead the army to preserve what he saw as human civilization and rights against barbarian attack. He found himself surrounded by men and women who had no understanding of his principles. Those closest to him betrayed him. Nevertheless, he found his way not only to forgive but also to love his betrayers. His statement of faith is given in his personal journal, usually called the *Meditations*.

The content of the faith of Aurelius, like that of all Stoics, is simple. It starts with the belief that the universe is lawful, knowable, and evolving. In referring to the ultimate, lawful, rational, and evolving principle of the universe, Marcus Aurelius refers to it as *God* or *Nature,* using these terms interchangeably. From his belief

he derives a natural law view of morality that gives him the strength to act in terms of universal principles of justice in a seemingly unjust world. It also gives him the peace that comes from sensing oneself as a finite part of an infinite whole.

With regard to the place of the individual in the cosmos, Aurelius says:

> Whether the universe is [a concourse of] atoms, or nature [is a system], let this first be established, that I am a part of the whole which is governed by nature; next, I am in a manner intimately related to the parts which are of the same kind with myself. For remembering this, inasmuch as I am a part, I shall be discontented with none of the things which are assigned to me out of the whole; for nothing is injurious to the part, if it is for the advantage of the whole (Aurelius, 1937, p. 275).

The intimate relationship of the individual with the whole of nature underlies the ethics of Aurelius: "Inasmuch as I am in a manner intimately related to the parts which are of the same kind with myself, I shall do nothing unsocial, but I shall rather direct myself to the things which are of the same kind with myself, and I shall turn all my efforts to the common interest, and divert them from the contrary" (Aurelius, 1937, p. 276).

Aurelius' principles of conduct flow from his ethical–ontological view. He says:

> [I]t is no way right to be offended with men, but it is thy duty to care for them and to bear with them gently; and yet to remember that thy departure will be not from men who have the same principles as thyself.
>
> He who does wrong does wrong against himself. He who acts unjustly acts unjustly to himself, because he makes himself bad.
>
> He often acts unjustly who does not do a certain thing; not only he who does a certain thing.
>
> Thy present opinion founded on understanding, and thy present conduct directed to social good, and thy present disposition of contentment with everything which happens—that is enough (Aurelius, 1937, p. 266).

Marcus Aurelius thus represents a version of natural law thinking in which principles of justice are in harmony with or parallel to the larger cosmic order. In expressing his cosmic perspective in such simple, even stark, terms, he succeeds in illuminating how, in any culture, a person with the courage and thoughtfulness to think through the human condition can achieve moral and spiritual maturity.

Spinoza's Theory of Natural Law

Another version of the achievement of a cosmic perspective on morality is evident in Spinoza's theory of natural law. Spinoza's ethical views, described in his *Ethics* (1930), were firmly grounded on a natural science psychology that was a great ancestor of Freud's rigorously deterministic theory. It was also grounded on a rational moral and political philosophy of a *natural rights* social contract variety. His ethical system had no less a purpose than the development of a coherent scheme that if followed would make all people free or happy.

Spinoza states that experience has convinced him that none of the objects that people usually set before themselves can yield complete satisfaction of desire. Pleasure, power, and wealth—all fail to serve as a source of permanent, unbroken enjoyment. They fail because of their nature. It is their nature to be perishable and

finite. Pleasures in activities sensed as unreal are not abiding. Hedonism is no solution for Spinoza because we need not only a life of pleasure but also a *real life*. According to Spinoza, self-realization is the fundamental striving of our nature, and to achieve self-realization is to *become real*.

If hedonism (taking our own pleasures as a primary object of concern) does not solve the central problem of life and its meaning, neither does morality nor altruism (taking the pleasures and pains of others as central concerns) fully solve these problems. Put differently, if we are to love others in a way satisfactory to themselves and others, it must be without possessiveness, domination, jealousy, or fear of loss. And how are we to do that? Spinoza says, "When I became convinced that things are good and evil, not in themselves, but only as our affections are aroused by them, I finally decided to ask whether there is a true good, one that gives its goodness of itself and by which alone our affections might be aroused; nay, rather, whether there were something which when found and possessed, could be kept forever with perfect and unbroken joy."

Spinoza is convinced that we cannot escape the dominion of our affections. We are the slaves of the love of something. The loves that enslave can be overcome only if there is and can be found an object that inspires a love that frees. If pleasure and power are not intrinsic ends, only some sort of love can be an intrinsic end. We only attain a stronger and more stable state of the self if we attain a stronger and more stable love of something. This love, Spinoza says, involves the love of something eternal and infinite. Can such an object be found? Spinoza thinks that we ought rather to ask, "What is the way to find it? What does trying to find it involve?" His answer is, "It involves the discovery of the union of the mind with the whole of nature." In other words, the ideal state of human nature is "that in which we know the union of man's mind with the whole of nature." What does Spinoza mean by this? It is self-evident that our bodies are a part of nature. It is not so clear to us that our minds are also a part of nature. But, Spinoza says, "Our mind is also a part of Nature; that is, Nature has an infinite power of thinking which contains subjectively the whole of Nature. The human mind is this power, not as infinite and perceiving the whole of nature, but as finite and perceiving only the human body."

How can this vision of reality be used to eliminate suffering and promote the growth of freedom and happiness? According to Spinoza, our normal joys are the results of our self-actualization, of activities in which our competence, power, and knowledge are enhanced, especially when our self-actualization is linked to the self-actualization of others. But ultimately our joy in self-actualization is crushed by our awareness that ourselves and the selves of others are only limited parts of a larger reality. As we first become aware of the larger reality that is the background of our activities, we are likely to be oppressed by a sense of the futility of all that we do and have and are. The *once-born* reaction to this sense of futility is to refocus on our own activities and the present in which they exist. We are bound to be miserable and unhappy, Spinoza thinks, as long as we are ignorant of our true place in nature.

Understanding of our place in nature provides the way to active acceptance and love of life. In part, Spinoza says, this depends on acceptance of events and our own actions as causally determined and acceptance of the limits of our power in

the face of Nature. In part, he says, it depends on more active love of Nature and sense of unity with it which comes with awareness of ourselves as part of Nature.

Spinoza is saying that if we understand Life or Nature, we cannot help but love it and all things in it. And if we love Life or Nature, we become capable of over-coming all the pains of life. The pains of life are caused by the disappointments or losses in our lives of particular people or aims. But if we are aware of the relation-ship of all people and things to the whole of Nature, then we continue to love the whole in spite of the disappointments or losses. For Spinoza, the demand for our survival can be met only by identification or union with something more eternal. This knowledge and love of Nature is a form of union. Our mind is part of a whole, Spinoza claims, and if we know and love the eternal, we ourselves are in some sense eternal.

The Relationship of Ontological Thought to Stages of Moral Judgment

I have argued philosophically that in order to avoid falling into the naturalistic fallacy, morality must be defined as an autonomous realm of discourse. I now wish to take up the psychological question of the relationship of ontological thought, such as that evidenced in the previous section, to stages of moral judgment. To do this, the functions of moral thinking and ontological thought must first be clarified. The function of moral or justice reasoning is to resolve competing claims among individuals on the basis of a norm or principle. The primary function of ontological thought is to address the issue of how morality and life's meaning fit within the context of one's relation to the universe, the transcendent, or sense of the whole.

In seeking to understand the reciprocal relationship of ontological thought to morality, Toulmin (1950) points out that the domain of moral reasoning is not fully self-enclosed but that moral questions can point beyond themselves to the onto-logical domain. He argues that if we continually ask for the reasons a particular norm (such as keeping a promise) should be upheld, we will, after a time, exhaust the possible moral reasons supporting the norm. We will find ourselves asking, "Why be moral at all?"—a question that can no longer be answered strictly on moral grounds. The "Why be moral?" question appears at the limit of moral inquiry and raises a new problem for consideration, namely, the fundamental meaningfulness of human activity. Toulmin states that the ontological problem is one in which the individual, finite and uncertain, seeks for assurance in the future.

It is important to note that the ontological response to the limit question of morality respects the integrity of the moral domain in a way in which other non-moral responses do not. The philosopher F. H. Bradley discusses the nature of the question, "Why be moral?" in a way that is helpful. He states that the question is reasonable but strange because, "We feel when we ask it, that we are wholly removed from the moral point of view" (Bradley, 1876/1962, p. 58). Bradley refutes the answer of ethical egoism by showing that attempts to base morality on nonmoral ends, such as pleasure, contradict the very meaning of morality. "To do good for its own sake is virtue, to do it for some ulterior end or object not itself good, is never virtue; and never to act but for the sake of an end, other than doing

well and right, is the mark of vice" (Bradley, 1876/1962, p. 62). Thus, the question makes no sense if we take it to mean, "What is the payoff for being moral?" The question, "Why be moral?" is a question about the meaningfulness of one's existence as a rational being.

Although the "Why be moral?" question may be raised philosophically, it is more commonly raised existentially when one is conflicted between the tension of one's duty and one's desire for happiness or between one's ethical ideals and the reality of injustice. Not only can we not justify being moral on the basis of a nonmoral end such as pleasure or divine reward, but human experience as epitomized in the figure of the suffering, upright Job also reveals that virtue, in the short run, may seem to go unrewarded.

Development to a cosmic perspective may offer a way of accepting reality as ultimately trustworthy in spite of the ambiguity occasioned by the seeming gap between the moral ideal and the real and by the existence of suffering. Ontological and ethical development to a cosmic perspective then addresses questions that arise at the boundary of moral reasoning. These questions ask in one form or another, "Why be moral?" Thus ontological questions presuppose moral structures but go beyond them in search for answers.

Fowler's Stages of Faith: Outlining Ontological Development

Over a number of years, James Fowler (1981) interviewed about 400 people aged four to 80 with the expectation of defining what he calls stages of faith that would broadly parallel the moral stages. Fowler's faith stages trace the structural development of a person's tacit view of the world. This development, referred to here as ontological development, is marked by structural changes in the view one has of the universe, or being, and one's relation to it.

Fowler defines faith broadly, as one's orientation to the ultimate environment in terms of what one values as being most relevant and important in life. In Judeo-Christian thought, the ultimate environment is defined as a personal God and his kingdom, which is the endpoint of human history. However, the ultimate environment need not be linked to a personal deity; it is also reflected in pantheistic or agnostic thought. Fowler thus distinguishes faith from religion. Faith is largely tacit, a universal quality of knowing and relating. Religion, however, is a particular expression of faith in which the nature of the ultimate environment is explicitly described in relation to God.

According to Fowler, the most developed stage of faith, Stage 6, Universalizing Faith, is a structure in which one experiences a oneness with the ultimate conditions of one's life and being.

> The persons best described by it have generated faith compositions in which their felt sense of an ultimate environment is inclusive of all being. They have become incarnators and actualizers of the spirit of an inclusive and fulfilled human community. . . . Their community is universal in extent. Particularities are cherished because they are vessels of the universal, and thereby valuable apart from any utilitarian considerations (Fowler, 1981, pp. 200–201).

Fowler points toward such figures as Martin Luther King, Mahatma Gandhi, Mother Teresa of Calcutta, Abraham Lincoln, and Dag Hammarskjold as exemplars of this most mature form of faith. By its description, his highest stage of ontological development, Universalizing Faith, can be generally equated with the moral metaphorical Stage 7.

Empirical Relationship Between Ontological Development and Stages of Moral Judgment

Fowler began his research with the expectation that faith stage development would broadly parallel the stages of moral development. In fact, research has indicated that there is a high empirical correlation between the two sets of stages. Shulik (1979) reports a correlation of .75 between independently made ratings of moral stage and of faith stage, a correlation almost as high as one would find between two alternative forms of the moral dilemma instrument. Beginning with a definition of religious stages as paralleling but going beyond moral stages, Power and I found 81 percent agreement between the moral and religious stages of 21 individuals who had been interviewed on morality and faith (Power & Kohlberg, 1980).

Although there are both theoretical and empirical correlations between the moral stages and Fowler's faith stages, it is uncertain what this means. Fowler's conception of faith stages is holistic and includes, as components of their definitions, Piagetian logical levels and the moral stages (Fowler, 1981, pp. 244–245). At the same time that Fowler's stage definitions include the moral stages, he conceives of his faith stages as being necessary for the grounding of a particular pattern of moral reasoning. In order to engage in making moral judgments, he claims a person must hold a broader system of beliefs and loyalties.

> Every moral perspective, at whatever level of development is anchored in a broader system or belief and loyalties. Every principle of moral action serves some center of value. Even the appeal to autonomy, rationality, and universality as justification for Stage 6 morality are not made *prior* to faith. Rather they are expressions of faith— expressions of trust in, and loyalty to, the valued attributes of autonomy and rationality and the valued ideal of a universal commonwealth of being. There is, I believe, always a faith framework encompassing and supporting the motive to be moral and the exercise of moral logic (Fowler, 1976, p. 209).

Fowler then argues that his stages of faith provide a more extensive framework for understanding moral motivation and accountability than the stages of moral judgment alone. He points out that one's commitments, loyalties, and sense of meaning in life inform the way in which one acts as a moral agent. In Fowler's approach to faith, no clear distinction may be drawn between one's stage of faith and one's stage of morality, because each moral stage presupposes faith even if such faith is tacit. Fowler is, I believe, correct in objecting that moral stages alone cannot provide a sufficient answer to such questions as, "Why be moral?" He is also correct in pointing to stages of faith as adding to our understanding of the person's actual moral decisions and actions. However, Fowler's broad definition of faith, which does not distinguish it from moral judgment, leads to confusions that make

the empirical study of the relationship of ontological development to morality difficult. The difficulty may lie, in part, in Fowler's assumption that his faith stages represent Piagetian structured wholes like the moral stages. This assumption needs to be questioned. I have addressed (Kohlberg, 1984, 1990) the issue of adult development research that remains within the strict Piagetian paradigm and research that does not, distinguishing between *hard structural* and *soft structural* stage models. Hard structural stages have all the formal properties Piaget attributed to them (and from which the equilibration model can be derived), whereas soft stages reflect qualitative age development, but need not have all the stage properties assumed by Piaget. Fowler's faith stage model falls in the latter category.

Hard- and *Soft-*Stage Models of Adult Development Research

It will be of interest to look at the five central criteria and two critical indicators distinguishing hard-stage and soft-stage models, using Piaget's logical stages and the moral stages as examples of the former. The first criterion proposed is that of universality. Hard stages are universal; the stages, as well as their sequence, can be found in every literate culture. Hard stages correspond not only to universal structures, but also to universal functions. In the intellectual and moral domains, logic and moral judgment are culturally universal functions of the mind.

In contrast, soft-stage development should not be looked upon as final phases in a universal, linear sequence. Although soft-stage development can be found in adulthood, such stages are optional, rather than necessary tracks of development. They represent reflective theories that individuals construct and thus are second order, or metamodes of reflection and not new structural forms. Therefore, although stages of logic and morality are culturally universal in that they address problems that face all human beings, stages of metaethical, religious, ontological, or epistemological philosophies are not. Movement in these stages is an option for individuals who are induced by their own personalities and life circumstances into those forms of reflection on life's meaning that soft stages represent. The development of advanced stages of reflective thought may depend more on unique personal experiences than on universal interactive experiences of logical and moral conflict assumed to lead to hard-stage development.

The second criterion of hard stages is that their structures embody operative reasoning. Piagetian structures of reasoning represent interiorized forms of action, or what Piaget calls *operations*. Empirically, this implies that the stages are related to individuals' actions with regard to the physical or social world. The moral stages, for example, relate to moral action in direct ways. The interiorized forms of action that they represent are prescriptive forms of role taking in concrete moral situations. The justice stages, then, represent the different operations of reciprocity, reversibility, equality, and universalizability. In both logical and moral judgment the operative functions of each stage constitute an equilibrated system. Each stage is a form of equilibration that provides resolutions to anomaly. The experience of resolution is the experience of closure within a system or a press toward consistency. In logico-mathematical reasoning, for example, there is a press for consis-

tency bound up with a notion of necessity. In the sociomoral domain, there is a press toward consistency bound up with a notion of oughtness or prescriptivity.

Conversely, soft stages represent theories rather than operations. They are qualitative levels; there is a differentiation as well as a hierarchy of reflectivity that can be identified. But as reflective and self-reflective forms of development, soft stages are not directly linked to action or to problem solving, as are hard stages of operative reasoning. Moreover, there is little or no evidence within any soft-stage model of a press toward consistency.

The third criterion of hard stages is the plausibility of distinguishing content from structure. Separating content from structure is a result of the identification of operations in a given domain. The current Colby and Kohlberg (1986) measurement of moral judgment involves a differentiation of the form of moral judgment from the content of the norm favored by individuals. An interview transcript is classified first by the content of the choice; second, by the content of the justification of that choice; and third, by the value content appealed to in the justification. Only after classifying content according to three content categories do we classify by stage or structure.

Differing from hard stages, soft-stage models do not appear strictly to separate the content of beliefs and theories from the forms of reasoning in any given domain. Typically, propounders of soft-stage models have not attempted to separate favored content from the structure of thought.

The fourth criterion of hard stages is that they be amenable to formalization within a rational normative model. A normative model constitutes a standard or regulative norm (as an established ideal) and has its foundation in human rationality. It must include a philosophical statement of an endpoint or most equilibrated stage. Hard stages represent what Habermas (1983) calls "rational reconstructions of ontogenesis" that presume some endpoint upon which rational agents could agree. The focus of Piaget and myself on morality as deontological justice springs, in part, from our concern with moral and ethical universality in moral judgment. For this reason I have focused particularly on stages of justice reasoning, since regardless of variation in ontological or religious beliefs or ideals of the good life, human beings must strive to achieve rational agreement on principles to resolve conflicting claims or rights.

Soft stages, however, cannot be formalized in a normative model. Development to the higher soft stages is optional. Moreover, although higher soft stages involve increased reflectivity, it is unclear whether some of the stages are of co-equal validity.

The fifth criterion of hard stages is the absence of an ego or a self in the construction of the stages. In studying moral judgment, I have followed Piaget in describing an *epistemic* subject. The epistemic subject is the rational moral subject abstracted from the larger, functioning ego of the self. Differing from hard stages, soft stages always seem to involve an integral concept of the self and of increased psychological self-awareness.

The first critical feature in the distinction between hard and soft stages concerns the relationship between the two. Hard stages are necessary but insufficient for soft stages. For example, Erdynast, Armon, and Nelson (1978) and Armon (1984) found

that fifth-stage moral reasoning is necessary but not sufficient for fifth-stage ideals of the good life. Broughton (1982) found Piaget's logical stages and the moral judgment stages to be necessary but not sufficient for his levels of metaphysical and epistemological thought. Similarly, Shulik, Kohlberg, and Higgins (Kohlberg, 1987) found moral stages to be necessary but not sufficient for Fowler's stages of faith. This relationship lends support to the notion that soft stages embody second order or metamodes of reflection; they represent reflections on the self's morality and logic.

The second critical feature in this distinction is that the terminus of many soft-stage sequences is some mystical, transcendental, postrational level. These levels move beyond a criterion of rationality or autonomy that is inherent in hard stages. In fact, the endpoint of all soft-stage sequences either works from James Mark Baldwin's hyperlogic to some notion of totality of unity or opts for the dialectical that transcends the subjective–objective distinction (Wallwork, 1982).

The reasons for the success of the Piagetian hard scheme in charting logical and moral development may be precisely the reasons that it will not be successful for charting the experience and wisdom of adulthood. Hard-stage models leave unanswered the great existential questions, including, "Why be moral?" The answers to these questions cannot be given within a rational logic of justice; that is, balancing the claims of individual egos. Such a rational logic cannot explain the unique characteristics of adult development, with its existential reflective theories and postconceptual experience.

Summary and Conclusion

In this chapter I have described the relation between morality and an ontological orientation that I have termed *Stage 7*. I have further distinguished this general orientation from operational moral reasoning in which one endeavors to reach equilibrated solutions to dilemmas of conflicting claims or rights. Research over the past 25 years reveals that there are distinct structural stages of such justice reasoning and that these stages form a hierarchical developmental sequence. However, although such reasoning indicates how concrete moral dilemmas can be resolved, they cannot provide *full* justification for choosing a particular course of action. Thus, not even the highest possible stage of justice reasoning can adequately answer the question, "Why be moral?"

This answer can be adequately resolved only at a more comprehensive cognitive level of morality, the level involving one's basic ethical–ontological orientation. It is only against this broader background that the justice operations of moral reasoning take holistic meaning in terms of one's total life. Moreover, the only ethical–ontological orientation that appears capable of generating a fully adequate resolution to ultimate moral questions ("Why be moral? Why be just in a world that is seemingly unjust?") is a cosmic perspective that cannot be structured solely on the basis of formal operational thought. Rather, this orientation appears also to rely upon some type of transcendental or mystical experience—experience of a level at which self and the universe seem unified. Such experience appears to be both nec-

essary in stimulating the shift to a cosmic perspective and instrumental in the structuring of its key features.

Having a cosmic perspective means that one experiences an intimate bond between oneself and the cosmos; one views things not so much from the standpoint of a distinct individual as from the standpoint of the universe as a whole. Some of the great moral philosophers appear to have held such a perspective, and available evidence indicates that it is attainable by those who undergo the appropriate kinds of experience (transcendental or mystical) and reflect upon them in specific ways.

It is because the structuring of a cosmic perspective is guided by reflective thinking, and because this thinking relies in part upon the self's particular and somewhat unique life experiences, that I do not consider it a *hard* developmental stage in the Piagetian sense. Thus, in achieving the fullest level of ethical development, hard stages serve as necessary but not sufficient conditions, and the developmental process must include maturation in reflective modes of thinking. At the most mature level, ethical life as a whole is most equilibrated, and there is a cognitive structure through which one experiences one's own ideas about the right and the just as reflecting basic patterns of the cosmos, and experiences one's ethical actions as expressions of natural law. Therefore, although the speculative philosophies of Marcus Aurelius and Spinoza that arise from and justify this cognitive structure are more diverse and less rigorous than moral stage theory (which is based in universal, primary-mode cognitive structures), they are not meaningless metaphysics, as positivism holds, but constructions essential for understanding the potential for human development in adulthood.

Acknowledgment

Portions of this chapter are reprinted from Kohlberg (1973a,b) and Kohlberg and Powers (1981) with permission from the publishers—Academic Press and Harper & Row, respectively.

It is somehow appropriate that in one of Dr. Kohlberg's last published works, he stands shoulder to shoulder with some of the great moral philosophers in reflecting on that level of thought from which ultimate moral questions can fully be answered. Dr. Kohlberg's original thinking, scholarship, and friendship will be deeply missed by those of us who have known and worked with him.

9

Moral Development Beyond Adolescence

Carol Gilligan, John Michael Murphy, and Mark B. Tappan

"Reason alone is sufficient to govern a rational creature," says one of the Houyhnhnms in *Gulliver's Travels* (Swift, 1726/1952), and like Gulliver, we are tempted to agree. Accustomed by the myriad of studies of Piaget to trace the growth of intelligence in the progression from the charming fallacies of childhood explanation to the irrefutable logic of adolescent thought, we readily equate cognitive development with the growth of logical thinking and see the formal operations of propositional logic as the apogee of human thought. "No person, can disobey reason, without giving up his claim to be a rational creature," warn the Houyhnhnms, and this inexorable logic becomes ever more compelling as Gulliver witnesses the order it sustains.

For in this land to which he has come, these amazing horses, whose self-chosen name proclaims them to be the "perfection of nature," have a rational solution for all of life's problems. Correcting the random disorder of nature with the measured constancy of reason, they rearrange children to make families alike, replacing loss, accepting death, and eliminating disagreement by decisions so rational as to be beyond dispute. Among these creatures "who cultivate reason," inequality vanishes and moral problems disappear, except of course for that of Gulliver—the "wonderful Yahoo that could speak like a Houyhnhnm"—who, being at once both rational and human, defies the categories of Houyhnhnm thought and so, in the end, is expelled from their land.

In this chapter we describe a similar moment that occurs in the course of human development when adolescents discover that the categories of their reason cannot encompass the facts of their experience. This is the time in cognitive development that Inhelder and Piaget (1958) describe as the "return to reality," the shift from a metaphysical to an empirical truth that charts the "path from adolescence to the true beginnings of adulthood" (p. 346). Then the contradictory pulls of logic and affect and the difficulty of their integration call into question Piaget's equation of reason with logical thinking, giving rise to a conflict that can be an occasion for further development.

208

Formal Logic and Intellectual Maturity: The Structure of Adolescent and Adult Thought

> Now, as we have come to see more clearly through Godel but knew long before, the ideal of a structure of all structures is unrealizable.
>
> Piaget, 1971, p. 142

Although Piaget (1967, 1971a, 1972; Inhelder & Piaget, 1958) sometimes stresses the difference between the adolescent's egocentric belief in the omniscient capacity of formal logic and the adult's more equilibrated "reason which reunites intelligence and affectivity" (1967, p. 80), the nature of this transformation has been largely left unexplored. Thus, it remains unclear how the structures of formal operations that permit bright 12-year-olds to solve the pendulum problem are transformed by the return to reality that Piaget claims is brought about by the responsibility of adult work. The increased interest in the nature of cognitive development in adulthood that has occurred during the past 20 years (see, for example, Commons, Richards, & Armon, 1984) fulfills, in part, the promise Piaget saw in such work, namely, to fill this gap by "elucidating from a cognitive point of view the passage from adolescence to adulthood" but also to "retroactively throw light on what we already think we know about earlier stages" (Piaget, 1972, pp. 9–10).

Questions about the development of formal operations and questions about the structural qualities of mature thought are thus conjoined. According to Labouvie-Vief (1979), "the ideal form of [development] has been seen [by Piaget] in the operative functioning of logical and mathematical group structures. The use of mathematico-logical tasks in the assessment of 'mature' cognitive has been derived, in turn, from these forms" (pp. 3–4). Consequently, Labouvie-Vief raises the question of whether the "Piagetian emphasis on formal logic as a criterion of adaptive maturity does not virtually guarantee the observation of adaptive failure and regression on either side of the adolescent apogee" (p. 2; cf. Labouvie-Vief, 1990).

One line of research points to a way out of this dilemma. Instead of assuming that the definition of mature cognition is already known and fully operationalized, a number of researchers have attempted to elucidate the structures of cognition used by adults in everyday life, with an eye toward describing the particular adaptiveness they may have (see Basseches, 1984a; Gilligan, 1977; Kitchener & King, 1981, 1990; Kramer & Woodruff, 1986; Labouvie-Vief & Hakim-Larson, in press; Labouvie-Vief, Hakim-Larson, & DeVoe, 1987; Riegel, 1973; Sinnott, 1975, 1989; Youniss, 1974). It is in this approach that our own work is grounded. For as Labouvie-Vief (1979) argues, "although the picture of intellectual maturity derived from [Inhelder and Piaget's] tests may be particularly germane in a school setting and at that stage of life, it may lack validity if applied to more mature adults and to new, non-academic settings" (p. 16; cf. Labouvie-Vief, 1985).

Thus, although it may be possible to generate "all possible combinations of propositions" (Piaget, 1967, p. 358) to Inhelder and Piaget's formal reasoning tasks in the laboratory, or even to solve all the logical problems encountered in the classroom, in the real-life situations faced by most adults such full formalism may be inadequate and even maladaptive. As Flavell (1977) suggests, "real problems with meaningful content are obviously more important in everyday human adaptation

[than abstract, wholly logical problems], and it is possible that these are the kinds of problems our cognitive apparatus has evolved to solve" (p. 116).

The demand, therefore, for formalization in reasoning may be a false standard for development. Such an interpretation is supported by a finding in the field of logic:

> The most important theorems limiting the formalization of logical thought are due to Godel. They are based on the fact that within any deductive system which includes arithmetic . . . it is possible to construct formulae—i.e., sentences—which are demonstrably undecidable within that system, and that such a sentence—the famous Godelian sentence—may say of itself that it is undecidable within the system (Polyani, 1958, p. 259).

According to Quine (1981), Godel's proof legitimates contradiction within the study of formal logic and is, because of its proof of formal undecidability, a "veridical paradox." Thus, Polyani (1958) observes that:

> This uncertainty can be eliminated for any particular deductive system by shifting it onto a wider system of axioms, within which we may be able to prove the consistency of the original system. But any such proof will still remain uncertain, in the sense that the consistency of the wider system will always remain undecidable (p. 259).

Such considerations have a direct bearing on research attempting to measure the attainment of formal operations, and, in fact, Godel's work was central to Piaget's (1970a) elaboration of the dialectical implications of his basic "structuralism:"

> Since Godel . . . the idea of a formal system of abstract structures is thereby transformed into that of the construction of a never completed whole, the limits of formalization constituting the grounds for incompleteness, or as we saw earlier, incompleteness being a necessary consequence of the fact that there is no "terminal" or "absolute" form because any content is form relative to some inferior content and any form the content for some higher form (p. 140).

The incompleteness of formal structures thus introduces a new element into the research on formal operations. The closed-system INRC logic that could generate all possible combinations is now qualified by a "certain openness," and a dialectic with "new knowledge," other legitimate points of view, and empirical reality is now required to demonstrate adequacy. These observations about the structure of formal systems led Piaget (1971a) to open his definitions of the structure of knowledge as well: "From Godel's conclusions there follow certain important insights as to the limits of formalization in general; in particular, it has been possible to show that there are, in addition to formalized levels of knowledge, distinct 'semi-formal' or 'semi-intuitive' levels which wait their turn so to say for formalization" (p. 35). Or as Polyani (1958) observes, "In the Godelian process we add to a formally undecided statement of ours a tacit interpretation of our own. . . . we establish something new by an inescapable act of our own, induced—but not performed—by formal operations" (p. 260).

Thus, the incompleteness of formal systems leads to an irremediable gap between the logical deduction and the assent of the person who chooses to affirm

it. The adequacy of a system of formal logic depends, then, as much on an awareness of the need to ground it within the context of the "next 'higher' theory" (Piaget, 1971a, p. 34) as on the demonstration of its completeness. It would seem, therefore, that the appropriate evaluation of a formal judgment would lie less in the
elegance of its formal justification than in a more open and dialectical process
involving contextualization and an openness to re-evaluation.

The implications of Godel's work for a theory of adult cognition have been
examined most fully by Labouvie-Vief (1979, 1985, 1990). She links Godel's proof
of the limits of a single perspective and the need for continued empirical verification in logic to the questions raised at the outset of this chapter about individual
cognitive development. In so doing she sketches a two-step progression of continuing cognitive development past the adolescent attainment of formal operations:

> [This progression begins with] a cognitive differentiation, namely, a realization that
> logic is merely a necessary condition and becomes a sufficient element of adult life
> only if subordinated to a hierarchically higher goal: social system maintenance. It is
> important then to distinguish between logic as a *goal* and logic as a *tool*. We propose
> that it is exactly this cognitive differentiation which brings with it the second step,
> the adult concerns with commitment, generativity, and social responsibility (Labou-
> vie-Vief, 1979, pp. 19–20).

The general outline of this progression can also be found in Piaget's discussion
of the reconciliation between formal logic and reality (Inhelder & Piaget, 1958; Piaget, 1967, 1972). In particular, the importance of the concern with social system
maintenance or, in Erikson's sense, with generativity, is expressed most clearly in
Piaget's (1967) observation that "[adult] personality . . . results from the submis-
sion or rather the autosubmission of the self to some kind of discipline. . . . In this
sense the person and the social relationship he engenders and maintains are interdependent" (p. 65).

The adult commitment to generating and maintaining interdependent systems
of social relationships, studied by students of ego development, has implications
for other areas of developmental psychology as well—particularly for moral development. Perry's (1970, 1981) work on intellectual and ethical development during
the college years makes this link most directly. He found evidence for a sequence
of development through nine "Positions," from the early absolutism of adolescent
logic, through its full flowering in the forms of multiplicity and relativism, to the
development of a new equilibrium of identity and epistemological commitment
within contextual relativism. Perry views the relativistic and postrelativistic positions (5–9) as adding "an advanced 'period' to Piaget's outline," or, in other words,
a post-formal-operational stage to the sequence of cognitive development.

For Perry (1970), an individual's attainment of this advanced period is dependent on a single epistemological paradigm shift beginning with the realization of
the contextual relativism of all knowledge. This, in turn, is based on an understanding of the limits of formal logic, which Perry refers to as "reason." In a passage
echoing those from *Gulliver's Travels* with which we began, he argues that

> Reason reveals relations within any given context; it can also compare one context
> with another on the basis of meta-contexts established for this purpose. But there is

a limit. In the end, reason itself remains reflexively relativistic, a property which turns reason back upon reason's own findings. In even its farthest reaches, then, reason will leave the thinker with several legitimate contexts and no way of choosing among them—no way at least that he can justify through reason alone. . . . If he is still to honor reason he must now also transcend it; he must affirm his own position from within himself in full awareness that reason can never completely justify him or assure him (pp. 135–136).

Thus, for Perry, the formally undecidable nature of human choice leads to an acknowledgment of the tacit component of thought referred to by Polyani and Piaget. In Perry's scheme, Polyani's tacit assent becomes affirmation, an act of commitment that "ushers in the period of responsibility" (p. 205).

In contrast to Perry's postformal scheme of intellectual and ethical development, Kohlberg's (1971, 1976, 1981, 1984a; see also Kohlberg & Ryncarz chapter in this volume) approach operationalizes a formal-logical model of cognitive and moral development. In Kohlberg's conception each Piagetian cognitive stage provides a necessary but not sufficient condition for a parallel moral stage. Thus, moral stages 1 and 2 in Kohlberg's scheme are based on successive substages of concrete operations, whereas moral stages 3 and 4 are based on early substages of formal operations (Kohlberg & Gilligan, 1971). Principled moral reasoning (stages 5 and 6), in particular, depends on the attainment of fully consolidated formal operations. Kohlberg (1976, 1984) claims, furthermore, that it is possible to assess moral reasoning in terms of its correspondence to a system of internal logic whose highest point relies on the propositional operations of logically reversible and universalizable "justice structures."

Yet Kohlberg's scheme repeatedly encounters difficulties when applied to samples of older adolescents and adults, in the form of a persistent finding of late adolescent and young adult regression from the highly logical stage 5 to mixed (4/5) or conventional (stage 4 or stage 3) scores. This problem was first noted by Kohlberg himself, as he followed his adolescent sample longitudinally into early adulthood. Kohlberg and Kramer (1969) reported the anomalous finding that 20 percent of Kohlberg's subjects seemed to have turned away from the compelling formal logic of his highest stages and regressed to a form of relativism or "hedonism" that resembled less complex forms of judgment. These findings ultimately led Kohlberg and his colleagues to undertake a complete revision of his scoring system in an effort to correct what he assumed was a confusion of content with form (see Colby & Kohlberg, 1987; Kohlberg, 1979, 1984; also Tappan, 1987, in press).

Rather than relaxing the formal requirements of his highest stages, however, Kohlberg has, if anything, increased them. Thus, although the rescoring of his own data by his revised system has virtually eliminated regression, it has also eliminated stage 6 and drastically reduced the incidence of stage 5 (Colby, Kohlberg, Gibbs, & Lieberman, 1983; Kohlberg, 1979, 1984). The situation with respect to moral development is thus analogous to that in cognitive development: By strict, formal criteria, very few adults appear to be mature. In a different longitudinal sample of bright, advantaged subjects, scored by the same coders using Kohlberg's revised manual, more than half of the 26 subjects scored at the fully principled level at one of the longitudinal testing points. Most of these subjects, however, later regressed from Kohlberg's highest stages, thus repeating with the new scoring system the very

violation of invariant sequence that it was designed to correct (Murphy & Gilligan, 1980).

When the same data were analyzed using a different scoring system based on Perry's (1970) scheme, however, longitudinal progression through a developmental sequence was clear. Since Perry's scheme is based on a progression from formal operations (positions 3 and 4—multiplicity) through a transitional crisis (position 5—relativism) to a post-formal-operational equilibrium in which the structures of cognition have been transformed (positions 6 and beyond—commitment in relativism), the Murphy and Gilligan (1980) findings of a developmental sequence with respect to Perry's scheme can be viewed as empirical support for a model of cognitive development that postulates progression in the transition from adolescence to adulthood toward more dialectical or contextual structures of thought.

Our use of Perry's scheme as a way to make sense of late adolescent moral development stemmed from our attempt to analyze the ways in which individuals at Kohlberg's highest levels applied their reasoning to the solution of their own real-life moral dilemmas. Our research began in 1970, when Gilligan set out to investigate the development of thinking about real-life experiences of moral conflict and choice (see Gilligan, 1977, 1982, 1986b, 1987a). The study that resulted was designed to describe the ways in which thinking about actual dilemmas differed from thinking about hypothetical dilemmas and to investigate the role of life experience in the process of moral development. By asking college students to describe moral dilemmas they had encountered and the ways in which they had come to resolve them, Gilligan began to identify the universe of dilemmas encountered by these students and to see the role that such encounters played in the evolution of their thought. The students' association of changes in their thinking with real-life experiences of conflict and choice then led to a naturalistic study of people who were facing a moral decision. Gilligan (1977) and Belenky (1978) interviewed women deciding whether to continue or abort a pregnancy and described the different forms of thinking that were brought to bear on the construction and resolution of that dilemma. In addition, Gilligan and Belenky (1980) described changes in thinking that were manifest on a one-year follow-up interview with these women, addressing the natural history and sequence of developmental transition and the conditions likely to precipitate or impede its occurrence (see also Gilligan, 1982).

The same transitional processes that appeared in the abortion decision study were also found among subjects in the college student study. Although a number of the students in that study did seem to meet or even exceed Kohlberg's rigorous criteria of formal logical structure at age 19, at ages 22 and 27 they began to indicate dissatisfaction with this logic as an adequate basis for understanding their own personal dilemmas of moral conflict and choice. Instead, their reasoning began to show different structural qualities, which, according to their own reports, emerged from experiences that had revealed to them the limitations of their earlier perspectives (see also Gilligan, 1982, Chap. 5).

In sum, *these* longitudinal data suggest that moral reasoning in its real-life context relies on cognitive structures other than those deriving solely from formal logic. In particular, Murphy's reinterviews of the college subjects at age 27 indicates that a developmental sequence can be traced from the perfection of logical systems

as a basis for moral reasoning in adolescence to the placing of these formal logical systems within the broader context of a more differentiated and dialectical moral understanding in adulthood. This chapter, then, describes aspects of our longitudinal study designed to elucidate the developmental transition from adolescence to adulthood by observing the nature of thinking about the "reality of things" (Piaget, 1967) and by analyzing the ways in which the growing experience of this reality can affect the development of thought.

The Philosopher and the "Dilemma of the Fact"

> Friendship and benevolence are the two principal virtues among the Houyhnhnms and these are not confined to particular objects, but universal to the whole race, for a stranger from the remotest part is equally treated with the nearest neighbor, and wherever he goes, looks upon himself as home.
>
> Swift, *Gulliver's Travels*

> Because I know that time is always time
> And place is always and only place
> And what is actual is actual only for one time
> And only for one place
> I rejoice that things are as they are . . .
> And pray to God to have mercy upon us.
>
> T. S. Eliot, *Ash Wednesday*

The two "philosophers" we will discuss in this section were college seniors at the time they agreed to participate in our study. They were part of a group of students who were chosen for study because they had shown particular interest in the study of morality, electing as sophomores to take a course, taught by Kohlberg, on moral and political choice. At the time of the course, their moral judgments were assessed by Kohlberg's standard method. We have chosen these two students for comparison here because they typify a pattern of developmental divergence that was evident in this sample as a whole.

Both students were philosophy majors whose judgment had, in their senior year, reached the highest level of Kohlberg's stage sequence. Philosopher 1's judgments of hypothetical dilemmas reflected a principled moral understanding that was scored at the highest of Kohlberg's stages (stage 5) in both his sophomore and senior years. At the beginning of his sophomore year, the judgments of Philosopher 2 were scored as transitional between conventional and principled morality (stage 4[5]), but by the end of his senior year they too had reached the fully principled stage. Thus, in their senior-year interviews, these two philosophers applied their principles of justice to the solution of Kohlberg's hypothetical dilemmas, proclaiming unequivocally the moral rightness of stealing a drug to save a life, and earning for their principled certainty the highest score of stage 5.

Our interviews, however, went beyond the standard Kohlberg procedure of assessing judgment of hypothetical dilemmas and posed, in addition, questions about moral conflicts that the students had experienced in the course of their lives, asking them to describe their thinking about these events. In this open-ended session of the interview on life experience, both students recounted involvement in

dilemmas of sexual infidelity and told of their difficulty in judging their actions. Philosopher 1 had broken a "mutual expectation" of honesty and fidelity in his relationship with a young woman he referred to as "Girl A" by not acknowledging to her that he had fallen in love with "Girl B." Philosopher 2's dilemma stemmed from the fact that the husband of the woman with whom he was involved had not been told about the affair. Although each student raised questions about the morality of his actions and the apparent discrepancy between his actions and his principles of justice, the questions in each case were different, and therein lies the basis for our comparison.

Philosopher 1 seems never to have questioned his belief that there was a right way to judge his dilemma. His problem stemmed rather from his uncertainty as to whether or not he was judging it correctly. Unclear as to whether he had violated his principles by acting toward Girl A as he did, he explains that

> Falling in love with Girl B made it hard for me to honor all of my commitments to Girl A, and it made it harder for me to always be as attentive to her as I really wanted to be, because I was preoccupied with somebody else. So, *it is difficult to sort out whether or not I was violating something.* I could make a case that I might believe (and I don't know whether I have, unconsciously or consciously) that I hadn't really grossly transgressed my principles, and then again I could construct another case that I maybe had in a few respects [emphasis added].

Attempting to reconstruct the facts of the dilemma in accordance with principles of trust, he suggests that he might in fact have respected the spirit of the agreement whose letter he had broken:

> How do I prevent myself from violating this first girl's trust, and I did that partly, and I didn't do it completely successfully . . . it was a question of her wanting not to be displaced in my feelings, and I think in some kind of sense I didn't do that. So I sort of honored her essential expectations, which was not that I tell her the truth so much as I not displace her with somebody else. *It's hard to know whether I did or not,* and sometimes I think I did and if I did, that would be a case where I could perhaps feel that I acted unjustly, if I did displace her, but I think that thinking about it, it is the kind of thing that had to end. And we were not doing that. And then it came time to do it, and I sort of had an extra impetus to do it because there was something else happening to me. And yet it did not seem to alter in an important way the course of things between the first girl and me. It did alter my treatment of her a little bit [emphasis added].

To resolve his quandary concerning the judgment of this dilemma, Philosopher 1 turns away from the contradictions that arise in his description of the event and focuses instead on questions of principle, asking, "What are her legitimate expectations of me and how do you define trust in principled terms?" He attributes the limitation of his current judgment in assessing the legitimacy of her expectations to his incomplete understanding of the principle of trust. Having initially endorsed the mutuality of trust, he nevertheless had acted "according to my estimation of where her interests lay instead of what her expectations were." Upon reflection, however, he seemed to feel that something was amiss in the expectation itself and questioned whether the "sort of trust and understanding we had was *the right one to have*" [emphasis added].

This student's philosophy, seemingly at odds with "facts" of his dilemma, is stretched to provide the judgment that he seeks. Convinced that a right answer exists and that eventually he will find the complete definition of trust, he believes that his discovery ultimately will determine the legitimacy of interpersonal expectations, establishing logical priorities to guide a just solution to this dilemma. Throughout his discussion, his concern remains with the internal consistency of his principles of justice, allowing him to reconstruct both his own actions and the other's expectations in his search for justification. His almost exclusive concern with logical consistency at the expense of verification, however, demonstrates cognitive immaturity of the type described by Piaget, Labouvie-Vief, and Perry, as well as the kind of closed formal structures discussed previously in relation to Godel's theorem.

Philosopher 2, in contrast, begins with an acknowledgment of moral violation. His principle was one of "obligation and if I see some kind of ongoing unjust situation, I have some kind of obligation to correct it in whatever way I see." Clearly, in his mind the husband of the woman with whom he was involved "should be told," since "otherwise he was not getting the information he needed to judge what his best interests should be in the situation." Putting himself in the husband's place, Philosopher 2 says simply, "I would have wanted to know." The injustice consisted in "his not knowing the full truth . . . I think the truth is an ultimate thing."

The complexity of the situation from the woman's perspective, however, complicated his judgment and confronted him with a dilemma. Overwhelmed by exams at school and illness in her family, she said she was unable to face the additional stress of informing her husband about the affair. Although she did intend to tell him, she was waiting for a more opportune time and thus resisted Philosopher 2's requests that she inform him. In the interim the husband discovered the affair. This unintended turn of events in fact resolved the dilemma, but the experience itself had a profound impact on Philosopher 2, shaking the foundations of his "moral system":

> So my dilemma was whether I should call the guy up and tell him what the situation was. I didn't, and *the fact that I didn't* has had a tremendous impact on my moral system. It did. It shook my belief and my justification of the belief that *I couldn't resolve the dilemma of the fact that I felt that someone should tell him.* . . . I did feel that there was some kind of truth issue involved here, higher than the issue of where the truth comes from—the kind of thing that no matter what happens, the other person should have full knowledge of what is going on, is fair. *And I didn't tell him* [emphasis added].

Left with a sense of moral compromise in not having acted in accordance with his principles, but realizing the possible consequences of such action for the woman for whom he cares, he seeks neither to alter the facts of the dilemma nor to equivocate about principles. Instead, he begins to re-examine the premises underlying these principles. In so doing he comes to question "whether there is a sense in which truth is relative, or is truth ever relative. That is an issue I have yet to resolve":

> What I learned was I became much less absolute. I was always aware of the kind of situation in which truth was not absolute. If a person comes up to me with a gun in

his hand, in that situation I never thought that the truth was that absolute. But with interpersonal situations that dealt with psychological realities and with psychological feelings, with emotions, I felt that the truth should win out in most situations. Then after that situation, I became more relativistic about it. As you can tell, right now, I have not worked out a principle that is satisfactory to me that would resolve that issue if it happened again tomorrow.

Unlike Philosopher 1, however, Philosopher 2 no longer is convinced that such a principle could ever be worked out:

I try to work out a system that would be fair to all persons involved . . . and I suppose the dilemma I have is the fact that—Rawls calls it the Blanket of Ignorance—the Veil of Ignorance—is not down. It is very difficult for me to be completely withdrawn from the situation and say if I was K. [the woman] or if I were T. [her husband], I would certainly want to know the truth. I feel there is no question about that. But if I were K., would I see what I wanted to do as being the right thing to do? And was her right to sanity, which I think was being jeopardized, less important than his right to know? That is a good moral dilemma—now you figure it out.

Thus, the relativism that has begun to erode his former claim to absolute knowledge of the "right thing to do" arises from his incipient awareness of the possible legitimacy of a different point of view.

As he begins to imagine alternative constructions of the dilemma that also have a claim to truth, his conception of truth itself begins to change, becoming, as he says, "more relativistic." No longer can he unequivocally defend the single "highhanded" perspective of his former moral judgments, and in the absence of this support the Rawlsian "Veil of Ignorance" falls, removing the basis, in Kohlberg's terms, for a principled moral resolution. As his experience leads him to see the moral legitimacy of other perspectives, Philosopher 2 begins to understand how the experience of others might lead them to the discovery of different truths. Finding the problem now in his former construction of the dilemma itself, he reconstructs it more broadly as a conflict of rights, but one that no longer reduces to a logically deductible moral solution.

Five years later, at age 27, this contextual relativism has invaded his hypothetical moral reasoning as well, causing his Kohlberg score to fall from the principled to the transitional level. His discovery that "experiences in my life tend to make simple solutions a lot more difficult to accept," colors his response to Kohlberg's dilemmas. The problem of judgment now occurs in two contexts that frame different aspects of the moral problem: the context of *justice,* in which he articulates the universal logic of fairness and reciprocity, and the context of *care,* in which he attends instead to the pressure of different dilemmas and the reality of different points of view. His resolution combines the absolute logic of a system of moral justification with a probabilistic contextual assessment of the likely consequences of choice. Thus, the right solution from a justice perspective, one that might be right "in an ideal world," may not, in fact, be the best solution in the actuality of time and place. The contextual morality of *responsibility* for the actual consequences of choice enters, therefore, into dialogue with the abstraction of *rights,* resulting in a judgment whose contradictory normative statements are scored as a mixture of Kohlberg's stages 4 and 5.

This change in the focus of Philosopher 2's moral concern can be interpreted in the light of our ongoing work, and, in fact, calls for a theoretical framework that distinguishes different dimensions of human relationship and on that basis differentiates two moral voices or orientations (see Gilligan, 1982, 1986a, 1987b; Gilligan, Brown, & Rogers, in press; Gilligan & Wiggins, 1987). A *justice* voice or perspective, often equated with moral reasoning, is recast as one way of speaking about or seeing moral problems and a *care* perspective is brought forward as a different voice or alternate frame. The distinction between justice and care as different voices or alternative perspectives is based empirically on the observation that a shift in the focus of a person's attention from concerns about justice to concerns about care changes his or her definition of what constitutes a moral problem. Thus, the same situation can be seen in different ways. Theoretically, the distinction between justice and care cuts across the familiar divisions between thinking and feeling, egoism and altruism, and theoretical and practical reasoning that have traditionally been key to moral theory. Instead, we call attention to the fact that all human relationships, public and private, can be characterized in terms of equality *and* in terms of attachment, and that both inequality and detachment constitute grounds for moral concern. Everyone, by virtue of being human, is vulnerable both to oppression and to abandonment, and the moral injunctions of justice and care— not to act unfairly toward others, and not to turn away from someone in need— capture these different concerns.

Seen in this light, Philosopher 2's dilemma arises from a conflict between perspectives. The fact that he did not call the husband contradicts his principles of justice. At the same time it shows his unwillingness to abandon K. or turn away from her concerns. Given the limitations of the situation, he sees no way to act that would be at once just and caring. His recognition of the genuine nature of this dilemma is reflected in his statement to the interviewer: "That is a good moral dilemma—now you figure it out."

Our interpretation, therefore, is that Philosopher 2's regression on Kohlberg's scale is an artifact of a new, more integrated and encompassing moral understanding where the care voice and the justice voice are in dialogue in a complex, dialectical way of thinking. This interpretation is supported by Philosopher 2's retrospective reflection, at age 27, on the dilemma he had reported five years earlier. Now the moral discussion "about who tells the truth and who doesn't" appears to him in a "very different perspective": as legitimate to the "justice approach" but ancillary to the "more fundamental issue" of the causes and consequences of infidelity. Focusing his discussion at age 27 on his understanding of why the situation arose in the first place and on the problem of life choice its occurrence presented, he attributes his previous unawareness of these issues to an "incredible amount of immaturity on my part," which he sees reflected in his "justice approach":

> The justice approach was really blinding me to a lot of issues. And, in a sense, I was trying to make it a justice issue, and it really blinded me to a lot of the realities of the problem. And now, being in a situation where, you know, married for a few years . . . it's a very different perspective to have on it. That it really wasn't a moral issue, that it was a moral issue, that part of it was, but that there were other things that I was not considering. [*What was the moral issue?*] I think that the moral issue was simply the matter of honesty and trust in the relationship. But even if that had

been fulfilled, we would have been left with the interpersonal dilemma of life choices, of what kind of relationship you want in your life. It could have been just as easily that [she] told her husband. So what? [You are] still left with the choice. And morality won't do you one bit of good in that situation.

Implicitly equating morality with the "justice approach," he now sees its illumination to have been "blinding," concealing from him the "realities of the problem"—the unresolved dilemma of choice. The perceived disparity between the justice solution (telling the truth to honor respect) and the remaining problems of responsibility and consequence leads him to the conclusion that the problem was at once both moral and not moral, and that the "moral" (i.e., justice) solution would not solve the problem (see also Brown, 1989). The moral question, therefore, becomes one of defining what is included in the moral domain, since the justice approach does not adequately address the concerns about care that are part of this life choice.

In our full sample, such a shift to a two-context or, in Perry's sense, "contextually relativistic" form of moral reasoning was prominent in a number of subjects between the ages of 22 and 27 (see Murphy & Gilligan, 1980). Its appearance was repeatedly tied to the experience of the "dilemma of the fact": that in the exigencies of life choice one moral perspective rarely could encompass the problem. It was precisely this problem of interpretive frames or moral perspectives that made the "right answer" no longer seem right, giving rise to such seemingly contradictory realizations as "I had violated my first principle of moral behavior, but I had made the right decision."

The addition of this second context for judgment has been consistently mistaken for a retreat from the adolescent cognitive apogee—in this case the justice principles of Kohlberg's highest stages. According to Kohlberg's (1984, Chap. 8) view that there are objective criteria of logical justification that make the moral principles of justice "best," adults who reason in terms of both justice and care may appear to be at the same developmental position as the moral equivocators or "relativists" whom he saw as in transition between stages 4 and 5. Thus, in the case of Philosopher 2, his two-context (i.e., contextual) judgments at age 27 receive a lower score in Kohlberg's system than his "principled" judgments at age 22. This finding of regression in Philosopher 2 was characteristic of our sample as a whole: two thirds of the students whose judgments had met Kohlberg's criteria for principled reasoning regressed in the transition from adolescence to adulthood (Murphy & Gilligan, 1980). In contrast to Kohlberg, we interpret this shift in reasoning not as regression but as reflecting a recognition of perspective that seems to be tied to experiences of relationship and the actualities of real-life moral conflict and choice (see also Gilligan, 1982; Tappan, 1987, 1989).

The Transition from Adolescence to Adulthood

They said to me, That's love, yes, yes, not a doubt, now you see how.... How easy it is. They said to me, That's friendship, yes, yes, no question, you've found it. They said to me, Here's the place, stop, raise your head and look at all that beauty. That order! They said to me, Come now, you're not

the brute beast, think upon these things and you'll see how all becomes clear. And simple! They said to me, What skilled attention they get, all these dying of their wounds.

Beckett, *Endgame*

I plot out in my mind what are the moral obligations, the rights, the duties, in that situation, and then the question is, "Is my choice based on those moral principles?" And I say to you, "Isn't it funny?"—because it is very difficult to answer.

Philosopher 2

Because the "ultimate welding of epistemological and moral issues" (Perry, 1970, p. 202) makes the act of knowing an act of commitment, the drama of late adolescent and adult development comes to center on the theme of responsibility. This theme, when it first appears in the encounter with adult dilemmas of irreversible choice, seems merely to be another figure on the familiar ground of logical justification. Perry's recognition of its capacity to revolutionize thinking and overturn the order of that landscape, however, extends our perspective on cognitive and moral development into the adult years.

The vision of a postconventional moral judgment impervious to the coercion of societal conventions and legal systems was the inspiration that led Kohlberg to seize on the logical power of adolescent reasoning and to forge from its operations of equality and reciprocity (i.e., reversibility) universal principles of justice, whose rationality was beyond dispute. In contrast, we see the strength of such moral resistance as arising from an act in relationship, which, in transcending the reflexivity of reason, can never be rationalized by logic alone.

From our perspective, the coercion of conventional morality lies not only in its social embeddedness, but also in its epistemological claim to an absolute and objective truth. When the recognition of truth as a human construction irrevocably binds the knower to the known, it topples the structure of conventional understanding by removing its epistemological base. One is then free to construct the truth of experience, but one is also responsible for the construction that one has made. The adequacy of any given understanding no longer can be established by logic alone, but depends on a continuing search for its empirical verification—a search that leads into relationship. The difference between the domains of hypothetical problem solving and actual life choice lies not in any distinction regarding the nature of logic or truth, but rather in the price of making mistakes. In this sense, then, our data confirm the tragic vision that knowledge is gained through the discovery of error, and thus involves acquaintance with sorrow and grief. In Perry's (1970) terms development itself becomes, therefore, "an act of moral courage" (p. 176).

Two lawyers tell, at age 27, of the conflict they faced in deciding between their responsibility to defend the individual rights of their client and their responsibility to maintain the system of justice, which they as lawyers also represent. In one instance this dilemma appears to engender the beginning realization of contextual relativism (the transition from Perry's position 4 to position 5) that is accompanied by a personal sense of moral retreat, whereas in the other it leads to a reconstruction of truth as an ongoing problem of commitment in relativism (Perry's position

6), a problem of seeing the consequences of action and taking responsibility for choice.

For one lawyer this dilemma arose when she was defending an insurance company against a claim brought by a person who had been injured in an accident (see also Gilligan, 1982, Chap. 5). When this person's attorney failed to put forward in evidence documents that were critical to his client's case, Lawyer 1 wondered whether she should tell him about the documents or simply remain silent about their omission:

What was the conflict for you?

The conflict was in knowing that in the best of all possible worlds we would just submit all documents and have it be a true fact-finding proceeding, instead of an adversary proceeding.

Would that be the right thing to do or was what you did the right thing to do?

Well, in the best of all possible worlds, I would have a different system. I would not have an adversary system.

Given the system we have . . . ?

Given the system we have, it was my duty to represent my client and to not do anything that would jeopardize my client's interests. And had I, in fact, put in that document, I might, in fact, be harming my client. And I thought that in the context of the system as it now works, I should not put in the document.

How did you feel about that decision?

I feel like it's too bad for our system. I really think, well, regardless of how meritorious the other person's claim is, it would be an ideal system to be able to bring all the evidence there is. But especially in the legal system, we have a complex system of weighing all the different possibilities and factors.

How did you know that was the right decision?

I don't think I knew it was right in the larger sense. In the larger sense, I don't think it was right. But in the circumstances that we are in, I think I just weighed the fact that I am supposed to be representing a client. I can't turn over every possible piece of evidence *that would hurt them.*

If you had to do it again, what would you do?

I would do the same thing.

You would do something you think is wrong again?

Well, it's wrong from a theoretical point of view. From a practical point of view, it was the only decision I could make.

This lawyer's reasoning is clearly logical. It also illustrates the way in which she has consciously subordinated individual rights to the "practical" constraints of the adversary system—a decision guided by her wish not to hurt her client and presumably herself. In her reasoning about this dilemma both justice and care concerns can be heard, and they seem to coexist unaltered side by side in an uneasy tension. As Perry's multiplistic (position 4) designation suggests, she would probably deny that either perspective was ultimately right or wrong.

Of the several subjects who score at Perry's higher positions of commitment in relativism, a second lawyer offers a particularly illustrative example. Within Kohlberg's framework his moral judgment scores regress from a pure stage 5 score at age 19 to a mixture of 5 with some 4 at 22, to an all-time low of 4(5) at 27. His scores in Perry's system on the same hypothetical dilemmas, however, show the opposite trend, beginning at position 4 at 19 to a mixture of 4 and 5 at 22, at an average of position 6 at age 27. This lawyer thus represents an excellent case for comparing these two divergent views of adult development.

Before examining his reasoning in action, however, let us first look at its context. Early in his interview at age 27, he describes how he had come to understand the limitations of his own point of view. In working for a consumer protection group when he was just out of college, he had spent a year "criticizing people, calling them scum, racketeers, crooks, low-life, etc." Then when he went to work for the district attorney's office in the same city, he gained access to secret files and learned that, "unbeknownst to me, the criticisms were probably unfounded because things were happening that I just didn't know about." He goes on to describe the way in which this experience changed his reasoning:

> I learned that there are always ten sides to every story, there is never just one. I guess I learned that it is relatively easy to criticize people, but then when you start to put yourself in their shoes, and you start to see the kind of pressures on them and their different perspectives and everything—I learned after a while to make very forceful and vehement, the best-reasoned criticisms I could of people, but always with the idea, always with the nagging doubt about whether it was correct or not. But I learned after a while to realize that [they] are big boys who can take care of themselves. That, especially in our society . . . there is a need for people to make strong and one-sided rejoinders. And I learned to appreciate the dialectic much more, and that is the best way to hash out decisions. And you should always be aware of this ambiguity and perhaps the fallacies in your own arguments and reasoning and doubts. You should always have that very healthy doubt about what you do and decisions you make. It keeps you honest.

Through his discovery of the limitations of his own perspective, and thereby his discovery of perspective, per se, this lawyer has come to rely on a different notion of honesty. His reasoning about the real-life dilemma that follows reveals how his notion of truth has been reconstructed. Whereas Lawyer 1 could attend only to the compromises that the adversary system forced on "the truth," Lawyer 2 has come to a different view of adversary truth and the system of legal justice.

The dilemma he recounts was his conflict over whether or not to prosecute someone on the basis of evidence that he thinks is "flimsy" and testimony that he has reason to believe might be perjured—whether to marshall the "tremendous power of state" and his own considerable skills to prosecute, and perhaps convict, someone who, as he so well knows, may turn out to be innocent:

How do you make decisions like that?

You have to weigh how bad the guy is, really how bad he is. And the degree to which the evidence is flimsy or whatever. You put all these things on a scale and you weigh them out, what good is going to be done—are you going to take a really bad guy out of society? At what expense? How badly are you going to

corrupt the system? If you are going to have a chance to counteract that, you know.

You mean by launching a full-scale case against him, will he be able to hire an attorney?

Yeah. Whether his attorney is going to have a chance to take measures to counteract the flimsy evidence or your questionable witness or whatever. To what extent are you violating his rights?

If the guy is really evil, why do you want him to have a good attorney?

Why do you want him to have rights?

But if you really believe he is evil . . . ?

Number one is whose decision it is. I don't think any one individual has the power to make those unilateral moral decisions in these particular situations. There is a system. Society has ultimately made these decisions and one has to pay a great deal of respect to society. And it is also something I have learned very much about—this thing I was telling you about before, this thing about, I am very much aware of how incomplete my information on any one thing is, any one situation or set of facts. I can think that some guy is a real terrible person who did the X, Y, Z murder, or something like that, and I could have it very much wrong. I have been very wrong in the past, very wrong. It is a check on my power. I guess I am very concerned about and sensitized to abuse of power, and I think that I should be checked just like everybody else. I have made a lot of mistakes and am going to make a lot more.

The major difference between Lawyer 2's thinking here and Lawyer 1's is that Lawyer 2 is clearly aware of the contextual relativity of all knowledge: "there are always ten sides to every story, there is never just one." Furthermore, he realizes that, given the relativity of the world, and faced with ambiguity and "nagging doubt," he nevertheless has to commit to a version of the "truth" that he can use to guide his life and his work. It is a truth, however, that he wants to be checked from time to time, so that he cannot abuse the power of such a truth, particularly when it is aligned with the force of the legal system. As such, he affirms the strength of his own perspective while at the same time acknowledging its limits. Recall Perry's description of this moment in development: "If he is still to honor reason he must now also transcend it; he must affirm his own position from within himself in full awareness that reason can never completely justify him or assure him" (1970, pp. 135–136).

Conclusion

In this chapter we have argued that intellectual and ethical development continues beyond adolescence and into adulthood through the shift from the metaphysics of logical justification to the psychology of everyday life—the empirical discovery of the irreversible consequences of choice. Our analysis is compatible with the interpretation that this return to reality requires a cognitive transformation from a formal to a dialectical mode of reasoning that can encompass the contradictions out

of which moral problems often arise (see also Basseches, 1980; Benack & Basseches, 1989). Although formal logic and principles of justice can free adolescent judgment from the binding constraints of societal convention, the actual constraints of choice—what Philosopher 2 calls the "realities of the problem"—impose a new context for decision that changes the dimensions of the moral problem. As Philosopher 2 reflects, "even if [principles of justice] had been fulfilled, we would have been left with the interpersonal dilemma of life choices . . . it could have been just as easily that [K.] told her husband. So what? [You are] still left with the choice." This realization restructures the understanding of moral choice from a problem of formal justification to a problem of what Perry calls "commitment in relativism"— or what Philosopher 2 calls the "interpersonal dilemma of life choices." This restructuring is based on the epistemological recognition of the ultimte fallibility of all knowledge, but it is also based on the recognition that life choices are made in a world of relationships. Thus, it forms the basis for an expanded adult ethic that encompasses empathy or compassion and tolerance or understanding, thereby joining respect with response in bringing morality into the context of human relationship (see also Gilligan, 1986a, 1986b, 1987b).

In the world of the Houyhnhnms, where the operation of reason is not "discoloured by passion or interest" ("they have no fondness for their colts or foals, but the care they take in educating them proceedeth entirely from the dictates of reason"), the rationality of the justice approach operates "[in entire agreement] with the sentiments of Socrates" (Swift, 1726/1952, pp. 165–166). The social order of that world, however, is maintained by breaking the tie to Gulliver, expelling the contradiction that he represents and the threat he poses to the order of the land. In the human world, though, when the bonds of relationship threaten to upset the order of reason and to compromise the operation of justice, a more inclusive understanding can be brought to bear.

In our attempt to reconnect a cognitive stage theory of development with data on late adolescent and adult thinking about real problems of conflict and choice, we have found it necessary to posit a different ideal of maturity to account for the transformations in thinking we have observed. These transformations arise out of the recognition of the paradoxical interdependence of self and relationship, which then overrides the pure logic of formal reason and replaces it with a more encompassing form of judgment, a polyphonic structure that is able to sustain the different voices of justice and care (see Gilligan, Brown, & Rogers, in press). Piaget (1967) envisioned that "reason which expresses the highest form of equilibrium [will] reunite intelligence and affectivity." We suggest, however, that to embrace the problem of contradiction rather than to expel it, like Gulliver, from the cognitive domain, reason must be reunited with relationship, thereby making feelings an inseparable part of human thought.

Acknowledgments

The research reported here was supported by grants from the Spencer Foundation, the William F. Milton Fund, and the small grants section of the National Institute of Mental Health

(#R03MH31571). We would like to thank Terry Deacon, John Gibbs, Donna Hulsizer, Dennis Norman, and Deanna Kuhn for their comments on earlier versions of this chapter, and Lynne Israelson and the editors of this volume for their editorial help and suggestions on the current version. Portions of this chapter represent a revisiting, in light of new work, of material that in its original form appeared in D. Kuhn (Ed.), *Intellectual development beyond childhood* (San Francisco: Jossey-Bass, 1979).

IV

THEORIES OF HIGHER STAGES
OF CONSCIOUSNESS
AND SELF DEVELOPMENT

Life After Formal Operations:
Implications for a Psychology of the Self

Emily Souvaine, Lisa L. Lahey,
and Robert Kegan

"Is there a stage of development beyond Piaget's formal operations?" The question is often asked by students of cognitive development in something of the same spirit of nonascertainability as the question, "Is there life after death?" The asker invites statements of *belief,* interesting more for what they reveal about the hopes and cosmology of the speakers than for their capacity to reveal anything of the unrevealable.

This chapter takes a different view. It regards formal operations as an evolutionary state, the outcome of a long-lived ontogenetic process that has a specifiable and ongoing logic. Although "formal operations" describes an evolutionary state of considerable organizing capacity and stability, these can be demonstrated logically and empirically to be vulnerable to the creative disequilibrium that eventuates in a new evolutionary state of still greater organizing capacity and stability. That is, "formal operations" can be shown *not* to qualify for candidacy as a necessary end state in the process of psychological evolution.

This chapter will be doing well, according to its own goals, if it shows how formal operations *cannot* be the necessary final stage of development, and suggests something of the form of a necessarily *next* evolutionary state. Although we were asked to write about an alternative *endpoint* in human development, we admit to dodging this request and reconstructing a more modest goal. It is *not* our intent to argue that this next evolutionary state must itself *be* the endpoint in development; in fact, we suspect that it too is something less than a perfectly equilibrated state and is thus itself vulnerable to adaptation.

At an intuitive level, the insufficiency of formal operations as an end state in development is suggested by making one's first research subject Jean Piaget himself. One cannot describe the totality of a system, including its boundaries and extremities, while one is still embedded in that system. It seems plausible that Piaget's ability to describe the formal operational system's very logic—that is, to describe the nature of its *systematicity,* rather than just its functional capacities—bespeaks his ability to stand somewhere "outside" the system. The ability to "stand outside" the system, to reflect *upon* it rather than for it to be the very means of one's own *reflecting,* is the essence of what it is to develop (Piaget, 1954; Werner,

1940). It may well also be the essence of what we really mean by "understanding," to "stand *under*," to hold or suspend, rather than to be "caught in" or "a part of." This is the basic "logic of development," a question of to what extent the elements of one's knowing and experiencing are *taken as object*, and so can be reflected upon, and to what extent one is *subject to* them in one's knowing and experiencing.

We are about to turn to a more rigorous explication of this logic as it is reflected in Piaget-the-theorist's "formal operations," but we cannot conclude this introduction without acknowledging that the same point (about Piaget-the-subject) that seems to launch the plausibility of an argument for a postformal state also casts a shadow on the likelihood of unexceptional people like ourselves to describe with anything approaching completeness the systematicity of that state. Since our investigations daily remind us that we spend the vast majority of our lives embedded in the *formal*-operational rational systems, the reader should understand that the qualified nature of this chapter's goals is appropriate. The authors come by their modesty honestly.

Our work concerns the implications of developmental states for the study of aspects of personality that include, but extend beyond "cognition" (Kegan, 1982, 1986a,b; Kegan & Lahey, 1983; Kegan, Noam, & Rogers, 1982; Lahey, 1986; Rogers & Kegan, 1989). We are interested in the meaning of developmental states, such as formal or "postformal" operations to the construction of internal and interpersonal psychological processes. It is in this bigger context of the psychological "self" that we have chosen to consider the meaning of development beyond formal operations. The present chapter, a speculative essay rooted in the kind of data we encounter in our own interview research, suggests (1) a unitary "deep structure" to formal operations, (2) necessary features of a deep structure *beyond* formal operations, and (3) the differing expressions of these structures in the organization of the psychological self, in general, and the individuals' construction of work and intimacy, in specific.

The Logic of Development

Whether we consider Werner's "orthogenetic principle" (1940) of increasing differentiation and integration or Piaget's notions of "decentration" and "re-equilibration" (1954) or any of several less explicit conceptions of development, a common evolutionary "rhythm" or movement emerges: When the organism develops, it undergoes a transformation by which the outgrown system of organization becomes a subsystem or element of the newly emerging system of organization. The old system (which was the way the organism was organized) is "differentiated" or "decentered" from what the organism has become, and the old system is "integrated" into the new system, which thus achieves a new equilibrial state. (The old system passes from the very principle of organization to *that which gets organized*.) This state is what is called a "stage" of development within the cognitive-developmental or constructive-developmental paradigm, of which Piaget is certainly a founding father (Kegan, 1982, 1986a,b; Rogers & Kegan, 1989). Working within this paradigm, Piaget described stages in the individual's mental construction of the physical world. What makes each of these (sensorimotor, preoperational, con-

crete operational, and formal operational) eras *stages* is not just that they arrive in a regular sequence but that each, including the prior organization as the basic element *to be organized* in the new system, consists in a new equilibrial state balancing *subject* (the principle of organizing) with *object* (that which gets organized). Each stage of development, then, more than an era or period in the life-span, is a living subject–object relation, the cognate or root of a qualitatively different system of *knowing*.

The idea that the person is a natural philosopher, which has received its most elegant empirical demonstration in the work of Piaget, has been empirically disaggregated into all the familiar divisions of philosophy: Piaget's work suggests the person is a natural *logician;* Kohlberg's (1969; see Kohlberg & Ryncarz chapter) suggests he or she is also a natural *ethicist;* Perry's (1970) and Broughton's (1975), a natural *epistemologist;* Fowler's (1981), a natural *theologian;* Parsons' (1983), a natural *aesthetician;* and Kegan's (1982, 1985, 1986a,b; Rogers & Kegan, 1989), a natural *ontologist.* All these theories describe stages of development, but each of the stages is undergirded by a living subject–object relation that is the essence of its "deep structure" (Kegan, 1982, 1985, 1986a,b; Rogers & Kegan, 1989).

What is the subject–object relation we suggest undergirds Piaget's formal operations? Table 10.1 is a simplified schematic of the subject–object relations implicit in each of Piaget's four stages. We would like to quickly (and inevitably crudely) rehearse these, if for no other reason than to give the reader a sense of the developmental or transformational approach we take to the subject–object relation. This will then clarify how the very idea of a postformal state gets understood by us, how we understand the very question of whether there is a stage of development beyond formal operations.

In the sensorimotor stage the infant is embedded in, or "subject" to, his or her actions and sensations, indeed his or her reflexes (e.g., the child is not able either to *interiorize* action in mental representation or to *control* reflexes [as in toileting]). What is "interiorized" or "controlled" has become "object," but for the infant nothing is yet object, which is another way of saying, as all developmental theories do, that the infant is "undifferentiated." A new balance (or dynamic equilibrium) is reached when actions and sensations are decentered from the very way of knowing (subject) and become elements in a new way of knowing (object). This new balance, which Piaget calls "preoperational" thinking, organizes (or takes as object) action and sensations, and is thus able to construct "perceptions," images of objects recognized as distinct from oneself. Although this evolution brings an end to the egocentric or boundariless state that makes no distinction between "me" and "not-me," preoperational thinking is *subject to* its own form of egocentricity. In being

Table 10.1 Subject–Object Balancing in Piaget's States of Cognitive Development

Stage	Subject ("Structure")	Object ("Content")
Sensorimotor	Action-sensations reflexes	None
Preoperational	Perceptions	Action-sensations reflexes
Concrete operational	"Reversibilities" (the "actual")	Perceptions
Formal operational	"Hypothetico-deduction" (the "possible")	Reversibilities (the "actual")

"subject to" the perceptions, this way of knowing is unable to distinguish between its perceptions of a thing and the thing itself. Rather than being able to "have" perceptions, it is embedded in them. Unable to "coordinate" or "organize" perceptions in space or in time, it cannot construct the "reversibilities" that are the essence of Piagetian "conservation" and concrete operations. "Coordinating" or "organizing" perceptions would mean being decentered *from* them, being able to take them as objects. Such a way of knowing would involve yet another qualitatively new subject–object equilibrium, one in which the "perceptions" are transformed from the very structure of knowing (subject) to an element (or object) of a new structure, which Piaget calls "concrete operations."

This new system of knowing, which grants to things their own properties distinct from the perceiver's perceptions of them, brings into being an organization of the physical world common to the school-going years of childhood. The world loses its preoperational lability or plasticity; things hold still, and their ascertainable dimensions become of interest to the scientistic preadolescent. But the very capacity to construct the reversibilities, overcoming the egocentricity of preoperational thought, brings into being yet a third kind of egocentricity or subjectivity that is expressed in the child's inability to *reflect upon* the concrete or the "actual" in abstract consideration of the "possible." For example, when the concrete operational child is presented with four beakers of colorless liquids and asked to figure out how to make a yellow liquid by mixing some number of some of the liquids, he proceeds haphazardly, hoping to hit upon the solution (Piaget, 1954). There is no "overall plan" in evidence. Or he may be presented with a group of metal rods that differ in all possible combinations of material, length, diameter, and shape of cross-section, and be asked what makes one rod more flexible than another (Piaget, 1954). He may experiment and declare that length is a factor, demonstrating his point with a long, small-diameter rod and a short, large-diameter rod. Asked about the difference in their diameters, since he says the difference is length but has used different diameters in his testing as well, he is likely to say that he chose them to make more emphatic the effect of differing lengths. What is happening here? The concrete operational child has no overall plan that constructs all possible ways of mixing the colorless liquids and does not isolate a single variable while holding all other factors constant, because he is subject to, or embedded in, the concrete in his construction of the physical world. An overall plan that can consider concrete events that have not yet happened requires a way of knowing the world in which the concrete moves over from the subject to the object of attention. If the reversibilities coordinate (take as "object") the perceptions for the evolutionary balance that is "concrete operations," the coordination of the reversibilities themselves distinguishes the renegotiated balance that Piaget calls "formal operations."

As before, what was the very context of meaning-making is integrated into a new context. How is it that the abstract reasoning that Piaget calls formal operations and that he often found emerging during adolescence is again a consequence of this same process of transformation? When a concrete child is asked how he knows the amount of liquid in the taller, thinner beaker is the same as in the shorter, wider beaker, he usually says something like, "You could just pour it back into the first beaker." Sometimes he says something like, "The level in this glass is

higher, but the glass is also skinnier, so it balances out." Both of these answers demonstrate the concrete operational ability to coordinate perceptions; they both demonstrate reversibility. But as Piaget says, they represent different kinds of reversibility. The first is the ability to see that if you reverse a process you get back to where you started from. (Piaget calls this kind of reversibility "negation" or "inversion" and represents it as $A + (-A) = 0$; it is the kind of coordination of perceptions that creates the notion of *classes* or *groups,* one-to-one correspondence, two points coordinated in *time*.) The second reversibility is the kind that recognizes that various adjustments can balance each other out, or that if one thing, in comparison to another, is greater in one way but lesser in another, the two things might be equivalent. (Piaget calls this kind of reversibility "reciprocity," and represents it as follows: If $A \leq B$ and $B \leq A$, then $A = B$. It is the kind of coordination of perceptions that creates the notion of *relations*, of two points coordinated in *space*.) When the new developmental balance is negotiated, both these kinds of reversibility move over from subject to object and are coordinated by the new subjectivity, which constructs what Piaget calls the "inverse of the reciprocal," a way of thinking that permits the reversibilities themselves to be reflected on, allows one to consider *relations* between *classes* and *classes* of *relations*, or, put another way, allows one to think about thought.

This new subjectivity can now construe the world propositionally, hypothetically, inferentially, abstractly. It can spin out an "overall plan" of which any given concrete event (e.g., a combination of beakers) is but an instance. Put most simply, this new balance makes "what is" just one instance of "what might be." This rebalancing, often the hallmark of adolescence, unhinges the concrete world. Where before the "actual" was everything, it falls away like the flats of a theater set, and a whole new world, a world the person never knew existed, is revealed. The actual becomes but one instance (and often a not very interesting instance) of the infinite array of the "possible." The underlying psychologic is transformed from the physical to the *meta*physical, and a whole new *way* of making meaning comes into being. Formal thought no longer must proceed from the actual to the theoretical. It can start right at the theoretical; it can transcend the earth and "go through air," like Daedalus the artificer (and Stephen Daedalus, the classic adolescent) escaping the cruel dominion of his island captivity. The formal thinker can ponder about situations contrary to fact; accept assumptions for the sake of argument; make hypotheses that can be expressed in terms of propositions and tested; leave the tangible, finite, and familiar for the infinitely large or the infinitely small; invent imaginary systems; become conscious of her own thinking; and reflect on her thinking in order to provide logical justification.

On the basis of this quick sketch of Piaget's stages as an evolution of subject–object relations, it should be clear that for us the question of development *beyond* formal operations is essentially framed this way: Is there a subject–object equilibrium in which whole structures of formal operations are taken as objects or elements of a new subjectivity? How would such a subject–object relation differently know the world? What is the egocentricity it corrects? We will address these questions in the context of a bigger question: What are the implications of formal and postformal knowing for the organization of the psychological self?

Formal Operations and the Self

As discussed, the authors' research and theoretical interests consider the meaning of subject–object relations to be a domain broader than the organizing of the physical world. We consider the meaning of subject–object relations to be the organizing of intrapersonal and interpersonal experiencing, what we call the "self." Consider, for example, the concrete operational eight-year-old's new ability to coordinate two points in space or time. Does this ability have consequences for the self? Might it give rise not only to the new ability to conserve quantity, but to the experience of ambivalence (two impulses held by the self simultaneously?) or the capacity to construct goals, purposes, enduring dispositions (two impulses held over time?) each also recognized as newly emergent in the eight-year-old (Kegan, 1982, 1985, 1986a,b; Rogers & Kegan, 1989)? The concrete operational child, in other words, may conserve not only physical objects, but the "self" as well. This is the time in development, for example, when the child constructs the concrete properties that attach to the category of the self ("I am tall," "a fast runner," "Catholic," "fond of preppie clothes," "a lover of seafood," "from Cleveland," etc.). Others are constructed as people one does things with, likes or does not like because of how they do or do not assist one in one's own plans, purposes, satisfactions, or self-definition. Alternately, the typical adolescent development of early-level formal operations (inverse of the reciprocal) is accompanied by the corresponding ability to *reflect upon* the concrete categorical appropriation of the self. With the ability to coordinate (take as object) classes and relations the self's properties are reported and experienced at a whole different level of self-reflectivity ("I get my feelings hurt easily," "I hate it when people make me feel guilty," etc.), and others are potential partners in the satisfactions and difficulties of mutually reciprocal relationships with the responsibilities, obligations, and expectations they entail.

A common shift in intrapersonal and interpersonal organizing that often takes place in *adulthood* (or between late adolescence and adulthood) seems to reflect the same underlying structures that distinguish what Colby (1975) calls "early formal operations" (the inverse of the reciprocal) from "full formal operations" (a single, integrated system; the so-called INRC group). The most common expression of this shift is a move away from defining the self in terms of the perceived expectations of valued others toward a more internally derived sense of purpose or direction. Experiencing in the earlier position is essentially co-owned and co-regulated. This self's strength lies in the capacity to coordinate two independent points of view simultaneously, thus bringing about a capacity, *inter*personally, for reciprocity, mutuality, and empathy; and *intra*personally, for intersubjectivity, "mood," and the experience of one's feelings as psychological states rather than social actions and interactions. The limit of this self is its inability to consult itself about its own psychological design and direction. It has always to look to others for this, essentially delegating to others, with whom it is merged, the power and responsibility to make the self a single whole system.

Although this organization of the self is frequently described as "interpersonally merged" because the recipients of this power and responsibility are frequently other *persons,* it is also possible for the self, organized in this balance, to make *ideas* rather than people the completers of a whole self. The same idealizations, confu-

sions of boundaries, embeddedness in, rather than authorship of, a whole system of explanation can be obtained with ideational *or* personal subjectivities. Described at a more abstract level, what the ideational or interpersonal versions of this self organization have in common is the same structure we see in "early formal operations," the "inverse of the reciprocal," which at once permits the new mutuality or reciprocity of experiencing but lacks the elaboration of a logically whole system contained within the self ("full formal operations").

The parallel to *full* formal operations in self organization is that capacity for personal autoregulation, autonomy, or identity that has been historically considered as maturity or the end state in implicit or explicit developmental theories from Freud (1916) to Rogers (1959). We will call this self organization "institutional," because it establishes the self as an administrator of a psychological institution (*in + statuere:* "to set up"; *statutum:* "law," "regulation," as in *statute* and *state.*). This "institutional self," which brings into being the self as a self-conscious system or form, has its cognitive manifestation in the full development of the formal operational system that Piaget describes. What makes that system formal most of all is the new way it relates to—or gives meaning to—concrete particulars. It transcends the concrete, subordinating it to general forms, abstracted, decontextualized organizations of the particular. The same evolution that disembeds personality from context-bound interpersonalism and brings the interpersonal under the governance of an internally consistent organization (identity) is most likely reflected in the evolution of the "formal" logic that "constructs relations and movements of particulars as governed by rules or laws that have an existence without reference to the contents of the particulars" (Basseches, 1984a,b). It may be the existence of these "abstracting rules," however unaware of them we are when we are firmly in the "institutional" balance, that permits us to be self-regulating, self-sustaining, self-naming.

Evolution Beyond the Institutional Self

Suggesting that there is qualitative development *beyond* psychological autonomy and philosophical formalism is itself somewhat controversial, as it flies in the face of cherished notions of maturity in psychological and philosophical (including scientific and mathematical) realms. It suggests in the domain of science that objectivity defined in terms of abstract principles and the independence of rules of order from the phenomena they govern may not be the fullest notion of maturity. And it suggests that highly differentiated psychological autonomy, independence, or "full formal operations" may not be the fullest picture of maturity in the domain of the person.

But the notion of "development beyond autonomy" certainly does not originate with us. In truth, it is an idea that has begun to call notions of maturity to account in every realm. Doubts about the possibility of "scientific autonomy"— the ability of the perceiver and the perceived to exist autonomously—are central to the story of modern physics, the theory of relativity, and the Heisenberg uncertainty principle. Doubt about psychological autonomy as the hallmark of personal

maturity has begun to surface in many quarters (Kaplan, 1976; Miller, 1976; Gilligan, 1982, 1986a,b, 1987b; Low, 1978), as have conceptions of a postformal stage of intellectual development (see Alexander, Druker, & Langer chapter; Basseches, 1984; Koplowitz, 1984, 1990).

Conceptions of postformal thought bear remarkable similarity to each other and are consistent with the notion of development—emergence from embeddedness, the whole becoming part of a new whole, reconstruction of a subject–object relation—presented here. Murphy and Gilligan (1980) found in their studies of post-college-age adults that some persons begin to question the limits of their abstracted forms or principles for intellectual solutions of moral problems. They do not feel any less that they alone must be the authors of their conceptions of what is true or right, but they begin to doubt whether it is possible to construct generalizable rules that, however internally consistent they may be, seem perilously to ignore the particulars they organize. They found these people evolving from a rather closed-system self-sufficiency to a "more open and dialectical process involving contextualization and an openness to reevaluation" (Gilligan & Murphy, 1979, p. 7). Among the central features of this new way of thinking seems to be a new orientation to contradiction and paradox. Rather than completely threatening the system, or mobilizing the need for resolution at all costs, the contradiction becomes more recognizable as contradiction; the orientation seems to shift to the relationship between poles in a paradox rather than a choice between the poles.

Koplowitz's conception is quite similar and complementary: "Formal operational thought is dualistic. It draws sharp distinctions between the knower and the known, between one object (or variable) and another, and between pairs of opposites (e.g., good and bad). In post-formal operational thought, the knower is seen as unified with the known, various objects (and variables) are seen as part of a continuum, and opposites are seen as poles of one concept" (1978, p. 32).

Basseches (1984a,b) studied interview protocols with adults and identified 24 distinguishable "schemata" (ways of thinking), the logic of each of which is carefully shown to be postformal. This logic Basseches calls "dialectical," and among its distinctive features are the following:

1. Rather than making the form or closed system ultimate, it orients to the relationship between systems.
2. It takes the relationship between systems as prior to, and constitutive of, the systems themselves.
3. It regards motion, process, and change (not forms and entities) as the irreducible and primary feature of reality; this differs, too, from seeing motion as the "behavior of entities whose essential nature remains fixed and unchanging" (p. 6).
4. Rather than orienting primarily to movement *in* a form, it orients to movement *through* forms.
5. Beyond grasping the nature of a form or a structured system, it "views forms in a larger context which includes relationships among forms, movement from one form to another, relationships of forms to the process of form construction or organizations" (p. 7).
6. Rather than having the experience of contradiction "happen to" it, it seeks

out contradiction and is not ultimately threatened by it; its organization does not exist solely for the purpose of driving out contradiction, but also recognizes its nourishment in it.

7. Rather than exercising its dynamics in a relatively closed, self-contained dichotomous system, its dynamism is between systems, oriented not to one pole or another but to the tension between them.

Such a "postformal" logic seems suggested in the *self*-organizations of those few of our subjects who appear to us not only to have constructed a coherent psychological system (or "form") but to have made the self the very context for *trans-formation*. For these persons the self appears to be no longer identified with a particular organization of itself, the basic axioms of which are unquestionable. The self is no longer founded on a single coherent identity which is internally consistent but self-sealing in the sense that all transaction or inquiry (introspectively and interpersonally) is constructed in such a way that regardless of how questions are settled, the basic premises of the self are preserved. In contrast to this now less glorified picture of psychological *autonomy,* persons constructing a *post*formal self seem to have moved beyond (or, more technically, "differentiated themselves from") the maintenance of the single closed system toward the interpenetration of systems and the very process of system reconstruction.

Recalling our earlier description of development as a process whereby the very principle of organization (or "subject") becomes element (or "object") of a new organization, it should be clear, theoretically at least, that a postinstitutional self will be able to "take" whole psychological systems "as object," coordinating them both within the self and between self and other, across time and space. Although such a description is admittedly highly abstract rendered in this language, we hope to demonstrate the way it illuminates the common features of an apparently disparate array of clearly specifiable abilities that seem to come together at a point in development beyond formal operations or the institutional self. These include the ability to reflect on one's basic premises and pursue evidence of their limitations, to be somehow qualitatively less defensive in relation to others, to recognize and tolerate paradox and contradiction, to sustain genuinely intimate interpersonal relations. In the following sections, we will present interview excerpts[1] of individuals talking about experiences in two different domains, those of work and of intimate relationships. We hope thus to illustrate how the common features in the two domains illuminate the differences between one self-logic (the institutional self) and another. We also hope to describe what we see as a gradual evolutionary process from the one to the next by illustrating the transition between the two. It is our sense that in each instance the common features of the paired excerpts in the two domains reflect a single subject–object distinction, making possible experiences that could not exist through an earlier self-system.

"Institutional" Constructions of Work and Love

The strength of the institutional self is its ability for self-regulation, its capacity to take personal responsibility for its self-owned and self-controlled psychological ini-

tiatives. The limitation of the institutional self lies in its being identified with the internal organization that it is responsible for running and regulating. Because there is no self independent of the institution to converse with, the institution is a sealed self-system: It lacks the ability to reflect upon or look onto those self-constructed, self-selected values, goals, and purposes. Being subject to this running (thereby cut off from the possibility of recognizing this limitation), the self is determined to continue managing itself as it is. The continued maintenance of the organization has become the very goal of the organization.

At the institutional balance, a supportive relationship between self and other is one that confirms the self's personal psychological autonomy—not in the sense of isolation or separation from others, but in the literal sense of "autonomy" as self-naming. These are relations that in some way allow for, and even celebrate, the meeting of each individual's self-constructed values, goals, and purposes. Individuals' value systems are interdependent to the extent that the institutional self can recognize the differing values or purposes of another and can encompass within the self's institution, the value of furthering the other's ability to exercise the administration of a separate self-system. Relationships in this context are as much about honoring a boundary constructed by the other for preservation of each person's self-system as they are about aiding each other in meeting one another's goals. Any act by the other that alters or threatens the exercising of this self-system is experienced as a violation to the self-regulating institutional self. How does this meaning system express itself in the more public context of work and in the more intimate context of love relationships?

In describing how he views his role as an editor, Sam illustrates a kind of sharing that typifies a work relationship between institutional selves:

> My writers constantly give me their work to read. The easier ones for me to respond to are the ones that I like right off the bat—they're the ones that are clear. I don't strain any to understand the ideas and I basically agree with most of what they've said. My responsibility to those writers is basically to back them up. You know, they've got my support to go ahead. It's a funny kind of approval. I mean they know how good their work is. It's not like they need me to say "this is good." But I say it anyway, because I know it's always satisfying to hear someone else tell you when they like what you've done. But then there are those pieces that I don't approve of, ones where I don't agree with what the person is saying, or how they're saying it, or something like that. I think my responsibility to those writers is the same as with the others—back them up. I try to let that person know that I respect her or his efforts, you know, to acknowledge the care that went into their work and the pride that comes from accomplishing something while also letting them know what I think is wrong about what they've done. I think my telling them what I don't agree with gives them the chance to go back to their drawing board and take it from there, to do what they choose to with the feedback I've given them. That's what I'd want someone to do with my work.

As editor, Sam sees his responsibility as supporting his writers in their work effort. "My responsibility is basically to back them up," he says. Support here has to do basically with respecting the authorship of his writer's ideas. Independent of Sam's evaluation, support essentially involves encouraging the other's ability to

exercise the administration of a separate self-system. More specifically, support is about honoring the creations of the writers, honoring their self-contained ability to produce those products, and honoring their independent capacity to evaluate themselves, or their selves' creations. Supporting some writers means that Sam applauds their work (for example, "I want to let them know that they've got my support to continue"). His "backing them up" in this way seems to be as much supporting their capacity to have worked out some idea by themselves as congratulating them on their actual product. His finding some aspect of backing them up as odd (for example, "It's not like they need me to say 'this is good' ") is evidence of his respect for others as their own authority, who, with their self-defining, self-depending, self-authoring capacities, can evaluate themselves.

Supporting other writers, those whose pieces he doesn't approve of, amounts to, again, congratulating those people on their being the originators of their purposes and meanings. Although he may not agree with their actual product, he nonetheless respects the authorship of their perspective. The way he offers them his negative feedback, allowing them, "to do what they choose to" with it, conveys this respect by placing the responsibility for reforming the ideas with the original author. Instead of acting in a unilateral way—for example, by telling those people what needs to be changed—he leaves it to them to "take it from there." In this way he communicates a basic trust in their capacity to judge for themselves what they want to do with his opinion. As such, he meets other people on their grounds, where they can remain the master in control of their product.

Sam's wanting to acknowledge the "care that went into their work and the pride that comes from accomplishing something" also illustrates a way he honors a product. This want seems expressive of a keen awareness of how personal one's work products are, that they are expressions of the self. His knowing that one's creation is so important is a knowing consistent with the institutional self whose identity is found in the exercise of maintaining its self-system. The self's construction of an idea and the formed idea itself are both expressions of this self's identity. As such, options for supporting other people include attending to their capabilities for being the originators of their work and/or attending to the actual outcomes of this work. By acknowledging the care that went into someone's work, Sam is confirming the self who is the creator of ideas, the writer herself. His remaining feedback is more addressing the product, the written and not the writer.

Sam sees himself as responsible both for backing up all his writers and for giving them his honest feedback. One way to understand his taking responsibility in these ways is to view them as characteristics of the role of all editors, a role that Sam steps into. Our perspective differs by seeing Sam as the designer of his responsibilities as editor; he is the source of his knowing how and what to tell his writers. His self-constructed view about how to support them best and about the quality of good writing is the basis for Sam's responses to the writers. Similarly, his ability to express to the writers his evaluation of their work, be it a positive or negative evaluation, suggests that Sam is not subject to their evaluations and expectations of him. His concern is with letting them know his opinion and how they should proceed (e.g., "go ahead" or "go back to the drawing board") and not with, for example, whether they approve of him. Sam's standard, and not anyone else's, is his

reference point. Sam gives the "go-ahead" to work that conforms to his definition of good writing, whereas he evaluates negatively the writing that does not meet his standards. Thus, the strength of Sam's meaning-making lies in his capacity to see himself as the originator of his own meaning and purposes, as well as in his seeing that others are in charge of their own meaning and purposes.

Sam's honoring of the integrity of the writer's work, regardless of whether he agrees with it, is simultaneously honoring his own integrity. That is, his construction of his responsibility to the writers is as much a responsibility to them as it is to himself. The way Sam goes about giving his negative feedback to others ensures that neither party's integrity will be disrupted, since no one gets confronted or directly challenged in the process. No one's work gets intruded on. As long as Sam's system keeps working smoothly, he is able to encourage his fellow workers to meet their own goals, values, and purposes. However, should his system be interfered with, then the limits of his meaning-making would be exposed. For example, we can imagine that, if a writer did not take into account Sam's negative feedback in their rewrite, Sam might decide not to allow that piece to be published. He has his standards for what constitutes good writing and he will continue to apply them. To apply, for example, the writer's standards instead of his own would amount to Sam's surrendering his own standards and values. When the self is ultimately invested in maintaining itself and when a choice that reflects that self-system must be made (as in Sam's case where what is published reflects the editor as well as the writer), then this choice is clear—the self's standards must prevail.

Such is the active defending of an institutional self. If Sam's system were not attacked directly, a limitation could still be seen in less immediately threatening circumstances, such as his evaluating of both himself and others. We imagine that if Sam were to tell us about his view of another person's standards for writing, he would use his own unquestioned standards to judge them. Like his evaluation of their writing, Sam's preference would tend to be those standards with which he agreed over those with which he disagreed. Without questioning the very standard he has (both for himself and others) or the ways that he uses them, his standards and consequential evaluations are bound to remain unchanged. As such, he is unlikely to discover ways that he is perhaps ineffective, unfair, or counterproductive or ways that he might enhance his perspective.

The price both Sam and the writer pay for his need to preserve his self-system is that their independent worlds remain independent and fundamentally unchanged. Instead of assuming that his standards are right, Sam could create a context where both his and the writer's perspective could be examined jointly, thereby testing his assumption about what makes for good writing. A possible product of such an exchange is that together the writer and Sam could define standards acceptable to both rather than each of them being in charge of their own ideas. Our suggestion is that such a different way of operating in one's work relations may not be simply a matter of temperament but the consequence of developmental position.

This way of constructing the relationship between self and other can be seen also in the domain of intimate relationships. Susan, in the following passage, reveals the criteria for a relationship with the institutional self when she talks about her relationships with her husband.

Last week my husband was telling me about an important feeling he had that was evidently very painful to him. I was trying to understand what was important for him so that I could help him, because I think my being an understanding, sympathetic listener is the way I can be most helpful to him. So I encouraged him to talk and I asked him some questions. Basically he did describe his experience, but I didn't really get a chance to respond to his description since he immediately asked me whether I would have felt hurt if I were in that situation myself. From what I understood of the situation, I was certain that I wouldn't have. But I couldn't tell him that because that would have been like my ignoring how he actually was hurt. And I certainly didn't want to do that! What I really wanted to do was to just let him know that I understood how he must have felt.

Susan's concern in her helping her husband seems to be about her wish to preserve the same kind of boundary that would be violated in Sam's view if he told others how they should rework their writing. Her construction of what is required in order to be helpful to her husband presumes a distinctness between them, a distinctness that, if it is to be bridged, requires that her husband tell her his experience. Susan's spanning this distinctness by understanding and responding to his experience seems to be at the heart of what being helpful means to her. Being helpful, being understanding, and being sympathetic are equated with providing a kind of company for her husband in his experience. From her statement, we can surmise that being an "understanding, sympathetic listener" basically amounts to her affirming her husband's experience of his sentiments. Her effort "to understand what was important" for her husband suggests an institutional self who honors his capacity to exercise his self-defined values.

In keeping with that effort, Susan seems to view a response that might be contrary to his as a violation of him. Telling him that she would not have felt the same way he did (e.g., "I was certain that I wouldn't have felt hurt if I were in the same situation") is unacceptable (e.g., "I couldn't tell him that"), because saying this does not preserve and honor his way of making sense of the experience. Again, her effort is to respect her husband's made-meaning.

A difference between Sam and Susan is revealed in their differing stances on the value of disagreeing with others. While Sam is committed to telling his writers when he disagrees with them, Susan views her disagreeing with her husband (e.g., telling him she would not have felt hurt if she were in the situation) as unhelpful. Differing in their ways of responding to others, so that Sam directly applies his standards to others' work whereas Susan appears invested in her husband's experiences and tries to keep her experiences out of the way, Sam and Susan are nonetheless fundamentally alike in that both are the chief designers of their values, purposes, and meanings. That is, Susan and Sam have theories, for example, about how to be effective as an editor or as a caring, helpful person. Just as Sam self-selects criteria for good writing and self-derives his method for supporting his writers, Susan is the author of her ideas about what and how to care for herself and others. In that way, Susan, like Sam, applies her standards to others.

Susan's capacity to be self-defining is the strength of her system, whereas her need to maintain that system is her limit. While Susan's understanding and sympathetic responses, coupled with her noncontradictory statements, result in confirming her husband's self-system, they simultaneously serve to maintain her own

self-system. For example, Susan never invites her husband to question her value that confirming his experience is the way she can be most helpful to him. The likely consequence of this is that Susan will not receive any information to support or disconfirm her value or theory of how to be helpful. Another example is found in Susan's not checking with her husband her assumption that he would negatively hear her telling him that she would have felt differently if she were in his situation. She assumes that he will hear this as "ignoring how he actually was hurt." Without dismissing the possibility of this interpretation, we can imagine alternative interpretations her husband could have constructed, some of which could even be positive (e.g., he might welcome hearing how someone *wouldn't* experience hurt). Without directly involving him in the workings of her system, without testing in any ways the accuracy of her assumptions and values about being helpful, she is bound only to discover exactly what she sets out to do. With no openness to bringing contradiction into either her own or her husband's experience, both systems thus remain self-sealed.

We hear how an institutional self might construct an intimate relationship in listening to Susan's concern for helping her husband. Intent on honoring his experience, Susan seeks to respond understandingly and sympathetically to him. Had he not disrupted her way of helping by asking for her interpretation, we imagine that she would have felt their exchange went quite smoothly, and successfully. Such success, from Susan's perspective, would lie in her letting her husband know that she heard and understood him. Her construction of success seems, therefore, to lie in her keeping their separate systems separate. Such success is not to suggest that Susan and her husband would not feel closer to each other as a consequence of the ways she responds to him. Indeed, we imagine both could experience quite powerfully each other's love through such a connection. Our point is that the strength of this way of knowing is that each person's self-defining self is given room to be exercised. In Susan's example she is able to keep exercising her self-defined system of care.

Both Sam and Susan are telling us something about the ways they construct their relationship to others. Although there are important differences in the ways they go about responding to others (Sam knowing to treat others as he does because he knows that is what he would want if he were in their situation; Susan responding to others by understanding their experiences from *their* perspectives), nonetheless both can be seen to live in a common psychologic. Both share the capacity to define themselves as well as to take responsibility for their individual selves. More specifically, they can both set their personal standards and be the primary source of evaluating themselves. Both are capable of also granting to others the same respect for the importance of their authoring of their perspectives.

Susan and Sam also share the inability to reflect upon the values or goals each has defined or to welcome in a relationship such reflection by another. That kind of reflection would be experienced as a lack of respect to the person whose sense of self comes from the exercise of self-definition. Reminiscent of Sam's relationship with his fellow workers, Susan and her husband cannot truly collaborate in their relationship. Each may help the other work on meeting the standards of his or her own self-system, but not in any way that questions how either defines or comes to

those standards. In both Sam's and Susan's world, such an effort would threaten the integrity of the self identified with the meeting of those standards and would violate the boundary that each works so naturally and so hard to preserve. A relationship between institutional selves is therefore a confirming of both individuals' autonomy with no effort or ability to transform either self-system.

Before we conclude this section we would like to point out what we think we have just done, and especially what we think we have not done. We normally use our framework as a lens to try to understand a whole individual in his activity of meaning-making. Here we focused on Sam's and Susan's descriptions of a single experience, not to explore the nature of his or her entire meaning-making, but to illustrate one distinction—that of institutional meaning-making—that our framework makes. Based on one excerpt of his and hers, we made generalizations that we mean to be about the institutional balance, *and not about Sam or Susan.* We will now follow our discussion of "Sam" and "Susan" with excerpts from different speakers, which again we use to characterize other balances. By focusing on the descriptions of the qualitatively different balances themselves, we are necessarily giving up following the dynamic experiences of real people. Thus, although an excerpt from an interview can be expressive of a person's made-meaning in one instance and hence can illustrate theoretical distinctions, it can never capture the activity or wholeness of that person's meaning-making. As such, our references to the interview excerpts using the speaker's name are by definition not expressive of a living person but of the particular balance we understand their words to illustrate. We speak of "Sam" and "Susan" as embodiments or "ideal types" of the institutional balance. Similarly, in later sections, "Mark" and "Michelle," "Donna" and "Dennis" serve as illustrations of other "ideal types" of made-meaning. We have made these static descriptions our focus in this chapter because our purpose is not to illustrate or discuss the developmental process but to distinguish between a subject–object balance representative of formal operations and a balance qualitatively beyond formal operations.

"Transitional" Constructions of Work and Love

As explained earlier in this chapter, the very nature of being subject to a system prevents the individual from reflecting upon the limits of that system. Thus, we would not expect Sam to be dissatisfied with his inability to reflect with a writer about how each comes to define good writing standards. Similarly, Susan cannot consider how her own feelings about what is helpful may affect how helpful she can be to her husband. If either Sam or Susan demonstrated this kind of reflective ability, we would suspect that they had begun to transcend the institutional balance.

The process of evolution from the institutional to the interindividual balance (like the evolution between all balances) begins with the individual's ability to reflect upon the limits of her institutional construction. When the individual begins not only to reflect upon the limits of the institutional balance, but to construct a new meaning in somehow addressing those limits, we see this as a fully transitional self-system. Because the transitional self is constructing this new meaning not in

and of itself, but in terms of improving the functioning of the earlier system, we see two meaning structures operating. The very existence of these two meaning structures alerts us to the transitional nature of the meaning-making.

In Michelle's description of a work experience, we see how the transitional self's capacities come from two meaning-structures.

> They asked such good questions, questions that were confronting of my views where I was learning. They asked questions which supported and made comments that helped me to see things that I had not seen. I felt it was, it was a successful lecture. . . . My view is it's terribly important for me to know and to learn when I'm wrong and when I have doubts, especially those that I'm not aware of, and those people were helping me to see that it's perfectly possible that I should be relatively bright and wrong and relatively bright and right, relatively right and not so bright. I mean all those, all those possibilities make good sense to me, and I need to know all of them because what if I were absolutely right and it was some sheer luck and it wasn't that I was particularly bright? I ought to learn that because it's terribly important for my sense of self-esteem for my worth to be based at some reality and not on a fiction that says I am not bright when I am—those combinations. So, I think the greatest sort of inner sense of competence is if my evaluations of myself, positive or negative, are confirmed by other people in ways which I can trust or disconfirm. It can be either way so that I learn.

Michelle tells us that this was a successful lecture. To understand how she experiences success, we look to see how she can reflect upon her own psychological system in order to question whether her evaluations of herself are valid. She says, "They asked such good questions, questions that were confronting of my views where I was learning. They asked questions which supported and made comments that helped me to see things I had not seen." Implicit in this statement is a recognition that she needs this experience of being questioned in order to learn. Unlike Sam, who sees his writers as capable of defining and evaluating their own standards for writing, Michelle tells us, "My view is it's terribly important for me to know and to learn when I'm wrong and when I have doubts. . . ." In this statement, we see Michelle reflecting on the limits of an institutional self. She seems to see how a closed system of self-evaluation could limit her ability to evaluate effectively her own performance. Michelle explains that she must have a way of knowing and learning when she is wrong. Essentially, she can take a perspective on her own exercising of her goals and values so as to perceive that she could blind herself to ways that she might be "wrong." Although Sam cannot see how his own definition of "good writing" might come up for questioning and therefore be enriched, Michelle cannot rest comfortably without creating a context in which her own premises and conclusions can be questioned. The creation of such a context is what alerts us to her construction of a self that is transitional between the institutional and interindividual balances.

Michelle tells us "those people were helping me to see that it's perfectly possible that I should be relatively bright and wrong and relatively bright and right, relatively right and not so bright . . . and I need to know all of them because what if I were absolutely right and it were some sheer luck and it wasn't that I was particularly bright? I ought to learn that because it's terribly important for my sense of self-esteem for my worth to be based at some reality and not on a fiction that says

I am not bright when I am—those combinations." We are inferring from this statement that Michelle is distinguishing between the actual ideas or answers that she produces and the reasoning or process by which she arrives at these ideas or products. An analogy might be the difference between her getting the right answer on a long division problem "by some sheer luck," and therefore never discovering that her method of dividing is "not so bright," or in the reverse, getting the wrong answer and never discovering that her method (except for some small error in, for example, subtraction) is "relatively bright." Essentially, then, helping Michelle to distinguish between "bright" and "right" can be viewed as providing feedback not only about the products she creates, but about her process of creating. To extend the long division analogy, she is inviting others to participate in the actual construction of how to solve the problem as well as to evaluate the way she did solve the problem. If a theory of how to perform long division were one of the premises of her psychological self-system, then she would be not only questioning her system, but reflecting on how others' self-systems might interact with hers to evaluate and perhaps transform the very premises of her own system.

That Michelle is engaging in such interaction seems clear when she says, "I think the greatest sort of inner sense of competence is if my evaluations of myself, positive or negative, are confirmed by other people in ways which I can trust or disconfirm, it can be either way so that I can learn." We infer then that it was a successful lecture, because it helped her to learn not only about the ideas she expounded in the lecture, but about the premises of her own system that constructed these ideas. Her ability to experience competence even if negative self-evaluations are confirmed demonstrates that she is not identified with the exercises of an independent, autonomous self-system; on the contrary, she is identified with the learning that comes from the interaction between such systems. If she learns from feedback that she is "not so right" or even "not so bright" in what she has said, her ultimate sense of self is not jeopardized, because the self that Michelle constructs is now identified with what she has learned.

Although we see how Michelle's construction of her experience transcends an institutional self, we also see the structure of the institutional self as still part of Michelle's meaning-making. We see that she can reflect not only upon her own process of creating, but also upon the functioning of others' systems so as to evaluate whether she can "trust or disconfirm" their contributions to an interaction. Remembering that she has said, "It's terribly important for me to know and to learn when I'm wrong," we infer that the purpose or the meaning she constructs for the interaction between systems is the ability to check her own independent evaluating and to detect erors that might result from its own potentially self-sealing properties. We can imagine, then, that if she could not find a way to "trust" or "disconfirm" their contributions to this interaction, then the interaction would have no value for her. If the interacting is brought into being to transform the limits of her independent self-system, then the interacting has no intrinsic value separate from its worth in terms of the transformation it is designed to effect. Although Michelle invites and welcomes others to participate in the defining and evaluating of her self-system (a construction of a post-institutional self), the purpose of the interaction exists in their participating in a process that has a product she can "trust or disconfirm" (a construction still characteristic of the institutional self). Here we

see the transitional nature of Michelle's self in the two different constructions that are present in her self-description.

The transitional self we see in Michelle's description of her experience is illustrated in the importance to her of detecting and correcting the errors of her own self-system (the emphasis on what she can learn) simultaneous with an ability to engage in an interaction between systems that transcends the functioning of any independent system. In other words, the ability to experience herself within the process of an interaction between systems reflects an interindividual construction of self, whereas the construction of the importance of perfecting the actual products of her own self-system reflects an institutional construction of self. Later in the chapter, we will explore the gestalt of a purely interindividual construction. What is relevant to the discussion here is how the existence of the two structures defines a self with an array of abilities qualitatively different from those of Sam and Susan.

The transitional construction of work and work relationships, as illustrated in this discussion of how Michelle experiences success, makes way for interactions between individuals, so that collaborative efforts can transcend the capacities of any one individual's perspective. When definitions of competence address a *process* of creating as well as the creations themselves, individuals and organizations can re-evaluate how they go about meeting values and goals, continually seeking to improve productivity, quality, and creativity. No longer ultimately invested in preserving the workplace as it is, the workers can engage one another and even those in other workplaces in a process of evolving and redesigning goals. The strength of this construction of work is its welcoming of others' perspectives, including negative and positive evaluations, as part of an important transformative process. The limitation of this investment in transformation, however, is that these others' perspectives are seen as valuable only in terms of the transformation itself. For example, those perspectives that might seek to advocate their investment in the goals and values as originally formulated may be seen as obstacles to the transformative process. Because the transformation is the ultimate value, anyone viewed as an obstacle to that transformation might be excluded from the defining and evaluating process. The very strength that allows the transitional self to include others in collaborative work can thus result in a concomitant excluding of those others whose investment in the original construction is ultimate.

If these abilities to collaborate with others in the workplace in a wholly new way are in fact a hallmark of a new subject–object distinction, we would expect to find parallel new abilities also within the domain of intimate relationships. In Mark's description of an experience of closeness with his wife, we hope to illustrate how we see such parallels:

My wife, A., and I can often bring each other a special insight and closeness. Recently, for example, she and I had been really stuck over her feelings about D., a woman I work with. We seemed to be unable to see how our own, as opposed to the other's, perspectives might be contributing to this mounting conflict. And the pain to both of us of her jealousy and my intolerance of that jealousy was very intense. Because I could not bear to add to that pain, I had decided not to share with A. my feelings about a blow-up D. and I had recently.

The recent conflict I referred to came up when A. overheard me telling a friend about the blow-up with D. What upset A. the most was that here was this relationship that she was worried about to begin with, and that my keeping silent about it only made her believe that she had reason to worry about it. A's telling me how mad she was really helped me to see how I was unintentionally hurting her. I realized that in my trying to protect her from more pain, that I still was hurting her. As we talked that through, a new upset was mounting in A. She wondered whether my decision indicated that I didn't trust her ability to grow or to change her ideas and feelings about D's and my relationship. Her asking that prompted me to consider that possibility. And it made a lot of sense to me, that my "kind" intent of protecting her wasn't kind at all, that such protecting perpetuated jealous feelings and offered no opportunities for change. So there was a way I was hurting both of us.

But by far the most exciting outcome of our working to understand my choice was that I realized, with A's help, that my contribution to the stuckness we had experienced around this topic could be related to my unwillingness to explore the possibility that it *is* a relationship that could threaten A's and my marriage. It was a wonderful reunion for us, a reexperience of our closeness together—we haven't yet resolved all the differences, but we have reawakened our faith in how our caring for each other helps us both to keep growing.

So what do you see as the resolution of this conflict?

Well, we haven't resolved it yet, but ultimately I imagine that each of us will see the error in the way we've been approaching this problem so that we will know how to prevent its being a problem. I may see how I am contributing to A's jealousy, and A may see that she doesn't need to be jealous of D in certain ways. Right now, it seems that if we are ready to explore where we are wrong, we will be able to resolve our conflicting feelings.

In Mark's description of an experience of closeness, we are immediately struck by how his experience of intimacy differs from that of Susan's in the last section. Whereas Susan experiences closeness in understanding and expressing her sympathy for her husband's perspective, Mark describes his frustration in finding that he and his wife A. cannot see beyond their own perspectives: He says, "She and I had been really stuck. . . . We seemed to be unable to see how our own, as opposed to the other's, perspective might be contributing to the mounting conflict." If Mark's construction of this experience were institutional, he could not report with frustration an inability to see beyond his own perspective; he would be identified with that perspective, just as he would experience his wife as identified with her perspective. Apparently, for Mark, the cause of the conflict is *not the difference in their perspectives,* but an experience of "stuckness" in a process that might otherwise help them to alter their perspectives. Whereas Susan's experience of intimacy causes her to keep her own views separate from those of her husband, Mark seems to experience closeness in finding a way to go beyond or to transform their separate views.

When Mark describes how he and his wife became unstuck, we see how his experience of intimacy is constructed from an ability to engage in an interaction

between his own and another self-system in order to transform the perspectives of both independent systems. He says,

> A's telling me how mad she was helped me to see how I was unintentionally hurting her. I realized that in my trying to protect her from more pain, that I still was hurting her. As we talked that through, a new upset was mounting in A. She wondered whether my decision indicated that I didn't trust her ability to grow or to change her ideas and feelings about D's and my relationship. Her asking that prompted me to consider that possibility. And it made a lot of sense to me, that my "kind" intent of protecting her wasn't kind at all, that such protecting perpetuated jealous feelings and offered no opportunities for change. So there was a way I was hurting both of us.

We see that Mark's experience of closeness comes in the sharing with his wife, in a joint reflection of how each came to hold the position that led to the conflict. By the very description he gives, we can see how he constructs this sharing in a way that allows him to reflect upon his own psychological self-system that originally defined keeping silent about his relationship with D. as protecting his wife A. We see that in engaging A's perspective, in considering how her psychological self-system viewed his "protecting" as an indication of his lack of faith in her, he is able to come to a new perspective, a transformation of his earlier view. His experience of joy can exist because A's "upset" at his earlier perspective *negatively evaluates a perspective of his with which he is no longer identified.* Able to take as object the "products" of his own institution, Mark is identified with the ability to engage with A. in transforming those "products." His ability to engage in that process is an illustration to us of meaning-making that transcends the institutional self.[2]

We can see, however, how Mark's meaning-making here is transitional and not fully interindividual when we consider his understanding of the purpose of this transforming process. He explains, "But by far the most exciting outcome . . . was that I realized, with A's help, that my contribution to the stuckness we had experienced . . . could be related to my unwillingness to explore the possibility that it *is* a relationship that could threaten A's and my marriage. . . . we haven't yet resolved all the differences, but we have reawakened our faith in how our caring for each other helps us both to keep growing." Here we see evidence again of how the interaction results in a transformed view: he is willing to consider newly that the relationship he viewed as benign could be a threat. Also apparent in this statement, however, is how his ultimate joy lies in the outcome of their exploration which promises to unfreeze a stuckness that had been a source of conflict. The result of their discussion is that he and A are no longer representing conflicting views: His reframing of his own intolerance of her jealousy causes him to lend a reasonableness to that jealousy. Thus, although we see how engaging in this interactive process reflects elements of the interindividual construction, we also see an emphasis on the importance of the resolution of their conflict as the purpose of their exploration. We imagine that had the outcome been equally transformative but less promising in terms of a resolution, Mark would not experience a comparable joy or closeness in having engaged his wife in this endeavor.

Reminiscent of Michelle's need to "trust" or "disconfirm" the evaluations of others so as to know whether she is "right" and/or "bright," Mark's purpose in

jointly exploring his perspective is the resolution of a conflict. We see in this purpose how an institutional self might come to reflect upon the limits of a sealed psychological system and engage a process *for the purpose of improving the functioning of the system.* While engaging in the transformative process evidences an interindividual construction, the emphasis on the product of that process testifies to a coexistent institutional construction. The emerging structure is being used on behalf of the older structure's purposes. What we see as a simultaneous existence of these two structures leads us to view Mark as illustrative of the transitional self.

We see Mark's construction of an intimate relationship as parallel to Michelle's construction of the working world. Just as Mark can seek to understand how his wife's perspective might reveal a misconception on his part, Michelle can seek others' negative evaluations to help detect errors in her own process of creating ideas. When the self is no longer identified with the products of its institution, both feelings and ideas become open for reconsideration and reframing. The other, whether a colleague or a loved one, can be viewed as the holder of a part of the self's own self-concept: Mark can see that in A's jealousy was an expression of his own unwillingness to consider how his relationship may be threatening the marriage. Michelle can see that in others' doubting of her ideas is an expression of her own "not so bright" creative process. Both individuals give evidence of how the transitional self can embrace the other as an expression of their own selves.

Just as the transitional self can transform the workplace, so can it transform the domain of intimate relationships. An experience of closeness or intimacy no longer needs to focus on preserving and embracing the other's experience as she describes it. Sharing can involve engaging in a process of growing together, of questioning and redefining values and hopes, of exploring as opposed to accepting differences. Although an institutional experience of closeness might involve helping the other to meet goals the self does not endorse, the transitional experience might exist in a context of examining how each came to hold such differing goals. Although the strength of this construction lies in the ability to engage one another in an enriching and ever-transforming process, the limitation lies in the emphasis on what is gained by such joint questioning. When the experience of intimacy comes in rejoicing in the transformations, the moments of stuckness and the frustrations of not transforming become difficult to share. If each experiences the other's engaging in the transforming as necessary to that intimacy, then an intimate other who becomes invested in one perspective can be experienced as distant and unintimate. Sharing or easing the pain of those moments can be impossible if one sees the other's inability to engage in an exploration as evidence of a lack of caring or closeness.

We see in this description how parallel are the features of the transformations the transitional self can effect in the domains of work and intimate relationships. On the one hand, perspectives can be included and welcomed in wholly new ways; goals and values can be questioned; and an emphasis on growing and sharing can replace an investment in confirming and accepting the status quo. On the other hand, the intimacy granted to such growing and sharing can result in an intolerance and rejection of others who cannot or do not participate in growing and sharing. We see the logic of this intolerance when we remember how the transitional self is brought into being through a dissatisfaction with the limits of the institutional world. It is quite possible, in ways reminiscent of transitions in infancy, childhood,

and adolescence, that what is *actually* being resisted, rejected, or excluded is more *the old self* than some other person, or aspect of another person. Because of the very tenuousness of its own hold on a new world, because its experience of this new world is valued in the ability to overcome the feared institutionality, the transitional self must adamantly resist any expressions of a closed system's constructions of meaning so threatening to its own new sense of self. When one begins to take a perspective on the paradox of engaging in a transforming process for the purpose of a future product, a gradual equilibrating process creates the interindividual self. In the following section we illustrate how we see this interindividual construction in the domains of work and intimate relationships.

Interindividual Constructions of Work and Love

The interindividual self takes a perspective on the transitional self's investment in transformation. This new subject–object distinction allows the self to see that the "products" of the transformative process are as subject to transformation as the products earlier identified with an institutional self. Recognizing then an inability to evaluate with certainty any one product or transformed product, the interindividual self constructs a new subjectivity that experiences self in the context of the interaction between systems. The evidence of the more equilibrated nature of this self lies in the lack of threat from, or intolerance toward, other perspectives. Whereas the transitional self evidences its disequilibrium in its inability to tolerate obstacles to its transforming endeavors, the interindividual self accepts such obstacles as expressions of the very nature of the interaction among all systems. All perspectives and all forms of meaning-making become elements *expressive of one's own self,* upon which one can reflect. The interindividual self is ultimately invested in the interacting between systems, each of which is seen as an expression of only one part of a larger whole. The only imaginable definition of the "whole" lies in the motion among these systems, with which the self is identified. This construction allows the self to see others and the self equally as expressions of a larger community to which both belong. Hence, this self knows the other as an expression of part of the self. No longer can cause and effect or two opposing sides of a conflict be identified within separable systems. One sees the self and the other as both the victim and the villain, product and process, lover and loved.

In the domains of work and intimate relationships we can see how the interindividual self is liberated from requiring that the other participate in reaching any particular outcome. While choosing to act toward certain values or goals, the interindividual knower can recognize others' opposition as an important expression of the meaning of these choices. For this self, striving for values and goals does not constitute overcoming the obstacles presented; rather, it involves experiencing these obstacles as an integral part of one's own action. Thus, in work and in love, the interindividual self can be responsible not only for striving to overcome pain and hurt but also for sharing the responsibility for causing and experiencing the pain and hurt.

In Dennis' description of an experience in teaching, we see illustrated an interindividual construction of the domain of work. Dennis described his recent expe-

rience of anxiety during a class he was teaching. Committed to a particular theory, he teaches this and other theories to his students. The group of students became stuck on a perspective they held, one they believed identified a contradiction in Dennis' theory. This perspective of the students prevented their being willing to inquire with Dennis into how the theory and their perspective conflicted. Just when Dennis had come to accept their unwillingness and move on, another student with whom he had worked raised a view that successfully invited the group stuck in one perspective to inquire into their reasoning and hers. The class then became able to continue interacting with Dennis and each other to examine their views of numbers of theories. The following excerpt comes at the end of a long discussion about what this experience meant to Dennis.

Did its having a successful outcome renew your faith in it in any way that an unsuccessful outcome would not have?

Well, um, I guess, I think the answer is sure. At the middle of this semester I, we, had a midterm evaluation of the course. Ninety participants were split almost exactly in half in terms of what they said—half found it one of the best courses that they had taken and half didn't like it at all and found it worthless. By the end of the course, I don't have an exact count, but I think, the vast majority thought it was worthwhile and I think this incident probably was—if you were going to point to one key incident that was it. There were a couple of other things as well that didn't have to do with me at all, but more with how I choreographed bringing in some other visitors who helped to confirm to them that it made sense to try out these ideas, and at the midterm my faith was shaken again. . . . I was feeling at the midterm, maybe I have been overambitious about the program and that I am trying to squeeze too much into too little, and for one reason or another, I just don't fit here and I ought to get out. I mean, I had, it is very easy to reawaken feelings of despair that what I am doing doesn't fit with the way the world works. Those had certainly been reawakened and I would say that this was, you know, that class period was probably the single key to making it work this year, and making it better than it has yet been here. But I mean, it reawakens my faith but I also think it sure leaves me in some state of suspension, because boy am I aware of how much it costs each time, boy am I more and more aware of how few people are having motivation to do this kind of thing, and therefore it still leaves the questions open as to whether all of this is serving a larger purpose.

Is it important to you to be keeping that question open, or is it a disappointment to you keeping that question open?

(*Laugh*) Well, obviously if I were absolutely consistent, it would be important to keep it open. That is, if I really believe in inquiry, that is the central question that I have, so I should keep it open. But in fact, I am very small in these matters, and I wish to hell I knew the answer to the questions and I was on the right side and fighting for truth and goodness and it was all clear and sure. I would love to know that I was on the right side and the winning side and what I have had for the first time seriously in the last few years, it has occurred to me that I might be on the right side and the losing side. And in that it really cosmically,

and socially, and politically may be a losing battle the question of whether one still wants to play it if that is the side one is on is a difficult question.

What I am inferring from all of this, and it may be quite a leap, is that this process of inquiring is in service of these values of truth and justice and the right side.

Well, that, that breaks the means, makes the means and ends seem too dichotomous, I mean, makes it sound like inquiry is the means to these other ends. So let me come back all the way on the other side and say while I would love to be on the side of truth and beauty and goodness, clearly there is certainly another part of me that does literally believe that the inquiring state is the awake state and that that is human destiny, so that the inquiry is actually the end as well as the means, and the closest we would ever get to truth so to speak would be to be so awake that the outer world is in question, my sensual world is in question, my cognitive world is in question and my so to speak purpose and intuitive world is in question all at the same time.

The actual outcome of the class Dennis had described is reminiscent of the kinds of transformation experienced by Michelle and Mark. The process of interacting had transformed a conflict between the students' view and his view. The interviewer's opening question, "Did its having a successful outcome renew your faith in any way that an unsuccessful outcome would not have?" probes to discover whether the transformation itself is constructed by Dennis as a transitional self's kind of ultimate test of his efforts as it might be for Mark or Michelle. Dennis' answer reflects a construction that does not grant an ultimate meaning to any one construction of this experience despite its successful outcome. On the one hand, he describes a perspective of a reawakening of faith in a process that can lead to encouraging others to participate in inquiry. On the other hand, Dennis presents the view that "it is easy to reawaken feelings of despair that what I am doing doesn't fit with the way the world works."

These feelings of despair acknowledge how others do not share "motivation to do this kind of thing" and consider "how much it costs each time," so as to ask himself whether his own actions are "serving a larger purpose." Dennis cannot ignore these aspects of the interaction as a transitional self might and must experience therefore not only hope but despair. For Dennis, all elements of this interacting are important in his experience. Thus, the outcome of transformation that reduced the conflict does not eliminate the tension of the earlier conflict, a tension he continues to experience as much as he experiences the joyful outcome. Dennis expresses this tension in his simultaneous acknowledging of renewed faith and questioning of the purpose of that faith.

Again probing for whether Dennis hopes to resolve this tension, the interviewer asks, "Is it important to you to be keeping that question open, or is it a disappointment . . . ?" We believe a transitional self is able to question a single perspective but seeks ultimately to resolve any discrepancy between a current product and the ideal goal. Dennis' response initially suggests to us that this resolution might be his intent. He acknowledges that he would like to reduce the self-questioning, to know that, "I was on the right side and fighting for truth and goodness and it was all clear and sure." If this wish were ultimately important to Dennis, we might liken him

to Michelle, whose goal in interacting with others is to be able to trust that her self-evaluations are based on reality.

The interviewer expresses such a transitional perspective by saying, "What I am inferring from this . . . is that this process of inquiring is in service of these values of truth and justice and the right side." In Dennis's response we see that he is not ultimately seeking any concrete embodiment of his values, that his ultimate purpose is not located in any product: "That makes the means and ends seem too dichotomous, I mean, makes it sound like inquiry is the means to these other ends." Essentially, in this statement Dennis is taking as object what we would see as a transitional construction, the desire to interact with others in order to realize ideal goals. The way that he rejects the interviewer's construction demonstrates his differentiation from the transitional self. As he explains, alternatively, how he does construct his purposes, we see how he has reintegrated this transitional perspective into his interindividual subjectivity. He elaborates on earlier statements in this way: "While I would love to be on the side of truth and beauty and goodness, clearly there is another part of me that does literally believe that the inquiring state is the awake state and that that is human destiny, so that the inquiry is actually the end as well as the means, and the closest we would ever get to truth so to speak would be to be so awake that the outer world is in question, my sensual world is in question, my cognitive world is in question and my so to speak purpose and intuitive world is in question all at the same time." Dennis does not deny that he would love to be sure of meeting his values. This element of the transitional construction is an important part of the interindividual self. In taking a perspective on this quest to be right and winning, he can experience the doubts that lead him to question himself and others continually. We see then that a part of him must always be reawakening doubts, being "so awake" that he is living rather than finding "truth."

Dennis apparently holds constantly in tension the ideal and the real, the successful outcome and the costs of that outcome, never allowing the recognition of the one to block the perception of the other. The side of him that does not want to play on the losing side is as central to this tension as the side that wants to keep seeking beauty and truth in the inquiring state. The side that feels the pain of the costs of his efforts is as significant as the side that rejoices in a victory for the inquiring purpose to which he commits himself. In his construction of self, then, is an ability to recognize the obstacles to his goals as part of himself, to see in the "stuckness" of others an important element of his own stuckness, an element for which he shares responsibility. If inquiry is "human destiny," then the others who participate are an expression of the self's own destiny to be interacting continually.

This ability to see the other as a part of oneself, and the ability to hold simultaneously the visions of the real and the ideal are features common to interindividual construction of the world of work. Different from the transitional construction of resolving "stuckness," the interindividual self can see in the obstacles to meeting goals a reminder of the need to question continually the goals themselves. Within the workplace no individual perspective need be excluded. Each contributes to the sense of community responsibility, so that no one worker can be isolated and blamed or credited for a success or failure. Moreover, each success contains failure and vice versa. This dialectical perspective can seek continually to reevaluate both

the objectives of the work community and the means of meeting those objectives while simultaneously striving to meet the goals that are currently defined. A commitment to a purpose is not seen as exclusive of questioning that purpose.

Just as the transitional construction of work has a parallel in the domain of intimate relationships, so does the interindividual self become a context for a whole new experience of closeness.

My husband S.'s father died recently, and I am still very sad, not only missing him, but sad about not having been able to be as close to S. in his experience as I would have liked. S.'s father died just before I was supposed to be matron-of-honor in my sister's wedding. We were faced with a decision we found very tough. Should I go with S. to share the loss and pain with him and his family, or should I still be in my sister's wedding and share with family and friends the joy of that day? We felt that no matter what we decided, we would end up hurting not only ourselves but also others whom we loved dearly. Eventually, we agreed that S. would go alone that day to join his family and that I would stay for my sister's wedding and join S. two days later. We felt very sad about not being together with both families, but agreed that it was the best solution we could come up with. Shortly after S. arrived at his mother's house, a series of conversations with his mother and brother brought up a whole wealth of new feelings and issues which made S. feel much less able to cope with my not being there both to participate in the discussions and to hear about his pain and confusion. As he was struggling with his feelings, he decided not to tell me about them over the phone because he felt he wanted to honor our decision and not make it difficult for me to participate joyfully in my sister's celebration. Although we did talk on the phone about missing each other, I had no idea how much his feelings had changed and how very lonely he was feeling. When I found out about this later, I was very hurt that he had not felt he could tell me about his loneliness.

So you wish he had told you so maybe you could have done things differently?

Well, I don't know whether we would have changed our decision. We might have, but probably not. What made me upset, a little hurt, even a little angry, was how I didn't even have the chance to share with S. what he was experiencing, how I was so very distant from what he was going through and didn't even know it. Maybe I was so involved in my sister's celebration and experiencing such vastly different emotions that I made him feel like he would be dampening my joy by telling me how he was suffering pain and confusion and missing me more intensely. So I guess as much as anything else, I'm upset at a price of our decision that we hadn't anticipated, how it may have made us unable to bridge a distance it helped us to create.

So, if you could do it differently now, is there anything you would change?

Well, I don't think I could prevent the pain. We are always having to hurt others and each other. I'd like to think, though, that by sharing with him his intense loneliness, I could somehow make that pain easier to bear. I think also he could make my sadness at the unanticipated price of our decision easier to bear by helping me to understand and share in his experience, by not trying to protect

me from his feelings. But it may be, as I said, that one of the costs of our decision, which we made as best we could, is that that kind of sharing couldn't happen at that time. I'd like to think that this experience can help us to check in with each other more carefully another time, and yet it was his love and caring which prompted S. not to check in with me. Maybe the best we can do is to share now with each other that love as well as the frustration, the pain, even the anger we may have felt at having been distant and to experience in this sharing the joy of having one another to reconnect with.

Donna's description of sadness and anger suggests an experience of intimacy reminiscent of Mark's in some ways. Just as Mark was able to see how his "protecting" A. from his relationship with D. was hurting A., Donna describes how S.'s honoring their earlier decision made her "very hurt that he had not felt he could tell me about his loneliness." As Mark could transform his own view as a result of engaging his wife in a sharing of perspectives, Donna can reflect upon S.'s and her experience to see how her own preoccupation elsewhere may have contributed to S.'s decision not to tell her about his experience. As Mark could see in A.'s jealousy an expression of his unwillingness to consider how his other relationship might be a threat, Donna could see in S.'s not telling her of his feelings an expression of her unavailability to perceive how his feelings might have changed. In illustrating how she can see the other as an expression of the self, Donna demonstrates to us that she can construct an interindividual perspective.

To understand how Donna's experience may differ from Mark's, how an institutional construction does not coexist with the interindividual, we examine what her experience of closeness is. For Mark, "the most exciting outcome" and what we infer as being his greatest experience of closeness comes in Mark's and his wife's being able to help one another to grow beyond perspectives that limit their growth and that create conflict. If this were Donna's experience of closeness, we imagine that she too would be excited to have discovered how an exploration of S.'s decision making and her feelings could lead both of them to a new understanding of what had happened and perhaps to a new faith in how their closeness will help them to prevent such occurrences from happening again.

To explore whether Donna's experience also seems to suggest a transitional self, the interviewer asks, "So, if you could do it differently now, is there anything you would change?" She answers,

Well, I don't think I could prevent the pain. . . . I'd like to think, though, that by sharing with him his intense loneliness, I could somehow make that pain easier to bear. I think also he could make my sadness at the unanticipated price of our decision easier to bear by helping me to understand and share in his experience, by not trying to protect me from his feelings. But it may be, as I said, that one of the costs of our decision, which we made as best we could, is that that kind of sharing couldn't happen at that time. I'd like to think this experience can help us to check in with each other more carefully another time, and yet it was his love and caring which prompted S. not to check in with me. Maybe the best we can do is to share now with each other that love as well as the frustration, the pain, even the anger we may have felt at having been distant and to experience in this sharing the joy of having one another to reconnect with.

In this description we see that Donna's experience of closeness has to do with a kind of sharing that she is now rejoicing in and that she was earlier upset and angry to be missing. While the interviewer pushes her twice to offer a solution to their earlier problem, Donna persists in her insistence that it is not an absence of distance and anger that she is seeking. Although she may strive to "check in with each other more carefully" and hope to avoid hurting, she accepts the inevitability that "we are always hurting others and each other." Her resignation to this inevitability does not detract either from her continued efforts to be close and caring or from her hurt and anger when these efforts fail.

What is clear is that her acceptance of the more negative feelings allows her to reconnect with S. to understand how the distance between them was even an expression of his love and to experience a joy in their now sharing all the feelings from which they had been distanced. Hers is a relationship apparently that can interact not only to transform the perspectives either might take (e.g., S.'s wish to protect her) but that can attend simultaneously to how those perspectives express an element of their relationship that can be shared as well as transformed.

Donna's ability to reflect upon the possible stuckness of their situation, to see how perhaps they may not be able to avoid hurt, reminds us of Dennis' attention to the reawakened feelings of despair as well as the reawakened faith due to a successful outcome. Just as truth for Dennis seems to be in the process of inquiry, intimacy for Donna seems to lie in the sharing itself of all kinds of feelings, not in any actual reconciliation or solution. Because the interindividual self can take as object any perspective, whether an initial or a transformed one, it is never fully identified with any one feeling, idea, or construction of a situation. Therefore, negative feelings like anger, frustration, and despair, even when they cannot be transformed, are no longer threats to the self. The transitional self can tolerate negative evaluations, even anger and hurt, because it is not identified solely with the products of its psychological system. It is able to consider how the anger or pain expresses an error that it can now correct.

What the transitional self *cannot* tolerate, however, is an inability to engage in the process that can correct the error. Because the interindividual self is no longer embedded in any need for transformation, it is free to pay a new kind of attention to those "errors" it cannot correct. Although Donna might be angry that S. did not share his feelings with her, she is able to take a perspective on that anger that does not demand either that he see how he could have shared his feelings or that she see why she should not be angry. The anger becomes to her as much an expression of their intimacy as the efforts she continues to make to prevent its future recurrence.

The strength of Donna's construction of the experience seems to lie in her ability not only to see how she contributes to what S. does but to see in the actual hurting an expression also of the loving. In the "best decision we could come up with" is the "unanticipated price" that the anger and hurt express. In the closeness she can experience now is also the distance and pain they experienced before. This ability to take a perspective on so many feelings and constructions does not distance Donna from those feelings. It enables her to experience and to share them more fully. When not being able to solve the problems of hurting and anger can itself be an expression of love, the self who is trying to express love does not need to fear the intensity of such emotions.

Donna's excerpt illustrates to us, then, how in the domain of intimate relationships the interindividual self can welcome a kind of sharing and fullness of experience too threatening to any less equilibrated self. When the villain is also the victim and vice versa and when the experience of love comes in the sharing, not in the ups and downs themselves, more durable closeness can be continually created and re-created. The suffering that is part of any intimacy is no less intense, perhaps is even more intense, but neither the self nor the relationship threatens to dissolve in the face of such suffering. Thus, the interindividual balance transforms, in similar ways, the domains of work and intimate relationships. The ability to experience oneself in the very process of interacting with others allows the self to engage others not as radically "other," but as expressions of the self's own experience and reciprocally to engage the self as participation in a human community. We find ourselves in others and others in ourselves. Oriented to a continuing transforming process, the interindividual self can still choose goals and values, can locate its own efforts in any one perspective, but it does not lose the ability to perceive the paradox of striving for a goal whose opposite is also expressed within the goal itself. Because the interindividual self is not identified with the goal it chooses, this recognition does not replace ideals with cynicism but rather lends a strength or courage to the self's acting and enduring.

Acknowledgment

The authors would like to make grateful acknowledgment of careful prepublication readings by Alfie Kohn and William Torbert.

Notes

1. Quoted speeches are used only to demonstrate our argument and the distinctions we make, not to prove the argument or the generality of the distinctions, so we will forgo here a discussion of the procedures we use for interviewing or coding. (We refer the interested reader to Lahey, Souvaine, Kegan, Goodman, & Felix, 1988.) Most of the speeches are excerpts from actual interviews; some are invented. In the interview excerpts, distinguishing features of the speaker's identity are altered to protect privacy.

2. We remind the reader that we are making generalizations about the developmental balance this person's excerpt illustrates, not about the person himself.

11

Reflections on Life-span Intelligence, Consciousness, and Ego Development

Juan Pascual-Leone

> At five years [the age is reached] for [the study of] the Scriptures . . . at twenty for the pursuit of the aim [in life], at thirty for strength, at forty for insight, at fifty for counsel, at sixty man attains old age. . . . (*Pirkey Avoth*, 1967, p. 95)

> What youth found and must find outside, the man of middle life must find in himself. (Jung, 1945/1953, p. 135)

> As soon as one thinks that the finger is the moon itself, one no longer wants to look in the direction the finger is pointing. (The Sutra of "The Perfect Awakening," Zen Keys/see Thich, 1974, p. 48)

The first two quotations given here illustrate the background of traditional beliefs, confirmed by recent empirical research, that motivate this chapter. During the late teens, 20s, and early 30s, most of us learn about life and learn our way in it as we develop our social awareness and social skills. In the process, each acquires a representation of himself as an individual, conscious person and as a person who is a member of many generic groups defined by roles. During the late 30s, the 40s, and 50s we tend to turn inward and develop a greater realization of our dispositions, values, competences, and contradictions, including those aspects heretofore suppressed. This new consciousness is analogous to the existential awareness described by Jaspers (1932/1970, 1935/1955, 1947/1959) and others.

The *Pirkey Avoth* (a collection of Jewish wisdom compiled over 1500 years ago) suggests that qualitative changes at the ages of 5, . . . 20, 30, 40, and 50 analogous to those observed in the developmental literature today were observed millennia ago. As this ancient text indicates, at age 40 or 50 such development often results in much deeper insight into human and social matters, and with it a special ability for counsel may evolve (e.g., Buhler, 1968; Dittmann-Kohli & Baltes chapter; Erikson, 1959, 1982; Fowler, 1981; Guttmann, 1977; Jung, 1931; Kohlberg & Shulik, 1984; Kohlberg & Ryncarz chapter; Neugarten, 1973).

In Jung's theory of the "individuation" process, intrapsychic change from the first to the second half of life is assumed to be related to organismic–biological determinants (Jung, 1945/1953, p. 124). This idea has been independently entertained by Scheler (1926/1961) and by contemporary personality researchers (e.g.,

Neugarten, 1973, p. 326). My reading of the literature suggests that these marked developmental changes are caused by one or more organismic–biological determinants, although these causes may not be the only ones. Life cycle stages and the developmental stages related to them (cf. Pascual-Leone, 1983) are currently interpreted as "overdetermined" (i.e., multidetermined in excess of the need) by a multiplicity of organismic and experiential factors (Baltes & Willis, 1977; Baltes, Dittmann-Kohli, & Dixon, 1984; Cytrynbaum, Blum, Patrick, Stein, Wadner, & Wilk, 1980; Willis & Baltes, 1980).

I present here the prolegomenon to a theory of adult ego development. This theory is testable and may be able to explicate in process-analytical terms the intuitions of theorists like Jung, Scheler, Jaspers, Neugarten, Bakan, Gilligan, or Fowler. I propose that with aging there is a physiological regression in certain organismic processes that actually leads to positive cognitive and personality changes that may not have occurred otherwise.

A second aim of the chapter is to discuss the possible emergence, within the ego–self organization, of a "transcendental self" that is different from the social-personal self currently recognized by cognitive-developmental psychologists. I should hasten to add that the term *transcendental self* is used as Kant or Husserl intended it and contains no mystical presuppositions (cf. Pascual-Leone, 1983). In the psychological sense, it refers to the highest self-control "center" that oversees the whole ego organization. I prefer to call it an *ultraself,* because the affix *ultra* etymologically means "beyond" or "more advanced but still of the same kind" (as in *ultramodern* or *ultraconservative*).

To facilitate the proper understanding of this "ultraself" notion and suggest the philosophical tradition that anticipated it, I will organize my presentation around a free interpretation of the work of two philosophers, Max Scheler and Karl Jaspers. Scheler's (and Uexkull's, 1926) pioneer work (on the structurally cumulative modes of organismic processing that emerge with evolution) can help to make clear the role of affect, intelligence, and self-structures in human cognition. Jaspers' modes of existential self development, which synthesize a long constructive-rationalist/ phenomenological tradition, provide us with a very suitable semantic analysis of the dimensions of experience organismically leading to the construction of an "ultraself."

Scheler's Conception of Human Nature

Max Scheler's (1926/1961) extraordinary book *Man's Place in Nature* anticipates some fundamental contributions of cognitive-developmental theory and existential phenomenology. Scheler puts forward a conception of man as the highest evolutionary stage of life's own structurally cumulative phylogenetic and psychogenetic construction of spiritual consciousness. Scheler sketches five states that follow a cumulative structural–ontological sequence (cf. Bunge, 1973; Hartmann, 1954). This sequence is cumulative because the functional modes (qualitative process structures) by which each stage is defined become incorporated into, and coordinated with, those of the next stage. Piaget independently introduced to modern developmental psychology this hierarchical approach of organizing stages.

There is, however, a major difference in the structural approaches of Piaget and Scheler. Piaget's (e.g., 1967) structural stage models are true precursors of the information-processing simulation models of cognitive science. They are exclusively intended to describe kinds of software, or functional structures, that are informational in the strong sense that they *in-form* (give form to) the figurative or operative *performance* of the subject. In his first theoretical synthesis, *La psychologie de l'intelligence,* Piaget (1947/1956) makes this important point absolutely clear.

In contrast, Scheler's programmatic stage models aim to describe a structurally cumulative hierarchy of *functional hardware* structures. Such hardware structures are not intended to reflect particular operative or figurative characteristics of situations in which they are applied, as are those of Piaget and cognitive science. Rather, they reflect different organismic endogenous resources that could be universally applied across such situations, as appropriate.

Scheler demarcates the resources indirectly, by recognizing ontologically distinct ways of human experiencing and reacting, which must be manifestations of irreducible processing modes. Scheler's irreducible modes are historical precursors of the silent-hardware stages that causally underlie Piaget's and other structural software stages. Thus, it is useful to discuss them as an introduction to this paper. Scheler distinguishes five such silent-resource modes: affective arousal, specific affective drives, associative memory, practical intelligence, and creative–spiritual intelligence. I examine them successively.

The Organismic Mode of Affective Arousal

The first ontological mode is the affective impulse or *affective arousal.* This is an organismic impulse to promote life's preservation. Scheler (1926/1961, 1973) believes that prior to the emergence of perceptual representations and consciousness, there are basic, purely organismic reactions to the *resistances* of the environment, reactions that *mark* current events as being organismically desirable or undesirable. This global affective impulse is for Scheler a basic sign of life. An elemental, purely affective, vital function (i.e., "equilibration"—a movement toward fulfillment of the species' biological project) exists in humans but is organismically complex and coordinated with other processing modes.[1]

The Instinctual Mode: Specific Affective Drives

According to Scheler, instincts are primary affective drives that constitute the progressive specification and differentiation of affective impulse and provide the organism's basic motivational organization. Primary specific affects are special signal systems that often are released by inner states of the organism and cause certain goals to emerge that lead to certain kinds of performance. Any such instinctive performance displays, says Scheler, four characteristics: (1) tacit goal direction toward the species' self-preservation rather than the individual's needs; (2) a temporal organization that follows an obligatory holistic sequence and rhythm that is largely intrinsically determined; (3) environmental circumstances releasing these basically hereditary drives, which are always generic, relational-pattern structures of the figurative or receptor-encoding variety, like Lorenz's (1982) innate releasing

mechanisms (clearly anticipated by Uexkull, 1926, 1952); and (4) relative stability independent of practice, even though variations (Piaget's "accommodations") can occur in performances as a result of experience.

Diffuse affective arousal and primary affective drives together constitute an innate, species-bound organization that holistically controls performance when higher modes of processing are absent. In turn, higher modes allow control of these initial affective–instinctual processes so that repeated practice ("habits") and organismically generated solutions ("intelligence") can also co-determine performance. Scheler's (and Uexkull's, 1926, 1957) idea of placing affective arousal and affective drives as the two phylogenetically older silent modes of processing implies that these simpler and automatic affective-processing systems are prior to and independent from cognitive processes. The idea that affective goals or "affective images" (cf. Pribram, 1971) can monitor the direction of cognition has, in some sense, been denied by Piagetians. Nevertheless, this notion has long been maintained by psychoanalysts, Jungians, ethologists, and certain developmentalists and has recently been taken up by personality–social psychologists (e.g., Zajonc, 1980).

The Associative Learning and Associative-Memory Mode

Scheler calls his third mode of processing "associative memory." The processes that Scheler tacitly considers here include habit-building, associative and content learning, as well as logical–structural learning of patterns and sets that develops slowly but progressively with repetition. He points out that these learning processes are guided by the pursuit of affective goals. He also emphasizes that learning from tradition through affectively driven *imitation* of other members of the species adds a further dimension to the determination of performance.

This new mode of *associative learning* weakens the power of instinctual forms and thus somewhat frees affect from its innate forms of manifestation. This freeing of affect from innate manifestations allows affective excesses, repressions, sublimations, and the gamut of affective transformations described by psychoanalysis. Associative learning and automatization can eventually make the individual and species predictable victims of this cumulation of habits when new or misleading situations arise that, in fact, require novel responses. To remedy these handicaps, "practical intelligence," the fourth mode of processing, emerges.

The Onset of Intelligence: Practical Intelligence Mode

Practical intelligence, the beginnings of superior cognition (Kant's "understanding"), appears in the ability to produce performances that manifestly correct the life-threatening excesses of instinctual–affective forms of reacting and of previous associative habits.

Intelligence, in contrast to simple perception, addresses *distal* objects and not *proximal* (i.e., sensorial–perceptual) ones. Distal objects are objective entities that emerge for the subject in his *praxis* (i.e., in his goal-directed activity addressed to the environment). They are *external packages of constraints* (i.e., *resistances*) that must be satisfied to attain the practical goals. The relations, causal or not, that objectively hold among distal objects are what Tolman and Brunswik (1935) have

called the "causal texture" of the environment and what Scheler and Piaget describe as "resistances." Intelligence is apt to recognize resistances that are favorable to a certain praxis (these are positive resistances—what Gibson, 1982, calls "affordances") as well as those that oppose this praxis and turn into obstacles (they are negative resistances).

Scheler defines intelligence by the conjunction of four essential characteristics: (1) Intelligent performance is intentional and anticipatory (cf. Husserl, 1954/1970); it involves adaptive action to meet "distal" goals in relation to objects of the environment. (2) It is not largely derived from previous trials but emerges as a discontinuity from the previous trial-and-error history. (3) It is a productive response produced to *novel* situations, new to both the species and the individual. (4) It emerges suddenly and is subjectively accompanied by a feeling of insight into a partly hidden nexus of relations relevant to the issues at hand.

Scheler states, "We call this intelligence 'practical' because it always aims at some action by means of which the organism obtains or misses a goal set by its drives" (1921/1961, p. 29). Since Scheler's modes are structurally cumulative, an individual endowed with practical intelligence would also be gifted with associative memory, primary affects, and affective arousal. Each cumulative organization of modes can be said to constitute an endogenous (hardware) stage underlying the functioning of the organism.

Defined as a stage, practical intelligence is the subject matter of Piaget's genetic-epistemological theory, as well as much of cognitive-developmental and cognitive-science research. In practice, however, research psychologists striving for empirical concreteness often attempt to reduce intelligence to associative memory. They want to reduce the essential innate ingredient of intelligence—*mental capacity,* that is, attentional energy, effort, or "fluid" intelligence (e.g., Johnson, Fabian, & Pascual-Leone, 1989; Pascual-Leone, 1970, 1980, 1983, 1984, 1987, in press; Pascual-Leone & Goodman, 1979; Pascual-Leone, Goodman, Ammon, & Subelman, 1978) to some kind of structural automatization (e.g., Hasher & Zacks, 1979).

Piaget's (1936/1952c) three-screen problem for testing the permanence and transperceptual invariance of hidden objects is perhaps the first cognitive landmark that unambiguously shows that practical intelligence is not reducible to associative learning. This illustration from infancy is relevant to adult development because the same hardware mechanisms of intelligence are found in the creative–spiritual intelligence of adulthood, albeit complicated by much learned experience. (For experimental evidence supporting the analyses that follow see Holloway, 1986; Holloway, Blake, & Pascual-Leone, 1987; Benson, 1989).

In this task the baby has to get the toy she wants, which has been hidden behind one of three screens—*A, B,* or *C*—that are accessible to her. The toy is first hidden behind *A,* and the 13-month-old can already reach for the toy by removing *A.* As a result, the baby should develop a mental habit or belief, that is, a scheme "(toy is behind *A*)" asserting where the toy is to be found. [The notation "(. . .)" symbolizes a scheme or mental structure that is semantically described by the statement written inside the parentheses.] Then the experimenter takes the toy again, hides it inside his hand, and brings it behind *A* while saying, "The toy! The toy!" But now, instead of leaving the toy behind *A,* he keeps the toy hidden and moves the hand

behind screen *B*, repeating the same routine. Then, without interruption, he moves his hand with the hidden toy behind screen *C*, where—while repeating aloud, "The toy! The toy!"—he drops it. A typical 13-month-old reacts to this situation by first removing screen *A*, looking for the toy. When she does so the habit-scheme "(toy is behind *A*)" controls her performance. She is, we could say, an associative-memory organism. In contrast, an 18- to 23-month-old baby directly searches *behind* C *for the toy without first searching behind* A *or* B. We can safely assume that she has acquired, during her prior daily experiences, a relational-learning scheme or *knowledge (K) structure* that in practical terms is equivalent to the following knowledge-expression: "(any object *X* is always found behind the obstacle-screen *Z*, where it disappears *last*)". If the baby would recognize the same relational patterns of experience across any concrete objects and concrete obstacles, she could easily learn this *K*-structure, but only provided that she can keep track simultaneously of four distinct aspects of the same experience: the knowledge relation *K*, the object *X*, the obstacle *Z*, and time of disappearance *T*-last. If she can do all this a *K*-structure "$K(X, Z, T\text{-last})$" corresponding to the same knowledge-expression will be formed as a scheme in her memory.

The availability of this *K*-structure can explain why the 23-month-old directly removes *C* to find the toy. The young child needs, besides the *K*-structure and the operative scheme for removing *C*, three additional schemes to achieve this end: the plan (the *executive*) to search for and find the toy; the remembrance that the hand carried the toy hidden in it; and the remembrance that the hand last disappeared behind screen *C*. For all this to happen three conditions must be met by the child's maturing hardware (i.e., her silent resources).

First, she must be able to "keep in mind" (in working memory) four distinct aspects of experience (four schemes) at the same time. This is made possible by the child's mental capacity, what I shall call her *M*-energy or operator.[2]

Second, to use the *K*-structure effectively "$K(X, Z, T\text{-last})$" in a *relevant non-automatized mental process* (i.e., a *"mediational process"*; see, e.g., Flavell, 1972; Kendler, 1979; Vygotsky, 1978; White, 1965), the child must be able to interrelate, in the here and now, the K-structure in question with three other schemes: the task executive "(search and find toy)," the idea that "(toy is hidden inside hand)," the idea that "(hand last disappeared behind *C*)." These four distinct schemes constitute the "causal texture" of the situation when she coordinates them by means of a *dynamic synthesis* (Pascual-Leone, 1980, 1984, 1987b), into a single *mediational process*. But she can coordinate these four schemes only when her *M*-operator resource simultaneously boosts them with activation. If there is not enough *M*-resource, the four schemes will fade away without dynamically interacting in the brain to synthesize performance, because these schemes are not strongly elicited by the here-and-now perceptual aspects of the situation. In contrast, if there is enough *M*-energy the mediational process in question will occur and with it the relevant performance. (A repetition of this process would eventually produce the corresponding mental *K-structure* via deliberate logical relational-pattern learning—the *LM* learning described later.)

Third, in addition to forming the mediational process explained previously, the child must actively inhibit the habit-scheme "(toy is behind *A*)," since otherwise

this *habit,* stronger than the just created mediational process, would prevent the process manifesting in performance. The resource used in this active inhibition of habits is a hardware "interrupt" facility that I call *I*-interruption operator (Pascual-Leone, 1983, 1984, 1987, in press; Pascual-Leone et al., 1978; Pascual-Leone, Johnson, Hameluck, Goodman, and Theodor, 1981). This example shows how the "causal texture" of a novel situation is discovered–invented by the subject via the creation of mental–mediational processes.

Notice that the better disguised (by misleading perceptual appearances) the true "causal texture" is, the greater quantity of the two hardware resources will be needed to generate mediational processes. Thus, even more so than practical intelligence, creative–spiritual intelligence should necessitate large amounts of *M*-energy and *I*-interruption, larger amounts than young children or apes, our close cousins, can provide.

Creative–Spiritual Intelligence or Personal "Spirit"

Scheler insists, as do modern researchers, that animals are quite capable of practical intelligence (i.e., mental–mediational processes) though to a lesser degree than humans. Scheler also identifies, however, a qualitatively distinct mode of processing unique to humans. Following the philosophical constructivist tradition, Scheler refers to this unique mode as "spirit." I refer to it as a *creative–spiritual* process. Scheler conceives of this personal spirit as the exclusive and most sophisticated achievement of the human brain. Through this processing model (which, coordinated with the lower modes, constitutes a new stage) a willful choice with regard to values becomes possible; with it the essential nature of objective reality can be more easily recognized and objective self-consciousness attained. At this level of development, the willful creation of new foundations and general principles in the humanities and knowledge-laden sciences can be more easily achieved. Cognitively refined affects and affectively attuned cognitions emerge, and this intricate coordination of affect and cognition gives rise to a new wisdom.

The ancient Greeks called this higher mode of processing *reason.* Kant (1781/1963) also called it "reason," contrasting it with "understanding" (that is, practical intelligence). Anticipating existential phenomenology (e.g., Jaspers, Heidegger, Ortega y Gasset, Sartre, Merleau-Ponty), Scheler posited that affective awareness of life *resistances* when experienced in a *detached* manner is at the origin of spiritual (i.e., ultraself) growth and valid cognition. Husserl (1954/1970a) called this manner of experiencing *phenomenological reduction.*

Scheler describes such phenomenological reduction as the mental attitude whereby the inferential and existential–affective aspects of objects or situations that offer resistances to praxis are *both made conscious and suspended.* Affects elicited by resistances are "suspended" in the sense of being tuned down to mere actualities by an aware but detached "releasement" (Heidegger, 1959/1966) from affects, toward a pure cognitive awareness of the ongoing situations. Heidegger called this heightened mental attitude *meditative thinking,* and he contrasted it with calculative thinking (i.e., practical intelligence), which constitutes a different sort of mindfulness. By adopting this meditative mental attitude, human intelligence can pro-

tect itself from the misleading biases caused by affects, while using affective impulses to increase the power and sensitivity of valid thinking. This blending of detached cognition with reduced but conscious affects facilitates the ontogenetic construction of creative–spiritual intelligence.

Simple and *superficial* states of meditative thinking occur spontaneously in most people at any age. Situations that engage attention in relaxed, unconcerned ways can lead to it, whether they involve a ritualized activity (e.g., praying, listening to or playing concert music, reading poetry, playing golf, knitting) or a purely natural activity (e.g., sitting outside to watch the sunset; taking a walk or a bath; quietly resting after a long, difficult effort).

Spontaneous *simple* states of meditative thinking can be facilitated in children by good parenting, which shelters the child from peremptory needs or discomforts while engaging her attention in relaxed ways. These states of subdued affects and heightened alertness facilitate mediational processes such as those that first reveal to a baby the "causal texture" of the three-screen problem.

Similar but *much deeper* states of meditative thinking, now focused on the "causal texture" of self- and life consciousness, can occur in adults. They are brought out by the subject's *own* mental attitude and result in the successive development of alternative modes of existential consciousness. Karl Jaspers (1935/1955, 1932/1970, 1947/1959) was the first to describe these modes. The first of these four creative–spiritual modes is self-awareness in everyday life (i.e., "empirical existence"). The second is self-awareness in the philosophical–conceptual formulation of experience (i.e., "conceptual existence"). The third is dialectical–relativistic self-awareness of alternative ways of "conceptual existences," now regarded as evolving totalities, and this I shall call "temporal existence." The fourth is the exploration of the ideal possibilities implicit in these evolving totalities, when explored by a deep meditative thinking. This is "meditative existence." The four modes of awareness, like the different alternatives of causal action open to the baby in the three-screen problem, are mutually contradictory, although they all reflect important necessary aspects of life in consciousness. Thus, the creative–spiritual intelligence of adults constructs the "causal texture" of life in consciousness using mediational processes similar to those that lead the baby to her first achievement of practical intelligence—similar but much further developed and deepened.

Phenomenological reduction or meditative thinking fosters cognitive growth and ego development at any age, from birth to maturity (cf. Alexander et al. chapter). A special aim of this chapter is to elaborate on this thesis for the adult years. The other aim is to interpret, in a current psychological idiom, the fundamental insights of Jaspers regarding self development. Jaspers' stages of self-realization serve to delineate and clarify Scheler's notion of creative–spiritual intelligence. Moreover, these stages of growth are important because they coincide with, and contribute considerable process-analytical clarification to, the subjective stages of adult development often described in the current literature. In the last sections of the chapter I use dialectical constructivist theorizing (cf. Pascual-Leone, 1980, 1987b, 1990) to explicate Jaspers' stages. Before turning to Jaspers, however, it is necessary to introduce some concepts from the theory of constructive operators.

The Constructive Operators of Intelligence

Elsewhere, I have proposed a dialectical constructivist theory that contains sufficient functional processes to explain human growth and the emergence of creative–spiritual intelligence (Ammon, 1977; Chapman, 1981; Johnson, Fabian, & Pascual-Leone, 1989; Pascual-Leone, 1969, 1970, 1976a,b, 1978, 1980, 1983, 1984, 1987, 1990 [in press]; Pascual-Leone & Goodman, 1979; Pascual-Leone, Goodman, Ammon, & Subelman, 1978; Pascual-Leone & Sparkman, 1980; Ribaupierre, 1983; Ribaupierre & Pascual-Leone, 1984; Vuyk, 1981). Therefore, a detailed description of the process theory and its empirical methods is omitted here; instead I focus primarily on some aspects particularly relevant to the issue of creative–spiritual intelligence. These aspects can help the reader to see, in general terms, how Scheler's evolutionary model, and Jasper's refined stage account of advanced creative–spiritual intelligence, can be interpreted in organismic process–analytical terms.

Embedded in the brain is a functional organization of processes that is causally responsible for mental or external performance. I call this hidden "psychological machinery" of the brain the *metasubject* (Pascual-Leone, 1976a, 1984, in press; Pascual-Leone & Goodman, 1979) to emphasize both its very active character and its holistic functioning as a dynamically evolving conglomerate of hardware and software. This conglomerate organization contains three sorts of modules: (1) cognitive–informational processes (i.e., cognitive *schemes* or structures that tell about environmental events, plans, objects, and contingencies); (2) affective–personal *schemes* (affects, values, personal structures) that tell about the organism's own needs and feelings; and (3) silent-hardware modules, *hardware operators* that serve to control and develop psychological functioning. The scientist can infer these modules from performances (and systematic error patterns!) repeatedly exhibited by the subject under study, within and across types of situations.

These functional modules, whether software schemes or hardware operators, are defined holistically by the releasing conditions that lead to their activation and by their organismic effects (i.e., the "computational" or associative details of their working are not specified). The biodynamic character of schemes explains their self-propelling effectiveness, which Piaget has called their "assimilation" function and others, after Husserl, call their "intentionality" or goal-directedness.

It is worthwhile to insist on the distinction between stored (innate or acquired) information, or "software," of the brain and the "hardware" needed for the use and translation of software into performance. I refer to the *software* modules as *schemes* (which include cognitive, affective, and personal schemes) and to the other modules as *silent-hardware operators*. Contrary to schemes, silent operators are *not* informational and thus can function universally across types of performance and situations. They are the hardware used to regulate the functioning of schemes and to change or update their information.

The progressively more advanced modes of processing that Scheler has postulated correspond to the emergence of these silent operators. Scheler's mode of "affective arousal" and "primary affects" correspond in humans to an *A* (affect) operator, that is, a general affective-arousal mechanism that modulates the reactivity of the specific affective schemes in the organism. Affective schemes are the

affects themselves, primary affects and their experientially differentiated descendants (cf. Zajonc, 1980; Buck, 1985).

Scheler's processing mode of "associative memory" corresponds to silent operators, which I refer to as content learning (*C-learning*) and logical-structural learning (*L-learning*). *C*-learning makes possible the remembering of *particular* or content-specific aspects of experience, as found in simple conditioning and perceptual learning. *L*-learning makes possible the remembering of generic-structural or patterned aspects of experience. *C*-learning, caused by the *C*-operator—a "hardware" capability that may predominate in the brain's right hemisphere—turns into structural *L*-learning with overlearning (e.g., Mandler, 1962). How *C*-learning turns into *L*-learning can be understood in the context of practical intelligence. The three-screen problem (see the preceding section "The Onset of Intelligence: Practical Intelligence Mode") illustrated how a mental process emerges as a dynamic synthesis with the help of *M*-energy.[3]

Other hardware operators are the *M*-operator and *I*-operator (i.e., interruption ability or active willful inhibition). In this theory, the *M*-operator functionally represents the endogenous capacity of the prefrontal lobe to energize or activate relevant executive (i.e., plans) and action (i.e., performance implementation) processes elsewhere in the cortex. This activation is likely to involve the descendant associative track to the subcortical reticular system and the "gate" back to the cortex provided by the thalamus (e.g., Fuster, 1980; Pascual-Leone, 1984, in press; Luria, 1973; Schiebel, 1981). The *M*-operator can be psychologically characterized as a limited reserve of mental–mediational energy that the dominant (most activated) executive schemes (i.e., those in charge of planning) can mobilize and allocate to action schemes, localized elsewhere in the cortex, for the implementation of the executive-planned performance. A result of this allocation of mental energy is that the activation level (Piaget's "assimilatory strength") of the schemes in question increases.

The *M*-operator can be appropriately understood as an innate functional component of Spearman's (1926/1953) general intelligence and Catell's fluid intelligence (cf. Pascual-Leone, 1970, 1983; Pascual-Leone & Goodman, 1979). Knowledge of this operator is important in process and task analysis for three reasons: (1) *Mediational* processes are instant coordinations of structures *not* strongly *LC*-learned or automatized (including tacit and/or conscious dialectical schemes) that have to be boosted with *M*-energy to cause performance. Their repetition rapidly produces *LM*-structures (see note 3) that, like the mediational processes, necessitate *M*-energy to be used in performance. (*LM*-structures could, if used very frequently in mediational processes, become automatized, that is, *LC*-structured, thus creating *LCLM*-structures that *do not* require *M*-power to be activated.) (2) The number of separate schemes that can be simultaneously boosted by *M*-energy to co-determine performance (this number we call *M-power*) has been shown to grow discontinuously but linearly with age up to 15 or 16 years (e.g., Pascual-Leone and Goodman, 1979; Johnson, Fabian, and Pascual-Leone, 1989; Pascual-Leone, 1970, 1978, 1980, 1983, 1987b; Ribaupierre, 1983). This discontinuous growth of *M*-power explains the transitions across Piaget's developmental stages; they are caused by the subject's inability to generate mediational processes (and thus acquire *LM*-structures) that demand more *M*-power than the subject possesses. (3) The likely

age-bound transitions across stages of adult development (Levinson, Darrow, Klein, Levinson, & McKee, 1978; see Levinson chapter) can be explained in part by a progressive difficulty in mobilizing energy from the M-reserve, which causes a relative lack of available M-energy (Pascual-Leone, 1983, 1984). Like the growing scarcity of gasoline to run large American-designed cars during the "oil crisis" of the 1970s, this lack of M-energy forces a remodeling of mental structures to make the life-and-work mental–mediational processing more M-efficient. These new structures, whether more comprehensive or more specialized (e.g., Baltes et al., 1984), are the cognitive–personal growth of later stages. Such a cognitive–personal growth is part of Scheler's creative–spiritual intelligence mode, which Jaspers has expanded.

Hardware operators other than M are needed to account for the processes of creative–spiritual intelligence. Of these I mention *only* the interruption ability, or I-operator. The I-operator is another capacity of the prefrontal lobe that complements the M-operator. This complementary function is an interrupt; it can actively inhibit the cortical processes that are not situationally relevant and therefore should not be boosted by M. When irrelevant processes are disactivated by I, relevant allocation of M-energy becomes easier and the ability of M-boosted schemes to override competing misleading schemes is greatly enhanced. Further, whenever it is convenient, a "wide-beam–narrow-beam" of attention can be obtained by canceling or strengthening the automatic I-interruption of unattended (not M-boosted) schemes that accompanies an act of M-allocation (Pascual-Leone, 1980, 1983, 1984, 1987 [in press]). In this manner, one can explain the phenomena of focal and selective attention as well as those of "working memory." The M- and I-operators can be used to cope effectively with situations and to develop schemes and structures requiring LM-learning or mental effort.

Structures of consciousness are a class of structures vital to the development of Scheler's creative–spiritual intelligence. Conscious structures are complex and encompassing. When boosted with M-energy, they create stable phenomenal organizations that practically relate past, present, and future within a single experiential horizon (cf. Carr, 1974; Ricoeur, 1967). From a dialectical constructivist viewpoint, full consciousness is not a capacity but the functional state of a very high M-activation in structures so comprehensive and encompassing that they can provide a well-developed referential *framework* for the person. The possibility of consciousness, of *pure consciousness* without a knowing self, prior to active states of thought, must be wired in the architecture (i.e., the hardware) of the brain (cf. Edelman & Mountcastle, 1982). For this reason and on the grounds of careful phenomenological analyses (e.g., Jaspers, 1932/1970; Sartre, 1957, 1943/1966), it can be safely assumed that this *pure* (self-less) function of consciousness *constitutes* (generates) the ego structures. It constitutes them by endowing certain informational (i.e., software) structures with intrinsic capabilities of consciousness. These are the ego structures. Thus, conscious structures are by definition ego structures. The culmination of this development of ego structures is the emergence within the person of an ultimate and purely intrinsic *ultraself* organization that can consciously monitor the subject's own life choices from within.

The concept of an *ultraself* or transcendental self (cf. Jaspers, 1932/1970; Sartre, 1957, 1943/1966) is still new in psychology. To show how it emerges out of the

coping efforts of an interpersonal self and how this self relates to the world-and Other-structures that are part of the ego repertoire is the issue now addressed.

The Ego Organization and the Collective Structures

The ego is the repertoire of all conscious structures. Consciousness is the functional state of experiencing that encompasses in the same mental mediation (or *M-centration*) the subject who has the experience, the object that is experienced, and the relation of knowing. The relation of knowing functionally interconnects the subject with the object of experience and gives rise to the meaning and "horizon" of knowledge (Husserl, 1954/1970a; Jaspers, 1932/1970). Ego structures are developed by means of mental effort and as a result of encompassing mental macro-decentrations. *Macro-decentrations* (Pascual-Leone, 1984) are attentional expansions from the present—the here and now—toward *both* the relevant future and past, so as to recall the complex and time-deep structures that are relevant to the knowing of the current situation; they are dynamic syntheses that restructure sets (segments) of external or mental experience.

In what follows, I shall present the outline of a model of the ego that is based on, and consistent with, the growing psychological literature on children's self development (e.g., Damon, 1983; Harter, 1983a; Selman, 1980). Since this chapter is focused on adult development, I will not review the child development literature here. Instead, I refer to classic sources on adult self-development, whether philosophical or psychoanalytical.

There are three main categories of ego structures: self structures; Other structures, which represent other persons; and world structures, which code the environment in terms of objects that are important to the self. Other and world structures basically create or *constitute* the *ego-milieu,* the subject's conscious life-world (cf. Carr, 1974; Husserl, 1954/1970a; Ricoeur, 1967). I call subordinate ego structures that interrelate self structures with world structures (which includes the structures of persons, but *only* as cognitive objects without affective–intersubjective experiencing) *ego-cognitive structures;* those that interrelate self structures with Other (i.e., intersubjective) structures and with the world, I call conscious collective structures, or *collectives.* A collective is the potentially conscious affective-and-cognitive functional structure(s) that in a subject represent a group or a community of persons, defined by the intersubjective roles that various types of persons play in it vis-à-vis each other.

A Modular Model of the Ego

There is no ego in the sense of an organismic "faculty" or homunculus (cf. Sartre, 1957, 1943/1966). The ego is only a particular collection of schemes that have two unique characteristics: first, the schemes have a disposition to become conscious, in the sense that they tend to control mental attention and the subject may be able to speak about their manifestations; second, these schemes carry information that deals with the coordination of complex cognitions and affects. Hence, they all pro-

vide an integrated general perspective about the subject and his/her environment. Though changing from one context to the next, some part of this collection of ego schemes is always present to monitor the show of consciousness from "behind the scenes." This is the phenomenological self (e.g., Hegel, 1929/1957; Husserl, 1954/1970a; Kant, 1781/1963; Sartre, 1943/1966), which develops in the context of continuous interactions with the other and the world and cannot be understood in isolation from them.[4] In fact, the ego must be understood as the set union of self structures, Other structures, and world structures.

As Table 11.1 shows, I have incorporated these observations in my model by distinguishing within the ego schemes two superordinate modalities: the ego-core, or interpersonal self, and the ego-milieu, or circumstances that include the Others, the world, values, and so on. As the Spanish philosopher Ortega y Gasset stated, "I am myself and my circumstances" (Ortega y Gasset, 1914/1961, p. 45). The self develops in interaction with the Other, and the Other represents a system of structures that must be regarded as part of the individual's ego.

Further, within the ego core a number of functional *categories* (i.e., qualitative modalities) are identified that represent different necessary aspects of the self. These categories integrate necessary distinctions (irreducible aspects) within the self that are often found in the literature. The *I-self* or *operative self* corresponds to Baldwin's (1908; cf. Mead, 1934; James, 1892/1966) "subjective self," where the "I" is the "doing" and "feeling" component of the self. The *Me-self* or *figurative self* is myself as a phenomenological–historical object. As Baldwin (1908) wrote, "Thus the self is, both for itself and also for others, a singular subjective inner pro-

Table 11.1 Categorical Organization of the Interpersonal Ego

	Ego-Core ("Actual" Self)	Collectives and Ego Cognition		Ego-Milieu (Circumstances)
I-self	(operative self: conscious interpersonal self, Jungian ego)		*Others*	(and other's perception of "actual" self, "ideal" self, and "ought" self)
	Agent (cognitive–pragmatic self, executive controls)	↔	*World*	(the environment as referrent of the ego's affective goals)
	Soul (empathic–affective self)		*Super-ego*	("ought" self: interdictions and prescriptions)
Me-self	(figurative self: historical–social self, self-as-object)			
Ego-synthesis	(self-evaluation, ethical conscience, self-consciousness, aesthetic awareness, ego-defenses, self-collectives, ego-cognition)	↔	*Ego-Ideal*	("ideal" self: self-projects, internalized mentors, and "special persons")
			Values	(Knowledge of affective reactions elicited by possible or future events, objects, persons, etc.)
Body-self	(somatic self, libidinal self)			
Identity	*Contextual-Identity* (Jung's "persona", situationally variable identity)		*Ideologies*	(conscious conventions and philosophies)
	Self-Identity (Jung's initial self, permanent identity)			

cess and also a generalized objective content" (p. 410). Other irreducible aspects of the self are also included in the model; of special interest are the "integrative" or *Ego-synthetic* executive function (e.g., French, 1952; Hegel, 1929/1957; Husserl, 1954/1970a; Neumann, 1949/1962) and the Body-self (e.g., Erikson, 1968b; Neumann, 1949/1962; Winnicott, 1969).

Each one of the ego-core categories should be functionally understood as some sort of "filing cabinet" or "transfer box" containing a number of *files* (alternative sets of schemes), *each geared to a different situation-specific context.* (The situation specificity of personality dispositions is well recognized—e.g., Endler, 1981.) For instance, inside the I-agent there are as many different varieties of self structures as there are kinds of contexts in which the I-agent acts. This is also true for each one of the other ego categories. Note that the Identity categories of Table 11.1 represent predicates of predicates (superpredicates) defined over the contents of all the other ego-core categories. At any given moment the contextual Identity (the "I" with which one currently identifies) *is the dominant activated file* (set of ego structures) in each and every filing category that is part of the self. As a function of life-span development, the schemes' commonalities across files (i.e., situation-specific contents) in all categories increase, thus adding to the definition of the subject's permanent self-Identity.

The various categories develop more or less concurrently with experience. In young persons the various files within each category and across categories are often mutually inconsistent; they correspond to different mutually inconsistent *partial-selves* that usually operate in different contexts but may eventually be needed together in the same context. To illustrate this point, consider the coordination of ego schemes that may be involved in learning to produce the suitable mixtures of mastery, dependency, attachment, and aggression needed to succeed in interpersonal dealings with such people as parents, mates, neighbors, subordinates, and bosses. Interaction with each of these kinds of Other requires a different behavioral formula, and the ego-synthesis function has to learn to combine I-agent and I-soul characteristics to produce them. The *I-agent,* the *competence-cognitive self,* is a partial-self focused on the social-cognitive aspects of dominance and mastery; its behavioral manifestation in a pure state may be what Bakan (1966) calls "Agency"; Baldwin (1908), "personal self"; and Buber (1923/1958), "I-It." The *I-Soul or empathic–affective self* is a partial-self often developed through the intimacy of loving others; its pure manifestation may be Bakan's "Communion," Baldwin's "social self," and Buber's "I-Thou." It is a modality of conduct reflecting an attitude of empathic experiencing of oneself and other persons or Nature as if they were part of the same holistic unit.

Clearly, different mixtures of I-agent and I-soul are needed to interact well with the boss, the mate, or the customer. A qualitative functional structure coordinating I-agent attitudes (e.g., power, dependence) with I-soul attitudes (e.g. love, aggression) will be needed. Mental effort—M-energy plus interruption ability—will be involved in the construction of this structure.

It is important to notice that self structures are found within both the ego-core and the ego-milieu. The ego-core self is the "true" or *actual self* with all its categories. The ego-milieu self is the "ideal" self (i.e., the ego-ideal category) and the "ought" self (i.e., super-ego category); they constitute a socially derived *marginal*

self that has often been called "false" self in the literature. As Higgins (1987) has emphasized, ego-core (that he calls "actual" self) and marginal self (i.e., the subject's own "ideal" and "ought" selves) are often contrasted, as are the "actual" self and the Other's perception of our "actual" self, our "ideal" self, and our "ought" self. Discrepancies found in these contrasting comparisons cause specific self emotions (disappointment, shame, fear, guilt, etc.) that serve to motivate growth of the ego-core (actual self) to integrate aspects of the marginal self; and growth of the marginal self to integrate aspects of the Other's evaluations of the self. These contrasting comparisons are carried out by means of collectives, that is, microsystems of intersubjective–interpersonal (and *intrapersonal–intrasubjective*) relations.

The Modular Structure of Interpersonal Relations: The Collective

To explain the psychogenetic relations that functionally link the ego-core self with its ego-milieu (including the relations among the various partial selves), I now describe a *natural elementary unit* of intersubjective–interpersonal structures: the *collective* (cf. Mead, 1934; Sartre, 1960). A *collective* is a complex superstructure that reflects semantic–pragmatic interrelations between or among persons *qua persons* (i.e., as sentient, more or less aware subjectivities). The interrelations they reflect are generally roles, exchange formulas, affective–personal dispositions, or social scripts. A *collective* can be structurally represented by a functor category or operative module such as *Roles* which are used vis-à-vis person-*subjects* (which I abbreviate as $(sub_1, sub_2, \ldots,$ etc., such as *self, Other, $\ldots$,* etc.) in accordance with prescriptions (conditions) stipulated by a *context* (which I abbreviate as *cx*). Thus:

$$\text{collective} = Roles\ (cx: sub_1, sub_2, \ldots)$$

Roles are adopted by actors $(sub_1, sub_2, \ldots)$ to communicate intersubjectively. The actors, or members of a collective, either are partial-self-entities of the ego-core (e.g., the I-self, Me-self, or Body-self) or are ego-milieu entities (e.g., different kinds of Other, the ego-ideal, or the super-ego). The context is that aspect of world structures that release roles (see Table 11.1).

In a collective, each person appears as a subject-prototype, a playwright's "character." Psychologically, each one of these person-prototypes, or interiorized "play characters," is represented by a person's model-object, or "frame" permanently stored in the subject's long-term memory. Model-objects, or "frames" (cf. Pascual-Leone et al., 1978), are multifaceted structural systems that stand for internalized representations of common distal objects that play a role in the subject's experience—from contextual objects (*obs*), such as pencils and restaurants, to personal objects, that is, *subjects* (*subs*), such as real or imaginary persons. I will use the terms *ob* and *sub,* respectively, as short names for this sort of internalized multifaceted model-object (Pascual-Leone, 1969, 1976b; 1983; 1984; Pascual-Leone et al., 1978). *A collective is a set of subs and contextual obs together with the systems of role operations that govern their interactions.* The intersubjective nature of interpersonal structures is clarified when regarded as instances of *collectives.* Although this is a controversial issue, there are good reasons to believe that the roots of collectives, no less than those of affects, are innate (e.g., Bowlby, 1981; Fromm, 1975; Lorenz, 1982; Trevarthen, 1980). Examples of collectives follow.

A first example is the innate interpersonal structure of the baby's attachment to the mother. Since this structure is not conscious in the baby, it is not part of his ego; it is nonetheless a precursor of later ego collectives. An unconscious precursor of ego collectives I call a *protocollective*. The sort of experiences that in infancy initiate the development of self, Other, and world—with their well-known aspects (e.g., baby-self, mother-Other, baby-world, baby-roles, mother-roles)—are organized into a protocollective represented by the expression "*role (cx: self, Other)*." In this expression *role* is a functional representation of the self's or Other's ways of interacting and communicating, through operations, acts, or attitudes; self and *Other* are subs. Finally, *cx*, the context, is the aspects of the world currently serving as releasers of roles. This operator-logic formalism serves to highlight the constructive complexity of a collective, since the psychogenesis of a collective often taxes the subject's mental effort (M-energy and I-interruption) as a function of the number of different generic types of Others (and/or self) necessarily involved in mutual interaction. The interactions described in the collective can be *binary* (as illustrated earlier, because they have to occur between two persons), *ternary, quaternary,* and so on. The mental energy needed for the L-learning of a collective should increase (up to a certain level) with the "ary" number of the collection in question (cf. Higgins, 1981). This is not the only possible source of complexity: a collective's complexity can also depend on the pattern of interaction that holds between or among its elements.

A simple example of ego collective is tacitly provided by Freud in his Oedipus complex (the male child's rivalry with the father vis-à-vis the mother). This complex provides an illustration of what happens when the constructive complexity of a to-be-developed collective is above the subject's M-power (cf. Fischer & Watson, 1981). As psychoanalytical theory emphasizes, three- to four-year-olds might, depending on the family dynamics, intensely experience the so-called Oedipus complex; but after five years this intensity decreases, and by seven to eight the manifestations of the complex may vanish. Disregarding the Freudian interpretation of these facts, the theory of constructive operators provides an explanation, because it has shown empirically that the M-energy of three- to four-year-olds can at most boost the executives elicited by the context plus one consciously mediated scheme; the M-energy of five- to six-year-olds can boost the context-elicited executives plus two consciously mediated schemes; and that of seven- to eight-year-olds can activate the executive plus three such schemes (Pascual-Leone, 1970, 1978; Pascual-Leone & Goodman, 1979).

In an ego collective directly abstracted from life situations, activation of executives is facilitated by the situational cues, so that the component "role (context . . .)" does not generally need to be boosted by M. From these premises three developmental predictions follow: (1) Children of three and four years cannot willfully (i.e., consciously and with deliberate intention) abstract any collective from their everyday experience, since their M-power cannot boost more than one conscious *sub* (personal subject representation) at a time. (2) The most complex collective easily accessible under these conditions to five- or six-year-olds is "role (cx: sub_1, sub_2)." In the Oedipal situation sub_1 and sub_2 are the personal subject-representations of any two terms of the "family triangle." (3) In contrast, seven- and eight-year-olds can willfully abstract from immediate experience collectives of the form: "role (cx: sub_1, sub_2, sub_3)." Thus the daily-life collective "role (context: self, mother, father)" is accessible to seven-year-olds but not to younger children.

If the whole family triangle cannot be incorporated within the same abstracted collective, the child will suffer affective confusions (not unlike the Gestaltist "field effect") between his role vis-à-vis mother and father's role vis-à-vis mother. The

child may affectively experience the father as causing the self's loss of mother's love (jealousy) and react with aggression. This should particularly be so in the case of the three- or four-year-old, who cannot consciously represent the qualitatively distinct relations between mother and self, and mother and father. Only at age seven, when the ego collective includes self, mother, and father, can the personal *subs* and the different roles they play among themselves be distinctly emphasized and coordinated. At this point confusion ceases and the "Oedipus complex"—expression of a cognitive limitation in the normal child—disappears; but only when the subject's "family triangle" collective has had in everyday life, a good chance to develop to a mature form (cf. Balint, 1977).

If a collective structure that incorporates all the necessary "characters" of a life "play" cannot be adequately encompassed by willful *M*-boosted representation, the self may not be able to adapt to or find its proper place in the "play." For this reason old people whose *M*-energy has diminished (or neurotics who allocate their *M*-energy improperly) may not be able to adapt to social changes without help.

It is important to notice that the conscious roles and values that an I-self develops within a given daily-life collective are greatly influenced by the kind of partial-self, the I-agent or the I-soul, that one predominantly uses in this context. If it is the I-agent, the themes of mastery versus incompetence, independence versus dependency will dominate, and the Other will be experienced as a separate individual whose will can oppose the self's will. The type of morality expressed, if good, will then be of justice and equality. If the predominant partial-self is the I-soul, the themes of love-attachment versus unattachment or aggression-hate-anger versus friendly-indifference will dominate instead, and the other will be experienced as a part of oneself, empathically in communion with goals that are "necessarily" common (Stewart, 1986). In this case, the moral mood will be of care, concern, and responsibility.

Four Experiential Determinants of Social-Ego Development and Transcendental-Ego Development

Structures provide *constraints* to guide performance in order to overcome the environment's resistances to the subject's actions. As long as new resistances are not encountered and praxis remains unchallenged, structures will not change or "accommodate" and new growth will not occur. Only when required will old structures adapt and give rise to new structures. Coordination or integration of new structures through learning can only occur when the new performance is adapted to the new circumstances because it embodies constraints that *overcome* (accept or correct) the circumstantial resistances.

There are four experiential determinants of ego development. First, *the growth and diversification of affective goals* is an ongoing determinant of ego development because praxis, and thus the resistances of reality, change as the subject's goals change. Second, *the richness and diversification of experience* will affect ego development because resistances change with new situations. Third, *existential awareness,* the willful *self-monitoring* of mental awareness in the direction of expanding the present toward the future and the past, is usually necessary to achieve new con-

scious means to overcome possible new resistances. Consequently, at every level the *development of existential awareness,* growth in self-conscious decentration (Piaget, 1947/1956, 1967), is a determinant of ego development. Fourth, *ego growth at any age is the result of overcoming (i.e., reversing or accepting) failures,* because structures do not change unless change is required.

Overcoming failure is best achieved by accepting errors and taking them as signals of resistances to be overcome, then initiating a *macro-decentration* (see Pascual-Leone, 1984) and an *active trial-and-error process* of increasing existential awareness in the context of praxis, to discover how to overcome the resistances. This principle of growth applies at all ages. At the highest level of development, transcendental-ego growth occurs through the existentially aware overcoming of "foundering" in the context of *ultimate limit situations* that cannot be avoided or apparently resolved—situations such as death, illness, irremediable oppression, tragic loss of time, aging, guilt, absolute failure, fear, and so on (Jaspers, 1932/1970; Latzel, 1981). The transcendental ego emerges and develops through mental coping in *ultimate limit situations.*[5]

Adult Stages of Ego Development and Jaspers' Existential Awareness

The four determinants of ego development, together with the silent-hardware changes described earlier, can help to clarify the *transitions* across ego-developmental stages that modern researchers have empirically found (e.g., Erikson, 1982; Fowler, 1981; Jung, 1931/1961; Kegan, 1982; see Souvaine, Lahey, & Kegan chapter; Kohlberg, 1981a; Labouvie-Vief, 1984; Levinson et al., 1978; Levinson chapter; Loevinger, 1976; Pascual-Leone, 1983; Snarey et al., 1983). This sequence is, despite excessive terminological and conceptual differences, surprisingly congruent across authors and congruent with the stages of existential awareness proposed by Jaspers in 1932 and, more explicitly, in 1935 (Jaspers, 1932/1970; 1935/1955). In what follows, I explain Jaspers' stages and *interpret them psychologically as optional mental-processing manifestations of biological hardware stages of human development.* As I present these endogenous stages, I will suggest how the experiential determinants and the silent-operator changes together provoke the transitions. In this account, I assume the theory of adult stages and the terminology I have introduced elsewhere (Pascual-Leone, 1983, 1984, 1987).

The Late-Formal or Existential-Self Stage

During the period from 17 to 25 years of age, in college or the workplace, people use their practical intelligence as well as their creative–spiritual intelligence to explore interpersonal relations in depth. In this way, affects and affective goals develop and diversify to become complex mediational systems. Two of these affect systems are of particular interest here: (1) the power system that is the main affective-driving source of the partial-self, called I-agent, which produces collectives exhibiting the justice-equality kind of morality (Kohlberg, 1981a); and (2) the love system, the main affective drive of the partial-self, called I-soul, which generates

collectives marked by the care–responsibility kind of morality (Gilligan, 1982; Lyons, 1983; Niebuhr, 1963; Stewart, 1986).

In these Late Formal years, a wealth of new experiences brings a great diversification in *often contradictory* affective goals. This diversification may stimulate the emergence of affective ego-systems and cognitive styles that restructure the personality. It also causes many often self-denied conflicts in situations where affective goals conjointly activate partial-self systems that have been developed locally but are incompatible. New ego structures may emerge from this *purely organismic* coping with conflicts and contradictions. These new ego structures are not interpersonally or socially derived, as were the concrete-operational ego structures. They are purely *intrapersonal;* they are, as Kant, Hegel, or Husserl would say, *transcendental structures* (cf. Carr, 1974; Pascual-Leone, 1983).

Thus, in the late formal years a new agency for *self-consciousness* (i.e., valid consciousness of consciousness) emerges that constitutes a *self-control center,* as Scheler thinks of it, of the interpersonal self. For reasons given earlier, I call this transcendental self the *ultraself.* As I will discuss later, there are four different ultraself modes of control or forms of existential awareness, which may emerge sequentially but function in coordination.

Table 11.2 illustrates how these four ultraself modes develop and how they are progressively coordinated with previously available self structures to constitute four different self-organizations characteristic of the four stages of adult development (Pascual-Leone, 1983).

Throughout childhood, with each hardware M-stage, a different level of ego organization emerges by coordinating the previous ego organization with the newly acquired modes of conscious processing. This dialectical ego-development "spiral" goes on (see Pascual-Leone, 1983, 1987, for more detailed discussion of why this process is dialectical). When the conscious-processing mode of *empirical existence* appears, it progressively coordinates with the ordinary adult's interpersonal self, schematized in Table 11.1, to generate the *existential self* that is *the* developmental option of the Late-Formal stage (17–25 years). The other modes emerge and are

Table 11.2 Four Ultraself Modes of Control (Forms of Existential Awareness) That Emerge Sequentially After the Adult Interpersonal Self Stage

Modes		Selves
↓		↓
late adolescent ego organization	→	ordinary adult interpersonal self
		↓
empirical existence	→	existential self
		↓
♂ conceptual existence	→	♂ predialectical (Duality) self
♀ temporal existence	→	♀ predialectical (Duality) self
		↓
♂ temporal existence ⎱ ♀ conceptual existence ⎰	→	dialectical (Trinity) self
		↓
meditative existence	→	realized (Quaternity) self

coordinated in a similar manner. Note that males and females do not usually develop these existential modes in the same order. I discuss these issues later.

Jaspers calls the first existential mode of awareness *empirical existence*. As in existential philosophy, "existence" refers here to a full awareness of being a solitary being-in-the-world who, to survive, must engage in uncertain praxis and endure in limit-situations. For Jaspers, *empirical existence* emerges with the experience of existential "foundering" in conflicts. Success in coping at this early stage leads to good life structuring and to control and self-confidence; failure in coping leads to a more or less hidden existential fear, to withdrawal of ambitions, life-structure dissatisfactions, and perhaps to a low-grade mood of "existentialist" hopelessness.

The Predialectical or Duality-Self Stage

By the close of the Late-Formal stage, after about 25 years of age, a wealth of refined affects and affective-executive goals (e.g., ambitions and alternative life-projects) and many specialized skills for coping in society and at work may have been developed (cf. Gould, 1972, 1979; Levinson et al., 1978). From 25 ($\pm$3) to about 35 years of age the person realizes that there are contradictions among his or her affects and cognitions, and in human interactions between personal goals and the Other's affectively empathized goals. The person copes by developing a life philosophy and more or less categorical and generic "theories" or "procedures" to meet with these reality resistances.

These practical and/or creative–spiritual philosophies and "theories" are typically constructed as "eternal," generic-prototype characterizations of an experiential domain. They typically exclude the temporal aspect of change and the individual-difference variabilities of the phenomena, because the person cannot cope otherwise with the informational overflow: One's mental effort, M- and I-resources, cannot afford more analytical processing. Jaspers (1932/1970; 1935/1955) names this mode of experiencing, which is characteristic of much of modern empiricist science and of classic rationalism, "consciousness-as-such," and I call it *conceptual existence.*

The *conceptual existence* mode of processing copes with each context domain by creating conceptualizations about the matter at hand expressed by way of scientific or cultural institutions, explicit belief systems, practices and objects (i.e., socially objectified reifications of thought that Hartmann, 1954, calls "objectified spirit" and Popper, 1974, calls the world-3 of objective spiritual realities). However, the constructions of *conceptual existence* are often too molar and idealized to encompass the richness and evolving diversity of the true *empirical existence.* Thus, the ways of processing of *empirical existence* and those of *conceptual existence,* although equally necessary for praxis, are mutually contradictory in their details. Their respective structures cannot be directly integrated. (This state of affairs will be the origin of dialectical thinking when the subject takes consciousness of the contradictions among modes of existential processing [cf. Pascual-Leone, 1983, 1987].)

Two separate ego subsystems or *partial-ultraselves,* one for *empirical existence* and the other for *conceptual existence,* must thus evolve to be coordinated into a

not fully conscious predialectical organization (cf. Pascual-Leone, 1983). Expression of this coordination between an empirical-existence-ultraself and a conceptual-existence-ultraself is the awareness of contradictions in life and within the ego, which the *predialectical self,* constituted by the interpersonal self and the two partial-ultraselves, possesses. When the existential self first attempts to cope with contradictions and with information overflow caused by a rich *empirical existence* within the ego's repertoire of conscious structures, it attempts to "chunk" the information by developing more abstract macro-decentration and macro-structures. This is the structuralist approach to developing *conceptual existence.*

These macro-conceptualizations are often sought by the existential self with the help of mentors (Levinson et al., 1978) who can serve as models and sources of advice and inspiration. A very special affective bond grows between the mentor and the disciple. The mentor becomes a *"transitional self-object"* of the disciple (a term introduced by Winnicott, 1969, in a different context).[6] The mentor is the chosen model of the to-be-developed conceptual mode of processing or control. While this conceptual existence mode is being developed, the mentor may come to fill the position of that mode *within the ego,* thus becoming an externalized partial-ultraself of the apprentice. The existential self and its mentor will thus maintain, during the construction process, the peculiar affective bond that later connects the partial-ultraselves to each other within the ego. This peculiar affective bond is what psychoanalysts call "transference." When the conceptual-existence partial-ultraself is fully developed, the mentor relationship may no longer be required.

In the mature predialectical self, the affective–cognitive interaction between these two partial-ultraselves functions, as it were, like a *purely intrapersonal (intrasubjective) collective* of partial-ultraselves that I call an *ultracollective.* This ultracollective is made up of the conceptual-existence-ultraself playing the role of "big brother–father" or of "big sister–mother" vis-à-vis the empirical-existence-ultraself, acting like a "son–daughter" in their interaction. This Duality self organizes, by means of special ego executives (*LM*-ultra-executives), the dual "parental–filial" communication that in praxis exists between the empirical-existence-ultraself and the conceptual-existence-ultraself. *The Duality* (i.e., predialectical) *self develops to serve the person's affective goals and is bound to be different with different affective systems in the person.*

A purely internal, agent-dominated Duality self is often found in men, and this is the one I have described thus far. In soul-dominated self systems, which often, but not only, occur in women, the conceptual-existence-ultraself of the predialectical self may maintain forever in a changed form the special affective bond with a "mentor" (i.e., a male or female spouse, friend, parent, or more senior co-worker) that may in practice be one *or several* persons in the life-world of the subject. In this case, the soul-dominated predialectical self will develop a style of cognitive-competence I-agent that treats the "mentor(s)" as a permanent constituent of the self's ultracollective. Therefore, it develops its agency skills and its *conceptual existence* to complement rather than replace the role that the mentor(s) play(s) in this ultracollective. *It is as if the mentor had become a permanent constituent of the ultracollective.* I refer to this development as the formation of a Duality self in the manner of an *externalized-ultracollective.*

An important developmental consequence of the externalized-ultracollective

mode of Duality self is worth discussing. When the "mentor" (i.e., the externalized self-object) plays in the externalized ultracollective a role of conceptual-existence-ultraself, the agency skills of the self develop complementarily and thus generate a dual temporal-existence partial-ultraself instead of a separate conceptual-existence partial-ultraself. This is diagrammed in Table 11.2. The net effect of this temporal-existence awareness that grows complementarily with the other's conceptual-exis-tence-ultraself is a heightened sensitivity to change and its time-distant conse-quences *for the other*. As a result of this development, whereas the agent-dominated predialectical self exhibits a morality of justice and equality (Kohlberg, 1981a), the soul-dominated predialectical self comes to have a morality of care and responsi-bility (Brabeck, 1983; Gilligan, 1982; Lyons, 1983; Niebuhr, 1963, Stewart, 1976).[7]

Both kinds of predialectical ultraself organizations—agent oriented and soul oriented—in fact coexist, although in different degrees, in men and women alike (e.g., Bakan, 1966; Brabeck, 1983; Buber, 1923/1958; Gilligan, 1982; Jung, 1951/1959; Lyons, 1983; Niebuhr, 1963). One could well say that the predialectical self develops separately (i.e., *in a nonintegrated way*) the two sorts of Duality selves—that of empirical-existence in coordination with conceptual-existence and that of empirical-existence in coordination with temporal-existence.

In one way or another, at the end of the Predialectical stage, individuals can be fully autonomous. Their conduct can be well monitored by an ultraself, either a purely internal Duality self or an externalized-ultracollective. This ultraself is built out of mediational structures that need M-energy and I-interruption resources to be functional. Since a refined and conceptually clear temporal awareness necessi-tates the internalized coordination of empirical existence, conceptual existence, and temporal existence, a fully developed existential experience of temporality is not yet available.

The Dialectical or Trinity-Self Stage

After the age of 35 or 40 years, the human psychological organism undergoes a crisis: a more or less abrupt decrement in the power of silent hardware operators. This crisis of "limited resources" renders many structures inoperative and may make the ultraself-control deficient. Anxiety—the organism's response to lack of control and to uncertainty or fear vis-à-vis the future—may appear, and a new pro-cess of re-equilibration begins that involves strong affective goals directed toward structural development and existential metamorphosis.

The main organismic instigators of this crisis are declines in the function of four hardware operators: M-energy, I-interruption, C-learning (unintended content-par-ticular learning—e.g., spontaneous cue learning), and the A-operator (affective arousal). These regressive processes are summarized as follows:

1. The mobilization of M-energy in the service of the Duality self (whether internal or externalized) becomes more difficult and requires higher affective arousal. Also, since M-allocation itself is a mindful process—the pre-executives and executives that monitor M-allocation themselves need attentional M-energy—the self-initiated allocation of M-energy may become inefficient.[8]

2. I-interruption ability may functionally decrease, and the ultraself may often find itself unable actively to inhibit task-irrelevant or misleading schemes that are

unexpectedly activated. As a result, partial-self systems and their *mutually contradictory* philosophies, "theories" and practices, that usually are controlled in situ by way of *I*-interruption, come into conflict. For instance, the professional man who is "married" to his work may begin to experience during working hours guilt resulting from neglected commitments to his spouse, children, or himself. Also, the married woman may experience ambitions and goals for herself that are no longer easily suppressed in the name of care and responsibility for husband and children.

3. The *C*-operator may decrease in power. As a result, the person may find that he or she forgets names, usually cued only by content-learning, and can neither learn new material nor remember new situational details without self-initiated (willful) learning preplanned by the ultraself and attentionally energized by *M* (self-mediated *LM*-learning).

4. The *A*-operator also decreases its drive. Emotions mellow and affects become more subtle. Consequently, affective arousal may decline at a time when *M*-allocation increasingly requires its services.

These four intrinsic and biologically prewired changes in the silent hardware resources explain, even in the absence of historical, sociological, or accidental external variables, the onset of a midlife crisis (e.g., Cytrynbaum et al., 1980; Gould, 1979; Levinson et al., 1978). Yet at the same time these hardware changes, like the metamorphosis of a caterpillar, open great possibilities for growth and qualitative change (cf. Baltes et al., 1984; Craik & Simon, 1980; Labouvie-Vief, 1981; Pascual-Leone, 1983). Now the conceptual-existence-ultraself mode of processing, although still capable of creative–spiritual intelligence, no longer suffices. Its complex holistic and/or situational models often demand too much *M*-energy to make their current application easy. Also, on the basis of greater life-world experience, these models now appear too idealized and schematic to satisfy a concerned, silent-resource deficient ultraself—an ultraself that can no longer guarantee easy control (*I*-interruption) of undesirable happenings or misleading schemes.

As the existential philosopher Ortega y Gasset (1914/1961, 1957) has emphasized, the creative–spiritual intelligence of humans is continuously looking with concern into the future and turning to the past for solutions and guidance. The more the future appears uncertain or uncontrollable, the more the classic static "theories" of *conceptual existence* may seem inadequate. Hence, the ultraself may increasingly focus attention on the process of temporal becoming in historical events and contradictions. The structural packaging or "chunking" (*LCLM* structures) of experience previously created by *conceptual existence* can still usefully serve to facilitate the conscious grasp of the temporal, but only if the ultraself gives up logical-formalist rigor and unnecessary precision (cf. Pascual-Leone, 1984, 1987).

As the focus turns to evolving totalities, the person begins to notice patterns of contradictory interacting "theories"; the ultraself begins to invent *dialectics* (e.g., Basseches, 1984a). As Lenin (1915/1977) wrote, "The splitting of a single whole and the cognition of its contradictory parts . . . is the essence . . . of dialectics" (p. 381). Jaspers (1932/1970; 1935/1955) called *spirit* this mode of processing, which focuses on the evolving totalities of *empirical existence*—totalities that *conceptual existence* first formulated as idealized and static. I call this mode of a personal

spirit, focused on temporal change and personal history, the consciousness of *temporal existence.*

With the growing importance of this mode of *temporal existence* (which might have begun in the previous stage for soul-dominated ultraselves) the ultraself becomes fully focused on the analysis of evolving totalities intuitively represented by relational–dynamic symbols, imaginal representations, or "ciphers" (Jaspers, 1932/1970; 1947/1959). In this way the person learns intuitively about human, individual and collective, history and about the openness to change (historicity) of society and of human creative–spiritual intelligence (cf. Carr, 1974; Jaspers, 1932/1970; Schlipp, 1981). This new mode of processing uses the "data" from the empirical-existence-ultraself and the theories from the conceptual-existence-ultraself as its own data but cannot be integrated with them: The three modes are semantically incommensurable and pragmatically contradictory. The ultraself has to organize itself again as an ultracollective coordinating the interpersonal-self structures with three partial-ultraselves: the empirical-existence ultraself, the conceptual-existence-ultraself, and the temporal-existence-ultraself. Dialectical rules and operations governing the partial-ultraselves interactions and use in self-control are developed. This new organization is the *dialectical self.* The explicit operations that coordinate its ultraself constituents with practical experience are *dialectical operations*—a new kind of operations that I have examined elsewhere (Pascual-Leone, 1983, 1987). Some clinical data support this analysis, which views the dialectical self as if it were a *Trinity self* or a three-term structural organization (Edinger, 1973; Jacobi, 1962; Jung, 1951).[9]

The Transcendental or Quaternity-Self Stage

Biological regression of the four silent resources may initially facilitate development of a temporal-existence-ultraself in the following ways. First, the difficult mobilization of *M*-energy weakens the capacity of conceptual existence to predict and control future events. With this foundering, a strong affective goal to develop a temporally oriented, rational reconstruction of life's evolving totalities appears. Second, the weakening of *I*-interruption forces the person to be open to experience and to "filter" less, so one can more easily notice excluded aspects of inner or outer experience that the "theories" of *conceptual existence* had not emphasized. Third, the weakening of content-particular learning facilitates the abstraction of invariant patterns in evolving totalities of "data" and "theories"—the forest is no longer lost for the trees. Finally, the attenuation of affective arousal makes the self-control attentional operations less biased by extraneous or minor affective goals, thus reducing distortion of the evolving totalities.

Though these silent-hardware regressions do not initially hinder real-life action processing, they will in time. After 55 or 60 years of age, the person *may* become inefficient, indecisive, or too rigid in making decisions under accelerated or unexpected conditions. Though first appearing during the Late Formal period, a class of cognitive operations that I call *transcendental operations* now comes to the fore.

Transcendental operations are a special form of dialectical operations that take the ego-core and ego-milieu structures as objects of knowledge or "theories" on

which the dialectical operations apply. It is the specific characteristic of transcendental operations that they apply only when the ego structures are not directly engaged in the action processing of real life. These structures are indirectly activated only in the context of remembrances, reflections, counsel, informal planning, or relaxed conversational exchange. Whereas ordinary dialectical operations emerge through action processing intermixed with executive processing in the midst of the life struggle, *transcendental operations emerge in the context of pure executive processing,* when action processing is not taking place (Pascual-Leone, 1983, 1984).

Under these conditions, sheltered from action and from rushed goal-directed thinking, a *meditative thinking* begins to appear (or becomes more frequent), which often uses transcendental operations. The thinker, absorbed in a spontaneously produced mental attitude of "phenomenological reduction" (see earlier), begins to explore freely, using the temporal existence mode of processing, life's or mind's evolving totalities. Feelings and evolving cognitions blend together in the meditative mood. History and the openness of these totalities are explored, and alternative possibilities that could have been or could evolve are entertained. Concrete events are often turned into ontological symbols and become the means for further reflection. Transcendental operations are dialectical operations of the second degree: dialectical operations performed on dialectical operations. During this process, feelings and affects become detached, and the thinker becomes fully aware that "theories" or experiential "data" *are not* the ultimate Reality, but symbols or ciphers of it (Jaspers, 1932/1970, 1947/1959). The thinker now knows, as the Zen saying goes, that the finger pointing to the moon is not the moon itself.

This sort of thinking and mental attitude, which Heidegger (1959/1966) called "releasement" to Reality, constitutes a new and final mode of processing developed by the ultraself organization. Jaspers calls it *Existenz;* I name it *meditative existence.* This mode of thinking develops a knowledge of foundations, often embedded in metaphysics and in what Scheler calls Ethos, where the ideal historical-developmental good and its counterpoint, the "ideal" evil, become vividly clear to an ultraego that has at last fully coordinated affect and cognition, past, present, future, and possible, into an open, freely interconnected, detached totality. I call *Realized self* the ultracollective coordinating the empirical-existence-ultraself, the conceptual-existence-ultraself, the temporal-existence-ultraself, and the meditative-existence-ultraself, with the interpersonal-self structures. The four existential modes of this realized self tempt one to call it a *Quaternity self.*

Jaspers, following Kant, calls this Quaternity organization "Reason." Jung (Edinger, 1973; Jung, 1951/1959), perhaps providing indirect empirical support for Jaspers' Quaternity-self conception of "Reason," has found that a Quaternity symbol appears late in self-realization in the dreams of patients and in the ancient esoteric literature. The openness of human history, human freedom, and Ethos in the face of an obscure Reality are now, according to Jaspers, better understood. The substantive ontological form of this "newly found" insight on the person's relation to Reality is strongly co-determined by the personal and cultural history of the tacit or explicit meditative seeker. The substance, therefore, of one's "new" philosophy—for example, religious or atheist, political revolutionary or conservative, philosophy of joy and hope or of mellowed "sadness" and "despair"—can vary and

may not be a good index of the ultraself's growth. Nevertheless, the similar functional structure and dialectical (rational or mystical) character of their beliefs, their aptitude to take alternative perspectives with equanimity, and their insightful detachment and attentive calm vis-à-vis the uncertainty of life's evolving totalities are signs (*ciphers,* Jaspers would say) of a Realized self.

Both Jaspers and Jung emphasize that *existential communication* between two humans in "mentoring," therapy, or in long-lasting companionship can foster ego-spiritual development. Similar ideas are conveyed in the Western tradition by the concept of spiritual apprenticeship and in the Eastern tradition by the concept of a guru. Jaspers, Heidegger, and the vast spiritual tradition of meditation insist that this effect can be greatly accelerated if existential communication is accompanied by systematic, solitary, meditative thinking. *Systematic* meditation differs from *free* meditative thinking or *meditative existence* primarily in that the object and method of thinking is prescribed and is relatively contentless from an intellectual viewpoint. As the work of Alexander (1981, 1982; see Alexander et al. chapter) and others (e.g., Maslow, 1976; Johnston, 1974) suggests, processes similar to those of free meditative thinking could occur through systematic meditation that fosters transitions across ultraself stages. The practical possibility of fostering transitions in ultraself growth should be of interest to those researchers who might otherwise neglect this chapter as an exercise in pure reason.

Conclusion

Guided by the work of Scheler, I have organized the first part of this chapter to show how a natural science, evolutionary analysis of organismic modes of functioning leads to the claim that humans, albeit similar to animals in practical intelligence, are capable of creative–spiritual intelligence—a form of intelligence that cannot be explained by current constructs in psychology. The development of this higher mode of functioning leads to the emergence of an *ultraself*—a conscious, purely organismic control-center utterly detached from the interpersonal self. The second part of the chapter pursues a process-analytical and developmental clarification of this ultraself by interpreting, in the current idiom, Jaspers profound analysis of human awareness. Jaspers' own four existential modes of processing are thus incorporated into constructivist process psychology, where they belong.

Children's silent-hardware stages and structural stages contrast sharply with the development of adult stages. Children's stages are caused by biogenetically timed progressive increments in M-energy (mental capacity), and as such they are strongly anchored in chronological age. It can be shown, using suitable tasks, that the structural stage level of a child is generally in correspondence with his silent-hardware stage level. This is often not so with adult stages. The transition from one adult stage to the next does not require a change in silent-hardware operators. Also, the hardware changes that do occur in adulthood involve decline rather than growth. Stage transitions can occur much earlier, perhaps in the Late-Formal or Predialectical period, if the experiential, personal-historical, and cultural conditions make it possible. They can also occur much later or never occur if sociocultural and historical-experiential factors hinder the transitions, as often happens in

our too competitive and overrushed culture. *In this case, the silent-hardware stage transitions should still take place at an age depending upon organismic-biological factors but the qualitative-structural stages of ego development would not emerge.* Chronological age is therefore a poor estimate of structural ego-developmental stages in adults. The adult structural stages must be defined independently of age, by their structurally cumulative characteristics.

For researchers who reject the possibility of structural stages in adulthood, there is an intriguing question: How is it that Jaspers' stages, when interpreted organismically, appear so congruent with many recently formulated stages of cognitive-existential adult development, such as those of Alexander et al. (see Alexander et al. chapter), Erikson (1982), Kohlberg (1981a; see Kohlberg & Ryncarz chapter), Labouvie-Vief (1984, 1990), Levinson (see Levinson chapter), Perry (1968), and others? This postulated congruence among adult-developmental theories clearly calls for investigation.

Acknowledgments

I am much indebted to Dr. Roger Bobillier for early discussions we had and to Lynn Stewart for early drafting of tape-recorded material. I owe to Dr. Janice Johnson and Dr. Charles Alexander invaluable editorial advice. I also owe editorial comments to Nancy Benson, Lynn Stewart, and Dr. Anik de Ribaupierre.

Theoretical work on affect, ego development, and moral development leading to this chapter was begun at the Institute of the Van Leer Jerusalem Foundation as a fellow of the foundation. The background empirical research informing this work and the chapter's preparation were supported by Grant A0234 from the Natural Science and Engineering Research Council of Canada.

Notes

1. *Equilibration* is a term used by Piaget, not Scheler. Here, and throughout the paper, I have abandoned terms used by Scheler and by Jaspers in favor of more contemporary psychological terminology. The probable loss in historical rigor is compensated by clarity and psychological relevance.

2. Readers familiar with my M-operator theory should observe that the counting of schemes in this example corresponds to the e scale of the M-power measure ($Mp = e + k$). The e scale develops during infancy. The k scale does not apply here, because the task is motivationally immediate, that is, it does not require executive planning, and responses are affectively driven (cf. Pascual-Leone et al., 1978).

3. By boosting schemes (perhaps C-schemes) M-energy causes them to coordinate into a pattern of brain coactivation that leads to a desirable praxis. With *few* repetitions an L-learned scheme complex acquired with the help of M emerges. This is an LM-structure (Pascual-Leone, 1976a, 1984; Pascual-Leone & Goodman, 1979). Notice that M should not be needed if the context strongly cues, and thus boosts with C-activation, all the constituent schemes involved and if no misleading or irrelevant scheme is activated. This context would be a *facilitating situation*. *Many* repetitions in this facilitating situation result in overlearning and thus patterning of the activated constituent schemes. This is what is currently called *automatization* (e.g., Hasher & Zacks, 1979). In my dialectical constructivist terminology, this is called LC-learning, because the C-operator applies first and then the L-operator applies on its product (Pascual-Leone & Goodman, 1979).

4. Rationalist philosophers and Jungians called ego what modern psychology currently refers to as self. I shall follow the modern usage and also refer to Jung's ego as self. Rationalist philosophers, Jungians, constructivist psychologists (e.g., Baldwin, 1908, 1894/1968; Piaget & Inhelder, 1966/1969), pragmatists (James, 1892/1966; Mead, 1934), and psychoanalysts (e.g., Guntrip, 1968; Rof Carballo, 1972; Winnicott, 1969) have all emphasized that this self develops through interactions with the social environment. Similar conceptions of the interpersonal self are implicit in Baldwin's (1908) important theory of the dialectical psychogenesis of the self and the "alter" (other self) and are also found in Mead (1934), Sullivan (1940/1953b), and the more recent psychoanalytical theory of the self–object relations (e.g., Eagle, 1984; Guntrip, 1968; Winnicott, 1969).

5. Every experience of enduring the unwanted resistances of a context of failure by means of meditative thinking is a *functional limit-situation*. This is so for as long as the subject does not succeed or give up. For this reason life hardships that are endured with existential awareness lead to remarkable growth in the self. But only *Ultimate* limit situations, the foundering with existential awareness in the face of *insurmountable but unavoidable* negative resistances, can lead the self into higher levels of transcendental (i.e., ultraself) development.

6. Winnicott (1969) described how the toddler internally constructs his first autonomous self (building beyond a protoself that is bonded to the mother). As the child gives up the heteronomous bonding to the mother, he symbolically transfers this bonding to some familiar "transitional object" (e.g., a blanket), which becomes a mother substitute and an externalized anticipation of the to-be-developed autonomous preschooler's self that is capable of willfully giving (not just receiving) responsible care.

7. The possibility of this externalized-ultracollective form of adult ego development has long been recognized by Jungians (e.g., Jung, 1953, 1954; Jacobi, 1967; Neumann, 1949/1962), and certain philosophers (Buber, 1923/1958; Niebuhr, 1963); it has recently been argued, in very different but no less clear terms by psychologists such as Bakan (1966) and Gilligan (1982).

8. As an after-the-fact illustration of this conclusion I should mention Ellen Langer's work (1982; 1989a,b, see Langer et al. chapter). Langer has shown that older adults sometimes *lack mindfulness* in the interpretation of situations and the organization of their conduct. This relative "mindlessness" results from a functional deficiency in mental mediation (a failure to apply, or to M-activate, mediational structures). Consistent with this interpretation of Langer's work, Jedrzkiewicz (1983) has shown in my laboratory that older adults have a deficiency in mobilizing their M-operator; other researchers have reached similar conclusions (e.g., Craik & Simon, 1980; Horn, 1982b). Thus, if mindfulness of performance is an index of the application of mediational intellective structures, mindlessness of performance (a simple associative style of functioning) in previously sophisticated subjects becomes symptomatic of a failure in mobilizing the M and I resources that intellective structures need.

9. Jung and his followers have found in the dreams and other materials of persons in advanced states of individuation the spontaneous emergence of Trinity symbols, which Jung relates to the Christian Trinity and interprets as a projection of psychological processes of self-development.

12

Growth of Higher Stages of Consciousness: Maharishi's Vedic Psychology of Human Development

C. N. Alexander, J. L. Davies, C. A. Dixon,
M. C. Dillbeck, S. M. Druker, R. M. Oetzel,
J. M. Muehlman, and D. W. Orme-Johnson

Do major qualitative advances in cognitive development occur after adolescence? Most contemporary psychologists would say they do not. In contrast, throughout the history of both Eastern and Western thought, one finds accounts describing the possibility of profound developmental transformations in adulthood. The most ancient and extensive of these descriptions is found in the Vedic tradition of India (Basham, 1959). In this chapter we propose that this ancient system, as recently formulated in the Vedic psychology of Maharishi Mahesh Yogi (1969, 1972; Orme-Johnson et al., in press), describes (1) a universally available sequence of "higher stages of consciousness" that dramatically extends beyond the ordinarily understood endpoint of human development and (2) the systematic means for their facilitation. In this chapter we will

1. Examine the higher stages as described in Maharishi's Vedic psychology (hereafter referred to as Vedic psychology) and demonstrate how they meet criteria for major qualitative advancement.
2. Discuss Vedic psychology's theory of "levels of mind" as an integrated hierarchy of discrete levels of cognitive functioning.
3. Propose a life-span model explaining how these levels of mind account for the unfoldment of the ordinary phases of development and, ultimately, for growth to higher stages of consciousness.
4. Propose a general mechanism of human development based on this model.
5. Review findings from experiments we have conducted to test developmental predictions arising from Vedic psychology (see Research Appendix).[1]

We begin with a brief review of developmental psychology's views on cognitive growth after adolescence and introduce criteria for its assessment.

Is There Development Beyond Adolescence?

One of the founders of contemporary developmental psychology, Jean Piaget (1972b), postulated that the endpoint of human development is a "formal operational" stage of abstract reasoning that is generally achieved by middle or late adolescence. Consistent with this chronological terminus, Loevinger et al. (1985) have found little evidence of change on their cognitive-structural measure of ego (or self) development during four years of college or after 18–20 years of age. Further, Flavell suggests that although cognitive transformations in childhood are "largely inevitable, momentous, directional, uniform and irreversible," dramatic "morphogenetic" changes meeting these five criteria do *not* typically take place in adulthood (Flavell, 1970, p. 274, 1984). A similar view is expressed by Dittmann-Kohli and Baltes; Levinson; and McGuinness, Pribram, and Pirnazar in this volume.

Why would such qualitative advances be generally lacking in adulthood? Flavell (1970, 1971a, 1985) straightforwardly asserts that the within-species uniformity of major childhood transformations results from momentous "biological–maturational" growth processes early in the life cycle. In fact, growth spurts in brain size (Epstein, 1974b, 1980), in the myelination of brain systems (Yakovlev & Lecours, 1967), and in concurrent synaptogenesis (Fischer, 1987; Goldman-Rakic, 1987) do tend to correspond to the normative ages at which cognitive stage development takes place during childhood. Piaget (Piaget & Inhelder, 1969, p. 154) proposed that physiological development provides a necessary but not sufficient condition for cognitive-structural development. If major neurophysiological development does generally come to a halt by late adolescence or early adulthood (Epstein, 1978; Tanner, 1970), it follows that the necessary physiological condition for further major cognitive advance is lacking.

Though fundamental physiological development and corresponding hierarchical ("vertical") cognitive advancement typically appear to "freeze" by age 25, new life experiences continue "horizontally" across the life span. This accruing of experience may result in an increase in "wisdom" later in the life cycle (e.g., Birren, 1990; Clayton & Birren, 1980; Dittmann-Kohli & Baltes chapter; Erikson, 1963; Levinson chapter; Sternberg, 1990). Nevertheless, accumulation of rich experience and adjustment to new societal demands do not generally promote major qualitative advances in cognition beyond formal operations nor substantially enhance "fluid intelligence" (Horn, 1982a,b).

However, several theorists do postulate that further qualitative advance in cognitive development can take place in adulthood, though it may be infrequently observed (e.g., Demetriou & Efklides, 1985; Fischer, Kenny, & Pipp chapter; Kitchener & King, 1981, 1990; Kramer, 1989, 1990; Labouvie-Vief & Hakim-Larson, 1989; Pascual-Leone chapter; Richards & Commons chapter, 1990; Sternberg & Downing, 1982). According to Richards and Commons (chapter), although these "postformal" models propose more complex patterns of operational thought, like formal operations, they are still "hypothetico-deductive" in nature. Also, these proposed higher stages do not appear to require further growth of the nervous system beyond late adolescence or early adulthood. Rather, their development seems to be based on optimizing use of available biological and corresponding cognitive resources.

Moreover, even the status of formal operations as a qualitatively distinct, universal late adolescent cognitive stage is currently being challenged (see review in Alexander, Druker, & Langer, introduction). Indeed, Flavell (1985) has asserted that there may be only one major developmental discontinuity: the shift between the sensorimotor schemes of infancy and representational thought processes beginning in the second year of life. He holds that while "qualitative trends" in growth continue, it is difficult to identify metamorphosislike hierarchical stage changes unambiguously within the representational period.

We propose that to classify as unambiguous qualitative advancement, adult growth not only should meet Flavell's (1970) original five criteria for fundamental change (see earlier), but also should satisfy the following requirements:

1. It should be at least as far beyond conceptual or representational thought as symbolic representation is beyond the sensorimotor domain of infancy (i.e., not merely an extension of formal operational thought). The subperiods of the sensorimotor period are superseded not simply by more complex forms of sensorimotor action but by a new mode of representation—the semiotic or symbolic function—which comes to regulate the domain of action. Similarly, fundamental development beyond the representational level should permit not only more effective conceptual thought but also the emergence of a purely postconceptual mode of knowing that comes to regulate the entire representational domain.

2. Such a fundamental qualitative advance in cognition, like the preceding one, would presumably require major neurophysiological maturation. Many researchers now hold that physiological development is even more important to cognitive development than Piaget, Kohlberg, and others initially recognized (e.g., Bornstein, 1988; Bower, 1982; Scarr & Kidd, 1983).

3. Postrepresentational development should resolve the fundamental epistemological and ontological constraint of the abstract reasoning (formal operational) level—that the reflective knower cannot directly know himself. The dawning capacity to think about thinking allows the adolescent consciously to "conceptualize . . . mental constructs as objects" (Elkind & Weiss, 1967). This new ability to represent the self abstractly as an object of contemplation may be a necessary condition for asking the critical question, "Who am I?" However, the major constraint of the abstract reasoning level is that while one can ask this question and attempt to answer it in terms of intellectual concepts, on the fundamental level of direct experience it cannot yet be resolved (cf. Chandler, 1975).

William James' (1890) relentless introspection about reflective or abstract thought led him to postulate that at this level one cannot directly experience an invariant self or "I," but only a series of "me's" about which one thinks. The essential epistemological problem is that the knower cannot simultaneously be both observer and observed. As folk psychology has expressed this dilemma, "knowing yourself is like trying to look into your own eyes." Higher-order forms of reflection may not resolve but, rather, may participate in this problem, because, like traditional homunculus (man in the head) models, they may lead to an "infinite regress of the self" (Russell, 1977; cf. Kramer, 1983). To observe a more abstract knower, a still more abstract observer would have to do the observing; and if he did, he could not, in principle, directly observe himself. Hence, further major qualitative development of the self could not take place within the representational domain

no matter how abstract it might be. Qualitatively distinct adult development should thus allow resolution of this conundrum and permit direct self-awareness.

4. Higher stages would be not only *non*representational but truly *post*representational. In accordance with the orthogenetic principle of development (Werner, 1957), the postrepresentational stages should become differentiated from and hierarchically integrated with the representational level. Thus, the capacity for conceptual thought would not be abandoned. Instead, the entire representational system—regardless of degree of abstractness or "multiple-loop" reflexivity (Miller, Kessel, & Flavell, 1970; Richards & Commons chapter)—would take on the status of a subsystem within, rather than the executor of, mental life. A postrepresentational level would be distinguishable from a prerepresentational level, because the latter would be unable to use symbolic (semiotic) processes, whereas the former would still employ the symbolic mode but subordinate it to an entirely new mode of knowing characterized by expanded capacities.

5. Postrepresentational stages should be "higher" not only in a purely structural sense but also in a functional sense. Higher stages should be more adaptive and stable ("equilibrated"), and more accurate ("veridical") and comprehensive ("decentered") in their knowledge of self and world (Elkind, 1979; Kohlberg, 1969; Piaget, 1977).

The Vedic Psychology of Higher Stages of Consciousness

Clearly, mainstream contemporary developmental psychology has not identified, nor has it established means to promote, such "momentous" changes in adulthood. In contrast, it is the explicit goal of Vedic psychology to promote such advanced stages of development of the knower (Maharishi, 1969; Dillbeck, 1983a; Orme-Johnson, 1988a). *Veda* is a Sanskrit word connoting complete or unified knowledge, which is said to be gained only at the highest level of development, when knower, known, and process of knowing are fully integrated (Maharishi, 1986, p. 26).

Vedic psychology has been chosen as a framework for discussing higher states of consciousness for several reasons:

1. While the Vedic literature has generally been difficult to comprehend for those outside this tradition, Maharishi presents this ancient knowledge in scientifically testable terms and has sought to relate its fundamental principles systematically to those investigated by the modern sciences (Chandler, 1987).

2. Vedic psychology (Maharishi, 1969) makes available a uniform set of procedures—the Transcendental Meditation (TM) and TM-Sidhi program—that are simple to practice, require no change in life-style or belief system, and are predicted to accelerate development of consciousness markedly without altering its basic form or sequence.

3. Large numbers have been instructed in this procedure across cultures (over 1 million in the United States and over 3 million worldwide) who are potentially available for scientific study. This has generated the largest existing body of empirical research investigating the impact of meditation techniques on human devel-

opment (Orme-Johnson & Farrow, 1977; Chalmers, Clements, Schenkluhn, & Weinless, in press, Vols. 2–4; Wallace, Orme-Johnson & Dillbeck, in press).

4. Vedic psychology has a decidedly developmental orientation. It delineates seven major states of consciousness (Maharishi, 1972). The daily cycle of waking, dreaming, and sleeping constitute the three ordinary changing states of consciousness. In addition, Vedic psychology describes an invariant sequence of three stable higher states of consciousness based upon experience of a purely nonconceptual fourth state of consciousness. Our life-span model proposes that these stable higher states constitute "postconceptual" higher stages of development that are consonant with, and dramatically extend, the Western "organismic model" of ontogenesis (Overton & Reese, 1973).

It is typically held that transcendental experience is transitory and accessed by only a privileged few (e.g., James, 1890; Maslow, 1964). In contrast, based upon Vedic psychology, we propose that these higher stages of consciousness naturally unfold in the course of "normal" adult development but that development "freezes" prematurely because accumulation of stress and lack of exposure to appropriate environmental support or developmental technologies. Thus, we suggest that to label such higher stages as "mystical" is a misnomer, for they "transcend" the representational domain in no more mystical a way than abstract thinking transcends the sensorimotor (or preoperational) activities of early childhood.

5. A critical concern in current cognitive psychology is the need to derive a taxonomy or architecture of mind that accounts for the structure and dynamics of the wide range of mental processes engaged in by the adult knower (e.g., Glass & Holyoak, 1986; Fodor, 1986; Norman, 1981). The construction of such a taxonomy is also crucial to the task of developmental psychology to identify an endstate of cognitive development. How narrowly or unidimensionally one conceives of cognitive processes and their capacity for integrated growth determines not only the breadth and upper boundary of development, but also one's formulations of all lower stages, which are invariably cast as sequential approximations of the final stage. Vedic psychology proposes such an architecture of increasingly abstract, functionally integrated faculties, or "levels of mind" (Maharishi, 1969; cf. Boyer, 1984).

This hierarchical sequence of intrinsic levels of mind appears to have considerable explanatory and predictive power. Based on this comprehensive theory of mind, we propose a model in which progressive unfoldment of these latent capacities underlies sequential unfoldment of ordinarily observed periods ("stages") and trends in human growth as well as further development of higher stages of consciousness. Although Vedic psychology has primarily focused on these latter higher stages, Maharishi has on several occasions also described the mechanics of growth during childhood in ways consistent with this model (e.g., Maharishi, 1978).

Levels of the Mind

Vedic psychology postulates that the mind is hierarchically structured in layers from gross to subtle: from highly active to settled, from concrete to abstract, and from diversified to unified (Maharishi, 1972). Maharishi specifies the following lev-

els of mind: the faculties of action and the senses, desire, the thinking mind, the discriminating intellect, feeling and intuition, and the individual ego (Maharishi, 1969; cf. Dillbeck, 1988, Orme-Johnson et al., in press). (Note that *mind* is used in two ways in Vedic psychology. It refers to the overall multilevel functioning of consciousness as well as to the specific level of thinking [apprehending and comparing] within that overall structure.) According to this theory, underlying the subtlest level of the individual knower and transcendental to it is the Self, an abstract, silent, completely unified field of consciousness, identified as the self-sufficient source of all mental processes:

> Self has two connotations: lower self and higher Self. The lower self is that aspect of the personality which deals only with the relative aspect of existence.... the mind that thinks, the intellect that decides, the ego that experiences. This lower self functions only in the relative states of existence—waking, dreaming, and deep sleep.... The higher Self is that aspect of the personality which never changes [the underlying unified state of consciousness]... the very basis of the entire field of relativity, including the lower self (Maharishi, 1969, p. 339).

As generally experienced in its active or excited states, consciousness is fragmented into the separate values of the active knower (ego), processes of knowing (levels of mind), and known (objects of experience), also referred to in Vedic psychology as *Rishi, Devata,* and *Chhandas,* respectively (Maharishi, 1986). Ultimately, Vedic psychology describes the essential, underlying nature of consciousness (the Self) as a silent, unified field of pure consciousness having no content other than itself. However, awareness is typically restricted so that the silent, unified nature of consciousness (referred to as *Samhita;* Maharishi, 1986) is hidden and only becomes fully available with the development of higher stages of consciousness. Ultimately, all processes of representation in the broadest sense—involving perception, thought, and feeling—are appreciated as fluctuations, or qualified states, of the underlying unqualified field of pure consciousness at their source (Maharishi, 1986).

We are usually aware of only the active levels of the mind engaged in thought and behavior. Thought proceeds as if "horizontally," mediated by language and symbolic content, moving from one idea to another. According to Vedic psychology, however, every thought has also undergone a "vertical" microgenesis from its unmanifest source in pure consciousness through more precipitated, concrete manifestations, until it finally becomes discernible to conscious awareness. According to Vedic psychology, the emergence of a thought from the least excited level of consciousness results from the interaction of sensory input with "the storehouse of impressions" (cf. long-term memory store) associated with the individual ego at the finest level of mind (Maharishi, 1969, p. 284). The thought comes to be experienced at a more or less precipitated level of its development, depending primarily on one's current period of cognitive development (see next section).

Thus, Vedic psychology posits a vast realm of subtle levels of mind or cognitive processing that typically lies outside the sphere of the ordinary waking state. The classic psychodynamic view was that the unconscious domain of mind was primarily a repository for more primitive processes or repressed thoughts and desires. Psychological order or organization must then be imposed from "above" by ratio-

nal processes or from "outside" through socialization. In contrast, Vedic psychology posits that these progressively subtler levels of mind display greater capacity to order and integrate experience. These deeper levels may typically lie outside of conscious awareness, not because they are primitive (or repressed) but because they operate at finer levels of excitation—comparable to finer time–distance scales or higher frequency modes—than those currently accessible to awareness.[2] Thus, deeper levels of mind would remain essentially preconscious until conscious awareness could function at a fine enough "resolution" or fast enough "shutter speed" to observe them.[3]

A Life-span Model of Development of Consciousness: General Features

We now describe our life-span developmental model for relating Vedic psychology's description of higher stages of consciousness to the ordinary phases of development described by contemporary developmental psychology. Broughton (1984) has argued that we must create theories that not only go beyond formal operations but "beyond Piaget." Since the endpoint we describe is dramatically beyond that considered by Piaget, it follows that it may be in order to reconceptualize both the steps and the mechanisms leading to that goal.

From the viewpoint of Vedic psychology, the entire developmental continuum investigated by contemporary psychology—including hypothesized "postformal" stages—occurs within the psychophysiological confines of ordinary waking consciousness (Alexander & Boyer, 1989; Dillbeck & Alexander, 1989). Thus, it is not surprising that qualitatively distinct cognitive stages may be difficult to discern within this period (cf. Flavell, 1985). According to Vedic psychology, only the qualitatively distinct psychophysiological experience of an entirely different major state of consciousness—pure or transcendental consciousness—provides the basis for major advances in adolescent–adult growth (see section on transcendental consciousness). Ultimately, whether the phases of development in childhood identified by Piaget (1970b), Bruner et al. (1966), Fischer (1980b), Case (1985), and others prove to be strict structured stages or simply to represent qualitative trends is an empirical question and beyond the scope of this chapter to determine. Therefore, here we will conservatively label them as developmental periods.

For our purposes what is significant is that within the ontogenesis of ordinary waking state (see Fig. 12.1), there is a striking correspondence between these general periods of development (listed across the top) and the capacities associated with the levels of mind, from gross to subtle, identified by Vedic psychology (listed down the left side).

-->

Figure 12.1 This developmental model proposes that shifting of the dominant locus of awareness through progressively deeper levels of mind underlies unfolding of commonly observed periods of development. Under optimal conditions (including exposure to appropriate developmental technologies) development will continue through the higher stages of consciousness described by Maharishi's Vedic psychology.

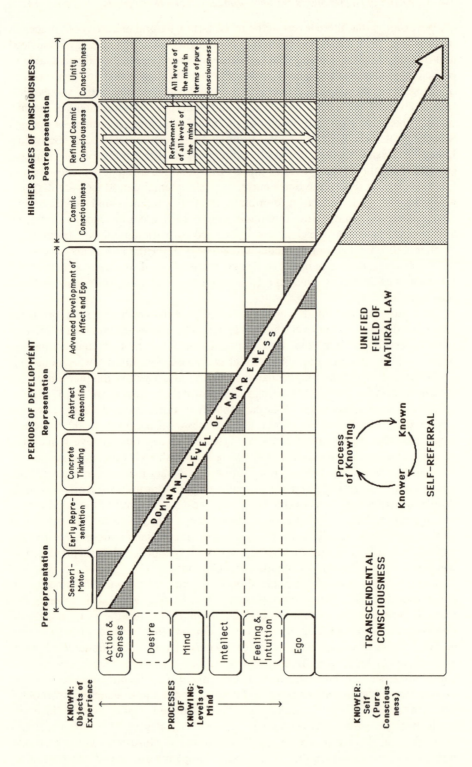

We propose that these levels of the mind form a natural hierarchy of "processes of knowing," with the forms (patterns) of thought and action strongly influenced and delimited by the most abstract structure of knowing functionally available to conscious awareness during each period. Further, we suggest that during the course of ontogenesis, the growing capacity to more fully activate and utilize successively subtler levels of mind corresponds with and underlies the unfoldment of the successive phases of cognitive development. The functioning of awareness through each progressively finer level may provide the "deep structure" (cf. Souvaine, Lahey, & Kegan chapter) for each sequentially higher expression of cognitive growth. If so, the deepest level of mind through which awareness predominantly functions would determine one's current developmental period (see the diagonal arrow in Fig. 12.1, indicating dominant level of awareness and corresponding developmental period). How this underlying cognitive competence is displayed, and in what particular areas, is also influenced by learning and skill training (cf. Fischer et al. chapter). In this model, though environmental factors are necessarily involved in the full unfoldment of deeper levels of mind, the basic structure and function of each level is inherent (cf. Pascual-Leone's chapter on "silent-hardware operators").[4]

According to our model, when awareness shifts to functioning primarily through a deeper mental level, this newly activated process of knowing is increasingly differentiated from the more expressed levels of thought and action and becomes the dominant locus of functional awareness. For example, when conscious awareness comes to function through the intellect in a reflective manner it provides the foundation for abstract reasoning such as formal operations (see Fig. 12.1). The reflective intellect, which involves the capacity to think about thinking, now represents the primary locus of conscious awareness. All the levels of the mind less subtle than the intellect are differentiated (solid lines separate the levels) and their contents can be taken as objects of knowing. Although their influence may be substantial, all the levels of mind more subtle or abstract than the intellect remain relatively undifferentiated and less available to conscious utilization and control (a dotted line separates these levels). However, because the levels of the mind constitute the inherent structure of consciousness, they all are to some extent active at all times and each contributes to every thought and partially undergirds every cognitive phase. (This is why in Fig. 12.1 all the levels of mind are represented or contained in each column of cognitive development.)

Our approach combines aspects of both epigenetic (Erikson, 1963) and hierarchical models of development (Loevinger, 1976; Piaget, 1970b). It is epigenetic in that all levels of mind are said to be inherent and grow together, with a different one in ascendency during any given period. On the other hand, our model is hierarchical, since, in an invariant sequence, increasingly abstract (subtle) levels serve as the primary locus of awareness and coordinate the less refined levels. Since it combines aspects of both approaches, this model may permit more satisfactory explanation of certain developmental findings. For example, concrete operational problems appear solvable at earlier ages than predicted if tasks are simplified and made more perceptually concrete (e.g., Bower, 1982; Bryant, 1974; Brown, Bransford, Ferrara, & Campione, 1983). This finding is consistent with our model because the faculties required to solve such problems are considered potentially

available at earlier ages but in a restricted condition that requires presentation in a manner accessible to the current level of mind through which awareness predominantly functions. According to this model, however, faculties associated with deeper levels of mind cannot be *fully* accessed before all prior levels are made available. Thus, as conscious awareness gains the capacity to function through ever deeper levels of mind, stable forms of cognitive functioning are gradually yielded as precipitates.

In this view, the ultimate status of the knower is always pure consciousness. However, in the process of experience, awareness becomes localized as the individual ego and identified with (i.e., unable to distance or distinguish itself clearly from) the processes of the current dominant level of mind. The ego can know itself and the world only indirectly through its processes of knowing—with knowledge about itself (the "me") constrained by the limits of the currently dominant level of mind.[5]

Ultimately, in the higher levels of development described by Vedic psychology, consciousness becomes fully integrated and self-referral, allowing direct Self knowledge. At all prior stages, however, the unbounded Self, in projecting itself through the currently available structure of the mind, becomes embedded in or restricted by the limits of that structure and hence assumes the status of a "bounded I," or self. Thus, the deep motive of development may be seen as the progressive rediscovery by the Self of its own inner nature as the basis for increasing perspective on and mastery over the subjective and objective world. The true status of the knower can be consciously appreciated only when awareness has finally transcended all the levels of mind to experience its source in pure consciousness—in which knower, known, and process of knowing have been unified in one wholeness of experience. In this self-referral fieldlike state, knower and known are no longer linked only indirectly through the excited, localized processes of knowing. The knower *is* the known, and hence Self knowledge is direct and immediate.

Mechanisms of the Model

How one views the endpoint of development influences one's understanding of the mechanics of development and vice versa. Flavell (1984, p. 188) has urged that the "what" (the domains) and "how" (the mechanics) of development be more broadly conceived. He suggests that some of the agents of our cognitive growth are *not* age-independent functional invariants; rather, they require development themselves and become available after a certain age or developmental level. Although all the levels of mind in our model are age-independent functional invariants in the sense that they all contribute during each period, there is also a sense in which they are not, since they become a dominant locus of conscious awareness only at certain points in development.

From our perspective, cognitive-structuralists such as Piaget (1972) have addressed themselves primarily to one domain of growth—development of the intellect. Further, while recognizing the contribution of other factors, they have tended to focus on a single corresponding developmental mechanism—the "operative" or analytic capacity of the intellect to resolve ("equilibrate") cognitive conflicts through active "construction" of new cognitive structures that more ade-

quately account for reality (for a more detailed review on developmental mechanisms see Alexander, Druker, & Langer, introduction). Gardner, Phelps, and Wolf (chapter) reach a similar conclusion; they argue that Piaget restricted himself to the study of "logico-mathematical intelligence" (or "paradigmatic thought"; Bruner, 1986). Piaget's special contribution has been to illuminate the functioning of the intellect (see the row corresponding to the intellect in Fig. 12.1) during the developmental periods through abstract reasoning. Indeed, he appears to reconstruct all prior stages and the mechanics of development in terms of successive approximation to his assumed endpoint: the achievement of full scientific reasoning at the abstract level of formal operationals. For example, even the infant is essentially portrayed as performing action experiments that will eventuate in the construction or theory of the permanent object (cf. Gardner, Phelps, & Wolf chapter).

Each of the other major approaches to development also tends to focus on a single developmental domain, thus emphasizing a different type of mechanism. In contrast, our model is multidimensional—integrating several major domains (rows in Fig. 12.1) and corresponding specialized mechanisms or mental faculties in its description of life-span development (columns) (see also Gardner et al. chapter). For instance, from the perspective of our model, the information-processing approach has focused primarily on the contribution of the processing capacities of the active thinking mind (row 3) across the various periods of development. Therefore, it has emphasized the contribution of such automatic or "figurative" functions as working memory, attention, and automization (e.g., Bjorkland, 1987; Siegler, 1986; Sternberg, 1984). Even when higher-order processes are introduced—such as executive control strategies (Case, 1985) and metacomponents (Sternberg, 1984)— they tend to be presented from the perspective of the mind as a thinking machine or computer. On the other hand, Erikson (1959) has emphasized the contribution of ego-synthetic processes across the life-span (row 6). Although this paper primarily compares and contrasts Vedic psychology's approach with that of cognitive-developmentalists, interesting comparisons can also be made, for example, with information-processing (Boyer, 1984) and ego-developmental approaches (Alexander & Jacoby, 1989).

Yet the question still arises, "Is there a primary mechanism that underlies development between levels of mind and across domains and periods of growth?" Vedic psychology proposes that this general mechanism is the "natural tendency of consciousness to evolve" (Maharishi, 1966, p. 55). We suggest this occurs through the very process of spontaneously shifting the dominant locus of awareness to progressively deeper levels of mind during psychophysiological development. Consistent with this view, Wohlwill (1973, p. 319) and Ryan and Deci (1985, p. 260) also posit a pre-existing disposition toward psychological development.

We propose that this general mechanism may account for the twin processes of differentiation and hierarchical integration that various thinkers have placed at the core of cognitive development (e.g., Langer, 1969; Werner, 1957). In our view, the shifting of awareness to function actively from each deeper level underlies the differentiation of this new mental structure from the prior levels of mind. Further, when awareness shifts from the cognitive structure in which it was previously

"embedded" (cf. Schachtel, 1959; Kegan, 1982) it becomes capable of hierarchically integrating and controlling all cognitive processes occurring at the prior level. Thus, this general mechanism for development *between* levels would sequentially activate specific cognitive functions primarily responsible for executing activities *within* each new period.

While emphasizing the contribution of intrinsic mental faculties to development, we also acknowledge the vital role of construction in the elaboration of these inherent structures and in the acquisition of context-specific skills (see Fischer, Kenny, & Pipp chapter). Indeed, elaboration and consolidation of these inherent structures are likely to account for the extensive period of time required for "within-stage" development observed by Flavell (1985) and others.

From our perspective, the structures of mind and body represent one integrated system (Maharishi, 1966, pp. 188–189). As William James recognized almost a century ago, there is a direct correspondence between the functioning of the mind and that of the nervous system. However, while James (1966, p. 18) emphasized the dependence of the "immediate condition of a state of consciousness" upon an "activity of some sort in the cerebral hemispheres," it is also apparent that one's physical state is profoundly affected by one's mental state (e.g., psychoneuroimmune responses, placebo effects, and psychosomatic illness: see Chopra, 1987, 1988; and Langer et al. chapter). Psychology and biology seek to understand the same organism but from different levels of analysis, which yield distinct yet complementary descriptions (e.g., Deci & Ryan, 1985, cf. Chopra, 1989). We have described the natural tendency for awareness to shift to deeper structures of mind as the general mechanism of development. At another level of analysis, biologists might describe this same process in terms of the inherent biological program of the organism to develop through a sequence of increasingly advanced stages of neurophysiological organization. While Vedic psychology emphasizes the unfoldment of mind, it recognizes that this unfoldment always involves a corresponding physiological reorganization as well.

Given the organism's inherent tendency toward psychophysiological growth and our claim that higher stages of consciousness represent the natural continuation of development in adulthood, why don't these higher stages inevitably unfold as did earlier developmental periods? We suggest these higher stages are, in principle, no less inevitable than earlier periods, but both depend on exposure to appropriate environmental support systems.

The inherent potential of the organism to survive and evolve assumes adequate environmental support (cf. Scarr-Salapatek, 1976). During every period the current level of psychophysiological development of the organism makes available certain potentialities for experience. However, only with requisite environmental support can these potentialities be actualized and yield permanent functional and organizational change in both the mind and nervous system. Without exposure to appropriate developmental technologies, or what Bruner (1972) referred to as "cultural amplifiers," cognitive and social development may be severely impeded. During the sensorimotor period, sustained interaction with an appropriate physical environment using the senses and motor organs appears to be a critical amplifier for the developmental achievements of this period. Selective deprivation in young ani-

mals (and unplanned deprivation in children) can lead to impaired physiological and perceptual development in the affected channels (e.g., Aslin & Banks, 1978; Hubel & Wiesel, 1963; Mitchell, 1981).

For the representational (symbolic) period of development, the most fundamental and universal developmental technology is language learning, or more broadly, symbol use. Though the capacity for language is inherent (Chomsky, 1972; Fodor, 1975), informal and formal instruction in language plays a major role in its development from soon after birth to adulthood (e.g., Cross, 1978; Karmiloff-Smith, 1979). Language is clearly a very powerful mechanism, or "medium," for the development of symbolic thought, particularly when language is understood in the broad sense to include symbolic play and other nonverbal forms of communication. Vygotsky (1962) emphasized the significance of language acquisition as a "secondary signal system" (cf. Pavlov, 1927) for freeing humans from reliance on the "primary (sensory) signal system" dominant in the animal world. Indeed, our entire formal educational system appears to be devoted to amplifying language and symbolic skills—reading, writing, and mathematics—in the service of conceptual development. With respect to development of abstract reasoning, Flavell (1971a, p. 123) states, "It has yet to be demonstrated that anything resembling formal operational, reflective, and speculative thinking can occur in the absence of a rich linguistic system. . . . Such a system might well be regarded as indispensable for complex and extended trains of thought."

Readiness for each shift to a deeper level requires that the functional changes of the current level of development are sufficiently stabilized and automatic such that conscious awareness is potentially freed to function predominantly through the next deeper level (cf. Csikszentmihalyi & Massimini, 1985, p. 127; Sternberg, 1984).[6] However, because awareness is habituated to functioning through the current level, increasingly abstract vehicles of experience and corresponding levels of environmental support may be required to redirect attention to act from more abstract levels. Thus, sequential exposure to "enactive" (sensorimotor), "iconic" (early representational), and "conceptual" cultural amplifiers (Bruner et al., 1966) may promote sequential redirection of attention through deeper levels—senses, representation, thinking mind and abstract intellect.

The Transcendental Meditation and TM-Sidhi Program as a Postlanguage Developmental Technology

Just as language learning is fundamental for promoting development beyond the sensorimotor level to the conceptual domain of ordinary adult thought, we propose that exposure to a postlanguage developmental technology—such as the Transcendental Meditation (TM) and TM-Sidhi program—may be at least as fundamental in facilitating development beyond the language-based conceptual level of thought to postconceptual higher stages of consciousness. The capacity for language use is inherent but actualized through participation in a linguistic environment; in a similar way, capacity to transcend the thinking process and act from a postconceptual perspective may be inherent but made available through systematic exposure to a postlanguage technology of consciousness. Just as language acquisition frees atten-

tion from the control of immediate sensory stimuli, a mechanism that promotes transcending of representation may be required to free attention from the habitual domination of symbolic thought.

The TM program is nonconceptual, in that it is not mediated in any way by the meaning of words (Maharishi, 1969, p. 471). Hence, it qualifies as a nonsemantic or non-language-based system. In contrast, any system of development through introspection or counseling relies on language for thought and communication. During TM, an effortless procedure involving use of a "mantra"—a specific sound utilized purely for its sound value without reference to any meaning—frees attention from the control of language and the semantically conditioned thinking process. During the practice, mental activity is said gradually to subside as increasingly refined levels of thought and feeling are experienced. This gives rise to the state of pure consciousness in which awareness is maintained, but all specific objects of attention (percepts, concepts, feelings) are systematically transcended, with the result that awareness becomes self-referral, or directly aware of itself (Maharishi, 1986, p. 27). The TM-Sidhi program is a more advanced procedure that Maharishi developed on the basis of the classical *Yoga Sutras* of Pantanjali (Aranya, 1977). This program trains the awareness to function effortlessly from the level of pure consciousness, in order to further accelerate growth and stabilization of higher stages of consciousness (Maharishi, 1986).

In the absence of an appropriate postlanguage developmental technology, psychological and corresponding physiological development typically appear to freeze during adolescence or early adulthood. We propose that in cultivating awareness to function from deeper levels of mind, such a technology "unfreezes" corresponding latent biological structures, thus providing the psychophysiological foundation for major, morphogenetic development in adulthood.

Although the process of transcending to experience pure consciousness is said to promote development during any period, Vedic psychology also describes accumulation of stress as a general phenomenon that may hinder or block growth at any point in the life cycle. In the psychodynamic literature, stress in the form of trauma has been perceived as a critical factor in the "fixation" or even "regression" of psychological development (e.g., Erikson, 1963). Maharishi (1972) describes stress more broadly as resulting from any "overload" on the functioning of the nervous system (and any level of mind), which remains in the organism in the form of biochemical or structural abnormality. For example, a simple photo flash may create a stress in the mechanisms of visual perception.

Sleep and dreaming are natural forms of rest which alleviate fatigue and tension, but they are not sufficient to neutralize more deep-rooted levels of stress (Chopra, 1987; Wallace, 1986). The consequent accumulation of stress may produce a chronically excited, disorderly, or "high-noise" style of functioning of the nervous system that impedes the natural ability to function through finer levels of mind. The process of transcending to a "least excited" state of pure consciousness during TM appears to "unfreeze" development by expanding awareness and, in the process, normalizing the nervous system from deep-rooted stresses that block further growth (see Research Appendix).

Thus, the gradual macrogenetic process of shifting awareness to deeper levels of mind in the course of psychophysiological development appears to be markedly

accelerated through the microgenetic process of transcending all the levels of mind during the TM technique. Such developmental advancement through TM has been observed even for populations otherwise recalcitrant to change, such as maximum security prisoners and the institutionalized elderly (Alexander, 1982; Alexander, Langer, Newman, Chandler, & Davies, 1989; see Research Appendix).

The Commonly Observed Periods of Development as Described by the Model

The primary purposes of our life-span model are (1) to describe how the unfoldment of underlying levels of mind as delineated by Vedic psychology may help to explain more fully the mechanics, sequence, and structure of the commonly observed periods of cognitive development and (2) to provide a developmental framework or context for understanding how subsequent adult development of higher states of consciousness represents a natural continuation and extension of the general process of development. In describing the sequential development of the knower (the "I") to its ultimate, unbounded status as the Self, we will identify specific changes in the relationship between knower, known, and process of knowing undergirding this process of growth. From the perspective of Vedic psychology, all knowledge is structured in consciousness—in the quality of the underlying relationship between knower, known, and process of knowing (Maharishi, 1972). This means that all knowledge in the domains of cognitive, social, and moral development is a function of the depth of unfoldment of conscious awareness as reflected in the comprehensiveness of this underlying tripartite structure.

Figure 12.1 illustrates the proposed relationship between levels of mind and major developmental periods. Although all levels of mind are said to function simultaneously, each period is characterized by the "dominance" of a given mental faculty in the conscious awareness of the knower.

Because the major focus of Vedic psychology (and this volume) is on more advanced stages, the earlier periods will be only briefly discussed.

Dominance of Faculties of Action and Sensation: The Sensorimotor Period

The newborn represents a primitive state of nervous system development. In the opening months of life, the first cortical area of the brain to mature is the motor strip, followed by the primary sensory cortex (Rose, 1973). Given at least minimal environmental support and opportunity to interact, during this period the most concrete faculties of mind are systematically engaged: These are the faculties of action[7] and the senses. The predominance of these faculties, functioning at their most expressed level, appears to underlie what Piaget and others have identified as the sensorimotor period.

What is the relationship between knower, known, and process of knowing at this first level of development? According to Vedic psychology, even the limited state of awareness of the infant is nothing but pure awareness functioning in a

highly restricted form. The Self (pure consciousness) is collapsed into the bounded structure of the self: The "I" or ego (knower) during this period acts on or senses (dominant process of knowing) nonpermanent objects of immediate sensation and action (known). Throughout most of this period, there is not a well-developed internal capacity to represent objects symbolically as permanent and as separate from other objects—be it a representation of the self (the "me") or any object in the environment. Thus, the self as known is not yet clearly differentiated from the environment. The "I" or ego tends to remain identified with its current sensations or actions. Apparently for the newborn, anything outside immediate experience does not exist—that is, there are no "permanent objects" (Kegan, 1982; Piaget, 1954).

However, consistent with our position that all levels of mind are intrinsic and always contribute to some degree to the child's experience, there is mounting evidence that the newborn is far better equipped psychobiologically than was previously realized (e.g., Banks & Salapatek, 1983). For example, soon after birth, infants demonstrate the ability to discriminate their own mother's voice from that of others (DeCasper & Feiffer, 1980) and to imitate simple movements (Meltzoff & Moore, 1983). Such findings imply a minimal ability to hold internal representations in memory in advance of substantial sensorimotor experience, which implies that the capacity for representations is not constructed but inherent within the organism. In any case, no amount of sensorimotor action would seem sufficient for "constructing" permanent objects in the absence of the capacity for already representing a mental image in memory that can be actively recalled even when its referent is removed from the sensory field (cf. Ginzberg & Opper, 1979, p. 63). The emergence of this ability may also begin much earlier than initially recognized: as early as eight or nine months (e.g., Mandler, 1984).

Dominance of Simple Representation and Desire: The Early Representational Period

According to our model, the symbolic function plays an increasing role in cognitive activity as the dominant locus of awareness gradually shifts from immediate action and sensation to a deeper representational level of mind. We propose that this shifting of awareness corresponds with normal physiological maturation and will naturally occur, provided there have been environmental opportunities for adequate cognitive experience. For instance, maturation of the cross-modal zones in the sensory cortex during the second through fourth years of life is considered critical to the development of the symbolic function (e.g., Geschwind, 1964). Further, Fischer (1987), extrapolating from existing data (Goldman-Rakic, 1987), conjectures that a spurt in concurrent synaptogenesis (around 18–21 months) may be involved in the more complex representational recall capacity required for full object permanence.

As the "I" or ego (knower) increasingly functions through simple representational processes, it comes to monitor objectively the domain of action and immediate sensation in which it was previously embedded. Actions and sensations are now internally organized through more stable perceptual–mental representations

and desires, which can also be outwardly expressed in the form of speech (verbal representation). At this level, the child can represent both himself and others as permanent objects of attention and desire (the known).

Vedic psychology (e.g., Maharishi, 1969) understands representation as arising from the interaction of senses and mind, and it views this interaction as largely mediated by desire. By virtue of desire, more abstract impulses of mind are given a direction through the senses and organs of action to execute goal-directed behavior. Thus, desire is seen as playing primarily a functional rather than a structural role in connecting the mind with the senses (and hence is enclosed in broken lines in Fig. 12.1). Thus, consistent with the Piagetian characterization of this period, our model views early representation more as a transition period.[8] The identification of the "I" with immediate desire and perception would account for the "egocentric" viewpoint typically associated with this period (Elkind, 1979). It is also for this reason that Loevinger (1976) would refer to this as the impulsive stage.

Dominance of Comparative Thinking Level of Mind: Concrete Thinking Period

Emergence of the deeper, comparative aspect of the thinking mind typically occurs during the five- to seven-year shift (White, 1970), which has been functionally related to myelination of the corpus callosum (Yakovlev & Lecours, 1967) and consolidation of left hemispheric dominance (e.g., Mount, Kagan, Hiatt, Reznick, & Szpak, 1981). Localization of language in the dominant hemisphere appears to correspond to dominance of the language-based thinking mind over simple perceptual–representational processes (cf. White, 1970). Rich exposure to informal language use and communication during this period may stimulate unfoldment of this underlying capacity.

During this shift, the primary association of the "I" (knower) shifts from desires and simple representation to the comparative thinking level of mind (dominant process of knowing), which generates classes and relations in terms of which the known is increasingly organized. Maharishi (1969) holds that the active thinking mind is responsible for apprehending, remembering, comparing, and conceptually organizing the multiplicity of perceptions to plan speech and action to fulfill desires. We suggest that during this period awareness "steps back" out of the simple representational screen of the mind and can now actively coordinate over time and space perceptions and concrete representations. As thought becomes more fully differentiated from sensory impressions and desire, egocentric behaviors resulting from confusion between these two domains naturally subside. The accompanying capacity to entertain and compare viewpoints further contributes to the reduction of egocentrism.

A milestone of this period is the achievement of "conservation" of quantity (Piaget, 1952b). Failure to conserve appears to result from perceptual centering on immediate spatial and temporal features of the stimulus array—for example, only seeing that a new beaker is taller. Successful conservation may result from association of awareness with the deeper comparative thinking mind. From this "decentered" perspective, percepts can be coordinated across space and time, enabling the recognition that the new beaker is both taller and narrower. This emergent ability

to de-embed from and coordinate representational stimuli over time may also contribute to substantial gains in constructive memory and metacognitive capacities observed during this period (e.g., Brown, Bransford, Ferrara, & Campione, 1983). Further, Vedic psychology (Maharishi, 1980) has proposed that the comparative thinking mind is responsible for the apprehension of part–whole relations, which would account for marked improvements in classification skills also found during this period.

The principal constraint of this period is that the child tends to be limited to thought about the actual or concrete world of his perceptions and desires. He is immediately embedded in the concrete thinking process and cannot operate upon it to generate more abstract forms of thought. Thus, though the knower can evaluate the outer world, he cannot systematically observe the internal mental processes through which this evaluation takes place.

Dominance of Reflective Intellect: Abstract Reasoning Period

During this period the primary locus of awareness shifts from the concrete thinking level to the level of the reflective intellect, which becomes the new dominant process of knowing. This enables the intellect to generate abstract thoughts from concrete representations and to operate on those abstract thoughts as new objects of knowledge.

The role of the intellect, according to Vedic psychology, is to discriminate, logically evaluate, and decide, bringing direction and order (and hence understanding) to the diverse and more outwardly oriented activity of the thinking mind. Maharishi (personal communication, August 23, 1980) describes the contribution of the intellect: "The exploration of nature in any field is fundamentally the same. The first examination is on the level of the senses. Then we inquire with the mind into the nature of the reality. Then the intellect begins to logically scrutinize this analysis and compartmentalizes it to identify layers of nonchange within change—rules [invariant principles]."

Although the functioning of the intellect is involved during every period of development, when awareness associates predominantly with the intellect, it provides the basis for abstract reasoning such as displayed in formal operations. The fundamental property of formal operations, from which Inhelder and Piaget (1958, pp. 254–255) derive all others, is the "subordination of reality to possibility," or the "concrete actual" to the "abstract hypothetical." From our perspective, this property derives from the intellect's emerging capacity to reflect consciously upon the contents of mind, rendering thoughts as possibilities rather than actualities in which the knower is immersed. The abstract operations of the intellect performed on more concrete operations of mind would appear to give rise to the "second-order operations" ("thinking about thinking") characteristic of formal operations (Piaget, 1950, p. 148).

The technical description of formal operations (Piaget, 1950) appears to cast this general process of abstract thinking too narrowly in terms of scientific problem solving and a specific logico-mathematical model (cf. Broughton, 1984). The apparently rare occurrence of formal operations in "nonliterate" cultures (e.g., Super, 1980) may be largely due to use of scientific–technical tests in societies that instead

display systematic reflective thinking in adaptive tasks more appropriate to their culture (e.g., Gladwin, 1970; Tulkin & Konner, 1973). More generally, the emergence of abstract thought appears to underlie the emergence of nascent "self-awareness" (Loevinger, 1976; Selman, 1980) and identity formation during adolescence and young adulthood (Erikson, 1968b; Gilligan, 1987b). It is only when internal mental states start to be reflected upon that the question "Who am I?" can arise as something more than simply distinguishing oneself by name or external characteristics from others. Eventually, at a more mature level of abstract reasoning, the intellect can construct a conceptually complex description of self and world with which the knower "conscientiously" identifies or adheres (Loevinger, 1976).

From the viewpoint of Vedic psychology, the primary constraint of this period is that while the intellect enables symbolic, reflective thought, it still does not permit direct awareness of Self (self-referral). The "I" can only know itself indirectly through a series of intellectual constructions or representations about itself as the "me" (James, 1890). This "dualism" is a universal design feature of language and symbolic representation of any kind (Hockett, 1960). The symbol always stands in for or refers to something else (the referent). The "me" (any thought or concept of the self) stands in for the self but is not the self. This is consistent with Broughton's view (1984, pp. 406–407) that thinking about thinking does not amount to true self-consciousness. The limits of the intellect are further reflected in the methods of conventional science, which, while making enormous progress in gaining objective knowledge of the laws of nature, has as yet made little progress in gaining equal understanding and mastery over subjective existence. The scientific enterprise has generally sought to exclude subjective existence (though with limited success; Hempel, 1966), rather than directly address it, and hence does not really answer the question, "Who am I?" which is essentially a subjective issue.

Resolution of the identity question by internalizing answers provided by others or society in terms of roles or values is not ultimately satisfying, as it really answers a different question—"what will I do (or believe)?" not "Who am I?" We suggest that one cannot go beyond such objectively defined conceptions of the self until the reflective intellect itself begins to be transcended. Complementary to the objective means of gaining scientific knowledge, systematic subjective means of gaining knowledge, such as the Transcendental Meditation technique, have been explicitly designed to foster transcending of the thinking process.

The Role of Feeling and Intuition in Development

According to Vedic psychology, feelings in the broad sense operate at and interconnect all levels of mind. However, they are particularly evident in the interface between mind and senses, and between the intellect and ego (see Fig. 12.1). In our model, during the early representational period, they function primarily as extrinsically motivated desires. At a more mature level of development, feelings function as delicate carriers of information, linking the intellect back to the intrinsic evolutionary motivation of the ego and ultimately to the inner Self. Feelings become more self-validating, and less dependent on validation through conscious intellectual analysis.

Maharishi (1969) describes feeling as a more "relaxed" state of the intellect. It

is flexible and relational (hence more sensitive to context and change) and involves a subtler, more rapid, holistic, intuitive mode of functioning, less dominated by linguistic expression and sequential formal reasoning. Mature feelings and intuition provide an internal ground for guiding the reflective intellect (cf. Maslow, 1968, on the "inner directedness" of self-actualizing people)—increasing the likelihood of creative insight in both the sciences and humanities (cf. Arlin, 1984, 1989, 1990; Dreyfus & Dreyfus, 1986).

It is widely recognized among life-span developmental psychologists that the advent of family and work relations during the adult years can stimulate further affective and personal growth and the integration of affect and cognition (e.g., Dittmann-Kohli & Baltes chapter; Erikson, 1959; Gilligan, Murphy, & Tappan chapter; Kramer, 1990; Labouvie-Vief, 1990; Levinson chapter; Orwoll & Perlmutter, 1990). Opinions differ, however, as to whether such change involves major qualitative transformations (cf. Flavell, 1970). Further, even those who propose "postformal" periods characterized by both expanded cognitive and affective capacities, generally agree that such growth is rarely achieved and still remains within the representational tier of development.

Several of these theorists have identified an initial postformal period, which Kramer (1983; 1989), Fowler (1981), Pascual-Leone (chapter), and Basseches (1984b) have labeled "dialectical operations." At this level, one is said to recognize the limitations of "closed-system" formal-operational reasoning that excludes sources of information that do not "fit" one's current world view (Labouvie-Vief, 1990). Apparently opposing conceptual systems can now be related to one another, and each can be applied as appropriate. Labouvie-Vief (1984) suggests that the logic of this postformal level is more flexible, containing within it and directing the more restricted logic of formal operations. In the interpersonal and affective domain, different viewpoints are no longer perceived as a source of threat (Souvaine et al. chapter). Others' values need not be collapsed to one's own; thus, intimacy is not at the expense of the "autonomy" of self and other (Loevinger, 1976).

According to our model, to the degree that such growth beyond the constraints of ordinary abstract reasoning takes place, it would be based on an increasing capacity for awareness to function from the subtler level of feeling and intuition.[9] Increasing differentiation and predominance of this deeper level of the mind would permit narrower conceptual processes of the reflective intellect to be viewed from a broader perspective. Because feelings are relational, when conscious awareness functions more from this level, it displays the flexibility necessary to appreciate and relate apparently opposing systems. Whereas logical reasoning functions to distill universal or general aspects of situations, feelings spontaneously take into account more of the richness of the immediate context and recognize that logic must be considered in relation to needs and responsibilities, and the uniqueness of the given situation (cf. Gilligan, Murphy, & Tappan chapter; Powell, 1984).

We recognize, alternatively, that affective and intellectual functioning can be conceived as semiautonomous domains (Zajonc, 1980, 1984), such that one could be developed intellectually but suffer emotional problems, and vice versa (cf. Loevinger, 1976). However, the hallmark of mature adult development is said to be that refined values of both affect and intellect are displayed in a relatively integrated manner (e.g., Gilligan, Murphy, & Tappan chapter; Labouvie-Vief, 1990). Why is

this more integrated style of functioning so rarely achieved? For example, as little as 1–2 percent of adults reach the "autonomous" level as measured by Loevinger (Cook-Greuter, 1990, in press). We suggest two major interrelated reasons. First, although our entire formal educational system is focused on the development of abstract reasoning, it lacks systematic means for experiencing and developing subtler levels of feeling and intuition that lie beyond the ordinary reasoning process. Second, as mentioned earlier, stress creates a "high noise" style of functioning of the nervous system that tends to block the unfoldment of deeper levels of mind. The more refined levels of feeling and ego are especially sensitive to the negative impact of stress. In the absence of a systematic means for eliminating stress accumulated at these subtler levels, it is difficult for conscious awareness to settle or "relax" sufficiently to function consistently from a deeper feeling level. Further, until these deep stresses are *fully* eliminated, emotion cannot be completely life-supporting and fully integrated with cognition, nor can intuition be consistently valid. Thus, affective development and ego development in adulthood tend to be fragmented and incomplete.

In contrast, Vedic psychology describes the potential for developing higher stages of consciousness characterized by fully stress-free functioning, based in a unified level of awareness that transcends all discrete modes of thinking and feeling. Development of these higher stages requires that conscious awareness regularly traverse mind, intellect, feeling, and ego to experience pure consciousness at their source. The repeated flow of awareness through each sequentially deeper mental faculty stimulates both their differentiation and integration. Maharishi predicts that under optimal conditions, including exposure to the TM and TM-Sidhi program, the integrated growth of these faculties should culminate in stabilization of the first higher stage of consciousness even within the student years. Thus, growth of intellect, feeling, and ego would be greatly accelerated and far more integrated than currently observed. Indeed, under such optimal conditions, it is predicted that growth of all faculties would be more rapid and holistic during childhood. (See Research Appendix for supporting evidence.)

The Role of the Individual Ego in Development

Vedic psychology locates the ego or bounded "I" at the subtlest level of individual functioning, closest to the silent, transcendental value of the unbounded Self. Maharishi states (1972, lesson 19), "The ego is that value of life which is most refined. The ego . . . is the experiencer in the individual life. . . . Ego understands, ego feels, ego thinks. That faculty of the ego which thinks is called the mind. That faculty of the ego which understands, discriminates, and decides is called the intellect. That faculty which feels—feeling, emotion—is called the heart."

The individual ego constitutes the interface between unbounded pure consciousness—the ultimate nature of the knower—and the current process of knowing. It is pure consciousness (the Self) which has become localized and qualified by functioning through the levels of mind and corresponding structures of the nervous system, giving rise to the bounded "I." As the active knower, the ego functions through these processes of knowing, integrating the aspects of the known into a coherent whole.

Although the ego performs general functions, it also reflects the distinctive character of the individual and hence differs from person to person. Each "I" is uniquely individualized or qualified by its enduring connection to the organized totality of impressions or memories (*Chitta*—Maharishi, 1969, p. 422) said to be stored at this finest level of individual awareness. According to Maharishi (1969, 1986), the ego provides the internal "reference point" and "organizing power" necessary for synthesis of information derived from all the levels of mind; its role is to sustain the integrity and evolution of the individual.

Several theorists have divided postformal growth into essentially two phases: the first allows seemingly opposing intellectual systems to be related to each other, the second fosters synthesis of these views into a single system (e.g., Kramer, 1983; Pascual-Leone chapter; Richards & Commons chapter). Kramer (1983, p. 93) suggests that whereas the former dialectical-type processes focus more upon the "immediate action environment," the latter synthetic processes permit "detached" reflection on life, the fruit of which is often referred to as wisdom (cf. Birren, 1990; Chandler with Holliday, 1990; Clayton & Birren, 1980; Csikszentmihalyi & Rathunde, 1990; Dittman-Kohli & Baltes chapter; Erikson, 1968b; Orwoll & Perlmutter, 1990; Pascual-Leone, 1990). There is general agreement that such growth is rarely achieved. (For example, less than 0.5 percent appear to reach Loevinger's final "integrated" level; Cook-Greuter, 1990, in press). Accordingly, one may assume, as Loevinger (1976, 1984) suggests, that theorists themselves are attempting to describe a level of which they may have some experience but lack the necessary perspective to describe objectively. In the absence of a clear framework for differentiation, elements of prior and higher periods often seem lumped together.

Our model suggests that to the degree such personal growth does occur in adulthood, it would result from increasing differentiation or development of the ego resulting in enhanced synthesizing capacity. On this basis, information provided through all other levels of mind could be more objectively appreciated and integrated. However, even in this relatively mature state, the ego still can only know itself indirectly through feelings (and the other levels of mind) and hence remains localized and constrained by the limits of that information. According to Vedic psychology, until the unbounded value of the Self, at the basis of the ego, is realized, the individual will always remain, to some extent, unfulfilled.

Higher Stages of Consciousness

According to Vedic psychology, all the periods of development thus far described would fall within the range of the ordinary waking state of consciousness (Maharishi, 1972; Orme-Johnson et al., in press). In contrast, higher stages of consciousness are said to be as qualitatively distinct from ordinary adult waking (and from each other) as waking is from the states of dreaming and deep sleep. On the one hand, we will see that development of these higher stages appears to involve the natural continuation of unfoldment of deeper mental structures. On the other hand, the higher stages can be viewed as dramatically "discontinuous" with (i.e., highly distinct from) prior periods of development. Just as the representational

periods follow the sensorimotor domain but are not reducible to it and hierarchically integrate it, so too the postrepresentational higher stages of consciousness are not reducible to and hierarchically integrate the representational domain.

We suggest that it is just this marked developmental discontinuity that makes these higher stages so difficult to comprehend by those who have not yet experienced them. Thus, it is not surprising that someone functioning from a baseline of abstract reasoning would view these postrepresentational stages as "altered" or nonordinary. Even within the representational tier of development, subjects at a particular cognitive or moral level cannot comprehend (though they may prefer) a level beyond their own (e.g., Rest, Turiel, & Kohlberg, 1969). In this sense, even an eight-year-old concrete operational child displaying conservation of continuous quantity (Piaget & Inhelder, 1969) could be regarded as essentially a "mystic" by a four-year-old preoperational child. For the latter, the container that is taller (though thinner) must have more liquid; and consensual agreement can be readily found among other four-year-olds (normal preoperational "scientists") using objective measures (e.g., rulers). For them, the statement that the shorter (though wider) container holds the same amount as the taller container would be nonsensical, and at worst delusional. The concrete operator's explanation—that there has just been an apparent change in amount but that nothing has really changed at all (liquid conserved)—is reminiscent of reports by individuals in higher stages of consciousness that the apparent ever-changing character of perceived objects is seen to be illusory once the ultimate nonchanging nature of reality is consistently experienced (conserved). Further, in communicating with people in higher stages of consciousness, there appears to be a directional asymmetry of comprehension characteristic of communication across all developmental periods: They can understand our logic but we cannot fathom the more unified, yet seemingly paradoxical, nature of their cognitions.

To make Vedic psychology's delineation of the four higher stages of consciousness more concrete and accessible, we have supplemented each description with first-person accounts from both current TM practitioners and exceptional individuals throughout Western history. Although it is beyond the scope of this chapter to provide a detailed content analysis of each report, we wish to make four general observations[10]:

1. The striking similarity among these current and historical accounts suggests that these are universally available experiences and not simply idiosyncratic to meditators, a function of shared mental set, or "Eastern" philosophical belief (see also Chandler, 1989; Pearson, in press).
2. The individuals themselves clearly view these experiences as discontinuous with ordinary modes of cognition.
3. Subjectively, they judge these experiences to be more developed, satisfying, and personally meaningful.
4. The four distinctive types of experience reflected in these accounts are highly consistent with Vedic psychology's conceptual delineation of higher states of consciousness. (However, it should be noted that these isolated experiences do not necessarily indicate that the person is permanently established in a higher stage of consciousness.)

Transcendental Consciousness

According to Vedic psychology, although *transcending* may be used broadly to refer to the process of shifting conscious awareness to finer levels of mind, *transcendental consciousness* refers exclusively to direct experience of the ultimate ground state of mind, pure consciousness, beyond the subtlest level of feeling or ego (Maharishi, 1969, p. 144). Maharishi (1976) describes systematic experience of transcendental consciousness during the TM technique:

> The Transcendental Meditation technique is an effortless procedure for allowing the excitations of the mind to gradually settle down until the least excited state of mind is reached. This is a state of inner wakefulness with no object of thought or perception, just pure consciousness, aware of its own unbounded nature. It is wholeness, aware of itself, devoid of differences, beyond the division of subject and object— transcendental consciousness (p. 123).

We describe this as a purely nonrepresentational state because it involves "no object of thought or perception"; in this state, processes of thinking ("excited" states of mind) no longer divide the knower from the known. According to our model, whereas emergence of the semiotic (symbolic) mode during the first year of life (Flavell, 1985) underlies development of the representational periods of development, experience of the purely self-referral mode of transcendental consciousness underlies development of the higher stages of consciousness described by Vedic psychology. This new mode permits consciousness to (1) know itself directly without symbolic mediation and (2) become completely differentiated from all prior levels of mind, including the individual ego.

Maharishi (1986) states that awareness becomes completely "self-referral" when "consciousness has nothing other than itself in its structure" (p. 27). He further explains: "Consciousness in its pure state, fully open to itself alone, experiences itself as this self-interacting reality of nature . . . consciousness knows itself to be the knower, the known, and the process of gaining knowledge—all three values simultaneously in one" (p. 40). In this experience, the divided state of the bounded self is transcended and the one unified Self is experienced as "I-ness," "amness," or "Being," unqualified and unchanged by active states of becoming, such as thought and feeling (Maharishi, 1972, lesson 19). Maharishi (1966) further describes Being in the language of the Vedic tradition: "Experience shows that Being is . . . *Sat-Chit-Ananda*—It is *Sat*, that which never changes; it is *Chit*, that which is consciousness; it is *Ananda*, that which is bliss . . . Being is the basis of life, that which gives it meaning and makes it fruitful" (pp. 28–29).

This experience of "bliss" is held to be the automatic consequence of attaining inner tranquility, of rediscovering the "Being of the Self": "This is the glory of the nature of the Self. Having come back home, the traveller finds peace. . . . This state of self-sufficiency leaves one steadfast in oneself, fulfilled in eternal contentment" (Maharishi, 1969, p. 424).

According to Vedic psychology, transcendental consciousness is a fourth major *state* of consciousness, as opposed to a stable *stage* of development, which can be temporarily experienced either alone (as during TM) or along with the active levels of mind and changing states of consciousness (Maharishi, 1972; Orme-Johnson, 1988b). Only when this silent, self-sufficient state is *permanently* maintained along

with waking, dreaming, and sleeping, does the first stable higher stage of consciousness dawn. Thus, during any developmental period, when awareness momentarily settles down to its least excited state, pure consciousness can be experienced. Nevertheless, in the absence of a systematic technology (such as TM) to culture this experience, those few individuals who frequently have experienced pure consciousness are already likely to function habitually at a subtle level of mind, in close "proximity" to the Self.

Such momentary transcendental-like experiences have been referred to by Maslow as "peak experiences." He conjectured that less than one in 1,000 adults have frequent peak experiences; in turn, full stabilization of a higher stage of consciousness appears to be an event of all but historic significance (cf. Bucke, 1969).[11] One reason for this may lie in an apparent inability to resolve an "existential dilemma" that may arise when initial episodes of spontaneous transcendence create a "yearning" for more such experiences. Then the "need to transcend [the ego's] limitations becomes evident . . . [but] the envisioned new way of perception cannot be consciously adopted because its essence is non-control" (Cook-Greuter, 1990).

Maharishi (1969) explains that mental effort cannot facilitate transcending because it is just that activity which keeps awareness localized or bound:

> The intensity of thought is very great at that subtle level of thinking where the mind is slipping out of thought and is about to lose the experience of the relative field. If the process is not disturbed and is allowed to go by itself in a very innocent manner, then the mind slips into the Self. If, on the other hand, pressure or force is applied in any way to check the mind or to control the process, the mind will be thrown off the course on which it is naturally set (p. 432).

Vedic psychology (Maharishi, 1966, pp. 52–56) emphasizes that it is just this process of systematically letting go of thought (effortless "noncontrol") through the TM technique that promotes regular transcendence and rapid stabilization of higher stages of consciousness.

According to our initial criteria, if experience of transcendental consciousness lays a foundation for major developmental advance, then it should also involve substantial physiological change. Indeed, transcendental consciousness has been described as a qualitatively distinct state of "restful alertness," as psychophysiologically different from ordinary adult waking as waking is from dreaming and deep sleep (Maharishi, 1966, p. 196; Wallace, 1970). A recent research review (Alexander, Cranson, Boyer, & Orme-Johnson, 1987; cf. Alexander & Larimore, in press) indicates that transcendental consciousness may be distinguishable from the three ordinary states of consciousness on over 20 psychophysiological parameters. For example, subjective experience of transcendental consciousness during TM (as indicated by button press) is highly correlated with heightened EEG coherence[12] across cortical regions and frequency bands, suggesting an increase in long-range spatial ordering and functional integration of the cortex (Badawi, Wallace, Orme-Johnson, & Rouzere, 1984; Farrow & Hebert, 1982). Further, in cross-sectional and longitudinal random-assignment experiments, increase in alpha EEG coherence was observed for TM practitioners but not for resting control subjects (e.g., Dillbeck & Bronson, 1981; Gaylord, Orme-Johnson, & Travis, 1989). Consistent with the view that enhanced structural and functional integration of the brain is a hall-

mark of advanced ontogenetic development (e.g., Werner, 1957; Yakovlev & Lecours, 1967), we find that higher alpha EEG coherence in frontal and central cortical regions in adolescents and adults is correlated with postmeditation behaviors indicative of continued growth, such as fluid intelligence, principled moral reasoning, concept formation, and creativity (e.g., Dillbeck, Orme-Johnson, & Wallace, 1981; Hernandez, 1988; Orme-Johnson & Haynes, 1981; Orme-Johnson, Wallace, Dillbeck, Alexander, & Ball, in press).

The proposal that transcendental consciousness as experienced during TM is distinctively characterized by both alertness and restfulness is further supported by the following findings. In comparison to simple relaxation, heightened alertness during TM is suggested by enhanced H-reflex motor neuron recovery, especially in subjects with clear self-report experience of transcendental consciousness (Haynes, Hebert, Reber, & Orme-Johnson, 1977); increased cortical blood flow (Jevning, Wilson, Smith, & Morton, 1978); and marked increase in plasma arginine vasopression, which is associated with improved learning and memory (O'Halloran, Jevning, Wilson, Skowsky, & Alexander, 1985). A distinctive simultaneous state of rest during transcendental consciousness is indicated by findings during TM of virtual respiratory suspensions (for up to 60 seconds) coinciding with self-report subperiods of transcendental consciousness (e.g., Farrow & Hebert, 1982; Kesterson, 1985); decreased minute ventilation (e.g., Wolkove et al., 1984); lower plasma cortisol (Jevning, Wilson, & Davidson, 1978); and increased serotonergic turnover (e.g., Bujatti & Riederer, 1976), in comparison to relaxation controls. The significance of the simultaneous deep state of rest experienced during transcendental consciousness is that it may neutralize the deep-rooted stresses that otherwise block further developmental advance.[13]

According to Vedic psychology (Orme-Johnson et al., in press), because the capacity to experience all the higher states of consciousness is inherent, under optimal circumstances, the mind and nervous system can temporarily assume a style of functioning that permits momentary experience of each of these states. Thus, levels of development well beyond one's own can be momentarily "glimpsed." However, without regular exposure to appropriate developmental technologies, the nervous system will generally lack the refinement and flexibility to sustain these new modes and therefore will tend to revert quickly to its prior style of functioning.

Experiences of Transcendental Consciousness. The first report comes from an advanced female TM practitioner in Kesterson's (1986) study who displayed periods of marked decline in respiration during her meditation practice. She begins by describing transcendental consciousness as a purely nonconceptual state—completely silent, devoid of thoughts. It is not, however, an absence of awareness, as during sleep. Instead, the knower is fully awake to her Self. She states that often during TM practice, "I experience a state of complete silence devoid of any motion, a state of unboundedness and total ease in deep relaxation. There are no thoughts, no feelings or any other sensations like weight or temperature. I just know 'I am.' There is no notion of time and space, but my mind is fully awake and perfectly clear. It is a very natural and simple state" (Alexander, Chandler, & Boyer, 1990).

Experience of transcendental consciousness during TM does not appear to depend upon prior mental set or expectation (e.g., Alexander, 1982), nor to require

long practice for its elicitation (Alexander, Langer et al., 1989). The following statement by a male practitioner suggests that this experience can occur during the first meditation session:

> I distinctly recall the day of instruction, my first clear experience of transcending. Following the instructions of the teacher without knowing what to expect, I began to drift down into deeper and deeper levels of relaxation, as if I were sinking into my chair. Then for some time, perhaps a minute or a few minutes, I experienced a silent, inner state of no thoughts, just pure awareness and nothing else; then again I became aware of my surroundings. It left me with a deep sense of ease, inner renewal and happiness (cited in Alexander, Chandler, & Boyer, 1990).

Next is an account of a developmental progression in the clarity of experience of pure consciousness by a long-term female practitioner who displayed numerous subperiods of virtual breath suspension and corresponding heightened EEG coherence during TM practice (Farrow & Hebert, 1982). Her description captures well the "restful alertness" quality of pure consciousness. She states that simultaneously awareness becomes fully expanded (i.e., alert) yet breathing virtually ceases (i.e., deep rest is gained):

> Then, with increased familiarity . . . the process of transcending became more and more natural. The whole physiology was by now accustomed to just slipping within, and at some point it would literally "click," and with that the awareness would become fully expanded, the breath would almost cease, the spine would become straight, and the lungs would cease to move. There would be no weight anywhere in the body, the whole physiology was at rest. At this point, I began to appreciate that this inner silence was not an emptiness but simply silent consciousness without content or activity, and I began to recognize in it the essence of my own self. Eventually, even the thin boundary that had previously divided individuality from this silent consciousness began to dissolve. The "I" as a separate entity just started to have no meaning. The boundary that I put on myself became like a mesh, a net, it became porous and then just dissolved, only unbroken pure consciousness or existence remained . . . the physiology after that state is incredible. It is like a power surge of complete purity, and great bliss and joyfulness are stirred from deep within.

There are striking similarities between the preceding descriptions and those reported by others at different times and places throughout Western history. Plotinus, an Alexandrian philosopher of the third century A.D., reports that he experienced a "self-transcendence" or "quietude" on many occasions (Katz, 1950, p. 157). He also emphasizes the tranquil, nonmoving, hence stable (i.e., nonchanging: *Sat*) quality of this purely nonconceptual experience. He states that one who had the experience "had attained unity and contained no difference . . . there was within him no movement, no anger, desire, reason, nor thought . . . he was tranquil, solitary, and unmoved. . . . He was indeed in a state of perfect stability, having, so to say, become stability itself" (p. 157).

The great early nineteenth-century German rationalist philosopher G. W. F. Hegel explicitly describes the self-referral nature of this transcendental experience of the unbounded Self. In contrast to the "finite I," he identifies an "infinite I" which is "the existence of a wholly abstract universality (1892, p. 39) . . . transcendent self-consciousness, which is identical with itself and infinite in

itself" (1892, p. 89). It is the imperturbable unity certain of its own truth" (1910, cited in Chandler, 1989).

The twentieth-century French playwright Eugene Ionesco (1971) describes the "immense serene joy" (i.e., bliss: *Ananda*) and "certainty of being" that spontaneously arises from this profound experience of becoming "one with the one essential reality":

> Once long ago, I was sometimes overcome by a sort of grace, a euphoria. It was as if, first of all, every motion, every reality was emptied of its content. After this, it was as if I found myself suddenly at the center of pure ineffable existence. I became one with the one essential reality, when along with an immense serene joy, I was overcome by what I might call the stupefaction of being, the certainty of being (pp. 150–151).

The early twentieth-century British social philosopher Edward Carpenter (1921) provides a vivid account of spontaneously transcending the thinking process of the "local self" to become fully identified with this "deeper Self" within:

> The Man at last lets Thought go, he glides below it into the quiet feeling, the quiet sense of his own identity with the self of other things—of the universe. He glides past the feeling into the very identity itself, where a glorious all-consciousness leaves no room for separate self-thoughts or emotions. He leans back in silence on that inner being, and bars off for a time every thought, every movement of the mind, every impulse to action, or whatever in the faintest degree may stand between him and That; and so there comes to him a sense of absolute repose, a consciousness of immense and universal power, such as completely transforms the world for him (p. 229) . . .
>
> This true Ego—this Self above and beyond the separate Me—to know it one must, as I say, become identified with it; and that is ultimately the only way of knowing it (pp. 229–230).

Finally, the nineteenth-century British poet Alfred Lord Tennyson in a letter of 1874 emphasizes that this transcendental experience of "boundless being" is not a nebulous or confused state, but is associated with "absolute clearness" of mind (1899):

> A kind of waking trance I have frequently had, quite up from boyhood, when I have been all alone . . . all at once, as it were out of the intensity of the consciousness of individuality, the individuality itself seemed to dissolve and fade away into boundless being, and this not a confused state, but the clearest of the clearest, the surest of the surest . . . utterly beyond words, . . . (p. 268).

These apparent experiences of transcendental consciousness are not restricted to philosophers and poets. Scientists such as Kepler, Maxwell, Einstein, and Schrödinger have written of them with equal eloquence (see Pearson, in press). Although all these individuals indicate that these experiences transformed their understanding of the ultimate nature of mind or reality, virtually none were able to maintain it on a permanent basis. Indeed, in the absence of a systematic means for its induction, some of these individuals (e.g., Ionesco) explicitly write of the frustration that can result from not being able to maintain this most "natural" and "simple state" (cf. Cook-Greuter, 1990).

Cosmic Consciousness

According to Vedic psychology, when awareness no longer alternates between identification with the bounded ego and the underlying Self and instead becomes permanently established in the experience of pure consciousness, the first stable, higher stage of consciousness is gained:

> This is the state of cosmic [i.e., unbounded] consciousness, where the Self has separated itself completely from the field of activity. . . . When . . . transcendental absolute Being [the nonchanging Self] is found in coexistence with the mind in relative existence, in the field of time, space, and causation, then the mastery of the higher Self is accomplished (Maharishi, 1969, p. 339).

The unbounded Self, in cosmic consciousness, is classically described as "nonattached," not in the sense of being withdrawn, but because it is no longer identified with or overshadowed by the boundaries of the changing values of thought, perception, and action (Maharishi, 1969, pp. 158–159), much as the concrete operational knower no longer shares the narrow attachment of a five-year-old to a single salient aspect of the stimulus array on conservation tasks.

From our developmental perspective, in cosmic consciousness, the Self has become fully differentiated from and hierarchically integrated with the most abstract activities of thinking, feeling, and even the ego itself. When experienced in isolation (as during TM), the self-referral state of transcendental consciousness is awake to itself alone. When pure consciousness is continuously maintained along with activity, then it also functions as a silent "witness," or observer, to that activity: "The activity assumed by an ignorant man to belong to himself—to the subjective personality that he calls himself [i.e., his mind, intellect, and ego]—does not belong to his real Self, for this, in its essential nature, is beyond activity. The Self, in its real nature, is only the silent witness of everything" (Maharishi, 1969, p. 98).

Although the individual ego—and all levels of mind—continues to function actively in cosmic consciousness, awareness is now primarily associated with the nonchanging, silent Self at the source of thought. Thus, we consider this stage postrepresentational not because representational thought processes are abandoned but because they now function as a subsystem within, rather than as the executor of, mental life.

When even the finest level of mind is completely transcended, consciousness assumes a unified field character allowing direct Self awareness. Thus, the primary constraint of the prior representational periods is overcome in that the question, "Who am I?" has been fully resolved. Self knowledge may now be said to be direct and complete. Knower, known, and process of knowing are unified in the unbroken, self-referral experience of pure consciousness. In terms of our life-span model, this process of differentiation of the Self culminates in what could be termed *subject permanence*—stable experience of the nonchanging Self as opposed to changing representations of the bounded self. From our perspective, this developmental milestone is even more significant than the emergence of object permanence during the transition from the prerepresentational level. This permanence of Self constitutes a radically new level of invariance providing a completely stable, expanded inner frame of reference.

Piaget (1977) proposed that each new cognitive stage should be increasingly equilibrated, and hence, more stable and flexible in application across time and situation. Nevertheless, even at the most advanced representational levels, this stability and flexibility are restricted to activity within the waking state. During sleep, the conceptual edifice of operational thought completely collapses and conscious awareness itself can no longer be sustained. Even within the waking state the capacity for abstract thought tends to be poorly utilized outside familiar domains of experience (Piaget, 1972) and is constrained by changes in mood and level of alertness.

In contrast, the self-referral capacity of the nonchanging Self permits continuous witnessing not only of the changing states of waking experience, but also of dreaming and sleep (for psychophysiological research on witnessing sleep, see the Research Appendix). It is the permanent, uninterrupted coexistence of transcendental consciousness along with waking, dreaming, and deep sleep that is said to define unambiguously the all-inclusive state of cosmic consciousness:

> After some time of alternating the fourth state [transcendental consciousness] with the other three, the nervous system becomes habituated to maintaining that state of [pure] awareness. . . . Then that state of awareness is maintained even during waking, dreaming, and sleeping. All the jerks and jolts of activity during waking, the rest of the night, or the delusive nature of dreams, all this is not able to overthrow the reality of the fourth state of consciousness; it is forever maintained (Maharishi, 1972).

If stress creates incoherent excited states of psychophysiological functioning that restrict awareness, it would follow that the unrestricted, least excited state of pure consciousness could only be fully maintained when the nervous system is freed from the influence of accumulated stress (Maharishi, 1969). Thus, neutralization of stress (as facilitated by the TM program) is considered critical in the development of higher stages of consciousness.

Behavior performed on the basis of this unrestricted, stress-free state of consciousness is said to be spontaneously effective and life-supporting (Maharishi, 1969, p. 291). From the perspective of our model, this dramatic gain in effectiveness with the shift of awareness to the postrepresentational domain is even greater than the earlier gain in effectiveness with the shift to the representational domain. The initial acquisition of sensorimotor functions (such as grasping, looking, walking) required a great deal of attention and effort. However, once these functions are reorganized from the deeper representational level, they operate in a highly efficient, coordinated, and virtually automatic fashion, requiring little effort or attention. Also, according to our model, when awareness shifts to functioning from the level of pure consciousness, all prior representational and related functions—even those of the individual ego—come to be performed in a highly efficient, coordinated, and effortless fashion.

Freedom from suffering, which is also said to characterize this stage, may result not only from absence of stress and consequent errors in behavior, but also from stabilization of the inherently "blissful" experience of "Being." Once this ultimate ground of satisfaction within the Self is consistently open to awareness, the individual is said to be truly autonomous, or self-sufficient. He is no longer dependent

on external sources of reinforcement for either contentment or self-identity, and thus experiences a state traditionally described as "liberation" (Dillbeck, 1983a,b).

Several postformal theorists suggest that there is increasing differentiation during development from initial symbiosis in the newborn to the uninvolved analytical reasoning of the formal operator, for whom thought itself becomes "objectified" and a "maximal distance between the thinker and the thought" is achieved (Cook-Greuter, 1990). A number of contributors to this volume (including Dittman-Kohli & Baltes, Gilligan et al., Souvaine et al., and Pascual-Leone) suggest that after this period, a process of reintegrating the knower with the known begins on the level of feelings, relationships, and living in the world. From the perspective of Vedic psychology, however, it is cosmic consciousness, not the reflective intellect, that represents the most abstract level of experience, involving greatest differentiation between the knower and objects known.

In cosmic consciousness, the entirely abstract field of pure consciousness, while unified *within* itself, is said to be completely separate or distanced from all values of the known *outside* the Self—including even the localized, individual ego. However, it is this most differentiated and self-sufficient state that also provides the basis for development of a more profound appreciation of others than was possible before; that is, self-knowledge provides the basis for knowledge of others (Maharishi, 1966, p. 217). This is similar to Erikson's (1968b) injunction that identity provides the basis for intimacy. To the degree that individual identity is stable and deep, there is a strong foundation for mutually fulfilling relationships with others, and identity is no longer threatened by intimacy.

In contrast to the identity of the bounded self, which is largely based on social roles and values (outwardly referring), identity in cosmic consciousness is based on direct experience of one's inner foundation in Being, or "amness," which is fully stable and self-referring and therefore not threatened by outward events. This allows a growth of intimacy with the environment that is completely unrestricted by self-protecting needs or motives and that characterizes development from cosmic consciousness to the stage of refined cosmic consciousness, and finally to a stage of complete unity between Self and world.

Unless otherwise stated, the following meditators' reports of growth of higher stages of consciousness are from the archives of Maharishi European Research University, which contains thousands of accounts reported during advanced TM and TM-Sidhi training courses (excerpted in Maharishi, 1976, pp. 76–85).

Growing Experiences of Cosmic Consciousness. An advanced male TM practitioner describes how experience of pure consciousness begins to be maintained outside of meditation practice: "Also, now, there is less of a contrast between activity and meditation. Sometimes during the day, with varying degrees of clarity, my awareness is this unbounded wholeness of my Self, quietly accompanying the thoughts and feelings in my daily life. It is not a mood or conception about myself, it is a natural state in which I am myself more fully." An advanced female meditator describes growth of cosmic consciousness in terms of stabilization of the "blissful evenness" of pure consciousness (cf. Plotinus' "perfect stability") and its benefits for activity:

The experience of [pure] bliss consciousness has become more clear, intense, and stable not only during meditation but also during activity. Now I find that a soft but strong feeling of blissful evenness is present most of the time. . . . This evenness is so deep and stable that it is able to maintain its status even in the face of great activity. Even when faced with great problems, this . . . evenness cushions one against all possible disruptions and makes all activity easy and enjoyable. . . . somehow my responsibilities seem to arrange themselves so that they can be accomplished with very little doing. In this way activity has become more and more effortless while leading to greater accomplishment.

Established in this inner blissful evenness of mind, one gradually becomes a silent "witness" not only to the activity of the waking state but also to dreaming and deep sleep. Another advanced TM practitioner states, "I have often clearly experienced pure consciousness or inner wakefulness continuing all throughout a nights' sleep, so that even though I was sleeping, inside I felt awake." An advanced male practitioner specifically describes witnessing dreams: "Often during dreaming I am awake inside, in a very peaceful, blissful state. Dreams come and go, thoughts about the dreams come and go, but I remain in a deeply peaceful state, completely separate from the dreams and the thoughts" (in Alexander, Cranson et al., 1987).

Another advanced male TM practitioner elaborates on the experience of witnessing deep sleep—held to be the most unambiguous indicator of growth of cosmic consciousness: "When it occurs, it is crystal clear—silence, wakefulness, dark, clear, and open. Silent and lively—like an amplifier turned on, but no sound" (in Alexander, 1988).

Although rarely occurring, growth of cosmic consciousness experiences also has been reported throughout Western history. The early twentieth-century phenomenologist Edmond Husserl (cf. Pascual-Leone chapter) at times seemed to experience pure consciousness as a "disinterested" or "transcendental spectator" (cf. concept of "witness") to the ordinary activity of the individual ego. He writes, "*I reach the ultimate experiential and cognitive perspective thinkable. In it I become the disinterested spectator of my natural and worldly ego and its life.* . . . The transcendental spectator . . . watches himself and sees himself; also as the previously world-immersed ego" (Husserl, 1950/1970b, p. 15).

Husserl's description of the transcendental spectator or knower as "above" and watching his ordinary ego is similar to Carpenter's earlier description of this "true Ego" as being "above and beyond the separate me." Both accounts support our developmental view that this experience represents a more mature state in which the Self, pure consciousness, is becoming differentiated from and hierarchically integrated with the ordinary functioning of the individual ego or self.

Further distinguishing this pure state of consciousness from the spatiotemporal bounded state of the limited ego, Husserl states, "Consciousness, considered in its *purity*, . . . must be reckoned as a *self-contained system of Being,* as a system of *Absolute Being.* . . . On the other side, the whole *spatio-temporal world* [and world immersed ego] . . . has the merely secondary, relative sense . . . (Husserl, 1913/1931, p. 153).

It is clear that Husserl believed that such a transcendental perspective yields a postconceptual, nonrelative way of knowing beyond the reflective, qualified

thought processes typical of adolescence or adulthood: "This is not a view, an interpretation of the world. Every view about, every opinion about the world has its ground in the pre-given world. It is from this very ground that I have freed myself..." (Husserl, 1936, p. 152).

The twentieth-century French poet and philosopher Romain Rolland (1931) also describes maintaining the experience of "Being" (the Self) along with the ordinary limited "personality." He states, "I have always lived two parallel lives—one the personality which consists of the combination of inherited elements, in a certain space and time—the other one of Being without face, without name, without place, without century, which is the very substance and breathes in all life" (pp. 107–108).

The experience of pure consciousness as a silent witness can be sustained not only during quiet moments but also along with dynamic activity. The contemporary woman athlete Billie Jean King (1974) describes such an experience during a tennis match and its value for spontaneous right action and personal fulfillment:

> I can almost feel it coming. It usually happens on one of those days when everything is just right.... It almost seems as though I'm able to transport myself beyond the turmoil on the court to some place of total peace and calm. Perfect shots extend into perfect matches.... I appreciate what my opponent is doing in a detached abstract way. Like an observer in the next room.... It is a perfect combination of [intense] action taking place in an atmosphere of total tranquility. When it happens I want to stop the match and grab the microphone and shout that's what it's all about, because it is. It's not the big prize I'm going to win at the end of the match or anything else. It's just having done something that's totally pure and having experienced the perfect emotion (p. 199).

In his journals, the nineteenth-century American essayist Henry David Thoreau reports on the apparent experience of pure consciousness (what he terms "infinite mind") during sleep: "I am conscious of having in my sleep transcended the limits of the individual.... As if in sleep our individual [mind] fell into the infinite mind, and at the moment of awakening, we found ourselves on the confines of the latter" (cited in Blake, 1929, p. 157).

If attainment of complete Self knowledge or awareness (even during sleep) is the goal of development, then development beyond cosmic consciousness would not seem likely. At this stage, however, a new possibility for growth arises. Once the Self is fully realized, it appears as completely separate from everything and everyone else. In contrast to the abstract inner wholeness of the Self, still only a comparatively superficial value of other selves and the outer world is appreciated. For this separateness to be overcome and a profound intimacy achieved, the same process of fathoming deeper levels of existence must take place with regard to others and the world as has already occurred in relation to the Self.

Refined Cosmic Consciousness

Just as the process of complete differentiation of the knower or Self took place in phases, Vedic psychology posits that subsequent unification of knower and the object known occurs through stepwise development. The first major stage in inte-

grating Self and non-Self is said to involve a profound refinement in perceptual appreciation of the subtlest values of objective reality—and hence is referred to as refined cosmic consciousness (Orme-Johnson et al., in press).

According to our life-span model, during growth from the sensorimotor period to cosmic consciousness, progressively deeper levels of mind are differentiated (senses, desire, etc.), but each continues to operate at its own characteristic level of refinement, while being hierarchically reorganized within an increasingly integrated whole. Thus, even in cosmic consciousness, sensory perception may remain on a comparatively superficial level though witnessed from the level of the Self (Maharishi, 1969). In growth to refined cosmic consciousness, all the processes of knowing are said to undergo further marked refinement and integration, until they function almost on the level of the Self, at the finest possible scale or level of excitation (see Fig. 12.1).

Quantum physics has established that physical existence is also hierarchically structured in "layers," from the gross level of macroscopic structures through more abstract molecular, atomic, and subatomic levels to underlying quantum fields. Although physical objects appear as discrete and separate at ordinary time and distance scales, quantum field theory has shown that at a subtler time and distance scales, these same objects may be more appropriately understood as fluctuations of underlying fields. Further, at successively finer time and distance scales the diversity and asymmetry of the physical universe diminishes until, ultimately, even the fundamental force and matter fields are said to become fully unified at the level of the supersymmetric unified field (Antomatis, Ellis, Hagelin, & Nanopoulous, 1988; Ross, 1984).

Similarly, according to Vedic psychology, although the knower is perceived as particulate and clearly separate from the localized objects known on the ordinary thinking level of mind, when all the faculties function from the subtlest possible level of mind, then a corresponding level of maximum refinement is appreciated in objective creation as well, and the rigid boundaries dividing subject and object begin to dissolve:

> When only the surface value of perception is open to our awareness, then the boundaries of the object are rigid and well-defined—the only qualities that are perceived are those which distinguish the object from the rest of the environment. However, when the unbounded awareness becomes established on the level of the conscious mind . . . then the perception naturally begins to appreciate deeper values of the object, until perception is so refined that the finest relative is capable of being spontaneously perceived on the gross, surface level (Maharishi, 1972, lesson 23).

By analogy, Maharishi (1972, lesson 23) likens the finest relative level of creation to the "colorless sap" in a plant, out of which root, stem, and leaves emerge and are structured. The finest relative level also may be comparable to the virtually nonlocal Planck scale in physics. The Planck scale is described as the finest possible time and distance scale beyond which space–time geometry becomes ill defined and assumes a fully unified field character (Ellis, Enqvist, Nanopoulous, & Werner, 1986). It is from this smallest scale that the separate expressions of natural law first emerge through "spontaneous symmetry breaking." Similarly, the unified field of consciousness (the Self) is said to lie beyond the subtlest level of mind, transcend-

ing the boundaries of time, space, and causation (Maharishi, 1969). Further, all diversified expressions of mind and matter are said to emerge from the finest relative level of creation at the meeting place between manifest creation and the completely unmanifest, nonchanging (or *absolute*) field of pure consciousness.

From the perspective of our developmental model, whereas differentiation of the Self in cosmic consciousness provides complete subject permanence, the further differentiation of the finest relative level provides the basis for a higher-order appreciation of invariance in the objective world than was achieved during the representational periods. In refined cosmic consciousness, the finest relative level is directly perceived and found to be fundamentally the same in all objects, mental or physical (Maharishi, 1972, lesson 23, p. 13). Further, its essential nature is conserved even as it is expressed or transformed into specific manifestations of mind or physical creation.

Appreciation of this finest level of creation may be understood in terms of development of the finest level not only of perception but also of feeling. Perception of finer values of an object (animate or inanimate) gives rise to greater joy in and love for the object, which in turn facilitates still deeper appreciation of the object:

> In such a state of integrated life [in refined cosmic consciousness] where behavior is in perfect harmony and . . . universal love for everything flows . . . every perception, the sound of every word, the touch of every little particle, and the smell of whatever may be, brings a tidal wave from the ocean of eternal bliss [the unified field of consciousness] (Maharishi, 1966, p. 250).

Although the identity established by the bounded self allowed some intimacy with other bounded selves (Erikson, 1968b), the identity based on the unbounded Self is said to allow development of a profound intimacy with others and with all of creation. Maharishi (1969) describes this growth of unrestricted love and appreciation:

> In this state of [cosmic] consciousness, the Self is experienced as separate from activity. This state of life in perfect non-attachment is based on bliss consciousness, by virtue of which the qualities of the heart have gained their most complete development. Universal love then dominates the heart. . . . The heart in its state of eternal contentment begins to move, and this begins to draw everything together and eliminate the gulf of separation between the Self and activity (p. 307).

Thus, the primary constraint of cosmic consciousness has been essentially overcome: the gap separating Self and non-Self has been narrowed to a "junction point" (Maharishi, 1985, p. 84). In cosmic consciousness the material world may still be viewed as essentially lifeless and inert. According to Vedic psychology, as one becomes more intimate with creation, the constraint of seeing things as not self or inert begins to disappear. The perspective of earlier stages, where one experienced only one's own kind as intelligent, now appears restricted. One comes to appreciate directly that "each layer of existence has its own nature, its own characteristic laws, or we could say, its own level of intelligence" (Maharishi, 1972, lesson 23) and that the "intelligence" of the finest relative level, responsible for mediating the expression of all more manifest levels of natural law, is almost infinite (Maharishi, 1969, p. 206).

In cosmic consciousness, once awareness is no longer identified with the ego, authorship of action is no longer attributed to the bounded ego (action is no longer "ego-centric"), yet neither is it attributed to the Self, which remains a silent observer to activity. In growth to refined cosmic consciousness, all action (of the ego and environment) becomes appreciated as the expression of universal laws of nature operating from the finest level of existence (see Maharishi, 1969, p. 128).

Certain key concepts in the Western rationalist tradition of philosophy that have proved difficult to understand from a formal operational perspective may have been based on at least temporary experience of this level of reality. For example, Plato's "forms" (1961, p. 1177), Spinoza's "laws of nature," (1951, p. 83) and Whitehead's "eternal objects" (1969, p. 58) were also said to underlie more expressed values of both mind and matter and ultimately have their origin in a fully unified level of nature's intelligence.

According to Vedic psychology, the "stress-free" state of cosmic consciousness provides the basis for this refinement in capacity for feeling and perception and for a corresponding refinement in physiological functioning, particularly on the biochemical level (Orme-Johnson et al., in press; Walton et al., 1986). According to Maharishi (1969), once established in cosmic consciousness, relationships with others that spontaneously culture feelings of love or devotion may further promote growth to refined cosmic consciousness. This process of refinement is also said to be systematically cultured and stabilized through the advanced TM-Sidhi program (Gelderloos & Berg, 1989).

Refined cosmic consciousness also has been referred to by Maharishi as "God consciousness", because in this state, one is said to directly perceive and intimately appreciate not only the full grandeur of all levels of creation, but also the ongoing process of creation occurring at the junction point between manifest existence and its unmanifest origin. However, the striking parallels (observed earlier) between this most ancient subjective description and modern physics' objective account of the origin and mechanics of creation suggest that the same phenomenon is being investigated from two different viewpoints (see Hagelin, 1987, 1989). The former approach may be describing the direct subjective experience of the internal dynamics of intelligence governing the "laws of nature" now being mathematically inferred through the approach of modern science.

Ironically, although scientists functioning exclusively from the formal operational level tend to exclude the domain of subjectivity from consideration, some of the physicists who have made the most profound contributions to our understanding of the mechanics of physical creation have felt deeply that these two approaches are both complementary and required for a complete understanding of reality (including Einstein, cited in Bernstein, 1973, p. 15; Heisenberg, 1962; Schrödinger, 1967; and Wigner, 1960).

Growing Experience of Refined Cosmic Consciousness. An advanced female meditator describes the growth of refined cosmic consciousness primarily in terms of refinement of affect or feeling:

> The value of love and devotion is growing more every day . . . there is a great radiance in my heart. The heart [feeling] is many times like a window to the Self, like a vast ocean which contains all, and all is known through the heart [feeling].

There is bubbling bliss flowing and enlivening everything which I perceive. . . . I am perceiving finer and finer values of bliss and beauty. . . . The progression of bliss through me and onto the objects of perception was so overwhelming at first, but it seems that now it is not as overshadowing and is becoming more stabilized. All is getting . . . brighter and more blissful, until it seems that that would be all that there is.

Another female advanced TM practitioner describes growth of refined cosmic consciousness largely in terms of refinement of perception:

Generally, whenever I put my attention on an object (e.g., when looking at scenery out the window, or sitting in the kitchen), I become aware of the subtler qualities of the objects around me. For instance, when looking at a tree, I first become aware of the object as it is—a concrete form bound in space and time. But then I perceive finer aspects of the object co-existing along with its concrete expression. On this subtler level, objects are perceived as almost transparent structures of soft, satiny light (unlike harsher, normal day light) through which the very essence of life appears to flow. This flowing field of life underlies and permeates the objects of perception. Perceiving these finer aspects of creation completely nourishes the finest aspect of my own being (in Alexander & Boyer, 1989, p. 358).

The twentieth-century English poet Kathleen Raine (1975) describes a singular moment in which she also appeared to experience a refinement in perception of objects. She identifies a finer level of existence or what she terms a "finer matter," that is invariant across all "living forms," be they animal or mineral. (Her description also appears to contain elements of experience of growing unity—see final section.)

There was also a hyacinth growing in an amethyst glass; I was sitting alone. . . . All was stilled. I was looking at the hyacinth, and as I gazed at the form of its petals and the strength of their curve as they open and curl back to reveal the mysterious flower-centres with their anthers and eye-like hearts, abruptly I found that I was no longer looking *at* it, but *was* it; a distinct, indescribable, but in no way vague, still less emotional, shift of consciousness into the plant itself. . . . I dared scarcely to breathe, held in a kind of fine attention in which I could sense the very flow of life in the cells. I was not perceiving the flower but living it. I was aware of the life of the plant as a slow flow or circulation of a vital current of liquid light of the utmost purity. I could apprehend as a simple essence formal structure and dynamic process. This dynamic form was, as it seemed, of a spiritual not a material order; or of a finer matter, or of a matter itself perceived as spirit. There was nothing emotional about this experience, which was, on the contrary, an almost mathematical apprehension of a complex and organized whole, apprehended *as a whole*. This whole was living; and as such inspired a sense of immaculate holiness. Living form—that is how I can best name the essence or soul of the plant. By "living" I do not mean that which distinguishes animal from plant or plant from mineral, but rather a quality possessed by all these in their different degrees. Either everything is, in this sense, living, or nothing is; this negation being the view to which materialism continually tends; for lack, as I now knew, of the immediate apprehension of life, as life (p. 119).

The eighteenth-century rationalist philosopher J. G. Fichte (1800/1956) describes in more general terms an experience of refined perception: ". . . the universe appears before my eyes clothed in a more glorious form. The dead inert mass,

which only filled up space, has vanished: and in its place there flows onward, with the rushing music of mighty waves, an endless stream of life and power and action, which issues from the original Source of all life . . ." (pp. 150–151).

Although in refined cosmic consciousness the Self is lived together with appreciation of the full value of manifest creation, the two still remain distinct. The finest, most powerful levels of the subjective and objective universe are now appreciated, but they are still said to be witnessed by the Self as different from its own value. Thus, for growth of complete unification between Self, mind, and environment, one more step of integration is required.

The Highest Stage of Human Development: Unity Consciousness

According to Vedic psychology, at the highest stage of unity consciousness, "The Self, which held its identity as separate from all activity in the state of cosmic consciousness, finds everything in itself" (Maharishi, 1969, p. 307). At this level, even the process of experiencing the world is said to become fully self-referral: All levels of mind and objective reality are experienced in terms of the Self.

> . . . in that state, the ultimate value of the object, infinite and unmanifest, is made lively when the conscious mind, being lively in the unbounded value of awareness, falls on the object. The object is cognized in terms of the pure subjective value of unbounded, unmanifest awareness. . . . In this unified state of consciousness, the experiencer and the object of experience have both been brought to the same level of infinite value, and this encompasses the entire phenomenon of perception and action as well. The gulf between the knower and the object of his knowing has been bridged. . . . In this state, the full value of knowledge has been gained, and we can finally speak of complete knowledge (Maharishi, 1972, lesson 23, p. 9).

Thus, the slight separation between subject and object that remains in refined cosmic consciousness is now completely bridged. Cook-Greuter (1990), Kohlberg and Ryncarz (chapter), Fowler (1981), Koplowitz (1984, 1990), and Maslow (1976) posit a unified end state beyond abstract representational thought but have not specified stages in the growth of that unification, and hence may have collapsed into one description several distinct levels of growth toward complete unification. Vedic psychology identifies the following steps of unification: (1) temporary experience of a unified Self, which completely transcends the divisions between knower, known, and process of knowing (transcendental consciousness); (2) permanent maintenance of this internal unified Self along with the active, divided levels of mind and changing states of experience (cosmic consciousness); (3) appreciation of the finest value of the object, allowing profound intimacy or integration between Self and non-Self (refined cosmic consciousness); and ultimately, (4) experience of the unmanifest value of pure consciousness underlying and pervading all manifest values of mind and matter, resulting in complete unification of subject and object within the wholeness of the unified field of consciousness.

Even within unity consciousness, there is said to be a sequence of substages whereby first the primary object of attention, and then objects of secondary, ter-

tiary, and further levels of attention, are gradually appreciated in terms of the Self until a fully mature state of unity consciousness, referred to as "Brahman consciousness," is established. In this ultimate state of wholeness, the *Bhagavad Gita* says that one "sees the Self in all beings, and all beings in the Self" (Maharishi, 1969, p. 441). It is realized that within the Self is contained the unmanifest structure of all the laws of nature (all knowledge structures), referred to by Maharishi (1985, p. 78) as the "Veda"; further, all manifest creation is directly appreciated as an expression of the self-referral dynamics of this unified field of consciousness.

Cognitive developmentalists generally hold that each higher stage should provide the basis for more veridical perception of objective reality (e.g., Kohlberg, 1969; Piaget, 1977). This is achieved through location of progressively deeper invariances in the functioning of natural law—such as object permanence, conservation of quantity, and conservation of motion at the formal operational level. This trend appears to continue beyond abstract reasoning to include realization of the invariant value of the subject (Self); conservation of the finest objective level of natural law; and ultimately in unity consciousness, conservation of the unified field of consciousness across all its expressions in both subjective and objective existence.

By locating one fundamental unified field underlying all subjective and objective existence, Vedic psychology presents a parsimonious description of nature as essentially simple and integrated. The concept of the ultimate identity of human nature with the nature of the universe may be unfamiliar. This is because development of higher stages of consciousness may be required to comprehend fully this higher-order level of conservation, just as concrete representational development was required to appreciate the otherwise "mystical" concept of conservation of quantity. It may also appear anthropocentric to attribute consciousness or intelligence to nature. However, this would only be the case if we were attributing our own limited, individual intelligence to nature, as children do in "animistic" thinking (Piaget, 1929). We are suggesting that the opposite occurs in unity consciousness. Individual intelligence expands to accommodate or fully identify with the ultimate, inner dynamic structure or "intelligence" of nature: the self-interacting dynamics of the unified field of natural law (as partially "glimpsed" from an objective viewpoint by quantum field theory; Hagelin, 1987, 1989).

Such a unified view of nature may also appear foreign because of the way psychology has historically developed as a science. Modern psychology was originally modeled on the paradigms of experimental biology and physics. However, while physics soon afterward moved from a classical to a quantum mechanical paradigm, psychology maintained a concrete perspective based on everyday experience, as reflected in behaviorist and information-processing approaches. From a classical Newtonian view, unity consciousness would appear fanciful and not in accord with physical observation of discrete events localized in time and space. Quantum theorists, however, now generally agree that there is a completely abstract, unified field underlying all the diverse expressions of natural law, though the detailed formulation of competing unified field models is still subject to debate. Further, several theorists have recognized that consciousness is not outside this unified structure of nature (e.g., Hagelin, 1987, 1989; Josephson, 1980; Stapp, 1985). Wigner (1960),

for example, has pointed out that consciousness and objective reality are necessarily connected in that mathematical formulations can be subjectively derived (manmade) that perfectly predict the observable regularities of nature's functioning.

Symbol systems of mathematics, such as lie algebra and group theory, serve as powerful symbolic tools that permit scientists to at least intellectually posit the existence of a unified quantum field. However, everyday experience of the world even by most quantum physicists is still restricted to the classical level, confined within scales of space and time where knower and known are still separate. Hence, the scientist's theoretical deductions may far surpass his developmentally restricted direct experience of the universe. This mismatch of intellectual knowledge and experience may be responsible for the widespread difficulties in interpreting quantum mechanical and unified field theories in terms of everyday understanding of the world (e.g., Heisenberg, 1962). From the perspective of Vedic psychology a technology of consciousness is required for scientists to catch up experientially to and complete the theoretical map of the universe they have already begun to construct—allowing direct observation not only of the unity of physical creation, but of all subjective and objective life. Unity consciousness may then represent a natural state of integration of knowledge and experience, capable of resolving fundamental constraints of modern scientific understanding.

Although modern psychology emerged as an empirical effort to understand consciousness (James, 1890), in the absence of a reliable method for its direct investigation, research became restricted for methodological reasons (following the classical model of physics and the natural sciences) to observable behavior (Boring, 1950). Until recently, theory and research on consciousness were thus regarded as esoteric, even though the positing of a transcendental Self or pure consciousness was central to both the Western rationalist and Eastern philosophical traditions (see Chandler, 1989, cf. Pascual-Leone chapter). Following recent advances in cognitive psychology and neuroscience, psychologists have rediscovered the critical need for developing an understanding of consciousness (Hilgard, 1980; Mandler, 1985; Miller, 1981; Natsoulas, 1983; Pribram, 1986a; Sperry, 1987, 1988) despite continuing constraints inherent in objective research methods (Hempel, 1966). The requirement for direct, systematic methods of isolating consciousness for experimental observation may be met through technologies of consciousness as provided by Vedic psychology, permitting this constitutive issue of psychology to be more directly addressed.

According to Maharishi (1986), the TM-Sidhi techniques in particular provide a direct test of the proposition that subjective and objective reality derive from a single unified source. The techniques are said to culture the ability to think and act from the level of the unified field of consciousness to influence directly not only subjective states but the objective expressions of natural laws. In the process of accelerating growth to unity consciousness, these performances are thus predicted to create specific effects such as dramatic enhancement of mind–body coordination (Aranya, 1977) and a spontaneous orderly or "coherent" influence on physical phenomena and social events even at vast distances. Some of these effects would clearly seem to require a postformal capacity to influence directly laws of nature governing the objective world through the activity of consciousness alone (for research supporting such predictions, see, for example, Davies & Alexander, 1989;

Dillbeck, Banus, Polanzi, & Landrith, 1988; Dillbeck, Cavanaugh, Glen, Orme-Johnson, & Mittlefehldt, 1987; Orme-Johnson, Alexander, Davies, Chandler, & Larimore, 1988; Orme-Johnson & Gelderloos, 1988).

Even in cosmic consciousness, once conscious awareness is primarily identified with this unified field of natural law (and no longer constrained by stress), thought and action are said to function in "attunement" with the fundamental economy and evolutionary trend characteristic of natural law as a whole, and thus to be spontaneously "life supporting" for both the individual and environment (Maharishi, 1986; Druker, 1989; cf. Csikszentmihalyi & Rathunde, 1990). According to Maharishi (1977b, p. 14), in mature unity consciousness, when the laws of nature are directly experienced as different modes of excitation of one's own unbounded consciousness, then not only attunement with but "mastery" over all the laws of nature can be gained, allowing immediate fulfillment of intentions and goals.

The endpoint of a normative stage developmental model serves as a standard against which progress can be gauged (Kohlberg & Armon, 1984, p. 391). Piaget (1950, p. 6) describes development in terms of progressive achievement of intelligence, defined as the "form of equilibrium toward which all the (cognitive) structures tend." However, Piagetians and neo-Piagetians (e.g., Turiel, 1983) do not believe that complete equilibrium or a conflict-free state can ever be attained in interaction with the "real world." This conclusion may follow from the formal operator's experience of himself as separate from a complex, ever-changing environment to which he must continually adjust: Neither the subject nor object is directly knowable but only successively approximated through reflective processes.

Development of full intelligence or equilibration would appear to require the capacity for complete unification between Self, or consciousness, and the objective world. Only if the Self were realized as identical with the universe, sharing the same inherent dynamic structure, would there be no "adjustment" required for the apprehension of the one by the other. The Self would be found to be interacting with itself alone, thus allowing direct and complete knowledge.

According to Vedic psychology (Maharishi 1969, p. 439), this unity of subjective and objective existence experienced in mature unity consciousness constitutes not only the endpoint of development, but the ultimate nature of reality, which exists independently of one's ability to appreciate it. Mature unity consciousness is then qualitatively distinct from prior stages, which are said to represent partial or limited viewpoints en route to its attainment. In this state, the source and endpoint of development are found to be the same uncreated reality of pure consciousness, which also underlies all points in the course of development. Thus, in unity consciousness, the source, course, and goal of human development are realized to be ultimately the same.

Growing Experiences of Unity Consciousness. An advanced TM practitioner describes the developing experience of unity consciousness: ". . . a new reality seems to be dawning in my daily life. I feel an underlying continuum of quiet bliss and fullness, of infinite and universal love. Often the deep silence of my Self seems all-pervading, everywhere the same. Objects seem transparent, and I perceive unboundedness, the unmanifest, in everything I see."

Another advanced meditator describes the apparent growth of this experience: "A continuum of awareness has become more predominant. The sense of events and time has given way to interconnectedness within a whole. Nothing can hide the Absolute [nonchanging pure consciousness] within everything. Everything seems to serve as a window to perceive its true nature within. . . . Activity is characterized more and more by the feeling of being sunk in the Absolute."

Finally, an advanced TM practitioner provides a more detailed account of growing unity consciousness—mind, body, and environment are experienced as expressions of the Self:

> During activity everything is in terms of Self—wholeness permeates creation. Any movement or perception within that wholeness is just a wave of bliss, a realization of my Self. . . . Just as in a flower, the petals, stem, leaves, and all the parts are interconnected and form a whole—everything I perceive is interconnected, a part of that wholeness. My Self, activity, and what I am interacting with, as well as one object with another, all seem to be connected through perception. Body and environment are not separated. It seems all of creation constitutes the fluctuations of my body and consciousness. . . . When I go for a walk. . . . Everything I experience on the walk is an exploration of my Self. It is as if I am discovering a new part of my Self, which is in terms of space and time.

The nineteenth-century French novelist Gustave Flaubert, apparently on several occasions, had unity consciousness-type experiences in which the gap between knower and objects known was closed:

> It is true, often I have felt that something bigger than myself was fusing with my being. . . . It was like an immense harmony engulfing your soul with marvelous palpitations, and you felt in its plenitude an inexpressible comprehension of the unrevealed wholeness of things; the interval between you and the object, like an abyss closing, grew narrower and narrower, until the difference vanished, because you both were bathed in infinity; you penetrated each other equally, and a subtle current passed from you into matter while the life of the elements slowly pervaded you, rising like a sap; one degree more, and you would become nature, or nature become you. . . . Immortality, boundlessness, infinity, I have all that, I am that! (cited in Jephcott, 1972, p. 31).

Apparently, on the basis of his own glimpses of unity consciousness-type experience (Chandler, 1989), the great early nineteenth-century German rationalist philosopher G. W. F. Hegel concluded that, ultimately, pure consciousness constitutes the essential nature of all objective as well as subjective existence: ". . . existence and self-consciousness are the same being, the same not as a matter of comparison, but really and truly in and for themselves . . . (1910/1949, p. 276). . . . [consciousness is] the pure essential being of things as well as their aspect of difference . . . consciousness declaring itself as this certainty of being all reality, of being both itself and its objects (1910/1949, p. 279). For Hegel this represented the ultimate goal of human knowing, for it permits us to ". . . divest the objective world that stands opposed to us of its strangeness, and as the phrase is, to find ourselves at home in it: which means no more than to trace the objective world back to . . . our innermost self" (1892, p. 335).

Conclusion: Meeting Criteria for Postformal Development

We are now in a position to consider whether the higher stages of consciousness as described by Maharishi's Vedic psychology, in principle, meet criteria for major qualitative advance posed at the beginning of the chapter:

1. Higher stages of consciousness appear to be at least as far beyond the representational domain of development as representation is beyond the sensorimotor domain of infancy. Just as the representational or semiotic mode provides the foundation for symbolic thought, the self-referral, nonrepresentational mode of pure consciousness provides the foundation for postconceptual development.

2. Experience of pure consciousness is associated with major psychophysiological changes, which, when stabilized, may provide the basis for development of higher stages of consciousness (see Research Appendix).

3. Maintenance of the self-referral experience of pure consciousness in the higher stages of consciousness resolves the fundamental constraint of the abstract reasoning level: that the "I" of experience is not directly knowable (see preceding personal accounts).

4. In accordance with Werner's (1957) orthogenetic principle of development, cosmic consciousness constitutes a major "hierarchical" advance beyond the representational tier, because at this stage pure consciousness appears to be fully differentiated from and hierarchically integrated with (as a silent witness to) even the most abstract representational processes involving the intellect, feeling, and ego.

5. Experiences of higher stages of consciousness are empirically associated with a wide range of functional changes indicative of greater personal fulfillment and increased adaptability and efficacy in thought and behavior (see Research Appendix; Orme-Johnson, 1988a,b). From the perspective of our life-span model, unity consciousness is a fully "equilibrated" developmental endpoint in which one gains direct "veridical" perception of the unity of existence underlying and pervading both subjectivity and objectivity. Thus, at this highest level, the subject–object split (of which the mind–body problem is a special case; cf. Pribram, 1986a) appears to be fully resolved.

These higher stages of consciousness also meet Flavell's (1970) original five criteria for major "morphogenetic" change. They are:

1. *Momentous*—they involve fundamental transformations in experience of self, other, time, space, and causality, which resolve major problems confronted within the representational domain.

2. *Directional*—the three higher stages of consciousness emerge in an invariant sequence that reflects increasing unification of self and world.

3. *Uniform*—not only is this sequence of higher stages described as uniform within Maharishi's Vedic psychology, but related accounts of pure consciousness and glimpses of higher stages of consciousness (see preceding

accounts) have been described throughout human history and across Eastern and Western cultures (cf. Bucke, 1969; Huxley, 1945; James, 1902; Wilber, Engler, & Brown, 1986).

4. *Irreversible*—in contrast to temporary experience of the state of pure consciousness, a higher stage of consciousness is said to be attained only when fully stabilized. Stage regression is presumably ruled out in that development of higher stages of consciousness is held to correspond to major changes in brain functioning (e.g., Orme-Johnson, Wallace et al., in press), which when stabilized are as difficult to reverse as prior stages of brain growth.

5. *Largely inevitable*—development of earlier stages appears inevitable, given exposure to appropriate environmental conditions or "cultural amplifiers" (Bruner, 1972) such as language learning. Similarly, we propose that higher stages of consciousness naturally unfold, given regular exposure to an appropriate environment of support or developmental technology. The TM and TM-Sidhi program appears to fulfill this requirement and thus provides a means for unfreezing and bringing to completion the normal course of ontogenetic development (see Research Appendix).

While on conceptual grounds, the higher stages of consciousness proposed by Maharishi's Vedic psychology meet criteria for genuine postformal development, it is clearly necessary to engage in systematic research to test empirically predictions arising from our model. Some of the major findings of this ongoing research program are summarized in the Research Appendix.

RESEARCH APPENDIX
Testing the Life-span Model of Growth to Higher Stages of Consciousness

Our developmental model proposes that (1) the general mechanism of shifting the dominant locus of awareness to progressively deeper levels of mind provides the foundation for corresponding periods of growth across ages and developmental levels; (2) accumulation of stress impedes this development; and (3) insofar as the TM and TM-Sidhi program accelerates the process of transcending all the levels of mind and neutralizing stress, it should enhance growth at any age or stage of development. Specifically, we have predicted and observed cognitive, personality, and psychophysiological changes that suggest that the process of transcending through TM may promote growth across four major developmental transitions identified in our life-span model: from dominance of simple representation to dominance of the concrete thinking mind; from dominance of the thinking mind to dominance of the reflective intellect; from dominance of the reflective intellect to advanced functioning of affect and ego; and, ultimately, to growth of higher stages of consciousness.

These predictions have been consistently supported in a series of cross-sectional and longitudinal studies conducted with such diverse populations as pre- and early-school-age children, maximum security prisoners, normal adolescents and young

adults, and the institutionalized elderly. The results of these studies and their implications for our model of development are considered here.

The Children Studies: Stimulating Growth from Early Representation to Concrete Thinking

To assess initially whether the TM program enhances rate of development from the early representational period (corresponding to immediate representation and desire) to the concrete thinking period (corresponding to dominance of the active thinking mind), two cross-sectional studies and a longitudinal study were conducted with children from 4 to 11 years of age. These studies evaluated the capacity for "conservation"—a hallmark of the concrete thinking period—as well as other indicators of cognitive development. Ordinarily, consolidation of the concrete operational ability to conserve requires 5 to 7 years. Thus, accelerated consolidation of conservation through the TM technique would indicate a more rapid transition to the level of the concrete thinking mind in our model.

Alexander, Kurth, Travis, Warner, and Alexander (in press) compared 45 children practicing the Children's TM technique (mean age = 7.4 years) to 47 matched controls (mean age = 7.2 years) on a standardized series of conservation tasks of graded difficulty (Goldschmidt & Bentler, 1968). The TM subjects solved significantly more conservation problems than did controls even when adjusting for possible demographic differences between the two groups on age, grade, gender, and parental socioeconomic status.

Warner (1986) extended these findings under more rigorous conditions. Sixty children practicing the TM program (mean = 7.8 years) were compared to 75 controls (mean = 7.9 years) similar in demographic profile. A more demanding series of conservation tasks was employed, and administered in reverse order, from difficult to easy to minimize a learning effect. Controlling for age and verbal and performance IQ, the TM subjects again solved significantly more conservation problems. Warner also found higher levels of information-processing capacity, reflectivity, and cognitive flexibility in the TM subjects. Length of time practicing this technique was significantly correlated with level of performance on these measures. In addition, Gelderloos, Lockie, and Chuttoorgoon (1987) observed greater field independence on cognitive-perceptual tasks in meditating children ($n = 48$) ages 7–11 years than matched controls ($n = 34$).

Dixon (1989) confirmed and further extended these earlier findings in a six-month longitudinal study. Thirty-seven preschool children (mean age 4.46 years), who learned the Children's TM technique immediately following pretest, were compared to 29 demographically similar control subjects (mean age 4.42 years) from two progressive preschools. Conservation of number and mass and a measure of egocentrism were used to assess development of concrete reasoning. Three additional measures were used to assess psychological differentiation—field independence, human figure drawing, and sustained attention and vigilance. Controlling for age, gender, previous preschool experience, parents' socio-economic status, and parents' educational level, Dixon found that subjects who regularly practiced the

Children's TM technique showed greater development on these factors over the 6-month experimental period. Using linear trend analysis to compare controls and 3 levels of regularity of practice, she found that degree of regularity significantly predicted degree of improvement on both developmental factors and on an overall index of general intelligence.

The children's TM technique is not structured to foster transcending to pure consciousness as does the technique for adults. Rather, in terms of our life-span model, this practice may promote shifting of the young child's awareness from centering upon immediate desires and percepts to association with the deeper level of the active thinking mind. Through accelerated stabilization of this more abstract and comprehensive level, this technique appears to foster the capacity to coordinate simultaneously, and thus conserve, increasingly complex features of the stimulus array. The "vertical" expansion of awareness resulting from this perspective shift may also account for the expanded information-processing capacity as well as increased general intelligence, cognitive reflectivity, flexibility, field independence, and overall psychological differentiation observed in these meditating children. Consistent with these findings, longitudinal testing indicates that older children practicing this program improve significantly on standard tests of language, reading, and mathematics over a one-year period in comparison to population norms (Nidich, Nidich, & Rainforth, 1986).

The Prison Studies: Stimulating Growth from Concrete Thinking to Abstract Reflection

A critical test of the capacity of transcending to "unfreeze" human growth was provided by assessing the impact of the TM program on development in adult prisoners. Inmates have proved highly recalcitrant to change, regardless of the treatment they receive (e.g., Sechrest, White, & Brown, 1979).

The principal developmental measure employed was Loevinger's (1976, 1984) ego or self-development scale, which is said to assess holistic structural change in cognitive complexity, character, and social development. We predicted that Loevinger's scale may provide outer behavioral "signs" of internal shifts in self-organization that may result from association of the awareness of the knower (the ego) with progressively deeper levels of the mind. Ego development typically freezes by around 18–20 years of age or by the end of formal education (Loevinger et al., 1985; Redmore & Loevinger, 1979).

In two samples (total $n = 90$) of maximum security prisoners followed over a one-year period, both long-term and new TM subjects significantly improved by one step on ego development in comparison to wait-list controls, dropouts, and those not interested in learning TM (controlling for pretest scores and demographic covariates). None of the four other treatment groups followed longitudinally changed significantly on this measure (Alexander, 1982). On the average, regular new meditators (who scored at a concrete operational level at pretest) improved from the "conformist" stage of ego development (corresponding to dominance of concrete thinking) to the "self-aware" level (corresponding to the onset of reflective

functioning of the intellect); and regular advanced meditators shifted from the self-aware level to a "conscientious" stage (corresponding to a mature form of abstract reflection).

This advance of one step for the new meditators over a year period substantially exceeds that for college students over a four-year period (Loevinger et al., 1985), yet at an age (26–29 years) and education level (ninth grade) where such changes are unlikely to occur. Assuming that the advanced TM subjects started at a comparable ego level to the new TM group, they advanced a mean of two steps during less than three years. It was also predicted that through regular transcending, stresses blocking continued development would be neutralized. This was suggested by both a significant decline in stress-related pathological symptoms and an increase in subjective experiences of higher states of consciousness in regular meditators compared to the four other treatment groups. Finally, these internal changes appeared to translate into long-term behavior consequences as indicated by a one-third lower recidivism (return) rate among TM inmates released from prison over a 3.5-year period in comparison to the other four programs, controlling for relevant demographic variables. The preceding finding of reduced recidivism in inmates practicing TM has been more recently replicated over a six-year period (Bleick & Abrams, 1987; see also Abrams & Siegel, 1978; Dillbeck & Abrams, 1987; Gore, Abrams, & Ellis, in press).

Studies in Young Adults: Advanced Affective and Ego Development

A review of over 20 published studies (involving approximately 7000 subjects) indicated that the highest average ego development level obtained in any adult sample was the "conscientious" stage (Chandler, in preparation). Furthermore, no interventions to facilitate ego development have succeeded in stimulating growth beyond the conscientious level; indeed, adults initially scoring at (or above) this stage tend to regress in their score by posttest. A longitudinal study (Chandler, in preparation; Alexander, Dixon, Chandler, & Davies, in press) compared change in ego development over an 11-year period in graduates from Maharishi International University (MIU), where the TM program is incorporated into the college curriculum, to change in graduates from three well-known universities offering standard curricula (see Adams & Shea, 1978; Loevinger et al., 1985). From the pool of respondents from each of the control universities, students were matched as closely as possible with MIU graduates on gender, pretest age, and college class (i.e., cohort group). All subjects (total $n = 136$) were at least 19 years of age at pretest during the late 1970's. Most MIU graduates were currently regular in TM practice; most control subjects also indicated that they currently practiced some form of self-development, stress-management, or exercise program for promoting physical and mental health (although none practiced TM). All tests were scored by a highly expert rater (who had previously scored over 3000 protocols) blind to experimental design and subjects' group affiliation.

At pretest, the MIU sample already scored at the conscientious level with con-

trol samples scoring at about the same level or somewhat lower. Over the intervening period, MIU graduates crossed the apparent conscientious stage barrier, significantly increasing (on adjusted change score) by almost one step to the "individualistic" level, in contrast to the control samples which remained relatively unchanged (or regressed slightly in score). Whereas at pretest 9 percent of the MIU sample scored at Loevinger's highest "autonomous" and "integrated" stages, at posttest 38 percent reached these two highest stages. In contrast, only 1 percent of the control college samples scored at these two highest stages at both pre- and posttest. In over 20 other studies, the maximum to achieve these two highest stages was only 9 percent. Furthermore, over the intervening period, the MIU graduates also significantly increased in use of principled moral reasoning as measured by the Defining Issues Test (Rest, 1975), and in capacity for intimacy as measured by the Thematic Apperception Test (McAdams, 1988). Enhancement of moral development in adolescents and young adults through TM practice has also been indicated by Nidich (1975) and Nidich, Ryncarz, Abrams, Orme-Johnson, & Wallace (1983).

The change in ego development among MIU graduates may be even an underestimate because Loevinger's instrument (using standard administration) was not specifically designed to be sensitive to subjects capable of responding at the highest levels of self-development. In a further study of 45 males with over 10 years of TM practice, subjects were given a standardized 18-item form of Loevinger's test with modified instructions sensitive to potential high level responders. Protocols were blind-scored by the same expert rater who scored the university samples. On the form with modified instructions, 87 percent of the sample scored above the conscientious level, with 36 percent scoring autonomous and 29 percent integrated. Typically, less than half of 1% of the adult population reaches the highest integrated level (Cook-Greuter, 1990). These final two stages are said to be characterized by balanced growth of affect and cognition and enhanced self-actualization (especially at the integrated stage; Cook-Greuter, in press). Previous studies with "normal" adult samples have indicated that use of modified instructions to enhance performance on Loevinger's test did not appreciably alter the proportion of subjects scoring at the highest stages of ego development.[14]

Aging and Elderly Studies:
Reversing Cognitive Declines

From our life-span perspective, the aging process itself and its deleterious side-effects may be primarily the consequence of a "freezing" of the underlying maturational process that is neither inevitable nor required (cf. Pascual-Leone chapter). It is when biological systems stop growing and adapting that they may become especially susceptible to the aging process (e.g., Timiras, 1978). Therefore, unfreezing psychophysiological development through transcending (and release of stress) during TM may slow or even reverse declines associated with aging.

Consistent with these predictions, in both cross-sectional and longitudinal studies (controlling for diet and exercise patterns), advanced TM practitioners of mid-

dle age or young adulthood appeared substantially younger biologically on the Morgan Scale (Morgan & Fevens, 1972) than their chronological age in comparison to short-term meditators, controls, or population norms (Toomey, Chalmers, & Clements, in press; Wallace, Dillbeck, Jacobe, & Harrington, 1982). Further, research suggests that transcending through the TM program may allow growth on a wide range of variables usually found to decline with age—including increase in alpha EEG coherence (Orme-Johnson & Haynes, 1981); blood flow to the brain (Jevning, Wilson, Smith, & Morton, 1978); and efficiency of neuroendocrine, cardiovascular, and certain cognitive functions (e.g., Cooper & Aygen, 1979; Dillbeck, 1982; Glaser et al., 1987; Werner, Wallace, Charles, Janssen, & Chalmers, 1986).

A longitudinal experiment was conducted to assess directly whether the TM program could promote extension of human life and reverse decrements in another population typically recalcitrant to change: the advanced elderly (Alexander, Langer et al., 1989). Seventy-three residents of eight homes for the elderly were randomly assigned to either the TM program, mindfulness training in active distinction making (Langer, 1982), a mental relaxation program modeled on TM (following Smith, 1976), or a no-treatment control. Each of the three treatment programs was practiced 20 minutes twice daily with eyes closed, and all instructors and subjects were provided with the same expectation of positive outcome.

Despite similarity of groups on pretest measures and expectations, over a three-month period the TM subjects improved most, followed by the mindfulness group, on systolic blood pressure, learning and cognitive flexibility, self-rating of behavioral flexibility and aging, and nurses' rating of mental health (after 18 months). The most striking finding was that after three years the survival rate (longevity) for the TM group was 100 percent and that for the mindfulness group was 87.5 percent, in contrast to significantly lower rates for the other conditions. The baseline rate of survival for the remaining elderly in these homes over the same period was only 62.6 percent ($n = 478$). This longevity result was consonant with Orme-Johnson's (1987) finding of marked reduction in health insurance utilization for major illnesses in over 2000 TM practitioners over a five-year period—especially in the over-40 age group—in comparison to control samples with similar demographic characteristics. Similarly, short-term longitudinal reductions in physical health problems and symptoms of stress, and increased cognitive efficiency and productivity on the job have been observed in adult practitioners of TM compared to matched controls from the same business settings (Alexander, Swanson, Rainforth, Carlisle, & Todd, in press).

Studies of Growth to Higher Stages of Consciousness

The TM program was specifically designed not just to promote transcending of the active levels of mind (including feeling and the ego) but to provide the direct self-referral experience of transcendental consciousness, and thus stimulate growth of higher stages of consciousness. To evaluate the predicted increase in frequency of pure consciousness experiences, at the basis of developing higher stages of consciousness, new methods of measurement had to be devised.

State of Consciousness Inventory

As a first step in this direction, the State of Consciousness Inventory (SCI) was designed to assess quantitatively frequency of higher state of consciousness experiences as described by Vedic psychology (Alexander, 1981, 1982), based on the supposition that individuals have temporary experiences of higher-state functioning before higher stages are stabilized (Maharishi, 1969). The inventory was psychometrically modeled on Rest's Defining Issues Test (1975) for measuring moral reasoning. Separate SCI scales were derived to measure pathological experiences, normal adult waking state, transcendental consciousness, and each higher stage from cosmic to unity consciousness. A misleading item scale (cf. Rest, 1975) was included to assess the subject's tendency to endorse misleading or grandiose statements. Following Jackson's (1970) model of employing "experts" in test construction, higher-state items were derived primarily from first-person statements of approximately 50 advanced practitioners of the TM program who reported frequent experiences of such states. Items were also drawn from accounts of such experiences throughout Western history. Items were made more appropriate by removing philosophical jargon and adjusting for word length and imbalances in social desirability. The results of studies applying the SCI (or single higher-state items) and their implications for our developmental model are summarized below.

Frequency and Structure of Experiences of Higher States
of Consciousness

We have proposed that experiences of higher states of consciousness are natural, albeit rarely occurring, phenomena and that TM increases their rate but does not alter their structure or sequence of unfoldment. In fact, a number of cross-sectional and longitudinal studies indicate that while nonmeditators infrequently report such states, TM does appear to enhance their occurrence (reviewed in Alexander, Boyer, & Alexander, 1987; see also Cranson, 1989). Also, rate and clarity of transcendental consciousness experiences during TM highly correlate with and appear to lead subsequent stabilization of pure consciousness experiences outside the practice (e.g., Jedrczak, Clements, & Alexander, 1989; Kesterson, 1986; Orme-Johnson, Clements, Haynes, & Badawi, 1977). Meditators do not score higher than nonmeditators on the misleading SCI scale, suggesting that these results are not attributable to response bias (e.g., Alexander, 1982). Further, reported rate of experience of each of the subsequent higher stages tends to be consistent with the developmental sequence proposed by Vedic psychology: Experience of pure consciousness along with activity occurs with greatest frequency, and unity consciousness-type experiences occur least often (Jedrczak, in press).

For both nonmeditating and meditating samples, factor analyses of the individual SCI items yield a conceptually meaningful higher state of consciousness factor that is empirically distinct from waking state and pathological experience factors and is consistent in its structure over a one-year period (Alexander, 1982). The underlying factor shared by these separate higher-state items may be the "ground state" of pure consciousness at the basis of all higher stages of consciousness. When different higher-state experiences weigh consistently on the same empirical factor

even among nonmeditators, it is unlikely that this pattern solely results from exposure to a shared belief system. Consistent with the SCI findings, samples of advanced TM practitioners also obtain higher scores than nonmeditating matched controls on Hood's (1975) experience scale, based on Stace's (1960) descriptions of transcendental-type experiences drawn from a variety of cultural traditions and historical epochs (Gelderloos & Beto, 1989). This finding underscores the apparent universality of higher-state experiences reported by these subjects.

Perhaps the most unambiguous subjective criterion of transition to the first higher stage, cosmic consciousness, is the experience of maintenance of pure consciousness even during the inertia of dreamless sleep. Reports of "witnessing" deep sleep are virtually absent in the psychological literature. However, 85 percent of a survey of advanced TM and TM-Sidhi practitioners at Maharishi International University (*n* = 235) reported this experience on an infrequent to regular basis (Orme-Johnson & Edwards, 1982). Consistent with this finding, 82.5 percent of meditating freshmen in a recent survey (*n* = 100) at the same university reported the experience of witnessing dreaming and/or deep sleep, as distinct from the more common experience of "lucid" dreaming (Gackenbach, Cranson, & Alexander, 1986). Lucid dreaming typically appears to involve increased cognitive and somatic arousal rather than maintenance of a silent, settled state of inner wakefulness, as during witnessing of dreaming (Alexander, Boyer, & Orme-Johnson, 1985; Gackenbach, Moorecroft, Alexander, & LaBerge, 1987).

Psychophysiological Correlates of Growth to Higher Stages of Consciousness

A criterion for substantial postformal development was that it involve major neurophysiological transformation. If transcendental or pure consciousness lays a foundation for development of higher stages of consciousness, then the "restful alert" state of transcendental consciousness is predicted to be as psychophysiologically distinct from ordinary adult waking as waking is from dreaming and deep sleep. As predicted, pure consciousness has been distinguished from these ordinarily experienced states on a wide range of psychophysiological measures. These results are summarized in the main text in the section on transcendental consciousness.

Enduring psychophysiological changes resulting from repeated experience of transcendental consciousness during TM are suggested by significantly lower baseline levels of spontaneous skin resistance responses, respiration rate, heart rate, and plasma lactate in TM practitioners outside of meditation practice as compared to control subjects (see meta-analysis by Dillbeck & Orme-Johnson, 1987). These findings suggest growing maintenance of the restful alert state of pure consciousness even during daily activity. This interpretation is supported by additional long-term psychophysiological changes observed in meditators during daily activity, including enhanced autonomic stability during mental tasks (Alexander, Swanson et al., in press; Gaylord, Orme-Johnson, & Travis, 1989); increased stability and efficiency of endocrine functions (Werner et al., 1986); maintenance of elevated arginine vasopressin before and after (as well as during) the TM practice (O'Halloran et al., 1985); maintenance of elevated EEG coherence during eyes-closed and eyes-

open rest (Farrow & Hebert, 1982; Levine, 1975); and more efficient EEG hemispheric lateralization during mental tasks requiring such hemispheric specialization (Bennet & Trinder, 1977).

Finally, there are preliminary psychophysiological data on maintaining the restful alert experience of pure consciousness—or witnessing—even during sleep. A pilot study of sleep in advanced TM practitioners showed that subjects who frequently report witnessing tended to exhibit simultaneously slow wave activity (associated with sleep) and rhythmic beta (associated with waking) in light sleep; and delta waves along with alpha spindles during deep sleep. Also, dream phases were shorter and less frequent for such subjects, and they required far less sleep at night than normal adults (Banquet & Sailhan, 1977; cf. Gackenbach, Moorecroft, Alexander, & La Berge, 1987). Recently Meirsman (1988) found that advanced TM and TM-Sidhi participants who reported witnessing sleep produced a significantly higher density of high-frequency rapid eye movements during REM sleep than did matched nonpracticing controls; this was associated with more abundant, higher-amplitude, and lower-frequency alpha waves and sleep spindles. These results were interpreted on the basis of prior research as indicating a more efficient and mature style of cerebral functioning and growth of capacity to maintain inner wakefulness during sleep. Further, as in Banquet & Sailhan's study, Meirsman's advanced subjects required less REM sleep, and less sleep overall, than controls. Also, Walton et al. (1988) recently reported a substantial correlation between frequency of experience of higher states of consciousness, including witnessing of sleep, and 5HIAA excretion (a serotonin metabolite associated with elevated mood states and decreased anxiety).

Personality and Cognitive-Perceptual Correlates of Growth to Higher Stages of Consciousness

A central criterion for postrepresentational stages is that they be "higher" in a functional as well as a structural way. If TM accelerates natural growth, then such positive functional changes associated with spontaneous experiences of higher states in nonmeditators should be identical to those resulting from systematic transcending in meditators. Indeed, greater frequency of higher-state experience for *both* meditators (outside the practice) and nonmeditators has been correlated with a wide range of similar positive personality, cognitive–perceptual, and behavioral outcomes associated with advanced human development (see Alexander, Boyer, & Alexander, 1987).

Experience of pure consciousness is predicted to accelerate growth of self-actualization as described by Maslow (e.g., Gelderloos, 1987). In several cross-sectional studies with *both* nonmeditating and meditating subjects, individuals who more frequently experienced pure consciousness during daily activity scored higher on self-actualization as measured by questionnaire or peer rating (see Alexander, Boyer, & Alexander, 1987). In contrast, it was found that frequency of nonordinary, high-imagery experiences during relaxation was not significantly associated with self-actualization (Davies, 1974).

Also, a number of longitudinal studies indicate that TM facilitates self-development in adolescents and young adults, as shown by self-actualization, ego devel-

opment, ego strength, personal identity, and self-concept (e.g., Alexander, 1982; Berg & Mulder, 1976; Gelderloos, 1987; Turnbull & Norris, 1982).

Moreover, as predicted, transcending through the TM technique appears to accelerate affective growth in adolescents and adults in comparison to appropriate control conditions on measures of emotional maturity (Brown, 1976; Overbeck, 1982), inner-directedness (Hjelle, 1974; Seeman, Nidich, & Banta, 1972), happiness (Childs, 1975; Geisler, 1978), and altruism (Nidich, Seeman, & Dreskin, 1973). Such enhancement in affective functioning also appears to underlie observed improvements in general capacity for warm interpersonal relations (Marcus, 1977), and for successful marital and work relations (Aron & Aron, 1982; Frew, 1974).

Furthermore, according to Vedic psychology, maintenance of pure consciousness at all times requires a stress-free nervous system; therefore, subjects who more frequently experience pure consciousness during activity should display fewer symptoms of stress. Several studies have shown that frequency of pure consciousness experience in meditating and nonmeditating samples is correlated with lower levels of psychopathology (e.g., Alexander, 1982; Davies, 1974). Reduction of psychological, biochemical, and health-related indicators of stress has been one of the most widely documented longitudinal changes associated with practice of TM (e.g., Eppley et al., 1989; Jevning, Wilson, Smith, & Morton, 1978; Orme-Johnson, 1987).

An often cited cognitive criterion for postformal development is that the rigid logic of formal problem solving be supplemented by an approach that also emphasizes the contribution of affect and intuition in constructive "problem finding" (e.g., Arlin, 1984, 1989, 1990). Consistent with this prediction, more frequent experience of pure consciousness in meditators and nonmeditators has been shown to correlate strongly with fluency, flexibility, and originality in creative thinking (e.g., Jedrczak, in press; Orme-Johnson & Haynes, 1981). Two studies also found a substantial association between frequency of pure consciousness experience and capacity for episodes of total attention or absorption (Alexander, 1978, 1982). This latter capacity appears to involve the ability to process information holistically through affective, attentional, and sensory channels rather than through propositional reasoning alone (Tellegen & Atkinson, 1974).

Again, longitudinal studies indicate that transcending through TM may enhance nonpropositional information processing and creative problem solving (e.g., Orme-Johnson & Haynes, 1981; Travis, 1979). Prospective studies also suggest that TM may stimulate change on several process-oriented cognitive functions that otherwise tend to become fixed in late adolescence—for example, fluid intelligence and choice-reaction time (e.g., Aron, Orme-Johnson, & Brubaker, 1981; Cranson, 1989; Dillbeck, Assimakis, Raimondi, Orme-Johnson, & Rowe, 1986; Holt, Caruso, & Riley, 1978); field independence (e.g., Pelletier, 1974); and perceptual flexibility (e.g., Dillbeck, 1982).

Conclusion

In several of our studies—especially in the prison and elderly experiments—the ordinary external environment minimally contributed to human growth. Yet even

in the absence of external enrichment (or controlling for it), the TM program—apparently through the mechanism of transcending—seemed capable of promoting growth across major developmental transitions as described by our model. These findings challenge a widely held tenet that quality of direct interaction with the external physical or social environment—from a learning theory, information processing, or Piagetian view—is necessarily the critical factor influencing cognitive growth.

In fact, even with application of enrichment or learning programs, structural-developmental change has been shown to be surprisingly resistant to lasting modification (e.g., Kuhn, 1974; Loevinger et al., 1985). Further, when training effects are observed, it is difficult to assess their validity because treatment is typically confounded with outcome measurement. For example, children will be trained on conservationlike tasks and then tested on closely related measures. In our experiments (with children, inmates, and the elderly), subjects received no external training with test-related materials or even with related concepts; instead, substantial change appeared to result from systematically turning attention inward to "enliven" intrinsically deeper levels of mind. Through optimizing the process of transcending and neutralizing stress, the TM and TM-Sidhi program appears to facilitate growth across all four major developmental junctures investigated. Thus, we propose that were such a technology widely introduced at the earliest appropriate time, development would not freeze prematurely and growth of higher stages of consciousness would appear as the inevitable consequence of normal human development.

Acknowledgment

We are pleased to acknowledge the following colleagues, who provided valuable editorial feedback on this chapter: Victoria Alexander, Robert Boyer, Melanie Brown, Ken Chandler, Rita Jacoby, Ellen Langer, Dan McAdams, Robert Oates, Juan Pascual-Leone, and Geoffrey Wells. We would also like to thank Ken Chandler and Craig Pearson for making available to us from their forthcoming publications, quotations from Western philosophy and literature on experiences of higher states of consciousness. Finally, we would like to express our gratitude to Maharishi Mahesh Yogi, whose Vedic psychology provided the theoretical foundation for this chapter.

Notes

1. Other investigators have also related different aspects of Eastern philosophical traditions to Western developmental psychology (e.g., Battista, 1978; Brown, 1977; Goleman, 1972; Hunt, 1984, 1989; Koplowitz, 1984, 1990; McClelland, 1979; Paranjpe, 1987; Shapiro & Walsh, 1984; Tart, 1975). Although independently drawn from a wide range of Eastern and Western traditions, Wilber's model, in particular, bears certain similarities to our own (e.g., Wilber, Engler, & Brown, 1986). Although there have been a few initial efforts to test some of these developmental theories, more substantial research is clearly required.

2. Consistent with the Vedic model, it is increasingly recognized that many cognitive and even ego-synthetic processes typically occur outside conscious awareness (e.g., Kohut, 1977; Marcel, 1983b; Shiffrin & Schneider, 1983).

3. Research on the perception of words presented at very short exposure times (e.g., Marcel, 1983a, 1983b) is consistent with this view. In these studies, words presented at intervals

too short for subjects consciously to detect their presence (sensory level) were discriminated at better than chance rates with respect to their internal graphic organization and semantic content (presumably at the early representational and thinking levels, respectively). In one study (Marcel, 1983a, experiment 1), the semantic content was found to be available at still shorter intervals than graphic representation, as would be predicted if meaning is mediated at a finer level than simple representation.

4. Several theorists (e.g., Beilin, 1971; Lenneberg, 1967; Wohlwill, 1973) have observed that the apparent universality, irreversibility, and so on, of at least lower stages of cognitive development would seem to be more parsimoniously explained through unfoldment of inherent mental and corresponding biological structures than through a process approaching pure cognitive construction. They emphasize that the positing of such inherent mental structures need not imply that they are in their final form at birth—they may follow a maturational time table, modulated by environmental interaction.

5. This is consistent with Marcus and Wurf's (1987) notion of the "working self-concept" as that subset of representations about oneself that are accessible at any given moment.

6. Sternberg (1984) makes a similar observation when he states that novel functions are processed centrally (require attention and serial processing), but when these functions become sufficiently practiced in the course of development, they are processed peripherally and automatically.

7. The five primary faculties of action or motor functions according to Vedic psychology are manipulation, locomotion, speech, elimination, and reproduction (Maharishi, 1969, p. 190).

8. As Flavell (1985) emphasizes, however, the representational achievements of this period anticipate in significant ways subsequent operational development.

9. However, the "finest level of feeling," which is held to lie at the very junction point with pure consciousness, is said to become systematically accessible only after awareness is already permanently identified with pure consciousness in the growth of refined cosmic consciousness (as described later).

10. For a consideration of methodological issues involved in such analysis of first-person accounts, see Forman (1990).

11. Fowler (1981), Koplowitz (1984), Kohlberg and Ryncarz (chapter) describe a "plateau"-like experience (Maslow, 1976) in which "peak experiences no longer have an out-of-this-world quality, they become a familiar experience" (Cook-Greuter, 1990). Insofar as these peaks have become familiar but pure consciousness is *not* clearly and permanently established as a 24-hour-a-day phenomenon (even during deep sleep; see next section), such apparent plateau experience would be transitional to full stabilization of the first higher stage of consciousness described by Vedic psychology.

12. EEG coherence is a measure of stability of phase angle between two EEG signals at a specified frequency (Orme-Johnson & Haynes, 1981).

13. Without addressing the distinctive simultaneous enhancement of alertness during transcendental consciousness, a review (Holmes, 1984) questioned whether meditation in general produced lower somatic arousal (i.e., deeper rest) than simple relaxation. However, a more recent quantitative meta-analysis (excluding non-TM studies) by Dillbeck and Orme-Johnson (1987) indicated that TM produces about twice the effect size of eyes-closed rest on reduced breath rate, plasma lactate, and increased basal skin resistance. Further, if simple or stylized relaxation reduced somatic arousal to the same degree as transcendental consciousness, then long-term effects of relaxation on psychological measures of stress reduction would presumably be equivalent to those produced by TM. Instead, a meta-analysis of over 100 studies indicated that the statistical effect size of TM on reduction of trait anxiety was again approximately twice as large as that associated with relaxation procedures or other forms of meditation (Eppley, Abrams, & Shear, 1989). Similar results were obtained in a meta-analysis on reduction of blood pressure through TM in comparison to other forms of meditation (Kuchera, 1987).

14. We are currently adding control groups that receive the same modified instruction. Thus far, subjects have served as their own controls. They were administered two independent 18-item forms in random order. The second form always had the modified instructions

encouraging them to report their "inner experience," and had fewer items per page to allow for longer responses. The advanced male TM practitioners scored markedly higher (2.2 steps) on the modified form. In contrast, previous studies with modified instructions showed only modest improvement (.5–.75 steps) and no gains at the highest levels of ego development. This suggests that modified instructions may yield such marked improvement in "performance" only (or especially) for subjects who already have an underlying high level of ego development "competence."

References

Abrams, A. I., & Siegel, L. M. (1978). The Transcendental Meditation program and rehabilitation at Folsom State Prison: A cross-validation study. *Criminal Justice and Behavior 5,* 3–20.

Adams, G. R., & Shea, J. A. (1974). The relationship between identity status, focus of control, and ego development. *Journal of Youth and Adolescence, 8* 81–89.

Adelson, J. (1972). Political imagination of the adolescent. In J. Kagan & R. Coles (Eds.), *Twelve to sixteen: Early adolescence.* New York: Norton.

Ader, R., & Cohen, C. (1982). Behaviorally conditioned immunosuppression and murine systemic lupus eurythemastosus. *Science, 215,* 1534–1536.

Adler, A. (1972). Mathematics and creativity. *The New Yorker,* February, 39–45.

Aebli, H. (1980). *Denken: Das Ordnen des Tuns: Kognitive Aspekte der Handlungstheorie* (Vol. 1). Stuttgart: Klett-Cotta.

Aebli, H. (1981). *Denken: Das Ordnen des Tuns: Denkprozesse* (Vol. 2). Stuttgart: Klett-Cotta.

Ahammer, I. M. (1979). *A positive growth model for adult development and aging.* Unpublished manuscript, University of Frankfurt, Frankfurt, West Germany.

Albert, S. (1978). Time, memory and affect: Experimental studies of the subjective past. In J. T. Fraser & N. Lawrence (Eds.), *The study of time* (Vol. 3). New York: Springer-Verlag.

Alexander, C. N. (1976, June). *On selected aspects of consciousness and human development.* Paper presented at the departmental seminar in social psychology, Department of Experimental Psychology, Oxford University, Oxford, England.

Alexander, C. N. (1981, April). *Theoretical and empirical implications of a stage of consciousness model for postformal operational development.* Paper presented at the Symposium on Post-Formal Cognition, Harvard University, Cambridge, MA.

Alexander, C. N. (1982). Ego development, personality and behavioral change in inmates practicing the Transcendental Meditation technique or participating in other programs: A cross-sectional and longitudinal study. (Doctoral dissertation, Harvard University.) *Dissertation Abstracts International, 43*(2), 539–B.

Alexander, C. N. (1988). A conceptual and phenomenological analysis of pure consciousness during sleep. *Lucidity Letter, 7*(4), 39–43.

Alexander, C. N., & Boyer, R. W. (1989). Seven states of consciousness: Unfolding the full potential of the cosmic psyche in individual life through Maharishi's Vedic psychology. *Modern Science and Vedic Science, 2,* 324–372.

Alexander, C. N., Boyer, R. W., & Alexander, V. K. (1987). Higher states of consciousness in the Vedic psychology of Maharishi Mahesh Yogi: A theoretical introduction and research review. *Modern Science and Vedic Science, 1,* 89–126.

Alexander, C. N., Boyer, R. W., & Orme-Johnson, D. W. (1985). Distinguishing between transcendental consciousness and lucidity. *Lucidity Letter, 4*(2), 68–85.

Alexander, C. N., Chandler, K., & Boyer, R. W. (1990). *Experience and understanding of pure consciousness in the Vedic Science of Maharishi Mahesh Yogi.* Prepublication manuscript, Maharishi International University. Department of Psychology, Fairfield, IA.

Alexander, C. N., Cranson, R. W., Boyer, R. W., & Orme-Johnson, D. W. (1987). Transcendental consciousness: A fourth state of consciousness beyond sleep, dreaming and waking. In J. Gackenbach (Ed.), *Sleep and dreams: A sourcebook* (pp. 282–315). New York: Garland.

Alexander, C. N., Dixon, C. A., Chandler, H. M., & Davies, J. L. (in press). Development of higher stages of consciousness in Maharishi's Vedic psychology: Theory and research. *Adult Development.*

Alexander, C. N., & Jacoby, R. (1989). *On the relationship between development of higher stages of consciousness and psychosocial development.* Prepublication manuscript. Maharishi International University, Fairfield, IA.

Alexander, C. N., Kurth, S. C., Travis, F., Warner, T., & Alexander, V. K. (in press). Cognitive stage development in children practicing the Transcendental Meditation program: Acquisition and consolidation of conservation. In R. A. Chalmers, G. Clements, H. Schenkluhn, & M. Weinless (Eds.), *Scientific research on Maharishi's Transcendental Meditation and TM-Sidhi programme: Collected papers* (Vol. 4, pp. 2352–2370). Vlodrop, The Netherlands: MVU Press.

Alexander, C. N., & Larimore, W. E. (in press). Distinguishing between Transcendental Meditation and sleep according to electrophysiological criteria: In R. Chalmers, G. Clements, H. Schenkluhn, & M. Weinless (Eds.), *Scientific Research on Maharishi's Transcendental Meditation and TM-Sidhi programme: Collected papers* (Vol. 3, pp. 1712–1719). Vlodrop, The Netherlands: MVU press.

Alexander, C. N., Langer, E., Newman, R., Chandler, H. M., & Davies, J. L. (1989). Transcendental Meditation, mindfulness and longevity: An experimental study with the elderly. *Journal of Personality and Social Psychology 57,* 950–964.

Alexander, C. N., Swanson, G., Rainforth, M., Carlisle, T., & Todd, C. (in press). The Transcendental Meditation program and business: A Prospective Study. In R. K. Wallace, D. W. Orme-Johnson, & M. C. Dillbeck (Eds.), *Scientific research on Maharishi's Transcendental Meditation and TM-Sidhi program: Collected papers* (Vol. 5, pp. 3141–3149). Fairfield, IA: MIU Press.

Allport, A. (1980). Attention and performance. In G. Claxton (Ed.), *New directions in cognitive psychology.* London: Routledge and Kegan Paul.

Ammon, P. R. (1977). Cognitive development and early childhood education. In H. L. Horn & P. A. Robinson (Eds.), *Psychological processes in early education.* New York: Academic Press.

Anastasi, A. (1970). On the formation of psychological traits. *American Psychologist, 25,* 899–910.

Anderson, J. R. (1982). Acquisition of cognitive skill. *Psychological Review, 89,* 369–406.

Anderson, R. M., Hunt, S. C., Vanderstoep, A., & Pribram, K. H. (1976). Object permanency and delayed response as spatial context in monkeys with frontal lesions. *Neuropsychologia, 14,* 481–490.

Antomatis, I., Ellis, J., Hagelin, J. S., & Nanopoulous, D. U. (1988). An improved SU5 × U1 model for the four dimensional string. *Physics Letters B, 208* (2).

Aranya, Swami Hariharananda (1977). *Yoga philosophy of Patanjali.* Calcutta, India: Calcutta University Press.

Arlin, P. K. (1975). Cognitive development in adulthood: A fifth stage? *Developmental Psychology, 11,* 602–606.

Arlin, P. K. (1977). Piagetian operations in problem finding. *Developmental Psychology, 13,* 247–298.

Arlin, P. K. (1984). Adolescent and adult thought: A structural interpretation. In M. L. Commons, F. A. Richards, & C. Armon (Eds.), *Beyond formal operations: Late adolescent and adult cognitive development* (pp. 258–271). New York: Praeger.

Arlin, P. K. (1989). Problem solving and problem finding in young artists and young scientists. *Adult Development, 1,* 197–216.

Arlin, P. K. (1990). Wisdom: The art of problem finding. In R. J. Sternberg (Ed.), *Wisdom: Its nature, origins and development.* New York: Cambridge University Press.

Armon, C. (1984). Ideals of the good life and moral judgment: Ethical reasoning across the life span. In M. L. Commons, F. A. Richards, & C. Armon (Eds.), *Beyond formal operations: Late adolescent and adult cognitive development* (pp. 357–380). New York: Praeger.

Armon, C. (1989). Individuality and autonomy in adult ethical reasoning. *Adult Development, 1,* 179–196.

Arnold, M. (1960). *Emotion and personality.* New York: Columbia University Press.

Aron, A., Orme-Johnson, D., & Brubaker, P. (1981). The Transcendental Meditation program in the college curriculum: A 4-year longitudinal study of effects on cognitive and affective functioning. *College Student Journal, 15*(2), 140–146.

Aron, E. N., & Aron, A. (1982). Transcendental Meditation program and marital adjustment. *Psychological Reports, 51,* 887–890.

Ashby, W. R. (1960). *Design for a brain: The origin of adaptive behavior* (2nd ed.). New York: Wiley.

Aslin, R. N., Alberts, J. R., & Peterson, M. R. (Eds.) (1981). *Development of perception: Psychobiological perspectives.* New York: Academic Press.

Aslin, R. N., & Banks, M. S. (1978). Early visual experience in humans: Evidence for a critical period in the development of binocular vision. In H. Sten-Schneider, H. Liebovitz, H. Pick, & H. Stevenson (Eds.), *Psychology: From basic research to practice.* New York: Plenum.

Astington, J. W., Harris, P. L., & Olson, D. R. (1988). *Developing theories of mind.* New York: Cambridge University Press.

Aurelius, Marcus (1937). The meditations of Marcus Aurelius (G. Long, Trans.). In G. W. Eliot (Ed.), *The Harvard classics: Plato, Epictetus and Marcus Aurelius.* New York: Collier.

Badawi, K., Wallace, R. K., Orme-Johnson, D., & Rouzere, A. M. (1984). Electrophysiologic characteristics of respiratory suspension periods occurring during the practice of the Transcendental Meditation program. *Psychosomatic Medicine, 46*(3), 267–276.

Badian, N. A. (1982). The prediction of good and poor reading before kindergarten entry: A four-year follow-up. *Journal of Special Education, 16,* 309–318.

Bakal, D. A. (1979). *Psychology and medicine: Psychobiological dimensions of health and illness.* New York: Springer.

Bakan, D. (1966). *The duality of human existence.* Chicago: Rand McNally.

Baldwin, J. M. (1906). *Thoughts and things or genetic logic* (3 vols.). New York: Macmillan.

Baldwin, J. M. (1908). *Thought and things: A study of the development and meaning of thought or genetic logic* (Vol. 2). New York: Macmillan.

Baldwin, J. M. (1968). *Mental development in the child and the race: Methods and processes.* New York: Kelley. (Originally published in 1894.)

Bales, R. F., & Cohen, S. P. (1979). *SYMLOG.* New York: The Free Press.

Balint, M. (1977). *Le défaut fondamental.* Paris: Petite Bibliothèque Payot.

Baltes, M. M., & Baltes, P. B. (Eds.). (1986). *The psychology of control and aging.* Hillsdale, NJ: Erlbaum.

Baltes, P. B. (1987). Theoretical propositions of life-span developmental psychology: On the dynamics between growth and decline. *Developmental Psychology, 23,* 611–626.

Baltes, P. B., & Baltes, M. M. (1980). Plasticity and variability in psychological aging: Methodological and theoretical issues. In G. Gurski (Ed.), *Determining the effects of aging on the central nervous system* (pp. 41–66). Berlin: Schering.

Baltes, P. B., & Dittmann-Kohli, F. (1982). Einige einführende Überlegungen zur Intelligenz im Erwachsenenalter. *Neue Sammlung, 22,* 261–278.

Baltes, P. B., Dittmann-Kohli, F., & Dixon, R. A. (1984). New perspectives on the development of intelligence in adulthood: Toward a dual-process conception and a model of selective optimization with compensation. In P. B. Baltes & O. G. Brim, Jr. (Eds.), *Life-span development and behavior* (Vol. 6, pp. 33–76). New York: Academic Press.

Baltes, P. B., & Kliegl, R. (1986). On the dynamics between growth and decline in the aging of intelligence and memory. In K. Poeck, H. J. Freund, & H. Gänshirt (Eds.), *Neurology Proceedings of the XIIIth World Congress of Neurology* (pp. 1–17). Heidelberg: Springer.

Baltes, P. B., & Labouvie, G. V. (1973). Adult development of intellectual performance: Description, explanation, and modification. In C. Eisdorfer & M. P. Lawton (Eds.),

The psychology of adult development and aging (pp. 157–219). Washington, DC. American Psychological Association.

Baltes, P. B., Reese, H. W., & Lipsitt, L. P. (1980). Life-span developmental psychology. *Annual Review of Psychology, 31*, 65–110.

Baltes, P. B., & Schaie, K. W. (1976). On the plasticity of intelligence in adulthood and old age: Where Horn and Donaldson fail. *American Psychologist, 31*, 720–725.

Baltes, P. B., & Smith, J. (1990). Towards a psychology of wisdom and its ontogenesis. In Sternberg, R. J. (Ed.) *Wisdom: Its nature, origins, and development.* New York: Cambridge University Press.

Baltes, P. B., & Willis, S. L. (1977). Toward psychological theories of aging and development. In J. E. Birren & K. W. Schaie (Eds.), *Handbook of the psychology of aging.* New York: Van Nostrand.

Baltes, P. B., & Willis, S. L. (1979a). The critical importance of appropriate methodology in the study of aging: The sample case of psychometric intelligence. In F. Hoffmeister & C. Miller (Eds.), *Brain function in old age* (pp. 164–187). Heidelberg: Springer.

Baltes, P. B., & Willis, S. L. (1979b). Life-span developmental psychology, cognitive functioning, and social policy. In M. W. Riley (Ed.), *Aging from birth to death: Interdisciplinary perspectives* (pp. 15–46). Boulder, CO: Westview.

Baltes, P. B., & Willis, S. L. (1982). Plasticity and enhancement of intellectual functioning in old age: Penn State's Adult Development and Enrichment Project (ADEPT). In F. I. M. Craik & S. E. Trehub (Eds.), *Aging and cognitive processes* (pp. 353–389). New York: Plenum.

Bamberger, J. (1978). Intuitive and formal musical knowing: Parables of cognitive dissonance. In S. S. Madeja (Ed.), *The arts, cognition, and basic skills.* St. Louis: CEMREL.

Bandura, A. (1982a). Self-efficacy in human agency. *American Psychologist, 37*, 122–147.

Bandura, A. (1982b). The psychology of chance encounters and life paths. *American Psychologist, 37*, 747–755.

Banks, M. S., & Salapatek, P. (1983). Infant visual perception. In M. M. Haith & J. J. Campos (Eds.), *Handbook of child psychology: Infancy and developmental biology (Vol. 2).* New York: Wiley.

Banquet, J. P., & Sailhan, M. (1977). Quantified EEG spectral analysis of sleep and Transcendental Meditation. In D. W. Orme-Johnson & J. T. Farrow (Eds.), *Scientific research on the Transcendental Meditation program: Collected papers (Vol. 1*, pp. 445–453). Rheinweiler, West Germany: MERU Press.

Basham, A. L. (1959). *The wonder that was India.* New York: Grove Press.

Basseches, M. A. (1980). Dialectical schemata: A framework for the empirical study of the development of dialectical thinking. *Human Development, 23*, 400–421.

Basseches, M. A. (1984a). *Dialectical thinking and adult development.* Norwood, NJ: Ablex Press.

Basseches, M. A. (1984b). Dialectical thinking as a metasystematic form of cognitive organization. In M. L. Commons, F. A. Richards, & C. Armon (Eds.), *Beyond formal operations: Late adolescent and adult cognitive development* (pp. 216–238). New York: Praeger.

Bates, E. (1979). *Emergence of symbols.* New York: Academic Press.

Battista, J. R. (1978). The science of consciousness. In K. S. Pope & J. L. Singer (Eds.), *The stream of consciousness.* New York: Plenum.

Bayley, N. (1970). Development of mental abilities. In P. Mussen (Ed.), *Carmichael's manual of child psychology* (Vol. 1, pp. 3–40). New York: Wiley.

Beckett, S. (1958) *Endgame.* New York: Grove Press.

Beilin, H. (1971). The development of physical concepts. In T. Mischell (Ed.), *Cognitive development and epistemology.* New York: Academic Press.

Beilin, H. (1983). The new functionalism and Piaget's program. In E. K. Scholnick (Ed.), *New trends in conceptual representation.* Hillsdale, NJ: Erlbaum.

Belenky, M. (1978). *Conflict and development: A longitudinal study of the impact of abortion decisions on moral judgements of adolescents and adult women.* Unpublished doctoral dissertation. Harvard University, Cambridge, MA.

Benack, S., & Basseches, M. A. (1989). Dialectical thinking and relativistic epistemology: Their relation in adult development. *Adult Development, 1,* 95–109.

Bennet, J. E., & Trinder, J. (1977) Hemispheric laterality and cognitive style associated with Transcendental Meditation. *Psychophysiology, 14,* 293–296.

Benson, N. (1989). *Mental capacity constraints on early symbolic processing—The origin of language from a cognitive perspective.* Doctoral dissertation, York University, Toronto, Ontario.

Beresford, M., Jedrczak, K., Toomey, M., & Clements, G. (in press). EEG coherence, age-related psychological variables, and the Transcendental Meditation and TM-Sidhi program. In R. A. Chalmers, G. Clements, H. Schenkluhn, & M. Weinless (Eds.), *Scientific research on the Transcendental Meditation and TM-Sidhi programme: Collected papers* (Vol. 3). Vlodrop, The Netherlands: MVU Press.

Berg, W. P., van den, & Mulder, B. (1977). Psychological research on the effects of the Transcendental Meditation technique on a number of personality variables. In D. W. Orme-Johnson & J. T. Farrow (Eds.), *Scientific research on the Transcendental Meditation program: Collected papers* (Vol. 1, pp. 428–433). Rheinweiler, West Germany: MERU Press.

Berlin, S. N., & Johnson, C. G. (1989). Women and Autonomy. *Psychiatry, 52,* 79–95.

Berndt, T. J. (1981). Relations between social cognition, nonsocial cognition, and social behavior: The case of friendship. In J. H. Flavell & L. Ross (Eds.), *Social cognitive development: Frontiers and possible futures* (pp. 176–199). Cambridge: Cambridge University Press.

Berne, E. (1961). *Transactional Analysis.* New York: Grove Press.

Bernstein, J. (1973). *Einstein.* New York: Fontana, William Collins, & Co.

Berry, J. (1981). Cultural systems and cognitive styles. In M. P. Friedman, J. P. Das, & N. O'Conner (Eds.), *Intelligence and learning* (pp. 395–405). New York: Plenum.

Bertanthal, B. I. (1981). The significance of developmental sequences for investigating the what and how of development. In K. W. Fischer (Ed.), *Cognitive development.* San Francisco: Jossey-Bass.

Beth, E. W., & Piaget, J. (1966). *Mathematical epistemology and psychology* (W. Mays, Trans.). New York: Gordon & Breach.

Bickhard, M. H. (1978). The nature of developmental stages. *Human Development, 21,* 217–233.

Bickhard, M. H. (1979). On necessary and specific capabilities in evolution and development. *Human Development, 22,* 217–224.

Biggs, J., & Collis, K. (1982). *A system for evaluating learning outcomes: The SOLO taxonomy.* New York: Academic Press.

Birren, J. E. (1969). *Age and decision strategies. Interdisciplinary topics in gerontology.* Basel: Karger.

Birren, J. E. (1990). Integration of approaches and viewpoints. In R. J. Sternberg (Ed.). *Wisdom: Its nature, origins, and development.* New York: Cambridge University Press.

Bjorklund, D. F. (1987). How age changes in knowledge base contribute to the development of children's memory: An interpretive review. *Developmental Review, 7,* 93–130.

Blachman, B. A. (1982, November). *Linguistic variables as predictors of kindergarten and first grade reading achievement.* Paper presented at the 33rd Annual Conference of the Orton Dyslexic Society, Baltimore, MD.

Blake, H. G. O. (Ed.), (1929). *Early Spring in Massachusetts. From the journal of Henry D. Thoreau.* Boston: Houghton Mifflin.

Blanchard-Fields, F. (1986). Reasoning on social dilemmas varying in emotional saliency: An adult developmental perspective. *Psychology and Aging, 1,* 325–333.

Bleick, C. R., & Abrams, A. I. (1987). The Transcendental Meditation program and criminal recidivism in California. *Journal of Criminal Justice, 15*(3), 211–230.

Block, J. (1971). *Lives through time.* Berkeley, CA: Bancroft.

Boesch, E. E. (1976). *Psychopathologie des Alltags.* Bern: Huber.

Bohm, D., & Hiley, B. (1975). On the intuitive understanding of nonlocatability as understood by quantum theory. *Foundations of Physics, 5,* 96–102.

Boole, G. (1854). *Laws of thought.* London: Walton & Maberly.

Boring, E. G. (1950). *A history of experimental psychology* (2nd ed.). Norwalk, CT: Appleton-Century-Crofts.

Bornstein, M. H. (Ed.). (1988). *Sensitive periods in development: Interdisciplinary perspectives.* Hillsdale, NJ: Erlbaum.

Botwinick, J. (1977). Intellectual abilities. In J. E. Birren & K. W. Schaie (Eds.), *Handbook of the psychology of aging* (pp. 560–605). New York: Van Nostrand Reinhold.

Bourbaki, N. (1939). *Eléments de mathématique.* Paris: Hermann.

Bower, G. (1975). Cognitive psychology: An introduction. In W. K. Estes (Ed.), *Handbook of learning and cognition* (pp. 25–80). Hillsdale, NJ: Erlbaum.

Bower, T. G. R. (1966). The visual world of infants. *ScientificAmerican, 215,* 80–92.

Bower, T. G. R. (1982). *Development in infancy* (2nd ed.). San Francisco: Freeman.

Bower, T. G. R., & Wishart, S. G. (1972). The effects of motor skill on object permanence. *Cognition, 1,* 165–172.

Bowlby, J. (1981). *Attachment and loss* (Vols. 1, 2, & 3). Middlesex, England: Penguin.

Boyer, R. W. (1984). Consciousness and attentional processes (Doctoral dissertation, University of Oklahoma). *Dissertation Abstracts International, 45*(5B).

Brabeck, M. (1983). Moral Judgment: Theory and research on differences between males and females. *Developmental Review 3,* 274–291.

Bradley, F. H. (1962). *Ethical studies.* New York: Oxford University Press. (Originally published in 1876.)

Brainerd, C. D. (1978). Learning research and Piagetian theory. In L. S. Siegel & C. J. Brainerd (Eds.), *Alternatives to Piaget: Critical essays on the theory.* New York: Academic Press.

Brainerd, C. J. (1978). *Piaget's theory of intelligence.* Englewood Cliffs, NJ: Prentice-Hall.

Braine, M. D. S. & Rumain, B. (1983). Logical reasoning. In J. H. Flavell & E. M. Markman (Eds.), *Handbook of child psychology: Cognitive development (Vol. 3).* New York: Wiley.

Brandtstädter, J. (1981). Entwicklung in Handlungskontexten: Aussichten für die entwicklungspcyhologische Theorienbildung und Anwendung. *Trierer Psychologische Berichte, 8*(8).

Brandstädter, J. (1984). Personal and social control over development: Some implications of an action perspective in life-span development psychology. In P. B. Baltes & O. G. Brim, Jr. (Eds.), *Life-span development and behavior* (Vol. 6, pp. 1–32). New York: Academic Press.

Bransford, J. D., Stein, B. S., Shelton, T. S., & Owings, R. A. (1981). Cognition and adaptation: The importance of learning to learn. In J. H. Harvey (Ed.), *Cognition, social behavior, and the environment* (pp. 93–110). Hillsdale, NJ: Erlbaum.

Brent, S. B. (1978), Individual specialization, collective adaptation, and rate of environmental change. *Human Development, 21,* 21–33.

Bridgewater, W., & Kurtz, S. (Eds.). (1963). *The Columbia encyclopedia.* New York: Columbia University Press.

Brim, O. G., Jr. (1974). *The sense of personal control over one's life.* Invited address to Divisions 7 and 8, at the 82nd Annual Convention of the American Psychological Association, New Orleans.

Brim, O. G., Jr. (1976). Theories of the male midlife crisis. *The Counseling Psychologist, 6,* 2–9.

Brim, O. G., Jr., & Ryff, C. D. (1980). On the properties of life events. In P. B. Baltes & O. G. Brim, Jr. (Eds.), *Life-span development and behavior* (Vol. 3, pp. 367–388). New York: Academic Press.

Bringuier, J. C. (1980). *Conversations with Piaget.* Chicago: University of Chicago Press.

Bronfenbrenner, U. (1979). *The ecology of human development.* Cambridge, MA: Harvard University Press.

Broughton, J. (1975). *The development of natural epistemology in adolescence and early adulthood.* Doctoral dissertation, Harvard University, Cambridge, MA.

Broughton, J. M. (1977). Beyond formal operations: Theoretical thought in adolescence. *Teachers College Record, 79*(1), 87–98.

Broughton, J. M. (1978). The development of concepts of self, mind, reality, and knowledge. In W. Damon (Ed.), *Social cognition.* San Francisco: Jossey-Bass.

Broughton, J. M. (1981a). The divided self in adolescence. *Human Development, 24,* 13–24.

Broughton, J. M. (1981b). Piaget's structural developmental psychology III. Function and the problem of knowledge. *Human Development, 24,* 257–285.

Broughton, J. M. (1982). Genetic logic and the developmental psychology of philosophical concepts. In J. M. Broughton & D. J. Freeman-Moir (Eds.), *The cognitive developmental psychology of James Mark Baldwin.* Norwood, NJ: Ablex.

Broughton, J. M. (1984). Not beyond formal operations but beyond Piaget. In M. L. Commons, F. A. Richards, & C. Armon (Eds.), *Beyond formal operations: Late adolescent and adult cognitive development* (pp. 395–411). New York: Praeger.

Brown, A. L. (1982). Learning and development: The problem of capability, access and induction. *Human Development, 25,* 89–115.

Brown, A. L., Bransford, J. D., Ferrara, R. A., & Campione, J. C. (1983). Learning, remembering and understanding. In J. H. Flavell & E. M. Markman (Eds.), *Handbook of child psychology: Cognitive development* (Vol. 3). New York: Wiley.

Brown, A. L., & French, L. (1979). The zone of potential development: Implications for intelligence testing in the year 2000. *Intelligence, 3,* 255–277.

Brown, D. P. (1977). A model for the levels of concentrative meditation. *International Journal of Clinical and Experimental Hypnosis, 25,* 236–273.

Brown, L. (1989). When is the moral problem not a moral problem. In C. Gilligan, N. Lyons & T. Hanmer (Eds.), *Making connections: Papers from the Emma Willard study.* Cambridge, MA: Center for the Study of Gender, Education and Human Development, Harvard University.

Brown, M. (1976) Higher education for higher consciousness: A study of students at Maharishi International University. (Doctoral dissertation, University of California at Berkeley). *Dissertation Abstracts International 38,* 2A.

Brown, R. (1973). *A first language.* Cambridge, MA: Harvard University Press.

Bruner, J. S. (1972). The nature and use of immaturity. *American Psychologist, 27,* 687–701.

Bruner, J. S. (1986). *Actual minds, possible worlds.* Cambridge, MA: Harvard University Press.

Bruner, J. S., Oliver, R. R., & Greenfield, P. M. (1966). *Studies in cognitive growth.* New York: Wiley.

Bryant, P. (1974). *Perception and understanding in young children.* London: Methuen.

Buber, M. (1958). *I and thou.* New York: Scribner. (Originally published in 1923.)

Buck, R. (1985). Prime theory: An integrated view of motivation and emotion. *Psychological Review, 92,* 389–413.

Bucke, R. M. (1969). *Cosmic consciousness: A study in the evolution of the human mind.* New York: Dutton. (Originally published in 1901.)

Buhler, C. (1968). The general structure of the human life cycle. In C. Buhler & F. Massarik (Eds.), *The course of human life: A study of goals in the humanistic perspective.* New York: Springer.

Bujatti, M., & Riederer, P. (1976). Serotonin, noradrenaline, dopamine metabolites in the Transcendental Meditation technique. *Journal of Neural Transmission, 39,* 257–267.

Bullock, D. (1981). On the current and potential scope of generative theories of cognitive development. In K. W. Fischer (Ed.), *Cognitive development.* San Francisco: Jossey-Bass.

Bunge, M. (1973). *Method, model and matter.* Dordecht, Holland: Reidel.

Bynum, T. W., Thomas, J. A., & Weitz, L. J. (1972), Truth function in formal operational thinking: Inhelder and Piaget's evidence. *Developmental Psychology, 40*(7), 129–132.

Calfee, R. C., Lindamood, P., & Lindamood, C. (1973). Acoustic-phonetic skills and reading: Kindergarten through twelfth grade. *Journal of Educational Psychology, 64,* 293–298.

Campell, A. (1980). *The sense of well-being in America.* New York: McGraw-Hill.

Campbell, J. (Ed.). (1971). *The portable Jung.* New York: Viking.

Campbell, R. L., & Richie, D. M. (1983). Problems in the theory of developmental sequences: Prerequisites and precursors. *Human Development, 26,* 156–172.

Cannon, W. B. (1942). Voodoo death. *American Anthropologist, 44,* 169–181.

Cantor, N., & Kihlstrom, J. F. (1987). *Personality and social intelligence.* Englewood Cliffs, NJ: Prentice-Hall.

Capon, N., & Kuhn, P. (1979). Logical reasoning in the supermarket: Adult females' use of proportional reasoning strategy in an everyday context. *Developmental Psychology, 15,* 450–452.

Carpenter, E. (1921) *The art of creation: Essays on the self and its power.* London: Allen & Unwin.

Carr, D. (1974). *Phenomenology and the problem of history.* Evanston, IL: Northwestern University Press.

Carver, C. S., & Scheier, M. F. (1982). Control theory: A useful conceptual framework for personality—social, clinical, and health research. *Psychological Bulletin, 92,* 111–135.

Case, R. (1980). The underlying mechanism of intellectual development. In J. R. Kirby & J. B. Gibbs (Eds.), *Cognition, development, and instruction.* New York: Academic Press.

Case, R. (1985). *Intellectual development: Birth to adulthood.* New York: Academic Press.

Cattell, R. (1971). *Abilities: Their structure, growth, and action.* Boston: Houghton Mifflin.

Chalmers, R. A., Clements, G., Schenkluhn, H., & Weinless, M. (Eds.). (in press). *Scientific research on Maharishi's Transcendental Meditation and TM-Sidhi programme: Collected papers* (Vols. 2–4). Vlodrop, The Netherlands: MVU Press.

Chandler, H. M. (in preparation). *The growth of wisdom through the TM and TM-Sidhi program: A ten-year longitudinal study of Maharishi International University alumni and controls.* (Doctoral dissertation) Maharishi International University, Fairfield, IA.

Chandler, K. (1987). Modern science and Vedic Science: An introduction. *Modern Science and Vedic Science, 1*(1), 5–26.

Chandler, K. (1989). *Experience and understanding of higher states of consciousness in light of Maharishi's Vedic Science.* Prepublication manuscript. Maharishi International University, Fairfield, IA.

Chandler, M. J. (1975). Relativism and the problem of epistemological loneliness. *Human Development, 18,* 171–180.

Chandler, M. J., & Holliday, S. (1990). Wisdom in a post-apocalyptic age. In R. J. Sternberg (Ed.) *Wisdom: Its nature, origins and development.* New York: Cambridge University Press.

Chanowitz, B., & Langer, E. (1981). Premature cognitive commitment. *Journal of Personality and Social Psychology, 41,* 1051–1063.

Chapman, L. J., & Chapman, J. P. (1967). Genesis of popular but erroneous psychodiagnostic categories. *Journal of Abnormal Psychology, 72,* 193–204.

Chapman, M. (1981). Pascual-Leone's theory of constructive cooperators: An introduction. *Human Development, 24,* 145–155.

Chapman, M. (1982). Action and interaction: The study of social cognition in Germany and the U.S. *Human Development, 25,* 295–302.

Chapman, M. (1988). *Constructive Evolution: Origins and development of Piaget's thought.* New York: Cambridge University Press.

Chapman, M., & Skinner, E. A. (1985). Action in development/development in action. In M. Frese & J. Sabini (Eds.), *Goal-directed behavior: Psychological theory and research on action.* Hillsdale, NJ: Erlbaum.

Charlesworth, W. R. (1966). Persistence of orienting and attending behavior in infants as a function of stimulus-locus uncertainty. *Child Development, 37,* 473–491.

Charlesworth, W. R. (1979). Ethology: Understanding the other half of intelligence. In M. von Cranach, K. Foppa, W. Lepenies, & D. Ploog (Eds.), *Human ethology* (pp. 578–594). Cambridge: Cambridge University Press.

Charlesworth, W. R. (1983). An ethological approach to cognitive development. In C. J. Brai-

nerd (Ed.), *Recent advances in cognitive-development theory* (pp. 273–258). New York: Springer.

Chew, P. (1976). *The inner world of the middle-aged man.* New York: Macmillan.

Chi, M. T. H. (1978). Knowledge structures and memory development. In R. S. Siegler (Ed.), *Children's thinking: What develops?* Hillsdale, NJ: Erlbaum.

Chi, M. T. H., & Glaser, R. (1980). The measurment of expertise: Analysis of the development of knowledge and skill as a basis for assessing achievement. In E. L. Baker & E. S. Quellmalz (Eds.), *Educational testing and evaluation: Design, analysis and policy.* Beverly Hills, CA: Sage.

Chi, M. T. H., Glaser, R., & Rees, E. (1983). Expertise in problem-solving. In R. Sternberg (Ed.), *Advances in the psychology of human intelligence* (pp. 7–76). Hillsdale, NJ: Erlbaum.

Childs, J. P. (1975) The use of the Transcendental Meditation program as a therapy with juvenile offenders. (Doctoral dissertation, University of Tennessee). *Dissertation Abstracts International 34,* 8A.

Chinen, A. B. (1990). Alfred North Whitehead and adult moral development. *Adult Development, 2. Models and methods in the study of adolescent and adult thought.*

Chomsky, N. (1965). *Aspects of the theory of syntax.* Cambridge, MA: MIT Press.

Chomsky, N. (1972). *Language and mind* (enlarged ed.). San Diego, CA: Harcourt Brace Jovanovich.

Chopra, D. (1987). *Creating health: Beyond prevention, toward perfection.* Boston: Houghton Mifflin.

Chopra, D. (1988). *The return of the Rishi.* Boston: Houghton Mifflin.

Chopra, D. (1989). *Quantum healing.* New York: Bantam.

Clausen, J. A. (1972). The life course of individuals. In M. W. Riley, M. Johnson, & A. Foner (Eds.), *Aging and society: A sociology of age stratification* (Vol. 3) (pp. 457–514). New York: Sage.

Clayton, V. (1975). Erikson's theory of human development as it applies to the aged: Wisdom as contradictory cognition. *Human Development, 18,* 119–128.

Clayton, V. (1982). Wisdom and intelligence: The nature and function of knowledge in the later years. *International Journal of Aging and Development, 15,* 315–323.

Clayton, V. P., & Birren, J. E. (1980). The development of wisdom across the life-span: A reexamination of an ancient topic. In P. B. Baltes & O. G. Brim, Jr. (Eds.), *Life-span development and behavior* (Vol. 3, pp. 103–135). New York: Academic Press.

Coan, R. W. (1977). *Hero, artist, sage, or saint?* New York: Columbia University Press.

Colby, A. (1975). *The relation between moral and cognitive development.* Unpublished manuscript, Harvard University, Cambridge, MA.

Colby, A., & Kohlberg, L. (1986). *The Measurement of Moral Judgment* (Vol. 1). New York: Cambridge University Press.

Colby, A., & Kohlberg, L. (1987). *The Measurement of Moral Judgment* (Vol. 2). New York: Cambridge University Press.

Colby, A., Kohlberg, L., Gibbs, J., & Lieberman, M. (1983). A longitudinal study of moral judgment. *Monographs of the Society for Research in Child Development, 48*(1, Serial No. 200).

Cole, M., & Means, B. (1981). *Comparative studies of how people think.* Cambridge, MA: Harvard University Press.

Cole, M., & Scribner, S. (1974). *Culture and thought: A psychological introduction.* New York: Wiley.

Cole, M., Sharp, D., & Lave, J. (1976). The cognitive consequences of education: Some empirical evidence of theoretical misgivings. *The Urban Review, 9,* 218–233.

Cole, S. (1979). Age and scientific performance. *American Journal of Sociology, 84,* 958–977.

Coleman, W. (1977). *Biology in the nineteenth century: Problems of form, function, and transformation.* Cambridge, MA: Cambridge University Press.

Commons, M. L., Armon, C., Kohlberg, L., Richards, F. A., Grotzer, T. A., & Sinnott, J. D. (Eds.). (1990). *Adult Development, 2, Models and methods in the study of adolescent and adult thought.* New York: Praeger.

Commons, M. L., & Hallinan, P. W. with Fong, W., & McCarthy, K. (1989). Intelligent pattern recognition: Hierarchical organization of concepts and hierarchies. In M. L. Commons, R. J. Herrnstein, S. M. Kosslyn, & D. B. Mumford (Eds.), *Quantitative Analyses of Behavior, 9, Computational and clinical approaches to pattern recognition and concept formation.*

Commons, M. L., & Richards, F. A. (1978). *The structural analytic stage of development: A Piagetian postformal stage.* Paper presented at the Annual Meeting of the Western Psychological Association, San Francisco.

Commons, M. L., & Richards, F. A. (1984a). A general model of stage theory. In M. L. Commons, F. A. Richards, & C. Armon (Eds.), *Beyond formal operations: Late adolescent and adult cognitive development* (pp. 120–140). New York: Praeger.

Commons, M. L., & Richards, F. A. (1984b). Applying the general stage model. In M. L. Commons, F. A. Richards, and C. Armon (Eds.), *Beyond formal operations: Late adolescent and adult cognitive development* (pp. 141–157). New York: Praeger.

Commons, M. L., Richards, F. A., & Armon, C. (1984). *Beyond formal operations: Late adolescent and adult cognitive development.* New York: Praeger.

Commons, M. L., Richards, F. A., & Kuhn, D. (1982). Systematic and metasystematic reasoning: A case for levels of reasoning beyond Piaget's stage of formal operations. *Child Development, 53,* 1058–1068.

Commons, M. L., Sinnott, J. D., Richards, F. A., & Armon, C. (Eds.). (1989). *Adult development, 1, Comparisons and applications of adolescent and adult developmental models.* New York: Praeger.

Cook-Greuter, S. R. (1990). Maps for living: Ego development stages from symbiosis to conscious universal embeddedness. *Adult Development, 2.*

Cook-Greuter, S. R. (in press). Defining and measuring post-conventional ego stages, especially stages 5/6 and 6. *Adult Development.*

Cooper, M. J., & Aygen, M. M. (1979). Transcendental Meditation in the management of hypercholesterolemia. *Journal of Human Stress, 4,* 24–27.

Cowan, P. A. (1978). *Piaget: With feeling.* New York: Holt, Rinehart & Winston.

Craik, F., & Simon, E. (1980). Age difference in memory: The role of attention and depth of processing. In L. Poon, J. Fozard, L. Cermak, D. Arenberg, & L. Thompson (Eds.), *New directions in memory and aging.* Hillsdale, NJ: Erlbaum.

Craik, K. H., & Sarbin, T. R. (1963). Effect of covert alterations of clock rate upon time estimations and personal tempo. *Journal of Perceptual Motor Skills, 16,* 597–610.

Cranson, R. W. (1989) Intelligence and the growth of intelligence in Maharishi's Vedic Psychology and twentieth century psychology. (Doctoral dissertation, Maharishi International University). *Dissertation Abstracts International.*

Cross, T. G. (1978). Mother's speech and its associations with rate of linguistic development in young children. In N. Waterson & C. Snow (Eds.), *The development of communication.* New York: Wiley.

Csikszentmihalyi, M. *Beyond boredom and anxiety.* (1975). San Francisco: Jossey-Bass.

Csikszentmihalyi, M., & Massimini, F. (1985). On the psychological selection of biocultural information. *New ideas in psychology, 3*(2), 115–138.

Csikszentmihalyi, M. & Rathunde (1990). The psychology of wisdom: An evolutionary interpretation. In R. J. Sternberg (Ed). *Wisdom: Its nature, origins and development.* New York: Cambridge University Press.

Curley, E. M. (1969). *Spinoza's metaphysics: An essay in interpretation.* Cambridge, MA: Harvard University Press.

Curtiss, S., Fromkin V., Krashen S., Rigler, D. & Rigler M. (1974). The linguistic development of Genie. *Language, 50,* 544.

Cytrynbaum, S., Blum, L., Patrick, R., Stein, J., Wadner, D., & Wilk, C. (1980). Midlife development: Personality and social systems perspective. In L. Poon (Ed.), *Aging in the 1980s.* Washington, D.C.: American Psychological Association.

Damon, W. (1983). *Social personality development.* New York: Norton.

Damon, W., & Hart, D. (1988). *Self-understanding in childhood and adolescence.* New York: Cambridge University Press.

Darwin, C. (1855). *On the origin of the species.* London: Murray.

Darwin, C. (1877). A biographical sketch. *Mind,* July, pp. 285–295.

Darwin, C. (1897). *Expressions of the emotions in man and animals.* Norwalk, CT: Appleton-Century-Crofts.

Davidson, L., McKernon, P., & Gardner, H. (1981). The acquisition of song: A developmental approach. *Documentary report of the Ann Arbor Symposium: Application of psychology to the teaching and learning of music.* Reston, VA: Music Educators National Conference.

Davies, J. (1974). Transcendental Meditation: Its nature, effects, and relation to psychotherapy and self-actualization. In D. W. Orme-Johnson & J. T. Farrow (Eds.), *Scientific research on the Transcendental Meditation program: Collected papers,* (Vol. 1, pp. 449–452). Rheinweiler, West Germany: MERU Press.

Davies, J. L., Alexander, C. N. (1989). Alleviating political violence through enhancing coherence in collective consciousness: Impact assessment analysis of the Lebanon War. *Proceedings of the American Political Science Association Meeting.*

De Casper, A. J., & Fifer, W. P. (1980). Of human bonding: Newborns prefer their mother's voice. *Science, 208,* 1174–1176.

Deci, E. L., & Ryan, R. M. (1985). *Intrinsic motivation and self-determination in human behavior.* New York: Plenum.

Deci, E. L. (1980). *The psychology of self-determination.* Lexington, MA: Lexington.

Decker, S. N., & DeFries, J. C. (1980). Cognitive abilities in families with reading disabled children. *Journal of Learning Disabilities, 13,* 517–522.

DeLong H. (1970). *A profile of mathematical logic.* Reading, MA: Addison-Wesley.

Demetriou, A., & Efklides, A. (1985). Structure and sequence of formal and postformal thought: General patterns and individual differences. *Child Development, 56*(4), 1062–1091.

Denmark, F. L. (1980). *Psychology, the leading edge.* New York: New York Academy of Sciences.

Denney, N. W. (1979). Problem solving in later adulthood: Intervention research. In P. B. Baltes & O. G. Brim, Jr. (Eds.), *Life-span development and behavior* (Vol. 2, pp. 37–66). New York: Academic Press.

de Vries, R. (1969). Constancy of generic identity in the years three to six. *Monographs of the Society for Research in Child Development, 34*(3).

Dewey, J., and Tufts, J. H. (1932). *Ethics* (rev. ed.). New York: Holt, Rinehart & Winston.

Dillbeck, M. C. (1982). Meditation and flexibility of visual perception and verbal problem solving. *Memory and Cognition, 10*(3), 207–215.

Dillbeck, M. C. (1983a). The Vedic psychology of the Bhagavad-Gita. *Psychologia, 26,* 62–72.

Dillbeck, M. C. (1983b). Testing the Vedic psychology of the Bhagavad-Gita. *Psychologia, 26,* 232–240.

Dillbeck, M. C. (1988). The self-interacting dynamics of consciousness as the source of the creative process in nature and in human life. *Modern Science and Vedic Science, 2,*(3) 245–278.

Dillbeck, M. C., & Abrams, A. I. (1987). The application of the Transcendental Meditation program in corrections. *International Journal of Comparative and Applied Criminal Justice,* 11, 111–132.

Dillbeck, M. C., & Alexander, C. N. (1989). Higher states of consciousness: Maharishi Mahesh Yogi's Psychology of human development. *Journal of Mind and Behavior, 10,* 4, 307–334.

Dillbeck, M. C., Assimakis, P. O., Raimondi, D., Orme-Johnson, D. W., & Rowe, R. (1986). Longitudinal effects of the Transcendental Meditation and TM-Sidhi program on cognitive ability and cognitive style. *Perceptual and Motor Skills, 62,* 721–738.

Dillbeck, M. C., Banus, C. B., Polanzi, C., & Landrith, G. S., III (1988). Test of a field model of consciousness and social change: The Transcendental Meditation and TM-Sidhi program and decreased urban crime. *The Journal of Mind and Behavior, 9,* 457–485.

Dillbeck, M. C., & Bronson, E. C. (1981). Short-term longitudinal effects of the Transcen-

dental Meditation technique on EEG power and coherence. *International Journal of Neuroscience, 15,* 151-157.

Dillbeck, M. C., Cavanaugh, K. L., Glen, T., Orme-Johnson, D. W., & Mittlefehldt, V. (1987). Effects of the Transcendental Meditation and TM-Sidhi program on quality of life indicators: Consciousness as a field. *The Journal of Mind and Behavior, 8,* 67-104.

Dillbeck, M. C. & Orme-Johnson, D. W. (1987). Physiological differences between Transcendental Meditation and rest. *American Psychologist, 42,* 879-881.

Dillbeck, M. C., Orme-Johnson, D. W., & Wallace, R. K. (1981). Frontal EEG coherence, H-reflex recovery, concept learning, and the TM-Sidhi program. *International Journal of Neuroscience, 15,* 151-157.

Dillbeck, M. C., & Vesley, S. A. (1986). Participation in the Transcendental Meditation Program and frontal EEG coherence during concept learning. *International Journal of Neuroscience, 15,* 44-55.

Dittmann, F. (1973). *Kultur und Leistung.* Saarbrücken: Verlag der SSIP-Schriften.

Dittmann, F. (1978, August). *Soziale Kompetenz in interpersonellen Beziehungen.* Konstanz: Universität Konstanz, Zentrum I Bildungsforschung, (Arbeitsbericht 8).

Dittmann-Kohli, F. (1980). Menschenbildung: Fähigkeiten für den Umgang mit sich selbst und anderen. In G. Grohs, J. Schwerdtfeger, & T. Strom (Eds.), *Kulturelle Identität im Wandel: Beiträge zum Verhältnis von Bildung, Entwicklung, Religion* (pp. 119-128). Stuttgart: Klett-Cotta.

Dittmann-Kohli, F. (1981a). Die Bedeutung psychologischer Konzepte für Bildungsprogramme in der dritten Welt. *Zeitschrift für Pädagogik* (Suppl. 16), 77-96.

Dittmann-Kohli, F. (1981b). Learning how to learn: A psychological approach to self-directed learning. *Education, 24,* 23-33.

Dittmann-Kohli, F. (1982). Theoretische Grundlagen der Analyse von Lebensbewältigung und Umwelt. In F. Dittmann-Kohli, N. Schreiber, & F. Möller, *Lebenswelt und Lebensbewältigung* (pp. 1-125). Konstanz, West Germany: Universität Konstanz, Sonderforschungsbereich 23, Forschungsbericht 35.

Dittmann-Kohli, F. (1983). Intelligenzförderung im höheren Erwachsenenalter. *Unterrichtswissenschaft, 4,* 361-369.

Dittmann-Kohli, F. (1984a). Weisheit als mögliches Ergebnis der Intelligenzentwicklung im Erwachsenenalter. *Sprache und Kognition, 2,* 112-132.

Dittmann-Kohli, F. (1984b). Die Bewältigung von Entwicklungsaufgaben bei Lehrlingen: Analyse- und Interventionsgesichtspunkte. In E. Olbrich & E. Todt (Eds.), *Coping im Jugendalter* (pp. 227-267). Berlin, West Germany: Springer.

Dittmann-Kohli, F. (1986). Problem identification and definition as important aspects of adolescent's coping with normative life tasks. In R. K. Silbereisen, K. Eyferth, & G. Rudinger (Eds.), *Development as action in context* (pp. 19-37). Berlin, West Germany: Springer.

Dittmann-Kohli, F. (1987). Intelligenz im Alter: Sind die üblichen Testaufgaben ausreichend? *Zeitschrift für Sozialisationsforschung und Erziehungssoziologie, 2,* 84-100.

Dittmann-Kohli, F. (1988). Sinndimensionen des Lebens im frühen und späten Erwachsenenalter. In H.-W. Bierhoff & R. Nienhaus (Eds.), *Beiträge zur Psychogerontologie.* (pp. 73-115). Marburg: Universität Marburg.

Dittmann-Kohli, F. (1989). Erfolgreiches Altern aus subjektiver Sicht. In M. M. Baltes, M. Kohli, & K. Sames (Eds.), *Erfolgreiches Altern: Bedingungen und Variationen.* Bern: Huber. In press.

Dittmann-Kohli, F. (1990). Self and meaning of life: Central domains of personality development in adulthood. In T. Rapoport, E. Ben-Ari & H. Haste (Eds.) *Changing lives, lives in change: Interdisciplinary study of the life course.* In press.

Dittmann-Kohli, F., Schreiber, N. & Möller, F., (1982). *Lebenswelt und Lebensbewältigung.* Konstanz, West Germany: Universitat Konstanz, Sonderforschungsbereich 23, Forschungsbericht 35.

Dixon, C. (1989). Consciousness and cognitive development: *A six-month longitudinal study of four-year-old children practicing Transcendental Meditation.* (Doctoral dissertation, Maharishi International University). *Dissertation Abstracts International.*

Dixon, R. A., & Baltes, P. B. (1986). Toward life-span research on the functions and pragmatics of intelligence. In R. J. Sternberg & R. K. Wagner (Eds.), *Practical intelligence: Origins of competence in the everyday world* (pp. 203–235). New York: Cambridge University Press.

Dörner, D. (1976). *Problemlösen als Informationsverarbeitung.* Stuttgart: Kohlhammer.

Dörner, D. (1982). The ecological conditions of thinking. In D. R. Griffin (Ed.), *Animal mind—human mind.* Berlin: Life Sciences Research Report 21, Dahlem-Konferenzen: Springer.

Dörner, D. (1983). Denken, Problemlösen und Intelligenz. In G. Lüer (Ed.), *Bericht über den 33. Kongress der Deutschen Gesellschaft für Psychologie in Mainz 1982,* Göttingen: Hogrefe.

Dörner, D., & Reither, F. (1978). Über das Problemlösen in sehr komplexen Realitätsbereichen. *Zeitschrift für Experimentelle und Angewandte Psychologie, 15,* 527–551.

Drabkin, I. E., & Drake, S. (1960). *Galileo Galilei on motion and on mechanics.* Madison: University of Wisconsin Press.

Drake, S. (1970). *Galileo studies: Personality, tradition and revolution.* Ann Arbor: University of Michigan Press.

Dreyfus, H. C., & Dreyfus, S. E. (1986). *Mind over machine: The power of human intuition and expertise in the era of computers.* New York: The Free Press.

Druker, S. M. (1989). *Unified Field based ethics: Vedic psychology's description of a highest stage of moral development.* Manuscript submitted for publication.

Dustman, R. E., & Beck, E. C. (1969). The effects of maturation and aging on the waveform of visually evoked potentials. *Electroencephalography and Clinical Neurophysiology, 265,* 2–11.

Eagle, M. N. (1984). *Recent developments in psychoanalysis.* New York: McGraw-Hill.

Eckensberger, L. H., & Silbereisen, R. K. (Eds.). (1980). *SozialeKognitionen: Modelle, Theorien, Methoden, Anwendung.* Stuttgart: Klett-Cotta.

Eddington, A. (1958). *The nature of the physical world.* Ann Arbor, MI: University of Michigan Press.

Edelman, G. M., & Mountcastle, V. B. (1982). *The mindful brain.* Cambridge, MA: MIT Press.

Edelstein, W., & Noam, G. (1982). Regulatory structures of the self and "postformal" stages in adulthood. *Human Development, 25,* 407–422.

Edinger, E. (1973). *Ego and archetype.* Baltimore: Penguin.

Eichorn, D. H., Hunt, J. W., & Honzik, M. P. (1981). Experience, personality, and IQ: Adolescence to middle age. In D. H. Eichorn, J. A. Clausen, N. Haan, M. P. Honzik, & P. H. Mussen (Eds.), *Present and past in middle life* (pp. 89–116). New York: Academic Press.

Einstein, A. (1950). *The meaning of relativity.* Princeton, NJ: Princeton University Press.

Ekman, P. (1979). About brows: Emotional and conversational signals. In M. Cranach, K. Poppa, W. Lepenies, & D. Ploog (Eds.), *Human ethology.* New York: Cambridge University Press.

Eliot, T. S. (1978). *Ash Wednesday.* New York: Putnam. (Originally published in 1930.)

Elkind, D. (1979). Cognitive development and psychopathology: Observations on egocentrism and ego defense. In D. Elkind, *The child and society.* New York: Oxford University Press.

Elkind, D., & Weiss, J. (1967). Studies in perceptual development: III. Perceptual exploration. *Child Development, 38,* 553–561.

Ellis, K., Enqvist, K., Nanopoulous, D. V., & Zwimer, N. F. (1986). Aspects of the super-unification of strong, electro-weak, and gravitational interaction. *Nuclear Physics 3, 276,* 14–70.

Emde, R., Gaensbauer, T., & Harmon, R. (1976). Emotional expression in infancy: A biobehavioral study. *Psychological Issues, 10*(37).

Endler, N. S. (1981). Interactionism comes of age. In M. P. Zanna, E. T. Higgins, & C. P. Herman (Eds.), *Consistency in social behavior: The Ontario Symposium* (Vol. 2). Hillsdale, NJ: Erlbaum.

Enriques, F. (1929). *The historic development of logic.* New York: Holt, Rinehart & Winston.

Eppley, K., Abrams, A., & Shear, J. (1989). *The differential effects of relaxation techniques on trait anxiety: A meta-analysis. Journal of Clinical Psychology, 45,* 6, 957–974.

Epstein, H. T. (1974a). Phrenoblysis: Special brain and mind growth periods. *Developmental Psychobiology, 7,* 207–224.

Epstein, H. T. (1974b). Phrenoblysis: Special brain and mind growth periods. II. Human mental development. *Developmental Psychobiology, 7,* 217–228.

Epstein, H. T. (1978). Growth spurts during brain development: Implications for educational policy and practice. In J. S. Chall & A. F. Mirsky (Eds.), *Education and the brain.* Chicago: University of Chicago Press.

Epstein, H. T. (1980). EEG developmental stages. *Developmental Psychobiology, 13,* 629–631.

Erdynast, A., Armon, C. and Nelson, J. (1978). Cognitive-developmental conceptions of the true and the beautiful. *Proceedings of the 8th Annual Conference of Piaget and the Helping Professions.* Los Angeles: University of California Press.

Ericsson, K. A. & Crutcher, R. J. (in press). The nature of exceptional performance. In P. B. Baltes, D. L. Featherman, & R. M. Lerner (Eds.), *Life-span development and behavior* (Vol. 10). Hillsdale, NJ: Erlbaum.

Erikson, E. H. (1950). *Childhood and society.* New York: Norton.

Erikson, E. H. (1958). *Young man Luther.* New York: Norton.

Erikson, E. H. (1959). Identity and the life cycle. *Psychological Issues Monograph, 1.*

Erikson, E. H. (1963). *Childhood and Society.* New York: Norton.

Erikson, E. H. (1968a). Life cycle. In *International encyclopedia of the social sciences. 9,* 286–292 New York: The Free Press.

Erikson, E. H. (1968b). *Identity, youth and crisis.* New York: Norton.

Erikson, E. H. (1969). *Gandhi's truth.* New York: Norton.

Erikson, E. H. (Ed.) (1978). *Adulthood.* New York: Norton.

Erikson, E. H. (1982). *The life cycle completed: A review.* New York: Norton.

Erlich, G. C. (1984). *Family themes and Hawthorne's fiction: The tenacious web.* New Brunswick, N.J: Rutgers University Press.

Farrell, M. P., & Rosenberg, S. D. (1981). *Men at midlife.* Boston: Auburn.

Farrow, J. T., & Hebert, J. R. (1982). Breath suspension during the Transcendental Meditation technique. *Psychosomatic Medicine, 44*(2), 133–153.

Featherman, D. L. (1980). Schooling and occupational careers: Constancy and change in worldly success. In O. G. Brim, Jr., & J. Kagan (Eds.), (pp. 675–738). *Constancy and change in human development.* Cambridge, MA: Harvard University Press.

Featherman, D. L. (1983). Life-span perspectives in social science research. In P. B. Baltes & O. G. Brim, Jr. (Eds.), *Life-span development and behavior* (Vol. 5, pp. 1–59). New York: Academic Press.

Feldman, D. H. (1980). *Beyond universals in cognitive development.* Norwood, NJ: Ablex.

Fengler, A. P. (1976, October). *Productivity and representation: The elderly legislator in state politics.* Paper presented at the Meeting of the Gerontological Society, New York.

Feuer, L. (1974). *Einstein and the generations of science.* New York: Basic Books.

Feuerstein, R. (1979). *The dynamic assessment of retarded performers: The learning potential assessment device, theory, instruments, and techniques.* Baltimore: University Park.

Fichte, J. G. (1956) In R. M. Chrisholm (Ed.), *The vocation of man.* Indianapolis: Bobbs-Merrill.

Filene, P. G. (1985). The "secret desire" of Lincoln Steffens. *Harvard Magazine,* Sept–Oct., pp. 72A–H.

Fischer, K. W. (1980a). Learning as the development of organized behavior. *Journal of Structural Learning, 3,* 253–267.

Fischer, K. W. (1980b). A theory of cognitive development: The control and construction of hierarchies of skills. *Psychological Review, 87,* 477–531.

Fischer, K. W. (1987). Relations between brain and cognitive development. *Child Development, 57,* 623–632.

Fischer, K. W., & Bullock, D. (1981). Patterns of data: Sequence, synchrony, and constraint

in cognitive development. In K. W. Fischer (Ed.), *Cognitive development.* San Francisco: Jossey-Bass.

Fischer, K. W., & Bullock, D. (1984). Cognitive development in middle childhood: Conclusions and new directions. In W. A. Collins (Ed.), *Development during middle childhood: The years from six to twelve.* Washington, DC: National Academy Press.

Fischer, K. W., & Corrigan, R. (1981). A skill approach to language development. In R. E. Stark (Ed.), *Language behavior in infancy and early childhood.* Amsterdam: Elsevier/ North Holland.

Fischer, K. W., & Elmendorf, D. (1986). Becoming a different person: Transformations in personality and social behavior. In M. Perlmutter (Ed.), *Minnesota symposium on child psychology* (vol. 18, pp. 137–178). Hillsdale, N.J.: Erlbaum.

Fischer, K. W., & Farrar, M. J. (1987). Generalizations about generalization: How a theory of skill development explains both generality and specificity. *International Journal of Psychology, 22,* 643–677.

Fischer, K. W., Hand, H. H., & Russell, S. L. (1984). The development of abstractions in adolescence and adulthood. In M. L. Commons, F. A. Richards, & C. Armon (Eds.), *Beyond formal operations: Late adolescent and adult cognitive development* (pp. 43–73). New York: Praeger.

Fischer, K. W., & Kenny, S. L. (1986). The environmental conditions for discontinuities in the development of abstractions. In R. Mines & K. Kitchener (Eds.), *Adult cognitive development: Methods and models* (pp. 57–75). New York: Praeger.

Fischer, K. W., Kenny, S. L., & Rose, S. (1987). *Levels and variations in the development of arithmetic concepts.* Manuscript in preparation. Harvard University, Cambridge, MA.

Fischer, K. W., & Lamborn, S. (1989). Mechanisms of variation in developmental levels: Cognitive and emotional transitions during adolescence. In A. de Ribaupierre (Ed.), *Transition mechanisms in child development.* New York: Cambridge University Press.

Fischer, K. W., & Pipp, S. L. (1984). Processes of cognitive development: Optimal level and skill acquisition. In R. J. Sternberg (Ed.), *Mechanisms of cognitive development.* San Francisco: Freeman.

Fischer, K. W., Pipp, S. L., & Bullock, D. (1984). Detecting discontinuities in development: Method and measurement. In R. Harmon & R. Emde (Eds.), *Continuities and discontinuities in development.* New York: Plenum.

Fischer, K. W., & Silvern, L. (1985). Stages and individual differences in cognitive development. *Annual Review of Psychology, 36,* 613–648.

Fischer, K., and Watson, M. (1981). Explaining the Oedipus conflict. In K. W. Fischer (Ed.), *Cognitive development* (pp. 79–92). San Francisco: Jossey-Bass.

Fitzgerald, J. M. (1980). Learning and development: Mutual bases in a dialectical perspective. *Human Development, 23,* 376–381.

Flavell, J. H. (1963). *The developmental psychology of Jean Piaget.* New York: Van Nostrand Reinhold.

Flavell, J. H. (1970). Cognitive changes in adulthood. In L. R. Goulet & P. B. Baltes (Eds.), *Life-span developmental psychology: Research and theory.* New York: Academic Press.

Flavell, J. H. (1971a). Comments on Beilin's "The development of physical concepts." In T. Mischel (Ed.), *Cognitive development and epistemology.* New York: Academic Press.

Flavell, J. H. (1971b). Stage-related properties of cognitive development. *Cognitive Psychology, 2,* 421–453.

Flavell, J. H. (1972). An analysis of cognitive-developmental sequences. *Genetic Psychology Monographs, 86,* 279–350.

Flavell, J. H. (1977). *Cognitive development.* Englewood Cliffs, NJ: Prentice-Hall.

Flavell, J. H. (1982). On cognitive development. *Child Development, 53,* 1–10.

Flavell, J. H. (1983). Structures, stages, and sequences in cognitive development. In W. A. Collins (Ed.), *Minnesota symposium on child psychology* (Vol. 15). Hillsdale, NJ: Erlbaum.

Flavell, J. H. (1984). Discussion. In R. J. Sternberg (Ed.), *Mechanisms of cognitive development.* San Francisco: Freeman.

Flavell, J. H. (1985). *Cognitive development* (2nd ed.). Englewood Cliffs, NJ: Prentice-Hall.

Flavell, J. H., and Wohlwill, J. F. (1969). Formal and functional aspects of cognitive development. In D. Elkind & J. H. Flavell (Eds.), *Studies in cognitive development: Essays in honor of Jean Piaget*. New York: Oxford University Press.

Flechsig, K. H. (1980). Learning how to learn: Historical background and psychological perspectives in Germany. In E. A. Yoloye & K. F. Flechsig (Eds.), *Educational research for development* (pp. 170–183). Bonn: German Foundation of International Development.

Fodor, J. A. (1986). The modularity of the mind. In Z. W. Pylyshyn & W. Demopoulos (Eds.). *Meaning and cognitive structures: Issues in the computational theory of mind*. Norwood, N.J.: Ablex Publishers.

Fodor, J. A. (1975). *The language of thought*. New York: Crowell.

Fodor, J. A. (1983). *The modularity of mind*. Cambridge, MA: MIT Press.

Ford, D. (1982). *The organization and development of human behavior: An open systems approach*. Unpublished manuscript, Pennsylvania State University, College of Human Development, University Park, PA.

Ford, M. E., & Ford, D. H. (Eds.). (1987). *Humans as self-constructing living systems: Putting the framework to work*. Hillsdale, NJ: Erlbaum.

Ford, M. E., & Tisak, M. S. (1983). A further search for social intelligence. *Journal of Educational Psychology, 75*, 196–206.

Forman, R. K. C. (1990). *The problem of pure consciousness*. New York: Oxford University Press.

Fourcher, L. A. (1981). A developmental scheme is a bad dialectic. *Human Development, 24,* `172–198.

Fowler, J. (1976). Stages in faith: The structural developmental approach. In T. Hennessey (Ed.), *Values and moral development*. New York: Paulist Press.

Fowler, J. (1981). *Stages of faith: The psychology of human development and the quest for meaning*. New York: Harper & Row.

Fraisse, P. (1964). *The psychology of time*. London: Eyre & Spottiswoode.

Frankenhaeuser, M. (1979). Psychoneuro-endocrine approaches to the study of emotion as related to stress and coping. In H. E. Howe (Ed.), *1978 Nebraska Symposium on Motivation*. Lincoln: University of Nebraska Press.

Frege, G. (1950). *The Foundations of Arithmetic* (J. L. Austin, Trans.). Oxford: Oxford University Press.

French, T. M. (1952). *The integration of behavior: Basic postulates* (Vol. 1). Chicago: University of Chicago Press.

Freud, S. (1930). *Civilization and its discontents*. London: Hogarth.

Freud, S. (1949). *An outline of psychoanalysis* (J. Strachey, Tr.). New York: Norton.

Freud, S. (1963). *Introductory lectures on psychoanalysis: Standard edition* (Vols. 15 & 16). London: Hogarth Press. (Originally published in 1916–1917.)

Frew, D. R. (1974). Transcendental Meditation and productivity. *Academy of Management Journal, 17,* pp. 362–368.

Fromm, E. (1975). *The anatomy of human destructiveness*. Greenwich, CT: Fawcett.

Funk, J. D. (1982). Beethoven: A transpersonal analysis. *ReVision, 5,* 1.

Funk, J. D. (1983). Music and fourfold vision. *ReVision, 6,* 1.

Funk, J. D. (1989). Postformal cognitive theory and developmental stages of musical composition. *Adult Development, 1. Comparisons and Applications of Adolescent and Adult Developmental Models,* 3–30.

Furth, H. G. (1981). *Piaget and knowledge: Theoretical formulations* (2nd ed.). Chicago: University of Chicago Press.

Fuster, (1980). *The prefrontal cortex*. New York: Raven Press.

Gackenbach, J., Cranson, R., & Alexander, C. N. (1986). Lucid dreaming, witnessing dreaming, and the Transcendental Meditation technique: A developmental relationship. *Lucidity Letter, 5*(2), 34–41.

Gackenbach, J., & LaBerge, S. (1988) *Conscious mind, sleeping brain*. New York: Plenum.

Gackenbach, J., Moorecroft, W., Alexander, C. N., & LaBerge, S. (1987). Physiological correlates of consciousness during sleep in a single TM practitioner. *Sleep Research, 16,* 230.

Gallistel, C. R. (1980). *The organization of action: A new synthesis.* Hillsdale, NJ: Erlbaum.

Gardner, H. (1979). Developmental psychology after Piaget: An approach in terms of symbolization. *Human Development, 22,* 73–88.

Gardner, H. (1980a). *Artful scribbles.* New York: Basic Books.

Gardner, H. (1980b). Cognition comes of age. Introduction to M. Piatelli-Palmarini (Ed.), *On language and learning.* Cambridge, MA: Harvard University Press.

Gardner, H. (1981). *The quest for mind: Piaget, Levi-Strauss, and the structuralist movement* (2nd ed.). Chicago: University of Chicago Press.

Gardner, H. (1982a). *Art, mind, and brain.* New York: Basic Books.

Gardner, H. (1982b). *Developmental Psychology* (2nd ed.). Boston: Little, Brown.

Gardner, H. (1983). *Frames of mind.* New York: Basic Books.

Gardner, H. (1984). The development of competence in culturally-defined domains. In R. Shweder & R. Levine (Eds.), *Culture theory.* New York: Cambridge University Press.

Gardner, H., & Winner, E. (1982). First intimations of artistry. In S. Strauss (Ed.), *U-shaped behavioral growth.* New York: Academic Press.

Gardner, H., & Wolf, D. (1979). First drawings: Notes on the relationships between perception and production in the visual arts. In C. Nodine & D. Fisher (Eds.), *Perception and pictorial representation* (pp. 361–387). New York: Praeger.

Gardner, H., & Wolf, D. (1983). Waves and streams of symbolization. In D. R. Rogers & J. A. Sloboda (Eds.), *The acquisition of symbolic skills.* London: Plenum.

Gasparski, W. (1969). Zum Effizienzbegriff. *Kommunikation, 5,* 81–98.

Gaylord, C., Orme-Johnson, D., Travis, F. (1989). The effects of Transcendental Meditation and progressive muscle relaxation on EEG coherence, stress reactivity and mental health in black adults. *International Journal of Neuroscience, 46,* 77–86.

Gehmacher, E. (1975). *Lebensmanagment: Planungswissenschaft für die individuelle Daseinsgestaltung.* Stuttgart: Seewald.

Geisler, M. (1978). Therapeutische Wirkungen der Transzendentaltn Meditation auf Drogenkonsumenten. *Zeitschrift fur klinische Psychologie 7,*4: 235–255.

Gelderloos, P. (1987). *Valuation and Transcendental Meditation.* Lelystad, The Netherlands: Soma Scientific Publisher.

Gelderloos, P., & Berg, W. P., van den (1989). Maharishi's TM-Sidhi program: Participating in the infinite creativity of nature to enlighten the totality of the cosmic psyche in all aspects of life. *Modern Science and Vedic Science, 2*(4), 373–412.

Gelderloos, P., & Beto, Z. H. A. D. (1989). The Transcendental Meditation and TM-Sidhi program and reported experiences of transcendental consciousness. *Psychologia, 32*(2), 91–103.

Gelderloos, P., Lockie & Chuttoorgoon (1987). Field independence of students at Maharishi School of the Age of Enlightenment and a Montessori school. *Perceptual and Motor Skills, 65,* 613–614.

Gelman, R., & Gallistel, R. (1978). *The child's understanding of number.* Cambridge, MA: Harvard University Press.

Gelman, R., & Spelke, E. (1981). The development of thoughts about animate and inanimate objects: Implications for research on social cognition. In J. H. Flavell & L. Ross (Eds.), *Social cognitive development: Frontiers and possible futures* (pp. 43–66). Cambridge: Cambridge University Press.

Geschwind, N. (1964). The development of the brain and the evolution of language. *Monograph Series on Languages and Linguistics, 17,* 155–169.

Getzels, J., & Csikszentmihalyi, M. (1976). *The creative vision.* New York: Wiley.

Ghiselin, B. (1952). *The creative process.* New York: Mentor.

Gibson, E. J. (1982). The concept of affordances in development: The renascence of functionalism. In W. A. Collins (Ed.), *Minnesota Symposia on Child Development* (Vol. 15). Hillsdale, NJ: Erlbaum.

Gibson, E. J., & Spelke, E. S. (1983). The development of perception. In J. H. Flavell & E. M. Markman (Eds.), *Handbook of child psychology: Cognitive development* (Vol. 3). New York: Wiley.

Gilligan, C. (1977). In a different voice: Women's conceptions of self and of morality. *Harvard Educational Review, 47,* 481–517.

Gilligan, C. (1982). *In a different voice: Psychological theory and women's development.* Cambridge, MA: Harvard University Press.

Gilligan, C. (1986a). Remapping the moral domain: New images of the self in relationship. In T. C. Heller, M. Sosna, & D. Wellberry (Eds.), *Reconstructing individualism: Autonomy, individuality and the self in Western thought.* Stanford, CA: Stanford University Press.

Gilligan, C. (1986b) Exit-voice dilemmas in adolescent development. In A. Forley, M. McPherson, & G. O'Donnell (Eds.), *Development, democracy, and the art of trespassing: Essays in honor of Albert O. Hirschman.* Notre Dame, IN: University of Notre Dame Press.

Gilligan, C. (1987a). Moral orientation and moral development. In E. F. Kittay and D. T. Meyers (Eds.) *Women and moral theory.* Totowa, NJ: Rowman and Littlefield.

Gilligan, C. (1987b). Adolescent development reconsidered. In C. E. Irwin (Ed.), *Adolescent social behavior and health.* San Francisco: Jossey-Bass.

Gilligan, C., & Belenky, M. (1980). A naturalistic study of abortion decisions. In R. Selman, & R. Yardo (Eds.), *Clinical-developmental psychology.* San Francisco: Jossey-Bass.

Gilligan, C., Brown, L., & Rogers, A. (in press). Psyche embedded: A place for body, relationships, and culture in personality theory. In A. Rabin (Ed.), *Studying persons and lives.* New York: Springer-Verlag.

Gilligan, C., & Murphy, J. M. (1979). Development from adolescence to adulthood: The philosopher and the dilemma of the fact. In D. Kuhn (Ed.), *Intellectual development beyond childhood.* San Francisco: Jossey-Bass.

Gilligan, C., & Wiggins, G. (1987). The origins of morality in early childhood relationships. In J. Kagan & S. Lamb (Eds.), *The emergence of morality in young children.* Chicago: The University of Chicago Press.

Gilligan, J. (1976). Psychoanalytic theory and morality. In T. Licona (Ed.), *Moral development and behavior.* New York: Holt, Rinehart & Winston.

Ginzburg, H., & Opper, S. (1979). *Piaget's theory of intellectual development: An introduction* (2nd ed.). Englewood Cliffs, NJ: Prentice-Hall.

Ginzburg, H., & Opper, S. (1988). *Piaget's theory of intellectual development: An introduction* (3rd ed.). Englewood Cliffs, NJ: Prentice-Hall.

Gladwin, T. (1970). *East is a big bird.* Cambridge, MA: Harvard University Press.

Glaser, J. L., Brind, J. L., Eisner, M., Vogelman, J., Dillbeck, M., Chopra, D., & Wallace, R. K. (1987). Elevated serum dehydro-3-epiandrosterone sulfate levels in older practitioners of the Transcendental Meditation and TM-Sidhi programs. *Proceedings of the American Aging Association, 17,* 5.

Glaser, R. (1981). The future of testing: A research agenda for cognitive psychology and psychometrics. *American Psychologist, 36,* 923–936.

Glass, A. L., & Holyoak, K. J. (1986). *Cognition.* New York: Random House.

Globerson, T. (1986). When do structural changes underlie behavioral changes? In I. Levin (Ed.), *Stage and structure: Reopening the debate.* Norwood, NJ: Ablex.

Golan, N. (1981). *Passing through transitions.* NY: The Free Press.

Goldman-Rakic, P. (1987). Connectionist theory and the biological basis of cognitive development. *Child Development, 58,* 601–622.

Goldschmidt, M. I., & Bentler, P. M. (1968). *Manual: Concept assessment kit-conservation.* San Diego: Educational and Industrial Testing Service.

Goleman, D. (1972). The Buddha on meditation and states of consciousness. *Journal of Transpersonal Psychology, 4,* 1–44, 151–210.

Gollin, E. S. (Ed.). (1981). *Developmental plasticity: Behavioral and biological aspects of variations in development.* New York: Academic Press.

Gooden, W. E. (1980). "Development of Black Men in Early Adulthood." (Doctoral dissertation, Yale University). New Haven, CT.

Goodman, G. S. (1980). Picture memory: How the action schema affects retention. *Cognitive Psychology, 12,* 473–495.

Gore, S. W., Abrams, A., & Ellis, G. (in press). The effect of statewide implementation of the Maharishi Technology of the Unified Field in the Vermont Department of Corrections. In R. A. Chalmers, G. Clements, H. Schenkluhn, & M. Weinless (Eds.), *Scientific research on Maharishi's Transcendental Meditation and TM-Sidhi programme: Collected papers* (Vol. 4, pp. 2453–2472). Vlodrop, The Netherlands: MVU Press.

Gottlieb, D. E., Taylor, S. E., & Ruderman, A. (1977). Cognitive bases of children's moral judgments. *Developmental Psychology, 12,* 473–495.

Gould, R. L. (1972). The phases of adult life: A study in developmental psychology. *The American Journal of Psychiatry, 129,* 521–531.

Gould, R. L. (1979). *Transformations: Growth and change in adult life.* New York: Simon & Schuster.

Gould, S. J. (1981). *The mismeasure of man.* New York: Norton.

Gould, S. J. (1984). Transformations during early and middle adult years. In N. J. Smelser & E. H. Erikson (Eds.), *Themes of work and love in adulthood.* Cambridge, MA: Harvard University Press.

Govinda, L. A. (1961). *Die psychologische Haltung der frühbuddhistischen Philosophie.* Wiesbaden: Löwit.

Greenacre, P. (1959). Play in relation to the creative imagination. *Psychoanalytic study of the child.* New York: International Universities Press.

Grossberg, S. (1980). How does a brain build a cognitive code? *Psychological Review, 87,* 1–51.

Gruber, H. E. (1973). Courage and cognitive growth in children and scientists. In M. Schwebel & J. Ralph (Eds.), *Piaget in the classroom* (pp. 73–105). New York: Basic Books.

Gruber, H. E. (1980). And the bush was not consumed: The evolving systems approach to creativity. In S. Modgil & C. Modgil (Eds.), *Towards a Theory of Psychological Development.* N.F.E.R.

Gruber, H. E. (1981). *Darwin on man* (2nd ed.). Chicago: University of Chicago Press.

Gruber, H. E. (1984). The emergence of a sense of purpose: A cognitive study of young Darwin. In M. L. Commons, F. A. Richards, & C. Armon (Eds.), *Beyond formal operations: Late adolescent and adult cognitive development* (pp. 3–27). New York: Praeger.

Guilford, J. P. (1959). Three faces of intellect. *American Psychologist, 14,* 469–479.

Guntrip, H. (1968). Schizoid phenomena, object-relations and the self. London: Hogarth.

Guttmann, D. (1977). The cross-cultural perspective: Notes toward a comparative psychology of aging. In J. E. Birren & K. W. Schaie (Eds.), *Handbook of the psychology of aging.* New York: Van Nostrand Reinhold.

Haas, H., Fink, H., & Hartfelder, G. (1963). The placebo problem. *Psycho-Pharmacology Service Centre Bulletin,* 1–65.

Habermas, J. (1979). *Communication and the evolution of society.* Boston: Beacon.

Habermas, J. (1983). Interpretive social science vs. hermeaneutics. In N. Haan, R. Bellah, P. Rabinow, & W. Sullivan, (Eds.), *Social science as moral inquiry.* New York: Columbia University Press.

Hacker, W. (1978). *Allgemeine Arbeits- und Ingenieurpsychologie.* Berlin: Huber.

Hagelin, J. (1987). Is consciousness the unified field: A field theorist's perspective. *Modern Science and Vedic Science, 1*(1), 29–87.

Hagelin, J. (1990). Restructuring physics from its foundation in light of Maharishi's Vedic Science. *Modern Science and Vedic Science, 3,* 1.

Hall, G. S. (1922). *Senescence: The last half of life.* Norwalk, CT: Appleton-Century-Crofts.

Hand, H. H. (1982). The development of concepts of social interaction: Children's understanding of nice and mean. (Doctoral dissertation, University of Denver). *Dissertation Abstracts International, 42*(11), 4578B. University Microfilms No. DA8209747.

Hand, H. H., & Fischer, K. W. (1981, August). *The development of concepts of intentionality*

and responsibility in adolescence. Paper presented at the Sixth Biennial Meeting of the International Society for the Study of Behavioral Development, Toronto, Ontario.

Harber, K. D., & Hartley, A. A. (1983). Meaningfulness and problem-solving performance by younger and older adults. *Experimental Aging Research, 9,* 93–95.

Hareven, T. K., & Adams, K. (Eds). (1982). *Aging and life course transitions: An interdisciplinary perspective.* New York: Guilford.

Harter, S. (1983a). Development perspectives on the self-system. In P. H. Mussen & E. M. Heatherington (Eds.), *Handbook of Child psychology: Socialization, personality, and social development* (Vol. 4). New York: Wiley.

Harter, S. (1983b). Children's understanding of multiple emotions: A cognitive-developmental approach. In W. F. Overton (Ed.), *The relationship between social and cognitive development.* Hillsdale, NJ: Erlbaum.

Hartmann, N. (1954). *La nueva ontología* (E. Estiu, Trans.). Buenos Aires: Editorial Sudamericana.

Hasher, L., & Zacks, R. T. (1979). Automatic and effortful processes in memory. *Journal of Experimental Psychology: General, 108,* 356–388.

Haynes, C. T., Hebert, J. R., Reber, W., & Orme-Johnson, D. W. (1977). The psychophysiology of advanced participants in the Transcendental Meditation program: Correlations of EEG coherence, creativity, H-reflex recovery, and experience of transcendental consciousness. In D. W. Orme-Johnson & J. T. Farrow (Eds.), *Scientific research on the Transcendental Meditation program: Collected papers* (Vol. 1) (pp. 208–212). Rheinweiler, West Germany: MERU Press.

Heckhausen, H. (1980). *Motivation und Handeln.* Berlin: Springer.

Heckhausen, H. (1986). Achievement and motivation through the life span. In A. Sorensen, F. Weinert, & L. Sherrod (Eds.), *Human development and the life course* (pp. 445–466). Hillsdale, NJ: Erlbaum.

Hegel, G. W. F. (1892). *The logic of Hegel* (2nd ed. rev.) (W. Wallace, Trans.). Oxford: Oxford University Press.

Hegel, G. W. F. (1910). *Phenomenology of mind* (2nd ed. rev.) (J. B. Baillie, Trans.) London: George Allen and Unwin.

Hegel, G. W. F. (1957). J. Loewenberg (Ed.), *Hegel selections.* New York: Scribner. (Originally published in 1929.)

Hegel, G. W. F. (1979). *Phenomenology of spirit* (V. Miller, Trans.). Oxford: Oxford University Press. (Originally published in 1807.)

Heidbreder, E. (1933). *Seven psychologies.* Norwalk, CT: Appleton-Century-Crofts.

Heidegger, M. (1962). *Being and time.* New York: Harper & Row.

Heidegger, M. (1966). *Discourse on thinking.* (J. M. Anderson & E. H. Freund, Trans.). New York: Harper & Row. (Originally published in 1959.)

Heisenberg, W. (1962). *Physics and philosophy: The revolution in modern science.* New York: Harper & Row.

Helmholtz, H. L. F. (1950). *Uber der ursprund und Bedeuting die Geometrischen Axiome.* Berlin: Comenius. (Originally published in 1866.)

Helson, R., Mitchell, V., Hart, B. (1985). The lives of women who become autonomous. *Journal of Personality, 53,* 257–285.

Hempel, C. G. (1966). *Philosophy of natural science.* Englewood Cliffs, NJ: Prentice-Hall.

Henley, N. M. (1977). *Body politics: Power, sex, and nonverbal communication.* Englewood Cliffs, NJ: Prentice-Hall.

Herbert, J. I. (1985). Adult psychosocial development: *The evolution of the individual life structure of black male entrepreneurs.* (Doctoral dissertation, Yale University).

Hernandez, R. S. (1988). *The effects of task condition on the correlation of EEG coherence and full scale IQ.* (Doctoral dissertation, Maharishi International University). *Dissertation Abstracts International.* 49 (8B).

Higgins, E. T. (1981). Role taking and social judgement: Alternative developmental perspectives and processes. In J. H. Flavell and L. Ross (Eds.), *Social cognitive development: Frontiers and possible futures.* Cambridge: Cambridge University Press.

Higgins, E. T. (1987). Self-discrepancy: A theory relating self and affect. *Psychological Review, 94,* 319–340.

Hilgard, E. R. (1980). Consciousness in contemporary psychology. *Annual Review of Psychology, 31,* 1–26.

Hinde, R. A. (1974). *Biological bases of human social behavior.* New York: McGraw-Hill.

Hjelle, L. A. (1974). Transcendental Meditation and psychological health. *Perceptual and Motor Skills 39,* 623–628.

Hockett, C. F. (1960). The origin of speech. *Scientific American,* September, 88–96.

Hoff, E., Lappe, L., & Lempert, W. (1982). Sozialisationstheoretische Ueberlegungen zur Analyse von Arbeit, Betrieb und Beruf. *Soziale Welt, 33,* 508–536.

Hofstadter, D. (1980). *Goedel, Escher, Bach: An eternal golden braid.* New York: Vintage Books.

Holliday, S. G., & Chandler, M. J. (1986). Wisdom: Explorations in adult competence. In J. A. Meacham (Ed.), *Contributions to human development* (Vol. 17, pp. 1–96). Basel: Karger.

Holloway, R. (1986). *Mental capacity, language and play: A neoPiagetian exploratory study of aspects of cognitive development from 6 to 20 months.* Unpublished Doctoral Dissertation, York University, Toronto.

Holloway, R., Blake, J., & Pascual-Leone, J. (1987). *Relations between cognitive and communicative abilities in infancy.* Unpublished manuscript, York University, Toronto.

Holmes, D. S. (1984). Meditation and somatic arousal reduction: A review of experimental evidence. *American Psychologist, 39*(1), 1–10.

Holt, J. (1980). *An adult development psychobiography of C. G. Jung.* Unpublished senior thesis, Yale University School of Medicine, New Haven, CT.

Holt, W. R., Caruso, J. L., & Riley, J. B. (1978). Transcendental Meditation vs pseudo-meditation on visual choice reaction time. *Perceptual and Motor Skills, 46,* 726.

Hood, R. W., Jr. (1975). The construction and preliminary validation of a measure of reported mystical experience. *Journal for the Scientific Study of Religion, 14,* 29–41.

Horn, J. L. (1970). Organization of data on life-span development of human abilities. In L. R. Goulet & P. B. Baltes (Eds.), *Life-span developmental psychology: Research and theory* (pp. 423–466). New York: Academic Press.

Horn, J. L. (1976). Human abilities: A review of research and theory in the early 1970s. *Annual Review of Psychology, 27,* 437–486.

Horn, J. L. (1977). Personality and ability theory. In R. B. Cattell & R. M. Dreger (Eds.), *Handbook of modern personality theory* (pp. 139–165). New York: Wiley.

Horn, J. L. (1982a). The aging of human abilities. In B. B. Wolman (Ed.), *Handbook of developmental psychology* (pp. 847–870). Englewood Cliffs, NJ: Prentice-Hall.

Horn, J. L. (1982b). The theory of fluid and crystallized intelligence in relation to concepts of cognitive psychology and aging in adulthood. In F. I. M. Craik & S. Trehub (Eds.), *Aging and cognitive processes* (pp. 237–278). New York: Plenum.

Horn, J. L., & Donaldson, G. (1976). On the myth of intellectual decline in adulthood. *American Psychologist, 31,* 701–719.

Howe, M. J. A. (1982). Biographical evidence and the development of outstanding individuals. *American Psychologist, 37,* 1071–1081.

Hoyer, W. J. (1984, September). *Cognitive expertise is knowing what to do next.* Paper presented at the Workshop on Intellectual Functioning, Social Structure, and Aging. National Institute of Aging, Bethesda, MD.

Hubel, D. H., & Wiesel, T. N. (1953). Single-cell responses in striate cortex of kittens deprived of vision in one eye. *Journal of Neurophysiology, 26,* 1003–1017.

Hubel, D. H., & Wiesel, T. N. (1963). Shape and arrangement of columns in cat's striate cortex. *Journal of Physiology* (London), *165,* 559–568.

Hunt, H. (1984). A cognitive psychology of mystical and altered state experience. *Perceptual and Motor Skills, 58,* 467–513.

Hunt, H. (1989). *Multiplicity of dreams.* New Haven, CT: Yale University Press.

Husserl, E. (1931). *Ideas* (W. R. B. Gibson, Trans.). London: George Allen and Unwin. (Originally published in 1913.)

Husserl, E. (1962). *Ideas: General introduction to pure phenomenology* (W. R. Boyle, Trans.). New York: Collier Books.

Husserl, E. (1970a). *The crisis of European sciences and transcendental phenomenology.* Evanston, IL: Northwestern University Press. (Originally published in 1954.)

Husserl, E. (1970b). *Paris Lectures* (P. Koestenbaun, Trans.). The Hague: Nijhoff. (Originally published in 1950.)

Huttenlocher, P. (1970). Synaptic density in human frontal cortex—developmental changes and effects of aging. *Brain Research, 163,* 195–205.

Huttenlocher, P. (1979). Synaptic density in human frontal cortex—developmental changes and effects of aging. *Brain Research, 163,* 195–205.

Huttenlocher, P., de Courten, C., Garey, L. J., & van der Loos, H. (1982). Synaptogenesis in human visual cortex—evidence for synapse elimination during normal development. *Neuroscience Letters, 33,* 247–252.

Huxley, A. (1945). *The perennial philosophy.* New York: Harper & Row.

Ikels, C. (1980). The coming of age in Chinese society: Traditional patterns and contemporary Hong Kong. In C. L. Fry (Ed.), *Aging in culture and society.* New York: Praeger.

Inhelder, B. (Ed.) (1977). *Epistémologie Génétique et Equilibration.* Neufchatel et Paris: Delachaux et Niestlé.

Inhelder, B., & Piaget, J. (1958). *The growth of logical thinking from childhood to adolescence.* (A. Parsons & S. Seagrim, Trans.). New York: Basic Books. (Originally published in 1955.)

Ionesco, E. (1971). *Present past past present: A personal memoir.* New York: Grove Press.

Izard, C. E. (1979). Emotions as motivations: An evolutionary-developmental perspective.. In H. E. Howe (Ed.), *1978 Nebraska Symposium on Motivation.* Lincoln: University of Nebraska Press.

Jackson, D. N. (1970). A sequential system of personality scale development. In C. D. Spielberger (Ed.), *Current topics in clinical and community psychology* (Vol. 2). New York: Academic Press.

Jacobi, J. (1962). *The psychology of C. G. Jung.* New Haven: Yale University Press. (Originally published in 1942.)

Jacobi, J. (1967). *The way of individuation* (R. F. C. Hull, Trans.). New York: Meridian. (Originally published in 1965.)

Jäger, A. O. (1967). *Dimensionen der Intelligenz.* Göttingen: Verlag für Psychologie.

Jäger, A. O. (1982). Mehrmodale Klassifikation von Intelligenzleistungen: Experimentell kontrollierte Weiterentwicklung eines deskriptiven Intelligenzstrukturmodells. *Diagnostica, 28,* 195–225.

Jahoda, G. (1979). On the nature of difficulties in spatial-perceptional tasks: Ethnic and sex differences. *British Journal of Psychology, 70,* 351–363.

James, W. (1890). *The principles of psychology* (Vol. 1). New York: Holt.

James, W. (1902). *The varieties of religious experience.* New York: Longmans, Green.

James, W. (1966). *Psychology: Briefer course.* New York: Collier.

Jaques, E., with Gibson, R. O. & Isaac, D. J. (1978). *Levels of abstraction in logic and human action.* London: Heinemann.

Jaspers, K. (1954). *Way to wisdom* (R. Manheim, Trans.). New Haven: Yale University Press. (Originally published in 1951.)

Jaspers, K. (1955). *Reason and existenz* (W. Earle, Trans.). New York: Noonday. (Originally published in 1935.)

Jaspers, K. (1959). *Truth and symbol* (J. T. Wilde, W. Kolback & W. Kummel, Trans.). New Haven: College and University Press. (Originally published in 1947.)

Jaspers, K. (1970). *Philosophy* (Vols. 2 & 3) (E. B. Ashton, Trans.). Chicago: University of Chicago Press. (Originally published in 1932.)

Jeans, J. (1981). *Physics and philosophy.* New York: Dover. (Originally published in 1943.)

Jedrczak, A. (in press). Psychological correlates of experiences of higher states of consciousness in subjects practicing the Transcendental Meditation and TM-Sidhi programme. In R. A. Chalmers, G. Clements, H. Schenkluhn, & M. Weinless (Eds.), *Scientific research on Maharishi's Transcendental Meditation and TM-Sidhi programme:*

Collected papers (Vol. 3, pp. 1960–1964). Vlodrop, The Netherlands: MVU Press.

Jedrczak, A., Clements, G., & Alexander, C. N. (1989). *Frequency and correlates of higher states of consciousness in subjects practicing the Transcendental Meditation and TM-Sidhi program.* Prepublication manuscript, MERU Research Institute, Mentmore, Buckinghamshire, England.

Jedrzkiewicz, J. A. (1983). *Adult development and mental effort: A neo-Piagetian experimental analysis.* Master's thesis, York University, Toronto, Ontario.

Jephcott, E. F. N. (1972). *Proust and Rilke: The literature of expanded consciousness.* New York: Barnes and Noble Books.

Jevning, R., Wilson, A. F., & Davidson, J. M. (1978). Adrenal-cortical activity during meditation. *Hormones and Behavior, 10*(1), 54–60.

Jevning, R., Wilson, A. F., Smith, W. R., & Morton, M. E. (1978). Redistribution of blood flow in acute hypometabolic behavior. *American Journal of Physiology, 235*(1), R89–R92.

John, E. R. (1977). *Functional neuroscience: Neurometrics* (Vol. 2). Hillsdale, NJ: Erlbaum.

Johnson, J., Fabian, V., & Pascual-Leone, J. (1989). Quantitative hardware-stages that constrain language development. *Human Development, 32,* 245–271.

Johnston, W. (1974). *Silent Music: The science of meditation.* New York: Harper & Row.

Jolly, A. (1972). *The evolution of primate behavior.* New York: Macmillan.

Josephson, B. D. (1980). Some hypotheses concerning the role of consciousness in nature. In B. D. Josephson & V. S. Ramachandran (Eds.), *Consciousness and the physical world.* Oxford: Pergamon Press.

Jung, C. G. (1931). *Essais de psychologie analytique* (Y. LeLay, Trans.). Paris: Librairie Stock.

Jung, C. G. (1933). *Modern man in search of a soul.* San Diego: Harcourt Brace Jovanovich.

Jung, C. G. (1953). *Psychological reflections: An anthology of the writings of C. G. Jung* (J. Jacobi, Ed.). New York: Harper. (Originally published in 1945.)

Jung, C. G. (1954). *La psicología de la transferencia* (J. K. Albert, Trans.). Buenos Aires: Editorial Paidos.

Jung, C. G. (1959). *The aion: Researches into the phenomenology of the self.* In H. Read, M. Fordham, and G. Adler (Eds.), *The collected works of C. G. Jung: Bolligen series XX,* Vol. 9, Pt. 2. New York: Pantheon Books. (Originally published in 1951).

Jung, C. G. (1961). The stages of life. In *Modern man in search of a soul.* London: Routledge & Kegan Paul. (Originally published in 1931.)

Jung, C. G., von Franz, M. L., Henderson, J. L., Jacobi, J., & Jaffe, A. (1964). *Man and his symbols.* New York: Doubleday.

Kagan, J. (1979). Overview: Perspectives on human infancy. In J. Osofsky (Ed.), *Handbook of infant development.* New York: Wiley.

Kagan, J. (1982). *Psychological research on the human infant: An evaluative summary.* New York: W. T. Grant Foundation.

Kahn, R. L., & Antonucci, T. C. (1980). Convoys over the life courses: Attachment, roles, and social support. In P. B. Baltes & O. G. Brim, Jr. (Eds.), *Life-span development and behavior* (Vol. 3, pp. 253–286). New York: Academic Press.

Kahneman, D., Slovic, P., & Tversky, A. (1982). *Judgement under uncertainty: Heuristics and biases.* New York: Cambridge University Press.

Kaminski, G. (1981). Überlegungen zur Funktion von Handlungstheorien in der Psychologie. In H. Lenk (Ed.), *Handlungstheorien interdisziplinär* (Vol. 3, pp. 93–121). Munich: Fink.

Kant, I. (1956). *Critique of practical reason.* Indianapolis: Bobbs-Merrill. (Originally published in 1788.)

Kant, I. (1963). *Critique of pure reason.* (N. Kemp Smith, Trans.). London: Macmillan. (Originally published in 1781.)

Kant, I. (1975). *Foundations of the metaphysics of morals.* Indianapolis: Bobbs-Merrill. (Originally published in 1785.)

Kaplan, A. (1976). Androgyny as a model of mental health for women. In A. G. Kaplan & J. P. Bean (Eds.), *Beyond sex-role stereotypes.* Boston: Little, Brown.

Karmiloff-Smith, A. (1979). A functional approach to child language: A study of determiners and reference. *Cambridge Studies in Linguistics, 24.*

Katz, J. (Trans.). (1950). *The Philosophy of Plotinus: Representative books from the Enneads.* New York: Appleton-Century-Crofts.

Katz, R. (1982). *Boiling energy: Community healing among the Kalahari Kung.* Cambridge, MA: Harvard University Press.

Keating, D. R. (1978). A search for social intelligence. *Journal of Educational Psychology, 70,* 218–233.

Keating, D. P., & Clark, D. V. (1980). Development of physical and social reasoning in adolescence. *Developmental Psychology, 16,* 23–30.

Keats, J. A., Collis, K. F., & Halford, G. S. (Eds.), (1978). *Cognitive development: Research based on a neo-Piagetian approach.* New York: Wiley.

Kegan, R. (1982). *The evolving self.* Cambridge, MA: Harvard University Press.

Kegan, R. (1984). The loss of Pete's dragon: Transformation in the development of the self during the years five to seven. In R. Leahy (Ed.), *The development of the self.* New York: Academic Press.

Kegan, R. (1986a). Kohlberg and the psychology of ego development. In S. Modgil & C. Modgil (Eds.), *Lawrence Kohlberg: Consensus and controversy.* Philadelphia: Falmer.

Kegan, R. (1986b). The child behind the mask: Sociopathy as developmental delay. In W. H. Reid, et al. (Eds.), *Unmasking the Psychopath.* New York: Norton.

Kegan, R., Noam, G., & Rogers, L. (1982). The psychologic of emotion: A neo-Piagetian view. In D. Cicchetti & P. Hesse (Eds.), *Emotional development.* San Francisco: Jossey-Bass.

Kegan, R., & Lahey, L. L. (1983). Adult leadership and adult development: A constructivist view. In B. Kellerman (Ed.), *Leadership: Multidisciplinary perspectives.* Englewood Cliffs, NJ: Prentice-Hall.

Kellerman, B. L. (1975). *Willy Brandt: Portrait of the leader as young politician.* Doctoral dissertation, Yale University, New Haven, CT.

Kendler, T. S. (1979). The development of discrimination learning: A levels-of-functioning explanation. In H. W. Reese & L. P. Lipsitt (Eds.), *Advances in child development and behavior* (Vol. 13). New York: Academic Press.

Kenny, S. L. (1983). Developmental discontinuities in childhood and adolescence. In K. W. Fischer (Ed.), *Levels and transitions in children's development.* San Francisco: Jossey-Bass.

Kesterson, J. (1986). Changes in respiratory control pattern during the practice of the Transcendental Meditation technique. (Doctoral dissertation, Maharishi International University). *Dissertation Abstracts International, 47,* 4337B.

Kihlstrom, J. F., & Cantor, N. (1984). Mental representations of the self. *Advances in Experimental Social Psychology, 17,* 1–47.

King, B. J., & Chapin, K. (1974). *Billie Jean.* New York: Harper & Row.

King, Martin Luther, Jr., (1976). Letter from Birmingham Jail. In F. Schulke, (Ed.), *Martin Luther King, Jr.: A documentary . . . Montgomery to Memphis.* New York: Norton. (Originally published in 1963.)

Kitchener, K. S. (1982). Human development and the college campus: Sequences and tasks. In G. R. Hanson (Ed.), *Measuring student development.* San Francisco: Jossey-Bass.

Kitchener, K. S. (1983). Cognition, metacognition, and epistemic cognition: A three-level model of cognitive processing. *Human Development, 26,* 222–232.

Kitchener, K. S., & Brenner, H. G. (1990). Wisdom and reflective judgment: Knowing in the face of uncertainty. In R. J. Sternberg (Ed.), *Wisdom: Its nature, origins, and development.* New York: Cambridge University Press.

Kitchener, K. S., & King, P. M. (1981). Reflective judgement: Concepts of justification and their relationship to age and education. *Journal of Applied Developmental Psychology, 2,* 89–116.

Kitchener, K. S., & King, P. M. (1990). The reflective judgement model: Ten years of research. *Adult Development, 2.*

Kitchener, K. S., & Kitchener, R. F. (1981). The development of natural rationality: Can formal operations account for it? In J. A. Meachan & N. R. Santilli (Eds.), *Social development in youth: Structure and content.* Basel: Karger.

Klahr, D. (1984). Transition processes in qualitative development. In R. J. Sternberg (Ed.) *Mechanisms of cognitive development.* New York: Freeman.

Klahr, D., & Wallace, J. G. (1976). *Cognitive development: An information processing view.* Hillsdale, NJ: Erlbaum.

Kliegl, R., & Baltes, P. B. (1987). Theory-guided analysis of mechanisms of development and aging through testing-the-limits and research on expertise. In C. Schooler & K. W. Schaie (Eds.), *Social structure and individual aging processes* (pp. 95–119). Norwood, NJ: Ablex.

Koestler, A. (1964). *The act of creation.* London: Hutchinson.

Kogan, N. (1976). *Cognitive style in infancy and early childhood.* Hillsdale, NJ: Erlbaum.

Kohlberg, L. (1969). Stage and sequence: The cognitive developmental approach to socialization. In D. A. Goslin, (Ed.), *Handbook of socialization theory and research.* New York: Rand McNally.

Kohlberg, L. (1971). From is to ought. In T. Mishel (Ed.), *Cognitive development and epistemology.* New York: Academic Press.

Kohlberg, L. (1973a). Continuities in childhood and adult moral development revisited. In P. B. Baltes and K. W. Schaie (Eds.), *Life-Span developmental psychology: Personality and socialization.* New York: Academic Press.

Kohlberg, L. (1973b). Stages and aging in moral development: Some speculations. *Gerontologist, 13.*

Kohlberg, L. (1974). Education, moral development and faith. *Journal of Moral Education, 4,* 5–16.

Kohlberg, L. (1976). Moral stages and moralization: The cognitive-developmental approach. In T. Lickona (Ed.), *Moral development and behavior.* New York: Holt, Rinehart & Winston.

Kohlberg, L. (1979). The meaning and measurement of moral development. *Heinz Werner Memorial Lectures,* April. Worcester, MA: Clark University.

Kohlberg, L. (1981a). *Essays in moral development: The philosophy of moral development* (Vol. 1). New York: Harper & Row.

Kohlberg, L. (1981b). The Meaning and measurement of moral development. *The Heinz Werner Lecture Series* (Vol. 13). Worcester, MA: Clark University Press.

Kohlberg, L. (1984). *Essays in moral development: The psychology of moral development—Moral stages, their nature and validity* (Vol. 2). New York: Harper & Row.

Kohlberg, L. (1986). A current statement on some theoretical issues. In S. Modgil & C. Modgil (Eds.), *Lawrence Kohlberg: Consensus and controversy.* Philadelphia: Falmer.

Kohlberg, L. (1987). *Essays in moral development: Ethical stages—Moral development through the life cycle* (Vol. 3). New York: Harper & Row.

Kohlberg, L. (1990). Which postformal levels are stages? *Adult Development, 2.*

Kohlberg, L., and Armon, C. (1984). Three types of stage models used in the study of adult development. In M. L. Commons, F. A. Richards, & C. Armon (Eds.), *Beyond formal operations: Late adolescent and adult cognitive development* (pp. 383–394). New York: Praeger.

Kohlberg, L., & Colby, A. (1978). *Assessing moral stages: A manual.* Unpublished manuscript, Harvard University, Cambridge, MA.

Kohlberg, L., & Gilligan, C. (1971). The adolescent as a philosopher: The discovery of the self in a post conventional world. *Daedalus, 100,* 1051–1086.

Kohlberg, L., & Kramer, R. (1969). Continuities and discontinuities in childhood and adult moral development. *Human Development, 12,* 93–120.

Kohlberg, L., Levine, C., and Hewer, A. (1983). Moral stages: A current formulation and a response to critics. *Contributions to human development, 10.* Basel: Karger.

Kohlberg, L., & Powers, C. (1981). Moral development, religious thinking, and the question

of a seventh stage. In L. Kohlberg (Ed.), *Essays of moral development*. San Francisco: Harper & Row.

Kohlberg, L., & Shulik, R. (1984). The aging person as philosopher: Moral development in the adult years. In L. Kohlberg (Ed.), *Essays on moral development: The psychology of moral development—Moral stages, their nature and validity* (Vol. 2). New York: Harper & Row.

Kohli, M. (1977). Lebenslauf und Lebensmitte. *Kölner Zeitschrift für Soziologie und Sozialpsychologie, 29,* 625–656.

Kohli, M. (1986). Social organization and subjective construction of the life-course. In A. Sorensen, F. Weinert, & L. Sherrod (Eds.), *Human development and the life course* (pp. 271–292). Hillsdale, NJ: Erlbaum.

Kohn, M. L., & Schooler, R. C. (1978). The reciprocal effects of the substantive complexity of work and intellectual flexibility: A longitudinal assessment. *American Journal of Sociology, 84,* 24–52.

Kohut, H. (1977). *The restoration of the self.* New York: International University Press.

Koplowitz, H. (1978). *Unitary thought: a projection beyond Piaget's formal-operations stage.* Toronto: Addiction Research Foundation.

Koplowitz, H. (1984). A projection beyond Piaget's formal operational stage. In M. Commons, F. Richards, & C. Armon (Eds.), *Beyond formal operations: Late adolescent and adult cognitive development* (pp. 272–295). New York: Praeger.

Koplowitz, H. (1990). Unitary consciousness and the highest development of mind: The relationship between spiritual development and cognitive development. *Adult Development, 2.*

Kossakowski, A., Kühn, H., Lompscher, J., & Rosenfeld, G. (Eds.). (1977). *Psychologische Grundlagen der Persönlichkeitsentwicklung im psychologischen Prozess.* Köln: Pahl-Rugenstein.

Kossakowski, A., & Otto, K. (1977). Persönlichkeit-Tätigkeit-psychische Entwicklung. In A. Kossakowski, H. Kühn, J. Lompscher, & G. Rosenfeld (Eds.), *Psychologische Grundlagen der Persönlichkeitsentwicklung im psychologischen Prozess* (pp. 17–63). Köln: Pahl-Rugenstein.

Kramer, D. A. (1983). Post-formal operations? A need for further conceptualization, *Human Development, 26,* 91–105.

Kramer, D. A. (1989). Development of an awareness of contradictions across the lifespan and the question of postformal operations. *Adult Development, 1,* 133–159.

Kramer, D. A. (1990). Conceptualizing wisdom: The primacy of affective-cognitive relations. In R. Sternberg (Ed.), *Wisdom: Its nature, origins and development.* New York: Cambridge University Press.

Kramer, D. A., & Woodruff, D. S. (1986). Relativistic and dialectic thought in three adult groups. *Human Development, 29,* 280–290.

Kranz, D. S., Grunberg, N. E., & Baum, A. (1985). Health psychology. *Annual Review of Psychology, 36,* 349–383.

Kranz, D. S., & Schulz, S. (1980). A model of life crisis, control and health outcomes: Cardiac rehabilitation and relocation of the elderly. In A. Baum & J. E. Singer (Eds.), *Advances in environmental psychology: Application of personal control* (Vol. 2). Hillsdale, NJ: Erlbaum.

Kroener, S. (1975). Concept attainment in normal and hyperactive boys as a function of stimulus complexity and type of instructions. *Dissertation Abstracts International, 36,* 1913.

Kuchera, M. M. (1987). The effectiveness of meditation techniques to reduce blood pressure levels: A meta-analysis. (Doctoral dissertation, Loyola University). *Dissertation Abstracts International 47,* (11b) 4639.

Kuhn, D. (1974). Inducing development experimentally: Comments on a research paradigm. *Developmental Psychology, 10,* 590–600.

Kuhn, D., & Meacham, J. A. (Eds.) (1983). *On the development of developmental Psychology.* Basel: Karger.

Kuhn, D., & Phelps, E. (1982). The development of problem-solving strategies. In L. P. Lip-

sitt & C. C. Spiker (Eds.), *Advances in child development and behavior* (Vol. 17). New York: Academic Press.

Kuhn, T. S. (1972). *The structure of scientific revolutions* (2nd ed.). Chicago: University of Chicago Press.

Kummer, H. (1971). *Primate societies: Group techniques of ecological adaptation.* Chicago: Aldine.

Kuypers, J. A., & Bengtson, V. L. (1973). Social breakdown and competence. *Human Development, 16,* 181–201.

Laboratory of Comparative Human Cognition. (1982). Culture and intelligence. In R. J. Sternberg (Ed.), *Handbook of human intelligence* (pp. 642–722). Cambridge: Cambridge University Press.

Labouvie-Vief, G. (1979). Uses of logic in life-span development: A theoretical note on adult cognition. *Human Development, 22.*

Labouvie-Vief, G. (1980). Beyond formal operations: Uses and limits of pure logic in life-span development. *Human Development, 23,* 141–161.

Labouvie-Vief, G. (1981). Proactive and reactive aspects of constructive growth and aging in life-span prospective. In R. M. Lerner & N. S. Busch-Rossnagel (Eds.), *Individuals as producers of their development: A life-span perspective.* New York: Academic Press.

Labouvie-Vief, G. (1982). Growth and aging in life-span perspective. *Human Development, 25,* 65–78.

Labouvie-Vief, G. (1984). Logic and self-regulation from youth to maturity: A model. In M. L. Commons, F. A. Richards, & C. Armon (Eds.), *Beyond formal operations: Late adolescent and adult cognitive development* (pp. 158–179). New York: Praeger.

Labouvie-Vief, G. (1985). Intelligence and cognition. In J. E. Birren & K. W. Schaie (Eds.), *Handbook of the psychology of aging* (2nd ed., pp. 500–530). New York: Van Nostrand Reinhold.

Labouvie-Vief, G. (1990). Modes of knowledge and the organization of development. *Adult Development, 2.*

Labouvie-Vief, G., & Blanchard-Fields, F. (1982). Cognitive ageing and psychological growth. *Ageing and Society, 2,* 183–209.

Labouvie-Vief, G., Hakim-Larson, J., & DeVoe, M. (1987). *The language of self-regulation: A life-span view.* Prepublication manuscript, Wayne State University, Detroit, MI.

Labouvie-Vief, G., & Hakim-Larson, G. (1989). Developmental shifts in adult thought. In S. Hunter & M. Sundrel (Eds.), *Midlife myths.* Newbury Park, CA: Sage.

Lachman, M. E. (1985). Personal efficacy in middle and old age: Differential and normative patterns of change. In G. H. Elder, Jr. (Ed.), *Life-course dynamics: 1968 to the 1980s* (pp. 188–213). Ithaca, NY: Cornell University Press.

Lahey, L. (1986). *Males' and females' construction of conflict in work and love.* Doctoral dissertation, Harvard University, Cambridge, MA.

Lahey, L., Souvaine, E., Kegan, R., Goodman, R., & Felix, S. (1988). *The subject-object interview, a guide to its administration and interpretation.* Unpublished manuscript. Subject-Object Research Group, Harvard University, Cambridge, MA.

Lamarck, J. B. P. A. M. (1873). *Philosophie Zoologique.* Leipzig: Abel.

Lamborn, S. D., & Fischer, K. W. (1988). Optimal and functional levels in cognitive development: The individual's developmental range. *Newsletter of the International Society for the Study of Behavioral Development,* Fall.

Langdale, S., & Gilligan, C. (1980). *The contribution of women's thought to developmental psychology.* Washington, D.C.: National Institute of Education Report.

Langer, E. (1982). Old age: An artifact? In S. Kiesler & J. McGaugh (Eds.), *Aging: Biology and behavior* (pp. 255–281). New York: Academic Press.

Langer, E. (1989a). *Mindfulness.* Reading, MA: Addison-Wesley.

Langer, E. (1989b). Minding matters. In L. Berkowitz (Ed.), *Advances in Experimental Social Psychology.* New York: Academic Press, *6,* 211–226.

Langer, E., Beck, P., Janoff-Bulman, R., & Timko, C. (1984a). Long-term effects of a memory-improvement strategy in late adulthood. *Academic Psychology Bulletin, 6,* 211–226.

Langer, E., Beck, P., Janoff-Bulman, R. and Timko, C. (1984b). The relationship between

cognitive deprivation and longevity in senile and non-senile elderly populations. *Academic Psychology Bulletin.*

Langer, E., Dillon, M., Kurtz, R., & Katz, M. (1989). *Believing is seeing: Using mindlessness to improve vision.* Prepublication manuscript, Harvard University, Cambridge, MA.

Langer, E., Janis, I. L., & Wolfer, J. A. (1975). Reduction of psychological stress in surgical patients, *Journal of Experimental Social Psychology, 11,* 155–165.

Langer, E., Stoddard, T., Park, K., & Brown, J. (1989). *Validating a mindfulness/mindlessness scale.* Prepublication manuscript, Harvard University, Cambridge, MA.

Langer, E., Perlmuter, L., Chanowitz, B. & Rubin, R. (1988). *Two new applications of mindlessness theory: Aging and alcoholism. Journal of Aging Studies, 2,* 289–299.

Langer, E., & Piper, P. (1987). The prevention of mindlessness. *Journal of Personality and Social Psychology, 53,* 280–287.

Langer, E., & Rodin, J. (1976). The effects of enhanced personal responsibility for the aged: A field experiment in an institutional setting. *Journal of Personality and Social Psychology, 34,* 191–198.

Langer, E., Rodin, J, Beck P., Weinman, C., & Spitzer, L. (1979). Environmental determinants of memory improvement in late adulthood. *Journal of Personality and Social Psychology, 17*(11), 2003–2013.

Langer, J. (1969). *Theories of development.* New York: Holt, Rinehart & Winston.

Langer, J., Wapner, S., & Werner, H. (1961). The effect of danger upon the experience of time, *American Journal of Psychology, 74,* 94.

Langer, S. K. (1942). *Philosophy in a new key.* Cambridge, MA: Harvard University Press.

Laplace, P. S. (1809). *The system of the world* (J. Pond, Trans.). London: Phillips.

Lassonde, M., Ptito, M., & Pribram, K. H. (1981). Intracerebral influences on the microstructure of visual cortex. *Experimental Brain Research, 43,* 131–144.

Latzel, E. (1981). The concept of ultimate situation in Jaspers' philosophy. In P. A. Schilpp (Ed.), *The philosophy of Karl Jaspers.* La Salle, IL: Open Court.

Lawler, R. W. (1981). The progressive construction of mind (one child's learning addition). *Cognitive Science, 5,* 1–30.

Lazarus, R. S., Folkman, S., & Gruer, R. (1985). Stress and adaptation outcomes. *American Psychologist, 40,* 770–779.

Leibniz, G. W. (1768). *Opera Omnia* (L. Deutens, Ed.). Geneva: Deutens.

Leibniz, G. W. (1875). *Die Philosphische Schriften.* Berlin: Gerhardt.

Lenin, V. I. (1977). On the question of dialectics. In K. Marx, F. Engels, & V. I. Lenin, *On dialectical materialism.* Moscow: Progress. (Originally published in 1915.)

Lenk, H. (1981). *Handlungstheorien—interdisziplinar* (Vol. 3). Munich: Fink Verlag.

Lenneberg, E. H. (1967). *The biological foundations of language.* New York: Wiley.

Leondar, B. (1971). The arts in alternative schools: Some observations. *Journal of Aesthetic Education, 5,* 75–92.

Leontjew, A. (1979). *Tätigkeit, Bewusstsein, Persönlichkeit.* Berlin: VEB Verlag Volk and Wissen.

Lerner, R. M., & Busch-Rossnagel, N. A. (1981). Individuals as producers of their development: Conceptual and empirical bases. In R. M. Lerner & N. A. Busch-Rossnagel (Eds.), *Individuals as producers of their development* (pp. 1–36). New York: Academic Press.

Levinson, D. J. (1977). The mid-life transition. *Psychiatry, 40,* 99–112.

Levinson, D. J. (1980). Toward a conception of the adult life course. In N. J. Smelser & E. H. Erikson (Eds.), *Themes of love and work in adulthood* (pp. 265–290). Cambridge, MA: Harvard University Press.

Levinson, D. J. (1981). Explorations in biography. In A. L. Rabin, J. Aronoff, A. M. Barclay, & R. A. Zucker (Eds.), *Further explorations in personality* (pp. 44–79). New York: Wiley.

Levinson, D. J. (1984). The career is in the life structure, the life structure is in the career: An adult development perspective. In M. B. Arthur, L. Bailyn, D. J. Levinson, & H. Shepard, *Working with careers* (pp. 49–74). New York: Columbia University, School of Business.

Levinson, D. J. (1986). A conception of adult development. *American Psychologist, 41,* 3–13.

Levinson, D. J. (in press). *The seasons of a woman's life.* New York: Knopf.

Levinson, D. J., with Darrow, C. N., Klein, E. B., Levinson, M. H., & McKee, B. (1978). *The seasons of a man's life.* New York: Knopf.

Levinson, D. J., & Gooden, W. E. (1985). The life cycle. In H. I. Kaplan, & B. J. Sadock (Eds.), *Comprehensive textbook of psychiatry* (4th ed.) (pp. 1–13). Baltimore: Williams & Wilkins.

Lewis, P. R. & Lobban, M. C. (1957). Dissociation of diurnal rhythms in human subjects living on abnormal time routines. *Quarterly Journal of Experimental Physiology, 42,* 371.

Liben, L. S., & Golbeck, S. L. (1984). Performance on Piagetian horizontality and verticality tasks: Sex-related differences in knowledge of relevant physical phenomena. *Developmental Psychology, 30,* 595–606.

Liberman, I. Y., & Mann, V. (1981). Should reading instruction and remediation vary with the sex of the child? In A. Ansara, N. Geshwind, A. Galaburda, M. Albert, & N. Gartrell (Eds.), *Sex differences in dyslexia* (pp. 151–168). Towson, MD: Orton Dyslexia Society.

Linn, M. C., & Siegal, H. (1984). Postformal reasoning: A philosophical model. In M. L. Commons, F. A. Richards, & C. Armon (Eds.), *Beyond formal operations: Late adolescent and adult cognitive development* (pp. 239–257). New York: Praeger.

Locke, J. (1966). *On the Conduct of the Understanding.* New York: Teachers College Press.

Lockett, D. W. (1980, April). *The relationship between levels of cognitive development and ego development in adult women.* Paper presented at the Sixth Biennial Southeastern Conference on Human Development, Alexandria, Va.

Loevinger, J. (1976). *Ego development: Conceptions and theories.* San Francisco: Jossey-Bass.

Loevinger, J. (1984). On the self and mediating behavior. In R. A. Zucker, J. Arnoff, & A. I. Rabin (Eds.), *Personality and the prediction of behavior.* Orlando, FL: Academic Press.

Loevinger, J., Cohn, L. D., Bonneville, L. P., Redmore, C. D., Streich, D. D., & Sargent, M. (1985). Ego development in college. *Journal of Personality and Social psychology, 48,* 947–962.

Lorenz, K. (1966). The role of Gestalt perception in animal and human behavior. In L. L. Whyte (Ed.), *Aspects of form.* Bloomington, IN: Midland.

Lorenz, K. Z. (1982). *The foundations of ethology.* New York: Simon & Schuster.

Lovejoy, A. O. (1942). *The great chain of being: A study of the history of an idea.* Cambridge, MA: Harvard University Press.

Low, N. S. (1978, May). *The mother-daughter relationship in adulthood.* Paper presented to the Annual Meeting of the Massachusetts Psychological Association.

Lowenthal, M. F., Thurnher, M., & Chiriboga, D. (1975). *Four stages of life: A comparative study of women and men facing transitions.* San Francisco: Jossey-Bass.

Luria, A. R. (1973). *The working brain.* Middlesex: Penguin.

Lurie, A. (1982). No one asked me to write a novel. *New York Times Book Review,* June 6.

Lyons, N. (1983). Two perspectives: On self, relationships, and morality. *Harvard Educational Review, 53,* 125–145.

Mach, E. (1906). *Space and geometry in the light of physiological, psychological and physical inquiry* (T. J. McCormack, Trans.). Chicago: Open Court. (Originally published in 1868.)

Mackenna, S. (1934). *The essence of Plotinus.* New York: Oxford University Press.

Macmurray, J. (1938). *Reason and emotion.* New York: Appleton-Century.

Macmurray, J. (1978). *The self as agent.* Atlantic Highlands, NJ: Humanities Press (Originally published in 1957.)

Macmurray, J. (1979). *Persons in relation.* Atlantic Highlands, NJ: Humanities Press (Originally published in 1961.)

MacWhinney, B. (1978). The acquisition of morphophonology. *Monographs of the Society for Research in Child Development, 43* (1–2, Serial No. 174).

Madhavananda, Swami. (1970). *Vivekachudamuni of Shri Shankaracharya.* Calcutta, India: Advaita Ashrama.

Maharishi Mahesh Yogi. (1966). *The science of being and art of living.* Los Angeles: International SRM.

Maharishi Mahesh Yogi. (1969). *On the Bhagavad-Gita: A new translation and commentary.* Harmondsworth, Middlesex, England: Penguin.

Maharishi Mahesh Yogi. (1972). *The Science of Creative Intelligence.* Los Angeles: MIU Press.

Maharishi Mahesh Yogi. (1976). *Creating an ideal society: A global undertaking.* Rheinweiler, West Germany: MERU Press.

Maharishi Mahesh Yogi. (1977). Inaugural address. In *First World Assembly on law, justice and rehabilitation.* Rheinweiler, West Germany: MERU Press

Maharishi Mahesh Yogi. (1978). Inaugural address. In *International Conference on EEG and perception in higher states of consciousness.* MERU, Seelisburg, Switzerland.

Maharishi Mahesh Yogi. (1980). *Levels of the mind.* Series of lectures given at the First International Conference on Vedic Science, New Delhi, India.

Maharishi Mahesh Yogi. (1977). Inaugural address. In *First World Assembly on law, justice and rehabilitation.* Rheinweiler, West Germany: MERU Press

Maharishi Mahesh Yogi. (1986). *Life supported by natural law.* Washington DC: Age of Enlightenment Press.

Mahler, M. S., Pine, F., & Bergman, A. (1975). *The psychological birth of the human infant.* New York: Basic Books.

Malthus, T. (1798). *An essay on the principle of population, as it affects the future improvement of society.* London: Johnson.

Mandler, G. (1962). From association to structure. *Psychological Review, 69,* 415–427.

Mandler, G. (1983, June). *Consciousness: Its function and construction.* La Jolla, CA: University of California, San Diego, Center for Human Information Processing (CHIP 117).

Mandler, G. (1985). *Cognitive psychology.* Hillsdale, NJ: Erlbaum.

Mandler, J. M. (1984). Representation and recall in infancy. In M. Moscovitch (Ed.), *Infant memory.* New York: Plenum.

Marcel, A. J. (1983a). Conscious and unconscious perception: Experiments on visual masking and word recognition. *Cognitive Psychology, 15,* 197–237.

Marcel, A. J. (1983b). Conscious and unconscious perception: An approach to the relations between phenomenal experience and perceptual processes. *Cognitive Psychology, 15,* 238–300.

Marcia, J. E. (1976). Identity six years after: A follow-up study. *Journal of Youth and Adolescence, 5,* 145–160.

Marcus, H., & Wurf, E. (1987). The dynamic self-concept: A social psychological perspective. *Annual Review of Psychology, 38,* 299–337.

Marcus, S. V. (1977). The influence of the Transcendental Meditation program on the marital dyad. Doctoral theses (abstract), California School of Professional Psychology, Fresno, CA. *Dissertation Abstracts International, 38*(8), 3895-B.

Martarano, S. C. (1977). A developmental analysis of performance on Piaget's formal operations tasks. *Developmental Psychology, 13,* 666–672.

Marx, K., Engels, F., & Lenin, V. I. (1977). *On dialectical materialism.* Moscow: Progress.

Maslow, A. H. (1964). *Religions, values, and peak-experiences.* Columbus, Ohio: Ohio State University Press.

Maslow, A. H. (1968). *Toward a psychology of being* (2nd ed.). New York: Van Nostrand Reinhold.

Maslow, A. H. (1972). The plateau experience. *Journal of Transpersonal Psychology, 2,* 107–121.

Maslow, A. H. (1976). *Farther reaches of human nature.* New York: Viking.

Matousek, M., & Petersen, I. (1973). Frequency analysis of the EEG in normal children and adolescents. In P. Kellaway & I. Petersen (Eds.), *Automation of clinical electroencephalography.* New York: Raven.

Maxwell, J. C. (1871). *Theory of Heat.* London: Longmans & Green.

Mayer, K. U., & Müller, W. (1986). The development of the state and the structure of the life course. In A. Sorensen, F. Weinert, & L. Sherrod (Eds.), *Human development and the life course* (pp. 707–741). Hillsdale, NJ: Erlbaum.

McAdams, D. P. (1988). *Power, intimacy, and the life story: Personalogical inquiries into identity.* New York: Dorsey Press.

McCall, R. B., Eichorn, D. H., & Hogarty, P. S. (1977). Transitions in early mental development. *Monographs of the Society for Research in Child Development, 42*(5, Serial No. 150).

McCall, R. B. (1979). The development of intellectual functioning in infancy and the prediction of later I.Q. In J. Osofsky (Ed.), *Handbook of infant development.* New York: Wiley.

McCall, R. B., Meyers, E. D., Jr., Hartman, J., & Roche, A. F. (1983). Developmental changes in head circumference and mental performance growth rates: A test of Epstein's phrenoblysis hypothesis. *Developmental Psychobiology, 16,* 457–468.

McCarthy, T. (1979). *The critical theory of Jergen Habermas.* Cambridge, MA: MIT Press.

McClelland, D. C. (1976). *Power: The inner experience.* New York: Irvingston.

McGuinness, D. (1981). Auditory and motor aspect of language development in males and females. In A. Ansara, N. Geschwind, A. Galaburda, M. Albert, N. Gartrell (Eds.), *Sex differences in dyslexia* (pp. 55–72). Towson, MD: Orton Dyslexia Society.

McGuinness, D. (1985). *When children don't learn.* New York: Basic Books.

McGuinness, D., & Brabyn, L. (1984). In search of visual spatial ability. Part I. Visual Systems. *Journal of Mental Imagery, 8,* 1–12.

McGuinness, D., & Pribram, K. H. (1978). The origins of sensory bias in the development of gender differences in perception and cognition. In M. Bortner (Ed.), *Cognitive growth and development: Essays in memory of Herbert G. Birch* (pp. 3–56). New York: Brunner/Mazel.

Meacham, J. A. (1982). Wisdom and the context of knowledge: Knowing that one doesn't know. In D. Kuhn & J. A. Meacham (Eds.), *On the development of developmental psychology* (pp. 111–134). Basel: Karger.

Meacham, J. A. (1990). The loss of wisdom. In R. J. Sternberg (Ed.), *Wisdom: Its nature, origins and development.* New York: Cambridge University Press.

Mead, G. H. (1934). *Mind, self, and society.* Chicago: University of Chicago Press.

Mead, M. (1978). *Culture and commitment.* Garden City, NY: Anchor.

Mehan, H. (1981). Social constructivism in psychology and sociology. *The Quarterly Newsletter of the Laboratory of Human Cognition, 3,* 71–77.

Meichenbaum, D. (1980). A cognitive behavioral perspective on intelligence. *Intelligence, 4,* 271–283.

Meirsman, J. M. R. (1988). Neurophysiological order in the REM sleep of participants in the Transcendental Meditation and TM-Sidhi program. In R. K. Wallace, D. W. Orme-Johnson, & M. C. Dillbeck (Eds.) *Scientific research on the Transcendental Meditation and TM-Sidhi program: Collected papers* (Vol. 5). Fairfield, IA. MIU Press.

Meltzoff, A. N., & Moore, M. K. (1977). Imitation of facial and manual gestures by human neonates. *Science, 198,* 800–802.

Meltzoff, A. N., & Moore, M. K. (1983). Newborn infants imitate adult facial gestures. *Child Development, 54,* 702–709.

Mendelsohn, R. M. (1987). *The I of consciousness: Development from birth to maturity.* New York: Plenum.

Meyer, J. (1986). The institutionalization of the life course. In A. Sorensen, F. Weinert, & L. Sherrod (Eds.), *Human development and the life course* (pp. 199–216). Hillsdale, NJ: Erlbaum.

Miller, G. A. (1981). Trends and debates in cognitive psychology. *Cognition, 10,* 215–225.

Miller, J. B. (1976). *Toward a new psychology of women.* Boston: Beacon.

Miller, P. H., Kessel, F. S., & Flavell, J. H. (1970). Thinking about people thinking: A study of social cognitive development. *Child Development, 41,* 613–623.

Mitchell, D. E. (1981). Sensitive periods in visual development. In R. N. Aslin, J. R. Alberts,

& M. R. Peterson (Eds.), *Development of perception: Psychobiological perspectives: The visual system* (Vol. 2). New York: Academic Press.

Morgan, R. F., & Fevens, S. K. (1972). Reliability of the Adult Growth Examination: A standardized test of individual aging. *Perceptual and Motor Skills, 34,* 415–419.

Mount, R., Kagan, J., Hiatt, S., Reznick, J. S., & Szpak, M. (1981). *Right visual preference correlates with early language development.* Paper presented at the Society for Research in Child Development, Boston.

Murphy, J. M. & Gilligan, C. (1980). Moral development in late adolescense and adulthood: A critique and reconstruction of Kohlberg's theory, *Human Development, 23,* 77–104.

Nagel, E., & Newman, J. R. (1958). *Godel's Proof.* New York: New York University Press.

Natsoulas, T. (1983). Concepts of consciousness. *The Journal of Mind and Behavior, 4*(1), 13–59.

Neimark, E. D. (1975). Intellectual development during adolescence. In F. D. Horowitz (Ed.), *Review of child development research* (Vol. 4). Chicago: University of Chicago Press.

Nelson, K. (1973). Structure and strategy in learning to talk. *Monographs of the Society for Research in Child Development, 38* (whole issue).

Neugarten, B. L. (1968a). Adult personality: Toward a psychology of the life cycle. In B. L. Neugarten (Ed.), *Middle age and aging: Reader in social psychology* (pp. 137–147). Chicago: University of Chicago Press.

Neugarten, B. L. (1968b). The awareness of middle age. In B. L. Neugarten (Ed.), *Middle age and aging: Reader in social psychology* (pp. 93–98). Chicago: University of Chicago Press.

Neugarten, B. L. (1973). Personality change in late life: A developmental perspective. In C. Eisdorfer & M. P. Lawton (Eds.), *Psychology of adult development and aging* (pp. 311–335). Washington, D.C.: American Psychological Association.

Neugarten, B. L., Crotty, W. J., & Tobin, S. S. (1964). Personality types in an aged population. In B. Neugarten (Ed.), *Personality in middle and late life.* New York: Atherton.

Neumann, E. (1962). *The origins and history of consciousness* (Vols. 1–2) (R. C. F. Hull, Trans.) New York: Harper & Row. (Originally published in 1949.)

Newell, A., & Simon, H. (1972). *Human problem solving.* Englewood Cliffs, NJ: Prentice-Hall.

Newton, I. (1960). *Mathematical principles of natural philosophy and his system of the world* (A. Motte, Trans.; revised F. Cajori) Berkeley: University of California Press.

Newton, P. M. (1984). Samuel Johnson's breakdown and recovery in middle age: A life-span developmental approach to mental illness and its cure. *International Review of Psycho-analysis, 11,* 93–118.

Nidich, S. I. (1975). A study of the relationship of the Transcendental Meditation program to Kohlberg's stages of moral reasoning. (Doctoral dissertation, University of Cincinnati). *Dissertation Abstracts International, 36,* 4361–4362.

Nidich, S. I., Nidich, R. J., & Rainforth, M. V. (1986). School effectiveness: Achievement gains at Maharishi School of the Age of Enlightenment. *Education, 107*(1), 49–54.

Nidich, S. I., Ryncarz, R. A., Abrams, A. I., Orme-Johnson, D. W., & Wallace, R. K. (1983). Kohlbergian cosmic perspective responses, EEG coherence, and the Transcendental Meditation and TM-Sidhi program. *Journal of Moral Education, 12*(3), 166–173.

Nidich, S., Seeman, N., & Dreskin, T. (1973). Influence of Transcendental Meditation: A replication. *Journal of Counseling Psychology, 20,* 565–566.

Niebuhr, H. F. (1963). *The responsible self.* New York: Harper & Row.

Nisbett, R., & Ross, L. (1980). *Human inference and shortcomings of social judgment.* Englewood Cliffs, NJ: Prentice-Hall.

Noam, G., & Kegan, R. (1981). *Social cognition and psychodynamics: Towards a clinical-developmental psychology.* Unpublished manuscript, Harvard University, Cambridge, MA.

Norman, D. A. (1981). Twelve issues for cognitive science. In D. A. Norman (Ed.), *Perspectives in cognitive science.* Hillsdale, NJ: Erlbaum.

Norman, D. A., & Shallice, T. (1975). *Attention to action: Willed and automatic control of*

behavior. La Jolla, CA: University of California, Center for Human Information Processing, December, 1980 (CHIP 99).

Norris, J. E. (1979, November). *Social cognition in adulthood: Perceiving the complexity of others*. Paper presented at the Meeting of the Gerontological Society, Washington, D.C.

Nuttin, J. (1984). *Motivation, planning, and action*. Hillsdale, NJ: Erlbaum.

O'Brien, D., & Overton, W. F. (1982). Conditional reasoning and the competence–performance issue: A developmental analysis of a training task. *Journal of Experimental Child Psychology, 34*, 274–290.

O'Halloran, J. P., Jevning, R. A., Wilson, A. F., Skowsky, R., & Alexander, C. N. (1985). Hormonal control in a state of decreased activation: Potentiation of arginine vasopressin secretion. *Physiology and Behavior, 35*, 591–595.

Onions, C. T. (1965). *The shorter Oxford English dictionary on historical principles* (3rd ed.). London: Oxford University Press.

Oppenheim, A., & Willsky, A. (1983). *Signals and systems*. Englewood Cliffs, NJ: Prentice-Hall.

Orme-Johnson, D. W. (1987). Reduced health insurance utilization through the Transcendental Meditation program. *Psychosomatic Medicine, 49*, 493–507.

Orme-Johnson, D. W. (1988a). The cosmic psyche—an introduction to Maharishi's Vedic Psychology: The fulfillment of modern psychology. *Modern Science and Vedic Science, 2*, 113–163.

Orme-Johnson, D. W. (1988b). The cosmic psyche as the unified source of creation: Verification through scientific principles, direct experience, and scientific research. *Modern Science and Vedic Science, 2*, 165–221.

Orme-Johnson, D. W., Alexander, C. N., Davies, J. C., Chandler, H. & Larimore, W. (1988). Peace project in the Middle East: Effects of the Maharishi Technology of the Unified Field on conflict and quality of life in Israel and Lebanon. *Journal of Conflict Resolution, 32*, 776–812.

Orme-Johnson, D. W., Clements, G., Haynes, C. T., & Badawi, K. (1977). Higher states of consciousness: EEG coherence, creativity, and experiences of the sidhis. In D. W. Orme-Johnson & J. T. Farrow (Eds.), *Scientific research on the Transcendental Meditation program: Collected papers* (Vol. 1, pp. 705–712). Rheinweiler, West Germany: MERU Press.

Orme-Johnson, D. W., Dillbeck, M. C., Alexander, C. N., Gelderloos, P., Boyer, R. W., Charleston, D. E., van den Berg, W., & Dillbeck, S. (in press). *The Vedic psychology of Maharishi Mahesh Yogi: Fulfillment of modern psychology*. Fairfield, IA: MIU Press.

Orme-Johnson, D. W., & Edwards, C. (1982). *Subjective experiences of stabilized pure consciousness*. Unpublished manuscript, Maharishi International University, Fairfield, IA.

Orme-Johnson, D. W. & Farrow, J. T. (Eds.) (1977). *Scientific research on the Transcendental Meditation program: Collected Papers* (Vol. 1). Rheinweiler, W. Germany: MERU Press.

Orme-Johnson, D. W., & Gelderloos, P. (1988). Topographic EEG brain map during yogic flying. *International Journal of Neuroscience, 38*, 427–434.

Orme-Johnson, D. W., & Haynes, C. T. (1981). EEG phase coherence, pure consciousness, creativity, and TM-Sidhi experiences. *International Journal of Neuroscience, 13*, 211–217.

Orme-Johnson, D. W., Wallace, R. K., Dillbeck, M. C., Alexander, C. N., & Ball, O. E. (in press). Improved functional organization of the brain through the Maharishi Technology of the Unified Field as indicated by changes in EEG coherence and its cognitive correlates: A proposed model of higher states of consciousness. In R. A. Chalmers, G. Clements, H. Schenkluhn, & M. Weinless (Eds.), *Scientific research on Maharishi's Transcendental Meditation and TM-Sidhi programme: Collected papers.* (Vol. 4, pp. 2245–2265). Vlodrop, the Netherlands: MVU Press.

Orne, J. E. (1969). *Time, Experience, and Behavior*. London: Iliffe Books.

Ortega y Gasset, J. (1957). Pasado y provenir para el hombre actual. In Griaule, H. Baruk, M. Merleau-Ponty, R. Romains Danielou, & J. Ortega y Gasset (Eds.), *Hombre y cultura en el siglo xx*. Madrid: Ediciones Guadarrama.

Ortega y Gasset, J. (1958). *Man and crisis*. New York: Norton. (Originally published in 1933.)

Ortega y Gasset, J. (1961). *Meditaciones del Quijote*. Madrid: Alianza Editorial. (Originally published in 1914.)

Orwoll, L. & Perlmutter, M. (1990). Wisdom and the study of wise persons. In R. J. Sternberg (Ed.). *Wisdom: Its nature, origins and development*. New York: Cambridge University Press.

Overbeck, K. D. (1982). Auswirkungen der Technik der Transzendentalen Meditation (TM) auf die psychische und psychosomatische Befindlichkeit. *Psychotherapie-Psychosomatik Medizinische Psychologie, 32*(6), 188–192.

Overton, W. F., & Reese, H. W. (1973). Models of development: Methodological implications. In J. R. Nesselroade & H. W. Reese (Eds.), *Life-span developmental psychology*. New York: Academic Press.

Paranjpe, A. C. (1987). The self beyond cognition, action, pain and pleasure: An Eastern perspective. In K. Yardley & T. Honeff (Eds.), *Self and identity: Psychosocial perspectives*. New York: Wiley.

Park, K., & Langer, E. (1987). *Psychology in context: The observer paradigm*. Prepublication manuscript, Harvard University, Cambridge, MA.

Parsons, M. (1983). Baldwin and aesthetic development. In J. M. Broughton & D. J. Freeman-Noir (Eds.), *The foundations of cognitive developmental psychology*. Norwood, NJ: Ablex Press.

Pascual-Leone, J. (1969). *Cognitive development and cognitive style: A general psychological integration*. Doctoral dissertation, University of Geneva, Geneva, Switzerland.

Pascual-Leone, J. (1970). A mathematical model for the transition rule in Piaget's developmental stages. *Acta Psychologica, 32*, 301–345.

Pascual-Leone, J. (1976a). Metasubjective problems of constructive cognition: Forms of knowing and their psychological mechanism. *Canadian Psychological Review, 17,* 110–125. (Errata: *Canadian Psychological Review, 17,* 307).

Pascual-Leone, J. (1976b). On learning and development, Piagetian-style: I. A reply to Lefebvre-Pinard. *Canadian Psychological Review, 17,* 270–288.

Pascual-Leone, J. (1978). Compounds, confounds, and models in developmental information processing: A reply to Trabasso and Foellinger. *Journal of Experimental Child Psychology, 26,* 18–40.

Pascual-Leone, J. (1980). Constructive problems for constructive theories: The current relevance of Piaget's work and a critique of information-processing simulation psychology. In R. Kluwe & H. Spada (Eds.), *Developmental modes of thinking*. New York: Academic Press.

Pascual-Leone, J. (1983). Growing into human maturity: Toward a metasubjective theory of adulthood stages. In P. B. Baltes & O. G. Brim (Eds.), *Life-span development and behavior* (Vol. 5, pp. 118–156). New York: Academic Press.

Pascual-Leone, J. (1984). Attention, dialectic, and mental effort: Towards an organismic theory of life stages. In M. L. Commons, F. A. Richards, & C. Armon (Eds.), *Beyond formal operations: Late adolescent and adult cognitive development* (pp. 182–215). New York: Praeger.

Pascual-Leone, J. (1987). Organismic processes for neo-Piagetian theories: A dialectical causal account of cognitive development. *International Journal of Psychology,* special issue.

Pascual-Leone, J. (1990). An essay on wisdom: Toward symbolic processes that make it possible. In R. J. Sternberg (Ed.), *Wisdom: Its nature, origins, and development*. New York: Cambridge University Press.

Pascual-Leone, J. (in press). An organismic process model of Witkin's Field-Dependence-Independence. In T. Globerson (Ed.), *Cognitive style and cognitive development*. Norwood, NJ: Ablex.

Pascual-Leone, J., & Goodman, D. (1979). Intelligence and experience: A neo-Piagetian approach. *Instructional Science, 8,* 301–367.

Pascual-Leone, J., Goodman, D. R., Ammon, P., & Subelman, I. (1978). Piagetian theory and neo-Piagetian analysis as psychological guides in education. In J. M. Gallagher & J. Easley (Eds.), *Knowledge and development: Piaget and education* (Vol. 2). New York: Plenum.

Pascual-Leone, J., Johnson, J., Hameluck, D., Goodman, D., & Theodor, L. I. (1981). Interruption effects in backward pattern masking: The neglected role of fixation stimuli. *Proceedings of the Third Annual Conference of the Cognitive Science Society.* Berkeley, CA.

Pascual-Leone, J., & Smith, J. (1969). The encoding and decoding of symbols by children: A new experimental paradigm and a neo-Piagetian model. *Journal of Experimental Child Psychology, 8,* 328–355.

Pascual-Leone, J., & Sparkman, E. (1980). The dialectics of empiricism and rationalism: A last methodological reply to Trabasso. *Journal of Experimental Child Psychology, 29,* 88–101.

Patrick, C. (1935). Creative thought in poets. *Archives of Psychology,* No. 178.

Pavlov, I. (1927). *Conditioned reflexes.* New York: Dover.

Peano, G. (1894). *Notations de logique mathématique.* Turin: Guadagin.

Pearson, C. (in press). *Moments of Heaven.* Fairfield, IA: MIU Press.

Pelletier, K. R. (1974). Influence of Transcendental Meditation upon autokinetic perception. *Perceptual and Motor Skills, 39,* 1031–1034.

Pelletier, K. R. (1977). *Mind as healer, mind as slayer.* New York: Dell.

Penner, W. J., Zingle, H. W., Dyck, R., & Truch, S. (1974). Does an in depth Transcendental Meditation course effect change in the personalities of the participants? *Western Psychologist, 4,* 104–111.

Perkins, D. N. (1981). *The mind's best work.* Cambridge, MA: Harvard University Press.

Perry, J., & Slemp, S. R. (1980). Differences among three adult age groups in their attitudes toward self and others. *Journal of Genetic Psychology, 136,* 275–279.

Perry, W. (1981). Cognitive and ethical growth: The making of meaning. In A. Chickering (Ed.), *The modern American college.* San Francisco: Jossey-Bass.

Perry, W. B. (1970). *Forms of intellectual and ethical development in the college years.* New York: Holt, Rinehart & Winston.

Piaget, J. (1929). *The child's conception of the world.* San Diego: Harcourt Brace Jovanovich.

Piaget, J. (1941). Le mécanisme du développement mental et les lois du groupement des opérations. *Archives de Psychologie, Génève, 28,* 215–285.

Piaget, J. (1948). *The moral judgment of the child.* New York: The Free Press. (Originally published in 1932.)

Piaget, J. (1950). *The psychology of intelligence* (M. Percy & D. E. Berlyne, Trans.). London: Routledge & Kegan Paul. (Originally published in 1947.)

Piaget, J. (1952a). Autobiography. In E. G. Boring, H. S. Langfeld, H. Warner, & R. M. Yerkes (Eds.), *A history of psychology in autobiography* (Vol. 4). Worcester, MA: Clark University Press.

Piaget, J. (1952b). *The child's conception of number.* New York: Humanities.

Piaget, J. (1952c). *The origins of intelligence in children.* New York: Norton. (Originally published in 1936.)

Piaget, J. (1953). *Logic and psychology* (W. Mays & F. Whitehead, Trans.). New York: Basic Books.

Piaget, J. (1954). *The construction of reality in the child.* New York: Basic Books. (Originally published in 1937.)

Piaget, J. (1956). *La psychologie de l'intelligence.* Paris: Librarie Armand Colin, 1956. (Originally published in 1947).

Piaget, J. (1957). Logique et équilibre dans les comportements du sujet. *Etudes d'Epistémologie Génétique, 2,* 27–118.

Piaget, J. (1962). *Play, dreams, and imitation in childhood.* New York: Norton.

Piaget, J. (1967). *Six psychological studies.* New York: Random House.

Piaget, J. (1970a). *Structuralism*. New York: Basic Books.

Piaget, J. (1970b). Piaget's theory. In P. H. Mussen (Ed.), *Carmichael's manual of child psychology* (Vol. 1). New York: Wiley.

Piaget, J. (1971a). *Biology and knowledge*. Chicago: University of Chicago Press.

Piaget, J. (1971b). The theory of stages in cognitive development. In D. R. Green, M. P. Ford, & G. B. Flamer (Eds.), *Measurement and Piaget*. New York: McGraw-Hill.

Piaget, J. (1971c). *Insights and illusions of philosophy*. New York: World Publishing.

Piaget, J. (1972). Intellectual evolution from adolescence to adulthood. *Human Development, 15*, 1–12.

Piaget, J. (1976). *The grasp of consciousness: Action and concept in the young child*. Cambridge, MA: Harvard University Press.

Piaget, J. (1977). *The development of thought: Equilibration of cognitive structures*. New York: Viking.

Piaget, J. (1980). *Experiments in contradiction*. Chicago: University of Chicago Press.

Piaget, J. (1985). *The Equilibration of Cognitive Structures* (T. Brown & K. Thampy, Trans.). Chicago: University of Chicago Press. (Originally published in 1975.)

Piaget, J., & Inhelder, B. (1969). *The psychology of the child*. New York: Basic Books. (Originally published in 1966.)

Piper, A., & Langer, E. (1984). Aging and mindful control. In M. Baltes & P. Baltes (Eds.), *Aging and Control*. Hillsdale, NJ: Erlbaum.

Pirandello, L. (1964). Six characters in search of an author. In R. W. Corrigan (Ed.), *The modern theater*. New York: Macmillan.

Pirkey, Avoth (1967). *The chapters of the fathers* (S. R. Hirsch, Trans.). New York: Feldheim.

Plato. (1961). *The collected dialogues of Plato* (E. Hamilton & H. Cairns, Eds.). New York: Pantheon.

Plotinus (1956). *The Enneads* (S. Mackennu, Trans.) (2nd rev. ed.). London: Faber & Faber.

Polanyi, M. (1958). *Personal knowledge*. Chicago: University of Chicago Press.

Popper, K. (1974). *Objective knowledge*. Oxford: Oxford University Press.

Powell, P. M. (1980). Advanced social role-taking and cognitive development in gifted adults. *International Journal of Aging and Human Development, 11*, 177–192.

Powell, P. M. (1984). Stage 4A: Category operations and interactive empathy. In M. L. Commons, F. A. Richards, & C. Armon (Eds.), *Beyond formal operations: Late adolescent and adult cognitive development* (pp. 326–339). New York: Praeger.

Power, C., & Kohlberg, L. (1980). Religion, morality, and ego development. In J. Fowler & A. Vergote (Eds.), *Toward moral and religious maturity*. Morristown, NJ: Silver-Burdett.

Pribram, K. H. (1969). Neural servosystems and the structure of personality. *Journal of Nervous and Mental Diseases, 149*, 30–39.

Pribram, K. H. (1971). *Languages of the brain: experimental paradoxes and principles in neuropsychology*. Englewood-Cliffs, NJ: Prentice-Hall.

Pribram, K. H. (1982). *Languages of the brain: Experimental paradoxes and principles in neuropsychology*. Englewood Cliffs, NJ: Prentice-Hall.

Pribram, K. H. (1986a). The cognitive revolution and mind/brain issues. *American Psychologist, 41*, 507–520.

Pribram, K. H. (1986b). The subdivisions of the frontal cortex revisited. In E. Perecman (Ed.), *The frontal lobes revisited* (pp. 11–39). New York: IRBN Press.

Pribram, K. H. (1990). *Brain and perception holonomy and structure in figural processing*. Hillsdale, NJ: Lawrence Erlbaum Associates.

Pribram, K. H., & Gill, M. M. (1976). *Freud's "Project" re-assessed: Preface to contemporary cognitive theory and neuropsychology*. New York: Basic Books.

Pribram, K. H., & McGuinness, D. (1975). Arousal, activation and effort in the control of attention. *Psychological Review, 82*, 116–149.

Pribram, K. H., & Melges, F. T. (1969). Psychophysiological basis of emotion. In P. J. Vinkey & G. S. Gruyn (Eds.) *Handbook of Clinical Neurology* (Vol 3.) (pp. 316–342). Amsterdam: North-Holland.

Prigogine, I., & Stengers, I. (1984). *Order out of chaos*. London: Heineman.

Quine, W. V. (1981). *Theories and things.* Cambridge, MA: Harvard University Press.

Radhakrishan, S., & Moore, C. A. (1957). *A sourcebook in Indian philosophy.* Princeton, NJ: Princeton University Press.

Raine, K. (1975). *The land unknown.* New York: Braziller.

Rakic, P., Bourgeois, J.-P., Eckenhoff, M. F., Zecevic, N., & Goldman-Rakic, P. (1986). Concurrent overproduction of synapses in diverse regions of the primate cerebral cortex. *Science, 232,* 232–235.

Redmore, C. D., & Loevinger, J. (1979). Ego development in adolescence: Longitudinal studies. *Journal of Youth and Adolescence, 8,* 1–20.

Riegel, K. (1973). Dialectic operations: The final period of cognitive development. *Human Development, 16,* 346–370.

Reinert, G. (1970). Comparative factor analytic studies of intelligence throughout the human life-span. In L. G. Goulet & P. B. Baltes (Eds.), *Life-span developmental psychology: Research and theory* (pp. 467–484). New York: Academic Press.

Reither, F. (1981). About thinking and acting of experts in complex situations. *Simulation and Games, 12,* 125–140.

Resnick, L. B. (1976). *The nature of intelligence.* Hillsdale, NJ: Erlbaum.

Rest, J. R. (1975). Longitudinal study of the Defining Issues Test of moral judgement: A strategy for analyzing developmental change. *Developmental Psychology, 11,* 738–748.

Rest, J. R. (1983). Morality. In P. H. Mussen (Ed.), *Handbook of child psychology.* Vol. 3: *Cognitive development* (J. H. Flavell & E. M. Markman, Eds., pp. 556–629). New York: Wiley.

Rest, J. R., Turiel, E., & Kohlberg, L. (1969). Level of moral development as a determinant of preference and comprehension of moral judgement made by others. *Journal of Personality, 37,* 225–252.

Ribaupierre, A. (1983). Un modèle néo-Piagetian du développement: La théorie des opérateurs constructifs de Pascual-Leone. *Cahiers de Psychologie Cognitive, 3,* 327–356.

Ribaupierre, A. de, & Pascual-Leone, J. (1984). Pour une intégration des méthodes en psychologie: Approches experimentales, psychologénétiques et differentielles. *L'Année Psychologique, 84,* 227–250.

Richards, F. A. (1990a). Equilibration models and the framework of postformal cognition. *Adult Development, 2, Models and methods in the study of adolescent and adult thought.*

Richards, F. A. (1990b). Detecting metasystematic, systematic, and lower stage relations: An empirical investigation of postformal cognitive development. *Adult Development, 2, Models and methods in the study of adolescent and adult thought.*

Richards, F. A., & Commons, M. L. (1990). Applying signal detection theory to measure subject sensitivity to metasystematic, systematic and lower developmental stage signals. *Adult Development, 2, Models and methods in the study of adolescent and adult thought.*

Ricoeur, P. (1967). *Husserl: An analysis of his phenomenology.* Evanston, IL: Northwestern University Press, 1967.

Ricoeur, P. (1970). *Freud and philosophy: An essay on interpretation.* New Haven, CT: Yale University Press.

Riley, M. W. (1983). Age strata in social systems. In R. H. Binstock & E. Shanas (Eds.), *Handbook of aging and the social sciences* (rev. ed, pp. 369–411). New York: Van Nostrand Reinhold.

Roberts, P., & Newton, P. N. (1987). Levinsonian studies of women's adult development. *Psychology and Aging, 2,* 154–163.

Rodin, J. & Langer, E. (1977). Long-term effects of a control-relevant intervention among the institutionalized aged. *Journal of Personality and Social Psychology, 35,* 897–902.

Rodin, J. & Langer, E. (1980). Aging labels: the decline of control and the fall of self-esteem. *Journal of Social Issues, 36,* 12–29.

Rof Carballo, J. (1972). *Biología & psicoanalisis.* Bilbao, Spain: Desclee de Brouwer.

Rogers, C. (1959). A theory of therapy, personality, and interpersonal relationships as devel-

oped in the client-centered framework. In S. Koch (Ed.), *Psychology: A study of science: Formulations of the person and the social context* (Vol. 3). New York: McGraw-Hill.

Rogers, L. and Kegan, R. (1989). " 'Mental Growth' and 'Mental Health' as Distinct Concepts in the Study of Developmental Psychopathology." In D. Keating and H. Rosen (Eds.), *Constructivist Approaches to Psychopathology*. Hillsdale, NJ: Erlbaum. (1989 in press).

Rolland, R. (1931). *Empedocle d'Argrigente L'Eclair de Spinoza*. Paris: Editions du Sublier.

Rose, S. (1973). *The conscious brain*. New York: Knopf.

Rosen, C. (1972). *The classical style*. New York: Norton.

Rosenthal, R., Archer, D., DiMatteo, M. R., Koivumaki, J. H., & Rogers, P. L. (1974). Body talk and tone of voice: Language without words. *Psychology Today*, September, 63–64.

Rosow, I. (1976). Status and role change through the life span. In R. H. Binstock & E. Shanas (Eds.), *Handbook of aging and the social sciences* (pp. 457–482). New York: Van Nostrand Reinhold.

Ross, D. (1977). *Aristotle*. London: Methuen.

Ross, G. G. (1984). *Grand unified theories*. Menlo Park, CA: Benjamin/Cummings.

Ross, L. (1978). *Shortcomings of the intuitive psychologist. Cognitive theories in social psychology*. L. Berkowitz (Ed.). (University of Wisconsin, Department of Psychology). Academic Press, New York.

Rowe, J. W., & Kahn, R. L. (1987). Human aging: Usual and successful. *Science, 273*, 143–149.

Rozin, P. (1976). The evolution of intelligence and access to the cognitive unconscious. In J. M. Sprague and A. A. Epstein (Ed.) *Progress in psychology and physiological psychology*. New York: Academic Press.

Rubin, S., & Wolf, D. (1979). The development of maybe: The evolution of social roles into narrative roles. *New Directions of Child Development, 6*, 15–28.

Rumelhart, D. E., & Norman, D. A. (1978). Accretion, tuning, and restructuring: Tree modes of learning. In J. W. Cotton & R. Klatzky (Eds.), *Semantic factors in cognition* (pp. 37–53). Hillsdale, NJ: Erlbaum.

Russell, B. (1977). *The problems of philosophy*. London: Oxford University Press.

Russin, J. E. (1989). "Stages of Adult Development in Black, Professional Women." In Reginald C. Jones (Ed.), *Black Adult Development and Aging*. Berkeley, CA: Cobb & Henry.

Ryan, R. M., & Deci, E. L. (1985). The "third selective paradigm" and the role of human motivation in cultural and biological selection: A response to Csikszentmihalyi and Massimini. *New Ideas in Psychology, 3*(3), 259–264.

Sartre, J.-P. (1957). *The transcendence of the ego*. New York: Noonday.

Sartre, J.-P. (1960). *Critique de la raison dialectique: Théorie des ensembles pratiques* (Vol. 1). Paris: Gallimard.

Sartre, J. P. (1966). *Being and nothingness* (H. E. Baines, Trans.). New York: Washington Square Press. (Originally published in 1943.)

Scarf, M. (1980). *Unfinished business*. New York: Ballantine.

Scarlett, G., & Wolf, D. (1979). When it's only make believe: The construction of a boundary between fantasy and reality in storytelling. *New Directions in Child Development, 6*, 29–40.

Scarr, S., & Weinberg, R. A. (1978). The influence of "family background" on intellectual attainment. *American Sociological Review, 43*, 674–692.

Scarr-Salapatek, S. (1976). An evolutionary perspective on infant intelligence: Species patterns and individual variations. In M. Lewis (Ed.), *The origins of intelligence: Infancy and early childhood*. New York: Plenum.

Scarr, S., & Kidd, J. (1983). Developmental behavioral genetics. In M. M. Hait & J. J. Campos (Eds), *Handbook of child psychology: Infancy and developmental psychobiology* (Vol. 2) (pp. 345–433). New York: Wiley.

Schachtel, E. (1959). *Metamorphosis.* New York: Basic Books.

Schafer, R. (1981). *Narrative actions in psychoanalysis.* Worcester, MA: Clark University Press.

Schaie, K. W. (1977/78). Toward a stage theory of adult cognitive development. *Journal of Aging and Human Development, 8,* 129–138.

Schaie, K. W. (1979). The primary mental abilities in adulthood: An exploration in the development of psychometric intelligence. In P. B. Baltes, & O. G. Brim, Jr. (Eds.), *Life-span development and behavior* (Vol. 2, pp. 67–115). New York: Academic Press.

Schank, R. C., & Abelson, R. P. (1977). *Scripts, plans, goals, and understanding.* Hillsdale, NJ: Erlbaum.

Scheler, M. (1961). *Man's place in nature* (H. Meyerhoff, Trans.). Boston: Beacon. (Originally published in 1926.)

Scheler, M. (1973). *Selected philosophical essays.* (D. Lachterman, Trans.). Evanston, IL: Northwestern University Press.

Schiebel, A. B. (1981). The problem of selective attention: A possible structural substrate. In O. Pompeiano & C. A. Marsan (Eds.), *Brain mechanisms of perceptual awareness and purposeful behavior* (Vol. 8). New York: Raven.

Schiffin, R. M., & Schneider, W. (1983). Controlled and automatic human information processing: II. Perceptual learning, automatic attending, and a general theory. *Psychological Review, 84*(2), 127–189.

Schlipp, P. A. (Ed.) (1981). *The philosophy of Karl Jaspers.* La Salle, IL: Open Court.

Schlossberg, N. K. (1984). *Counseling adults in transition.* New York: Springer.

Schoenwald, R. L. (1965). *Nineteenth century thought: The discovery of change.* Englewood Cliffs, NJ: Prentice-Hall.

Schrödinger, E. (1967). *Mind and matter* (Vol. 1). New York: Cambridge University Press.

Schulz, R. (1976). Effects of control and predictability on the psychological well-being of the institutionalized aged. *Journal of Personality and Social Psychology, 33,* 563–573.

Scriven, M. (1980). Prescriptive and descriptive approaches to problem solving. In D. T. Tuma & F. Reif (Eds.), *Problem solving and education: Issues in teaching and research* (pp. 127–140). Hillsdale, NJ: Erlbaum.

Sechrest, L., White, S. O., & Bronn, E. D. (Eds.). (1979). *The rehabilitation of criminal offenders: Problems and prospects.* Washington, DC: The National Research Council, National Academy of Science.

Seeman, W., Nidich, S., & Banta, T. (1972) Influence of Transcendental Meditation on a measure of self-actualization. *Journal of Counseling Psychology, 19,* 184–187.

Seligman, M. E. P. (1975). *Helplessness: On Depression, Development, and Death.* San Francisco: W. H. Freeman and Co.

Seligman, M. E. P., & Elder. (1986). Learned helplessness and life-span development. In A. Sorensen, F. Weinhert, & L. Sherrod (Eds.), *Human development and the life course.* Hillsdale, NJ: Erlbaum.

Selman, R. L. (1976). Social-cognitive understanding: A guide to educational and clinical practice. In T. Lickona (Ed.), *Moral development and behavior: Theory, research and social issues.* New York: Holt, Rinehart & Winston.

Selman, R. L. (1980). *The growth of interpersonal understanding: Developmental and clinical analyses.* New York: Academic Press.

Selye, H. (1974). *Stress without distress.* Philadelphia: Lippincott.

Selye, H. (1976). *Stress in health and disease.* Woburn, MA: Butterworth.

Seung, T. K. (1982). *Structuralism and hermeneutics.* New York: Columbia University Press.

Shanan, J., & Sagiv, R. (1982). Sex differences in intellectual performance during middle age. *Human Development, 25,* 24–33.

Shapiro, D. H., & Walsh, R. N. (Eds.). (1984). *Meditation: Classic and contemporary perspectives.* Hawthorne, NY: Aldine.

Shaw, R., & Bransford, J. (1977). Introduction: Psychological approaches to the problem of knowledge. In R. Shaw & J. Bransford (Eds.), *Perceiving, acting, and knowing* (pp. 1–42). New York: Wiley.

Shulik, R. (1979). *Faith development, moral development, and old age: An assessment of Fowler's faith development paradigm.* (Doctoral dissertation, University of Chicago, Chicago IL).

Siegler, R. S. (1981). Developmental sequences within and between concepts. *Monographs of the Society for Research in Child Development, 46*(2, Serial No. 189).

Siegler, R. S. (1983). Information processing approaches to cognitive development. In W. Kessen (Ed.), *Handbook of child psychology: History, theory and methods* (Vol. 1). New York: Wiley.

Siegler, R. S. (1986). *Children's thinking.* Englewood Cliffs, NJ: Prentice-Hall.

Siegler, R. S. (1989). Mechanisms of cognitive development. *Annual Review of Psychology, 40,* 353–79.

Sinnott, J. D. (1975) Everyday thinking and Piagetian operativity in adults. *Human Development, 18,* 346–370.

Sinnott, J. D. (1984). Post-formal reasoning: The relativistic stage. In M. L. Commons, F. A. Richards, & C. Armon (Eds.), *Beyond Formal Operations: Late adolescent and adult cognitive development* (pp. 298–325). New York: Praeger.

Sinnott, J. D. (1989) Lifespan relativistic postformal thought: Methodology and data from everyday problem solving studies. *Adult Development, 1, Comparisons and applications of adolescent and adult developmental models.*

Smedslund, J. (1961). The acquisition of conservation of substance and weight in children. *Scandinavian Journal of Psychology, 12,* 11–20.

Smelser, N. J. (1980). Vicissitudes of work and love in Anglo-American society. In N. J. Smelser & E. H. Erikson (Eds.), *Themes of work and love in adulthood.* Cambridge, MA: Harvard University Press.

Smith, J., & Baltes, P. B. (in press). A study of wisdom-related knowledge: Age/cohort differences in responses to life planning problems. *Developmental Psychology.*

Smith, J., Dixon, R. A., & Baltes, P. B. (in press). Expertise in life planning: A new research approach to investigating aspects of wisdom. In M. L. Commons, J. D. Sinnott, F. A. Richards, & C. Armon (Eds.), *Beyond formal operations II: Comparisons and applications of adolescent and adult developmental models.* New York: Praeger.

Smith, J. C. (1976). Psychotherapeutic effects of Transcendental Meditation with controls for expectation of relief and daily sitting. *Journal of Consulting and Clinical Psychology, 44,* 630–637.

Smith, M. B. (1968). Competence and socialization. In J. A. Clausen (Ed.), *Socialization and society* (pp. 270–320). Boston: Little, Brown.

Smith, S. D. (1982, November). *The search for a dominantly inherited form of dyslexia.* Paper presented at the 33rd Annual Conference of the Orton Society. Baltimore.

Snarey, J., Kohlberg, L., & Noam, G. (1983). Ego development in perspective: Structural stage, functional phase, and cultural age-period models. *Developmental Review, 3,* 303–338.

Sowarka, D. (1989). Weisheit und weise Personen: Common-Sense-Konzepte älterer Menschen. *Zeitschrift für Entwicklungspsychologie und Pädagogische Psychologie, 21,* 87–109.

Spearman, H. S. (1953). *The abilities of man.* London: Macmillan. (Originally published in 1926.)

Sperry, R. W. (1987). Structure and significance of the consciousness revolution. *The Journal of Mind and Behavior, 8,* 37–66.

Sperry, R. W. (1988). Psychology's mentalist paradigm and the religion/science tension. *American Psychologist, 43,* 8, 607–613.

Spevak, A. A., & Pribram, K. H. (1973). A decisional analysis of the effects of limbic lesions on learning in monkeys. *Journal of Comparative Physiological Psychology, 82*(2), 211–226.

Spinelli, D. N., & Pribram, K. H. (1966). Changes in visual recovery functions produced by temporal lobe stimulations in monkeys. *Electroencephalography and Clinical Neurophysiology, 20,* 44–49.

Spinelli, D. N., & Pribram, K. H. (1967). Changes in visual recovery functions and unit activity produced by frontal and temporal cortex stimulation. *Electroencephalography and Clinical Neurophysiology, 22,* 143–149.

Spinoza, B. (1930). Ethics. In J. Wild (Ed.), *Spinoza selections.* New York: Scribners.

Spinoza, B. (1951). *Theologico-political treatise and political treatise* (R. H. M. Elwes, Trans.). New York: Dover.

Spivack, G., Platt, J. J., & Shure, M. B. (1976). *The problem-solving approach to adjustment.* San Francisco: Jossey-Bass.

Sprockhoff, J. F. (1979). Die Alten im alten Indien. *Saeculum: Jahrbuch für Universalgeschichte, 30,* 375–433.

Sroufe, L. A. (1979a). Socioemotional development. In J. D. Osofsky (Ed.), *Handbook of infant development.* New York: Wiley.

Sroufe, L. A. (1979b). The coherence of individual development. *American Psychologist, 34,* 834–841.

Stace, W. T. (1960). *Mysticism and philosophy.* Philadelphia: Lippincott.

Stapp, H. P. (1985). Consciousness and values in the quantum universe. *Foundations of Physics, 15*(1), 35–47.

Staude, J. R. (Ed.). (1981). *Wisdom and age.* Berkeley, CA: Ross.

Staudinger, U. (1989). *The study of life review: An approach to the investigation of intellectual development across the life span.* Berlin: Max Planck Institute for Human Development and Education, Studien und Berichte 47.

Sternberg, R. J. (1980). Sketch of a componential subtheory of human intelligence. *The Behavioral and Brain Sciences, 3,* 573–584.

Sternberg, R. J. (1981). Toward a unified componential theory of human intelligence: I. Fluid ability. In M. P. Friedman, J. P. Das, & N. O'Conner (Eds.), *Intelligence and learning* (pp. 327–344). New York: Plenum.

Sternberg, R. J. (1982). The nature of intelligence. *New York University Education Quarterly, 12,* 10–17.

Sternberg, R. J. (Ed.) (1984). *Mechanisms of cognitive development.* New York: Freeman.

Sternberg, R. J. (1984). Mechanisms of cognitive development: A componential approach. In R. J. Sternberg (Ed.), *Mechanisms of cognitive development.* New York: Freeman.

Sternberg, R. J. (Ed.) (1990). *Wisdom: Its nature, origins, and development.* New York: Cambridge University Press.

Sternberg, R. J., Berg, Cynthia A. (1987). What are theories of adult intellectual development theories of. In C. Schooler & K. W. Schaie (Eds.), *Cognitive functioning and social structure over the life course* (pp. 3–23). Norwood, NJ: Ablex.

Sternberg, R. J., Conway, B. E., Ketron, J. L., & Bernstein, M. (1981). People's conceptions of intelligence. *Journal of Personality and Social Psychology, 41,* 37–55.

Sternberg, R. J., & Detterman, D. K. (Eds.). (1979). *Human intelligence.* Norwood, NJ: Ablex.

Sternberg, R. J., & Downing, C. J. (1982). The development of higher-order reasoning in adolescence. *Child Development, 53,* 209–221.

Sternberg, R. J., & Powell, J. S. (1983). The development of intelligence. In J. H. Flavell & M. Markman (Eds.), *Handbook of child psychology: Cognitive development* (Vol. 3). New York: Wiley.

Sterns, H. L., & Sanders, R. E. (1980). Training and education of the elderly. In R. R. Turner & W. H. Reese (Eds.), *Life-span developmental psychology: Intervention* (pp. 307–330). New York: Academic Press.

Stewart, W. (1976). *A psychosocial study of the formation of the early adult life structure in women.* Doctoral dissertation, Teachers College, Columbia University, New York.

Stewart, L. A. (1986). *A metasubjective analysis of the development of moral reasoning.* Doctoral dissertation, York University, Toronto, Ontario.

Stone, C. A., & Day, M. C. (1980). Competence and performance models and the characterization of formal operational skills. *Human Development, 23,* 323–353.

Strauss, S. (Ed.) (1982). *U-shaped behavioral growth.* New York: Academic Press.

Strauss, S., & Stavy, R. (1979). U-shaped behavioral growth: Implications for theories of development. In W. W. Hartup (Ed.), *Review of child development research* (Vol. 6). Chicago: University of Chicago Press.

Stravinsky, I., Craft R. (1966). *Themes and Episodes.* New York: Knopf.

Sugarman, S. (1987). *Piaget's construction of the child's reality.* New York: Cambridge University Press.

Sullivan, H. S. (1953a). *The interpersonal theory of psychiatry.* New York: Norton.

Sullivan, H. S. (1953b). *Conceptions of modern psychiatry.* New York: Norton. (Originally published in 1940.)

Super, C. M. (1980). Cognitive development: Looking across at growing up. In C. M. Super & S. Harkness (Eds.). *New directions for child development: Anthropological perspective on child development.* San Francisco: Jossey-Bass.

Surber, C. F., & Czesh, S. M. (1984). Reversible operations in the balance scale task. *Journal of Experimental Child Psychology, 38,* 254–274.

Surman, O. S., Gottlieb, S. K., Hackett, T. P., & Silverberg, E. L. (1973). Hypnosis in the treatment of warts. *Archives of General Psychiatry, 28,* 439–441.

Swift, J. (1952). *Gulliver's Travels.* Chicago: Encyclopedia Britannica. (Originally published in 1726.)

Tallal, P., & Stark, R. (1982). Perceptual/motor profiles of reading impaired children with or without concomitant oral language deficits. *Annals of Dyslexia, 32,* 163–176.

Tanner, J. M. (1970). Physical growth. In P. H. Mussen (Ed.), *Carmichael's manual of child psychology* (Vol. 1). New York: Wiley.

Tappan, M. (1987). *Hermeneutics and moral development: A developmental analysis of short-term change in moral functioning during late adolescence.* Doctoral dissertation, Harvard University, Cambridge, MA.

Tappan, M. (in preparation). The development of justice reasoning during young adulthood: A three-dimension model. *Adult Development, 3.*

Tappan, M. (in press a). Stories lived and stories told: The narrative structure of late adolescent moral development. *Human Development, 32,* 300–315.

Tart, C. T. (1975). *States of consciousness.* New York: Dutton.

Taylor, C. W., & Barron, F. (1966). *Scientific creativity: Its recognition and development.* New York: Science Editions.

Taylor, S. (1981). *Seven women: Life structure evolution in early adulthood.* Unpublished Doctoral Dissertation. City University of New York.

Taylor, S. E. (1986). *Health psychology.* New York: Random House.

Telang, K. R. (Trans.) (1970). The Bhagavadgita. In F. Max Muller (Ed.), *Sacred books of the east* (Vol. 8). Delhi: Motilal Banarsidas.

Tellegen, A., & Atkinson, G. (1974). Openness to absorbing and self-altering experiences ("absorption"), a trait related to hypnotic susceptibility. *Journal of Abnormal Psychology, 83,* 268–277.

Tennyson, H. (1899). *Alfred, Lord Tennyson: A memoir by his son* (new ed.). London: Macmillan.

Thatcher, R. W., Walker, R. A., & Giudice, S. (1987). Human cerebral hemispheres develop at different rates and ages. *Science, 236,* 1110–1113.

Thich, N. H. (1974). *Zen keys.* New York: Doubleday.

Thomae, H. (1968). *Das Individuum und seine Welt.* Göttingen: Hogrefe.

Thomae, H. (1983). *Alternsstile und Alternsschicksale.* Bern: Huber.

Thomas, H., Jamison, W., & Hummel, D. D. (1973). Observation is insufficient for discovering that the surface of still water is invariantly horizontal. *Science, 181,* 173–174.

Thoreau, H. D. (1929). In H. G. O. Blake (Ed.), *Early spring in Massachusetts and summer: From the journal of Henry D. Thoreau.* Boston: Houghton Mifflin.

Thorndike, E. L. (1920). Intelligence and its uses. *Harper's Magazine. 140,* 227–235.

Timiras, P. S. (1978). Biological perspectives on aging. *American Scientist, 66,* 605–613.

Tolman, E., & Brunswik, F. (1935). The organism and the causal texture of the environment. *Psychological Review, 42,* 434–77.

Tomaszewski, T. (1978). *Tätigkeit und Bewusstsein*. Weinheim: Beltz.

Tomaszewski, T. (1981). Struktur, Funktion and Steuerungsmechanismen menschlicher Tätigkeit. In T. Tomaszweski (Ed.), *Zur Psychologie der Tätigkeit*. Berlin: VEB Deutscher Verlag der Wissenschaften.

Tomkins, S. S. (1979). Script theory: Differential magnification of affects. In H. E. Howe (Ed.), *1978 Nebraska Symposium on Motivation*. Lincoln: University of Nebraska Press.

Toomey, M., Chalmers, R., & Clements, G. (in press). The Transcendental Meditation and TM-Sidhi programme and reversal of the ageing process: A longitudinal study. In R. A. Chalmers, G. Clements, H. Schenkluhn, & M. Weinless (Eds.), *Scientific research on Maharishi's Transcendental Meditation and TM-Sidhi programme: Collected papers* (Vol. 3, pp. 1878–1883). Vlodrop, The Netherlands: MVU Press.

Torrance, E. P. (1965). *Rewarding creative behavior*. Englewood Cliffs, NJ: Prentice Hall.

Tough, A. (1971). *The adult's learning projects*. Toronto: The Ontario Institute for Studies in Education.

Toulmin, S. (1950). *An examination of the place of reason in ethics*. Cambridge, England: Cambridge University Press.

Toulmin, S., & Feldman, C. (1976) Logic and the theory of mind. *Nebraska Symposium on Motivation, 23*.

Travis, F. (1979). Creative thinking and the Transcendental Meditation technique. *The Journal of Creative Behavior, 13*(3), 169–180.

Trevarthen, C. (1980). The Foundations of Intersubjectivity: Development of Interpersonal and Cooperative Understanding in Infants. In D. R. Olson (Ed.), *The Social Foundations of Language and Thought*. New York: Norton.

Trevarthen, C. (1986). Development of inter-subjective motor control in infants. In M. G. Wade and H. T. A. Whiting, *Motor Development Control* (pp. 209–261). Dordrecht: Martinus Nijhoff.

Trower, P. (1980). How to lose friends and influence nobody: An analysis of social failure. In W. T. Singleton, P. Spurgeon, & R. B. Stammers (Eds.), *The analysis of social skill* (pp. 257–274). New York: Plenum.

Tuchman, B. W. (1978). *A distant mirror: The calamitous 14th century*. New York: Ballantine.

Tulkin, S. R., & Konner, M. J. (1973). Alternative conception of intellectual functioning. *Human Development, 16*, 33–52.

Turiel, E. (1983). *The development of social knowledge: Morality and convention*. Cambridge, MA: Cambridge University Press.

Turnbull, M. J., & Norris, H. (1982). Effects of Transcendental Meditation on self-identity indices and personality. *British Journal of Psychology, 73*, 57–68.

Tversky, A., & Kahneman, D. (1973). Availability: A heuristic for judging frequency and probability. *Cognitive Psychology, 5*, 207–232.

Uexkull, J. V. (1926). *Theoretical biology*. San Diego: Harcourt Brace Jovanovich.

Uexkull, J. V. (1952). A stroll through the world of animals and men. In C. H. Schiller (Ed.), *Instinctive behavior*. New York: International Universities Press, 1952. (Originally published in 1934.)

Ullian, D. Z. (1981). The child's construction of gender: Anatomy as destiny. In E. K. Shapiro & E. Weber (Eds.), *Cognitive and affective growth*. Hillsdale, NJ: Erlbaum.

Ungerleider, L. G., Ganz, L., & Pribram, K. H. (1977). Size constancy in Rhesus monkeys: Effects of pulvinar, prestriate, and inferotemporal lesions. *Experimental Brain Research, 27*, 251–269.

Uzgiris, I. C., & Hunt, J. McV. (1975). *Assessment in infancy: Ordinal scales of psychological development*. Urbana, IL: University of Illinois Press.

Vaillant, G. (1977). *Adaptation to life*. Boston: Little, Brown.

Van Gennep, A. (1960). *The rites of passage*. Chicago: University of Chicago Press. (Original published in 1908.)

Volpert, W. (1980). Zur Erforschung effektiver innerer Modelle. In W. Hacker & H. Raum (Eds.), *Optimierung von kognitiven Arbeitsanforderungen* (pp. 21–31). Bern: Huber.

Volpert, W. (1982). The model of the hierarchical-sequential organization of action. In W. Hacker, W. Volpert, & M. von Cranach (Eds.), *Cognitive and motivational aspects of action* (pp. 35–51). Berlin: VEB Deutscher Verlag der Wissenschaften.

Von Cranach, M., Kalbermatten, U., Indermühle, K., & Gugler, B. (1980). *Zielgerichtetes Handeln*. Bern: Huber.

Vuyk, R. (1981). *Overview and critique of Piaget's genetic epistemology 1965–1980*. (Vol. 1–2). New York: Academic Press.

Vygotsky, L. S. (1962). *Thought and language*. Cambridge, MA: MIT Press. (Originally published in 1934.)

Vygotsky, L. S. (1978). The development of higher psychological processes. In M. Cole, V. John-Steiner, S. Scribner, & E. Souberman (Eds.), *Mind in society* (pp. 79–119). Cambridge, MA: Harvard University Press.

Waddington, C. H. (1975). *The evolution of an evolutionist*. Edinburgh: Edinburgh University Press.

Wallace, R. K. (1970). Physiological effects of Transcendental Meditation. *Science, 167*, 1751–1754.

Wallace, R. K. (1986). *The Maharishi Technology of the Unified Field: The neurophysiology of enlightenment*. Fairfield, IA: MIU Press.

Wallace, R. K., Dillbeck, M. C., Jacobe, E., & Harrington, B. (1982). The effects of the Transcendental Meditation and TM-Sidhi program on the aging process. *International Journal of Neuroscience, 16*, 53–58.

Wallace, R. K., Mills, P., Orme-Johnson, D. W., Dillbeck, M. C., & Jacobe, E. (1983). Modification of the paired H-reflex through the Transcendental Meditation and TM-Sidhi program. *Experimental Neurology, 79*, 77–86.

Wallace, R. K., Orme-Johnson, D. W., & Dillbeck, M. C. (Eds.). (in press). *Scientific research on Maharishi's Transcendental Meditation and TM-Sidhi program*. Collected Papers. (Vol. 5). Fairfield, IA: MIU Press.

Wallach, M., & Kogan, N. (1965). *Modes of thinking in young children*. New York: Holt, Rinehart and Winston.

Wallwork, W. (1982). Religious Development. In J. M. Broughton, & D. J. Freeman-Moir (Eds.), *The cognitive developmental psychology of James Mark Baldwin*. Norwood, NJ: Ablex.

Walton, K. G., Gelderloos, P., Macrae, P., Goddard, P., Pugh, N. D. C., Maclean, C. & Alexander, C. N. (1988). Urinary excretion of the serotonin metabolite 5-hydroxyindoleacetic acid (5-HIAA) correlates positively with alertness and health [abstract]. *The Journal of the Iowa Academy of Science, 95*(1), A53.

Walton, K. G., McCorkle, T., Hansen, T., MacLean, L., Wallace, R. K., Leni, J., & Meyerson, J. R. (1986). "Substance M" a serotonin modulator candidate from human urine? In Y. H. Ehrlich, R. H. Lenox, E. Korecki, & W. Berry (Eds.), *Advances in experimental medicine and biology: Molecular mechanisms of neural responsiveness*. New York: Plenum.

Warner, T. (1986). Transcendental Meditation and developmental advancement: Mediating abilities and conservation performance. (Doctoral dissertation, York University, Toronto, Ontario). *Dissertation Abstracts International 47* (08-B) 3358.

Watson, M. W. (1981). The development of social roles: A sequence of social-cognitive development. In K. W. Fischer (Ed.), *Cognitive development*. San Francisco: Jossey-Bass.

Watson, M. W., & Fischer, K. W. (1980). Development of social roles in elicited and spontaneous behavior during the preschool years. *Developmental Psychology, 16*, 483–494.

Weber, M. (1958) Politics as Vocation. In C. W. Mills (Eds.), *From Max Weber*. New York: Oxford University Press.

Weinert, F., & Kluwe, R. H. (Eds.). (1984). *Metakognition, Motivation und Lernen*. Stuttgart: Kohlhammer.

Weiss, E. (1950). *Principles of psychodynamics*. New York: Grune & Stratton.

Weiss, P. (1969). The living system: Determinism stratified. In A. Koestle & J. R. Smythies (Eds.) *Beyond reductionism*. London: Hutchinson.

Weisz, J. R. (1983). Can I control it? The pursuit of veridical answers across the life span. In P. B. Baltes & O. G. Brim, Jr. (Eds.), *Life-span development and behavior* (Vol. 5, pp. 233–300). New York: Academic Press.

Werner, H. (1940). *Comparative psychology of mental development* New York: Harper & Row.

Werner, H. (1957). The concept of development from a comparative and organismic point of view. In D. Harris (Ed.), *The concept of development* (pp. 125–148). Minneapolis: University of Minnesota Press.

Werner, H., & Kaplan, B. (1963). *Symbol Formation.* New York: Wiley.

Werner, O., Wallace, R. K., Charles, B., Janssen, G., & Chalmers, R. (1986). Long-term endocrinologic changes in subjects practicing the Transcendental Meditation (TM) and TM-Sidhi program. *Psychosomatic Medicine, 48*(1), 59–66.

White, R. W. (1952). *Lives in progress.* New York: Holt, Rinehart & Winston.

White, R. W. (1974). Strategies of adaptation: An attempt at systematic description. In G. V. Coelho, D. A. Hamburg, & J. E. Adams (Eds.), *Coping and adaptation* (pp. 47–68). New York: Basic Books.

White, S. H. (1965). Evidence for a hierarchical arrangement of learning processes. In L. P. Lipsitt & C. C. Spiker (Eds.), *Advance in child development behavior* (Vol. 2). New York: Academic Press.

White, S. H. (1970). Some general outlines of the matrix of developmental changes between five and seven years. *Bulletin of the Orton Society, 20,* 41–57.

Whitehead, A. M. (1938). *Modes of thought.* New York: Macmillan.

Whitehead, A. N. (1969). *Process and reality: An essay in cosmology.* New York: The Free Press.

Wigner, E. (1960). The unreasonable effectiveness of mathematics in the natural sciences. *Communications and Pure Applied Mathematics, 13,* 1–14.

Wilber, K., Engler, J., & Brown, D. P. (1986). *Transformations in consciousness: Conventional and contemplative perspectives on development.* Boston: Shambala, New Science Library.

Wilensky, R. (1981). Meta-planning: Representing and using knowledge about planning in problem-solving and natural language understanding. *Cognitive Science, 5,* 197–233.

Willis, S. L., & Baltes, P. B. (1980). Intelligence in adulthood and aging: Contemporary issues. In L. W. Poon (Ed.), *Aging in the 1980's: Psychological issues* (pp. 260–272). Washington, D.C.: American Psychological Association.

Winnicott, D. W. (1965). *The Maturational processes and the facilitating environment.* London: Hogarth.

Winnicott, D. W. (1969). *De la pédiatrie à la psychanalyse.* Paris: Petite Bibliothèque Payot.

Wittgenstein, L. (1965). *The blue and brown books.* New York: Harper & Row.

Wittgenstein, L. (1968). *Philosophical investigations.* Oxford: Blackwell.

Wohlwill, J. F. (1973). *The study of behavioral development.* New York: Academic Press.

Wolf, D., & Gardner, H. (1979). Style and sequence in early symbolic play. In N. R. Smith & M. B. Franklin (Eds.), *Symbolic functioning in children.* Hillsdale, N.J.: Lawrence Erlbaum.

Wolf, D., & Gardner, H. (1981). On the structure of early symbolization. In R. Schiefelbush & D. Bricker (Eds.), *Early Language: Acquisition and Intervention.* Baltimore: University Park Press.

Wolkove, N., Kreisman, H., Darragh, D., Cohen, C., & Frank, H. (1984). Effect of Transcendental Meditation on breathing and respiratory control. *Journal of Applied Physiology: Respiratory, Environmental and Exercise Physiology, 56*(3), 607–612.

Yakovlev, P., & Lecours, A. R. (1967). The myelogenetic cycles of regional maturation of the brain. In A. Minkowski (Ed.), *Regional development of the brain in early life.* Oxford: Blackwell & Mott.

Youniss, J. (1974). Operations and everyday thinking. *Human Development, 17,* 386–391.

Zajonc, R. B. (1980). Feeling and thinking: Preferences need no inferences. *American Psychologist, 35,* 151–175.

Zajonc, R. B. (1984). On the primacy of affect. *American Psychologist, 39,* 117–123.

Zieleniewski, J. (1966). Die Leistungsfähigkeit des Handelns. In K. Alsleben & W. Wehrstedt (Eds.), *Praxeologie* (pp. 35–70). Quickborn: Verlag Schnelle.

Zimmerman, B. J., & Blom, D. E. (1983). On resolving conflicting views of cognitive conflict. *Developmental Review, 3,* 62–72.

About the Editors

Charles N. Alexander received his B.A. (Magna Cum Laude, Phi Beta Kappa), M.A., and Ph.D. in developmental and personality psychology from Harvard University. He was a predoctoral fellow in experimental psychology at Oxford University and a postdoctoral fellow in psychology at Harvard University where he was also a member of the Division on Aging of the Faculty of Medicine. Dr. Alexander is currently Professor and Associate Chairman of the Department of Psychology and graduate faculty member in the doctoral programs in Psychology and the Neuroscience of Human Consciousness at Maharishi International University. He conducts research on cognitive and self development across the life span (especially in adults) and on the phenomenology and psychophysiology of higher states of consciousness.

Ellen J. Langer received her Ph.D. from Yale University in social psychology. She is currently Professor of Psychology and chair of the doctoral program in Social Psychology at Harvard University where she is also a member of the Division on Aging of the Faculty of Medicine. Dr. Langer was the 1988 recipient of the American Psychological Association Distinguished Contributions of Psychology in the Public Interest Award. Also, she has been a Guggenheim Fellow and served on several advisory committees for the National Academy of Science, including the Committee on Biology, Behavior, and Aging. Her most recent book is entitled *Mindfulness.* Her research focuses on reversing cognitive and performance decrements in the areas of aging, health, education, and the workplace.

Contributors

Charles N. Alexander
Department of Psychology
Maharishi International University
Fairfield, IA 52556

Paul B. Baltes
Max Planck Institute for Human
  Development and Education
Lentzeallee 94
D-1000 Berlin 33
West Germany

Benzion Chanowitz
Department of Psychology
Brooklyn College, CUNY
Brooklyn, NY 11210

Michael L. Commons
Department of Psychology
Harvard University
Cambridge, MA 02138

John L. Davies
Center for International Development and
  Conflict Management
University of Maryland
College Park, MD 02742

Michael C. Dillbeck
Department of Psychology
Maharishi International University
Fairfield, IA 52556

Freya Dittmann-Kohli
Max Planck Institute for Human
  Development and Education
Lentzeallee 94
D-1000 Berlin 33
West Germany

Carol A. Dixon
Department of Psychology
Maharishi International University
Fairfield, IA 52556

Steven M. Druker
713 Hampden Place
Pacific Palisades, CA 90272

Kurt W. Fischer
Graduate School of Education
Harvard University
Appian Way
Cambridge, MA 02138

Howard Gardner
Project Zero
Graduate School of Education
Harvard University
Appian Way
Cambridge, MA 02138

Carol Gilligan
Human Development
Graduate School of Education
Harvard University
Appian Way
Cambridge, MA 02138

Stephen Jacobs
ATT. American TransTech
8000 Bay Meadows Way
Jacksonville, FL 32256

Robert Kegan
Graduate School of Education
Harvard University ·
Appian Way
Cambridge, MA 02138

Massachusetts School of Professional
  Psychology
Dedham, MA

The Clinical-Development Institute
Belmont, MA

Sheryl L. Kenny
628 Owens
Crowley, TX 76036

Lawrence Kohlberg (deceased)
Department of Psychology
Harvard University
Cambridge, MA 02138

Lisa L. Lahey
Minds at Work
396 Concord Avenue
Belmont, MA 02178

Ellen J. Langer
Department of Psychology
Harvard University
Cambridge, MA 02138

Daniel J. Levinson
Department of Psychiatry
Yale University School of Medicine
New Haven, CT 06519

Diane McGuinness
Department of Psychology
University of South Florida
Fort Myers, FL 33919

John M. Muehlman
Department of Psychology
Maharishi International University
Fairfield, IA 52556

J. Michael Murphy
Child Psychiatry Service
ACC 725
Massachusetts General Hospital
Boston, MA 02114

Roberta M. Oetzel
4090 Orme Street
Palo Alto, CA 94306

David W. Orme-Johnson
Department of Psychology
Maharishi International University
Fairfield, IA 52556

Mark Palmerino
The Cambridge Consortium Inc.
Waltham, MA 02154

Juan Pascual-Leone
Department of Psychology
York University
Downsview, Ontario M3J 1P3
Canada

Erin Phelps
Murray Research Center
Radcliffe College
Cambridge, MA 02138

Sandra L. Pipp
Applied Developmental Program
Psychology Department
University of Colorado
Boulder, CO 80302

Marian Pirnazar
827 32nd Avenue
San Francisco, CA 94121

Karl H. Pribram
Center for Brain Research and
    Informational Sciences
Department of Psychology
Radford University
Radford, VA 24142

Francis A. Richards
Department of Human Development
Cornell University
Ithaca, New York 14853

Rhode Island Department of Education

Mark Rhodes
5960 5th Avenue South
St. Petersburg, FL 33707

Robert A. Ryncarz
121 Garden Street
Cambridge, MA 02138

Emily Souvaine
Souvaine & Associates
44C Irving Street
Cambridge, MA 02138

Mark B. Tappan
Graduate School of Education
Harvard University
Appian Way
Cambridge, MA 02138

Philip Thayer
29 Concord Avenue #305
Cambridge, MA 02138

Dennie Wolf
Project Zero
Graduate School of Education
Harvard University
Appian Way
Cambridge, MA 02138

Name Index

391

Subject Index

Abilities approach, 139
Abstract schema, 103
Abstraction. *See also* Formal operations
  arithmetic tasks, 168–75
  brain-growth hypothesis, 175–78
  developmental spurts, 162–87
  levels, 168–75
  postformal period criteria, 29–31
Abstract reasoning
  effects of Transcendental Meditation (TM) program on, 331–32, 336
  in model based on Maharishi's Vedic psychology, 303–4
Academic intelligence, 73
Accommodation, 6, 261
Achievement motivation
  and intellectual development, 67
  time orientation, 125
Action, Piaget's epistemology, 100–103
"Action space," 61
Action theory, 61–63, 78
Activation, neural mechanisms, 101–2
"Actual" self, 271–72
Addition skills, 168–75
Adolescence, creativity, 92
Adolescing, 51
Affective arousal mode, 260, 266, 279
Affective drives, 260–61, 266
Affective functioning. *See also* Feeling
  effect of Transcendental Meditation program on, 337–38
  implications for self-development, 229–57
  integrated with cognition, 209, 305
"Affordances," 262
Age-linked stages, 43, 52, 105–8, 111
Aging, 114–36
  effect of Transcendental Meditation program on, 333–34
  and intelligence, environment, 66
  mindlessness/mindfulness, 116–19, 134
  mindset experiment, 127–34
  nonsequential development, 114–36
  time perception, 124–27
Alpha EEG, 310–11, 336–37
Alpha mechanism, 112
Analog mapping, 88
Animal intelligence, 264
Arithmetic skills
  discontinuities, 167–68, 172–75

  levels, 168–75
  spurt criteria, 172–75
Arousal, neural mechanisms, 101
Artificial intelligence, 82
Assimilation, 6, 266–67
Associative memory, 261
Attachment–separateness polarity, 48–49
"Attunement," 326
Auditory thresholds, 132
Automatization, 261, 284
Autonomy, 235–37, 305–6
Autoregulation, 99–100

Belief systems, 67
Bending rods experiment, 151–52
Beta mechanism, 112
Beyond formal operations. *See* Postformal development
Biological factors. *See also* Hardware modules
  brain-growth hypothesis, 175–78
  and cognitive stages, 6, 8–9, 30–31, 159
  comparative analysis, 23–25
  in development of consciousness, 296–99, 310–11, 336–37, 339–40
Bliss consciousness, 309, 312–13, 315–17, 320, 322
Boolean connectives, 145–46
Buddhist philosophy, wisdom, 68

Care perspective, 17–18, 217–18
Categorization, 105
Category operations, 158
"Causal texture," 265
Causality, 151–53
Chhandas, 291
Chitta, 307
"Chunking," 60, 106
Classification
  in model based on Vedic psychology, 303
  Piaget's theory, 143–45
Cluster hypothesis, 174
Cognition
  and aging, 117
  effect of Transcendental Meditation program on, 330–33, 337–38
  hierarchical theories, 15
  Piagetian theory, 4–9, 102–13
  stage theory critique, 103–13